Revolution In the
Development of
Capitalism

for BK

200-1
202, 203 sqq
215-16
221-2 sqq
248 sqq
280 sqq
324 sqq

Revolution In the Development of Capitalism

The Coming of the English Revolution

Mark Gould

University of California Press

Berkeley   Los Angeles   London

For my Parents and in memory
of my sister; they have all shared
the capacity to mandate
high standards while providing
unconditional support

University of California Press
Berkeley and Los Angeles, California

University of California Press, Ltd.
London, England

Copyright © 1987 by the Regents of the
University of California

Library of Congress Cataloging-in-Publication Data

Gould, Mark.
    Revolution in the development of capitalism.

    Bibliography: p.
    Includes index.
    1. Social structure—England—History—
17th century.   2. England—Social conditions—17th
century.   3. Revolutions—England—History—
17th century.   I. Title.
HN398.E5G68   1987   305'.0942   86-11310
ISBN 0-520-05693-0 (alk. paper)
ISBN 0-520-06101-2 (pbk.)

Printed in the United States of America

1   2   3   4   5   6   7   8   9

Contents

Never pretend that the things you haven't got are not worth having.
—*Virginia Woolf,*
quoted in Norman Rosen,
"The Ordeal of Rebecca
Harding," *New York Times
Book Review* (15 April 73),
p. 39.

Abbreviations Used in Text

A	adaptive subsystem, economy
C	consumer support
C_a	economic consumer support (L—[product]→ A)
C_g	political support (I—[product]→ G)
C_i	leadership responsibility (G—[product]→ I)
C_l	commitment to the production of goods (A—[product]→ L)
DA	deviant aggression
DC	deviant conflict
DI	deviant innovation
DR	deviant retreatism
G	goal-attainment subsystem, polity
I	integrative subsystem, societal community, *and* investment
I_a	economic investment, allocation of fluid resources (G—[product]→ A)
I_g	authorization of powers of office (L—[product]→ G)
I_i	value-based claims to loyalties (L—[product]→ I)
I_l	commitments to common value (I—[product]→ L)
L	pattern-maintenance subsystem, latency subsystem
LB_g	legitimizing belief for political disorder
LB_i	legitimizing belief for integrative disorder
M_a	money
M_{ad}	money demanded
M_{ah}	demand for money to hold, standards for allocation of resources (I—[factor]→ A)
M_{as}	money supplied
M_{at}	transactions demand for money
M_d	medium demanded
M_g	power
M_{gd}	power demanded

M_{gh} allocation of surplus product (A—[factor] → G)

M_{gs} power supplied

M_{gt} transactions demand for power

M_h definition of allocatable medium resources, demand for medium to hold

M_i influence

M_{ih} assertions for claims for resources (A—[factor] → I)

M_{it} transactions demand for influence

M_l value-commitments or real commitments

M_{lh} operative responsibility (G—[factor] → L)

M_{lt} transactions demand for commitments

M_s medium supplied

M_t transactions demand for medium

N   constituent intent

N_a labor capacity (L—[factor] → A)

N_g interest demands (I—[factor] → G)

N_i policy decisions (G—[factor] → I)

N_l consumer income (A—[factor] → L)

NB_g neutralizing belief for political disorder

NB_i neutralizing belief for integrative disorder

O   definition of opportunity

O_a opportunity for effectiveness (G—[factor] → A)

O_g legitimation of authority (L—[factor] → G) *and* opportunity structure for political disorder.

O_i commitment to valued association (L—[factor] → I) *and* opportunity structure for integrative disorder

O_l justifications for allocation of loyalties (I—[factor] → L)

P_g precipitating factor for political disorder

P_i precipitating factor for integrative disorder

r   rate of opportunity

r_a interest rate, inverse of rate of economic opportunity

r_g rate of alienation, inverse of rate of legitimation

r_i rate of alienation from commitment to valued association

r_l rate of distrust

REVOF   faciliatory rebellion, a revolution seeking to redefine role structures within the polity

REVOG   rebellion, a revolution seeking to redefine collectivity structures within the polity

REVON   normative revolution, a revolution seeking to redefine normative structures within the polity

REVOV   total revolution, a revolution seeking to redefine value patterns within the polity

S   savings *and* structural strain

S_a economic savings (A—[factor]→ G), extent delimited by ranking of claims (I—[product]→ A)

S_g operative responsibility (G—[factor]→ L), extent delimited by control of productivity and services (A—[product]→ G)

S_i justification for allocations of loyalties (I—[factor]→ L), extent delimited by grounds for justification of claims (A—[product]→ I)

S_l commitment to valued association (L—[factor]→ I), extent delimited by moral responsibility for the collective interest (G—[product]→ L)

SF   strain at the level of facilities

SG   strain at the level of goals

SN   strain at the level of norms

SV   strain at the level of values

X_g social control of political disorders

X_i social control of integrative disorders

Y   subsystem output, income

Y_a economic output (A—[product]→ L, A—[product]→ G); income (A—[factor]→ L, A—[factor]→ G)

Y_g political output (G—[product]→ I, G—[product]→ L); income (G—[factor]→ I, G—[factor]→ L)

Preface

This book is an examination of seventeenth-century English social structure; specifically, an attempt to explain the genesis of revolution within that social structure and to speculate on the consequences of revolution for the transformation of it. My arguments are nested within three overlapping theoretical frameworks—functional, structural, and developmental—and implicitly this essay is an argument that viable sociological theory must be articulated along these three dimensions (see Gould 1985).

Chapter 1 briefly outlines certain of the conceptual tools and theoretical assumptions that serve as a foundation for the work that follows.

Chapters 2 and 3 formulate propositions that I label societal universals. They are delimited in the context of a functionally defined conceptual schema and are intended to be valid for all societal systems. This means that both the concepts and the propositions are very abstract and require considerable specification before they can be used in concrete historical analysis. Chapter 2 analyzes the conditions determining the level of production within economic and political subsystems and analyzes the conditions of stability for these subsystems. Chapter 3 concentrates on theory that specifies the necessary and sufficient conditions for the occurrence of four types of political revolution.

Chapter 4 formulates a model of prerevolutionary English social structure. It specifies the patterned constraints operative within this social structure and analyzes the tendencies that these constraints define. I call this social structure a "manufacturing social formation," as it finds its foundation in that stage of economic development, in both industry and agriculture, which Marx labeled manufacture. In other words, the limits of variation within this type of society are determined by that mode of economic production (a stage of capitalism) called manufacture. In early seventeenth-century England the manufacturing economy was interpenetrated with a rationalizing value orientation and regulated by a patrimonial political structure. This structural model, unlike the functional theories of chapters 2 and 3, is valid for only one type of social structure, that definitive of stage four in the development of societal systems.

I argue in chapter 4, and the argument is continued less formally in chapter 6, that these tendencies generate certain of the variables necessary for the genesis of one type of political revolution. In other words, the internal tendencies of a manufacturing social formation generate the variables specified in the theory of internal disorder (chap. 3) which generate a "rebellion" (REVOG), a revolution that seeks to transform the collectivity structure of the political system.

Chapters 5 through 7 constitute a historical examination of the English revolutions of the seventeenth century, concentrating on the period from 1640–49. By using the theoretical tools developed in the preceding sections of the book I endeavor to explain the genesis of three substages in the English Revolution from 1640–49. It is largely in terms of this empirical analysis that the work must be evaluated, and it is the success of this analysis, insofar as it is successful, which justifies the book as a whole.

Chapter 8 presents a stage sequence model of social development, a model defined so as to be applicable not simply to societies but to all social (and action) systems. I argue that the structural model outlined in chapter 4 defines one stage of this sequence, for societal systems.

Chapter 9, the most speculative section of the essay, argues that the English revolutions of the seventeenth century led to the creation of political conditions that, in conjunction with the natural and now politically accepted tendencies of a rationalized manufacturing system, allowed for the genesis of machine capitalism, a capitalism based on the extraction of relative surplus value. In other words, placing the structural model of chapter 4 within the context of the developmental model of chapter 8 allows for a tentative assessment of the potential for societal transformation in early seventeenth-century English society.

Much of what follows in this essay involves an articulation of technical theory; some readers may find it difficult reading. I want to suggest three alternative strategies for reading the following chapters. Once the reader has completed this preface she may begin at one of three points. She may proceed directly to chapter 1 and read sequentially; she may proceed to chapter 1 and then skip to chapter 5; or she may simply begin at chapter 5.

The fifth, sixth, and seventh chapters in the essay attempt to explain the English revolutions from 1640–49. They are written, insofar as this was possible, in an accessible terminology, in a vocabulary that presupposes little or no sociological background, and which assumes very little knowledge of the historical context. At the same time I try to tie this discussion to the other sections of the book, and especially to chapter 3, which delimits the theoretical framework from which the theory in chapters 5 through 7 is derived.

The advantage of reading chapter 1 prior to chapter 5 is that it will provide a cursory knowledge of the conceptual underpinnings of the essay. In addition, it outlines some of the assumptions that structure chapters 5 through 7. The advantage of reading consecutively from chapter 1 to chapter 9 is that the theoretical apparatus that molds the essay will then be transparent. The disadvantage is that this theory (and especially chap. 2) is not easily digestible, and might best be swallowed in small doses. I recommend that the sociologically timid begin with the preface, try chapter 1 and then proceed to chapter 5 through 7; retreat to chapter 3, to 2, and then go on to 4, 8, and 9. For the sociologically initiated, the chapters are correctly ordered.

Metatheory

A usual methodological position among empirical social scientists is that a scientific theory must be capable of falsification. In other words it must be propositional, and these propositions must be such that a specifiable body of data might show them to be in error.[1] This set of assumptions is almost diametrically opposed to the "facts."

At least within the social sciences (my only concern) it is almost impossible to falsify a proposition. Propositions can only be verified within the context of a given range of data which they usually aid in creating. Imagine a case of apparent falsification: I argue if x, then y. You present a case x', not y'. There are two interpretations open in this circumstance: the first admits that the theory is in error; the second argues that the operationalization of the terms was invalid, and thus empirically we are not dealing with x and/or y. Formally, there is no way to decide which interpretation is correct.

In their methods courses social scientists are taught about the validity of operationalizations. An index on a social survey is a valid operationalization of a concept if it "really identifies or measures" that concept. But in fact the only useful image of validity is "context validity." You know that the concept is accurately measured because your theory works. In other words, the concepts in the theory are assumed to be validly operationalized when the theory is verified; when the theory is falsified there is no way of determining whether the concepts were validly measured or not.[2]

In the natural sciences the problem is much less serious as there are accepted ways of operationalizing a significant portion of the concepts used by these scientists. Natural scientists will assume the validity of an operationalization when it has resulted in the formulation of valid propositions, and when a new proposition is falsified they will have a tendency to reject the proposition (see Gould 1977:25ff.). More important, natural scientists are able to formulate viable theory because they are usually dealing with phenomena that may be experimentally manipulated or which have the property of being relatively unchangeable in the face of human study. One must move into the fringe of these disciplines before the raised issue becomes a serious problem.

In the social sciences, however, we have to admit that we do not have a generally accepted theory to work from. Although we know much about how social structures operate, it is clear to most observers that the question is not why we know so much but why it is that we know so little about social processes. It is necessary, in my opinion, that we recognize that there are social structural reasons why we know relatively so little, and it is essential that we adopt a strategy of work which is realistic within the conditions we now confront.[3]

It is plausible to argue that "truth" is produced within a realm of scientific practice where doing science consists in the articulation and evaluation (verification via controlled observation and experimentation) of scientific theory. Here a determinate and autonomous product, knowledge, emerges from the realm of scientific practice. The question is whether this image of scientific practice is a legitimate one for both the natural and the social sciences.

In physics, for example, it is clear that an autonomous institutional framework for doing science may exist, and that practice within this framework may produce (true) knowledge. It is then legitimate to speak of the application of this knowledge (within, for example, the capitalist mode of economic production). In the social sciences, however, even if theory is articulated within a scientific problematic (whatever this might be) there is no autonomous realm of evaluation.

It is difficult to see how an autonomous realm of social scientific practice might emerge. For social science the production of scientific knowledge is possible only within the context of political action and thus only within the realm of the concomitant production of a political product. In other words, insofar as social scientific theory studies actual social processes the evaluation of that theory is inextricably bound up with the goal-oriented transformation of those processes. There is no way to imagine a case of the autonomous production of (true) social knowledge without impinging on the lives of those studied. The doing of social science will require the evaluation of the consequences of scientifically guided political action and thus the double production of knowledge and implementation of goals. The production of (true) social knowledge is always implicated in the political application of that knowledge (cf. Althusser, in Althusser and Balibar 1970:59), and thus is always subject to distortion by the constraints that limit political action within any society (see chap. 4, below; and Habermas 1970:146; 1975).

Social scientific practice, therefore, must occur within an institutional framework isomorphic with (or more realistically, analogous to) the one that guarantees the scientificity of, for example, physics. But this framework will characterize the society within which social scientific practice occurs. Distortions inherent in nonscientific criteria for making decisions inhibit the possibility of social scientific practice. Within a capitalist social structure, for example, scientifically grounded practice would continually violate the system's internal constraints, which are grounded in an interest in profit, not truth.

This is not the place for an elaboration of the notion of an equitable society, that mode of social organization which would mandate scientifically grounded practice (Gould 1977; and chap. 8, below). Very briefly, it will involve the structuring of political actions in quasi-experimental terms, where the differentiation of roles among actors will be effected based on the relevant performance capacity of those actors. There will be no attempt to efface the theoretical skills of political leaders, but the theory they articulate will be subject to free and unimpeded discussion (see Habermas 1970) and to democratic control. When acted on, this theory must be subject to the evaluation of those on whom these actions impinge; it will be evaluated by those with the expertise to assess its consequences, an expertise grounded in the experience of those consequences. Both theory and theorist will be evaluated in terms of the empirical consequences of these theoretically guided interventions, and ultimate control will rest in the hands of those in a position of expertise, the people "suffering" the effects of the actions.

The social sciences are capable of emerging only in situations where their scientificity is guaranteed, only within institutional structures that necessitate scientifically redeemable choices. But as the social sciences deal with the structures of society, these extant structures will have to be transformed. It is within the context of this transformation, guided by political associations organized according to equitable principles, that a viable social science will emerge.

Within a completed equitable society, political interests will be defined in terms of a quest for truth and will not be grounded in class position. In Marxist terms this society is labeled "communist" and results in the elimination of the state. Once classes are eliminated, the state is no longer necessary. There is no longer a need for a differentiated structure to protect the particular interests of a class dictatorship, a dictatorship of the bourgeoisie, in capitalism, or of the proletariat, in socialism. In an equitable society political practice will be guided by the universal interest, truth, and actualized within democratic structures so that a degeneration from this goal—and thus from the principle of unanimity—will lead to a backsliding into the decisionistic determination of goals by the majority.

Whether or not these assertions are accepted in this dogmatic form, they do frame the work that follows.[4] If one is cognizant of the absence of an appropriate institutional context or other equally severe limitations on our current socially structured capacity to evaluate social scientific theory, certain consequences must be recognized. This book is intended, for example, as a very preliminary attempt to construct theory, not to verify it. I assume nonetheless that some level of theoretical development may occur—has occurred in relative isolation from "experimental practice"—and that it is important to endeavor honestly to confront theory with historical materials. Even if these materials—always capable of many interpretations and always fragmentary and imprecise— cannot falsify theory, their intelligent and honest use can help us to correct our more obvious errors.

It is clear that the empirical materials included here will not support the weight they are asked to carry. The theory is complex, often abstract, and incapable of proper evaluation within the context of one case study. In writing this book I was constantly aware of two things: how little I know about the many issues, both theoretical and historical, relevant to my discussion; and that it would be impossible to gain mastery over the materials necessary to make this book empirically adequate. For example, to draw an adequate portrait of a mode of economic production in England one should have mastered the literature dealing with the different manifestations of this stage of economic development in different countries within the same historical conjuncture, and at different stages in the development of the world system. In addition one wants to grasp the preceding and following stages of economic development, at least for England, and preferably for numerous countries. If one adds political, legal, cultural, and other systems, all relevant to the analysis that follows, the mind boggles at the prospect. And I have said nothing about the relevant bodies of theory.

What is to be done? The answer is, I think, reasonably simple. That it is impossible for one person to gain command of the materials necessary to analyze one concrete situation in a theoretically sophisticated fashion is obvious; but in a sense this impossibility is what theory is all about. Only when the knowledge of innumerable social scientists and historians is codified within a shared body of theory, theory built up, however tentatively, by the detailed knowledge of these practitioners, will it be possible for any to practice his or her profession in a way that will further the development of this theory. The problem is a bit like the famous hermeneutic circle: one must first know what a fragment of a text means in order to decipher its meaning, but the whole point of analyzing the text is to construct the structure of meaning within which the text is intelligible. There is no logical resolution to this dilemma—one must simply begin, but within the context of a considered study of both the relevant history and theory.

In effect the point of this book is not found in any of its arguments; rather, the point is the mode of argumentation. The medium is the message. I am trying to convince my reader that the body of theory within which this work is delimited, my own amalgam of the classical and Marxist traditions of social thought, provides us with a means of entry into our circle. I am suggesting that in this amalgam we have a foundation upon which we may begin contructing a viable body of social theory, a social theory capable of helping us to define the potentialities inherent in our social world.

It will be apparent in the pages that follow that I have used a general theoretical framework to guide my empirical research. Insofar as the abstractions I have used allow us to reconceptualize the findings of others in their empirical studies, I have endeavored to learn from their results. I have been able to evaluate the theoretical import of past historical research in realms very different from my own concerns for my own theoretical and empirical questions. Although there are surely innumerable studies that are relevant to my work which have remained unconsulted, it is my belief that the conscious use of a theoretical framework has helped to demolish intuitive and often erroneous preconceptions, while leaving a more cogent and I hope more accurate set of preconceptions.

Insofar as this codification of past research can occur, the general theory I discuss in this book—theory formulated using abstract, functionally defined concepts—can guide our research by helping us to avoid certain erroneous formulations and by directing us to theoretically interesting problems. In other words, it orients the researcher to problems outside her immediate concerns and enables historians to evaluate propositions applicable to their own empirical interests. It aids the historian in contributing to the explanation of events interesting to others, events about which she may have no immediate knowledge.

If one type of abstraction allows us to treat political processes from many societies within one framework, enabling the researcher concerned with the English Revolution of the 1640s to learn from research on the French Revolution of 1789, another type allows the researcher concerned with political phenomena to learn from studies of the economy. These conceptualizations have reference to social systems; for example, they treat economic and political systems alike in certain respects. A measure of our success in doing this is our ability to glean knowledge about the polity from theories formulated to explain economic phenomena. A general theoretical framework allows us to determine when two theories are saying the same thing; or from a different perspective, allows us to determine when two empirical studies, perhaps about widely different political systems, perhaps about different types of social systems, are saying the same thing. Sometimes we will find out that two theories that should be congruent are not, and on occasion we will be able to modify one so as to improve its explanatory adequacy.

Implicit in these arguments is the necessity of talking to one's colleagues. Insofar as we are able to speak the same language we should do so, for only in discussing our ideas with one another will it be possible to come near the limitations of our social circumstances. These discussions will possess adequate breadth only when a discussion of the English Revolution occurs at a sufficient level of abstraction and formality to allow for broad comparisons with other revolutionary phenomena. I will thus be more formal than historians usually like, not to forestall discussion but rather to aid in the beginnings of a wider discussion.

This book attempts a contribution to this task by articulating a theory relevant to the problems discussed and capable of surviving my own logical and empirical scrutiny. Whether this book actually makes a contribution will depend on its capacity to survive such scrutiny from the reader.

Strategy

It does not sound as strange now as it did when this project was initiated to indicate that one is working within a tradition defined by both Marxist and classical theory. There has been so much work within the past several years attempting to link Marx with Freud or systems analysis perspectives that the notion of doing so is at least comprehensible. This acceptance has freed me from any form of discursive justification for making the linkage (see Gould 1981c). I decided at a very early point that this work would have to be evaluated as a systematically articulated body of empirical theory, and not in terms of the use it makes of any theoretical authority.

I have taken one advantage from drawing on well-known sources. Where possible, as a means of more rapid and lucid exposition, I have tied my work to these sources. This has the danger of allowing an ill-conceived evaluation of what I write in terms of its fidelity to Marx or Weber or whomever, but the compensating advantage of accessibility seemed to outweigh the possibility of evaluation in terms of the wrong criteria, or even of misinterpretation based on a failure to note my divergences from these texts. I thus draw explicitly on Marx, Weber, Piaget, and Parsons.[5]

More important is the way I deal with historical sources. As a student one is always taught to deal with a text as a whole, to refrain from taking things out of context. In this book I have frequently violated this tenet. I have often taken a bit of information from a source and used it to support an argument with which the original author might well disagree. There are two dangers in this: the first involves the potential for misinterpreting one's authorities; the second, which is related, involves selecting materials because they fit one's preconceptions rather than because they are accurate representations of the accumulated historical sources.

Another problem, much like these, involves what logicians refer to as the fallacy of arguing from authority. One accepts what are in fact unsubstantiated statements owing to one's trust in the judgment of the historian cited, or, less generously, because they support one's preconceptions. The problem is that one often implicitly rejects statements made by historians whose credentials are equally solid.

There are two possible avenues of escape from these dilemmas. The first involves a systematic reconstruction of all data presented. This is the best solution, but one that is clearly impossible. There is no systematic history in this sense, at least not for the seventeenth century. There is no self-contained set of numbers whose manipulation allows for the explanation of 70 percent of the variance. By the criteria of any decent sociological methods course, let alone of natural science, there is no viable history.

The second escape route would involve turning this book into a study of the historiography of the period. One might carefully consider the different arguments, weigh the evidence presented for different points of view, and carefully defend one's own conclusions. In a sense this was done in determining which authority to cite, but to have put it in writing would have been to alter the entire nature of this book.

Failing to adopt either of these routes implied another quandary.

Often I found myself dependent on an argument that was not adequately substantiated in the author's text, but which I nonetheless tentatively accepted. Here I had two choices: I could either present her materials in considerable detail, criticizing their inadequacies; or I could simply quote her summary of these materials, with the understanding that my reader might consult the original text. I have generally adopted the latter tactic, but this has entailed the double problem of arguing from authority—Mary Smith the famous historian has concluded *x*, therefore it must be so—in a situation where this authority was not acceptable in the face of criticism.

In more contemporary work one can often base arguments on statistics. But statistics, even at their best, may be unreliable (Morgenstern 1965); those available for the seventeenth century are like intelligence reports coming from a double agent. In order to weed out reliable information from unreliable, in order to interpret the information one has, it is necessary to filter it through a set of assumptions that are not based on that information. There is a tendency to accept information confirming what one already believes, for this is the information that "must be" reliable, and to discount as unreliable what conflicts with one's preconceptions. Thus it is the preconceptions that rule, not the information (cf. Smith 1973).[6]

There remains no minimally adequate solution to these predicaments. I have tried to relate a coherent picture of the events to an (at least partial and tentative) evaluation of the theory presented.[7] I attempted to do this impartially, but it is clear that from many other points of view I have been very partial indeed. I have tried not to discount opposing materials, although I have ignored some sources that only appear to contradict my arguments, but which actually rest on misconceptions of their own arguments or their own data. The conclusion is inescapable, however, that this book is an act of theory construction, that its success will be determined by the dialogue it engenders between sociologists and historians (not only historians of England), and that an intelligent person will view what I have to argue with caution and circumspection.

These comments do not, I believe, affect certain apparently arbitrary points in the construction of this work. The selection of England as a case and the determination to focus on England in the abstract were, for example, not arbitrary decisions. England was selected as she was the first country to develop machine capitalism, and with it, the accoutrements of stage five, the social structure typified by organic solidarity. It was in England's case that one could study the leading edge of the transformation of one stage of societal development into another. Each other point of transition was different, and was in some fundamental way affected by England's prior crossing of this barrier.[8]

The second point, concerning the "world system," is more difficult. There clearly was a "world system" in the seventeenth century, but it was not one that determined England's development. England affected this system, and as far as there came to be a "world system" relevant to the development of capitalism in England, it was largely of her own creation. The system of which Wallerstein (1974) writes existed; the description he provides of it in terms of a capitalist division of labor in the sixteenth and early seventeenth centuries is largely of his own imagination.

There are two easy ways of perceiving Wallerstein's fundamental errors: the first involves a theoretical analysis of Wallerstein's book, which shows that it is based on utilitarian assumptions (see Parsons 1949; Gould 1981*b*, 1981*c*; Brenner 1977). If only barriers would disappear capitalism would be generated, as actors would act "rationally." He provides no explanation of the social structure that was capitalism, and within which "rational" profit maximization was necessary. Second, England created the markets for her goods via three mechanisms: most important, internal markets were created with the development of manufacture (see chap. 4, below; and Lenin 1960ff: vol. 3); externally, markets were created owing to the superiority of her productive techniques and political system. Her political strength was manifest both in terms of her capacity to open up and to create markets and in terms of her capacity to control her budding working class. The control over workers was made easier by the success of manufacture in agriculture; by 1650 sufficient grain was produced to yield a stagnant price for grain over the next years; this in turn helped create an internal market for "industry." Thus the second feudalism in eastern Europe, itself unexplained by Wallerstein, was relatively unimportant to England at just that point when her economy began its secular growth within the manufacturing system.[9]

Acknowledgments

This book has had a very long gestation period and many organizations and individuals have aided in its completion. The British

Library possesses not only the best collection of materials available for the study of seventeenth-century England; just as important, its location in the British Museum allows for extraordinarily pleasant breaks from one's work. The museum houses a bas-relief of a wounded Assyrian lion and she became my special companion on many a rainy day. Widener Library at Harvard University has a remarkable collection of books, journals, and pamphlets relevant to this book. I greatly miss having this collection near at hand. Finally, though Haverford College's Magill Library houses only a small collection of material concerned with seventeenth-century England, it is the home of a group of people who work very hard to make the small size of the library a virtue instead of a vice. I am grateful to the staffs of all three of these libraries.

During the period I have been working on this book I have received grants relevant to it from the National Institute of Health and from Haverford College, which awarded me two Whitehead Grants for Faculty Development.

Chapter two of this book is an amended version of an essay originally published in Jan Loubser, Rainer Baum, Andrew Effrat and Victor Lidz (eds.). *Explorations in General Theory in Social Science*. It is used in this revised form with the kind permission of the publisher, Macmillan.

While an undergraduate at Reed College I took for granted the time and energy certain of my professors devoted to my queries. When I joined the faculty of a small liberal arts college I came to realize the sacrifices involved in this devotion. At Reed, John Pock helped me to learn how to define a social scientific problem and convinced me of the virtues of doing social *science*. John Tomsich helped me to learn how to evaluate works of history and nurtured my desire to do historical sociology. Howard Jolly was the best teacher of social theory I have ever known. He led me to the vocation of doing theory.

I have been reading the work of Talcott Parsons for over twenty years and I argued with him about that work and other matters for more than ten years. It will be obvious to the reader that the corpus of Parsonian sociology has left its mark on virtually every page of this book. I believe that Parsons was the most important social theorist of his generation, but I am especially grateful that he was my teacher and my friend.

During my sojourn at Harvard Barrington Moore Jr. was a source of consistent support and assistance. Perhaps because he disagrees so fundamentally with much of what I do in this essay, his questions were always provocative and helpful. He helped me to define the standards that I have tried to meet in this book.

Three of my other teachers helped me to mold the arguments that constitute this book: Kenneth Arrow's insistence that my argument required a structural distinction between manufacture and machine capitalism led to my writing chapter 4. Karl Deutsch served as an early sounding board for and critic of the arguments in chapter 3. Judith Shklar forced me to take texts seriously; while talking to me about Hegel, she was never reticent in expressing her skepticism about social science. I wish that I believed this book would convince her otherwise.

Daniel Bell was co-opted as a member of my dissertation committee near the end of that project. He read that manuscript closely and made numerous suggestions leading to its improvement and thus to the improvement of this book. I remain grateful to him for taking seriously a mode of doing sociology very different from his own.

Jeff Alexander encouraged me to submit this book to the University of California Press during the period when he edited a series for the Press. His comments on the manuscript were detailed and very valuable in helping me to clarify my arguments and mode of presentation.

Jürgen Habermas spent a semester at Haverford and I a semester at the Max-Planck-Institut in Starnberg while this book was being written. His work, more than the work of any of his generation, manifests an understanding of the scope and nature of the task in constructing social theory and contains invaluable suggestions about how to proceed. The questions he poses are in my opinion the correct ones and the fact that someone of his intellectual and moral stature understands the issues in a way analogous to my own point of view has periodically renewed my faith in the necessity of working in the direction I have followed.

One of the great virtues of living in Philadelphia has been contact with friends and colleagues in the area. There is no way that I can convey what I have learned from Renée Fox, Willy DeCraemer, Victor Lidz, and Harold Bershady. Whatever sensitivity I might demonstrate in an analysis of value patterns must largely be credited to them.

If I had known Michael Weinstein when I began this book, it would be stronger than it is today. His economist's skepticism over the type of theory this book attempts, when coupled with a friend's willingness to explore issues of concern to me, will no doubt lead to my reformulation of some of what I've said here and to clearer work in the future.

The Haverford College Sociology-Anthropology Department has put up with me for more than ten years. The intellectual support of my two departmental colleagues has been invaluable. Wyatt MacGaffey has frequently forced me to rethink or to better defend my positions. His comments on chapter 3 were very helpful. Bill Hohenstein, the other Haverford sociologist, has developed, from very different origins, a perspective that is complementary to my own. I am grateful to him for sharing his own work with me and for his continued faith in my work.

I have known Frank Domurad since seventh grade. The fact that he grew up to be a historian has been a considerable consolation to me, as there has always been at least one historian who has treated my work seriously and explored its utility in his own research. He has been for me an exemplar of the historians on whose writings this book builds; it is to their often brilliant work that I am most indebted.

For well over fifteen years my students at Harvard, Radcliffe, Haverford, and Bryn Mawr Colleges have been exposed to the ideas and arguments contained in these pages. Their intelligence coupled with their sympathy and critical judgment created for me a standard of excellence which is much higher than any colleague might reasonably demand. If I have not always fulfilled their expectations, this essay is much the better because I have tried to make it worthy of them.

There have been many friends and two dogs (Yoboseyo and Träger) who have served as distractions from the writing of this book. While some might argue that without them it would have been completed long ago, in fact without them it would never have been completed.

I am not always very skillful in letting Anita Kaplan know what she means to me. I hope that she understands, even if I don't have the words to express what I feel.

While working in a sociology-anthropology department with two colleagues who do field work, I have come to view the people of seventeenth-century England as my "tribe." They have caused me much frustration and given me enormous pleasure. The best of them built the foundation for much that is valuable in our world.

I. A Sociological Foundation

This chapter introduces briefly, but I hope coherently, the rudiments of the theoretical framework used throughout this book. If this chapter is clear, it should make the entire work accessible to historians and laypersons as well as to professional sociologists. My aim is not to provide a rigorous introduction to the conceptual bases of my theory but only to make the following discussions comprehensible.

Overtly or covertly, abstract concepts are used in all historical research. This is apparent in comparative essays dealing with two or more societies. There it is usually obvious to both the researcher and to her audience that in speaking of, for example, the English and the French revolutions, a concept, *revolution*, will have been introduced into the discussion. This is not primarily because of the similarities between the two revolutions, but rather because each is historically unique. Even if it were possible to describe each and every characteristic of a specific historical case, to speak of two cases under one heading involves the use of abstractions, concepts that transcend historical specificity. Further, to speak solely of the English Revolution involves the use of the same abstraction, and necessarily involves an implicit set of comparisons, however much emphasis might be laid on historical specifics.

It is neither possible nor desirable to be exhaustive in our descriptions. When speaking of Cromwell I will not be concerned with his molecular composition—conceptualized within a theoretical framework clearly irrelevant to my concerns—but rather with his social roles, and perhaps with his personality. To speak of Cromwell is to use abstract terms, to abstract from the phenomena. The question is not whether abstractions will appear in our analysis. The question is which abstractions we shall use. Will we use them consciously to at least partially control the biases they must introduce into our analysis? Will we endeavor to skew these biases in the direction of theoretical, scientific explanations? (see Parsons 1967:chap. 3; Lidz 1981).

Concepts are neither true nor false; rather they are useful (or not useful) for a specific type of analysis. A concept is good not because it is valid but because it helps, when used as an element in a proposition, to elucidate a relationship. It is my belief that within the social sciences the most useful concepts have three foci, what I refer to as functional, structural (interactional), and developmental dimensions.

Units conceptualized for sociological analysis must be defined in terms of the consequences of their actions for the social system of reference when that social system is taken as a whole. Our task is not to identify a set of seemingly "objective" properties of the unit: "the objective forms of all social phenomena change constantly in the course of their ceaseless dialectical interactions with each other. The intelligibility of objects develops in proportion as we grasp their function in the totality to which they belong" (Lukacs 1971: 13). The proletariat, for example, must be defined with reference to the consequences of its actions for the capitalist system; the proletariat cannot be defined by noncontextual, objective attributes.[1]

The second focus of each conceptualization must be interactional. This involves the identification of the unit's relational network, its interactions with other units at the same level of analysis. Within certain contexts this may involve the specification of the organizational patterns within which these interactions occur, and hence this conceptual frame of reference is often referred to as "structural."[2] The proletariat is defined within the context of its interactions with the bourgeoisie.

The final focus of good social concepts is developmental. This involves a consideration of the potential for structural transformation inherent in the unit and forces us to categorize it within the context of this potential for development, and within the context of its past transformations. In other words, it is essential that we are able to conceptualize the stages of development for our units, and in analyzing a particular manifestation of that unit, we must characterize it as falling within one or another of these stages. (A stage sequence model is presented in chap. 8, below.) One asks with regard to a particular proletariat, at which stage in its development as a class is it to be found? Within a highly simplified two-stage model, is it a class in itself or a class for itself?

The second level of conceptualization, the structural, deals with patterns of social interaction, where violation of the pattern implies (in the ideal case) a negative sanction (see below in this chap.; and Durkheim 1964 : 424). These patterns may be differentiated according to the stage of social development arrived at by the system under analysis; that is, each stage is said to be constituted by a specific structural pattern.

This book will analyze these structures within the context of a more general functional frame of reference. This does not involve functional, teleological explanations, but rather the provision of a coherent, analytically defined set of concepts within which it is possible to discuss social interactions. Functional analysis is, to use the economists' term, a form of macroanalysis (Ackley 1961 : chap. 20). Units are categorized according to the consequences of their actions for the system as a whole, without reference to their organizational characteristics. Thus the level of production for an economy consists in the sum of the production of all producing units within the given economic system, from independent artisans to General Motors.

Structural and functional analyses are congruent insofar as our discussion relates solely to one stage of social (here almost always societal) development. Here, in dealing with concrete social formations (see chap. 4 n. 1, below), we restrict ourselves to discussing organizations characteristic of a particular stage. For example, so long as one discusses economically productive units only as they are organized in a capitalist fashion and ignores those productive units not so organized, even if found within the most highly developed capitalist economy, one's discussion will be congruent in its structural and functional dimensions. For here all productive units within the discussion will be, by definition, of one type, and thus an aggregative analysis, summing these units, will not differ from a structuralist analysis, as the integrity of the organization is maintained in both cases.

Structural and functional analysis will differ in those cases where an analysis of a concrete social system is undertaken. As noted, functional analysis will treat all productive organizations alike, owing to their common functionally defined consequences for the economy under examination. A structural analysis of the same system will focus on the tendencies constituted by specific patterns of interaction between economic units. Both abstract from the concrete system, but the procedure of abstraction differs in the two cases. The focus of a functional analysis necessitates that the functional concepts be defined at a level of abstraction enabling them to encompass all varieties of social organization which might fall within their purview. The focus of a structural analysis involves the introduction of concepts that allow the articulation of an underlying structure, a structure not apparent on an examination of appearances.

While structural analyses are couched in a functionalist frame-work—the units are defined, in part, in terms of the consequences of their actions for the total system—they also involve the speci-fication of an organizational context. They are therefore defined more narrowly than their functionalist counterparts. Propositions using functionalist concepts are "societal universals," meant to be valid for all societies (see chaps. 2 and 3); propositions using struc-tural concepts are meant to be valid only for the type of society to which they refer (see chap. 4). Functionally defined theory is valid for all stages of societal development; structuralist theory is valid for only one specific stage.

The specification of functionally defined categories does not im-ply any one-to-one correspondence with social structures. There are three reasons for this. First, a given social structure may fulfill more than one function. For example, in many "primitive" societies kinship collectivities perform both economic and socialization functions. Second, two or more types of structures may fulfill one function. In many contemporary societies different types of orga-nizations are involved in the production of consumer goods. Third, the functional model elaborated in the pages that follow involves a nesting process. It concerns the categorization of social processes within a social system compartmentalized by four functional prob-lems; each of these problems is viewed as definitive of a type of social system. In addition it is assumed that each of these subsys-tems is in turn divisible according to these same functional prob-lems. Thus within any subsystem there is the possibility of a social structure being located within more than one functional categoriza-tion. For example, some collectivities will be categorized, according to the consequences of their actions for the entire system, in the economy. But in addition, within the economy (treated as a func-tionally defined subsystem) they will be categorized within the pol-ity, owing to the consequences of their actions for the economy.

This series of subsystem levels bars any unique correspondence between a functional category and a social structure.

This book deals with social structures and processes within a functional frame of reference. There are three types of social processes relevant to our discussion. The first is defined by, constituted as, the social structure. This is the group of social interactions that are organized as sanctioned social patterns and which are stable in form for the period of analysis. The second process involves aspects of a system equilibrium. The third involves transformations of social structure, alterations in previously stable patterns of inter-action.

Social structures involve the patterned articulation of four types of components. In any social system values (V) are the component that reaches the highest level of generality. "Values state in general terms the desirable end states which act as a guide to human endeavor; they are so general in their reference that they do not specify kinds of norms, kinds of organization, or kinds of facilities which are required to realize these ends" (Smelser 1962:25). In the ideal case societal values are internalized by all members of the society; they define the good society; they are a definition of the desirable, not necessarily of the desired.

Parsons has commented that

> values are, for sociological purposes, deliberately defined at a level of generality higher than that of goals—they [values] are *directions* of action rather than specific objectives, the latter depending on the particular character of the situation in which the system is placed as well as its values and structure as a system. (Parsons 1960:172)

> The component of *norms* [italics mine] is the set of universalistic rules ... which define expectations for the performance of classes of differentiated units within the system—collectivities, or roles, as the case may be; and values are the normative patterns defining, in universalistic terms, the pattern of desirable orientation for the system as a whole, independent of specification of situation or of differentiated function within the system. (Parsons 1961b:43–44)

Parsons has elsewhere remarked,

> in one respect, they [norms] are derived from the evaluative judgements that have been institutionalized in the value system; but independently of this component, they also include, as is clear in the case of legal systems, three other specifications. The first specifies the categories of

units to which the norm applies; this is the problem of jurisdiction. The second specifies what the consequences will be to the unit that conforms and to the unit that does not conform to the requirements of the norm (variations in degree are, of course, possible); this is the problem of sanctions or enforcement. Finally, the third specifies that the meaning of the norm shall be interpreted in the light of the character and the situations of the units to which it applies; this constitutes the problem of interpretation, which is roughly equivalent to the appellate function in law.   (Parsons 1967:9)

There is some terminological and substantive confusion regarding the remaining two components. Smelser has commented,

By themselves values and norms do not determine the *form of organization* of human action. They supply certain general ends and general rules; they do not specify, however, who will be the agents in the pursuit of valued ends, how the actions of these agents will be structured into concrete roles and organizations, and how they will be rewarded for responsible participation in these roles and organizations.... Most of what sociologists call "social organization" or "social structure"— families, churches, hospitals, government agencies, business firms, associations, political parties—is specified by this third component of "mobilization of motivation into organized action." Furthermore, around this component we find the operative play of rewards, such as wealth, power, and prestige, which accrue as a result of effective performance in roles and organizations.   (Smelser 1962:27–28)

In Smelser's work this classification is substituted for one of Parsons's categories, the *collectivity*. Collectivities involve higher levels of interaction or the potential for interaction among two or more actors within a common normative framework. It is within the context of these collectivity structures that sanctions are mobilized which serve as incentives to comply with socially defined expectations.

Smelser's category of situational facilities involves those aspects of the actor's environment which she "utilizes as means; these include knowledge of the environment, predictability of consequences of action, and tools and skills" (Smelser 1962:24–25). Very simply, the mobilization component concerns the definition of socially defined goals, while the facility component involves the means, the instrumentalities used to obtain those goals.

It is important to note that the same concrete object can be both a facility or a reward. Role performances, for example, are the normatively regulated participation of actors in social interactions with specifiable role partners. Depending on the situation under examination, they may be considered to be either the limiting case of a collectivity or to be instrumentalities in the pursuit of some social goal. For most purposes in the discussions that follow, I will use the term *collectivity* as a parallel to mobilization mechanism, and the term *role* as a parallel to facilities. These comments should remind us that we are working with analytical constructs and not with phenomenological descriptions.

It is important to note that, in Parsons's words,

> *Any* concrete structural unit of a social system is always a combination of all four components—the present classification involves *components, not types*. We often speak of a role or collectivity as if it were a concrete entity, but this is, strictly speaking, elliptical. There is no collectivity without member roles and, vice versa, no role which is not part of a collectivity. Nor is there a role or collectivity which is not "regulated" by norms and characterized by a commitment to value patterns.... Nevertheless, the four categories or components are, in the nature of the case, independently variable. Knowing the value pattern of a collectivity does not, for example, make it possible to deduce its role-composition. Cases in which the contents of two or more types of components vary together so that the content of one can be deduced directly from another are special and limiting, not general, cases. (Parsons 1966:19)

Social structures involve the patterned interrelationships between these four components. Parsons has commented that the structure of social systems consists in the normative patterns that are institutionalized within that system (e.g., Parsons 1967:2–8). It is my belief that this view, at times contradicted by Parsons himself, is in error; Parsons's own ambivalence concerning this point is seen in the following quotation:

> the structure of any empirical system may be treated as consisting in (1) *units*, such as the particle or the cell, and (2) *patterned relations* among units, such as relative distances, "organization" into tissues and organs....
>
> In social structure the element of "patterned relation" is clearly *in part* [italics mine] "normative." ...
>
> The proposition [is] that the relational patterns of social systems *are normative* [italics mine], which is to say that they *consist in* [italics mine] institutionalized normative culture ... the structure of social systems in general *consists in* institutionalized patterns of normative culture. (Parsons 1961c:223–24)

Social structures ought to be seen as the underlying patterns that guide interrelationships between units, and violations of these patterns involve, in the ideal case, some form of negative sanction; but these patterns are not necessarily normative, and in fact they can contravene explicit norms extant within a social system. The most obvious example is the competitive constraint within atomistic market situations. Only in certain circumstances are its patterns explicitly formulated in normative terms, a fact emphasized by Weber. It remains the case, however, that the absence of a normative component in this one respect—for example, regarding rational economic behavior—does not involve the absence of a more generalized normative component within the society; the norms of contract still underlie market behaviors.

Parsons's comments about normative social structures are more appropriate concerning a specific type of social structure, institutions. Institutional structures are, in the context of this book, legitimized normative patterns defining regularized expectations for actors in situations where the requisite facilities for performance are provided and where conforming performance is, in the idealized case, rewarded and "disorder" (motivated actions in violation of the norm component of any institutional structure) negatively sanctioned.

Legitimation involves the appraisal of social actions within the context defined by the values common in the system of reference. If we take the cultural system to be definitive of a societal logic of intelligibility, the legitimation of actions involves their subsumption under social values in ways acceptable within the system of cultural symbols. This implies that norms are legitimized by higher-level values. The constraint that an institution's norms constitute comes from their relation to the society's values; in Durkheim's terms, the force of the norm lies in its relation to the collective conscience.[3]

When rules are legitimized by the society's value system, they are accepted as moral obligations. This means that legitimized norms are internalized in the personality of the actor and her adherence to them is not attributable to reason. Internal constraint involves the "exercise of moral authority through the *conscience* of the individual" (Parsons 1967:29).[4] At the social level this involves the institutionalization of the norms. When these norms have reference to differentiated institutional structures, their appellation is often used elliptically as synonymous with the entire institutional complex (values, norms, collectivities, and roles).

I mentioned above that not all social structures are institutions in this sense. In addition, it is essential to emphasize that much, if not most, human action is not social in this sense. If we simplify our discussion by referring solely to the norm components of social and cultural systems, social norms refer to the definition of right or wrong action, while cultural norms define sense or nonsense in human action; they are norms of intelligibility (cf. Durkheim 1965 : 30 and n. 20). Perhaps a simple example will clarify this distinction. If I meet a stranger on the street and suddenly draw a gun and shoot her, my action is in violation of both social and cultural norms; it is both wrong and unintelligible. If we are having a vicious fight over a position in a queue, and she calls me a fool, and I then draw my gun and shoot her, my action is wrong but intelligible. If I walk up to a stranger and suddenly begin shouting nursery rhymes in her ear, my action is culturally unintelligible but not socially wrong.

It is clear that in this sense much human action is culturally, not socially, mediated.[5] It is also clear that social action is also culturally mediated. This book is almost entirely concerned with social action, action within the context of social structures. I will have little need to refer to "subinstitutional," culturally but not socially mediated action.

My concern will be with social action, action that takes place in the context of social systems. Very simply, social systems are a series of interrelationships among actors which maintain a boundary and are open (interchange with an environment). "A boundary means simply that a theoretically and empirically significant difference between structures and processes internal to the system and those external to it exists and tends to be maintained" (Parsons 1961*b*: 36). Social systems are analytically defined, as we are concerned only with the social aspects of this interaction. For example, the human individual as a personality system and behavioral organism is seen simply as a support of social positions.[6]

> For any system of reference, functional problems are those concerning the conditions of the maintenance and/or development of the interchanges with environing systems, both inputs from them and outputs to them. Functional significance may be determined by the simple criterion of the dysfunctional consequences of failure, deficit, or excess of an input to a receiving system.   (Parsons 1968*b*: 460)

The same is true of functionally defined social subsystems; they maintain boundaries and are open. For units within these subsystems, the primary environments with which they interact are the other social subsystems.

Each of the four components of social action serves as the locus of a functionally defined social subsystem. It will help us to gain an intuitive understanding of these subsystems if we imagine a simple society, a small-scale monadic system in which there is no differentiation between units. Strictly speaking, this society would involve no role differentiation, and thus no sexual differentiation, and this reminds us that we are constructing it within our imaginations. In such a system there would be no difference between 1) values, as definitions of the desirable system, 2) norms, as expectations differentiated by function, and 3) the collectivity, as the focus of value implementation within concrete situations. Further, if we carry our abstraction to its limit and imagine away nonsocial factors—for example, what are from this point of view the idiosyncratic aspects of human personality—there is only one value, one norm, and thus one goal within our imaginary society; the actions of the collectivity are directed toward the implementation of that goal. Variations in external environments are irrelevant to the system, for in all environments it seeks to realize its goal, which is the same as its value, which is the same as its norm. In this situation there is no possible question about the allocation of facilities, for with one goal all facilities become instruments used in attaining it.

This absurd picture provides us with the basis to understand the functional imperatives Parsons has formulated. Any form of structural differentiation within our system—that is, the existence of a social system—will give rise to a discrepancy between values and norms. While values relate to the definition of the desirable for the entire system, and in the ideal case are internalized by each member of the system, norms specify expectations that are different for differentiated units within the system.

With the differentiation of values and norms it is easy to see that two separate functional imperatives must be present. The first concerns the maintenance of social values for all system units and the transmission of these values to all new system members. The second concerns the coordination and harmonization of the actions of the differentiated units. Parsons refers to the first as the function of pattern maintenance (L) and the second as integration (I). The first has reference to Durkheim's mechanical solidarity, the second to his organic solidarity (see Durkheim 1964; Parsons 1967: chap. 1; 1968a).

Actions with pattern-maintenance and integrative consequences concern processes internal to the system, L at an intraunit and I at an interunit level. Goals involve directional changes to meet discrepancies between the "needs" of system units in interchanging with some environment; this might be a social or cultural environment, or perhaps the personalities of system members. Collectivities are the foci of mobilization procedures to ensure attainment of collective goals, and it is safe to assume that any differentiation among collectivities will yield a differentiation among normative expectations regarding collective actions and collective goals. This division leads to the definition of the function of goal attainment (G).

The appearance of multiple goals within the system immediately makes apparent another functional problem, the allocation of means or facilities in the attainment of social goals. If two or more goals are present in a system the question of cost in the allocation of facilities is always manifest, although its content will be found to vary depending on the culture and social values of the system under examination. The functional consequences of processes concerned with the allocation of instrumentalities for goal attainment are referred to by Parsons as falling within the adaptive subsystem (A).

It should be obvious that these four functional areas correspond to the four structural units described above. Those social processes categorized within the L subsystem are concerned with the definition, transmission, maintenance, and transformation of social values. Processes within the I subsystem are involved with the regulation of the interaction among system units, and thus with the articulation of social norms. Mobilization for the attainment of social goals (G) occurs within collectivities; processes within the adaptive subsystem (A) are involved in the provision and allocation of facilities, including role performances, necessary for the attainment of collective goals.

While this parallelism is obvious, it is necessary to add a word of warning. These functional categories are used to classify social actions in terms of their consequences for the system under examination. Insofar as these actions are regularized or structured they are very likely to involve all four of the components of social action. A quotation from Parsons earlier in this chapter indicated that these structural units were components, not types, and it is essential to realize that the units categorized within each of the four functionally defined subsystems involve all four components, even though actions within the subsystems are differentiated, in part, by the orientation taken toward the components. In other words, while each structural unit involves all four components, these units may be differentiated in terms of the consequences of their actions for one or another of these components. While values, norms, collectivities, and roles are all relevant to processes within L, these processes possess a different relation to social values than processes categorized in A.

It is Parsons's belief that these four functional categories are useful in the analysis of all living systems, and most particularly in the analysis of what he calls "human action."[7] He divides action systems into four functional subsystems: L, the cultural system; I, the social system; G, the personality system; and A, the behavioral organism (Parsons 1977). These systems are viewed as independent but interdependent (1949:25 n. 2).

Our concern in the present work is at a different level of analysis. Almost the entire discussion is concerned with social systems, especially with societal systems. "A society is a type of social system, in any universe of social systems, which attains the highest level of self-sufficiency as a system in relation to its environments" (Parsons 1966:9ff.). While this brief definition is not, for many purposes, adequate, here it will suffice. At this level our concern is with the four societal subsystems; these are functionally defined analytical categorizations: A, the economy; G, the polity; I, the societal community; and L, which has no simple cognate.[8]

The question is often raised as to why there are only four subsystems identified. Here I will give only the most pragmatic answers. First, it is obvious that at least these four are necessary to provide an adequate analysis. This should be apparent even from the cursory discussion provided above. Second, it is necessary to have a determinate number of subsystems in order to begin an analysis of their interactions. Third, it is possible to specify innumerable aspects of a social system within these simple categories when they are nested within one another. Finally, and perhaps most important, these four categories seem to have great heuristic value. They provide a simple framework within which it seems possible to say important things about social action. After reading the present work the reader will be in a better position to judge for herself.

Parsons believes that institutions differentiate along functional lines; that is, that organizational complexes come to specialize in processes categorizable according to these four functions. Whether

this is correct or not, it is true that such complexes are often identifiable in terms of their primary consequences for the society.
Using normative structures as a shorthand, these are property-
contract in A, authority in G, stratification-legal systems in I, and
"religious"-kinship systems in L.[9] When we come to formulate
propositions dealing with these subsystems, we will find that dedif-
ferentiations between categorized structures are paralleled by a lack
of differentiation among the conditions generating, for example,
disorder in any one subsystem (see chap. 3, below; and Gould
1977).

The units categorized in each of these functional subsystems are
viewed as independent, yet interdependent (see Parsons 1949:25
n. 2). This means that they interrelate with one another in specifiable ways, but none is viewed as the determinant of any of the
others. This does not imply that each subsystem (speaking elliptically; we should in fact refer to the structures categorized within
each subsystem) stands in the same relation to all of the others, as
in, for example, certain neoclassical models of the economy. On the
contrary, the subsystems are viewed as standing toward one
another in a cybernetic hierarchy of control.

A cybernetic system is made up of at least two parts, one said to
be high in information, the other high in "energy." In this system
the first controls the second, while the second conditions the first.
Perhaps the easiest example to visualize is a thermostatically controlled heating unit. The thermostat controls the heating motor,
turning it on when the temperature falls below the specified level,
but the motor conditions the thermostat. The unit will function
only within a certain range—specified by the system's "energy"
potential. If the temperature falls below the motor's range, setting
the thermostat higher will have no effect on the controlled temperature. The thermostat controls, but only within the range of variation delimited by the energy potential of the heating motor.

Social systems are organized in the same general fashion. Some
units are higher in "energy," while others are higher in information.
Within a society, working toward the cybernetically controlling
system, the organization is as follows: the economy (A), the polity
(G), the societal community (I), and the latency subsystem (L). Thus
the economy is said to condition the polity—or less elliptically,
organizations in the economy provide adaptive resources to the
organizations in the polity, resources that are the conditions of

effective political action—and the polity controls the economy—political organizations lay down broad goals within which economic organizations function.

The utility of this type of conceptualization is manifest only when we are able to specify, in at least a rudimentary fashion, the resources provided by one subsystem to the others, and are able to understand these resources as the conditions or controls of social actions. Parsons has attempted to do this within the context of an interchange paradigm that shows the inputs and outputs from each subsystem to every other system. (This schema is discussed in chap. 2 below and in Gould 1976.) Here I want to make only one comment: the word *control* should not be allowed to become misleading. I use the term like Freud did when he spoke of the ego controlling the id. In his famous analogy, the ego is the rider on the horse, the id.

> The horse supplies the locomotive energy, while the rider has the privilege of deciding on the goal and of guiding the powerful animal's movement. But only too often there arises between the ego and the id the not precisely ideal situation of the rider being obliged to guide the horse along the path by which it itself wants to go.   (Freud 1965:77)

It can come to pass that the final decision as to where to go is made by the id, not by the ego. The word *control* is used in its specific cybernetic meaning, not as a synonym for *effective determinant*.

One of the concerns of this book will be the structural constraints on subsystem organization which limit the variability of its outputs to other subsystems, and thus condition or control the actions of those other subsystems within a range of variability which might contrast with the wishes of, for example, political decision makers.

We will find an additional set of concepts of great use in this task of analyzing structural constraints: the generalized media of communication. In Luhmann's terms, these media transmit selections from alter to ego.

> Media, then, solve the problem of double contingency through transmission of reduced complexity. They employ their selection pattern as a motive to accept the reduction, so that people join with others in a narrow world of common understandings, complementary expectations, and determinable issues.   (1976:512)

These media are symbolic mechanisms of communication, analogous in certain respects to language. A code defines for each medium what is acceptable as a message (money, power, influence [reputation], and value-commitments [love]) (Parsons 1969:pt. 4; Luhmann 1974, 1976, 1979; Loubser et al. 1976; Gould 1977). This code is the institutionalized base of the medium; for example, power flows within an institutionalized authority structure. The code defines the limits of acceptable "communication," of acceptable pressure of ego on alter.[10]

These media may be said to have value in exchange but not in use. For example, money may serve to mobilize resources, to be exchanged for use values, but money itself has no use value. Only in the limiting case, in which the symbolic content of the medium disappears, may it be said to have a value in use. In this instance it is reduced to its security base; for example, where power is reduced to force (Parsons 1967:chap. 9).

Within this context only one additional point need be made concerning these media. Their capacity to mobilize resources, not simply to reduce complexity but to enhance alternatives, is dependent on their stable functioning within their subsystem of reference (money in the economy, power in the polity, influence and reputation in the societal community, and value commitments and love in the latency subsystem). This stability is dependent, in the simplest terms, on a balance between inputs of real and symbolic resources to the subsystem of reference. A situation where the symbolic scope of the medium (factors controlling its operation) exceeds its resource base (conditioning factors) will involve an inflation of the medium; ego will have the "right" to pressure alter but this pressure will go unheeded. In situations where the resource base of the medium exeeds its symbolic scope, a medium deflation will occur. Here the term *pressure* takes on a more literal sense, and ego retains an illegitimate capacity to obtain her articulated goals. Both the controlling and conditioning factors may be nested within determinate social structures, so their variability will not be arbitrary.

We will discover in the following pages that when the media are systematically conceptualized within a functional model of societal structure and process, an analysis of their stability is crucial in explaining the genesis of social disorder. The following chapter begins this analysis.[11]

2. Systems Analysis, Macrosociology, and the Generalized Media of Social Action

> The object of our analysis is, not to provide a machine, or a method of blind manipulation, which will furnish an infallible answer, but to provide ourselves with an organized and orderly method of thinking out particular problems; and, after we have reached a provisional conclusion by isolating the complicating factors one by one, we then have to go back on ourselves and allow, as well as we can, for the probable interactions of the factors amongst themselves. This is the nature of economic thinking. Any other way of applying our formal principles of thought (without which, however, we shall be lost in the wood) will lead us into error.
>
> (Keynes 1965:297)

Theory utilizing functionally defined concepts formulates societal (social) universals, propositions intended to be valid for all societies. Premised on the understanding that any social system requires specifiable resources to function adequately, it asks about the consequences of the "withdrawal," for whatever reason, of one or more of the functionally defined inputs. No claim is made that the resources are always present; rather, questions are asked about the consequences of the relative dearth or plethora of one or another of these inputs.[1]

A theory of internal disorder may be formulated in the context of these simple questions. It is possible to enunciate a theory of subsystem output for each of the four functionally defined subsystems Parsons has identified. Determinant consequences occur when inputs to any of these subsystems fall out of balance. For example, if the "real" inputs to the polity exceed in scope the symbolic inputs to that subsystem, a deflation of power will occur. In this situation "governmental" coercion will be used in an attempt to maintain order. Power deflation will channel a possible social disorder toward the political subsystem.

A theory of internal disorder couples an analysis of imbalances affecting the generalized media of social action (including money, power, influence, and value commitments) with a theory of social strain. Each of the four functionally defined subsystems provides factors of production to the other three subsystems (facilities from A, motivational resources from G, normative justifications from I, and evaluative legitimations from L); an imbalance stemming from any of these inputs will generate social strain for the receiving subsystem. Depending on the location of strain, disorders will be directed at one or another of the components of social action (role relationships, collectivities, norms, and values). The disorder will be directed toward the affected subsystem depending on the location of the medium imbalance. For example, a strain affecting goals when coupled with a deflation of power will generate a political disorder (revolution or riot) directed to the collectivity structure of the polity. (The theory of internal disorder is presented in chap. 3.)

Using a functional theory of subsystem production will also allow us to assess the consequences of the uneven development of societal subsystems. Thus we will discover (in chap. 4) that one source of disorder within subsystems is the unbalanced development of, for example, economic and political structures. Any theory that allows for the differentiated and independent (even if interdependent) development of societal subsystems must formulate hypotheses concerning the limitations of their autonomy if the system as a whole is to reproduce itself. This chapter and the next formulate a theory that allows for the precise specification of those limitations.

In this chapter I use a modified version of the interchange paradigm developed by Talcott Parsons. In it I seek to accomplish two goals. Contrary to criticisms of Parsons's work, which often view it as a collection of concepts of no significance in the formulation of explanatory theory, this chapter demonstrates that those concepts may be interrelated to formulate highly generalized propositions about production in the four social subsystems. This task is consonant with Parsons's aspiration, but no one has previously accomplished it. Second, I show that the balance of inputs to each subsystem defines the criterion for the stable functioning of that subsystem. As I have already noted, later in this essay I use this finding to generate propositions concerning the consequences of

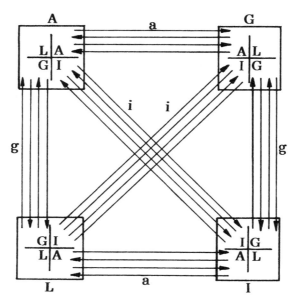

Figure 1. The Economy and Society paradigm.
Adapted from Parsons and Smelser, 1956:68.

uneven development among societal subsystems. Thus perhaps for the first time the notion of contradiction within social systems is given a determinant analytical meaning (see chap. 4).

Each of the four subsystems Parsons describes may be understood as providing resources enabling the entire system to meet a particular set of functionally defined exigencies; for example, economic resources enable a society to meet adaptive needs. This is a tautology, as units are categorized within the adaptive subsystem (at the societal level, the economy) because they have adaptive consequences for the system under examination. Further, the adaptive resources produced within the economy are allocated to the other three subsystems, enabling them to perform their respective tasks. Thus the adaptive subsystem provides adaptive resources to the adaptive subsectors of the goal-attainment, integrative, and pattern-maintenance subsystems.[2] Figure 1 illustrates this in a simplified version of the revised interchange paradigm (see Gould 1976). An adequate supply of these economic resources to the polity, for example, is necessary in order for it to fulfill its goal-attainment tasks.[3]

I will develop the theory of subsystem output within the context of an intrasocietal analysis. In this exposition I will not be concerned with interchanges between societies and will only be peripherally concerned with the interchanges between a society as a social system and the other three action subsystems (culture, personality, and the "behavioral organism") which make up a major portion of its nonsocial environment. Nor will I discuss questions of development in this context. Thus while I view the social system as open—spatially and temporally—in this chapter I have limited my perspective to the internal relationships within any one societal system, within the context of a given stage of development, and generally, from a short-term, comparative-static perspective.

There are a few simple distinctions that the reader should bear in mind when reading this chapter: (1) Each social subsystem is seen as processing factor inputs from the three other subsystems in order to produce product outputs. The factor inputs are "real" resources; that is, they are defined in terms of the medium centered in the sending subsystem. For example, labor capacity is a factor of economic production, derived from the latency subsystem. It is a form of commitment (the generalized medium centered in L), not a form of money (the generalized medium centered in A). Conversely, wages are paid to workers; they are a factor output from the economy to the latency subsystem. They are defined within a monetary metric; they are not a form of value commitment.

(2) Factor inputs to any subsystem are combined in a value-added process to generate product outputs. Product outputs are defined in terms of the medium centered in the receiving subsystem. Thus consumer goods are a "real" output from the economy, defined in terms of the economic commitment to produce; they are paid for with money, but they are not themselves a form of money.

(3) Factor inputs are, in general, interchanged for income, which is returned to its source subsystem in exchange for that subsystem's product output. Thus *income* may refer to both a factor output and a product input; for example, to wage income and consumer support, the latter being a form of income for economically productive units.

(4) The terms *input* and *output* are always relative to the subsys-

tem under examination. A particular output from one perspective is always an input from the converse perspective.

The presentation that follows is incomplete in numerous ways:
(1) I have not provided operational definitions of concepts, and further, many of the concepts are better termed search devices. They are less precisely stated with regard to inclusion and exclusion criteria than I am capable of now. This strategy has been adopted to avoid premature closure and, frankly, to enable "cheating." "Cheating" allows for the avoidance of premature falsification of a proposition by changing the categorization of the empirical materials examined. To take a crude example: If examining a specific revolutionary movement leads to the conclusion that the hypothesized determining (independent) variables for a revolutionary coup d'etat are present, yet the actual revolution falls outside the boundaries of the conceptualized dependent variable, it is permissible to redefine the notion of a coup d'etat to include the historical case. This redefinition allows for the apparent confirmation of the proposition.

The checks on this seemingly arbitrary procedure occur in examining the next coup d'etat similarly defined (and this definition must be rigorously drawn), and in determining if one's propositions lead to correct explanations and avoid incorrect ones.

The redefinition of variables is commonplace in survey research work. There "cheating" involves the redrawing of boundaries within the scales defining (i.e., measuring) variables, in order to strengthen statistical relationships. In survey research work, "cheating" is too often not recognized, as I would have it, as an aspect of theory construction; instead it is often erroneously viewed as an aspect of theory verification.

We must be wary of throwing out good propositions simply because we do not completely understand their exact conceptual references prior to digging into diverse empirical, historically specific materials (see DeJouvenal 1962:114). We should recognize that essays like this chapter, stated at high levels of generality, remain of limited value until used within many historical contexts. This chapter is intended as a guide to our research; the theory I enunciate will gain in precision as it is used and evaluated in diverse empirical situations. As it stands I think that it can (along with the theory of internal disorder presented in chap. 3) codify much research. For this to happen, however, we must be prepared to use it flexibly and to modify it in light of our empirical findings. (For more on "cheating" see the first few pages of chap. 3.)

(2) In addition, the theory identifies only the major determinants of subsystem output and ignores auxiliary determinants, as expressed, for example, within interchanges not under examination. Any predictions from the theory will therefore be crude and assume the ceteris paribus condition. The alleviation of this problem would entail the specification of numerous middle-range theories, a task that must be left undone in this context.

(3) Related to these problems and in part derived from them is my indication of only the direction of interrelationships, not their exact nature. Further specification involves processes of disaggregation, structural analysis, and historical particularization. While some specification occurs in the following chapters, I hope that this chapter is sufficiently precise and suggestive to generate error and solicit commentary.

Subsystem Inputs: Product

This essay is predicated on Parsons's realization that it is possible to treat diverse social processes as social (sub)systems. Parsons believed that it is possible to formulate propositions applicable to the functioning of all social subsystems. Each subsystem may be seen as a mechanism of production and the level and stability of this production should be explicable. In this chapter I specify a series of interrelationships between inputs to a given social subsystem and the product output of that subsystem. This theory may be stated at various levels of complexity and with various degrees of completeness. Here I will be brief and will therefore be very schematic. In introducing the theory my discussion is very abstract, focusing on the three product inputs to any societal subsystem.[4] Initially I seek to outline certain general implications that may be drawn from well-known and basic economic theory. Later in the chapter I make this discussion specific to the economy itself and then to the polity.

The level of media input ("expenditure") provided for each subsystem is dependent on the balance between saving (S), the amount of media withheld from current consumer support (C), and the amount invested (I), the amount of media used to add value to future production. (The appendix of the end of this chapter is a guide to

the symbols used; for a discussion of the media see the last pages of
chap. 1 and the references I have cited on those pages.) My central
concern will be to explicate the relationships between subsystem
production, output (Y) and various allocations in the spending of
subsystem-derived income (Y).

There are two perspectives that we might adopt regarding the
support the consumer provides the producing subsystem. In the
aggregate, her consumption input (what I call consumer support)
provides the resources, the income, enabling subsystem units to
generate their product. With regard to individual units, the consumer provides support to particular productive enterprises—
which can be analyzed at many levels of specificity; for example,
within the economy by industry, or by firm within the context of an
industry, or between industries providing interchangeable products. Products consumed (the product output from the subsystem of
reference to the consuming subsystem) are utilized within the context of the time period under analysis (although even with this
period delimited it is often difficult to draw an exact line between
consumer and investment goods).

Savings refers to the total income derived from a subsystem
withheld from current consumption, and so defines the total of subsystem resources that might be made available for purposes of investment. Savings is thus a measure of income not used in current
support of the subsystem, while investment refers to nonconsump-
tion utilization of income. Investment involves the allocation of
media resources (a form of support) toward the addition (over a
specifiable period) to the value of produced capital, produce reserved for further production.[5] Investment is therefore equivalent
to the total value of subsystem production minus product consumed. Likewise, since the value of subsystem output is equivalent
to subsystem income, actual investment will be equivalent to actual
savings. Both savings and investments are equivalent to total product minus consumed product; savings plus consumption is equivalent to subsystem-derived income ($C + I = Y$; $C + S = Y$; $I = S$).

Subsystem Product Inputs:
Specified to the Economy

Thus far, while using terminology drawn from the discipline of
economics, I have endeavored to couch my discussion in general

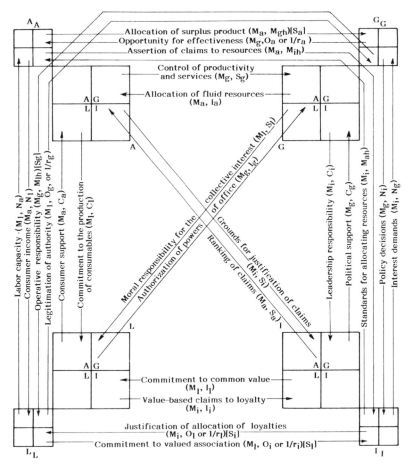

Figure 2. Revised interchange paradigm.

KEY:

All symbols are explicated in the appendix to this chapter or in footnote 52.

Inner exchanges are product exchanges; outer exchanges are factor exchanges.

The *first symbol in each parenthesis* refers to the medium in control of the output. The *second symbol* refers to the discussions within part two of this chapter. For example: "Value based claims to loyalty (M_i, I_i)" refers to (Influence, Investment input to integrative subsystem). The reader will note some overlap in terminology, e.g., "I," for integrative subsystem and investment. These overlaps were unavoidable unless standard conventions were thrown to the winds. Meanings should be clear within contexts.

terms, to encompass product inputs to all four societal subsystems. In order to make what follows a bit more concrete I will make these terms specific to the economy and identify their location within the interchange paradigm Parsons has developed. Figure 2 represents my reworking of Parsons's paradigm; its logic is explained in some detail in Gould 1976:470–78. Later, in elaborating the theory, I will return to the more general formulations.

Economic consumption (C_a) concerns the product input of monetarily defined resources to the economy from the latency subsystem ($L \rightarrow A$). Economic investment (I_a) refers to the monetary product input from the polity to the economy ($G \rightarrow A$), what Parsons has termed "allocation of fluid resources, financial." Economic saving (S_a) is a two-pronged concept, in the first instance referring to the "ranking of claims" between money allocated toward consumption and money withheld from current consumption and thus available for purposes of investment. Second, it concerns those resources actually made available within the context of an investment market, those resources not hoarded. Functionally the first occurs across the $I \longleftrightarrow A$ boundary as the product input to A, a definition of the rate of surplus value, the second across the $G \longleftrightarrow A$ boundary as the factor input to G, what I will call the allocation of surplus product.

The preceding is in need of clarification. First, for the reader familiar with Parsons: At the $G \longleftrightarrow A$ boundary, the product input from G to A concerns the allocation of liquid capital; the specification of funds in particular uses, including hoarded cash, occurs *within* the economy, at $A_G \longleftrightarrow A_A$ (see Parsons and Smelser 1956: 123ff., 210ff.). Saving is viewed as dependent on the allocation of income within the economy—as Keynes would have it—and is not specifically concerned with intralatency decisions. It involves, therefore, questions of business saving as well as saving by wage earners; it further involves the much-debated "forced saving," and saving enforced by the government. The question is one of solvency, the coordination standard of money in A, not pattern consistency, the coordination standard of commitments in L. Insofar as the former is relevant to latency decisions it is concerned with the allocation of funds within the consumer's budget; thus dissaving can occur within the context of the $A \longleftrightarrow L$ boundary. I assume, therefore, that hoarded cash remains within the economy, not within the latency subsystem.

For the reader familiar with Marx, I view the factor output from A to L as involving the monetary payment equivalent to the value of labor power (while recognizing the ambiguity of this social and cultural definition within the Marxian framework, and treating it as if it were applicable outside the structure of a capitalist economy; see Gould 1981a). Marx's variable capital is treated here, for simplicity's sake, as a segment of the money income allocated to L and returned in consumer expenditure. But not all consumption stems from what Parsons calls "wage income"—although all wage income is consumed. Some consumption derives from an allocation of surplus value (or more generally and thus more accurately in this context, "surplus product"), for example, from transfer payments drawn from government taxes or conspicuous consumption drawn from sources including profits and rents (revenue). Both of these examples involve an allocation of funds via G—(product) → A—(factor) → L, although various levels of dedifferentiation may be manifest. I have therefore labeled the A → L factor output "consumer income," a category including but extending beyond the monetary payment for labor power (or more generally, labor capacity).

The boundary interchange at I ⟷ A is obscure in the economic literature. The factor output from A to I clearly refers in part to economically necessary costs of sales and distribution; in part, however, it includes the costs of advertising and publicity that do no more than waste income; some part of these are costs of production and some are waste.[6] In any case, it does not involve the actual export of income across this boundary.

Total economic product is a summation of the real (nonmonetary) products at A → L and A → G (not all of which actually cross the boundaries), and total economic income is the sum of the factor (monetary) outputs at the same boundaries (not all of which actually cross the boundaries). The factor output from A to I concerns rational, nonrational, and irrational assertions of claims for funds, but not the actual provision of income (which involves the hiring of labor capacity and the actual export of surplus product). The product output from the economy to the societal community (A—[product] → I) concerns the justification of the allocation of claims within the societal community, between individualistic demands and more general loyalties. It does not concern the aggregate scope of economic production, only its possible uses.[7]

Thus at the I ⟷ A boundary questions of the scope of economic output are not at issue—although the scope can be and usually is influenced by what occurs at this boundary. Rather, issues concerning the allocation of available resources to "make good" the symbolic definition of scope are of paramount importance. (See the discussion of inflation and deflation further on in this chapter)[8]

Economic output is equivalent in value to total income, which is equivalent to consumption plus investment, and/or consumption plus savings. Thus within the context of the theory, income is either defined, across the I ⟷ A boundary, as available for (1) consumption that occurs across the A ⟷ L boundary (A—[factor]→ L—[product]→ A), or (2) savings at the G ⟷ A boundary (A—[factor]→ G + hoard, i.e., the allocation of surplus plus whatever is hoarded in A). In the simplest case all the surplus will be allocated to investment purposes; surplus value would be equal to value saved equal to value invested. In the more complicated reality, the government allocates certain of it to its own labor force as wage income (here there is a dedifferentiation between the economy and the polity). Certain of it is transferred to others for the purpose of consumption, certain of it is consumed by political groups (here there is a dedifferentiation between the polity and the latency subsystems),[9] and certain of it is utilized as revenue by capitalists, renters, and their agents (or their equivalents in noncapitalist social formations). Nonetheless, income is allocated for either consumption or savings. The equivalence between savings and investment appears over the A ⟷ G boundary in money allocated to the polity which is not utilized for purposes of consumption (either by transfer or by dedifferentiation); in Keynesian terms only the surplus of tax is properly called "savings," or more generally, the surplus not redistributed as consumer income.

It is now possible to explicate a simple model of income determination. At this point let us view investment as constant with regard to income, and view saving as positively related to income. In this case figure 3 can be constructed.

The intersection of the saving and investment curves determines the equilibrium level of economic output. This level of equilibrium output may also be seen by examining the intersection of the aggregate support curve ($C_a + I_a$) with the 45° line ($C_a + S_a$). The actual slope of the curves produced will be determined by the structural characteristics of the system under examination, as will the dis-

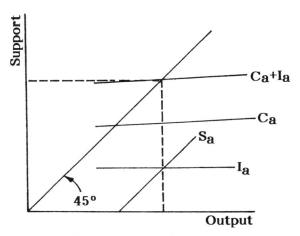

Figure 3. The determination of aggregate equilibrium output.

aggregated character of the terms used.[10] But in any case, the point of equality between savings and investment should determine the level of output and income.

We can make verbal sense out of this if we first imagine a case in which output exceeds the point marked by the equilibrium; here intended aggregate saving will exceed intended aggregate investment. Some firms will find themselves incapable of selling produced goods and inventories will begin to accumulate. These firms will be forced to curtail production, thus curtailing aggregate output and intended saving.

If output should fall below the presumed equilibrium point, intended investment would exceed intended saving. Here there will occur, for some firms, an involuntary disinvestment—for example, the selling of inventories. Aggregate intended support (consumption plus investment) will exceed output, generating pressures for an increase in output (and an actual increase, assuming the availability of the necessary factors of production). Only at the equilibrium point does aggregate support equal aggregate output; only here is a stable level of output specified.[11]

In the last paragraph mention was made of aggregate support, conceptualized as the addition of intended aggregate consumer support to intended aggregate investment to form the $C_a + I_a$ schedule in figure 3. The reader will note that the intersection of the $C_a + I_a$ curve with the 45° line determines an output equivalent to the equilibrium point where desired savings equals desired investment. Here total output equals total spending (aggregate demand equals aggregate supply), and aggregate savings equals aggregate investment.

In concluding this segment of the chapter I will introduce only one further economic concept, the multiplier. This term is used to denote the numerical coefficient that shows the ultimate change in output and income which results from a change in spending, for example, a shift upward in the investment curve. The general formula for this relationship is as follows:

$$\text{Change in output} = \frac{1}{\text{MPS}_a} \times \text{change in investment}$$

$$= \frac{1}{1 - \text{MPC}_a} \times \text{change in investment}$$

where MPS_a (Keynes's marginal propensity to save) indicates what percentage of an increase in income will be allocated to savings instead of consumption, and MPC_a (marginal propensity to consume) indicates what percentage of the increase in aggregate income will be allocated to consumption ($\text{MPC}_a + \text{MPS}_a = 1$). Unlike some economists I define these terms solely in terms of aggregate measures and make no psychological assumptions concerning them. Again, the actual arithmetical value of the curves is determined by the structural conditions within any given economy.[12]

A simple example shows that if the MPS_a is one-fifth, a $10 billion shift in the investment curve, at any level of output, would increase output by $5 \times \$10$ billion. Likewise, a shift upward in the savings curve of $10 billion will decrease output by $50 billion; this is equivalent to saying that a shift downward of $10 billion in consumer support, at any level of income, has occurred, with the consequent fall in output.[13]

The shift upward in the saving schedule is often referred to as the "paradox of thrift," for thrift ultimately yields both a decrease in output and, if we drop the assumption of a horizontal investment schedule—introducing a more realistic schedule showing a positive relationship between output and investment (fig. 4)—a decrease in aggregate savings. Conversely, an increase in the consumption

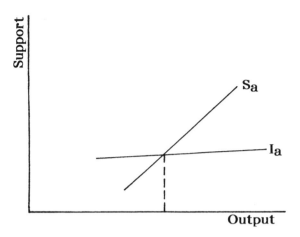

Figure 4. Equilibrium of saving and investment
showing both as positive functions of output
(income).

schedule—a decrease in the savings schedule—yields an increase in
output and an increase in savings. This paradox will reappear in my
discussion of the polity and is very important to bear in mind.

Subsystem Inputs: Factor

If we now execute a mental shift and go back to the level of
generality referring to any subsystem, it will be possible to elaborate on our theory. Here the terminology I have adopted is not
drawn from economics, and therefore this discussion will perhaps
be a bit more difficult to follow than the previous analyses. The
following discussion focuses on the factor inputs to any given
subsystem and the interrelationships among the six (product and
factor) inputs to that subsystem as they affect output.

One of these factor inputs involves a specification of intent, one
a definition of resources, and the last a definition of opportunity.
Three varieties of the first, constituent intent, are labor capacity,
interest demands, and policy decisions. Marshall defines "*labour* as
any exertion of mind or body undergone partly or wholly with a
view to some good other than the pleasure derived directly from the
work. And if we had to make a fresh start it would be best to regard
all labour as productive except that which failed to promote the

aim towards which it was directed, and so produced no utility"
(1920:65). Easton tells us that "a demand may be defined as an
expression of opinion that an authoritative allocation with regard
to a particular subject matter should or should not be made by
those responsible for doing so" (1965:38).[14] Parsons defines policy
decisions as "the process of altering priorities in such a way that the
new pattern comes to be binding on the collectivity" (1967:321).
All of these resources involve the specification of constituent
intentionality.[15] All, however, are objectified in exchange; all may
be generalized, and within the system we call "democratic capitalism," all are alienated.

I will call this factor of production (including labor capacity,
interest demands, and policy decisions) "constitutent intent" (N). It
involves a factor input to the subsystem of reference (for example,
an input of labor capacity to the economy [L—(factor) → A]), defined in "real terms," that is, defined in terms of a medium other
than that centered in the subsystem of reference. This input is the
"real" measure of value produced and embodied within the subsystem's intrinsic satisfiers, the product outputs purchased with
media input, with the product outputs of other subsystems.

It is important to recognize that in a capitalist social
formation—and here I paraphrase Marcuse's discussion of Hegel's
viewpoint concerning labor—the intention of the individual (any
unit under examination) fails to guarantee that her wants will be
attended to. A force alien to the individual, over which she remains
powerless, determines whether or not her needs will be fulfilled.
The value of the product of such intentional action is independent
of the individual and is subject to constant change (Marcuse 1960:
58).

To continue the paraphrase: The particular intention becomes a
universal one in the process of exchange; it becomes a commodity.
The universality also transforms the subject, the constituent, and
her individual activity. She is forced to set aside her particular facul-
ties and desires. Nothing counts but the distribution of the product
of intention; nothing counts but abstract and universal intention.[16]

It should be apparent that constituent intention is not a homo-
geneous quality; neither, however, are any of its specifications:
labor capacity, interest demands, and policy decisions. Just as certain
forms of labor capacity command more income—in certain social
situations—so with interest demands and policy decisions. An important task, one that lies beyond the boundaries of this essay,

is the development of a theory of distribution applicable to these inputs, disaggregated by unit (individuals, occupational groupings, racially or ethnically defined collectivities, classes, and so on). Here we will concern ourselves only with aggregate inputs of intent.[17]

The second factor input concerns the definition of allocable media resources available for actual utilization within the subsystem (M_h). It defines one component of the "demand for the media," the amount to be held in the context of various levels of acceptable opportunity within the system. A relatively high level of opportunity (defined by the third factor input) implies a relatively low inducement to part with the medium in question; the second factor input is thus concerned with the hoarding of media resources, that subsystem asset with the greatest liquidity.

In other words, the second factor input specifies the allocational priorities of the demand for the medium of reference. One aspect of this concerns the structure of the response (in the monetary case, the slope of the "speculative demand for money curve") to available opportunities (defined in monetary theory by "the interest rate"). Another component of "liquidity preference" is defined by the transactions demand for the medium (M_t) and is dependent on the level of output and income generated by the subsystem in which the medium is centrally located. An excess of produced output will be equivalent in value to the excess of the relevant medium demanded.

The last factor input concerns the availability of acceptable opportunities. The varieties of opportunity and the indices thereof differ according to the subsystem of reference. All concern, however, a definition of the directionality of attitudes toward production within the subsystem. All define the return expected for the provision of media to the subsector encompassing "banking" functions for the subsystem under discussion and all serve to balance the amount of each medium held with the amount of the medium supplied.

Subsystem Factor Inputs: Specified to the Economy

It is possible to specify each of these variables as factor inputs to the economy. The first, constituent intent, becomes, as has already been noted, the input of labor capacity (L—[factor]$\rightarrow$ A, N_a). The second, the definition of available resources, concerns what Parsons has labeled "standards for the allocation of resources" (I—[factor] → A), or, more precisely within economic theory, it partially defines the structure of the demand for money, the slope of the "speculative demand for money," that aspect of liquidity preference which is correlated with acceptable opportunities for the use of money (M_{ah}).[18]

The last factor input to the economy (G—[factor] → A) Parsons has labeled "opportunity for effectiveness." In specifying this within the conceptualizations available in academic economic theory we enter into an area of controversy and confusion. I am concerned with the determinants of investment and the demand for money. Here I can only summarize: one index of opportunity is contained in the notion of "the interest rate" (see Parsons and Smelser 1956: 63–64, 75–76), and it seems reasonable, at this level of schematism, to outline a model assuming one interest rate within the economy.

Second, opportunity must involve some measure of the possibility of profitable investment. This factor may itself involve a number of components, varying from wealth effects to the levels of security and return obtainable from banks and in various types of investments. Third, the level of opportunity can encompass questions related to political incentives to invest, for example, the availability of subsidies or tax incentives. More generally, such factors concern the political reallocation of income. Finally, at least from our restricted point of view, public policies may be of broader relevance than simple political incentives; these vary from one or another form of governmental regulation to overt (or covert) imperialism, involving, for example, direct or indirect opportunities for investment and the control of markets and materials. All of these define the relative position of units within the system.

In the following discussion I will deal with only one variable across this boundary: the interest rate, treated as an index of opportunity. An increase in the interest rate (r_a) measures a decrease in opportunity for productive, profitable investment (O_g). I assume, with tongue in cheek, that the other components of opportunity will appear in the measure of interest, which is a way of saying that implicitly they do appear in the slopes of the curves I will draw.[19]

It is possible to discuss the relationships among the six inputs to the economy in two market contexts: a production market and a

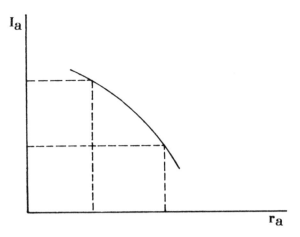

Figure 5. Investment and interest rate.

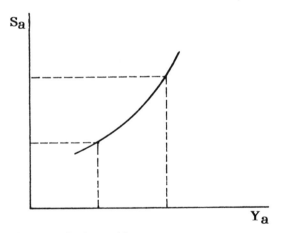

Figure 6. Saving and income.

money market. I will only make an abbreviated reference to a third market, for labor capacity. My comments are brief and nonrigorous, suited more to the inexact nature of the discussion that follow than to the (apparently) rigorous discussions in which economists engage.[20]

Figures 5 and 6 represent the relations between investment (I_a) and the rate of interest (r_a), and savings (S_a) and income (Y_a).

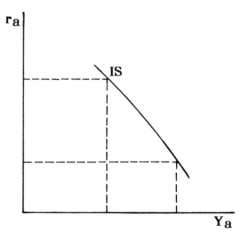

Figure 7. Combinations of Y_a and r_a which
yield an equality of I_a and S_a (given the I_a
$[r_a]$ and S_a $[Y_a]$ functions).

I assume unless I indicate otherwise the parameters M_a, the money supply, and P_a, the price level, as given. I often obscure distinctions between real measures and monetary measures.

Investment is taken as a decreasing function of the interest rate, an increasing function of opportunity; saving is taken as an increasing function of income. Figure 7 shows the Hicks IS curve. It represents the combinations of income and interest rates that equilibrate the real sector of the economy, those points where savings equals investment, where consumption plus investment equals income. It is downward sloping; as the rate of interest falls investment rises, income rises, and therefore saving rises.

Figures 8 and 9 represent the relations between the demand for money and income and the rate of interest. The transaction demand (M_{at}) is an increasing function of income; the demand for money to hold (M_{ah})[21]—comparable to Keynes's speculative demand—is a decreasing function of the interest rate. In other words, as opportunity increases (i.e., as the interest rate falls) it is reasonable to trade influence for money (at I $\longleftrightarrow$ A money becomes relatively more attractive). In addition, since the reward for relinquishing money (r_a) decreases, hoarding becomes more attractive.

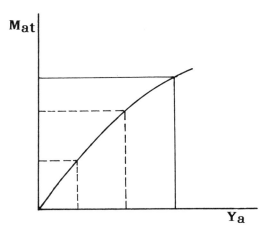

Figure 8. Transactions demand for money.

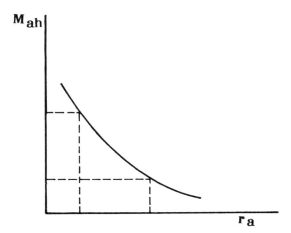

Figure 9. Demand for holding, "speculative demand" for money.

The LM curve, figure 10, represents those combinations of income and interest rate which result in an equilibrium of the money market, when the money supplied equals the money demanded ($M_{as} = M_{ad}$) and when the parameters remain as follows: the stock of money is fixed and the price level is given. The LM curve is upward sloping; at high levels of income more money will be re-

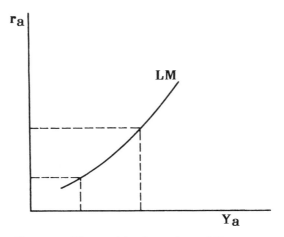

Figure 10. The combinations of r_a and Y_a
which yield an equality of M_{as} and M_{ad} for a
given stock of money and a given price level.

quired for transactions, leaving less for holding and necessitating a
rise in interest rates to induce those holding money to part with it.

Figure 11 shows the IS and the LM curves on the Y_a, r_a plane.
The intersection of the two curves displays the income and interest
rate that balances both the monetary and the real sectors. It identifies the level of subsystem output which equilibrates the factor and
product markets for the economic subsystem, the level at which
utilized real factors secured with money balance the input of
money, secured in exchange for real products, "intrinsic satisfiers."
The utility of this model is that it identifies, using only a few equations, key positions in the interrelationship of these inputs, and
specifies the importance of the variable of opportunity in linking
the two market contexts.

To display the model fully, especially the effects of monetary
considerations on the thus far excluded factor input, labor capacity
would require a detailed elaboration of the IS-LM model. For our
purposes it will be sufficient if we treat the demand for labor capacity as an increasing function of output. If we draw this relationship
in figure 12 below the IS-LM curves, the specification of output
determines the amount of labor demanded. A major thrust of Keynes's work was, of course, that at the equilibrium level not all labor
capacity available need be utilized.[22]

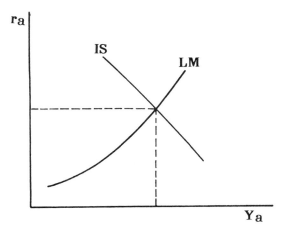

Figure 11. The equilibrium of money and production markets.

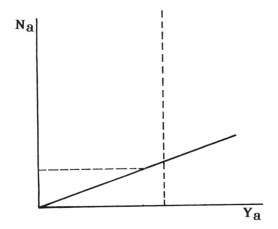

Figure 12. Labor and Income.

Variations in the parameters of the model can be indicated in the context of this analysis, and predictions generated as to the resultant effects on other variables. It should be remembered that the variables within the theory are mutually determined and that all of the variables are interdependent. With this in mind let us take the example of an increase in the propensity to invest, or a decrease in the propensity to save; the latter is of course equivalent to an increase in the propensity to consume, $1 - MPS_a$. In the former case, the I_a curve in figure 5 shifts upward and to the right; in the latter, the S_a curve in figure 6 shifts downward and to the right. In figures 7 and 11 these changes result in an upward and rightward shift of the IS curve, and an increase in r_a and/or Y_a—depending on the slope of the curves. Here, unlike the simple multiplier model outlined previously, part of the expansion is absorbed in higher interest rates and only part in an increase in income.[23]

It is also possible to vary the supply of money in an IS-LM analysis.[24] Very simply, an increase in the supply of money (or a downward shift in the M_{ah} schedule) will pull the LM curve out and to the right; such an increase yields an increase in Y_a and a decrease in r_a, as well as yielding an increase in investment, consumption, and saving.

Subsystem Product Inputs:
The Polity

I have now outlined a general framework within which it is possible to discuss subsystem output as it relates to the interrelationships among factor and product inputs to the subsystem. To do this I generalized the basic national income model used in contemporary macroeconomics, making it abstract enough to encompass all four societal subsystems. Then I placed the economic case within the social system interchange paradigm I've taken and modified from Parsons (see Gould 1976:470–78). I will now make the theory specific to the polity, and show how it is possible to generate propositions of some interest concerning the inputs to that subsystem. The discussion will be easier to follow if we begin by looking at the three product inputs to the polity: political support ($I \rightarrow G$, C_g), control of productivity and services ($A \rightarrow G$, S_g), and authorization of powers of office ($L \rightarrow G$, I_g).

In the aggregate, political support (a form of consumer support, C) concerns the product input (defined in terms of power) to the polity at the $I \longleftrightarrow G$ boundary. It provides the resources, the income, enabling political units to regenerate consumed products. With regard to individual units, the consumer provides support to individual collectivities, for example to one or another party in an election. This is the provision of diffuse yet contingent support for units assuming leadership responsibility. The source of support derives from the factor output from G to I, policy decisions.[25] Thus the scope of support in any given time period is delimited by the income of power from the polity to the societal community. Subsequently this support can be expanded, but the primary leverage for expansion is investment, which often stems from the political "banking system," located in L, not in either G or I (see Parsons 1967:338–45).

Political investment (I_g) refers to the power (product) input from the latency subsystem to the polity. This input has been labeled by Parsons "the legality of powers of office." I change this phrase to "authorization of powers of office," for I am concerned not so much with delimiting the code of the political authority system but rather with the actual specification of the permission to use authority within classifiable types of situations. While the definition of the particulars of usage is an intrapolity decision, the investment input to the polity delimits the scope of discretion within which authorized units may act.[26]

Both political consumption and investment (authorization) involve the allocation of subsystem-derived income in support of units classified within the polity. Consumption refers to the satisfaction of "immediate wants" (within the time period of reference), and investment involves the allocation of power in the generation of legitimate political institutions to be used in the production of future outputs.[27]

Political saving (S_g) is dependent on the allocation of income within the polity, not within the societal community. It refers to the total of political income withheld from the societal community and thus not available for current consumer support. Like economic saving, S_g is a two-pronged concept; first, referring to the definition of the total of subsystem resources that might be made available for investment, and second, defining those resources actually made available for political authorization (I_g), those resources not hoarded. The first occurs across the G $\longleftrightarrow$ A boundary as the product input to the polity. It specifies the economic resources (services and productivity) over which the polity can exercise political control. The second occurs across the L $\longleftrightarrow$ G boundary as the factor input to L, the assumption of operative responsibility.

Control over services and productivity indicates the allocation of political control over economic processes, exchanged for inputs of monetary resources. "This has often been put as presenting to political organization the 'problem' of *mobilization* of adequate manpower [and economic productivity] to meet its obligations in the society or attain its collective goals" (Parsons 1969:479). Such resources are used in the assumption of operative responsibility within the system, unless the input is hoarded. A resource is hoarded "when qualified members of the labor force simply refuse to accept 'opportunities for effectiveness' [within the polity] and remain passive so far as contributions to collective goal-attainment are concerned" (Parsons 1969:480). If a resource is hoarded, available economic productivity is not allocated in the attainment of collective goals.[28]

The reader conversant with the Parsonian interchange paradigm will have noted modifications across the G ⟷ A boundary. In this presentation the control of both productivity and services is relinquished across the product interchange. The control of productivity indicates "not managerial control of particular plants ... but control of a share of general productivity of the economy through market mechanisms, without the specification of particulars" (Parsons 1967:349; this definition may be expanded to include social formations where the economy is not controlled by market mechanisms). I do not mean to refer to a factor of effectiveness, but to the "political control" (via mechanisms of banking and credit, among others; see Parsons 1967:304) over productive capacity and over the increased potential for generating economic output (see Parsons and Smelser 1956:72; Parsons 1969:487–88, for Parsons's views). This product output includes control over those components of services which economists have come to label "human capital," but I do not view all services as passing into the control of the polity.[29] Rather a service is in the first instance an economic, occupational category.[30] In the second place services should be categorized in terms of their consequences, or function, implying in many instances a dedifferentiation in the noneconomic case;[31] only those services that pass into the control of the polity are considered at this boundary.

The control of productivity and services is granted in exchange for the monetary investment input—at the product boundaries— while the provision of opportunities is exchanged for the allocation of monetarily defined economic surplus—at the factor boundaries.[32] The input of surplus is a factor component of effectiveness, providing monetary resources to the polity. One would predict, therefore, that opportunity would not be allocated equally between units, across the G $\longleftrightarrow$ A boundary, unless those units are "monetarily equal."[33]

Total political product is the sum of the real (nonpower) products at G $\rightarrow$ I and G $\rightarrow$ L (even if not all of this output actually crosses these boundaries), while total political income is the sum of the factor (power) outputs at the same boundaries (not all of which cross the boundaries). Thus political power is divided between power used in current policy decisions (G—[factor] $\rightarrow$ I) and power withheld and potentially available to construct the political infrastructure (political capital). Total investment (I_g), political authorization (L—[product] $\rightarrow$ G), is limited by the scope of savings (S_g), operative responsibility (G—[factor] $\rightarrow$ L). In each period, in other words, political income and output are equivalent to the sum of current consumption (C_g), political support for current policy decisions (I—[product] $\rightarrow$ G), and investment, the authorization of powers of office (L—[product] $\rightarrow$ G).

Actual authorization (I_g) is equivalent to actual operative responsibility (S_g). The extent of *ex post* investment is defined by the actual scope of the political control of economic resources (S_g). It should thus be apparent that political income is equivalent in value to political investment plus political consumption and/or political consumption plus political saving. Political income is allocated either for consumption (G—[factor] $\rightarrow$ I—[product] $\rightarrow$ G) or as saving (G—[factor] $\rightarrow$ L), to be utilized for investment (L—[product] $\rightarrow$ G) or hoarded in G, as saving and as investment.

It is now possible to present a simple theory of the determinants of political production and income. Political production in a specifiable period is the sum of the real (nonpower) outputs from the polity to the societal community and the latency subsystem—leadership responsibility and moral responsibility for the collective interest. The factor outputs from the polity which return as income supporting political action are operative responsibility (to L) and policy decisions (to I), both measured in terms of power. The two product outputs from the polity are the intrinsic satisfiers exchanged for incomes of support (consumption = political support [from I] and investment = authorization [from L]).[34]

Parallel to the presentation of the economic model let us begin discussing political relationships by treating investment (authorization) as constant with regard to income, and saving (control over productivity and services in operative responsibility) as positively related to income. Figure 13 represents these relationships.[35] Within the context of any single stage of political development an increase in income will yield a greater proportional increase in savings; that is, the MPS_g (marginal propensity to save) will be greater than the APS_g (average propensity to save). The reason for this is that an increase in the scope of political output will necessitate the greater proportional allocation of power resources to police functions, paralleled by a greater input of authorization for powers of office. The intersection of the authorization and savings curves,[36] and the intersection of the aggregate support (authorization plus political support) curve with the 45° line $(C_g + S_g)$, is the equilibrium condition determining the level of political output.

Once it is formulated in this fashion, it is easy to make verbal sense out of my hypothesis. Assume for a moment that output exceeds the place marked by the equilibrium condition. In this case intended aggregate saving will exceed intended aggregate investment; that is, the provision and utilization of economic resources in the assumption of operative responsibility (and not transferred to the societal community) will be greater than the authorized powers of office. In this case the assumed level of leadership responsibility will not meet with the requisite level of support. Thus, in a situation analogous to the economic, some political production will be curtailed, decreasing the level of aggregate output and intended saving. That is, a decrease in the input of politically controlled economic resources and in the assumption of operative responsibility will occur.[37]

If output and income fall below the hypothesized equilibrium condition, intended investment, authorization, would be in excess of intended saving, the assumption of operative responsibility. In other words, aggregate intended support (consumption plus investment, political support plus the authorization of powers of office) will exceed output, and will generate pressures for an increase in output. Only at the equilibrium condition will aggregate intended output be equal to aggregate intended support; only at this point will an equilibrium be generated.

This model, like the macroeconomic model, is constructed so that intended aggregate political support plus intended aggregate authorization form the $C_g + I_g$ schedule in figure 13. The 45° line

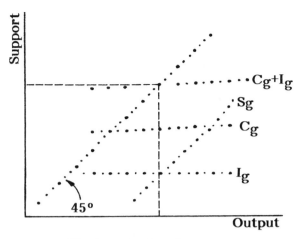

Figure 13. The determination of aggregate
equilibrium political output.

measuring aggregate income, support plus saving, intersects the
aggregate support line at the point where desired saving equals
desired investment; here total output equals total support, and
aggregate saving equals aggregate investment.

Without the generation of ratio scales measuring power, a strict
numerical analysis of the multiplier becomes impossible. If I outline
the form it would take, it is because the approximation is theoretically interesting, even if difficult to carry out in practice. (Once the
graphs are drawn, lines approximating the actual data can, of
course, be fitted to the distributions.) Here the multiplier can be
viewed as the numerical coefficient approximating the ultimate
change in output and income which results from a change in support, for example, a shift upward in the investment curve. The
general formula for this relationship is identical to the economic
multiplier:

$$\text{Change in output} = \frac{1}{\text{MPS}_g} \times \text{change in investment}$$

$$= \frac{1}{1 - \text{MPC}_g} \times \text{change in investment}$$

where MPS_g indicates what percentage of the increased income will
be allocated to savings (operative responsibility) instead of con-

sumption ($MPC_g + MPS_g = 1$). As in the economic case, I define these terms in aggregate measures, making no psychological assumptions. The actual arithmetical values of the curves—as approximated—will be determined by the structural properties of the polity under examination.

The important point for us to note is that an increase in the scope of authorized power generates an increase in the scope of political output far greater than might appear at first glance. The reverberations of this increase in political investment are magnified in inverse proportion to the new power income allocated for operative responsibility, MPS_g. The less allocated toward contingent consumer support (political support), the less the magnification of the increase in the scope of defined powers.

As in the economic case, there is a political "paradox of thrift." A shift upward in the saving schedule will decrease output a commensurate amount. In other words, a simple increase in the political control of economic resources for police functions will decrease, not increase, output. Such a shift will also yield, where investment varies positively with output, a decrease in aggregate saving. Conversely, an increase in the consumption schedule ($I \rightarrow G$), a decrease in the saving schedule ($G \rightarrow L$), generates an increase in output and an increase in aggregate savings.

It is worth pausing for a moment to draw two conclusions from this analysis. We are in a position to begin evaluating two of the most important problems of classical normative theory in light of the results of a systematic body of theory, and to help explain a wide variety of empirical findings in the process. In the first instance, the analysis above provides the basis for understanding the foundation for the expansion of state power. Institutional transformations, including those brought on by revolutions, may result in increases of effective support which reverberate within the system owing to the "multiplier effect." This circumstance will be discussed in chapter 9 of this book.

Although the simple use of organizational and often repressive resources in maintaining order may in the short run yield an increased "acceptance" of authority, in the longer run it will yield a deterioration in the scope of political output and a diminution of the very powers those in authority sought to maximize (see chap. 5, below). While there is no way within this aggregate model to identify the effect of an increase in political saving, relative to other uses of power, on specific units in the system, it is possible to say that for the entire political system the morality that preaches "law and order" is, in the long run, inimical to order through law. The "conservative" who emphasizes "law and order" will under certain conditions get it, although she will narrow the scope of what is politically enforceable; in other conditions she may create a deflation of power severe enough to generate political disorder.[38] Wisdom lies with those who attempt to alleviate the disorder through the generation of political support through meeting the interest demands of the constituencies involved.

Subsystem Factor Inputs: The Polity

It is now possible to introduce the factor inputs to the polity. The first concerns the "specification of intent"—interest demands, the factor input from the societal community (I—[factor] $\rightarrow$ G, N_g). Interest demands

> is conceived to be the primary basis on which leadership elements of the polity are put in a position, through the use of their influence, to appeal for political support.... Thus we conclude that knowing constituents' wants, as well as partly "shaping them" through leadership initiative ... is a crucial factor in political effectiveness. As such, however, it must be combined, with some approach to "optimization," with other factors ... From this analysis it is perfectly clear that it is neither desirable nor realistically possible for political leadership, in governmental ... collectivities, to attempt to "satisfy" all demands or wishes of its constituents. (Parsons 1969:490–91)

Thus interest demands are a factor input of influence definitive of the value of the polity's product. As in the case of labor capacity, the individual unit's intent does not guarantee the satisfaction of her desires. The structure of control over output differs markedly in various types of polities and so the degree of the alienation of intent differs depending on the social formation under examination.

The second factor input to the polity concerns the allocation of economic, monetarily controlled resources (A—[factor] $\rightarrow$ G, M_{gh}). In a capitalist social formation this includes a component of surplus value, which provides the primary economic basis for political action. But in capitalist social formations it may also include a component of the workers' value of labor power. In the latter case, services provided by the state partially define the bundle of resources included in the definition of the value of labor power (see Gould 1981*a*). In both of these cases the primary vehicle for this input is taxation.

This second factor input thus specifies the monetary resources available to finance political output. It defines the structure—in the figures, the slope—of one aspect of the demand for power as a medium of exchange, that aspect that responds to fluctuations in opportunity and legitimacy. If political legitimacy is high it is reasonable to trade money for power and thus more power is demanded. In addition, there is a "transactions demand for power" (M_{gt}) dependent on the level of output generated by the polity. An excess of political product will be equivalent in value to the excess of power held.

The final factor input delimits the evaluational status of the political system and thus serves as an index of attitude toward the legitimacy of the system (L—[factor] $\rightarrow$ G, O_g). There are many possible indices of legitimacy; perhaps the most important is the rate of perceived alienation from the values implemented within the political system (r_g).[39] An increase in political alienation marks a decrease in legitimacy for the political structures. The rate of political alienation serves as an index of political legitimacy in much the same way that the rate of interest serves as an index of economic opportunity.

The rate of alienation is indicative of the value of the stock of political capital or powers of office within the polity. Greater alienation, relative to any office, implies that the true domain of power (the number of persons who view pronouncements as binding or the scope of pronouncements accepted as binding) is lessened. This implies an increase in the number of units adopting a calculating attitude toward the political order, and thus an increase in the rate of alienation indicates that political productivity must increase in order to justify the current level of political authorization. Conversely, as the rate of alienation falls, less payment is required to induce authorization of powers, but because power becomes more valuable, more of it will be hoarded. The rate of alienation is therefore, as we will see below, the link balancing the market for power and the market for political product.[40]

As in the case of the economy I will discuss the interrelationships

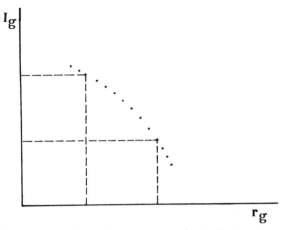

Figure 14. Political investment (authorization)
and the rate of alienation.

between the discussed political variables in two "market" contexts:
a production and a power "market." I will only make a passing
reference to the "market" for constituent intent, interest demands.

Figure 14 represents the relations between authorization (I_g) and
legitimacy (O_g); in order to avoid confusion and to maintain analogous relationships to the economic case, O_g will be represented in
the figures by an index of political alienation, r_g, which varies inversely with legitimacy. Authorization decreases with an increase in
alienation and increases with an increase in granted legitimacy.

Figure 15 displays the relationships between the assumption of
operative responsibility (S_g) and income (Y_g). Unless indicated
otherwise the parameters M_g, the amount of power in circulation,
and P_g, the ratio of power to the capacity to secure binding obligations and therefore political intrinsic satisfiers, are given.[41] The
scope of assumed operative responsibility increases with political
income.

Figure 16 is a modified version of the IS curve, as specified to the
polity. It represents the variations of income and legitimacy which
equilibrate the real sector of the polity. The curve shown is downward sloping; with increases in opportunity (increases in legitimacy, decreases in the rate of political alienation), investment rises
(the scope of authorization is enlarged), the scope of output and
income broadens and therefore saving increases (the scope of

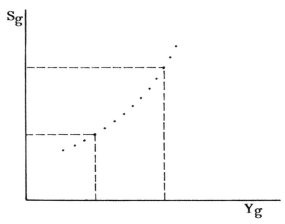

Figure 15. Political saving and political income.

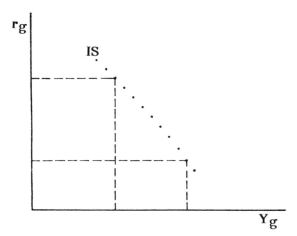

Figure 16. Combinations of Y_g and r_g which yield
and equality of I_g and S_g (given the I_g [r_g] and S_g [Y_g]
functions).

assumed operative responsibility grows). Figure 16 does not identify any single level of equilibrium; rather it demarcates a series of
positions where political saving balances political investment, a
series of possible political outputs. To find a single equilibrium
position requires a discussion of the market for power.

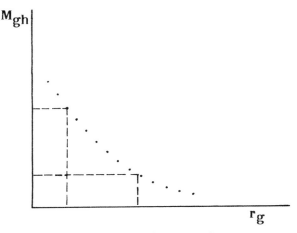

Figure 17. Allocation of surplus economic resources.

Figure 17 displays the relation between the definition of available resources and the level of opportunity. The input of monetary resources (M_{gh}) varies positively with the level of legitimacy, negatively with the rate of political alienation (r_g). As political opportunity increases it becomes more attractive for units to trade off monetary resources for the access to power; power becomes a more secure resource to hold, and increases in relative value. As the level of legitimacy rises, the level of hoarded power grows.

As legitimacy and opportunity grow, less positive sanction is needed to induce units to make power available for transactions. The autonomous level of investment varies positively with the level of legitimacy; as legitimacy increases, investment increases. Also, power becomes more valuable relative to money as its legitimacy grows, and the trading of money for power increases. This power is held, not made available for transactions or made available within the investment market. It becomes apparent that legitimacy symbols set a balance between production and power markets, as we will see in figure 20.

If the reader refers back to the discussion of the economy she will find a strikingly parallel set of circumstances. However, in the economic case it is influence that is traded for money. An increase in the flow of influence generates an increase in the demand for money to hold. In that instance as in this, I categorize hoarded media in the

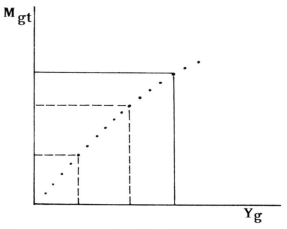

Figure 18. "Transactions demand" for power.

system of immediate reference: money in the economy, power in the polity.

Figure 18 represents the transactions demand for power (M_{gt}) as increasing with income. An increase in income from the polity will generate an increase in the number of political transactions and thus an increase in the demand for power, to be utilized in those transactions.

The LM curve in figure 19 displays those combinations of income and legitimacy which result in an equilibrium of the power market, where the total amount of power equals the power demanded ($M_{gs} = M_{gd}$), and where our parameters are a fixed amount of power controlled and a fixed ratio between the amount of power controlled and the capacity to secure the available intrinsic satisfiers. The LM curve slopes upward. At high levels of income more power is required for transactions leaving less for holding, yielding a decrease in opportunity (the legitimacy of the available fringe opportunities will be less secure than those closer to the center of the power system) and an increase in return for parting with money. In other words, an increase in the rate of political alienation implies that a greater reward will have to be offered to individuals in order to induce them to make held power available within the investment market.

Figure 20 represents the political IS-LM curves. On this figure

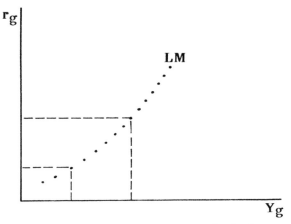

Figure 19. For a given stock of power and a fixed ratio between the amount of power controlled and the capacity to secure available intrinsic satisfiers, the combinations of r_g and Y_g which yield an equality of M_{gs} and M_{gd}.

the intersection of the two curves identifies the level of political output and political legitimacy which equilibrates the two market systems. Figure 20 also identifies the aggregate measure of interest demands which will be fulfilled; the output specified by the IS-LM curves determines the scope of interest demands met, but not, as I have mentioned before, which interest demands are fulfilled.[42] Figure 20 thus specifies the level of subsystem output which exemplifies a balance between the factor and product inputs to the polity.

It is possible, of course, to vary the parameters in the model and to generate predictions of effect upon the other variables. As in the economic case, all of the variables are mutually determined and interdependent.

An increase in the inducement to invest, the aggregate level of authorization at any level of opportunity, or a decrease in the propensity to save, a smaller assumption of operative responsibility at any level of output and consequently the provision ·and utilization of a relatively greater proportion of income for consumption, or political support, involves the following reactions: In the former case the I_g curve in figure 14 shifts upward and to the right; in the

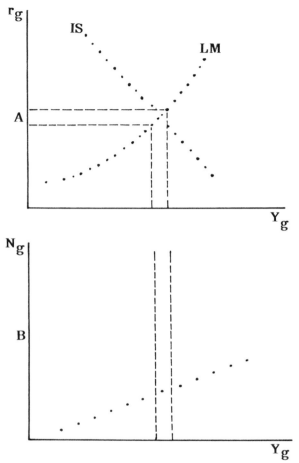

Figure 20. (A) The equilibrium of power and production markets; (B) Scope of implemented interest demands.

latter case the S_g curve in figure 15 shifts downward and to the
right. In figures 16 and 20, either of these changes would result in
an upward and rightward shift in the IS curve, yielding an increase
in r_g and/or Y_g, a decrease in political legitimacy and/or an increase
in output (depending upon the slope of the curve). Unlike the simpler multiplier model proposed previously, part of the expansion of
output and income will be swallowed by a growth in the sense of
political alienation, a decrease in legitimacy.

In the short run the decrease in legitimacy can be countered with an increase in the amount of power within the system. This could involve, for example, a redefinition of the assets that might come under political control or an inclusion of previously excluded persons within the jurisdiction of control. In any case, it involves an increase in the generalized capacity to command binding obligations, and if the power is not inflated, to secure the performance of these obligations.

An increase in the amount of power within the system or a decrease in the M_{gh} schedule (the level of economic surplus provided to the polity at each level of legitimacy) shifts the LM curve (in figs. 19 and 11) out and to the right, yielding an increase in Y_g and a decrease in r_g, and in addition, an increase in the authorized powers of office, in the level of political support, and in the assumed control of productivity and services in the assumption of police powers. These effects retain their meaning only if an inflation of the medium can be avoided. It is to this issue that I turn in a few paragraphs.

As should be apparent, the historical analysis of any society might place it anywhere along the curves I have drawn or might affect the shape of those curves. Let me note two examples whose economic analogies have received much attention. The first is the so-called "classical case," wherein there are relatively high levels of investment and saving and the relationship between a decrease in legitimacy and the demand for power is low. In this situation an increased inducement to invest or consume will result in little change in income and a relatively large change (downward) in the legitimacy of authority (an increase in the rate of political alienation). On the other hand, an increase in the amount of power will yield a large effect in the scope of political income and output, as shown by the movement of the LM curve outward and to the right. This situation is typified graphically when the equilibrium point lies along a nearly vertical segment of the LM curve; that is, where the IS curve intersects with the LM curve along a nearly vertical segment of the latter.

The converse case is represented for the economy in the Keynesian discussion of the "liquidity trap"; here levels of investment and saving are low, unmet interest demands generally high. The equilibrium point is found on the nearly horizontal section of the LM curve, or the entire curve may be horizontal, and thus a movement upward in the authorization schedule (a movement of the curve, not along it) will result in little increase in alienation and a great increase in income. This would involve an upward and rightward shift of the IS curve. An increase in the supply of power (a shift to the right in the LM curve) would involve only a slight increase in income, and a slight reduction in the level of political alienation.[43] Thus the impact of an expansion of power might well differ markedly according to the historical context.

Inflation and Deflation

In discussing imbalances in the media I am again entering an area of much controversy in contemporary economic theory. I will once again limit my arguments to basic points generally accepted in the context of short-term analysis. Rather than taking the space to elaborate on the specifics of the economic case, I will focus on a discussion of the polity, interspersing comments applicable to all the generalized media.

A medium may be said to be inflated when its symbolic scope exceeds or is growing more rapidly than its capacity to command real resources. Such a situation will be manifest where the accepted credit standing of the units commanding the medium exceeds their capacity to control the income of the medium withheld from current consumption, where investment exceeds savings, or where the total of aggregate support exceeds total real output. "True inflation" is the situation where an increase in support produces no increase in output, but simply raises the cost per unit output in full proportion to the increase in the scope of support (see Keynes 1965:303). At this point an expansion of the amount of the symbolic medium will produce no increase in real output and will be purely inflationary.

Power inflation is the situation wherein the scope of the powers of office exceeds the capacity to implement binding decisions; this is a situation where the polity would provide relatively less in intrinsic satisfiers for the same amount of power. Power inflation will be manifest if granted authorization of the powers of office exceeds control over economic resources by the polity and if in a situation of rising support the potential to assume operative responsibility is held constant, decreases, or rises more slowly.

Support inflation may be portrayed within the context of the IS-LM diagram, although the portrayal is awkward. Therefore I

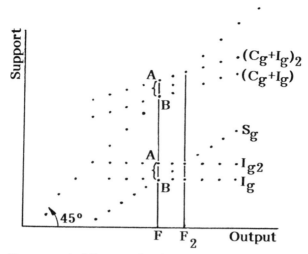

Figure 21. A shift upward in the political investment schedule and the inflationary gap.

begin with a simple example using the product interchange model. In figure 21 we see political consumption, investment, and savings plotted on an income and expenditure axis. Point F marks the equilibrium level of output and also the level of interest demands fulfilled.

Let us assume that there occurs an increase in the political investment schedule, owing for example to a constitutional expansion of the powers of selected offices.[44] This is shown by the upward movement of the aggregate support curve, $(C_g + I_g)_2$, and the investment curve, I_{g2}. Output will increase to F_2 and accepted interest demands to F_2. It is possible that both F and F_2 mark situations comparable to "full employment equilibria," where the difference between the interest demands $(F_2 - F)$ is equivalent to demands induced by the polity, a situation of "low full demand" and "high full demand." (In the economy this is a situation in which persons are induced into the labor market). It is also possible, however, owing to circumstances explicable only in an examination of the societal community, that F marked the total level of interest demands extractable from the public. Stated differently, F_2 would mark a situation where certain outputs from the polity were not adequately justified by inputs of demand (see Parsons 1969:490). In this instance we confront an inflationary gap (A − B), a situation where the excess of support will generate an inflationary spiral until curtailed by an increase of political alienation. This spiral can be halted (this can be plotted on fig. 21 but is not shown) by a decrease in the political support schedule and an increase in the saving schedule (the political control of economic resources in the assumption of operative responsibility). In the latter case the new point of intersection would be to the left of F_2; the inflationary gap would close when the level of output once again reached point F.

An expansion of power will generate similar inflationary pressures. If, on figure 20, a shift in the LM curve out and to the right increases political output beyond the level adequately justified by the input of interest demands, an inflationary push will be generated. Assuming a situation of true inflation, with no real increase in output, the fall in the value of power would be halted when the decrease in symbolic value approximated the increase in the amount of power.[45]

If both an expansion of power and a shift upward in the inducement to invest curve occur simultaneously, the pressures are compounded. This latter case is not unlikely; an increase in the political authorization schedule will generate an increase in output (even assuming no inflation) only by leading to an increase in political alienation. A remedy for the latter might be found in the increase in the amount of power within the system, perhaps through an extension of the franchise. Clearly a more complete model would specify the conditions under which any medium would undergo expansion, and just as clearly, such an explanation would broaden our focus beyond a single subsystem.

The interchange model provides us with a framework within which to trace certain effects of a medium inflation. The effects of an inflation of power are manifest in the power outputs from the polity. Policy decisions are called into question; if the medium is inflated their bindingness is dubious; and further, if the medium is inflated the capacity of politically categorized collectivities to maintain effective organizational control and, in the extreme, to wield effective force, the security base of power (see Parsons 1967: chap. 9), is also called into question across the G→L boundary, in the implementation of operative responsibility. The ability of the government to enforce its decrees is doubtful when power is inflated, when its symbolic scope exceeds its effective base. (Examples of these situations are analyzed in chaps. 4 and 5, below.)

A simple example will also display the value of the interchange paradigm in this regard. An inflation of money will involve an alteration in the A factor input to G. Ceteris paribus, as money inflates it becomes less valuable relative to power, thus it is more likely to be traded off for power. The M_{gh} curve will shift upward, moving the LM curve in and to the left. This will generate a decrease in Y_g, political income, and an increase in r_g, the rate of political alienation, and more generally, a contraction of the entire political subsystem. Knowledge of the conditions in one subsystem often enables us to generate predictions concerning other subsystems.

A major qualification of the points in the last paragraphs must be added. In speaking of money inflation an economist usually expects to find an upward change in the general price level, not an increase in prices in one sector (perhaps coupled with a smaller decrease in others). Admittedly, however, sectorial inflation occurs, when prices remain stable in other sectors (see Schultze 1959, 1967 : 108–9). Sectorial inflation is even more common in the polity. Power is often inflated for certain collectivities, for certain uses and not others. Let me elucidate by way of an example (also see the discussion in chaps. 3, 5, and 6, below).

The successful use of power depends on the combinatorial addition of inputs to the polity. Within a value-added model (see chap. 3, below) we can view a balance of I, A, and L resource inputs as the necessary and sufficient condition for the actual implementation of political output without engendering disequilibrium. It is possible, within any given set of conditions, to identify a maximum "real output" from the polity in terms of the limits of the resources available to it. Within this framework the limit on the scope of the control of economic productivity and services available in the assumption of operative responsibility is a primary conditioning variable (in the cybernetic sense).

An elected communist government in a nation with a capitalist economy would hold inflated power. Such a government would be incapable of implementing policy decisions essential to the generation of a communist social formation, even if there was political support for such a program. Unless it were drastically to alter the capitalist character of the economy, eliminating profit as the criterion of economic success and requisitioning control over economic resources in an attempt to restructure the economy, it would be unable to secure the necessary control of economic resources to assume the operative responsibility for the implementation of essential programs. In other words, it would be unable to secure the required economic inputs to make good its promises within the context of leadership responsibility, as the extent of its capacity to assume operative responsibility (real, not inflated) is defined by its control over productivity and services. A government unwilling to abide by the conditions of action delimited by the economic system extant in capitalist countries would be in a position of cybernetic control with an energy system refusing to respond to inputs of information. This is one aspect of what Marx meant by the dictatorship of the bourgeoisie,[46] that class in control of the economy in a capitalist social formation.[47]

In this hypothetical situation[48] those who support the government in its anticapitalist policies do so with inflated power; that is, the government is incapable of generating the resources to make its decisions binding and, relatively, their support is for a lesser scope of leadership responsibility (see Parsons 1967:342). Those who oppose the government in these policies may well be able to use their power with greater effect elsewhere, and their power is not necessarily inflated. (Not being able to purchase a specific painting because it has already been sold, or has increased in price, does not mean that money is inflated for the actor; likewise, not being in control of some decision does not necessarily mean that power is inflated for the actor when he turns to some other issue. If, however, the power [or money] the actor controls is only used in one sector of the polity [or economy], and that sector is where the inflation has occurred, perhaps as a consequence of her support, then the medium as she utilizes it is inflated.) In certain situations power may be inflated with regard to only some sectors of the polity. The same sectorial breakdown in the effects of inflation is also present in circumstances of deflation.

"In the field of power it [deflation] is toward progressively increasing reliance on strict authority and coercive sanctions, culminating in the threat and use of physical force" (Parsons 1967:382). A deflationary situation for part of the polity occurs when the assumption of operative responsibility exceeds the authorized powers of office, or when political output exceeds the input of support. Diagrammatically, in the aggregate, if the saving schedule shifts upward, moving the aggregate support curve ($C_g + I_g$) downward (in figure 22) we have a situation of a deflationary gap (A − B), and

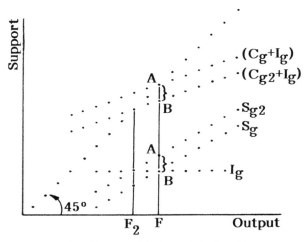

Figure 22. A shift upward in the political saving schedule and the deflationary gap.

would predict decreasing output and greater demands for binding decisions, "to which the demander has some kind of right but which ... [are] out of line with the normal expectations of operation of the system" (Parsons 1967:291).

Deflation is a situation in which the economic resources are present to increase the scope of political output, but aggregate intended support falls short of the intended output at which all justifiable interest demands would be met. It becomes a situation in which individuals demand power to hold, but this power is in danger of losing its symbolic nature, and as a result, the appeal to force becomes a method of coercion. The capacity to command force in the implementation of operative responsibility is present for the scope of output extant prior to the deflationary downswing in output. In deflation, power is more valuable, but within a limited scope of discretion; its distinction from "real," intrinsic satisfiers can become blurred, and political barter may well develop.[49]

In cases of acute deflation, the situation becomes too complex to be dealt with adequately in an aggregate model. Paradoxically, depending on the location of the deflation, it can result in an inflationary spiral. If the government in power attempts to enforce a scope of output for which it is unable to generate sufficient support—if, for example, it enunciates policy decisions that are in violation of the interest demands of some segment of the public and which those persons believe to be in violation of authorized powers—then the equilibrium of the system will be impaired. In such a situation those individuals in deflated sectors of the polity—those who, for example, view the excess political output as unauthorized—will withdraw their affirmations of legitimacy from the system and will adopt a calculating attitude toward presumptively binding decisions,[50] obeying when it is in their interest to obey, disobeying when it is in their interest to disobey (see chaps. 3, 5, and 6, below).

If these segments of the society are numerous enough, or under conditions of normalcy are in key social positions—for example they make up the governmental bureaucracy, including the army and police, or are in crucial positions in control of the economy— then a situation of inflation may occur, wherein previously acceptable and authorized powers of office are incapable of implementation because of the lack of resources in the assumption of operative responsibility. A situation of inflation will exist alongside a situation of deflation. (This is the situation of a communist government trying to rule in a country with a capitalist economy and is similar to the portrait painted in chap. 4 of early seventeenth-century England.) The deflation in one sector of the polity curtails saving to a level below the authorized powers of incumbent officials. If the situation becomes one of coercion, the incumbents might not be capable of enforcing their decrees.[51]

Conclusion

I hope this chapter demonstrates that a systematically articulated explanatory theory may be developed about subsystem production. While this goal was implicit in Parsons's project, neither he nor anyone else has previously accomplished it. Second, I hope to have demonstrated that the balance of inputs into any subsystem defines the equilibrium condition for that subsystem.[52] This finding serves as the foundation on which the remainder of this book is constructed.

Theory using functionally defined concepts formulates societal (social) universals, propositions intended to be valid for all societies. Premised on the understanding that any system requires specifiable resources to function adequately, it asks about the consequences of the withdrawal, for whatever reason, of one or more of the functionally defined inputs. It is this question that has dominated this chapter. In the next chapter we will see that a theory of internal disorder may be formulated within the context of this theory. In chapter 4 I will use the findings I have developed, there specified for a concrete historical situation, to generate propositions concerning the consequences of uneven development among societal subsystems. The notion of contradiction between societal subsystems will be given a determinant analytical meaning within the context of a concrete historical situation.

Appendix

A   Adaptive subsystem, economy

C   Consumer support

C_a Economic consumer support (L—[product] → A)

C_g Political support (I—[product] → G)

G   Goal-attainment subsystem, polity

I   Integrative subsystem, societal community, *and* investment

I_a Economic investment, allocation of fluid resources (G—[product] → A)

I_g Authorization of powers of office (L—[product] → G)

L   Pattern maintenance subsystem, latency subsystem

M_a Money

M_{ad} Money demanded

M_{ah} Demand for money to hold, standards for allocation of resources (I—[factor] → A)

M_{as} Money supplied

M_{at} Transactions demand for money

M_d Medium demanded

M_g Power

M_{gd} Power demanded

M_{gh} Allocation of surplus product (A—[factor] → G)

M_{gs} Power supplied

M_{gt} Transactions demand for power

M_h Definition of allocatable medium resources, demand for medium to hold

M_i Influence

M_l Value commitments or real commitments

M_s Medium supplied

M_t Transactions demand for medium

N   Constituent intent

N_a Labor capacity (L—[factor] → A)

N_g Interest Demands (I—[factor] → G)

O   Definition of opportunity

O_a Opportunity for economic effectiveness (G—[factor] → A)

O_g Legitimation of authority (L—[factor] → G)

r   Rate of opportunity

r_a Interest rate, inverse of rate of economic opportunity

r_g Rate of alienation, inverse of rate of legitimation

S   Saving

S_a Economic saving (A—[factor] → G, extent delimited by ranking of claims (I—[product] → A)

S_g Operative responsibility (G—[factor] → L), extent delimited by control of productivity and services (A—[product] → G)

Y   Subsystem output, income

Y_a Economic output $(A—[\text{product}]\rightarrow L,\ A—[\text{product}]\rightarrow G)$; income $(A—[\text{factor}]\rightarrow L,\ A—[\text{factor}]\rightarrow G)$

Y_g Political output $(G—[\text{product}]\rightarrow I,\ G—[\text{product}]\rightarrow L)$; income $(G—[\text{factor}]\rightarrow I,\ G—[\text{factor}]\rightarrow L)$

3. Toward a Theory of Internal Disorder

This chapter presents a theory of internal disorder. In trying to explain the genesis of disorder in social systems I attempt to answer the following questions: What determines whether disorderly acts will be committed, or somewhat differently, under what conditions will actors take part in such acts? What determines what type of disorder will occur, and whether disorderly actions will become a regularized activity for the participants?

The theory presented here is meant to be applicable to all societal systems. I refer to such propositions as "societal universals." This chapter attempts to specify the necessary and sufficient conditions for the occurrence of various types of disorder and to delimit a framework in which additional varieties of disorder might be conceptualized and their occurrence explained. I focus on disorderly events and their preconditions; I do not attempt to understand the long-term consequences of these events, or to understand the structural tendencies within a specific type of society which generate their preconditions. In order to accomplish these two related tasks, it is necessary to explore the structure of various types of societal systems and to investigate the developmental patterns involved in the transformation of one type of society into another (see chaps. 4 and 8, below).

The careful reader will notice in reading this chapter that many of the concepts are imperfectly defined. She will think of examples of strain that might fit into one of two categories and she will rightly criticize the author for allowing this ambiguity to remain. But while this criticism is valid, at least some of the ambiguity is intentional and, I believe, necessary in any preliminary attempt at theory construction. This work straddles a line between the theoretical closure implicit in a series of organized propositions and the diffuseness of not yet operationalized or tightly defined concepts. It is my belief that researchers using the framework outlined will be able to identify and isolate the specified types of disorder and to identify the generating conditions of those disorders. In so doing they will provide examples of the variables outlined in the pages to follow, and these empirical studies will enable us to refine the conceptualizations in nonarbitrary, determined directions.

Implicit in this strategy is a tactic I call "cheating." In a paper presenting a tentative statement of a theoretical framework, much depends on the coherence of argument and on the plausibility of my contentions to those familiar with relevant empirical materials. The process of refinement, especially the tightening of definitions, can only come with the use of the framework. On occasion it is justifiable to modify concepts rather than to treat a negative case as falsifying a proposition. The sole restraint on the modification of definitions ("cheating") in an attempt to save one's propositions is the necessity to be consistent in such modifications. If it is determined, for example, that a historical case of wage decrease under conditions XYZ is a case of strain at the level of facilities (because the manifested reaction appears to be a form of "deviant innovation"), then the next case of wage decrease under the same conditions cannot be categorized as strain at the level of goals (because in this instance the reaction appears to fall within the category of "deviant aggression"). If this contradiction occurs we will be forced to modify the propositional structure of the theory, but our modifications will be guided by solid research, and our research guided by a coherent theoretical orientation.[1]

Internal Disorder: A Preliminary Definition

I define internal disorders as motivated actions in violation of the normative component of any institutionalized structure.[2] If the disorder is to be labeled internal, these actions must be carried out by members of the collectivity system under examination; outsiders may take part in such actions only if it is clear that the main thrust behind the events is domestic.[3] Acts of disorder are in violation of a legitimized normative structure, but this does *not* preclude the possibility that such actions are conforming within some other collectivity, for instance, a societal subculture.

The following theory of internal disorder attempts to systematically integrate and develop earlier theories of deviance and collective behavior.[4] In this presentation I concentrate on deviance and revolution. A brief explanation of how these two partial theories fit within the more general framework is in order as a preface to an exposition of a theory of deviant action.

Internal disorders may be categorized within a three-axis framework. First, the disorder will be directed toward the institutional structure centering within one of the four subsystems (as identified by Parsons) of the society under discussion:[5] adaptation, property-contract; goal attainment, authority; integration, stratification-legal system; and latency, "religion."[6] Second, the disorder will be directed at one or more units of social action within the institutional structure attacked, at values, norms, collectivities, or situational facilities. Third, disorders are classified as to whether they attempt to restructure the institution under attack. Is the disorder solely negative or does it demand a positive redefinition within the extant system?

The following are the necessary and sufficient conditions for the occurrence of an internal disorder within some segment of a population examined: strain, an open illegitimate opportunity structure, two aspects of a neutralizing belief structure (neutralizing the actors' orientations to specific performances and deflation in one of the generalized media), and a precipitating factor. If a counter-subculture is to be formed, a set of legitimizing beliefs must be institutionalized in the group, and if the subculture is to be successful in an attempt to redefine a unit of social action, a situation of media inflation must ensue (in the same media where the deflationary situation was earlier or is concurrently observed) and the capacity to build a new institutional structure must be present.

The disorderly movement will be directed toward the institutional structure within which the medium deflation occurs: money, property-contract; power, authority; influence, stratification-legal system; and value commitments, "religion." The type of strain extant among the participants determines the level of action within the institutional structure that will be attacked: strain at the level of facilities, situational facilities; strain at the level of goals, collectivities; strain at the level of norms, norms; strain at the level of values, values. Whether or not the movement seeks to redefine the component of social action attacked depends on one component of the

TYPE OF STRAIN PRESENT WITHIN THE SYSTEM	COMPONENT AT WHICH DISORDER IS DIRECTED	IS THE COMPONENT REDEFINED?	MEDIA DEFLATED			
			Money	Power	Influence	Value–Commitments
At the level of values	values	yes		Total Revolution REVOV		
		no		RIOTV	Deviant Retreatism DR	
At the level of norms	norms	yes		Normative Revolution REVON		
		no		RIOTN	Deviant Conflict DC	
At the level of goals	collectivities	yes		Rebellion REVOG		
		no		RIOTG	Deviant Aggression DA	
At the level of facilities	facility-roles	yes		"Facilitory Rebellion" REVOF		
		no		RIOTF	Deviant Innovation DI	

Figure 23.

movement's legitimizing belief structure, the orienting belief (see fig. 23).

It is essential to underscore the importance of the statements in the last paragraph. The framework outlined in this chapter provides a basis for technical definitions of the various types of internal disorder, and it is important that these definitions are not isolated from the categorizations of the variables said to lead to internal disorder. Drawing on the concepts developed by Parsons and Smelser, we can show that there is a relation between the location of strain within a societal system and the social structural target of the disorderly response; further, we can relate the direction of the response toward, for example, the political or legal-stratification systems to a malfunctioning of one of the symbolic media of action, power, or influence. We thus have a framework that allows us to provide theoretically informed definitions of various types of internal disorder, and which relates these categorizations to systematically analyzed preconditions for their occurrence, possibilities dependent on the previous enunciation of a coherent conceptual framework.[7] With an examination of two variables (strain and deflation) it is now possible to isolate important components of an explanation of the occurrence of an extraordinarily diverse set of phenomena. It will also prove possible in later work to show how these forms of disorder are related to similar institutionally acceptable social actions, and to discriminate between the preconditions of these two types of social action.

It is for these reasons that I use the Parsonian interchange framework (see figs. 1 and 2). It is possible, within the context of this still rudimentary paradigm, to begin (1) to locate and systematically define the variables relevant to the occurrence of internal disorder and (2) to isolate the mutual dependencies between these variables and between the various types of disorder. In this chapter I will not discuss these questions in detail, but I will make reference to the locale of the variables in terms of the interchange framework. The great utility of the framework is only apparent in a reasonably systematic analysis of some societal (or other social) system, and it may seem that my references are gratuitous in the context of this work; they are included as guidelines for future research. (For discussions of the interchange paradigm, see Parsons and Smelser 1956; Parsons et al. 1961:30–85; Parsons 1969:chaps. 1, 2, 9, 13–17; Parsons and Platt 1973; and chap. 2, above.)

Within this schema, deviance is the type of disorder which focuses on the integrative subsystem, and which does not attempt to redefine the unit of social action at which it is directed. "We define deviant behavior as [motivated] behavior which violates institutionalized expectations [institutionalized norms, norms legitimized by institutionalized values]—that is, expectations which are shared and recognized as legitimate within ... [the integrative sub]-system."[8] Implicit in this definition is the view that there are mechanisms in the system which will react to a known act of deviance through the application of some sanction.[9] The act is regarded as deviant relative to the norms violated, and thus deviant within the system where those norms are institutionalized. I have not precluded the possibility that the deviance could be a conforming act within some other system, for instance a deviant subculture, but only emphasized that the actor must be a member of the system in which the deviant act was committed.

A Theory of Deviant Action

The scheme used to organize the determinants of deviant action is a value-added model. Its key element is that

> every stage in the value-added process ... is a necessary condition for the appropriate and effective addition of value in the next stage. The sufficient condition for the final ... [outcome], moreover, is the combination of *every* necessary condition, according to a definite pattern.... As the value-added process develops, it allows for progressively fewer outcomes other than the one we wish to explain.   (Smelser 1962:14)

The variables in the model are not necessarily ordered in time. The first variable in the model need not be present prior to the second; what the model tells us is that the second variable will only add value, or become relevant to the predicted outcome, when the first variable is present. In this model we are dealing with a series of independent yet interdependent variables, ordered in terms of their effect on the final outcome to be predicted but not necessarily ordered in linear time.

The model that follows is organized along a cybernetic hierarchy, where conditions high in "energy" precede controls high in "information." Over one hundred years ago Marx and Engels pointed out that unless the material conditions for revolutions are present, it is immaterial whether the ideas of revolution have been expressed (Marx and Engels 1964:50–51, cf. 61). But the logic of the value-added differs from the logic of Marx's theoretical arguments and adheres to Weber's on one important point. For Marx the presence of the material conditions of revolution necessarily would give rise to those ideas also necessary as preconditions for its occurrence. For Weber, while the material components are seen as the conditions of social transformation, ideational factors are seen as autonomous from those conditions, although interrelated with them. In the value-added model the relative independence of the variables is maintained; there is no determination in the last instance, only a series of prior limiting conditions. Thus every variable in a value-added theory is a necessary condition for the occurrence of some outcome, but only together do they encompass the necessary and sufficient conditions for the outcome. It is important to recognize that each of these variables may be overdetermined.

If we assume that XYZ are the necessary and sufficient conditions for event A, the phenomenon of overdetermination is not manifest in the case where XY (or XZ, or YZ) are the sufficient conditions for event A. In that case the earlier theory is simply erroneous; Z (or Y, or X) is not a necessary condition for the occurrence of A. A is overdetermined in the presence of x_1x_2yz, where y activates variable Y and z activates variable Z, and either x_1 or x_2, both present, would suffice to activate variable X. In this latter case variable X is said to be overdetermined because there are at least two substantive processes categorizable within its purview, either of which alone would activate the variable (within some proposition), both of which are present. Occurrences of this sort are very frequent in actual historical situations.

The problem of overdetermination is made much more difficult owing to the practical and theoretical problem of specifying exactly when a variable is activated. In practice, I fear, sociologists too often make this determination when the dependent variable appears on the scene; this "fudging" occurs in both historical and survey research work. Often there can be no distinction between determination and overdetermination with regard to a given variable, but this is a weakness in our ability to operationalize our concepts. (Such problems are implicit, among others, in Althusser's discussions, 1970:chap. 3.)

If we hold to the basic value-added model, the presence of each variable, no matter how limited, when grouped with all the other variables implies the dependent result, even if the sociologist's limiting case occurs, the restriction of the result to one individual's behavior. To predict the size of the resultant movement it is necessary to quantify each variable, and to specify an equation that will weight the relative combinatorial effects of the various independent variables, to formulate a schema that will predict both the occurrence or nonoccurrence of an event, and if the former, its size. Such a weighted model becomes more important in the study of disorder which attempts to restructure some social structural component, for here the strength and size of the movement may help to determine its chances of success. Even if such a formula cannot be stated at this time, the logic implicit in its enunciation must be articulated in the theory developed.

What follows is an attempt to identify the necessary and sufficient conditions for the occurrence of deviant action.

Structural Strain

At least since Merton's first paper on anomie and deviant behavior (1957 [1938]:chap. 4), sociologists have been concerned with the categorization of strain, and with parallel categorizations of deviance.[10] This theorizing reached an important point with the publication of Cloward and Ohlin's work (1960). In the transition from Merton to Cloward and Ohlin major changes were made: dealing with the restricted area of juvenile delinquency in the United States, Cloward and Ohlin concentrate on only one variety of strain, the stress experienced by lower-class youths oriented toward economic improvement and facing a closed legitimate opportunity structure. Depending on the illegitimate opportunity structure that confronts them, these youths can respond in one of three ways. If this structure is open, they may enter into a criminal subculture. If they live in a disorganized system (e.g., a slum that does not provide connections to an illegitimate structure), they are deprived of both conventional and criminal opportunities; their response in this situation may be the violent behavior displayed in the conflict gang. Finally, Cloward and Ohlin discuss the formation of the retreatist subculture, a grouping made up of those who fail in both legitimate and illegitimate structures and who drop out of both systems.

There are definite problems in this construction, problems created in a conceptual confusion between opportunity structures and "strain". In fact, Cloward and Ohlin outline three types of strain, and within situations characterized by these three impairments they have outlined why deviance developed into a specific reaction. They begin by discussing the lower-class youths who face a condition of strain due to an attempt to improve their economic position. Their response to strain—a strain I prefer to view more generally as a condition of uncertainty concerning the sufficiency of means to attain some socially defined goal—comes in the form of activities within the framework of a criminal subculture, activities of utilitarian benefit. Their discussion of this subculture is well constructed; very briefly, strain leads actors to seek some means to obtain the desired facility, in this instance money, and their illegitimate opportunity structure channels them into a criminal gang. But when Cloward and Ohlin discuss the conflict subculture their mode of explanation subtly changes. They ignore the fact that a disorganized system is poorly integrated in terms of its normative structure, and further, that this disorganization constitutes a new type of strain within the system. In reality, I believe, the conflict gang is one of many possible responses to a situation of normative strain. The specific type of response is limited by the illegitimate opportunity structure located within the system. The illegitimate opportunity structure found in many disorganized slums is, of course, encompassed by the traditions of the conflict gang.

Cloward and Ohlin's discussion of the retreatist subculture is marred by difficulties similar to those that mark their treatment of the conflict gang. In this instance they ignore their implicit suggestion that these deviants are withdrawing from society due to their rejection of the values of that society. This strain on the level of values is the immediate condition of stress to which the retreatist responds. As in the case of strain on the level of norms and facilities, withdrawal is guided by the illegitimate opportunity structures available to the actor. In lower-class areas, they argue, this structure is often found among those who seek the "kick," perhaps through the use of narcotics.[11]

Before rephrasing in a more systematic and general fashion this discussion drawn from Cloward and Ohlin, I want to add one further example of strain. This stress and the parallel response among lower-class adolescents is discussed by Cohen (1955). It involves a condition of strain in which actors perceive themselves at a disadvantage relative to middle-class youths in their opportunity to achieve the rewards they seek.[12] The response is an aggressive, nonutilitarian, negativistic attack on property (and perhaps person). The specifics of the response are once again delimited by the illegitimate opportunity structure confronted.

A Brief Systematic Restatement. Following Smelser, I "shall define strain as an impairment of the relations among and consequently inadequate functioning of the components of social action" (1962:47). Strain is a necessary but not sufficient condition for the occurrence of deviant action. The location of strain in one of the four components of social action (values, norms, mobilization mechanisms [goals], and facilities) sets limits on the type of deviant action which is possible. (On the components of social action, see Smelser 1962.)

The position outlined here, that the location of strain within the system sets limits on the type of resulting deviance and, more generally, disorder, runs counter to Smelser's (with regard to collective behavior) that "any kind of strain may be a determinant of any kind of collective behavior" (1962:49), and counter to Cloward and Ohlin's view that "the pressures that lead to deviant patterns do not necessarily determine the particular pattern of deviance that results" (1960:40; for a clarification of their position, see 41). On the contrary, I argue that each type of strain limits the developing reaction to a limited category of responses (to be outlined below).

As I pointed out above, owing to their limitation of perspective Cloward and Ohlin discuss only one form of strain and three possible responses. In their theory, the individual's opportunity structure determines which type of deviance will result from anomie; I, on the other hand, list four classes of deviance and argue that depending on the location of strain in the system, only one of these four sets of responses is possible. The illegitimate opportunity structure helps condition the specific response within any one of these four categories.

Smelser's problem is more complex; his error stems from too narrow a categorization of responses.[13] Had he classified the responses to strain both in terms of functionally categorized institutionalized structures and in terms of components of social action in each of the functionally categorized institutions, he would, I believe, have seen that while the focus of strain is *not* relevant to the direction of the response toward a specific functionally categorized

institution, it *is* relevant to the direction of the response with regard
to the component of social action attacked, whatever the functional
system.[14] Which subsystem is attacked is conditioned by the location of a medium deflation within the system.[15]

The first kind of strain is on situational facilities (SF); it involves
a "condition of *ambiguity* as to the adequacy of means for a given
goal" (Smelser 1962: 51). This type of strain is nearly equivalent to
Merton's "anomie." Anomie, says Merton, results "when there is
an acute disjunction between the cultural norms and goals and the
socially structured capacities of members of the group to act in
accord with them." (See Merton 1957: 162. I would, however, substitute "social" for the phrase "the cultural norms and" in Merton's
definition, as I use the term *cultural norm* to signify a component of
the symbolic meaning system which stands above social goals on
the cybernetic scale.)

I am of course primarily concerned with actors in their social
capacity, where goals are defined within the context of the collectivity structures in which actors are placed. It is useful, therefore, to
place this discussion within the context of Parsons's interchange
paradigm.[16] Within this model, strain at the level of facilities is
located at the factor outputs from an adaptive subsystem (or subsector) to the receiving subsystem (or subsector). The capacity of
some collectivity members to implement their socially defined goals
is impaired by some disjunction in the provision of adequate adaptive (at the societal level, economic) resources. It is obvious that a
meaningful description of such strain is dependent on an analysis of
the structural organization of the concrete situation under discussion.

The interchange model Parsons has elaborated is an aggregate
model. All performances with certain consequences for the social
system are categorized in X position. In an analysis of the roots of
disorder it is often necessary to disaggregate the phenomena so classified, a disaggregation in accord with their structural organization.
Thus while for "Keynesian" purposes it might be useful to determine that there has been a sharp decrease in personal income within
American society, for an analysis of the possibilities of an increase
in disorder, and especially if we are concerned with the locale of
that disorder, it will be necessary to understand how that decrease
has been distributed across social groupings. While it might be
possible to construct a "rate of crime" table based on a "rate of SF"

table, such a set of predictions would be much better grouped if distribution figures on SF were available.

We might further be misled by aggregate figures in a case like the following: there has been a marked increase in the variables necessary for some form of disorder but the incidence of the various conditions do not overlap; for instance, strain is focused on group A while that group is not affected by a deflation of influence. In addition, it is often necessary to have data on the stock of facilities already possessed by the affected social units. The definitions, as stated, seem to imply that simple flow data would be sufficient; this is so only as a first approximation.

The deviant response associated with this form of strain may be termed, following Merton, innovation (DI). This response implies a rational, utilitarian innovation to obtain the facilities necessary to achieve the desired goal. This innovation will be termed deviant when and if it results in acts that violate the institutionalized normative order located within the integrative subsystem under examination. SF is a necessary but not sufficient condition for DI.[17]

A second kind of strain, SG, occurs at the level of goals (for Smelser, at the level of motivational mechanisms).

> The mobilization series characterizes the generation of human motivation and its channeling into organizations and roles. This series is also the seat of rewards ... for the responsible fulfillment of role behavior into which motivation is channeled. Strain, therefore, involves a relation between responsible performance in roles and the rewards which accrue thereby.   (Smelser 1962:54)

This form of strain can be described in a brief discussion of the concept of relative deprivation. When an actor is measuring herself against a reference group (or in the limiting case, a reference individual) that serves as a "comparison group," she evaluates her position relative to the people who are members of that group. She feels relatively deprived when in comparing her situation with theirs, she views them as gleaning greater rewards than she obtains for like performances. When this deprivation is socially structured, when a number of persons as members of some social group feel relatively deprived in comparable situations, SG is manifest as a sociological variable.

In an analysis using the Parsonian interchange framework, SG is manifest in impairments of the factor outputs from goal-attainment subsystems (or subsectors). The concept of relative deprivation is taken as narrowly referring to the allocation of "politically" defined resources (in Parsons's functional definition of *political*), in whatever sphere of activity. This would seem to exclude relative deprivation concerning adaptive facilities. Although I believe that this is realistic, I want to add two very important caveats.

The first concerns the difficulty in differentiating between these variables in concrete historical, empirical cases. It requires careful analysis to determine the appropriate categorization. For example, is the exclusion of some ethnic or religious groups from certain occupational roles a form of SF or SG or both? This question is impossible to answer without a comprehensive knowledge of their alternative opportunities to gain monetary facilities, without an awareness of their value systems (in the sense of the desirable, not the desired), and so on.

Second, our definitions are by no means airtight. It is clear that the dissection of specific cases will involve not only a process of categorization but also a process of redefinition. This is the procedure referred to above as "cheating."

The deviant response to SG, provided the other preconditions for deviance are present, may be termed deviant aggression (DA). DA consists in a nonutilitarian attack upon property (or perhaps person).[18] SG is a necessary but not sufficient condition for DA.

"Normative strain is discussed frequently under headings such as 'role strain,' 'role conflict,' and 'cross pressures'" (Smelser 1962:59). Parsons has defined *role conflict* as "the exposure of the actor to conflicting sets of legitimized role expectations such that complete fulfillment of both is realistically impossible" (Parsons 1951:280; cf. Gross et al. 1958, especially p. 248 and chap. 17). This definition of role conflict[19] is broad enough to encompass the other two concepts, role strain and cross pressures, but perhaps the best summary term linking the three concepts is *role ambiguity*. Role ambiguity includes not only situations in which the actor feels herself confronted with incompatible expectations (cf. Gross et al. 1958:249) but also situations in which the expectations to which she is expected to conform are not specific or detailed (cf. Parsons 1951:249; McClosky and Schaar 1965:14–30). This norm ambiguity is discussed by Bay under the rubric of "anomie,"[20] "the disintegration of authoritative norms and institutions" (Bay 1965:75). SN, strain at the level of norms, thus implies a confusion with regard to expectations; a confusion created either by a proliferation of norms or a dearth of norms relevant to a specific situation (cf. Bay 1965:276).

Within the interchange model this strain involves the factor outputs from the integrative subsystem or integrative subsectors. It might, for example, concern irreconcilable interest demands on some political organization or conflicting claims on monetary resources defined by zero-sum constraints. In situations controlled by a symbolic medium, influence is the relevant focus of concern in identifying SN, and this strain can appear where there is a paucity of influence available to effect some social performance.

The deviant response associated with this form of strain is deviant conflict (DC), antagonistic behavior directed toward other persons, usually in a situation of mutual contention. DC involves clashes regarding incompatible actions and must be differentiated from acts of violent personal crime, but the distinction may be ambiguous. The key to DA is a nonutilitarian outburst; to DC, a hostile action within a situation of social conflict.

The most commonly discussed form of DC is the "conflict gang" (for example, see Cloward and Ohlin 1960: especially pp. 171–78; Yablonsky 1966; Short and Strodbeck 1965; Downes 1966). In most of these discussions the authors speak of a dissociation from the norms of the society that surrounds gang members. Often this dissociation is forced on youths owing to the fact that they live in a "disorganized" neighborhood, in an area of low normative integration (cf. Kobrin 1951). Such individuals are unable to isolate a set of norms to follow, either legitimate or illegitimate norms, and are thus predisposed to turn to one or another form of contentious action, to DC.

Such actions are deviant when in violation of the institutionalized normative system in the integrative subsystem under examination. SN is a necessary but not sufficient condition for the occurrence of DC.

The final form of strain occurs at the level of values (SV). This disjunction can be conceptualized as an ideological alienation in which actors are ambivalent toward or consciously reject what they believe are the dominant institutionalized values of their society. (This type of strain and one reaction to it are discussed at great length in Gould 1967; see also Kenniston 1965). Within the interchange paradigm this variety of strain is located at the factor outputs from the latency subsystem (subsectors). It involves impediments to the making and actualization of certain types of value commitment (see Parsons 1969:chap. 16), involving, for example, the perceived legitimacy of economic, political, or associational ties.

The deviant response connected with this form of strain may be termed, again following Merton, retreatism (DR). Retreatism involves the withdrawal from actions accepted as institutionally legitimate within the system and becomes deviant when coupled with actions in violation of the norms institutionalized within the examined integrative subsystem (or subsector). SV is a necessary but not sufficient condition for the occurrence of DR.

Cohen has argued that "the crucial condition for the emergence of cultural forms [deviant subcultures] is the existence, *in effective interaction with one another, of a number of actors with similar problems of adjustment*" (1955:59). The extent of strain within a system contributes to the likelihood of the emergence of a subculture of deviance or a deviant subculture. Should a deviant subculture emerge, it will provide the necessary resources to initiate newcomers into the normative structure that must be understood before deviant acts can be successfully performed. The existence of widespread strain is not a necessary condition for individual, atomistic deviance, but if neutralizing and legitimizing beliefs are to be created on a group level (see below) and if widespread deviance is to ensue and be regularized, widespread strain is a necessary condition for its emergence.[21]

Opportunity Structure (O_i)

Given a situation of strain regarding one of the components of social action, deviance need not result. Structural strain is at most a necessary condition for the occurrence of deviant behavior. Within the logic of the value-added model, other determinants must be present if the resulting outcome is to be behavior that violates the institutionalized norms of the integrative system under scrutiny. The second factor that must be present in an "illegitimate opportunity structure."

Such a structure may be conceptualized as the presence of the necessary facilities to perform deviant actions; within the interchange system, once we locate the deviance, this involves access to alternative adaptive inputs to the subsystem (subsector) where the deviance occurs; that is, alternative resources from the A subsystem (subsector). The specifics of this structure are thus dependent on what type of deviance we wish to explain, or from a different point of view, the specifics of this structure condition what type of deviance will occur. The opportunity structure helps determine the explicit response to strain. Depending on the type of strain manifested the response is limited to its cognate reaction (e.g., SF implies DI), but within the boundaries of that deviant classification (DI, DA, DC, DR) the specific type of deviant action to be selected depends on the opportunity structure.

Some forms of deviance demand the availability of specific physical facilities, tangible objects needed to perform the deviant actions. The availability of these objects is thus a necessary prerequisite for the occurrence of certain forms of deviant action. It should not be assumed that such facilities are interchangeable. For example, there are many individuals who will try marijuana but not LSD, owing to the fact that they have generated a neutral attitude toward the former drug but view the latter as dangerous (see Gould 1967). Needless to say, an actor's position within a social and cultural milieu will largely determine the availability of the facilities necessary for the deviant action to occur. This remains the case even when the facilities are not material, and when new adaptations are created. Even here the opportunity structure constrains the possible deviant outcomes.[22]

At this point we confront two situations: the first concerns the creation of a new subculture centered around deviant activities; the second concerns socialization into an already existing subculture. Widespread strain and access to an illegitimate opportunity structure are preconditions for the development of the subculture. Neutralizing beliefs allow for its generation and an emergent ideology may be formed (or adopted) to help reduce the dissonance generated in the commission of deviant acts and leading to the institutionalization of deviant patterns. Once the subculture is formed, its members are able to socialize new recruits. The newcomers will progress through the same stages as the originators of the deviant response, but the mechanisms of indoctrination may differ considerably from the original pattern of subcultural growth.

In the case of socialization into the already existing structure, a crucial aspect of the illegitimate opportunity structure is contact with those already engaged in acts of deviance. As Sutherland long ago pointed out, "criminal behavior is learned in interaction with other persons in a process of communication" (1956:8). Here the mobilization of new recruits from the subculture of deviance into the deviant subculture is of major importance, but so also is the extension of the subculture of deviance. We shall see below that parallel phenomena occur within the context of a subculture of revolution and a revolutionary subculture.

What we have said concerning the illegitimate opportunity structure remains very abstract; in order to provide a realistic analysis of the opportunity structure confronting some social group we need to begin assessing its place within the context of an extant social organization. In many cases the rudiments of such an analysis can be performed by analyzing the group within the context of the Parsonian interchange framework, thus assessing the facilities it has available in its most immediate interchange networks. Often this analysis will have to be at a subsystem level and be restricted to a given locality of interaction, as against an analysis on the level of the societal system. In an analysis of revolutionary movements, in which we are concerned with the potential of some organization to redefine some aspect of the governmental structure, the opposite is often the case.

Neutralizing Belief (NB_i)

Matza has challenged Cloward and Ohlin's discussion of the deviant subculture on two central points: (1) he claims that Cloward and Ohlin err in speaking of a *deviant subculture*, a group "in which certain forms of ... [deviant] activity are essential requirements for the performance of the dominant roles supported by the subculture" (Cloward and Ohlin 1960:7). Taking issue with this conceptualization, he argues that deviance takes place within the context of a *subculture of deviance*, within "a setting in which the commission of ... [deviant acts] is common knowledge among a group of" individuals (Matza 1964:33). The major point of difference between the two views concerns the content of the belief systems found in the two types of subcultures. The deviant subculture encompasses an ideology that legitimizes the commission of specified deviant acts, and which seems to imply that these acts will be regularly committed. The subculture of deviance, on the other hand, only tolerates deviant behavior. It encompasses an ideology that justifies deviance, but only under rigorously defined conditions. It supplies an excuse for one who has committed a deviant act, but not a legitimation for committing that act.

(2) Matza complains that Cloward and Ohlin's theory requires too much deviance; if their theory were correct, "delinquency would be more permanent and less transient, more pervasive and less intermittent than is apparently the case" (Matza 1964:22).[23] Matza's alternative is the view of the deviant in a state of drift. The member of a subculture of deviance is in a position where she is "neither compelled nor committed to deeds nor freely choosing them; neither different in any simple or fundamental sense from the law abiding, nor the same" (28). Legal norms are neutralized by the drifter, but she does not surrender her allegiance to them. Her drift is described relative to the laws she violates.

These two views, that the deviant legitimizes her norm-violating action or that, on the contrary, she temporarily neutralizes the norm she violates (thus excusing her deviance) seem to contradict one another, but in fact they do not. To eliminate the apparent contradiction and to resolve the argument one need only view the process leading to the formation of a deviant subculture as occurring within the boundaries of the subculture of deviance. If this last perspective is accurate, the actor passes through a series of stages: one of the necessary conditions for the commission of deviant acts is the creation of a set of neutralizing beliefs. These beliefs enable an actor to violate certain norms, but if she is to continue to violate these norms regularly, she must construct or adopt some set of beliefs which not only excuse deviance but which legitimize it and perhaps demand it (cf. Parsons 1969:chap. 16). One situation wherein these beliefs develop is the deviant subculture.[24]

Both the deviant subculture and the subculture of deviance can exist in the same system at the same time. The member of the deviant subculture will have passed through the stage wherein she was a member of the wider, more inclusive subculture of deviance. Once the actor has committed a deviant act, if she is to continue to behave in a deviant manner with some regularity (see Gould 1967:95–110), she must accept or create an ideology that legitimizes her deviance; this ideology will be in opposition to the normative standards of her society, but in the case of deviance it will not demand a redefinition of those norms. The actors who adopt this legitimizing set of beliefs will make up the core group within a subculture of deviance; they will be the deviant subculture.

It is my view that given any of the above discussed forms of strain and an open illegitimate opportunity structure, one cannot always expect a deviant reaction. The next component of the value-added schema is the neutralizing belief (NB_i): the development of a set of beliefs which imply (at the societal level) a calculating orientation toward the institutionalized legal system, and a non-negative attitude toward specific deviant acts, acts that might combat structural strain. Placed in a situation of strain, confronting an open illegitimate opportunity structure, and covered by a neutralizing belief system, an actor is in a state of drift where, given the specific opportunity, she will commit a deviant act, a state that permits her to become a primary deviant. (On primary and secondary deviation see Lemert 1964, 1967:chap. 3. For differing though related discussions of drift and neutralizing beliefs, consult Sykes and Matza 1957; Matza and Sykes 1961; Matza 1964; Matza 1969.)

The primary component of a neutralizing belief is thus the development of what Gross calls an expedient orientation toward normative expectations (see Gross et al. 1958: chap. 17 for a discussion that has inspired important components of my analysis). Once this orientation is assumed, an actor, when given the opportunity to violate an institutionalized norm, will be primarily concerned with the relative sanctions derived from deviance versus conformity, and less concerned about the legitimacy of the two expectations.

Moving away from a social psychological to a sociological perspective, it is possible to conceptualize the advent of a neutralizing belief within the context of the interchange paradigm. With regard to integrative phenomena, the generation of a calculating attitude toward the institutionalized normative system (at the societal level, the legal system) is an aspect of a deflation of influence.

"Influence is a way of having an effect on the attitudes and opinions of others through intentional (though not necessarily rational) action—the effect may or may not be to change the opinion or to prevent a possible change" (Parsons 1969:406).

"Influence ... consists of appeals for certain types of action in the interest of an integrative unit-collective solidarity" (Parsons 1969:446). An actor, in "attempting to influence" another, must justify her assertions.

With reference to items of information, justification is necessary, since influence is a symbolic medium. The function of justification is not actually to verify the items, but to provide the basis for the communicator's *right* to state them without alter's needing to verify them; for example, ego may be a technically competent "authority" in the field. With reference to intention, justification may be regulated by various aspects of status that are regularly invoked to indicate that such intentions should prove trustworthy when stated by persons in the category in question. A very important category of the justification of influence is what is ordinarily meant by "reputation." (Parsons 1969:417–18)

More generally, an actor's ability to influence another depends upon her prestige in the other's eyes; the degree to which this prestige may be generalized depends upon the values institutionalized in the system under examination. In some cases, prestige allows an actor to control in a diffuse body of situations; in some systems prestige is situation-specific (see Parsons 1969:chap. 15, postscript).

The major mode of pressure[25] which is specifically legal and which is used within the legal system in influence.[26] An indicator of influence deflation is the actor's refusal to accept legal pronouncements as justified owing simply to the fact that they are "law." Law is no longer acceptable solely in terms of the presumed prestige accorded to the legal system and its constituent components. When such a deflation occurs, an actor must be persuaded to obey the law (Parsons 1969:chap. 15, postscript). In a situation of influence deflation, an actor would be primarily concerned with the relative sanctions she would derive from deviance versus conformity, and less concerned with the supposed right inherent in the law.

A deflation of influence will thus result in one of two phenomena, or perhaps in both. In the first instance, appeals will be made to the security base of influence, types of knowledge relevant to the specifics of the situation at hand. This is a situation where one actor demands that another put up or shut up; she is no longer willing to accept the status position of the other as definitive of the other's capacity to make decisions. Second, recourse to a situation of barter might occur. Here the intrinsic satisfiers of influence (the product outputs of the integrative subsystem [subsector]) are directly exchanged—if you support my leadership in sphere x, I will support your leadership in sphere y. (On both of these points see Parsons 1969:chap. 15, postscript.) A third possibility involves the dedifferentiation between influence and other media systems, most particularly power. Even when this dedifferentiation does not occur, the effects of influence deflation are transmitted to other subsystems via factor outputs from the integrative subsystem. In either case, dedifferentiation or simple transmission of effect, there is a possibility that force, the security base of power (see Parsons 1967:chap. 9; Gould 1976), will be used to enforce norms normally controlled by influence.[27]

In chapter 2 I discussed a framework isolating the generating conditions of media imbalances, including a simple model formulating certain of the generating conditions of monetary inflation and deflation and power inflation and deflation. In that chapter, I mentioned cognate variables definable within the context of Parsons's interchange paradigm and applicable to the case of influence. Here I can only provide a series of assertions derived from the argument of that chapter.

There are many sets of conditions under which such a deflation of influence will occur. One is comparable to the economic "paradox of thrift." If we view the three product inputs to the integrative subsector as parallel to consumer support, investment, and savings to the economy,[28] value-based claims to loyalty (I_i) occupy a position cognate to the allocation of investment funds; the assumption of leadership responsibility (C_i) a position cognate to consumer support; and grounds for the justification of claims (S_i) defines the level of influence savings, the allocation of loyalties (S_i), in a way similar to how the ranking of claims specifies the level of economic surplus allocated to savings.

A shift upward in the curve indicating the relationship between the grounds justifying loyalties and integrative solidarity will yield a decrease in solidarity, not an increase. As in the economic situation, where an increase in the savings curve will generate a deflationary situation, this increase in "savings" will generate a deflation of influence, and assuming a positive relationship between influence investment and integrative solidarity (as shown in fig. 24), a decrease in the scope of value-based claims to loyalty. Thus the effective scope of integrative norms, norms supported by a working consensus, will shrink.

A similar form of deflation may occur where the scope of policy decisions (N_i) increases beyond the equilibrium level of justifiable loyalties (S_i) and value-based claims to loyalties (I_i). In this case there will be a set of policy decisions that generate a deflationary gap. These decisions are therefore not acceptable within the context of the evaluations of some units within the system, units that will

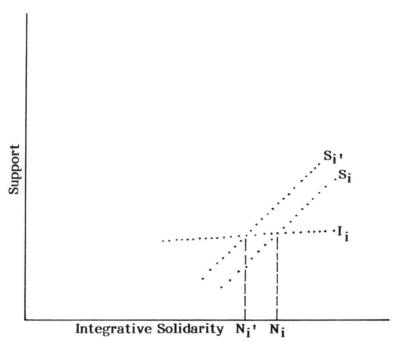

Figure 24. The determination of aggregate equilibrium integrative output, solidarity.

adopt a calculating orientation to such policies. These policies will either fall into disuse, will be justified in terms of the security base of influence (knowledge relating to performance capacity), or will involve an imbalance in the power system and thus an attempt to enforce the decisions. In formal terms, these decisions are comparable to unemployed labor power (N_a), constituent intentions that are present within the system but which do not have an impact on its productivity.

The second aspect of the neutralizing belief is the development of a nonnegative point of view with regard to the specific type of deviation under discussion; that is, the actor must feel that she will not suffer adverse sanctions due to her particular violation. One finds, for example, many individuals who will rob a large company but not a single person; they have at least a neutral attitude toward the former, but find the latter abhorrent. Here we refer to neutral orientations that are specific to the actual acts involved in the commission of whatever type of deviance is under scrutiny. Implicit in this neutral view is a positive attitude towards those forms of deviance which will serve as relevant responses to specific kinds of strain. In consequence, in table 1 drift is seen as derivative from a positive sanction regarding some deviant action (even if the actor's attitude to the activity itself is neutral) and a deflation of influence.

Assuming the prior existence of strain and an open illegitimate opportunity structure, we can conceptualize the determinants of drift in the following paradigm:

Table 1.

	Influence	
	Normal	Deflated
+	conformity	drift
0 or −	conformity	conformity re this action, possible drift re another

Sanctions regarding some deviant action: + = reward, − = negative sanction, 0 = neutral.

We are conceptualizing a situation in which an actor is confronted with the alternative between conforming to some norm or violating it, and where the appropriate strain and opportunity structures are present. The expectation defined by the norm is either legitimate (a balance within the influence system) or illegitimate (deflation). The sanctions involved in undertaking some specific action in violation of the norm are positively, negatively, or ambivalently perceived. We would expect an actor who had adopted a calculating attitude toward the normative system (deflation) and viewed the possible violation in a positive or a neutral light to be in a state of drift. The individual who has accepted obedience to the normative structure as a moral obligation should continue to conform to its norms, even if she views the violation as yielding a positive reward, and especially if she views it negatively. The individual who is in a situation of influence deflation but views the commission of some specific act from a negative perspective can be expected to conform to the norm governing it, but might violate that norm in the commission of other deviant actions that she feels will yield positive sanctions.[29]

It is in the situation of influence deflation that the import of criminal sanctions is manifest. The first resource the legal system possesses lies in the attempt to justify a norm with information and knowledge relevant to a definition of the collective interest of the system and system members under examination. If this fails, an attempt to enforce the law is usually made, implying a dedifferentiation of the power and influence systems, or at least the use of power or its security base, force, within the jurisdiction of the influence system. These constraints are relevant in our model insofar as they change the perceived balance between negative and positive sanctions for the actor who has assumed a calculating orientation. The certainty of the application of a negative sanction commensurate to the possible benefits obtained in the deviance is the most adequate deterrent. If and when the norm is defensible within the cultural norms of the actors, this sanction can be made apparent via the transmission of information within the context of the influence system, even if deflated, with perhaps greater results than those obtained in many coercive power systems (cf. Gould 1967:chap. 5).

Precipitating Factor (P_i)

Strain, an open illegitimate opportunity structure, and a set of neutralizing beliefs create a state of drift, but will not produce deviant behavior. In addition, each actor facing these conditions must confront a situation that offers her the chance to commit a deviant act. A precipitating factor, the specific set of events or the specific event that gives the actor an immediate opportunity to commit an act of deviance, is a necessary condition prior to the commission of an action in violation of the integrative subsystem's normative structure. If an individual is in a state of drift, the immediate opportunity to perform a deviant act should be accepted if the calculus of constraints is favorable. Obviously, in the case of an actor's deviance occurring via a pattern of "differential association," precipitating factors will often be consciously created by members of the deviant subculture in order to entice members of the subculture of deviance into the actual commission of deviant acts.

For Smelser, precipitating factors are events that "initiate or exaggerate a condition of strain," or give concrete substance to generalized beliefs, or redefine a situation of structural conduciveness (see Smelser 1962:17, 352–53). In other words, the precipitating factor serves to specify or accentuate some other variable within the

context of a concrete situation. In our terms it might simply be the
provision of a concrete opportunity to use some illegal drug—
handing a friend a marijuana joint at a party, perhaps under the
assumption that she already smokes. But while this type of precipitant is easily isolated in the concrete, it has proven impossible to
isolate in the abstract. We are thus often incapable of predicting
which specific events or types of events will act as precipitating factors, even though we are almost always capable of identifying them
after they have produced their results. In this case as in so many
others, hindsight alerts us that something is present, but does not
immediately tell us what that something is. The variable must be
treated, however, because there are many situations in which deviance does not occur simply because there was no precipitant.

Legitimizing Belief (LB_i)

I have now specified the necessary and sufficient conditions
under which deviant actions will be committed, the conditions
underlying primary deviation. Festinger has argued that "dissonance almost always exists after a decision has been made between
two or more alternatives" (1962:261). This implies that an actor
who chooses to commit a deviant act will find herself experiencing
dissonance.[30] And further, "identical dissonance in a large number
of people may be created when an event occurs which is so compel-
ling as to produce a uniform reaction in everyone" (Festinger
1962:262). Thus in situations where a large number of individuals
commit the same deviant act, similar dissonance may be widespread. In these situations, similar dissonance may "compel" a uniform reaction in a large percentage of the people affected.

It is reasonable to argue that if an actor is to continue to perform
deviant acts, a set of legitimizing beliefs must be developed to reduce the dissonance created by her actions. The termination of
deviance is, of course, an alternative method of reducing the dissonance. For those in whom legitimizing beliefs are developed,
it is possible to conceptualize the content of belief in terms of the
paradigm developed in the discussion of the neutralizing belief.
With the development of a set of legitimizing beliefs we can speak
of the genesis of secondary deviance.

The legitimizing belief will consist in the attitude that the specific
act of deviance the actor has committed was not illegitimate. In

addition, she must feel that positive rewards will accrue to her due to her deviant performance. Conversely, I would expect a secondary deviant to minimize the rewards she would be able to obtain by conforming to the recognized laws of her society. She will legitimize deviant acts that she views as rewarding.

In those instances where numerous individuals experience similar dissonance, I would expect them to settle on similar modes of reducing dissonance. In systems where the pressures leading to deviance are widespread I expect a deviant subculture to be formed. As Festinger has stated, "social support is particularly easy to obtain when a rather large number of persons who associate together are all in the same situation—that is, they all have the same dissonance between cognitions which can be reduced in the same manner" (1962:192). In forming legitimizing beliefs, two other factors must be considered: (1) I would expect new deviants to spend more time with their fellow deviants than they had previous to their own violation, and (2) I would expect that many of these individuals would attempt to convince others that the correct attitude toward this specific form of deviance is embodied in their legitimizing beliefs. Proselytizing should be fairly widespread. Such proselytizing, unless it evolves into a "norm-oriented movement," will not lead to an attempt to redefine the societal legal structure but only to attempts to convince others of the legitimacy of specific violations. It will lead, in other words, to a deviant subculture, within a subculture of deviance.

Thus the core group of a subculture of deviance, that is, "a setting in which the commission of ... [deviance] is common knowledge among a group of" actors (Matza 1962:33), is a deviant subculture, a group "in which certain forms of ... [deviant] activity are essential requirements for the performance of the dominant roles supported by the subculture" (Cloward and Ohlin 1960:7). The subculture of deviance includes drifters and primary and secondary deviants; the deviant subculture includes only secondary deviants. The subculture of deviance includes those who have progressed in the value-added schema to the point of holding neutralizing beliefs; the deviant subculture includes those who hold legitimizing beliefs. (An extensive discussion of one type of deviant subculture, that associated with the use of psychedelic drugs in the late 1960s, is found in Gould 1967:67–74, 101–10.)

Social Control (X_i)

The study of social control is the study of those counter-determinants which prevent, interrupt, deflect, or inhibit the accumulation of the determinants just reviewed. For purposes of analysis it is convenient to divide social controls into two broad types: (a) Those social controls which minimize ... strain [close an illegitimate opportunity structure, or stabilize an influence system—perhaps by eliminating the law that has been violated]. In a broad sense these controls *prevent* the occurrence of an episode of ... [deviant action], because they attack very nonspecific determinants. (b) Those social controls which are mobilized only *after* ... [the occurrence of acts of deviance].... To assess the effectiveness of the second kind of social controls, we shall ask how the appropriate agencies of control—the police, the courts, the press, the religious authorities, the community leaders, etc.—behave in the face of a potential or actual outburst of [deviant action].   (Smelser 1962:17)

(Smelser is, of course, speaking about collective behavior, thus the discontinuity in the quotation.)

A detailed study of societal mechanisms of social control is essential in aiding our understanding of the development of deviant subcultures. Certainly the reaction of society to the commission of deviant acts is an important variable in determining whether the actor will become a secondary deviant,[31] and the societal reaction may determine whether deviance will be sustainable as a regularized pursuit within a subcultural context.

It is also important to note that actions taken by social control agencies often have unintended consequences. The most widely discussed in the literature is the generation of a deviant identity, the stigmatization of the actor as a deviant. But from a more sociological perspective, it is often possible to note how the actions of social control agencies generate or intensify the variables that lead to the commission of deviant acts. Sometimes this occurs while the agency seeks to eliminate these very variables, or rather the substantive "problems" seen as the causes of deviance; often this occurs as a consequence of actions not directed toward these variables at all, actions taken in ignorance of their import.

Another unintended consequence might be labeled "symptom substitution." This occurs when the social control authorities convince a deviant population, by whatever tactics, that the sanctions to be derived from the commission of some action are negative. In this case they have eliminated one component of the neutralizing belief structure and moved the actor from the upper right corner (drift) to the lower right corner (conformity re this action, drift re another) in the paradigm in table 1. If an alternative form of deviance, with all other preconditions equivalent, is available, and if this alternative provides a positive sanction, the actor is likely to be back in the upper right corner (drift) prepared to engage in the new action whenever the immediate occasion arises. Such situations of "symptom substitution" are frequent among the users of various illicit drugs.

This is not the place to discuss social control mechanisms, but I want to make two suggestions concerning that study. The first is that the reactions of social control agencies can often be studied within the context of the framework articulated above as a theory of deviance. While it is true that the interactions of deviant and "police" are frequently routinized, often they occur in an area of institutional confusion, and often the reaction is taken in lieu of pressures similar to those confronting the deviant. This phenomenon has consistently been noted in the study of police reactions to many other forms of disorder, for example, the various forms of riots, and parallels can be found in the study of deviance. Often in these cases the social control agents are acting in violation of the rules they are "sworn to uphold."

Second, all regularized, unpunished deviance occurs within the context of an inflation of influence, even if this inflation is a localized phenomenon within the subsystem under analysis. In this situation (to simplify greatly) the symbolic content of influence exceeds the real potential for exerting pressure via the utilization of the medium; this can occur where the request for "trust" exceeds the actual performance capacity of those whose status enables them to legitimately make such a request. This phenomenon is analyzable within the context of the interchange framework referred to in the discussion of the neutralizing belief.[32]

Revolution

A Theory of Revolutionary Action

I define revolutionary actions as motivated actions that abrogate the institutionalized authority code within a polity and are guided by a belief (an ideology) in an attempt to redefine and restructure one or another of the components of social action in that polity. This attempt to redefine some aspect of the authority structure rests on the application of violence,[33] and depends on this mechanism until routinized within a normative structure.[34]

While revolutionary acts are in violation of the normative component of the institutionalized authority system, I do not exclude actions that are conforming and nondisruptive within some other collectivity, but only emphasize that the revolutionaries must be members of the system in which the revolutionary acts occurred, and thus are liable to the authority structure within that system.[35] (Outsiders may take part in the movement, e.g., mercenary troops, so long as it is clear that the main thrust of the movement is indigenous.)

It is important to note that while revolutions imply the violation of norms institutionalized within the authority structure, these violations need not involve the use of force. Often the first application of force comes from the resisting authorities. As Tilly points out, in the modern European record repressive agents like police and soldiers are "the most consistent initiators and performers of collective violence" (Tilly 1975:515). Either the revolutionaries or the counterrevolutionaries may attempt to ensure their control through the use of force, but most often those previously in control of the power system will resort to force as the power system becomes deflated (see Parsons 1969:chap. 9; Tilly 1975:515). We will see that this deflation is a necessary condition leading to revolution.

It is necessary to distinguish between revolutionary actions and revolutions. The former are acts of disorder defined by the actors as relevant to the overthrow and ultimate reconstruction of some component of the political authority structure. These actions are considered revolutionary because of their aim and because of their abrogation of the authority code; they need not, and often do not, lead to actual revolution.

Revolutions may and generally do involve actions the effects of which are not in accord with the desires or expectations of the participants. They are defined in terms of the actual result, the violent (not necessarily forcible) redefinition of one or more aspects of the institutionalized authority structure. But some ambiguity remains in this characterization of revolutionary actions as against revolutions because we customarily define attempts to violently restructure the political system, even if failed, as revolutions. Clearly there is a threshold where revolutionary actions are concentrated on the actual attempt to seize power and thus become part of a revolution, whether it fails or succeeds.

Tilly has defined the circumstances that we might adopt as definitive of the onset of revolution:

> In order for a situation to produce multiple sovereignty and thus become revolutionary, commitments to some alternative claimant must be activated in the face of prohibitions or contrary directives from the government. The moment at which some men belonging to members of the alternative coalition seize control over some portion of the government [polity] and other men not previously attached to the coalition honor their directives marks the beginning of a revolution.   (Tilly 1975:530)

In other words, the revolution begins when nonparticipants honor the directives of the revolutionaries as against those of the government, whether the revolutionaries succeed or are crushed at some future time.

In many instances actors may participate in actions that are not directed toward a redefinition of the polity but which are important in such a redefinition (e.g., the various forms of riot: actions comparable to deviance, only directed toward the political system; or "revolutionary activities" directed toward local rather than national governmental units). The generating conditions of these acts are related to their immediate, not long-term consequences. These immediate consequences may involve the genesis of some precondition of revolution; thus their relevance for our discussion. Further, many revolutions are complicated processes, involving sequential and overlapping phases. In identifying generating conditions it is absolutely essential to distinguish between these phases.

It is therefore necessary to analyze the generating conditions leading to the revolutionary actions of various collectivities within a society, and simultaneously to analyze the consequences of those actions for the system as a whole and for other collectivities. In doing this it becomes obvious that major revolutions are complex, multifaceted events and that summary appellations—"The French Revolution"—often mask the multiple revolutions and other disorders occurring concurrently or following one on the other.[36]

In viewing any society we must attempt to isolate a series of revolutionary potentialities inherent in its structure.[37] Five types of

potential may be briefly characterized as follows: (1) the potential
for the occurrence of revolutionary action; (2) the possibility of the
legitimization of these actions within a revolutionary subculture;
(3) the potential for the restructuring of some component of the
institutionalized authority structure; (4) the possibility of the institutionalization of a new structure; (5) the likelihood of the new
structure bearing a "family resemblance" to the one envisioned by
the revolutionaries.

In what follows I emphasize the rudiments of an explanation of
the first two potentialities, or more accurately of the actions associated with them, and make reference to the third. The final two possibilities can only be dealt with within the context of a model of
societal development.

Regarding numbers (4) and (5), we must be concerned with the
chances of the revolutionaries successfully mobilizing the resources
to restructure some component of the political system. This possibility can be assessed, in a very rudimentary fashion, within the
context of the interchange system: Do the revolutionaries possess
the capabilities to mobilize the inputs to the subsector attacked?
Second, we must attempt to discern whether the type of system they
desire to establish is viable within the context of the society in
which they live and if they have the capacity to restructure that
society. To do this a stage sequence model of societal development
is necessary, specifying the structural characteristics of each stage
and isolating the consequences of modes of progression not within
the developmental pattern outlined. This requires an analysis of the
society, not simply the political system (see chap. 4 and 8 below;
Gould 1985; cf. Lenin 1960ff.:vol. 3).

The next paragraphs outline the necessary and sufficient conditions for the occurrence of revolutionary actions. In this context I
attempt little more than to show the fit of this partial theory within
the theory of disorder.

Structural Strain (S)

The strain component in the generation of revolutionary actions
is the same as described in the discussion of deviance, only here,
owing to a combination with other variables, the possible reactions
differ. Substantively, of course, the manifestations of strain may
differ. It is especially important to note that while strain is rife in all
social systems, the systemic impairment of the relationships among

social units at a level commensurate with widespread dissatisfaction and response is not always present. An analysis of the conditions that lead to the genesis of this type of impairment would take us beyond this middle-range theory and into a theory of social development, and an analysis of the tendencies within specific stages of development. Here I limit my remarks to a brief elucidation of the possible responses to each variety of strain.

SF. Reaction to this type of strain, assuming the presence of the other variables, involves an attempt to work within the context of the collectivity structures extant within the system in redefining the actual content of the roles involved. Thus it involves the "misuse" of existing collectivities in the political misappropriation of adaptive resources, an attempt to redefine the facility-role component of the institutionalized authority structure, but not the collectivity or normative component of that structure. An example would be the revolt of the aristocrats in France in the late 1780s. (The classic and now controversial discussion is Lefebvre 1947:pt. I.) Here, within the context of existing collectivities (primarily the *parlements*) the aristocrats, with widespread "popular support," attempted to redefine the facility base of the political system. Louis XVI commented with regard to one of these actions that "if he yielded, the monarchy would be converted into 'an aristocracy of magistrates, which would be as contrary to the rights and interests of the nation, as to his own sovereign prerogatives'" (Goodwin 1966:36).

Similar situations were present in the first phase of both the Russian Revolution of 1917 and the English Revolution of 1640. In the latter case, the Long Parliament in its first one and one-half sessions attempted to assert its control over facilities previously under the control of the king. He, in response, reaffirmed his control over these resources, although he eventually yielded under severe pressure.[38] The important point to remember in this and other situations is that in misusing a set of collectivity structures, the participants in this type of revolution generate a second focus of political authority in their attempt to exert control over some set of political questions, and they call upon societal members to obey their directives, often labeling those who obey "citizens" while refusing this appellation to the disobedient.

In each instance, a "facilitory rebellion" (a revolution at the level of facilities, REVOF) is in violation of the normative component of the institutionalized authority structure. This violation involves a redefinition of the role arrangements within one of the collectivities that constitute the extant political system.

SG. Strain at the level of goals, when coupled with the other necessary variables, leads to an attempt to redefine the collectivity structure of the polity. This involves a seizure of control over what Easton has labeled the "government," as against the "regime" (focusing on political norms) and the "political community" (focusing on political values). A major focus of this sphere of political responsibility, the "government," involves the specification and implementation of executive decisions and the ultimate control over "police" powers.

There are many substantive types of rebellions (revolutions at the level of goals, REVOG), including most coup d'etats. Here only the actors in charge of governmental collectivities are changed; the norms and values that cybernetically control these collectivities remain intact. Thus even if the transfer of power is between two antagonistic parties, it is easy to isolate and specify the type of revolution which has occurred or which is attempted.

More difficult to identify are those rebellions that lead to the formation of "provisional governments," either in name or in fact. Frequent examples of this phenomenon are found in 1848, and also in the Constituent Assembly in the Great French Revolution, the Provisional Government of the Great Russian Revolution, and the rule of the English Parliamentarians in the English Revolution. In these cases no explicit attempt is made to revise the type of regime extant in the polity, but the redefinition of the collectivity component manifests sufficient discontinuity with the previous system that normative readjustments are inevitable, unless the revolution backslides into something resembling a simple change of personnel within the previously extant normative structure. Thus while rebellions may result in the termination of the constitution of the previous regime, they are not directed in an attempt to redefine it. Where resistance is generated from the previous incumbents, however, a situation of normative strain stemming from the multiple expectations that result from multiple sovereignty is inevitable—at least for certain portions of the societal community. (See Trotsky's brilliant discussion, 1967, 1:chap. XI). So long as the ultimate control over coercive mechanisms lies in disputed hands, normative strain is likely to be generated within the system, and with normative strain, pressures toward the next type of revolution.

SG is a necessary but insufficient condition for the development of a movement seeking a rebellion, REVOG, a movement seeking to redefine the collectivity structure of the authority system.

SN. A disorderly reaction to strain at the level of norms, when directed toward the political system, gives rise to a "normative revolution," or REVON (a revolution at the level of norms). A movement so directed will seek to redefine the political regime, which is constituted by the norms of the authority structure, the codes within the political system definitive of the justifiable rights and duties of offices. Such a movement often involves the redefinition of the political constitution of the society; it seeks to replace the old set of rules regulating political processes with a new code and therefore to radically modify the content and form of those processes. In a strictly defined REVON, the new constitution will be legitimized in terms of the prior, presumably still acceptable political values.

Revolutions of this type are less frequent than those already discussed. The establishment of the legislative assembly and a Republic under the control of the Gironde, in the French Revolution; the establishment of Kerensky's Republic in the Russian Revolution; and Cromwell's Commonwealth in the English Revolution are three well-known examples. In each of these revolutions there was an abolition of the monarchy and the institution of a republic, but each retained the core of the political values of the past. It is important to note that in all of these cases there were further attempts to extend the scope of the revolution into the sphere of values; in part these attempts were accelerated and facilitated by the major institutional changes within the normative revolution. A redefinition of the norms used to justify political actions may well reflect on the values that are utilized to legitimize those actions. SN is a necessary but not sufficient condition for the generation of a movement seeking a normative revolution, a REVON.

SV. Strain at the level of values may give rise to a movement attempting to redefine the pattern of political evaluation. This movement is aimed at the fundamental values that legitimize the political structure under examination, the evaluations definitive of the "good polity" (cf. Smelser 1962:25). Such a movement may involve components of the society's "civil religion" (Bellah 1967) or definitions of the national community. It always concerns the value nexus that cybernetically controls the political system. Following Johnson (1966), I label these movements "total revolutions," REVOV (revolutions at the level of values).[39]

These are the revolutions most commonly associated with "social revolutions,"[40] but the two are differentiable. In this chapter I am only concerned with political revolutions, even when they form a part of larger social movements and even when they have effects upon these more general transformations.

The Bolshevik and Jacobin phases of the Russian and French Revolutions fall within the category REVOV. The Leveller movement within the English Revolution was crushed before it had the opportunity to effect this type of redefinition. SV is a necessary but insufficient condition for the occurrence of a movement seeking a "total revolution," REVOV.

There are many categorizations of revolution, and many attempts to specify the conditions leading to revolution, but few attempts to specify correlations between the two. In fact, most researchers have either identified one basic type of strain as generating revolution in general or else they have specified many types of strain leading to a given revolution. What I attempt to do is differentiate between the types of strain and isolate their relationships to the types of revolution. A structural analysis of a prerevolutionary society should show that there is a differential tendency for a given type of strain to be manifested in specific social groups. If this analysis can be successfully carried out and the locale of each type of strain isolated, we have the basis of an explanation, or prediction, of the type of revolutionary actions, if any, in which a group is likely to engage. Further, we will have laid the foundation for the explanation of the various stages within a revolution, insofar as revolutions pass through the four types enumerated.

One of the reasons it has been so difficult to isolate the causes of any given revolution has been that this differentiation between the types of strain and the types of revolution has not been made in a systematic fashion. A researcher might well have fixed on a relevant type of strain but examined it in connection with the wrong group, or in connection with the wrong phase of a revolution, falsely arguing for its irrelevance or conversely finding it relevant for one phase of a revolution and assuming its relevance for all revolutions. It is essential that we learn that many of the events that we label with a single word or phrase are really complex in their internal structure, and that the conditions leading to one aspect or component of them often differ from those leading to another. In many instances, only with the independent, if interdependent, genesis of various factors will their effects interrelate to generate some emergent phenomenon. Revolutions are not the only social actions to which these strictures apply; other examples include religious reformations, transformations in the structure of science, and economic changes—for example, the Industrial Revolution.

Opportunity Structure (O_g)

In discussing the illegitimate opportunity structure it is necessary to be clear in specifying what we wish to elucidate. As long as our interest is confined to the generation of a climate within which revolutions might grow—a subculture of revolution—and the organization of a core group within a revolutionary movement— a revolutionary subculture—the discussion can closely parallel the earlier one for deviance. If we are concerned with the actuality of a revolution, the issue becomes much more complex.

In the first case, the generation of a revolutionary movement, the opportunity structure can be conceptualized as the availability of the necessary facilities to perform the revolutionary actions. If our concern is not the socialization of new recruits into an extant structure but the first actions in the genesis of the movement, these early actions will not be revolutionary; rather, they will be riotous—that form of disorder which is in violation of the code component of the authority structure but which makes no attempt to restructure any component of the polity; a form of disorder which is not aimed at such a redefinition.[41] As in the case of deviance, the specifics of the illegitimate opportunity structure are dependent on the type of riot or revolution one wishes to explain, or conversely, the nature of the illegitimate opportunity structure determines the specifics of the movement one might predict. We have said that the type of strain present in the system will determine the type of movement to be generated, but the tactics of that movement will be largely dependent on the illegitimate opportunity structures available within the system. Clearly, a group dominating extant governmental organizations will adopt different tactics than a group with no access to such organizations. Access to governmental organizations is a necessary component of the opportunity structure for REVOF, and this tells us a great deal about these revolutionaries within the context of any society.

Widespread strain, an illegitimate opportunity structure, and a set of neutralizing beliefs are conditions for the occurrence of political disorders. With their occurrence a subculture of riot or revolution may form, and if ideologically directed toward a redefinition of some component of the authority structure, a revolutionary subculture. Once formed, such a subculture can actively engage in the recruitment of new partisans; the possibilities of its formation are dependent on the mutual interactions that occur among those actors exposed to a given form of strain. As in the case of deviance, we are dealing with learned behavior, and one component of the illegitimate opportunity structure is contact with individuals either susceptible to the commission of revolutionary actions (those in a state of drift; see below, the discussion of neutralizing beliefs) or members of a revolutionary subculture. It is therefore usual for the formation of the subcultures to occur within the context of previous organizational ties; there is considerable evidence that these ties serve as a basis of political mobilization, and if they are broken revolutionary activities become less likely.

In certain situations, symbolic mechanisms of communication can serve as partial substitutes for direct contact. It is not a coincidence that Arendt dates the onset of ideological revolutions in the postprinting world of early modern Europe. (The reader need only glance through a small selection of the Thomason collection of tracts published during the English Revolution, from 1640 to 1660, to appreciate the ideological fervor generated by and leading to revolutionary activities. Thousands of these tracts are housed in the British Museum.) Further, the quality of transportation systems has a direct impact on the articulation of political movements. These factors concern the infrastructure enabling the allocation of facilities (material and ideational) necessary for widespread revolutionary disorder.

Newcomers to revolutionary actions will progress through the same stages as the originators of the response, but the mechanisms of passage may differ. For one thing, the extant subculture may manipulate the variables under examination, thus necessitating, or at least making possible, a revolutionary response. This is a process of the mobilization of new recruits from the subculture of revolution into a revolutionary subculture. One component of this mobilization can be the generation of an illegitimate opportunity structure, opening the way to participation in revolutionary actions. It is important to note again that this mobilization often uses the previous social ties among the disaffected (cf. Selznick 1960).

The illegitimate opportunity structure involves access to adaptive resources necessary in the commission of revolutionary actions, and perhaps the regularization of such actions within a revolutionary subculture. The question of whether this revolutionary subculture will have the potential to restructure some component of the polity concerns not only whether it is able to mobilize the resources to maintain its existence as an autonomous subsystem within the society, but also whether it has the capacity to mobilize the adaptive resources necessary for the performance of the actions demanded by the political system of the society as a whole. In societies of relative freedom or of weak enforcement capabilities, the ability to form a revolutionary subculture may not imply the capacity to mobilize the resources necessary to control some aspect of the political system.

With regard to the opportunities for the institutionalization of the revolution and the likelihood of the new structure bearing a family resemblance to the one envisioned by the revolutionaries, I will make only one comment. In locating the structure to be redefined within the interchange schema, one has identified the necessary inputs relevant to the institutionalization of an alternative structure. One might begin the search for an illegitimate opportunity structure that allows the institutionalization of a new structural component within the political subsystem by examining the capacity of the revolutionary subculture to mobilize alternative sources of these inputs. Alternatively one might ask about the capacity of the revolutionary subculture to capture the current sources of these inputs. In either case, the relevant adaptive inputs should be emphasized.

To give a crude but accurate example, one of the major components of the illegitimate opportunity structure for successful revolutionary actions concerns the capacity of the revolutionaries to mobilize monetary resources and human services. It is obvious that access to these adaptive resources will vary depending on the social background of the revolutionaries. Certain groups will control key positions in the economy and will be able to mobilize economic resources for their revolutionary actions; others will be forced, owing to their social positions, to either mold their revolutionary actions into channels acceptable to those who control the economy, and viable within the context of the constraints delimited by the type of economic structure, or they will be forced to take control of the economy and/or redefine the economic structure, or they will fail as the political system disintegrates in their hands. The constraints are much less severe when we limit ourselves to an inquiry into the genesis of revolutionary movements. In either case, however, it is clear that this capacity cannot be analyzed in isolation from the type of justifying and legitimizing orientations the revolutionaries adopt, as the provision of adaptive resources is interrelated with the level of support from the societal community and the political authorization, from the latency subsystem, generated by the revolution.

Neutralizing Belief (NB$_g$)

One of the most virulent controversies among those who seek to make revolutions and among those who seek to analyze them concerns the question of spontaneity versus organization. It has appeared in many guises and has involved discussions of many issues: the role of intellectuals in making revolutions, the role of leadership in revolutions, the manipulation necessary or not necessary in order to make a revolution, whether revolutions are inevitable or must be made, among many others. But basically the question is always the same: Does the revolution occur because of the spontaneous actions of the masses, or owing to the coherent plans of a small organization? (the difference between "circumstances" and "plot"; cf. Brinton 1965:77–86). Though many investigators argue that both types of revolutions occur, only a few have argued that both views are correct and both incorrect. These arguments— which run through the Marxist-Leninist tradition and receive their most incisive formulations in Lenin's writings—indicate that both a relatively small revolutionary cadre and a considerably larger group available for mobilization or neutral towards revolutionary actions must be present in any revolutionary situation.[42]

With the development of the neutralizing belief, actors are set in a state of drift. They form the generally nonhostile or even sympathetic subculture of revolution which surrounds the revolutionary subculture, the revolutionary cadre. The latter group, committed to a legitimizing belief structure, forms the revolutionary core, with the former group, "neutralized" and in a state of drift, forming the revolutionary periphery. Those in the subculture of revolution are likely to commit revolutionary actions if convinced that they will in consequence derive some benefit, and if given the specific opportunity to do so.

As in the case of deviance, this neutralizing belief system is multifaceted. Here, however, it includes a calculating orientation toward the power system, not the societal influence system (see Parsons 1969:chaps. 13–17; my discussion assumes a familiarity with the Parsonian concept of power). In this situation power is deflated, political decisions are not accepted as binding, and recourse is had to coercive sanctions. In such cases, units within the deflated political sectors will adopt an expedient orientation toward the authority structure, no longer automatically accepting its decisions.

I have discussed a model within which it is possible to isolate the generating conditions of the deflation of power in chapter 2, and I will not repeat that discussion here. But I do want to briefly refer to the context in which I treat an oft-noted but little understood phenomenon in the genesis of revolutions. If we simplify our model, we can point to the three product inputs to the polity as the focus of our analysis; they are comparable to the three product inputs to the economy: political support from the societal community (C_g) parallels consumer support (C_a); the authorization of powers of office (I_g) parallels the allocation of fluid resources, investment (I_a); and the scope of control over productivity and services delimits the extent of operative responsibility (S_g) in the same fashion as the ranking of claims delimits the extent of economic surplus saved (S_a). The parallels extend into a model that identifies the level of political production at the equilibrium point between the scope of authorized powers and the scope of operative responsibility. (A less elementary model incorporating the factor inputs to the polity is examined in chap. 2, above.)

The one situation of deflation that I want to note involves a political "paradox of thrift." A shift upward in the saving schedule, as shown in fig. 25, will decrease output, and where investment varies positively with output, decrease the authorized powers of office. What we see here is an increase in the political control of economic resources leading not to an increase in political control but rather to

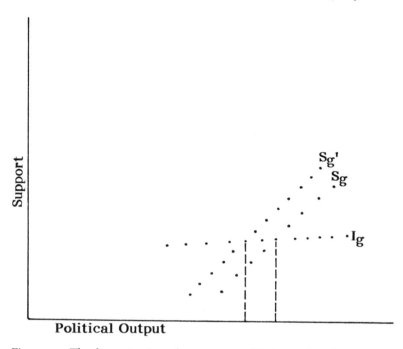

Figure 25. The determination of aggregate equilibrium political output.

a decrease in the scope of that control; this is a phenomenon that often occurs in revolutionary situations, where it is often coupled with an attempt to enforce powers in excess of those authorized.

Quite simply, in a case of power deflation the real resources within a power system exceed the accepted symbolic definition of the scope of that system. In these cases, the "men of power" will resort to the security base of the medium, force. They will seek to enforce their decisions. This is true of all polities, including democracies. And this is one basis of what Marx referred to as the dictatorship of the bourgeoisie and the dictatorship of the proletariat. Marx argued that in a capitalist system, the "rules of the game" protect the interests of the bourgeoisie as a class and that any class acting in defiance of those rules, in violation of the authority code, would be forced to conform. The extent of the freedom such a system allows is always defined by such a code, and if the code does in fact favor one class, it is acceptable to refer to the system as a dictatorship of that class, even if the actual wielders of power are not class members, even if the system is "democratically controlled" (see chap. 2 especially n. 72, above). It is within this context that Lenin's strictures concerning the organization and discipline of a revolutionary party must be understood. His vision was not accurate solely in the context of Tsarist Russia, but within the context of any "dictatorship" where the revolutionaries represent an excluded class.

In a situation of power deflation, actors in those sectors of the society which are affected will adopt a calculating orientation toward the decisions of those in power. This is the first aspect of a revolutionary neutralizing belief; the second is constituted by a neutral orientation toward the specific revolutionary acts that might be called for by the revolutionary cadre, acts aimed at the institutionalized authority structure. When both components of the neutralizing belief are joined to strain and an open illegitimate opportunity structure, some set of actors will be in a state of drift. In this state, a framework identical to the paradigm in table 1 is applicable, excepting that the relevant medium is now power, not influence. In a state of drift an actor, if confronted with a specific opportunity and a favorable set of sanctions, will take part in riotous and/or revolutionary actions.[43]

Precipitating Factor (P_g)

Stone (1972a) refers to them as triggers, Johnson (1966) as accelerators, and Smelser (1962) as precipitating factors, the term I have chosen. In each instance the discussion of the authors, those cited and many others, informs us that this factor is the immediate precursor of revolutionary actions, the factor that accentuates one or more of the variables leading to revolutionary action or else removes some social control mechanism that has impeded such action. But no one tells us how to pinpoint what these elusive factors are in a general way. We are even warned, appropriately, that the precipitating factor may "overlap empirically with some of the broader background conditions" of strain and an open illegitimate opportunity structure (Smelser 1962:252; the second variable is mine, not Smelser's).

A precipitating factor provides the immediate impetus to engage in riotous or revolutionary actions.[44] It seems that this occurs by affecting some prior condition of these actions, accentuating strain past the breaking point, opening up some illegitimate opportunity structure, making a deflation of power manifest, or providing the ideological connection between some set of actions and the possible rewards necessary to alleviate a condition of strain, identifying a target of the reaction, or perhaps removing the coercive force used to stifle the disorderly acts. What is impossible to say at this point is whether the precipitating factor has an independent effect, differentiable from a simple substantive determination of one of the other variables within the schema. It is my supposition that it does, but I am not yet capable of identifying it in theoretical terms.

In any case, the precipitating factor is an occurrence that sets off riotous or revolutionary actions; either spontaneously among those in a situation of drift, or because it is used as a focus of mobilization by those in the revolutionary subculture. These actions will result in dissonance and then perhaps in the formation or acceptance of a set of legitimizing beliefs.

Legitimizing Belief (LB_g)

Earlier in this chapter I quoted Marx: "if these material elements of a complete revolution are not present ... then, as far as practical development is concerned, it is absolutely immaterial whether the *idea* of this revolution has been expressed a hundred times already, as the history of communism proves" (Marx and Engels 1964:50–51, cf. 61). The belief structures that are called upon to legitimize revolutionary actions may have been in existence prior to those actions, but only with the commission of acts in violation of the institutionalized authority code will these beliefs enable those within the revolutionary subculture to guide the actions of the potential revolutionaries within the subculture of revolution.[45]

"The group requires that each individual perform an irrevocable action" (Fanon 1966:67; cf. Lukacs 1971). Once an actor undertakes actions in violation of the institutionalized authority code, she must legitimize her actions or retreat into conformity, while perhaps justifying sporadic violations. When many actors in like situations act violently against the political system, the legitimations may cohere in the belief system of a revolutionary subculture. To speak more accurately, this subculture will become revolutionary as against riotous when one component of the legitimizing belief demands the restructuring of some component of the political system. Depending on the nature of the strain to which the group is responding, this will involve the facility-role complex, "facilitory rebellion" (REVOF); the collectivity structure, rebellion (REVOG); the norm structure, normative revolution (REVON); and/or the value structure, total revolution (REVOV).

All legitimizing belief systems must define the specific revolutionary actions undertaken as desirable in the context of attaining the sought-after transformation. Such actions must be seen as beneficial for the system as a whole even though they might be seen as dangerous for the individual performer. While such "suicidal" orientations are rarer within revolutionary movements than many have assumed, for this attitude to develop at all the belief systems that legitimize it must provide assurances of the eventual success of the movement of which they form a part. Such belief systems are almost always of a "charismatic" nature.

The term *charisma* has been used to characterize a diverse set of phenomena. Here it involves, in the first instance, a "religious" phenomenon. Charisma involves the mobilization of a cultural input (definition of a situation) within the social system in an attempt to expand, contract, or redefine the foundation of value commitments as a symbolic medium of social pressure (cf. Parsons 1969:chap. 16; Parsons and Platt 1973). A religious prophet is an individual who claims a personal relation with the "divine," with the ultimate source of meaning for a society, the individual who provides a unified and meaningful view of the world and who defines moral obligations as the duty of her followers. For Weber, "Prophets systematized religion with a view to unifying the relationship of man to the world, by reference to an ultimate and integrated value position" (1968, 2:460; cf. Shils 1961, 1965). The focus of charisma for value commitments is along the L-I boundary of the social system; drawing on the "definition of the situation" input to the society, the prophet seeks to regulate the "investment" input to the latency subsector.

Charisma can also have meaning in the context of a discussion of the economy, polity, or societal community. I view charisma as one determinant of where the focus of any generalized medium may be directed and how its scope might be regulated. It involves a relation between the value-commitments input to any subsystem and the investment input to that subsystem.[46] In the case of the polity these inputs can be captured by a revolutionary subculture and form the basis of a second system of sovereignty challenging the extant political structure. The charismatic leader thus broaches the divide between the political and latency systems. She demands obedience and legitimizes this demand in terms of a special relationship to that sphere that transcends ordinary political life. She appeals to the defining values of the "religion," however secularized, recognized by at least part of the populace, or to the values that define the destiny of the nation or another relevant social unit, in which case she might well help to create a "national religion." She demands obedience as a recognition of duty, as a recognition of moral obligation. Obedience is, however, conditional: she must prove herself; she must offer evidence of a close relationship with "the center," and in the political situation this implies the effective assumption of operative responsibility.

The routinization of political charisma involves the successful increase, decrease, or transfer of both the commitment and power inputs from the latency subsystem, but also a parallel increase, decrease, or transfer of the other inputs to the polity from the economy and societal community. The capacity to effect these transfers is one measure of the potential for the success of some revolutionary subculture that challenges the established political system. The more radical the challenge (moving upward in the cybernetic hierarchy: REVOF, REVOG, REVON, REVOV), the more components of the structure which will need redefinition.[47] This potentiality cannot be adequately assessed without a discussion of the requisites for a progression from stage to stage in a model of social development. But I would agree with Weber that the form of commitment system he labeled "the Protestant Ethic" was essential to the growth of capitalism, and would further agree with later commentators that it, or some functional equivalent, was a necessary component in the revolutions that helped to generate the political conditions within which capitalism could flourish (see chap. 4, below; and Gould 1981*b*).

When a revolution occurs, especially if it involves the widespread use of force, there is a possibility of it serving as the foundation of a new order. This is not because violence (as violation and as bloodshed) is praiseworthy, but because it is abhorrent within most value systems and therefore creates very strong levels of dissonance in many of those subjected to it (in any capacity), and therefore requires strong and definite legitimation. In such cases, a new political order may be founded upon the mythology of the revolution (Fanon 1966; Sorel 1961).

In summary, the revolutionary subculture exists as a core group within a broader subculture of revolution. It includes those who have legitimized the commission of revolutionary acts, and many who have devoted their lives to the revolution. This core is the cadre who will act within the setting of the "neutrals," those segments of the society in a state of drift. They seek to mobilize the drifters to engage in acts of revolution, and then help to legitimize the actions into commitments in order to routinize their support. In all revolutionary situations a revolutionary subculture, or many such groups, acts within the much more populous subculture of revolution.

Social Control (X_g)

Here my framework of analysis parallels the case of deviance, but with two modifications. In the first instance, there are two levels of control; both are relevant prior to and following revolutionary actions. The first concerns the ability of the authorities to prevent the formation of a subculture of revolution and revolutionary subcultures; the second, the prevention of a revolution. With regard to the first, I might make the commonplace comment that some degree of political freedom must be present within the system to allow the movement to develop, but this freedom must not be so broad with regard to the redressing of grievances (as defined by the movement's ideology) so as to allow for a nondisorderly settlement of the issues contested. It is likely, in other words, that the relationship between disorders and political repression is curvilinear; riotous and revolutionary actions will be few at very low levels of repression, will rise with an increase in repression, and past some point will shrink with an increase in the severity and effectiveness of the containment.

With the formation of a revolutionary subculture there is the possibility of the initiation of a revolution. If this group endeavors to move beyond the stage where it controls the political activity of its members and attempts to define itself as an essential component of the polity for the society as a whole, a revolution will have been initiated that must be met by the governmental organization. To assess the possibilities of success for this revolutionary subculture would be (1) to evaluate its internal organizational strengths and weaknesses and (2) to assess the position of the revolutionaries

within a given society in order to determine their capacity to mobilize political resources (the type depending on what variety of
revolution is under examination) against the institutionalized political structure.

With regard to the prevention of the revolution, reliance is not
on influence, as in the response to deviance, but primarily on
power, and in its deflated state, on coercive force. The possibility
of the authorities defeating the revolution depends on their ability
to prevent an inflationary spiral of power affecting the controls
necessary to crush it.[48] If, for example, units within the deflated sector control a significant segment of the service inputs to the polity,
their defection may well create a situation of inflation within the
system, leading perhaps to a collapse of the power structure.

This collapse is usually viewed in terms of the government's loss
of the army, and seen as a necessary prerequisite for the success of a
revolution. But it can extend beyond that to the entire administration. The king was very nearly powerless at the onset of the English
Revolution in 1640 because his "bureaucracy" was not under central control but rather in the hands of local notables. When these
notables supported the first revolutionary actions of the Parliament,
the king was impotent; only when a large number of them returned to the fold as the revolution attacked more basic components of the polity, and when he based his appeals on the accom-
plishments of the first revolution (REVOF) did the king have any
chance of organizing a resistance (see chap. 5).

If the issue becomes one of civil war it will be contested in a
sphere of deflation between two systems, and the system of greater
strength will triumph. One of the major components of strength
depends on how smoothly each combatant is able to run the power
system within its sphere of control, how successfully each will be
able to mobilize economic resources, political support, and political
legitimation; in sum, how successful each will be in mobilizing for
collective action.

Conclusion

I have covered considerable ground in this chapter, surveying
some points much more thoroughly than others. I want to conclude
by stressing one more aspect of revolutionary phenomena. This is
the importance of treating revolutions as social processes within a

developmental model, rather than as simple events. The model must include not only a portrayal of the role of revolution in societal development but also a portrayal of the development of the revolution. When this is done it is possible to show how revolutions progress up the cybernetic scale in a regular pattern of radicalization.[49]

I will not discuss this in detail here (see chap. 8, below) as that would involve a presentation of a developmental model, but I want to note three points. The first is that this progression involves not only a movement of effect, the type of revolution, but of cause, the conditions under which the revolution will occur. To identify this movement, it is necessary to recognize that revolutions involve many disparate phenomena. We must remember, for example, that many of the participants in a revolution will be engaging in actions that are properly classified as riots, and that the effect of their actions on the revolution may be the generation of one or another of the conditions we have specified as determinants for revolution.

It is important to realize that many of these actions, especially in the final two types of revolution, will not be the same type as the revolution they help to effect. Thus riots directed toward the facility or collectivity complex may be a component of REVOV: the indirect consequences of these riots in the redefining of the political structure may be directed by a small organizational center. Revolutions directed toward the collectivity structure of a local political system (and many of the actions in a revolution are directed toward local power centers, not toward the national polity) may have national consequences of a different order, even though conflicts may soon appear between the two sets of revolutionaries.

This leads to our second point. It is important to realize that the first revolutionary subculture will develop on an organizational base extant prior to its formation. As previously extant groups engage in revolutionary actions, they will form a revolutionary subculture challenging the power of the prior government. It is in this situation that we must begin to study the coalition formation and differentiation that occur as the revolution progresses. It is very important to understand the prior social structural basis of these coalitions; for example, the first Country organization in the English Revolution centering upon the local power of the notables and acting within the Parliament; then the activation of mercantile London and the "progressive gentry and yeomen" interests in the

"Presbyterian Parliament," first supported by, then opposed and crushed by grandee, "Independent" interests in the army, who were supported by a faction of the gentry in disoriented status positions (status inconsistency). The "Independents" then crushed their erstwhile supporters, the Leveller interests in the army, who were supported by some sect and some artisan collectivities. This summary is not adequate, but perhaps it does hint at the multifaceted interrelationships among stratification and economic, religious, and political actions. (See Trotsky 1967, 1: ch. XI; cf. Engels's erroneous parallels between the French and English revolutions in Marx and Engels 1975, 3:472–73. My own extended discussion follows in chaps. 5–7. The most sophisticated analyses of this kind of development within a revolution are Marx's, 1963, 1964.)

Third, we note when we utilize this schema that some revolutions do not undergo this progression but deal solely with one variety of movement, for example, coups d'etat. These are revolutions unimportant in European societal development, at least after the seventeenth century. Further, only after the sixteenth century were revolutions directed forward and not legitimized in terms of prior values. It is in the process of legitimizing total revolution that new sources of evaluation are called upon or generated. Tilly is probably correct in pointing out that when new groups seize power they legitimize the attack in terms of general values, while old groups defend and reinforce their power by recalling prior services and by enunciating the specifics on which their power is based (Tilly 1973:218).[50] It is important to remember that the working out of these processes can carry us well beyond the normally identified time limit of the revolution, and that the institutionalization of the revolution can take many years.

4. The Manufacturing Social Formation

In twenty years of the sixteenth century, still more in
one or two lifetimes, what had been a reasonable
money-rent might become quite unreasonable from the
landlord's point of view or indeed from any point of
view. The tenant got all the advantage of prices for his
produce doubled or trebled, the lord if he did not
cultivate got no more money to pay for his horses, his
Spanish gloves and his slashed Elizabethan doublet—or
even the rough clothes and rough living of a tiny rural
manor.

(Clapham 1949:205)

No man can be rich, but he must be rich either by his
own labours, or by the labours of other men helping
him. If a man have no help from his neighbour, he shall
never gather an estate of hundreds and thousands a
year. If other men help him to work, then are those
riches his neighbours' as well as his; for they be the
fruits of other men's labours as well as his own.

(Winstanley, as quoted in Brailsford 1961:661)

Whatever doubts may linger about the landowner's
position in the years before 1580, few can remain in
connection with the succeeding period up to 1620,
which saw a massive redistribution of income in favour
of the landed class: a redistribution which, in the final
analysis, was as much at the expense of the agricultural
wage-earner and consumer as of the tenant farmer.

(Bowden 1967:695)

In this chapter I outline a model of early seventeenth-century English social structure. I make no attempt at a descriptive portrait of prerevolutionary English society; instead, I present an analysis of the predominant "manufacturing" social formation and argue that this structure was constituted by tendencies that resulted in the seventeenth-century revolutions, especially the REVOGs (rebellions) of 1641–49 and 1688 (see chaps. 3 and 6). In other words I provide a model of the English social formation which reveals that its tendential development resulted in the generation of the variables leading to a REVOG. Although the variables within the theory of revolution (chap. 3) are defined with sufficient abstraction so as to be applicable to all societal systems, the model presented in this chapter applies only to societies at a certain stage of development, to the "manufacturing" social formations of stage four (see chap. 8).[1]

The argument of this chapter is simple. I contend that the pre-revolutionary English social formation may be conceptualized, to adopt Piaget's term, as a "stage of action," as a transitional stage. This type of social formation is characterized by a set of practices looking forward to the next stage of social development; further, it is the nature of such a stage that these actions are legitimized in terms of beliefs drawn from the previous stage. The transitional stage extant in early seventeenth-century England was constituted economically as a manufacturing structure both in town and country, which Marx treats as a form of capitalism, and by patrimonial political legitimation, which Weber treats as a form of traditionalism. The English revolutions of the seventeenth century were an outgrowth of internal, inherent movement of this manufacturing mode of economic production when controlled, as it was in England, by a set of rationalizing values, in contradiction to a political system legitimized within the context of traditional values; the revolutions mark the point where the continued transformation of the social formation became self-generating within a developing structure.[2]

The core of my argument in this chapter is straightforward. I contend that the English Revolution marks, not the transition between feudalism and capitalism, but a transition internal to that mode of economic production we characterize as capitalist. The resolution of the contradiction between a formally rational economic structure and a patrimonial political structure occurred as a consequence of the revolutions of the seventeenth century and resulted in the development of a stable political system in eighteenth-century England. This conclusion to the political disorders of the seventeenth century allowed for the natural development from a capitalism dominated by the extraction of absolute surplus value—manufacturing rooted in simple cooperation—to capitalism dominated by the extraction of relative surplus value—manufacturing dominated by complex cooperation and finally machine capitalism.

The incompatibility between two subsystems may be conceptualized on many levels and the quest for a theory of compatible structures is almost as old as social theory itself. In the following pages I will treat incompatibility as the inability of a subsystem to furnish the resources necessary to allow for the stable functioning of another subsystem. In making such judgments, which will rarely be presented in such boldfaced terms, I will rely on the arguments enunciated in chapter 2. There a theory of subsystem output was articulated which emphasized the balance between inputs to any subsystem as determinate of its stable functioning. Within the context of that theory, a deficiency of output from one subsystem to another can be specified and analyzed. The compatibility or contradiction between two subsystems may be analyzed and the contradictions between structures dominant or predominant within subsystems pinpointed.

I will thus be working within a functionally defined theory of contradiction. It is possible to go one step behind this level of theorization to ask questions concerning the nature of structures likely to prove compatible. Although I will make comments concerning such questions, I do not in this context formulate a theory of structural compatibility. Thus although I point out that a specific organizational complex in the English polity was incapable of allowing for efficient capital accumulation within a manufacturing economy, I do not formally generalize such statements. I do attempt to show that the tendential development of one subsystem may generate, and in prerevolutionary England that the tendential development of a specific economic structure did generate, contradictions between it and other societal subsystems.[3]

It is clear that there is no simple relationship between a democratic republic and capitalism, to take an obvious example, and that capitalist economic structures may be compatible with diverse types of political structures for significant periods of time. What we do not know is whether our characterizations of structure—for example, "a democratic republic"—are the "correct" ones (i.e., useful in formulating viable propositions); neither do we know the limits of this compatibility nor the effect on this compatibility of different historical and social systemic conjunctures. For example, does it matter whether we are dealing with England, the first capitalist country, or Germany, a late developer, or does it matter whether we are dealing with the United States, a dominant country within the world system, or Italy, a relatively dependent country? In addition we do not know the duration for which a compatibility might be maintained. Germany sustained considerable capitalist economic development with a basically patrimonial political system, albeit one with a formally rational bureaucracy. For how long was this connection possible?

While the theory presented in chapter 2 will aid in identifying compatible structures, it does not specify the exact conditions of a breakdown in, as against the unstable functioning of, a subsystem. For our purposes in this chapter, a breakdown will be associated with the genesis of internal disorder severe enough to lead to the transformation of the structure within one subsystem. Here, as I have already noted, I will be examining the genesis of the variables leading to a specific type of political revolution.

The concept of structure often has static connotations. It is therefore important to highlight certain aspects of my discussion. I emphasize that unlike the functional dimension of theory a structural model is in no sense descriptive. It is not aggregative and one may not view it, as one may under certain circumstances view a functional theory, as an abstraction from "simple descriptions" (see Gould 1981c).

The problem becomes how to know whether the structural model is an accurate representation of the society we are analyzing. In my opinion the simplest way to assure this, within the context of the problems discussed in this book and making no ontological assumptions, involves the recognition that a structure describes a tendency of development. Marx, for example, retains the Hegelian "notion" within the context of his analysis of each stage of social development. His characterizations of these stages are tendential, and the primary way to determine whether the analysis of a stage is empirically acceptable is to focus on this tendential movement.

It is important to differentiate between two things: the first may be labeled *predominance* and the second *dominance*. A specific social structure is predominant within a system when its tendencies create the sufficient conditions for the transition into the next stage of social development. A specific social structure is dominant within a stage when (1) its tendencies create the sufficient conditions for the transition into the next stage and (2) its pattern is tendentially extended to all social organizations within the system under examination. Dominance, with regard to an economic mode of production, implies that the mode of production will ultimately, at the limit that never arrives, subsume all productive relations within its structure. A predominant mode of production will coexist with other modes of production within the system in which it predominates. Both dominant and predominant systems generate the internal tendencies leading to the self-transformation of the system.

Transitional stages contain a predominant mode of economic production, while stages contain a dominant mode of economic production. In this chapter I analyze manufacture as a transitional stage, showing that it will under specifiable conditions develop into a machine capitalist system capable of dominating a social formation. In other words, I argue that the manufacturing structure predominated in the seventeenth-century English society. This does not mean that all economic structures in England might be so characterized nor does it mean that all economic organizations in England were subsumed in social relationships predominated by manufacturing. Rather it means that the logic of a manufacturing structure was such as to generate the conditions for its self-transformation, and the predominance of this structure within English society is demonstrated by the fact that this self-transformation occurred.

There are problems with this sort of analysis in that a tendency is just that; it involves the logic of progression within a stage, but is subject to countervailing pressures within the same logic, conjunctural imbalances and exogenous dislocations, and therefore the consequences of a tendency are difficult to pinpoint at a determinate spot along a linear, chronological scale. In fact, one of the central purposes of this book is to specify the complementary variables necessary for the tendential development of a manufacturing structure to "work itself out." In an analysis of contemporary social formations these problems are very difficult, and are resolvable only in the continued application of the model to the analysis of events as symptoms of this underlying syndrome and in actions guided by this analysis; the two masters of this were Freud and Lenin (see Gould, forthcoming). In historical research it is possible to isolate another form of check. If we focus on some consequential event or set of events occurring within the system under analysis, our structural model ought to be able to explain the genesis of the variables within a functional theory which explains the genesis of those events. While this check is by no means foolproof, it seems the best we can hope for in historical work. In any case, it is clear that one does not display the predominance of an economic structure by counting the number of times its units appear; this form of assessment denies the entire basis of the analysis I carry out. It negates the argument that a structure is a pattern of sanctioned constraints characterizing the social system of reference, but not necessarily descriptive of each unit in the system or even of each unit subsumed within the structure under examination.

It may help if I try to rephrase this argument: I am concerned to demonstrate that a specific social formation existed in prerevolutionary England. The existence of such a structure is difficult to prove, as it is not characterized primarily by phenomenological attributes but by the pattern it constitutes. This pattern may be deemed extant insofar as we are able to empirically isolate variables that will develop as a consequence of its existence. In the case under analysis, these variables are key determinants of a specific type of revolution. Even here it is difficult to make this determination in practice because a tendency is subject to dislocations of various sorts, some internal to its own structure. But in the case of a historical situation we can argue that the tendency, the structure, was manifest if it appears to have worked itself out to a sufficient degree to have generated the variables necessary for the revolution.

An important aspect of this analysis involves the way I try to integrate what I call societal universals and the structural model. The former specify the necessary and sufficient conditions for a revolution (see chap. 3, above). The latter characterizes a specific stage of societal development. It is possible to imagine circumstances wherein chance factors have generated the conditions for revolutions seemingly prohibited by structural tendencies (chance factors such as earthquakes, or, much more important, exogenous impingements on a society from other societies, factors systematized from another perspective). Here I make the argument that the variables leading to a revolution may have, and in the case of the English revolutions did have, internal sources of development.

Manufacture

The labor process as a form of social relation producing use-values is common to all societies. "It is the everlasting Nature-

imposed condition of human existence, and therefore is independent of every social phase of that existence, or rather, is common to
every such phase" (Marx 1967, 1:184). The organization of this
labor process and the mode of extracting or not extracting surplus
labor within it are variable and together they constitute crucial
aspects of the different modes of production dominant or predominant in the development of economic systems. In the capitalist
mode of production the laborer works under the control of the
capitalist, to whom she sells her labor power. The product, which
takes the form of a commodity, is the property of the capitalist, not
the laborer (Marx 1967, 1:184–185).

The general formula for capital is $M - C - M'$. In this circuit the
capitalist purchases two types of commodities which are combined
in the production of commodities. The money put forward is capital when used to purchase commodities that produce commodities
that embody a value greater than the value originally expended
($M' - M$). That part of capital which is represented by the means of
production—raw material, auxilliary material, and the instruments
of production—Marx calls constant capital. When incorporated in
the process of production it undergoes no quantitative change in
value.

That part of capital represented by labor power does undergo a
quantitative change in the process of production. In the $M - C - M'$
circuit, the capitalist purchases from her legal equal, the laborer,
the latter's labor power. Labor power, when treated as if it were a
commodity, has the capacity to produce a value greater than its
own value. It produces, in addition to the equivalent of its own
value, a surplus value. The part of capital used to hire labor power
Marx labels variable capital (see Marx 1967, 1:209).

Labor power is the only commodity with the capacity to produce
a value greater than its own value. The value of labor power is the
value of the socially and historically defined subsistence required
for its maintenance and reproduction (for a more precise discussion, see Gould 1981a:139–46); it is possible to imagine that a
value equivalent to this per diem cost might be produced by the
laborer in less than a full working day, in which case she would
produce a surplus value, a value in excess of the value of her own
labor power. Capitalism is the social relationship wherein the production of surplus value occurs.

$M - C$ represents the capitalist's purchase of commodities with
money capital. In $C - M'$, the sale of produced commodities for

money, M' is greater than M. The difference between M' and M, assuming as we will throughout that all commodities are sold at their value, is the surplus value produced by the laborers' living labor power.

The production process may be considered from two points of view, as labor process and as valorization process. In capitalist production the labor process, which yields use-values as its products, is a means to the valorization process, the production of surplus value. For the capitalist "the crux of the entire process is the exchange of *objectified labour* for *living labour*, of less *objectified labour* for more *living labour*. In the course of exchange an amount of labour objectified in money as a commodity is exchanged for an equal amount of labour objectified in living labour" (Marx 1976: 1009). It is this living labor, the labor power sold as if it were a commodity, at its value, which produces an exchange value greater than its own value. In the actual labor process the laborer productively consumes the object of his labor with the instruments of production. From the point of view of the valorization process, the means of production consume the worker. "Living labor does not realize itself in objective labour which thereby becomes its objective organ, but instead objective labour maintains and fortifies itself by drawing off living labour; it is thus that it becomes *value valorizing itself, capital*, and functions as such" (Marx 1976:988). The capitalist acts as a support in this process, assuming the social role assigned to her in the structure of production (Marx 1976:1022, 1027, 1054).

The social division of labor forms the foundation of all commodity production. Capital can only come into existence on the foundation of the circulation of commodities, but it is only with the development of capitalism that the commodity becomes the general form of all produce. The process of primitive accumulation, the starting point of the capitalist mode of production, involves the freeing of labor from previous ties of social and political dependency, of the often coercive separation of the laborer from the means of production, and of the accumulation of money and resources that become capital when conjoined with free labor in the production of surplus value. Capitalism always begins in a context defined by prior modes of production.

In the first stage of the development of capitalism, manufacturing, the labor process is formally subsumed under capital. The labor process becomes a means in the extraction of surplus value, an instrument in the capitalist valorization process. The capitalist is severed from direct production, assumes managerial responsibilities, and exploits the worker, but manufacturing is not characterized by a labor process of a specifically capitalist type, by the specifically capitalist mode of production. In effect the capitalist mode of production is in its most general form typified by the capitalist valorization process, but not necessarily by a distinct process of production.

Manufacturing, at least in its early stages, does not imply any alteration in the actual process of production.

> On the contrary, the fact is that capital subsumes the labour process as it finds it, that is to say, it takes over an *existing labour process*, developed by different and more archaic modes of production. And since that is the case it is evident that capital took over an available, established labour process. For example, handicraft or the form of agriculture corresponding to a small, independent peasant economy.   (Marx 1976:1021; I have altered what I assume is a typographical error in the text, cf. Marx 1971:194)

In manufacture a monetary relationship exists between the buyer and seller of labor power. The worker is formally free and is dependent on the capitalist only because the latter controls the conditions of the former's labor. Technologically the worker may conduct her labor process exactly as she did prior to this subordination, but now it is her labor that is consumed in the labor process and the capitalist has control over the commodity that is produced. Unlike handicraft production, where the master may also have controlled the conditions of production, in manufacturing, capital is not restricted in the form it may assume. A master's position is defined in terms of the trade she has mastered; her "capital" is tied to specific use-values, and the methods of production are traditionally defined. In manufacturing the use-value of the capital is theoretically irrelevant to the capitalist; her only concern is the surplus value produced.[4] In such circumstances the capitalist will be removed from the actual process of production and will assume the functions of capital, the appropriation and control of the labor of others and the selling of the products of that labor (Marx 1967, 1:308–9).

Marx distinguished between two forms of surplus value. If we assume a laboring day of eight hours, and assume that the value of simple labor power is equivalent to the value produced in four hours, the second four hours of simple labor is surplus and produces four hours of surplus value. This surplus value, produced by the prolongation of the working day beyond the point necessary to reproduce the labor power consumed, is absolute surplus value.

It is sometimes possible, by increasing the productivity of labor in those branches of production resulting in commodities incorporated into the value of labor power, to reduce necessary labor time. Thus if workers work eight hours per day, and if the number of working hours necessary to produce a value equivalent to the value of the bundle of commodities socially defined as necessary to maintain and reproduce consumed labor power is reduced to, for example, two hours of labor time (from four hours), the increment of value produced in the two hours shifted from necessary to surplus labor Marx calls relative surplus value. Relative surplus value obviously presupposes capitalist production and therefore the production of absolute surplus value (Marx 1967, 1:315, and 509–10; cf. Gould 1981*a*).

Manufacturing, when based on the formal subsumption of labor under capital, yields absolute surplus value. Machine capitalism revolutionizes the actual mode of the labor process and yields relative surplus value. The specifically capitalist mode of production *sui generis* is based on the extraction of relative surplus value; here there is a congruence between the actual process of production and the valorization process; it is here that the capitalist mode of production is dominant, while manufacturing only predominates. In machine capitalism there is a "real subsumption of labor under capital" (Marx 1976:1024ff., 1034ff.).

The development of manufacturing is itself a complex process. For my purposes I will be concerned whether it is carried out in terms of simple cooperation or cooperation based on a division of labor, whether it is able to generate relative surplus value, whether it is subject to the tendential law of the decline in the rate of profit, and, perhaps most important, I will argue that accumulation within the early stages of a manufacturing system is not mandated by the objective constraints of that system, but rather that accumulation depends on the control of a specific type of rationalizing ideology.

As noted above, manufacture is originally based on the formal subsumption of labor under capital. In industry, for example, it always rests on the handicrafts of the town and even more on the putting-out system in rural areas. As such it does not eradicate alternative modes of production nor does it sever industry from agriculture. Based on simple cooperation, it retains the previous labor process and fails to achieve dominance within the economy (Marx 1967: vol. 1, 429, 748). This stage of manufacturing, constituted by the capitalist valorization process but not revolutionizing the actual process of production, is not subject to the laws of capitalist accumulation.

Even in this first period, manufacturing is based on cooperation as a productive power of capital. At its most primitive level this cooperation induces no change in the actual productive process other than concentrating larger numbers of workers under one roof or coordinating the work of individual workers who ply their trade in their own dwellings. Later it may give rise to a situation in which the workers, either side by side or doing coordinated labor while they work at home, perform different but connected tasks in the production of commodities. "In the handicraft-like beginnings of manufacture, and in that kind of agriculture on a large scale, which corresponds to the epoch of manufacture ... simple cooperation is always the prevailing form, in those branches of production in which capital operates on a large scale, and division of labour and machinery play but a subordinate part" (Marx 1967, 1:335).

The latter type of simple cooperation, in which different tasks are performed by different workers, melds into manufacturing processes based on a more complex division of labor. In heterogeneous manufacture articles made separately are later fitted together; here, where the production of each part is separated from the rest, the labor process may be, and in its early stages usually was, farmed out to private homes, saving the capital outlay on a shop. In serial manufacture, commodities are produced in connected processes. These remain isolated from each other, but in most cases, Smith's example of the manufacture of the pin being the most famous, this process is best carried out under one roof. Serial manufacture transforms the labor process itself, and it covers the gap between the earliest capitalist production based solely on the formal subsumption of capital under labor and machine capitalism. In manufacture based on cooperation characterized by the division of labor, the value embedded in individual commodities may decrease, and thus relative as well as absolute surplus value may be extracted (see Marx 1967, 1:342–68).

At times Marx limits his characterization of manufacture to this latter form: "While simple co-operation leaves the mode of working by the individual for the most part unchanged, manufacture thoroughly revolutionizes it, and seizes labor-power by its very roots" (1967, 1:360). It is clear, however, that if the manufacturing period in both industry and agriculture is to be considered as encompassing the mid-sixteenth to the last third of the eighteenth century, it must include labor processes based on simple cooperation when these were formally subsumed under capital (Marx 1967, 1:322, 367).

Two distinctions are crucial here: (1) between (a) usurer's and merchant's capital situated in the interstices of precapitalist modes of production and (b) manufacture, and (2) between manufacture and the specifically capitalist mode of production. The first distinction concerns production formally subsumed under capital versus production "in which capital is to be found in certain specific, subordinate functions, but where it has not emerged as the direct purchaser of labour and as the immediate owner of the process of production, and where in consequence it has not yet succeeded in becoming the [pre]dominant force, capable of determining the form of society as a whole" (Marx 1976:1023). The two subordinate forms Marx has in mind are usurer's and merchant's capital.

> In such forms capital has not yet acquired the direct control of the labour-process. By the side of independent producers who carry on their handicrafts and agriculture in the traditional old-fashioned way, there stands the usurer or the merchant, with his usurer's capital or merchant's capital, feeding on them like a parasite. *The predominance* [my italics] in a society, *of this form of exploitation excludes the capitalist mode of production* [my italics]; to which mode, however, this form may serve as a transition, as it did towards the close of the middle ages. (Marx, 1967, 1:510)

These subordinate forms of exploitation are not based on the formal subsumption of labor under capital. "The immediate producer still performs the functions of selling his wares and making use of his own labour" (Marx 1976:1023). In dealing with merchant capital, outside the formal subsumption of labor under capital, the artisan sells commodities to a customer; she does not sell her labor power to a capitalist. While the line is often a fine one, it is important to draw it.

In manufacture based on simple cooperation and on the formal subsumption of labor under capital, absolute surplus value predominates. While any increase in the productivity of labor in the manufacture of the socially defined necessities making up the value of labor power may reduce the value of labor power and thus, under most circumstances, increase relative surplus value, clearly this is an ancillary process within this system. The value embedded in individual commodities (and therefore the price of those commodities) is not significantly decreased and the basis for competition not yet constituted.

Manufacture based on cooperation characterized by the division of labor implies a transformation of the labor process and the extraction of relative surplus value. But this form was still based on the predominance of circulating over fixed capital and it is debatable whether it, excluding machine capitalism, may be taken as representing the "specific capitalist mode of production." While predominant, manufacture, even of this developed form, was not dominant in the sense of constituting an ever-expanding mode of production liable to take over all productive processes. For this to happen, machine production had to develop. For our purposes, whatever terminological conventions we might wish to adopt, the second crucial distinction is between (1) manufacture based on the formal subsumption of labor, characterized by an incongruence between the valorization and labor processes, and the extraction of absolute surplus value; and (2) the specifically capitalist mode of production based on the real subsumption of labor, characterized by a congruence between the labor process and the valorization process, and the extraction of relative surplus value. When I use the term *manufacture*, unless otherwise noted I will be referring to a system characterized by the formal subsumption of labor under capital, the extraction of absolute but not relative surplus value, constant returns to scale, and thus incompletely developed competitive constraints.

Capital accumulation *may* occur within the context of a manufacturing system based on the formal subsumption of labor. Here, where absolute surplus value is extracted, accumulation grows either with the lengthening of the work day, or more clearly via an extension of production, where an increase in the volume of capital employed implies an increase in the number of persons employed, and thus an increase in the amount of surplus value extracted and available for reinvestment—accumulation via replication of producing units at constant returns to scale. It is still absolute surplus value that is extracted and, aside from a comparatively slight increase in relative surplus value which might occur indirectly via an intensification of the labor process, increases in turnover times, or via simple cooperation, only absolute surplus value. In this situation an increase in surplus value is paralleled by an increase in total capital invested, the rate of surplus value (s/v, surplus value/variable capital) and the rate of profit ($s/c + v$, surplus value/constant capital + variable capital) remain constant. Where the amount of surplus value is increased by an increase in the scale of production, where no or almost no increase in relative surplus value occurs, and where the rate of surplus value remains constant, I refer to the surplus value gleaned in accumulation as *iterative surplus value*. In such a system competitive constraints will not be articulated.

There are three modes of increasing the total amount of surplus value: additions to Marx's absolute and relative surplus values, both of which also involve an increase in the rate of surplus value, and what I have referred to as iterative surplus value. This last involves a multiplication of units within a productive organization, but it does not involve a direct extension of surplus labor time for the individual worker, neither via an increase in the total time nor via a decrease in necessary labor time. It amounts to a multiplication of absolute surplus value, that is, it is a type of absolute surplus value, generated via a multiplication of the units from which surplus value might be extracted.

In situations where greater absolute surplus value is extracted from a given unit of production the average rate of profit will increase. In situations of machine capitalism, where competition acts as a coercive mechanism, attempts will be made to increase labor productivity in order to garner surplus profits by selling commodities below their value. Here the individual value of commodities is below their social value and the capitalist is able to undercut the prices of her competition while still making above-average profits. Marx argues but does not demonstrate that in the long run this process will lower the average rate of profit for all capitalists, as the competitors catch up. But in increasing the productivity of labor in those industries whose commodities constitute the goods incorporated in the value of labor power, this process will also increase the relative surplus value extracted.[5]

Increases in productivity in machine capitalism come primarily through increased investment in fixed (a form of constant) capital. Marx argues that in this situation, motivated by competition, relative surplus value will increase, the absolute level of surplus value will increase, but owing to an even greater increase in the organic composition of capital, the ratio of constant to variable capital, the rate of profit will tendentially decrease. In other words, as increased investment in fixed capital occurs, a higher percentage of capital will be made up of "dead labor," labor previously embodied in commodities that have value incorporated into newly produced commodities, but which do not produce surplus value. As the percentage of living labor power decreases, even with a lesser increase in the rate of surplus value, the rate of profit will fall. Variable capital will shrink proportionately to constant capital (both fixed and circulating), and the denominator will increase more rapidly than the numerator in the rate of profit fraction $(s/c + v)$.

Increases in iterative surplus value under conditions of simple cooperation will leave both the rate of surplus value and the rate of profit stable, while increasing the amount of both. In situations of cooperation under a division of labor, productivity will increase, owing to the factor of production Marshall labeled "organization." Owning to an increase in relative surplus value and in the intensity of labor, the rate of surplus value will increase. It is likely, however, that the rate of profit will not decline, as the only major concomitant increase in constant capital will be the circulating capital embodied in raw materials; this decline appears not to have taken place. It is for this reason that production based on a complex division of labor may be predominant but is not dominant within an economic subsystem.

The important question to pose in this context concerns the nature of the mechanisms that lead to the increase in the number of productive units formally subsumed under capital, that is, which lead to capital accumulation in which iterative surplus value predominates. It is clear that the formal subsumption of labor under capital may occur in many conjunctures and that it did occur without becoming the predominant mode of production within a society (Marx 1973:505–6; Marx 1976:1022); I am concerned with the conditions of its predominance where its development is such as to control the tendential movement into the next stage of economic organization.

Marx informs us that the production of surplus value is the

absolute law of the capitalist mode of production. Use-values are produced solely as a means to the valorization of capital (e.g., Marx 1967, 1:618). Thus the aim of capitalism is production, and consumption is essential only because the value of produced commodities must be realized. Marx also informs us that production for production's sake, production as an end in itself, appears with the formal subsumption of labor under capital, when the exchange value of the product is the deciding factor in its production. "But this *inherent* tendency of capitalist production does not become *adequately realized*—it does not become *indispensable*, and that also means *technologically* indispensable—until the *specific mode of capitalist production* and hence the *real subsumption of labour under capital* has become a reality" (1976:1037). Only in the latter case is production severed from "needs laid down in advance." Here the law of value is fully developed, and accumulation is manifest in the form of concentration and centralization, and thus, Marx suggests, in an increase in the organic composition of capital. Capital accumulation becomes a necessity if an individual capitalist is to remain competitive and survive.

Marx further distinguishes between the use-values that enter into the productive process: "On the one hand, we find the material means of production, the *objective* conditions of production, and on the other hand, the active capacities for labour, labour-power expressing itself purposively: the *subjective* conditions of labour" (1976:980ff.). The capacity of each of these two sets of conditions to determine the nature of the productive process changes in the movement from manufacture to machine capitalism. "In Manufacture, the organization of the social labour-process is purely subjective; it is a combination of detail labourers; in its machinery system, Modern Industry has a productive organism that is purely objective, in which the labourer becomes a mere appendage to an already existing material condition of production" (Marx 1967, 1:386). We might add that in machine capitalism the capitalist is equally constrained by the objective conditions of production. She functions only as personified capital, just as the worker is labor personified: "the capitalist is just as enslaved by the relationships of capitalism as his opposite pole, the worker, albeit in a quite different manner" (Marx 1976:990).

In machine capitalism the extraction of relative surplus value through increases in productivity allows for the lowering of costs and prices. This process creates the coercive constraints of competition. "Free competition brings out the inherent laws of capitalist production, in the shape of external coercive laws having power over every individual capitalist" (Marx 1967, 1:270; cf. 316).[6] It is this competition that, in turn, coerces the capitalist into lowering the price of her product via the introduction of new productive techniques; it is competition that forces the generalization of these techniques and the resultant increase in relative surplus value, along with the tendency toward a decrease in the rate of profit (at least in the machine period). It is competition that forces production for production's sake, and incidentally creates the material conditions for the development of a new social order, while actualizing the law of capital accumulation (Marx 1967, 1:319 and 592).

This distinction between subjective motivation and objective constraint is crucial, but it must not be misunderstood. Marx does not argue that in machine capitalism the individual capitalist will necessarily follow the law of capital accumulation; rather he contends that determinate consequences will befall her if she fails to obey it. These consequences are enforced by competitive pressures. If the system is to function reasonably efficiently, a rationalizing ideology will emerge within the system motivating actions congruent to those required for survival. Thus capital accumulation will appear as voluntary and capitalists will be committed to it, perhaps even in situations where it is not required by competitive pressures. To say that the constraints within the system are "objective" does not imply that value commitments legitimizing action within the system are unimportant; rather it means that these commitments must be of a particular sort.

Where labor is formally subsumed under capital, competitive constraints are at most incompletely developed. In a strict sense, as manufacture approaches a system with constant returns to scale, they are not present at all. This means that capital accumulation is not mandated by the "objective constraints" in the mode of production. In consequence, various ideologies may prove to be consistent with manufacture, even ideologies that do not motivate capital accumulation (see Gould 1981*b*).

In manufacture, as we have seen, accumulation occurs within the context of iterative surplus value; accumulation implies the extension of production, the replication of production units (cf. Marx 1967, 1:612ff.). Accumulation in manufacture is not coerced by the inadequately realized tendency of capitalist production. While there may be motivations to lower costs to gain a competitive advantage, they are not inherent in the laws of capitalism within the context of the extraction of iterative surplus value, where competitive constraints are not in place. At this stage activities are subjectively motivated rather than "objectively constrained" for both the capitalist and the worker.

Marx explicitly recognizes this for the worker. Much of his discussion of primitive accumulation involves a specification of the conditions under which persons might be forced to work as wage labor. This argument is codified in his equation, at one point, of the subjective conditions of labor with the means of subsistence. The greater control over necessities maintained by the capitalist, the more firmly established the formal subsumption of labor under capital (1976:1026). He also emphasizes this point in his discussion of discipline problems under manufacturing. While it is clear that certain aspects of manufacture were structured with a view to giving control over the labor process to the capitalist (cf. Marglin 1974; Brighton Labour Process Group 1977), only with the development of machine capitalism was this control and the consequent discipline conclusively established (Marx 1967, 1:367–68; cf. Stone 1974; Braverman 1974; Burawoy 1985).

When it comes to providing an understanding of the subjective controls over the capitalist, Marx's arguments are less cogent. He indicates that the development of manufacture grounded in the real subsumption of labor under capital is a spontaneous formation, leaving us with the image of a chance mutation and the competitive advantage of natural selection.[7] But in addition he cogently discusses the ascetic values of the capitalist, the bourgeois virtue of reinvesting surplus value as capital instead of squandering it as revenue. "It will never do, therefore, to represent capitalist production as something which it is not, namely as production whose immediate purpose is enjoyment or the manufacture of the means of enjoyment for the capitalist. This would be overlooking its specific character, which is revealed in all its inner essence" (Marx 1967, 3:244; cf. 1:586).[8] Forgetting the philosophical flourish, this statement is intelligible only within the context of the real domination of labor by capital, the congruence between the valorization and labor processes, and the extraction of relative surplus value in competitive conditions. Within this context Marx's analysis of commodity fetishism makes perfect sense for all who are "supports" of the system. It is a mystification if applied to the first stage of manufacture, for it assumes a commitment to a form of rationality which had itself to be created.[9]

Fortunately Marx provides hints at the answer to this problem, and Weber comes very close to its solution. There are in Marx's writings scattered references to the importance of Protestantism, or more specifically Puritanism, in establishing the hegemony of capitalism. He tells us that Protestantism is the most fitting form of religion "for a society based upon the production of commodities, in which the producers in general enter into social relations with one another by treating their products as commodities and values, whereby they reduce their individual private labour to the standard of homogenous human labour" (1967, 1:79). He explicitly notes the importance of Protestantism in eliminating traditional holidays, and thereby regularizing the work schedule within economic production (1967, 1:276 n.2:cf. Thompson 1967; Thomas 1964). Most important, he recognized the relationship between English Puritanism ("and also Dutch Protestantism") and asceticism, self-denial, self-sacrifice, frugality, and contempt for mundane and fleeting pleasures (Marx 1973:232). Unfortunately he does not tie this religious ethic, which itself never effectively discussed, to the process of accumulation within a mode of production dominated by manufacture. For this linkage we must turn to Weber.

The logic of Weber's studies in comparative religion is as follows: a series of necessary and sufficient conditions for the genesis of capitalism may be established; these conditions, with the exception of one, a legitimizing ideology enforced with psychological sanctions, were found in a number of situations. In only one situation, northwest Europe from the sixteenth century, were all of the necessary and sufficient conditions present, including the requisite "ideational" control, and here we find the origins of capitalism. Unfortunately Weber does not adequately specify the nonideological conditions for the development of capitalism, nor does he explicitly identify and discuss them in his comparative work. I want to argue that one of these conditions was the presence of a manufacturing economy.[10]

Weber can be rescued from the possible problem of a circular definition of modern capitalism in terms of its ethic if one recognizes that the Protestant ethic had positive consequences for the development of capitalism only when it legitimized actions within a specific mode of production, manufacture, and when the predominance of manufacture and then the dominance of machine capitalism are taken as dependent variables.[11] The general point is also made by Marx; for example, in discussing the different impacts of an influx of money within two different types of economic structures (1973:233–5; cf. on merchant capital, 1967, 3:332–33). More generally, the point is made by Mao: "Does materialist dialectics exclude external causes? Not at all. It holds that external causes are the condition of change and internal causes are the basis of change, and that external causes become operative through internal causes. In a suitable temperature an egg changes into a chicken, but no temperature can change a stone into a chicken, because each has a different basis" (1965, 1:314).

The presence of ascetic Protestantism within a rudimentary manufacturing economy gave rise to capital accumulation and the predominance of that economy.[12] The presence of ascetic Protestantism in situations not characterized by a rudimentary manufacturing economy did not give rise to the predominance of manufacturing within the economy.[13]

Weber's main conclusion is that a modern capitalism seeking profit in terms of the rational organization of formally free labor, while dependent on a given economic foundation and on many other variables, developed only in the context of the rational ethical prophecy embedded in Calvinism. He demonstrates the effect of a certain set of religious commitments on the ethos of an economic system. He is not concerned with the theology of Protestantism, nor with its direct teachings concerning economic activities. Rather he analyzes the consequences of its teachings in the genesis of value commitments controlling these economic activities. He is at pains to argue the unintended consequences of Calvinism, and continually emphasizes the sanctions embedded in the pattern of commitments which enforced these commitments (see, e.g., Weber 1958: 97–98, 197 n. 12, 217 n. 3).

Weber emphasizes that rational action is relative to a particular point of view and embedded in a particular series of social relations. Rational action within the feudal mode of production or according to Catholic ethics differs from rational action in a manufacturing structure or according to Puritan ethics. It is not self-interest that concerns Weber, but formally rational action characterized by the calculation of profit. Such action was compatible with a nascent capitalism; an ethic demanding an inner-worldly asceticism, operative in another set of circumstances, would have another set of consequences. In a situation of nascent manufacture the inner-worldly asceticism embedded in the notion of a calling, demanding as a moral duty the fulfillment of obligations in worldly affairs, and emphasizing what later came to be called Methodism in their pursuit, gave rise to the spirit of capitalism, which entailed the rational acquisition of profit. This pursuit was sanctioned by the necessity of manifesting one's salvation; in a theological system defined by predestination, this resulted in the rational ordering of one's entire worldly life. The calculation of good deeds versus bad deeds was unacceptable when works were irrelevant to salvation; the certainty of salvation in faith was relevant only as an indicator of God's favor, and this certainty came in a totalistic judgement of one's self. A theology based on predestination was not the sole foundation of moral sanction; Weber especially notes the importance of church discipline. It clearly was important in the genesis of the pattern of commitments Weber discusses. (On value commitments and their sanctions see Parsons 1969: chap. 16.)

Weber differentiates between what I would label a manufacturing system legitimized by traditional values and one legitimized by rationalizing values. In the first instance the form of organization was capitalist (labor was formally subsumed under capital), "But it was traditionalistic business, if one considers the spirit which animated the entrepreneur: the traditional manner of life, the traditional rate of profit, the traditional amount of work, the traditional manner of regulating relationships with labour, and the essentially traditional circle of customers and the manner of attracting new ones" (1958:67). When the same organization is found in conjunction with the spirit of modern capitalism, that is, where the values that regulate its operation are specifications from the values of ascetic Protestantism, a process of rationalization occurs. This process resulted in capital accumulation via iterative surplus value, in extended reproduction. This occurred, Weber emphasizes, without necessarily modifying the form of organization or the nature of the labor process. But it changed the circumstances in which those touched by these businesses did business.

The development of this system, in which labor was formally subsumed under capital and the subjective control over the process was constituted by the spirit of capitalism, was autonomous in that while it drew on extant capital and labor (from the process of primitive accumulation) and extant markets, it also created the capital, labor, and markets it needed both domestically, and once it conquered the state, internationally. A manufacturing system legitimized by the values of the Protestant ethic was a self-sustaining system, operating in terms of the law of capital accumulation. This system was predominant in early seventeenth-century England; the narrowly economic foundation for it had existed elsewhere, but the manufacturing system predominated only when that foundation was interpenetrated with a formally rational, inner-worldly ethos.

It is essential to recognize that the Protestant ethic did not define a substantive orientation toward economic activities. Rather, in conjunction with a nascent manufacturing structure, it rationalized activities already extant. In other words, the logic of economic activities and thus the "structure of economic rationality" was defined by the manufacturing structure within which these values were assimilated. In rationalizing these activities, the Protestant ethic initiated a process leading to the predominance of manufacture within the English economy.

Let me emphasize again that an economic structure is a patterned set of constraints involving all four components of social action: roles, collectivities, norms, and values. The economy is the subsystem defined by the function of producing and distributing adaptive resources, at the societal level, but the organizations within the economy are partially constituted by a set of economic values, which are themselves independently variable. My point is that the pattern of value commitments definitive of a traditional religious structure when combined with a rudimentary manufacturing structure did not result in the predominance of that structure within the economy. The pattern of value commitments definitive of the Protestant ethic when combined with a rudimentary manufacturing structure did result in a controlled process of capital accumulation, in the first instance based on iterative surplus value, and in the predominance of the manufacturing structure.

Weber agreed with Marx that the capitalist system in its developed form was self-sustaining:

> The capitalistic economy of the present day is an immense cosmos into which the individual is born, and which presents itself to him, at least as an individual, as an unalterable order of things in which he must live. It

forces the individual, in so far as he is involved in the system of market relationships, to conform to capitalistic rules of action. The manufacturer who in the long run acts counter to these norms, will as inevitably be eliminated from the economic scene as the worker who cannot or will not adapt himself to them will be thrown into the streets without a job. (Weber 1958:54–55; see also 72, 181–82, and 282 n. 108)

This is Marx's machine capitalism, the dominant mode of production within the society where the real subsumption of labor under capital has occurred. In Weber's terms, "these are phenomena of a time in which modern capitalism has become dominant and has become emancipated from its old supports" (1958:72). What we must avoid is the error of explaining capital accumulation within a manufacturing system in terms of the constraints operative in machine capitalism. In manufacture, if extended reproduction was to occur, the controls definitive of the spirit of capitalism were necessary to motivate persons within the economic system and to assure the predominance of manufacture within the economy.[14]

Manufacturing in England

The period from roughly 1500 to 1640 in England marked the development of manufacture. During this period labor was formally subsumed under capital and the manufacturing system gained economic predominance. The first point it is essential to grasp about this process is that it occurred in both industry and agriculture.

Developmentally prior to manufacture a considerable social division of labor was found in English society. In part this involved a differentiation in agricultural production in various localities, and in part it was a consequence of the growth of merchant capital, involved in both domestic and international exchange.[15]

It is not our task to examine this division of labor. What we must trace is (1) the construction of a manufacturing system within the context of the division of labor and (2) the development of this division of labor, and the circulation of commodities consequent on its development, within the context of the development of manufacture. It is an important attribute of the latter that it is instrumental in creating markets for the realization of its own surplus value.

In the pages that follow I will illustrate the predominance of manufacture in the early modern English social formation. I do this in reference to standard histories of the period, within a context that will make plain, I hope, the structured constraints inherent in a manufacturing system, and thus the tendencies that define its predominance. The illustrations are not proof of that predominance; insofar as proof is possible it comes in showing that the variables that derive from the tendency and which generate a specific form of disorder did in fact manifest themselves, and that this manifestation occurred in those areas where the predominance of the manufacturing structures (in industry and agriculture) seems most clear.

The foundation of manufacture is the selling of labor power as if it were a commodity. It has been estimated that the percentage of laborers among the adult male population of England increased from approximately 25 to 33 percent in the reign of Henry VIII to approximately 47 percent in the late seventeenth century (Everitt 1966:56). The latter figure is based on Gregory King's calculations for the 1680s and 1690s; he classed 23 percent of the national population as "labouring people and outservants," and an additional 24 percent as "cottagers and paupers" (see Coleman 1956:283; Bowden 1967:598; Everitt 1967a:399; Lindert 1980; cf. Clapham 1949:212–13; Woodward 1981). MacPherson, also using King's figures, comments that "very nearly half the men were full-time wage-earners; if the cottagers are counted as part-time wage-earners, the proportion is over two-thirds" (1962:61; he provides the basis of his calculations on p. 301, where he indicates that he includes both male in-servants and common soldiers). Basing his calculations on various sources, Everitt states that in the Tudor and early Stuart periods the laboring population formed about one-quarter to one-third of the entire population of the countryside (1967a:398). Clarkson estimates that 50 percent or more of the population of towns were wage earners in the early sixteenth century, and that the percentage in rural areas approached this figure by the end of the seventeenth century, including both farm laborers and those employed in rural industry (1971:48).

Three reservations must be stated about these "data." They are very rough approximations and it is impossible to estimate the margin of error they manifest. Second, it is unclear how we ought to categorize women and children when discussing wage labor. Their work was crucial in manufacturing production, in both industry and agriculture, and it was sometimes subsumed within their husbands' and fathers' contracts. Third, we must not confuse wage labor with productive labor within a capitalist system. Productive laborers in capitalist modes of production sell their labor power as if it were a commodity, and as a consequence of this transaction produce surplus value. Not all wage laborers are productive laborers. For example, those who sold their labor as services, in exchange for revenue, were not productive laborers; they lived off the surplus value others created (revenue). They did not create surplus value themselves (Marx 1968, 1:addendum 12). Wage labor is much older than manufacture; our concern must be with the tendential development of productive labor within the manufacturing system. Even with these reservations, the cited figures seem to indicate that a considerable growth in the number of productive workers engaged in agriculture and industry was manifest throughout the sixteenth and seventeenth centuries.

It is important to recognize that there was no sharp distinction between industry and agriculture in early modern England (cf. Clarkson 1971:75; Grigg 1980:97; Berg et al. 1983:27–28; Wadsworth and Mann 1968:26); both may be characterized as manufacture and they developed together. Unlike feudalism, in which the country may be said to dominate the town, or capitalism, in which the town dominates the country, manufacture involved the parallel growth of town and country (Patten 1978:17; Wadsworth and Mann 1968:56; Kriedte, Medick, and Schlumbohm 1981:209 n. 50). Nonetheless, seventeenth-century England was an agricultural country. Even in 1650, only 20 percent of the laboring population worked in industrial manufacture; in addition, the expansion of industry was not rapid enough to absorb the ever-growing work force (Bowden 1967:598; Clay 1984, 1:30–31).

The early modern period was one of significant alterations in agricultural organization. During the 150 years preceding the political revolutions of the seventeenth century two trends stand out: the development of a rural proletariat made up of productive laborers and the separation of land ownership from farming. The latter occurred as large landowners stopped cultivating their own land and instead leased it to tenants to be exploited for profit. The former occurred in innumerable ways: most of the writing devoted to it has focused on enclosures for pasturage, which may have depopulated the countryside, and certainly separated many from direct control over the land and from rights to certain land previously held in common.[16] Here, rather than going over this material (see a recent discussion for Essex in Hunt 1983:chap. 2), I want to stress that enclosures were only one aspect of the development of agriculture based on manufacture: their presence may be taken as an indication of this development, but they did not exhaust the social structure that created the demand for productive wage labor.[17]

> It is no use asking whether people were better off as wage-earners than they had been as small farmers. As long as they could make a go of their farms, they held on to them. When they could no longer make a go of them, they had to chose other livelihoods. The alternative was thus not between a prosperous little farm and wage-work, but between starvation or pauperism and wage-work. The opportunity to go out to work for wages thus came as a godsend to those who could not make their livings as farmers.   (Kerridge 1973:148)

In fact, the opportunity to make their livings as wage earners was an integral part of the process that separated small farmers from their land.

In 1500 many laborers were the sons of men who controlled their own land; these children could expect to inherit land of their own, and wage labor (or servantry) was a temporary burden. Many laborers were supplementing incomes derived from lands in their possession. While it would be inaccurate to assume that these two intermediate statuses had disappeared by 1640, it appears that the share of land controlled by laborers declined between 1500 and 1640 (Everitt 1966:57; 1967a:400ff.) as the number of rural wage earners increased (Bowden 1967:598). In part this occurred via the process of enclosure (Everitt 1967a:406ff.), but other circumstances were also important.

Cottage farmers generally held less than two acres of land and comprised approximately one-fourth of the farmworking population (Everitt 1967a:420). Their fortunes varied at this time, but were usually connected with their rights in common (403). In all areas the basis of their farming was livestock, primarily cattle (413–14). Better-off cottage farmers were able to increase their stock, while poorer ones were squeezed out. The former almost always supplemented their income with wage labor, while the latter became mere wage workers. The decline of wealth of laborers was more striking in fielden than forest areas (424). "It was the conjunction of all three circumstances in woodland areas—[relatively]

large[r] holdings, generous commons and numerous by-employments—that enabled enterprising labourers to better their lot at a
time when the labouring community, as a whole, was being gra-
dually disinherited and impoverished" (425).

Nearly two-thirds of all laborers wealthy enough to leave an in-
ventory (i.e., those who formed a subgroup among cottagers) took
up some form of by-employment. In other words,

> whenever peasant industries were combined with agriculture, farm-
> workers tended to be relatively wealthy ... It was in regions where
> rural industries were divorced from agriculture ... or where they were
> absent altogether ... that labourers were very poor. The income which a
> working family derived from any particular by-employment may have
> been small; but it was often sufficient to pay the rent of their cottage-
> holding, and it enabled them to lay aside a small surplus against times of
> dearth or unemployment.   (Everitt 1967*a*:429)

Most of these by-employments were concerned with either forest or
woodland crafts, or with the spinning and weaving of flax, hemp,
or wool (425). Not surprisingly, these were concentrated in woodland areas given over to dairy or pasture farming, in areas where
"the local demand for agricultural labor was relatively slight, or at
best spasmodic" (Everitt 1967*a*:429).

Sharp has recently criticized the emphasis Everitt and Thirsk
have placed on by-employments. He has noted:

> Capitalists had come to dominate the broadcloth industry and the new-
> drapery—products, aimed at an export market, which demanded con-
> siderable investment in raw materials and in the distribution of the
> finished product.... In these sectors of the economy, the skilled man was
> a propertyless wage earner or pieceworker, depending for employment
> upon the clothier or ironmaster, and for his food, upon the market.
> (Sharp 1980:7)

Thus while "these cottagers [often] supplemented their wages by
exploiting the woods and pastures of the royal forests" (5), and
while they rioted to preserve these open commons, they are properly viewed as a rural proletariat, not as farmers engaging in by-
employments (260, chap. 6). Sharp emphasizes the dominance of
these "artisans" in the main manufacturing areas of the country (1,
269). I suspect that while he may draw too sharp a line between
those cottagers who engaged in by-employments and those wage
earners who supplemented their wage by grazing a few beasts on

pasture, the picture Sharp paints is progressively more accurate as our period advances, and in general, progressively more accurate the more developed industrial manufacture was in a region.

The most authoritative estimate of English population growth between 1541 and 1641 suggests an increase of over 80 percent (Wrigley and Schofield 1981: table 7.8, 208–9). This population growth, whether due to an increase in fertility as Wrigley and Schofield argue, or to a decrease in mortality as was at one time assumed, provided the foundation on which manufacture developed and expanded. Unlike in the thirteenth century, there was little indication of parcelization of lands in fielden areas. Instead, with the predominance of manufacture the burdens of this growth were shifted onto the shoulders of the landless, while "bigger farmers and rentier landlords did well" (Grigg 1980: 90).

It is important to note that this increase in population was not evenly distributed within the country. There was considerable movement of population from fielden to forest (and fenland) areas. In these areas forms of partible inheritance often allowed for the breaking down of holdings to the minimum size capable of supporting a family under population pressure and in the circumstances of a particular social environment (e.g., the existence of rights to common land and industrial employment). While differentiation between yeoman and laborer marked manufacture in agriculture within fielden areas, in forest areas an equality of subsistence often survived. In the latter areas an elastic supply of labor was available for use in industrial manufacture. Forest areas were, as we have seen, where the putting-out system of manufacture most often took hold (for this paragraph see Thirsk 1961, 1967, 1976, 1978; Jones 1974; Spufford 1974; Everitt 1967*a*; Wrightson 1982; Hunt 1983: 28ff.; Kriedte, Medick, and Schlumbohm 1981).

This labor was also very cheap. It was supplementary to the income of many families and because of the use of women and children only a family wage was provided. In other words, the value of labor power which we usually associate with a man's income was derived from the employment of the entire family (for a discussion of this issue in defining the value of labor power see Gould 1981*a*). While the prosperity of families often varied depending on their size, wages were never high and often assumed other family resources (for this paragraph see Bowden 1985: 5; Chapman 1972: 10; Coleman 1973: 9; Levine 1977; Pinchbeck 1981: 45,

121ff.; Thirsk 1978; Wadsworth and Mann 1968:11, 26; Kriedte, Medick, and Schlumbohm 1981).

It would be misleading to imply that most of the displaced persons, even among those who held on to a very little land, depended for sustenance on by-employments. Most laborers depended on work as wage laborers on a farm for the bulk of their income. These men and women, unless boarded on the farm, were usually expected to own their tools (for a useful discussion of servantry, see Kussmaul 1981). During this period there was an increasing specialization of tasks; this differentiation was most marked in fielden areas where many farms employed a "sizeable labor force," less so in forest areas where agricultural employment was not so abundant and where migration in search of industrial manufacturing employment was more common. (This paragraph is based on Everitt 1967a:430–43.)[18]

We might summarize the discussion so far by saying that the 150-year period preceding the English Revolution witnessed the progressive growth of a "specifically commercial nexus between masters and men" (Everitt 1967a:440); labor tended to become wage labor, to be dismissed or hired at the will of the "capitalist manufacturer." This process was integral to the development of manufacturing in both agriculture and industry. It now remains to sketch the structure of a manufacturing economy in order to further articulate the tendencies that defined its predominance in pre-revolutionary England and to make clearer how it involved both the displacement of persons from their land and at the same time the creation of opportunities for them to earn livings, as it resulted in the formal subsumption of labor under capital.

In feudal Europe rent was the primary mode of extracting surplus value. To take the simplest case, a peasant, in exchange for the right to use a plot of land, worked half time for the lord. In other words, three days each week she worked for herself, three days for her lord. Whatever the substance of the institutional arrangements that constituted this relationship, the peasants' surplus labor was under the control of the lord, even if transferred in kind or in money. The exploitation within this system was, as Marx points out, transparent, and effective control over the actions of the peasant rested not simply on economic mechanisms but also in political, legal, and religious structures, which interpenetrated the work situation. The need for these extra economic components of

surplus extraction was ultimately dependent on the fact that peasants controlled the means of production necessary to produce their
own subsistence.

In manufacture, rent occupies a different position. Here it becomes an extraction from total surplus value produced under the
subsumption of labor to capital; it serves as a payment for the differential productivity of one piece of land over another (no matter
on what basis this differential rests), or as a payment for the control
exercised over the land by its owner, a payment based on the in-
dispensability of land in all modes of production, and the control
over land as private property within most capitalist modes of
production.[19] In either instance, however, it becomes a payment
subtracted from the surplus value created by productive labor. Formally it makes no difference whether the payment is made (for
accounting purposes) to the farmer who also serves as a capitalist
or whether the payment is made to a landlord who rents land to the
farmer. In England the latter was most often the case; there developed the so-called tripartite division between landlord, tenant
farmer, and wage laborer.

This threefold division was rooted in the seventeenth century or
earlier, although the level of its development in the 1600–1650
period remains uncertain (see Holderness 1976:50; Kerridge
1973:76; Stone 1972*a*:68). Stone comments that large-scale demesne farming by the nobility was almost extinct by the outbreak of
the Civil War, and notes that by 1640 most were rentiers, and many
were absentee rentiers (1967:141–43; see Stone and Stone
1984:282–83; Tawney 1967:203–4). For them as for other large
landowners, "it was the large leasehold farm operated on commercial principles by the capitalist farmer which provided the best
opportunity for high rent" (Bowden 1967:689. Bowden does not
specify how he defines "large" in this context, but from his comments elsewhere, we may assume that it is a farm above 100 acres;
cf. 659; cf. Wrightson and Levine 1979:30; and more generally
Clarkson 1971:62ff.).

In either case, whether the farmers owned the land and thus received the rent themselves, or whether they leased the land and paid
rent to the landowner, the mechanisms of manufacture production
were the same. The landowner usually provided the fixed capital,
the tenant the circulating capital, and while the workers might have
owned their own implements, their labor was clearly incapable of

providing for their subsistence unless hired by the capitalist who controlled (even if in conjunction with a landlord) the means of agricultural production. Labor power was thus formally subsumed under capital and yielded absolute surplus value to be divided among the tenant and the landlord as profit and rent.

Levine has stated his understanding of the issues we are discussing as follows (I quote him at length as he is one of the few historians to point out the structural similarities between the organization of agriculture and industry during the period under examination):

> In Marx's categorical framework the nature of full-blown industrial capitalism is twofold: The worker is not only separated from the ownership of the means of production but also, and perhaps more important, he loses control over the labor process, becoming an extension of the machine that regulates *his* work. It is in the second sense that the industrial activity studied in this volume [*Family Formation in an Age of Nascent Capitalism*] does not yet fulfill Marx's definition. Rural industrial workers were indeed often reduced to proletarianization, but they almost never lost control over the pace of production [i.e., while labor was formally subsumed under capital, the real subsumption of labor under capital had not yet occurred]. Their skill was valued, not diluted as in later stages of capitalist industrialization. In agriculture, much the same process was under way when the peasantry were first dispossessed of their land and then, later, brought together as wage laborers working the farms of capitalist producers.... The important dimension of capitalist agriculture is that unlike other forms of market-oriented, large-scale commercial production it was based on a system of private property, wage labor, and concentrated units of production. This last point is of critical importance in discussing England where the spread of commercial, capitalist agriculture was accompanied by the disappearance of the small farmer. (Levine 1977:1–2)

(See also Wrightson and Levine 1979; Wrightson 1982; and for a more general discussion of the relevant theoretical issues, Goodman and Redclift 1981:chap. 3.)

Levine goes on to point out that while small independent landowners survived beyond the sixteenth- and seventeenth-century changes in agricultural organization, they survived "within an economic universe in which the classic triad of landlord, tenant farmer, and wage laborer exercised hegemony" (1977:2). In other words, in my terminology, agriculture organized as manufacture predominated. This entailed a sustained growth of production and in consequence a furthering of the division of labor within society.

There is considerable evidence that by 1650 English agricultural production had increased to a point that allowed for both a stabilization of price and a considerable increase in exports. John has commented that "what differentiates the century after the Restoration from other periods is the importance attached to the export trade as a palliative for the 'great redundancy of corn, cattle, butter, cheese and other commodities' which by then appeared" (John 1976:47). It is clear that the existence of a grain surplus preceded the growth of exports, which accelerated at the beginning of the eighteenth century (John 1976:47, 48, 60, and passim; see also Kerridge 1968:332; Thirsk 1978:161; Olsh 1977). Ormond has endeavored to demonstrate that in the second half of the seventeenth century English grain replaced Baltic grain in European markets. He refers to England's "vast grain surpluses" (Ormond 1975:37; see also Bogucka 1980). Both Ormond and John note the importance of grain bounties in stimulating exports from 1673 onward.

Although the importance of these claims and the numbers various authors use to substantiate them is in some doubt owing to the stabilization and then the decline of population after the 1650s, there is little controversy that production was more than sufficient to feed the English people. There is no controversy concerning the fact of considerably increased production from 1500 to 1640. This is perhaps confirmed by Wrigley and Schofield's demonstration that "the seventeenth century retained no vestige of the positive check [on population]." Instead preventive checks kept population in balance with growing resources. This coupled with "special factors" "both pushed prosperity to heights unusual by pre-industrial standards and prolonged the period of prosperity beyond the common span" (Wrigley and Schofield 1981:472, 473). It is instructive to compare Wrigley and Schofield's figure 11.7, a model of population for the seventeenth century, with those depicting earlier and later periods. It appears that the seventeenth century marked a turning point even for these demographers, where demographic variables no longer dominate social variables.

There is considerable controversy concerning the sources of increased production. Thirsk argues that "increased production had been achieved by the more intensive cultivation of land in the best corn growing areas (the result, in part, of heavier manuring with more animals), and by the conversion of some selected grasslands to corn—most successfully in drained fens and marshlands, but also in some forests and vales" (1978:161). In another essay she points out that the watering of meadows, along with most of the important innovations in grain-growing regions, was "associated with substantial farmers and the owners of great estates" (1976:78). Kerridge also emphasizes the import of what he calls "capital farms" in grain production (1973:74ff. and chap. 4). But it is apparently the case that significant innovations were possible even in open field lands, suggesting that they were at least sustainable, if not the norm, under farming conditions similar to those prevailing prior to their development (Havinden 1967; see also Spufford 1974). Kerridge acknowledges this within the context of developments on "capital farms" (1973:132–33). More important, he notes that "even in the capital-farm countries there always remained a gradation of farms from small to large" (1973:136).

Almost everyone sees convertible husbandry as an important innovation, but there is considerable controversy concerning its spread by the 1650s and its consequences. John feels that there is no evidence of a substantial rise in yield per acre in the southeast of England, London's breadbasket, and that increased production must therefore have involved an extension of production, "made possible by new techniques in farming" (1976:61). Grigg feels that regional specialization was the sole innovative source of a new-won efficiency in English agriculture in the later sixteenth century; he suggests that there were few innovations in farming until the second half of the seventeenth century. With regard to convertible husbandry he argues as follows:

> It has been claimed that the spread of the "up and down" husbandry led to considerable increases in crop yields. This is perhaps dubious; arable land under grass was rested, and the roots helped to improve the soil structure. It also gave extra grazing, but it was not until the introduction into England of pasture legumes—clover, trefoil and sainfoin—whose nodules helped bacteria to fix soil nitrogen, that ley farming could have contributed much to increased yields of following cereal crops. These, together with turnips, were not adopted until the second half of the seventeenth century. (1980:93, citing Jones 1967:157)

Bowden suggests that "the increase in the country's agricultural output in the two centuries before 1650 ... probably owed less to improvements in productivity than to extensions in the cultivated area" (1967:606, 679–80). This certainly involved increases in other than grain production. Increases in production could happen either via the migration of small producers (as in much encroachment; Everitt 1967a:406ff.) or the draining of fens; in either case this land was sooner or later drawn into the commercial nexus within which manufacture in agriculture was gaining predominance (cf. Jones 1968).[20]

Kerridge, however, has strenuously argued for substantial increases in productivity; these were not caused by mechanization, but mainly by up-and-down (convertible) husbandry. He sees the main achievements as occurring before 1673, but here his opinion is questioned by most other experts, including Grigg as quoted above (Kerridge 1968:328 and passim; for brief reviews of the controversy see Woodward 1971; Overton 1984). Because Kerridge associates these improvements with the collapse of agricultural prices (1973:129) and because this did not happen until the second half of the seventeenth century, it seems safe to side with other experts who would suggest that the transformations in productivity Kerridge describes gathered momentum only late in our period. (Thirsk, ed., 1985 provides a comprehensive overview of the period 1640–1750.)

In my opinion, during the period from 1500 to 1640 an increase in outputs did not stem primarily from heavy investments in capital. While certain innovative methods of farming gained wider acceptance during this period, the main source of increased profits seems to have been due to organizational change. Even Kerridge writes that "successful improvers reaped great profits, just as unsuccessful ones faced disastrous losses.... Even in the absence of any considerable technical improvement, when from a demesne let out to service tenants was created a capitalist farm worked by wage labor, the rewards were substantial" (Kerridge 1973:133–34; cf. Brenner 1976:61ff; Clay 1984, 1:chaps. 3–6; Woolf 1970:524; Jones 1967:14). In my terms Kerridge's "capitalist farm" seems to refer to manufacture.

It may help to illustrate the nature of the manufacturing structure by highlighting the consequences of crises on different sized producers. By the seventeenth century a crop failure affected farmers of varying sized holdings very differently. "Since the demand for bread was inelastic (i.e. only a little less was consumed when the price increased substantially), large grain-growers who produced for the market could expect to enjoy increased receipts in times of harvest failure" (Bowden 1967:625). For small farmers, especially those who consumed a significant part of their output and sold a surplus of grain to meet rents and other expenses, a crop failure was disastrous. These farmers might even have to purchase grain at exorbitant prices (Bowden 1967:625–26; cf. John 1960:250). In a series of calculations Bowden estimates that the mixed farmer's breakeven point was between 50 and 100 acres of land; below this several harvest failures would probably mean economic disaster; somewhere around this acreage, a general crop failure would mean a net increase in income. "The main reason for these differences in fortune was that the larger farmer, even if he were no more efficient than the small producer, had a proportionately greater marketable surplus.... Moreover, the assumption about equal efficiency is questionable, and although the large grower may have sown seed in the same quantities per acre as the subsistence farmer, there seems good reason to think that his yield per bushel of seed was in some cases much higher" (Bowden 1967:659, cf. Spufford 1974:83, 90).

Speaking more generally of the seventeenth-century economic crisis, Hobsbawm argues that crisis led to increased concentration both in agriculture and in industry (1967:33–35ff.). Whereas in the fourteenth century crisis had led to the dispersion of economic control, in the seventeenth century it led to concentration of control (1960:109; see Bowden 1985; Thirsk 1985c:xxiv; Clay 1984, 1:63, 97–99). This difference may not be traceable solely to organizational changes in economic structure, to the development of manufacture, but it is not coincidental that the process was the same in both agriculture and industry.

This process will be clarified if we construct a thought experiment. Imagine a market with one price for like commodities. Within this context grain will be sold at a market price determined by the least productive land in cultivation within the purview of this market, by the least productive soil necessary to meet the inelastic demand for grain which prevailed in seventeenth-century England. The differential rent produced on this least productive land was zero. "Surplus profits" were garnered in one of at least two ways: if the market price is set by the least productive land then all more productive land will garner a return in excess of the average rate of profit. (For England in the sixteenth and seventeenth centuries see Grigg 1980:87, 91.) Second, if more intensive than average cultivation occurs or if some new technique is introduced to raise productivity but the technique is not widely used, a surplus profit will develop (see Grigg 1980:92). The market price will still be set by the least productive soil in cultivation and the uneven spread of new techniques or new organizational forms will yield a surplus profit either by increasing the volume of commodities sold or by lowering the price of production.[21]

It should be obvious that those involved in intensive cultivation would make superior profits, but if markets were in excess of supply, those with moderate amounts of land, barring crises, might survive and perhaps even prosper. In the 100 years prior to the revolutions of the 1640s, rationalizing tenants, be they gentry or yeomen, if they had 50 acres or more of land, seem to have prospered (Clay 1984, 1:140).

This prosperity is not questioned by most authorities (the most obvious exception is Trevor-Roper 1953). There is considerable evidence suggesting large increases in landed incomes from the second half of the sixteenth century (Finch 1956; Simpson 1961; Stone 1965a). There is, however, even more evidence of the relative and absolute impoverishment of the laborer during this same period; landowners, especially after 1580, gained markedly at the expense of small tenants and those who worked the farms. By this time the social background of the landowner—gentry or peer— was not as significant as the nature of estate organization (Bowden 1967:695).

This period saw a continued inflation in agricultural prices, while the real costs of agricultural production tended to decrease (Bowden 1967:674; Portman 1974:138). "This margin, or surplus, was potentially available to the landlord as rent, though in practice all or part of it might be retained by the tenant" (Bowden 1967:674). In fact, both rent and profits seem to have increased.

"Insofar as there was a 'profit inflation' in the Tudor and early Stuart periods ... it must have been in agriculture and not in industry" (Bowden 1967:609; cf. Davis 1973b:105–106). Bowden had earlier commented concerning the lag in industrial prices behind agricultural prices, "as real wages fell, the proportion of income spent on industrial goods declined, while the proportion spent on foodstuffs and other essential items increased. Since agricultural prices kept ahead of most other prices, the class with largest proportionate increase in income must have been those agricultural producers who farmed primarily for the market" (607–8; see also Hill 1969*b*: 61ff.).

It is clear, as we have seen, that large farmers benefited more from high grain prices then did small farmers (John 1960: 226), but it also is clear that yeomen, if they farmed moderate amounts of land (say above 50 acres), if they were diligent, and if they adopted commercially sound procedures, might improve their position (see Campbell 1960; Stone 1966: 26). As Kerridge puts it, "The more successful farmers simply rose *en masse* into the ranks of the lesser gentry" (1973: 138). "The gradual formation of a class of wealthy peasants took place in three ways, through the buying up by well-to-do men of parts of their neighbours' properties, through the colonizing by villages of the unoccupied land surrounding them, and through the addition to the customary holdings of plots which had at one time been in the occupation of the lord, but which, for one reason or another, he found it more profitable to sell or lease to his tenants" (Tawney 1967: 78, 87). The foundation on which this process spread was the growth of commerce; commercial opportunities provided the context within which the formal subsumption of labor to capital might occur, and this possibility of exploiting the labor power of others enabled many smaller holders to improve their position. Thus there was a differentiation in the fielden countryside between those farmers who were growing richer and those who were becoming progressively more impoverished.

One of the determinants of the amount of surplus value available for distribution to the land- and capital-owning classes is the level of wages. The 150-year period from 1500 to 1650 saw a dramatic decrease in real wages to approximately 50 percent of their former real value. While many workers were able to supplement their wages with produce from a garden plot, most lived at a subsistence level. In times of dearth many, perhaps as many as one-third, would face starvation, as most who were without land spent 80 to 90 percent of their income on food. Under such circumstances the rate of exploitation, even without increases in relative surplus value, must have increased enormously during this 150-year period, and this is yet another indication of the growing predominance of manufacture.[22]

The period also witnessed a considerable increase in rents; in addition the surplus collected by those who farmed and owned the land was supplemented by the sale of timber and the exploitation of other resources on the land. In general rents rose according to the capacity of land to produce income, and it is clear that improvements on the land, even if made by tenants, increased the future rent that land might command (Kerridge 1973:142–43). When custom could be overcome the full benefit of differential rents was grasped (Tawney 1967:146–47, but cf. Bowden 1967:693) and often enough custom was overcome so that rents rose steadily after 1560; although a setback may have occurred in the 1620s, rents continued to rise until 1659 (Kerridge 1973:143; Kerridge 1953; cf. Stone 1972*a*:131; Stone 1967:194, 154ff.).

Bowden summarizes the evidence for this rise in rents and notes that rents were in general highest in those areas with an accessible market for produce (1967:689ff.). We would expect that high rents would be correlated with high profits; Kerridge comments:

> There can be little doubt that the profits of capitalist farmers increased in the course of the sixteenth and early seventeenth centuries. Even though the farmer's profit increment might be temporarily forfeited on the taking of a new lease, the rents paid by sitting tenants were static for long periods during which the price of their produce rose considerably. Even though the rents paid for new takings kept pace with prices, or even if they led them, the average rents paid by farmers as a whole lagged behind the prices of farm produce. Moreover, long leases enabled farmers to undertake improvements and increase their yields. All told, this would seem to have been a period of prosperity for the substantial cultivators. (1953:29; see Stone 1972*a*:68, 72ff.)

Under these circumstances it was possible for even the less efficient farmer-landowner to prosper.

The fact that in agriculture prices are set by the least productive land in use in order to meet market demand[23] means that the pressures of competition in agriculture differ from those in industry. Even if Kerridge is more right than his detractors, that is, even if there was considerable technical innovation using fixed capital in agriculture, this process did not establish sufficient competitive pressures to ruin the relatively less efficient capitalist farmer; the combination of surplus (rent and profit) might be divided differently for the less efficient than the more efficient farmers (if rents were equalized), but unless their efficiency was markedly inferior to their capitalist peers, they would survive, at least until the late seventeenth century. The same would be true for units of capitalist production characterized by differences in output per bushel of seed or per acre associated with increased size (see n. 18, this chap.).

In fact Kerridge agrees with the crucial conclusion I want to draw concerning the consolidation of manufacture prior to 1640.

> In cereal growing the small farm could not compete on equal terms with the large one. The small farmer had higher unit costs and so little money coming in that he could not wait and get the best prices for what he had to sell. As long as a seller's market kept corn prices high, all this did not matter so much, but later on, in the seventeenth century, especially towards the end of it, when a buyer's market developed and prices slumped, many small men had to throw up their farms. (Kerridge 1973:148)

Thus even if Kerridge's characterization of the situation is correct, competition does *not* constitute the motive for increasing production prior to 1650.

Kerridge need not search for an explanation for increasing production as he believes that "once an innovation had proved itself profitable, everyone wanted to take it up.... They were taken up rapidly because they were open for all to see.... To learn new techniques one had only to lean over the gate and gaze" (1973:131). "In short, the real cause of the agricultural revolution is that the improvers were given a chance" (1973:136). Kerridge's argument is purely "utilitarian" (Parsons 1949:chap. 2; Gould 1981c), assuming the very form of rationality which I've suggested it was necessary to create. (See n. 9, this chap. Brenner avoids falling into this trap only by assuming the existence of competition, which thus necessitates rational calculation and action; cf. 1977:75–77; 1982:98–100.)

In sum, the dynamic I have associated with manufacture as a mode of production is manifest in agriculture, yet we cannot assume that an "objective" tendency (apart from a rationalizing ideology) toward capital accumulation was present in agriculture. Prior to 1650, even under conditions leading to moderate increases in the organic composition of capital, capital accumulation had to be subjectively motivated.

The situation was, as has been suggested, somewhat different in the late seventeenth century. At this point a stabilization of population growth occurred, and a more widespread use of new techniques within new organizational forms was apparent.[24] Prices stabilized as the level of demand was reduced to the level of supply and vice versa. In other words, to break even required greater efficiency of production, in part because real wages began a slow movement upward. In these circumstances less efficient farmers had a harder time making do, whether their inefficiency was determined by poor soil or by the misuse of their soil or by organizational constraints (perhaps conditioned by too little soil). It is crucial, however, that we understand that this bind had two consequences: the first involved the reduction of the farmers' earnings. The second, which often but not always followed, meant their going under. As in the earlier period, such farmers often succumbed to the burden of debt. Here, however, this burden was exacerbated by competitive pressures that may have forced them, even in the best of years, to lower prices below those necessary for their survival.

The former situation is where the farmers continued to farm their own land (to take the most favorable, but not typical, case of the freeholder) but for returns not commensurate to the land's worth under capitalistic production. Here the farmers' income did not include a return for their ownership of the land, as their products fetched only prices commensurate with the value of their labor power were they to enter into wage labor. In other words, ground rent was abolished and the rewards to the farmers' (families) labor were reduced to the wage rates of formally free labor (Amin 1977:60). Marx comments about this situation as follows:

> The smallholding peasant's exploitation is not limited by the average profit on capital, in as much as he is a small capitalist; nor by the need for a rent, in as much as he is a landowner. The only absolute barrier he faced as a petty capitalist is the wage that he pays himself, after deducting his actual expenses. He cultivates his land as long as the price of the product is sufficient for him to cover this wage; and he often does so down to a physical minimum. (1981:941–42; see also 815, 829)

This process was essentially similar to the one Chayanov discovered in prerevolutionary Russia. As Amin has stated, the

> dominant capital wiped out rent, i.e., abolished landownership. It proletarianized the peasant worker. The latter certainly remained the formal owner of the land but was no longer its effective owner. On the

surface, the peasant remained a commodity producer who offered products on the market, but in actual fact, was a seller of labor power, this
sale being masked under the cover of commodity production. Thus the
peasant was actually *reduced to the status of a person working at home
under the domestic system* [my italics].   (Amin 1977:60, basing himself on Chayanov 1966. Cf. Kautsky 1970; Banaji 1976; Thorner 1962)

In other words, many but surely not all seemingly independent producers were akin to those formally subsumed under capital (or en-
cased within social relations dominated by mercantile capital). For
these persons and their families, and more so the more economically unfavorable their position, independence, such as it was, would
be a precarious circumstance (cf. the West Riding woollen
clothiers). In debt in order to raise a crop, their position became
ever more precarious as manufacture in agriculture developed from
simple to complex cooperation, and in time of harvest failure their
position might well become untenable. Their difficulties would certainly have worsened after 1650. Their failure would swell the
labor force as family members left the farm in search of other employment.

The precise timing of the "elimination" of the small holder is in
doubt.[25] The classic analysis (Johnson 1963) emphasizes the period
at the end of the seventeenth and the beginning of the eighteenth
centuries as the most critical one for small owners. Although this
has not been demonstrated conclusively (Thirsk 1963:xii; cf.
Cooper 1967), "no one has found fault with Johnson's main contention, that the decline of the small landowner began not at the
time of the Parliamentary enclosure movement, but at the beginning of the sixteenth century with the growth of commercial agriculture" (Thirsk 1963:vii; see Habakkuk 1965). In at least one
fielden area small farms were nearly wiped out (by debt, not competition) by the 1630s; more important, it is clear here and we
might suspect elsewhere that standard medieval holdings, in fact
any holdings below 40 acres, were in trouble well before 1650
(Spufford 1974:chaps. 3, 4). This is the crucial point: the development of manufacture in agriculture, and thus the formal subsumption of labor under capital, set in motion a process resulting in the
consolidation of holdings, the increase in surplus value allocated as
profit and rent to those who farmed the land and to those who
owned the land, and the progressive severing of labor from the
land. Capital accumulation did occur via the extension and inten-

sification of production. While these did not result in the domination of competitive pressures, in times of crisis the environment that they created put pressure on holders of less than 30 to 50 acres of land. These persons had difficulty surviving periods of crisis. This process of consolidation was essential in the creation of a class of landless or land-poor laborers:

> In the long run, the elimination of the small-holder helped to raise agricultural productivity, thus enabling the country to sustain population levels far higher than those that had brought disaster in the fourteenth century. But this benign outcome was not fully apparent until the reign of Charles II. In the shorter run ... the cannibalization of subsistence farms interacted with the natural population increase to swell the class of landless wage laborers. The entire county [Essex], as Wrightson and Levine remarked about the village of Terling, was "filling up at the bottom."   (Hunt 1983:40–41; Hunt provides a judicious discussion of this process in chap. 2.)

In other words, the rationalization of an incipient manufacturing structure in agriculture led to its growing predominance in seventeenth-century England and thus to an increase in surplus value garnered by the more efficient producers (however divided between tenant and landlord) so long as the level of supply did not overburden demand (Marx 1981:815). When, probably beginning to a significant extent during the second half of the seventeenth century, this supply and demand equation began to alter in favor of supply (increased productivity and production with a stable population), competitive pressures were exacerbated which made the position of the less efficient producer ever more precarious. It is important to remember that these competitive pressures were a consequence of the development of manufacture; they did not affect manufacturing production in agriculture in the first period of its development. Thus competitive pressures cannot explain the process of rationalization which they consolidated.

Tawney wrote many years ago that "The social problem in the sixteenth century was not a problem of wages, but of rents and fines, prices and usury, matters which concern the small holder or the small master craftsman as much as the wage earner. The 'working classes' were largely small property holders and small traders" (1967:23 n. 2; see Tawney 1972, 1962). He further noted that the lessees played in the economics of agriculture the same part played in industry by the capitalist clothier (1967:202). We can illustrate this economic process in greater detail if we turn to manufacture in industry. What I want to emphasize, however, is that the process was structurally the same in both agriculture and industry; the process involved the growing predominance of manufacture.[26]

We might begin by drawing a schematic distinction between the guild system, where the workers owned both the instruments and objects of production; the domestic system, where they owned the instruments but not the object of production; and the factory system, where they owned neither the instruments nor the objects of production (Lipson 1959:ix, 440). The transition from the first to the second paralleled the movement of industry from town to country (de Vries 1976:245–46; Mendels 1972), but we must be careful not to exaggerate this process, as much English manufacture remained within the orbit of the towns, often in suburbs to avoid guild restrictions.

Key questions in determining whether or not manufacture exists are (1) who controls the commodity produced and (2) whether or not the workers are wage laborers producing surplus value. The two are interrelated: in a guild system, where labor is not subsumed under capital, the artisans produce for a customer; in other words, they sell a commodity, not their labor power. In the domestic system, the artisans produce a commodity that is controlled by a capitalist; they sell their labor power to the capitalist. The dividing line is ambiguous but the transition is significant. In the guild system workers, even if divided in rank, control the process of production and the valorization process; in manufacture, workers have lost control over the valorization process and are progressively deprived of control over the labor process (cf. Lipson 1959:472–73).

A guild system might well be stratified into master and journeyman levels and the journeymen might function as wage laborers, but if the masters continued to work alongside their journeymen and if the masters' position is dependent on their own skill in the actual process of production, the guild system has not been transcended. In this system the producers, even as represented by the master, control the commodity. In the domestic system the functions of capitalist and worker are separated; the capitalist provides the raw materials, the worker provides the instruments of labor, and the capitalist owns the product. The worker functions as pro-

ductive labor within a capitalist system, producing surplus value
that is embodied in commodities owned by the capitalist (cf. Lipson
1956, 2:xxviff.).

Domestic industry was characterized by constant returns to
scale; that is, inputs and outputs increased in comparable pro-
portions. Innovations were primarily organizational (de Vries
1976:91; Grassby 1969:736–37), but they only marginally
affected the actual labor process. Mantoux comments that the
domestic system retained the industry of the Middle Ages almost
unchanged (1962:61). Labor remained the most important factor
of production, and thus attempts were made, with the cooperation
of the government, to control the level of wages (Coleman
1956:287; Hawkins 1973). While real wage levels were decreasing
during this period, the possibility of increasing relative surplus
value was slight, as concentrations of capital did not depend on
heavy outlays for fixed capital, improving productivity and thus
lowering the value of labor power.[27] The amount of fixed capital
was originally so insignificant as to be controlled by the laborers
themselves. As Clarkson has put it:

> The diversity of manufacturing in pre-industrial England was matched
> by a considerable uniformity in organization. Most manufactures oper-
> ated on a small scale, used little fixed capital and employed labour-
> intensive methods. Neither the nature of industrial technology nor the
> size of the market made extensive investment of capital necessary.
> Machinery was usually small and operated manually. Few production
> techniques required specialized buildings and when premises were
> needed to house machines or workers, or for warehouses, they could
> usually be rented cheaply.   (1971:97–98)

The largest employers were manufacturers who put workers to
work in the workers' own homes.

Cloth production, England's most important industry, was un-
affected by cost-saving innovations (Bowden 1967:608) and the
new draperies, a lighter fabric that gained in importance during the
first half of the seventeenth century, was more labor intensive than
the old draperies (Coleman 1969:423). Thus domestic industry
rested on older methods of production, productivity was low, and
there were only slim opportunities to improve it (Coleman 1956;
Cornfield 1973:200). Coleman goes so far as to write that "textiles
in general, not merely the English wool-using branch of the industry, were from roughly the fifteenth to the eighteenth centuries one

of the more technologically stagnant and conservative industries in European economic history" (1973:5; see also Patten 1978:58, 80; Kriedte, Medick, and Schlumbohm 1981:75, 88, 92, 95, 111–13, 136, 299 n. 5). He emphasizes that "rural putting-out industry evolved as an innovation in organisation, without drastic change in techniques; the industrial revolution brought drastic change in both techniques and organisation" (Coleman 1973:14). In other words, "the putting-out system by itself did not entail an increased labour productivity either. Rather, the putting-out capitalist adopted existing work-processes and tools" (Kriedte, Medick, and Schlumbohm 1981:111).

In the sixteenth century English cloth manufactures endeavored to sell dear, for example, by controlling overseas prices by monopolies. In the seventeenth century they realized the necessity of selling cheap (Supple 1959:147–48, 223). As Hobsbawm put it, the desire for profit was not enough; rather, capitalists must seek the greatest aggregate profit via "mass production." (1967:15–16). In this period, however, an increase in production resulted in the multiplication of units under the formal control of capital (Clay 1984, 2:97). Supple has written elsewhere that

> neither existing technology nor potential demand normally justified large-scale units of production, and the possibilities of cost-reduction by an expansion of output were severely limited. Correspondingly, industrial expansion more often took place by a multiplication of units of production and an increase in investment and the demand for labor, than by a relative increase in the allotment of capital and an increase in productivity. (1977:397)

Rowlands emphasizes that the metal industry as practiced in the Midlands as late as the middle of the eighteenth century involved an aggregation of small units, using methods unchanged from the Middle Ages. Yet "it is evident that this simple structure showed itself capable of sustained great expansion and growth" (1975:121). This is in accord with the more expansive picture painted by Patten about the seventeenth century: "Increases in the volume of production to meet increased demand at home or opportunities abroad were generally made by increasing the numbers of people working on the product involved" (1978:162). Thus "it was not ... the size but the number of enterprises which contributed to the multiplication of capital" (Kamen 1971:115).[28]

While there appears to have been relatively little innovation in productive technology, there were very considerable innovations in products:

> They generally pass unmentioned by modern economists interested in the historical process of growth and innovation. They were simply new fabrics, new designs, different colours, different finishes, changes in yarn, in weaves, in patterns.... More and more the market—influenced increasingly by shifts in fashion as more substitutes became available—dominated production. Textile manufacture provides the supreme example of the pre-industrial revolution multiproduct industry; and moreover, of a consumer-oriented industry, effecting little or no change for centuries in the basic techniques of its main production processes but frequently changing, in an almost infinite variety of small ways, the combination of inputs which determined the look, feel, finish, colour, pattern or weight of the final product—and by this route sometimes, though not necessarily, also affecting its cost and profitability. (Coleman 1973:9)

Thirsk has labeled this process "The Fantastical Folly of Fashion," in reference to the stocking knitting industry (1973).

More important, she has documented another element of the same process for a series of consumer industries dependent on the home market, which was "capable of absorbing a wide range of qualities.... As a result, goods at many different prices were available to every class of purchaser, and their sale did not depend upon the whim and fashion of one small section of the population. Everyone could find the price and quality that suited him" (1978:115–16). Shops spread and pedlars increased to a "prodigious number" after the Civil War. She sees a seventeenth-century mass market for consumer goods (122–25).

The necessity of mass production highlights a point of distinction between the guild and manufacturing systems. In the former, the masters' position within the enterprise, coupled with the specific nature of their "capital" and the traditional controls upon their capacity to expand (Marx 1967, 1:358) precluded extensive capital accumulation within the industrial sphere. Large-scale capital was either merchant or usury capital that when operative within a traditional economy precludes the development of a capitalist mode of production (Marx 1967, 1:510; this point runs throughout Weber's writings). In manufacture the possibility of capital accumulation via iterative surplus value became a reality. When freed from tradition controls and coupled with a rationalizing ideology, such accumulation was structured into the nature of the system.

The importance of labor as a factor of production and the constant returns to scale implied by the adoption of older technologies had two important consequences: increases in demand and production resulted in the multiplication of the number of workers needed. Home markets were relatively stable, growing, as we will see, with the spread of manufacture, but until at least 1650 severely retarded by the low wages earned by a significant body of the society. This, coupled with the fact that almost all enterprises involved a concentration of circulating but not fixed capital (Mendels 1972:255 and the sources he cites), may have implied that increases in capital accumulation were especially sensitive to foreign markets. The volatile nature and frequent disruption of those markets was exacerbated by the easy disinvestment possible in manufacturing industry. Supple has documented this process for the all-important cloth industry. We must be sensitive to its consequences in terms of the nature of the demands that manufacturing interests came to make on the government after the revolutions.[29]

While the domestic system had considerable disadvantages for the capitalist (see Lipson 1956, 2:55ff.), it also had considerable advantages. Workers were often formally in an autonomous position vis-à-vis the capitalist, functioning as independent producers. They lost this independence via two mechanisms: As they became indebted to their employers their capacity to make autonomous decisions concerning the allocation of their time was eliminated. In addition, as the growth of production was facilitated via an increase in the division of labor among workers, they lost their capacity to complete a finished product; as in agriculture, tasks became increasingly specialized (Clarkson 1971:100ff.; Hill 1969b:91; Brailsford 1961:102–3; Tawney 1962; Everitt 1967a:432).

Credit was the basis of almost all commercial production in the early seventeenth century. Borrowing and credit were pervasive in the rural society Spufford studied and those yeomen who lost their land appear to have done so because they fell into debt (1974:80ff.; see Clarkson 1971:149ff.). When farmers were able to mortgage their land and may have had to mortgage their land in order to bring in a crop, it was possible that they could lose their land, especially in time of harvest failure, and fall more directly under the control of capital (cf. Tawney 1967:138–39).

Mantoux describes the comparable plight of "independent" domestic workers; I quote the description of the process whereby they lost their implements. In a bad year, "he had to borrow, and who was the most likely person to lend if not the merchant who employed him? The merchant was generally willing to lend him money, but he needed security, and the readiest pledge was the weaver's loom which, after becoming the means of earning mere wages, now ceased to be the exclusive property of the producer. In this way, following on raw material, the implement in its turn fell into the capitalist's hands" (1962:64; see also Thirsk 1978:170; Wadsworth and Mann 1968:6). He places this process at the end of the seventeenth and beginning of the eighteenth centuries, when Johnson felt that small landowners lost their land. Whatever the exact timing, which varied by locality, it is clear that in both industry and agriculture a widespread process of class differentiation was occurring in the seventeenth century; the mechanism that powered this differentiation was manufacturing, as it represented a mode of the formal subsumption of labor under capital.

Wilson has argued that the years 1660 to 1700 in England saw a period of economic growth unique in the preindustrial society (1965:xii–xiii). If so, this development was clearly a continuation of processes originating in the preceding century; these preparations were made in both agriculture and in industry and entailed the very considerable diffusion of manufacture.

Lipson provides a long list of industries that were organized along capitalist lines; the most important was the woollen industry, but others are not to be discounted. He emphasizes in addition to textiles, coal, other forms of mining, and other industries involving relatively large capital investments. Clarkson tells us, however, that textiles, clothing, leather, metalworking, building, and the processing of food and drink accounted for about three-quarters of the urban work force, and for most nonagricultural rural employment. These, when organized as manufacture, required little investment in fixed capital (Lipson 1956, 2:xxviiiff.; Clarkson 1971:80; Thirsk 1978).[30]

In speaking of the period from 1603 to 1660, Wilson comments that "everywhere the nation's leading industry was household industry, full of rural cottage workers working for a capitalist who 'put out' materials to them and collected their product" (Wilson 1965:67). While manufacture was unevenly diffused through early seventeenth-century England, its grip was intensifying. Court tells us:

> Capitalism was beginning to strike its roots wide and deep in the Midlands in the seventeenth century. . . . The capitalist enterprise of that age in the Midlands grew very largely in and by a domestic production which did not weaken with capitalism's growth, but rather strengthened with its strength, both flourishing and expanding in mutually indispensable association, under the peculiar economic conditions of the time. The line between industrial capitalism and production of handicraft type therefore becomes difficult to draw. . . . What was important for the seventeenth century was exactly their close association and even interdependence. (1953:71–72)

The situation was similar in many other areas of the country. Although it is impossible to say how many persons were employed by domestic capitalists and of these how many worked to supplement "incomes" from agriculture, it appears that these domestic capitalists were by far the largest employers in industry (cf. Clarkson 1971:100; Wilson 1965:67).

The third, fourth, and fifth decades of the seventeenth century witnessed severe hardship in England. The conjunction of harvest failures and commercial depression resulted in extreme difficulties in a society where a significant part of the population lived on the margin of subsistence. This hardship was not generalized; its severity was partly because of the growing differentiations in wealth with the spread of manufacture. It points out how crucial the interrelationship between agriculture and industry was, and shows the importance for tendential economic growth of the predominance of manufacture in both of the economy's major sectors (see Bowden 1967:621; Hoskins 1953–54:98; Supple 1959:15ff., 55–57; Barnes 1961:3).

The interrelationships between agriculture and industry were many; most industry was based on the processing of agricultural products. "Down to the eighteenth century, it has been well said (Mathias 1959:xxi), manufacture [in industry] may be seen more significantly as processing the harvest than as something divorced from it" (Hill 1969b:21). "England's [industrial manufacture and] trade—in wool, leather, grain, hops, minerals—grew directly out of her land and farms" (Wilson 1965:36). In many instances industry had its roots in the land; in some instances those who took part in the one participated in the other. We have seen this for laborers;[31] it was also true for "capitalists." Court emphasizes this connection for the Midlands (1953:73–74), but it was also apparent elsewhere (see Habbakuk 1953; Everitt 1960:17; Willcox 1940:175). These interrelationships were both direct in the sense of one person having an unmediated interest in both sectors, and indirect in the sense that the profits of, for example, farmers and merchants were often interconnected (Kerridge 1973: 140). These interrelations often involved the formation of like interests among the manufacturers in agriculture and their counterparts in industry. We will see in this chapter and in chapters 5 and 6 how this commonality of interest united these different groups in opposition to the the Crown (Stone 1972a:69).

Jones, in presenting an argument "that developments on the production side of agriculture were indeed instrumental in bringing the earliest advanced countries to the brink of industrialization," comments about England that "the social mechanisms which permitted London to grow and rural industrial concentration to emerge did ensure that the [agricultural] surplus could be traded. In return the farm population received cash to spend on colonial wares and industrial consumer goods. They did not need to eat up the food surplus in home population growth" (1974:128, 130).

Bowden points out that a harvest failure resulted in an increase in grain prices and consequently in a decrease in the demand for manufactured goods; this effect might be intensified by a reduction in the demand for labor. Woollen goods were, Bowden argues, particularly susceptible to such effects, as clothing was the principal consumer good on which money might be saved in times of dearth (1967:626, 629ff.). Conversely, a good harvest, by decreasing the price of food, increased the real earnings of those who purchased food, and this included both nonagricultural and many agricultural workers, releasing a significant amount of purchasing power to be spent on manufactured goods (Supple 1959:16; Everitt 1967a: 418, 450).

I have already suggested that by 1650 England had an adequate grain supply and that grain prices began to stabilize (Brenner 1976:61ff.; John 1960; Jones 1967, 1974; Bowden 1967:605–6; 1985). Agricultural output had increased and this growth proved sufficiently self-sustaining to free persons to work in industry. After 1650, "rising agricultural production was increasing the supply of food and tending to reduce its price, though the preponderant effect was to release young people from agriculture" (Jones 1974:138). It may well be that the slowing down of population growth after 1650 allowed for the relative stagnation in agricultural prices, while organizational transformations continued at an only slightly increased rate (see Bowden 1967:605–6; cf. Clay 1984, 1:123, chap. 4; Bowden 1985:69). In any case, the prerequisites for industrial growth were maintained.

Many commentators have pointed out the importance of the "agricultural revolution" for English industrial growth. Some have argued that earlier periods of industrial development were retarded by the inability of agriculture to produce an adequate surplus; some have commented on the negative effects of importing grain susceptible to increasing costs, or on the parcelization of land which previously occurred in meeting rising demand (Jones 1967:4, citing Habakkuk and Deane, and 18; Jones 1968:617; 1974:chap. 5; Thompson 1966:517; Hobsbawm 1967:25–27; Hobsbawm 1960:106; Brenner 1976:61–75). It is clear that in England the corner was turned in agriculture and in industry together, owing to their mutual interpenetration and their congruence in structure. English economic growth was self-sustaining in the period prior to the industrial revolution. This self-sustaining development was based on the formal subsumption of labor to capital and the rationalization of this structure. Crises occurred, but though they slowed down this process they did not halt it (cf. Hobsbawm 1960:99–100).

Handicraft production involved the sale of commodities by the producer to a customer. If the customer was a direct consumer production had to be based on local markets; if the customer was a merchant, it might have involved sales within wider, perhaps even world, markets. In the latter case, it usually involved luxury goods. Manufacture was based on a social division of labor and on interregional markets. In the process of its growth it constructed national markets and often provided commodities for international markets (cf. Bücher 1968; Unwin 1957; Lenin 1960ff.: vol. 3; it is interesting that Lenin thought Bücher's book of sufficient interest that he translated into Russian the section devoted to the growth of a national economy; see Lenin 1960ff., 3:652 n. 119; and the n. on 550 for Lenin's criticisms of Bücher).

The seventeenth century saw in England the creation of interregional markets. Most manufacture was for the domestic market (Thirsk 1978:2, 136); even in 1841 "more than 40 per cent of industrial craftsmen in England were supplying exclusively local markets" (Clarkson 1971:117), and in the early seventeenth century, only woollen textiles had overseas markets of great importance. The seventeenth century saw a steady expansion of internal trade, and this expansion was accelerated by growing urbanization. The greater population concentration in the cities "upset the balance of communities hitherto largely self-supporting, and compelled them to depend upon market supplies" for sustenance (Everitt 1967b:564).

London was of particular importance in this process. Its demand for food was enormous and helped to effect the transformation of agriculture in the surrounding counties. By 1637 there was a carrying trade between London and all parts of the country. England was fortunate to be an island and also to be furnished with innumerable navigable rivers; much of her trade used either her coasts or her river system. Both developed considerably during the seventeenth century, with London often providing the stimulus. When the commodities finally appeared in towns, there was a growing series of retail shops in which they might be sold. (The above two paragraphs are based on Chartes 1977a, 1977b, 1985; Clarkson 1971:114ff.; Everitt 1969a:39; Everitt 1967b; Fisher 1935, 1948, 1968, 1971; Levine 1977:6; Patten 1978:177, 216, 222, 278; Thirsk 1978; Willan 1938, 1964, 1976; and Wrigley 1967.)

Everitt emphasizes the growth of private markets during the first part of the seventeenth century; he sees these as one aspect of the "great development in inland trade in England between 1570 and 1640" (Everitt 1969a:39). In his cautious appraisal of the changes in agricultural marketing from 1500 to 1640, he emphasizes the importance of the transformations of the second half of the period:

> On the whole, while the early sixteenth century was not a time of stagnation, the last seventy years of the period showed a sudden leap forward in the volume, organization, and impact of agricultural trading in the English economy. Rising prices, an expanding population, the growth of urban and industrial areas, the progress of agricultural specialization and enclosure all tended to stimulate agricultural trade; and these four forces were all exceptionally powerful in the latter half of the period. (Everitt 1967b:587)

"It is rather paradoxical to argue, as does Christopher Hill, that in this period there was at the same time 'a savage depression of the living standards of the lower half of the population' and also a considerable expansion of consumer purchasing power within the domestic economy" (Corfield 1973:200, quoting Hill 1969*b*:83). Perhaps this phenomenon is paradoxical, but it nonetheless appears to have occurred in just the way Hill describes (Corfield's citation for her discussion is to pages 65–69; Hill's discussion of this point follows the quotation cited, 83ff.). Imagine the following situation: If each of ten persons needs seven products, or use-values, to survive, and if each produces all seven products and in addition three others, no commodities exist and no exchange is necessary. If each person produces only one of the necessary products, she will have to enter into exchanges in order to obtain the other six. If we assume that she produces only a sufficient amount of that one product to exchange for the other six but not for the luxury products, or that she is paid only this amount for producing her one product, her standard of living will have declined but she will be forced to enter into exchanges in order to survive. Something like this happened in the development of manufacture, where the formal subsumption of labor under capital resulted, in its first stage, in the reduction of real income of the actual workers; it nonetheless left them needing to purchase commodities in order to survive, and thus it broadened the market for manufactured goods, both in agriculture and industry.

It would be erroneous to suggest that this process touched all families in seventeenth-century England, but a major point in the above discussion has been that this transformation was widespread; it affected and was effected by "small men." We are not speaking of large-scale enterprises producing luxury goods but of smaller-scale manufacturing producing for markets growing in scope and in depth (Thirsk 1978).

It is clear, as Hill among many others points out, that low wages retarded the development of England's home market (1969*b*:85), but because of transformations in economic structure, "much of the expanding internal demand for food and manufactured goods came from landless wage laborers, who though absolutely poorer had to purchase more because they no longer produced for themselves" (Hill 1966:24–25; 1969*b*:85).

During this entire period the home market for industrial com-

modities was wider than the world market.[32] The growth of these
markets was reflected in the equalization of prices throughout the
kingdom (de Vries 1976:246–47). Agriculture also saw a narrowing of price differentials in various markets, "this being a development which one would expect to occur as the market became wider
and better organized" (Bowden 1967:614; cf. John 1960:224–25;
and for 1640–1750 see Bowden 1985:27–29; Chartres 1985).

These tendencies, halting as they were, are indications of the development of manufacture in both industry and agriculture. They
allow one to succumb to the temptation "to see the seventeenth
century as the decisive period in the creation of a national market"
(Hobsbawn 1967:50–53). This fact is emphasized when we consider that the increase in real wages during the second half of the
century allowed for the continued development of agricultural markets, and in addition, fueled the growth of the market for industrial
commodities. What had been a cyclical phenomenon prior to this
period, moving with the level of the harvest, now became a tendency toward expanding purchasing power; this tendency, in part a
manifestation of the predominance of manufacturing in agriculture,
appears to have continued into the eighteenth century (Bowden
1967:626ff.; John 1967; Jones 1967:38; Jones 1974:129).

In this section I have outlined indications of the predominance of
manufacturing in early seventeenth-century England. This predominance is evidenced by the working out of those tendencies we
have seen to be associated with manufacture, tendencies connected
with the predominance of iterative surplus value as controlling the
economic valorization process and with the realization of this surplus value within the contexts of a developing exchange economy.
In its early stages this economy resulted in increased profits for both
agricultural and industrial manufactures, in increased rents for
landlords, and in decreased real incomes for the growing body of
wage earners. These latter were forced more and more to enter into
market relationships; the necessity of selling their labor power as a
commodity generated the necessity of purchasing needed use-values
as commodities.

Corfield comments that by the early 1640s "the English economy was not on the verge of take-off into a modern growth economy" (1973:202). She is correct, but she misses the point. The
argument is not that Stuart patrimonialism bound Prometheus; the
argument that I want to make is that this political system stood in

contradiction to the then-predominant manufacturing economy; once the political system had been removed the inherent tendencies within this economy slowly worked themselves out, and into the development of a manufacture based on a more complex division of labor and the extraction of relative surplus value, and more important, into machine capitalism.

Economy and Polity

It is important to emphasize one connection between the constraints placed on political action by the economy and the controls put on political action by the societal community and latency subsystem. In a system where political actions are justified in terms of their success and where support is forthcoming for the implementation of interest demands, the structure of the economy limits the scope of actions capable of generating political support, as this economic structure limits the scope of political actions capable of successful completion. These constraints may be of two types. The first is aggregative. Any economy will be capable of producing only so many adaptive resources at one time; this will limit the level of political output. Also, an economic structure limits the type of resources which might be successfully produced. Thus there are constraints within a feudal structure not applicable to a capitalist structure, and constraints within a capitalist structure which will not be applicable within a socialist structure.

If we assume a complementarity between the economy and polity of a society, we may assume under most circumstances that persons in the societal community will act instrumentally within the context of a given situation, and will not make demands on a political structure which that structure cannot fulfill. If actors within the polity endeavor to attain certain goals barred by economic constraints, their failure will be sufficient proof of the fact that they (and perhaps the party or structure they constitute) are not deserving of support. This is obviously to draw the picture too sharply, as support and failure may be complex issues, but where the economy and the polity are each capable of mutually providing the necessary resources for the stable functioning of the other subsystem, the natural consciousness of those embedded in the structures will involve a perspective congruent with successful adaptive and goal-attainment performances.

It is essential to point out that there is no simple universally defined position from which persons within the societal community
evaluate economic and political performance. Social positions are
structurally conditioned and controlled and may result in conflicting interests and perspectives. For example, while it is true that
satisfactory economic performance within a capitalist economy has
proven more important to workers than certain vulgar versions of
Marxian theory have implied, it is also true that there remains a
structurally defined contradiction between the workers' and the
capitalists' interests within the economy and within the polity.
These discrepant positions may provide the basis for a differential
evaluation of the same political action.

The situation was different in early seventeenth-century England.
Here a patrimonial political system was legitimized within traditional values (Weber 1968, 1:226ff.), but economic activities
were being carried out which were nontraditional. (For the logic of
this process see chap. 8, below.) In this context pressures were
placed on the political system which required an expansion of the
scope of its authority; these pressures were filtered through the extant structure of the political system, but their consequences were,
for a significant body of those included in the political nation,
evaluated in terms of an economic structure incompatible with the
state. To put it at its simplest level, the polity required additional
economic resources in order to meet demands placed on it, but the
allocation of the resources was not justified in terms of the positive
benefits derived from governmental policies, and in fact, these policies had negative effects within the economy. The governmental
policies were those of a patrimonial regime; the economy was one
of manufacture.

Patrimonial polities function within the context of traditional
values; that is, the ruler's powers are viewed as legitimate insofar as
they are traditional (Weber 1968, 3:1020).* These traditional beliefs do not entail the constant repetition of custom, but they do
necessitate a legitimation of innovation in terms of past practice. In
one sense, as we will see in chapter 8, these innovations result in the
discovery of the past as something other than a seamless web.

A crucial aspect of patrimonial authority involves its reaction to

---

* Unless otherwise noted, all subsequent page references in this section refer to
Weber 1968; pages 1–398 refer to vol. 1 and pages 941–1469 to vol. 3.

transformations within traditional social relations. The ruler "is considerably influenced by the well-founded apprehension that his own, especially his economic, interests would be badly hurt by any shock to traditional loyalty produced by groundless and 'unjust' interference with the traditional distribution of duties and rights. Here, too, the master's omnipotence toward the individual dependent is paralleled by his powerlessness in face of the group" (1011–2). In response to these innovations she seeks the consolidation of her political powers by including extrapatrimonial areas within the realm of her "patriarchal" power. To do this it is necessary to develop a set of "servants," an administration whose loyalty is to her, and whose use is at her discretion (231–32, 1013, 1022).

It is clear that "besides the army the coercive administrative apparatus available to the ruler was important for determining the size and quality of the enforceable demands" (1025). The ruler's capacity to develop such an administration was enhanced by economic transformations that developed autonomous classes existing within yet apart from extant social structures. The clearest examples of this type of group in the Occident are those occupying mercantile and financial positions in the interstices of a noncapitalist mode of production. Both Weber and Marx go to great lengths to inform us that these persons were not the ancestors of modern capitalism, but they were important in providing the resources on which a patrimonial administration, always dependent on the favors of the ruler, might be built (1092, 1094; see Takahashi 1976).

> The *liturgical* meeting of the ruler's political and economic needs is most highly developed in the patrimonial state.... For the ruler liturgical methods mean that he secures the fulfillment of obligations through the creation of heteronomous and often heterocephalous associations held accountable for them.... The most radical liturgical arrangement is the transfer to other vocational groups of this hereditary attachment: thus corporations, guilds and other vocational groups established, legalized or made compulsory by the ruler become liable for specific services or contributions of their members. In compensation and especially because of his own interest in preserving the subjects' economic capacity, the ruler customarily grants a monopoly on the respective economic pursuits and ties the individual and his heirs to the association, both with respect to their persons and their property. (1022–3)

Under such circumstances financiers and trade capitalists may flourish (1095); these and some industrial groups, granted monopolistic control, serve as the fiscal basis on which patrimonial authority might be constructed (1098).

Finance becomes a significant issue for all patrimonial states. "The obligations placed on sources of direct taxation tend both in amount and in kind to remain bound to tradition. At the same time there is complete freedom—and hence arbitrariness—in the determination of (a) fees and (b) of newly imposed obligations, and (c) in the organization of monopolies. This element of arbitrariness is at least claimed as a right" (238). This situation leads to a contradiction that often causes disturbance. On the one hand financial rationalization moves imperceptibly toward bureaucracy that resorts to systematic taxation; on the other hand, this results in innovations that violate tradition, while the legitimacy of the patrimonial ruler is founded on traditional values (1014, 1021, 1094).

As we move to consider the consequences of such a regime for manufacture, we must beware of an easily committed error. We must not assume that the manufacturing capitalists knew what was in their own interest. There were no guidelines for them to follow, at least not in England, and we must argue in terms of cause, not in terms of a *telos* that was unexpected and unpredictable, at least by the actors involved.

Traditionalism places serious obstacles in the way of formation of formally rational administrative processes. There is not only a tendency toward arbitrariness but also a tendency toward determinations grounded in substantive values, traditional values (239–40). "For all these reasons, under the dominance of a patrimonial regime only certain types of capitalism are able to develop: (a) capitalist trading, (b) capitalist tax farming, lease and sale of offices, (c) capitalist provision of supplies for the state and the financing of wars, (d) under certain circumstances, capitalist plantations and other colonial enterprises" (240). The situation is different for those forms of capitalist organization based on the systematic extraction of iterative surplus value, and thus a rational organization of free labor producing commodities for sale to private consumers, for they depend on the capacity to calculate the consequences of specific actions, and on the regularity and impersonality of the response to these actions.[33]

"Patrimonialism can resort to monopolistic want satisfaction, which in part may rely on profit-making enterprises, fee-taking or taxation. In this case, the development of markets is, according to the type of monopolies involved, more or less seriously limited by irrational factors. The important openings for profit are in the hands of the ruler and his administrative staff. Capitalism is thereby either directly obstructed, if the ruler maintains his own administration, or is diverted into political capitalism [which does not stand in the main line of continuity with the later autonomous capitalistic development], if there is tax farming, leasing or sale of offices, and capitalist provision for armies and administration" (238, and for the insert, 241). Although this form of government may substantively reinforce certain aspects of capitalist development, "as a rule, the negative aspect of this arbitrariness is dominant, because—and this is the major point—the patrimonial state lacks the political and procedural *predictability*, indispensable for capitalist development" (1094–5).

The development of manufacturing capitalism required a minimum of regulation, within the context of a stable structure of social expectation. If, as Weber suggests, the two bases of the rationalization of economic activity are "a basis for the calculability of obligations and of the extent of freedom which will be allowed private enterprise" (238), it is surely, as he also suggests, no coincidence that capitalism developed in England, where the rule of officials was minimized (1099, 1064) nor that the champions of manufacture "usually attempt to substitute bureaucratization or a plutocratic domination by *honoratiores*" in the place of a patrimonial administration (1091). These *honoratiores* were bound by a logic of decision which was sanctioned within the social context in which they were embedded, and although they were liable to pressures from the ruler or other sources favoring arbitrary decisions, they were sanctioned within norms defined by the interests of the notables in their own social structure. In early modern England their decisions were constrained within an emergent manufacturing structure; here the "*kadi* justice" of the Justices of the Peace, as of the common law courts, was not arbitrary, but was structured in the interests of the administrators and their class (1061). The relative autonomy of the political and legal structures from the economy allowed for a considerable reconciliation of ruling class interests within a calculable structure of formal controls. It was this arbitrary yet calculable structure that proved flexible enough to allow for capitalist development and strong enough to crush opposition to the process.

An apparently ideal situation for economic change involved the postrevolutionary retention of higher-order traditional values, within the context of which fundamental social structural alterations might be made. This traditional order helped to maintain social stability while the expropriators of the patrimonial state came to control the governmental administration, including the armed forces, as well as the institutional context of property and financial policy within which capitalist accumulation occurred.

Although patrimonialism may be said to be based on innovations legitimized within traditional beliefs, innovations were always in a precarious position under patrimonial rule. If your daily actions necessitate the violation of some rule, the police who refrain from arresting you will be able to exert considerable pressure on you. Either you create a countervailing power to repulse their power or you remove them from office, or you continue to live under a sword. New modes of acquisition are always under that sword within a patrimonial system, and even the privileged few are in a situation where the loss of favor brings ruin and destruction (1099).

Economy and Polity: 17th Century England

The Tudor monarchs might be said to have nationalized feudalism; they bequeathed to the Stuarts a unified state in which the crown held a monopoly over the use of force. In doing this they greatly expanded the court and central administration and their own powers of office. This process continued into the seventeenth century, but correlatively, the power of Parliament and of the king's greatest subjects also expanded. Judson explains this in terms of the growing power of the king's prerogative coupled with growing rights (especially of property) attributed to and claimed by the landowners represented in Parliament (1949:81–82).

Hexter has commented,

> What was new about Tudor policy lay not in the social theory at its base, but in its magnification of the active regulatory role of the royal government as the means by which society might approximate its own ideal.... The ideal of Tudor statesmen was organic: society was made up of members performing different functions for the common good. The ideal was also hierarchical: though all parts of the commonwealth were indispensable, they were not equal, but differed in degree and

excellence as well as in kind. The role of policy was to maintain and support good order as good order had been understood for several centuries—social peace and harmony in a status-based society. (1963:106, 108)

This led to a centralized policy of regulation, privilege, and supervision which sought to contain economic innovations within the context of traditional values, but now these values were imposed at a national level (109ff.). The Tudors, and later the Stuarts, acted to meet their perceived responsibilities vis-à-vis these innovations, to subordinate private gain to a hierarchical society and to their own somewhat inconsistent image of the public welfare. Whether these policies were benevolent or based on the fear of disorder (see Walter and Wrightson 1976), they were defined and articulated within a frame of reference which implied the subordination of the many to the few, and especially by the Stuarts they were articulated through the use of prerogative powers.

Charles I nurtured his authority; he carefully altered the coronation oath, promising to maintain the liberties and laws of the kingdom so long as they did not conflict with his prerogative (Wedgwood 1966b:60). He proceeded, during the personal rule, to endeavor to extend his patrimonial control over the entire breadth of England, bringing previously autonomous functions of provincial authorities under his supervision. In order to accomplish this, in conflict with Parliament, he endeavored to routinize the revenue due to him as the highest feudal lord and to enlarge the revenue gleaned within the scope of his undoubted prerogative powers. This revenue was essential if the crown was to adequately fulfill its functions as understood by Charles and his advisors.

In one sense, as we will see in chapter 8, the problem was to locate the validating principle definitive of the general welfare. Within a patrimonial state, the prerogative was essential.

There is meaning and significance in each of the terms employed [to describe it]. This power was absolute and not ordinary because it was not tied to, nor limited by, ordinary rules of procedure or by forms of action. It was regal or royal because it belonged most peculiarly and most intimately to the king. It was in fact inseparable from him and intrinsic to his sovereignty because without it there could be no royal government and no kingly sovereignty at all. It handled matters of state because only the king possessed the art and wisdom to deal with those affairs so integrally a part of this "estate." It was public and not private because it existed in order to enable the king to provide for the general and public welfare of all.   (Judson 1949:114–15)

All of this came into question as independent bases of interest emerged and were consolidated within the society, when, on the foundations laid by a manufacturing economy, a structurally independent societal community emerged, within which interests were capable of articulation. To put the matter much too schematically, within the economy certain claims for social resources were put forward, and these were translated into interest demands made of the polity [A—I—G]. These demands were grounded in the structure of possibility defined by the emerging manufacturing structure, and were in contradiction to the "normal" actions of a patrimonial state.[34]

In assessing the disjunction between the patrimonial polity and the emergent manufacturing economy in seventeenth-century England there are numerous points one might use as references. In the chapters that follow I write in considerable detail of how the contradictions between the two generated the variables leading to internal disorder. Here I will endeavor briefly to present the context within which the following chapters might be understood.

The first point needing emphasis concerns the nature of administrative control within a patrimonial state. If a nascent capitalism seeks to establish an administration of *honoratiores*, subject to the influence of their peers and liable to negative economic sanctions when acting against the interests of their class, a patrimonial regime seeks to establish an administration dependent on itself. This conflict was played out in both church and state during the personal rule of Charles I, as the king and his archbishop sought a reformation of church and state governance involving central and monarchical as against collegial or congregational control. This policy led to charges of favoritism and bias in the selection of clerics and counselors and amounted to an attempt to incorporate previously excluded positions within the "patrimonial household."

Actions such as these were perceived as having, in conjunction with more specific policy decisions, economic consequences. Everitt emphasizes that for most people most of the time, government scarcely existed (1969a:9–10), but in a state where economic policy often implied the generalization to the nation of the particularisms previously embedded in municipalities, and where the policies ran counter to the profit of those in certain social positions, conflicts arose (Heckscher 1955; Clarkson 1971:177, 206). In a society where mercantile interests had begun to feel the need for positive governmental policies, merchants felt "harassed politically and burdened financially for no concrete return" (Corfield 1973:213). What was worse, Stuart policies were inconsistent and made it impossible for anything resembling prediction or calculation concerning future prospects for profit (Corfield 1973:210–11, 215, and 217; Hawkins 1973:52; Tawney 1947:173–74; Hill 1966:56). Some have emphasized that Charles's policies were defensive, that mercantilism in England, at least prior to 1640, was not a systematic ideology (see Coleman ed. 1969); what was important, however, was the color of the spectacles through which these crises were perceived, and therefore the nature of the response taken toward them. These governmental responses were not the consistent manifestation of a coherently articulated policy, but they tended to interfere with autonomous economic activity; insofar as the crown's policies were consistent they moved in the direction of greater monarchical control.

A paradox arose in this situation. There was on the one hand an economic system in growing need of governmental assistance, both in the creation of opportunities and in the removal of obstacles. On the other hand there was a government whose interference with the economy was pervasive, was too often subservient to fiscal needs, and often sought to restrict the development of the very economic forces that were forcing its intervention. The court interfered with private interests and slowly crossed over the boundary that divided the rights of property from those of the prerogative; while this might be "accepted" if those persons violated were poor and politically impotent, it was not accepted when they constituted the very notables who were expected to enforce the policy decrees.

In a society where the economy was privately controlled and where economic decisions were decentralized, the crown's policies were simply an irritant; they were of sufficient breadth and consequence to alienate significant sections of the community, but they were insufficiently radical to undermine the economic position of that community. In other words, they ran counter to private interests as delimited within a mercantile-manufacturing structure, but they did not expropriate those interests. Thus not only did the contradiction continue, the bases of resistance to governmental policy remained intact.

The government did not seek to establish its own economic organizations but rather tried to bring extant organizations under its central control; this was done via a policy of monopolies which resulted in economic organizations dependent on the Crown and loyal to the Crown,[35] but at the expense of provoking the much stronger manufacturing interests hindered by the policy (Zagorin 1969:134–35). Monopolies were one of the policies, usually motivated by fiscal requirements, which were perceived as interferences from many economic positions and which were seen (whatever the Crown's motivation) as retarding economic progress. What was worse, these policies failed; they neither prevented internal disorder nor succeeded in routinizing the government's supply of money.

Charles interfered with manufacture in innumerable other ways; during depressions, for example, he sought to keep manufacturing capital operative, fearing the consequences of mass unemployment (Supple 1959:64, 109, 117, 234, 237; Hawkins 1973:54). At various times the Crown meddled with the currency or sought to seize bullion from the treasury. These or any one of a number of other heavy-handed maneuvers created widespread uncertainty and economic dislocation (cf. Supple 1959:125ff.).

Many of these policies were extended and their consequences exacerbated during the period of the personal rule. At this point Crown policy was not to restrain industry and agriculture so much as to control it, or to benefit from its violations of traditional standards. The policy against enclosure did not so much seek to retard the process as to make money from it. But like so many of Charles's policies, this one produced more aggravation and opposition than money (see, e.g., Clarendon 1888, 1:131). In an economy where governmental regulation was all-pervasive (Clarkson 1971:163ff.), where the government's right to regulate was not questioned (193), regulations were a means of reward and of social and economic policy, a way of controlling the economy, reaping fiscal benefit, and supporting government servants. These diverse aims proved incompatible (Ashton 1970:97–98).

Hawkins has pointed out that over a period of two or three generations the politically influential developed the outlines of a social policy that placed broad responsibilities on the shoulders of the central government. Within the context of a developing manufacturing economy in both agriculture and industry, this led to growing but conflicting policy demands concerning both domestic and international policy. These demands required considerable governmental intervention, but there was no commensurate willingness to support the consequent governmental regulation and control. There was no comparable growth of governmental administrative or financial capacity, and attempts to develop an efficient administration within the patrimonial governmental structure resulted in the growth and development of antagonisms toward the government. Under these circumstances a gap grew between the demands of society on the government and the capacity of the government to meet those demands.

In addition, this was "an age in which the formal ability to articulate policy had developed well beyond the administrative capacity to enforce it: an England all of whose economic regulations were fully in force would have been unrecognizable as well as unthinkable" (Supple 1959:252; for a comparison between England and France, see Nef 1957). But these regulations were available, and if the Crown had consolidated its administrative powers, they might well have been implemented. In any case, their existence coupled with attempts at their implementation created uncertainty where manufacturing capitalists wanted greater self-control. The Stuarts sought to bring industry and agriculture within their control, while the political nation sought to bring the Crown under its control (Corfield 1973:215). To allow the king to make economic decisions required that the nation trust the king, and although it is no doubt correct that if his policies had been to their liking he would have received their support, this was impossible without his ceasing to be their king, given how both the Tudors and Stuarts understood the obligations of their office and how the structure of the polity imposed these obligations upon them (cf. Judson 1949:146; Gardiner 1884, 6:215).

It is not possible, in my opinion, to demonstrate that the patrimonial monarchy was incapable of transforming itself to adapt to the new situation constituted by the predominance of manufacture. What one can argue and what I have tried to argue is that this adaptation would have involved a self-transformation of both the ruler and the structure of his rule. This argument recognizes that violence (as violation) is necessary in a revolution only if the old regime does not roll over and play (and stay) dead. For the reasons enunciated, the Stuarts were not likely to voluntarily transform the nature of the political system (see chaps. 5–7, below).

Consequences

In what has been said so far the impression has perhaps been left that the development of manufacture was evenly distributed throughout the country. This is not correct, and a very cursory examination of the nature of its geographical distribution will enable us to tie the elements of this chapter together.

In arguing that capital accumulation based on iterative surplus value is dependent on subjective controls, I do not mean to imply that every capitalist who so accumulated was an ascetic Protestant. On the contrary, what I wish to argue is that when within a given market situation a sufficient number of these capitalists are so motivated, the nature of the situation will be transformed. In its early stages there will be positions that are structurally autonomous from the manufacturing structure, a structure fundamentally unconstrained by the pressures of competition; nonetheless, rationalizing manufacturers will progressively dominate the activities of a higher percentage of productive positions within each relevant market situation (cf. Woolf 1970:526).[36]

It is very difficult to provide direct evidence supporting this contention. What it is possible to do is to broadly outline the distribution of manufacture and Puritanism. It is not coincidental, in my opinion, that the two overlap. It would be erroneous to contend that nascent manufacture was irrelevant to the consequent adherence to ascetic Protestant beliefs. Nonetheless, the two were independent, even if interdependent (see Parsons 1949:25 n. 2). I want to argue that where they were conjoined, nascent manufacture and Puritanism resulted in the predominance of manufacture. It is also no coincidence that these areas were the primary supports of Parliament during the Revolution.

Homans has noted that "a certain kind of society, a society of small villages and towns, half-industrial, half-agricultural, a society of cottage manufacture organized on a putting-out system, a society of clothiers and cloth workers, capitalists and craftsmen... [was] more liable to infection with a new religious movement [Puritanism] than the more purely agricultural society which remained in many parts of England" (1940:528). This relationship, although hard to document in any great detail, is noted by many others. Hill treats Puritanism as the religion of the industrious sort, and included within this group are those who had their feet on the ladder of prosperity and were endeavoring to improve their position within a commercial economy; they included yeomen, artisans, small and middling merchants (1969c: chap. 4, 227, 240), but in a society characterized by a progressive division between those who rose and fell within the social structure. He speaks of the "division among the gentry which takes place in the century before 1640, as a result of economic changes in the countryside. A growing section of the gentry began to engage in the clothing industry or in production for the market on their own estates, or developed trading connections in the City. By and large, over the country as a whole, religious radicalism was strongest in the economically advanced areas; and in these areas we find an increasing number of landowners supporting the new ideas, often from conviction, sometimes no doubt from mere coincidence of interests" (1971 : 55; cf. Everitt 1969a : 60; Hill 1963, 1972b; Stone 1972a : 99; 1966 : 43–44, Thirsk 1985a : 558; Zagorin 1969 : 185). These developed areas—very simply, in the south and east as against the less developed north and, in part, west—were the very areas that supported the REVOG within the English Revolution (Ashton 1978 : 79; Clarkson 1971 : 215–16; Hill 1980a : 132; Morrill 1979 : 83–84; Supple 1959 : 4–5; and chap. 6, below).

If we place the discussion contained in this chapter within the context of the models developed in chapters 2 and 3, it will be possible to see how a manufacturing structure gave rise to the variables leading to a REVOG, a revolution restructuring the collectivity component of the English polity. In the final section of this chapter I write of two of those variables, strain at the level of goals and deflation of power.

The Linkages between the Structural and Functional Theories

In order to grapple adequately with these questions we must focus our attention on three places: on both the economy and the societal community where strain at the level of goals was manifest, and on the polity in interaction with the other three societal subsystems to determine the bases for the deflation of power. It will help if I reformulate the analysis contained in this chapter in terms of the framework outlined in chapter 2. It will then be easier to see the linkages between the two theories.

Implicit in the analysis proposed in this chapter has been a functionally defined categorization of the components of any economic system. The argument has been that a particular organization of these components characterizes a manufacturing economy, in contradistinction to, for example, a feudal or machine capitalist economy. The terms in this discussion may be elliptically categorized as follows:[37]

A_{A_a}: the object of labor
A_{A_g}: the means of labor
A_{A_l} : labor capacity (in capitalism, labor power)
A_A : the means of production
A_G : the nonlaborer[38]
A_L : the distribution system

The missing two locations refer to the organizational mechanisms of the labor process (A_{A_i}) and the valorization process (A_I).[39] These categorizations are presented in figure 26.

As we have seen, within a manufacturing system there is a formal but not a real subsumption of labor under capital. In other words, the nonlaborer, the personification of capital, controls the valorization process but not the labor process. Surplus value is iterative, the capitalist having relatively little control over variations in its rate. The capitalist has, in other words, relatively little control over the level of productivity within the economy, and the capacity of the economy to expand is dependent on environmental circumstances.

We have seen that the instrumental activism mandated by ascetic Protestantism generated a dynamic toward expansion via a replication of units. But this expansion of production was subject to and dependent on political controls. The expansion of production was dependent on opportunities offered and the removal of constraints imposed by the political system. These constraints included governmental regulations and limited access to capital funds. Thus economic activity was in part controlled by governmental policies within the polity's fiscal subsector, including "banking mechanisms," and was dependent on the capacity of the government to open new markets and other opportunities outside the territory of England (G—[factor]$\rightarrow A$, and derivatively, G—[product]$\rightarrow A$).

In this situation, where there were tendencies leading to the expansion of economic production in a manufacturing system controlled by instrumentally activist values, political constraints on that growth involved strain at the level of goals (across the G—[factor] → A interchange). As we have seen in this chapter, these constraints existed and were recognized (see also chap. 6).

There was a possible route for coping with this strain: one basis on which interest demands from the societal community might be grounded is their justification in economic circumstances (A—[factor] → I and A—[product] → I, and consequently, I—[factor] → G). When these demands are regularized, because of their genesis within a determinate economic structure, a failure of governmental response is a socially structured strain at the level of goals (across the G—[factor] → I interchange). Within the context of Stuart patrimonialism such was the case, as governmental response was at best arbitrary and irregular. When during the period of the personal rule all mechanisms for exerting fiduciary control over governmental policy seemed to be severed, and when those policies seemed counter to interests grounded within a manufacturing economy, goal strain was exacerbated.

Thus in this system the arbitrary nature of governmental policies

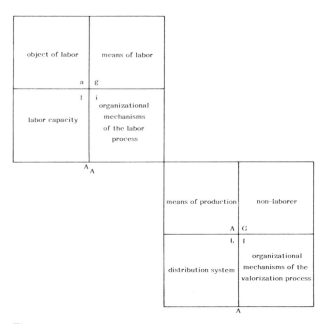

Figure 26.

conflicted with the systematic necessities generated within a manufacturing economic system controlled by rationalizing values. A
manufacturing economy is especially subject to such dislocations as
the labor process (A_A in fig. 26) is not controlled by capital. Where
the dynamic of economic growth is defined by the interpenetration
of the formal subsumption (but not the real subsumption) of labor
under capital and a system of rationalizing values, the dynamic of
the system is especially subject to political pressures (both positive
and negative). In mid-seventeenth-century England the input across
the G—[factor] → A boundary was in conflict with the imperatives
of the predominant economic structure, and thus in those areas
where this manufacturing structure was widespread, goal strain
was also widespread.

If we move on and present a schematic portrait of the political
system extant in early seventeenth-century England, we will see that
the executive controlled what we might label the "legitimation
process," but that he was debarred from control over the "authorization process." While he might be said to have possessed real
substantive control over the country's decisions he was barred
from a parallel formal control.

The terms in this discussion may be elliptically categorized (see
n. 36) as follows:

G_A : the administration
G_G : the executive
G_{G_a} : fiscal-"banking" process
G_{G_g} : executive-implementation process
G_{G_i} : policy decisions
G_I : fiduciary control

The missing two locations refer to the organizational mechanisms
of the legitimation process (G_{G_l}) and the authorization process
(G_L). These categorizations are presented in figure 27.

Within the patrimonial polity of the personal rule Charles controlled the mechanisms in the executive structure of the polity (G_G).
He was able to regulate the structure of opportunities available
within the economy in terms of fiscal policies, governmental regulations, foreign and trade policies, and so on (across the G—
[factor] → A interchange). In addition he was able to demand, and
to have these demands "legitimized" by the state-dominated religious organization, surplus value that was produced within the

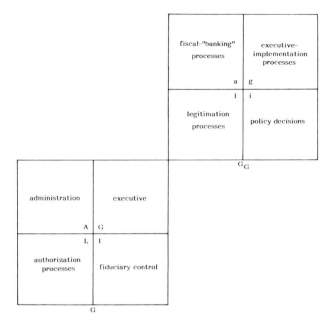

Figure 27.

economy (across the A—[factor] → G interchange). His attacks fell where the economy was most vulnerable (at A_A).

These impositions, necessitated in large measure as a response to the consequences of the structural changes within the economy, but exacerbated by the extravagance and incompetence of the Stuarts and at times aggravated by the needs of making war, were one factor in the genesis of power deflation. As we saw in chapter 2, an autonomous increase in the economic surplus controlled by the government will result in a decrease in political output.[40] This tendency was exacerbated by two others: the legitimation that the polity was able to assume came from a state-controlled church that was tainted in the eyes of many citizens, the group we loosely label Puritans. It was this same group that we found to be dispersed within England's predominant manufacturing structure. These persons called into question the efficacy of the official church's sanction for governmental actions. For them the "legitimacy" of the Church's legitimation of Charles's political policies was in doubt. Thus the capacity of the government to expand the scope of power within the system was, to say the least, limited.[41]

Direct demands came to be made on the economic resources and services of the nation. During the personal rule, "the thorough," administrative reforms within the counties demanded an exertion of time and effort from the political nation. At the outbreak of the Scottish Revolution, these demands were increased by the need to form an army. While it is true that the Crown, not controlling the "authorization structure" within the state, was not always capable of enforcing these impositions, they intensified the growing deflation of power.[42] This was especially the case within the manufacturing sectors of the economy. Here the goal strain across the G—[factor] → I interchange, coupled with the lowered "legitimacy" accorded to the Church's legitimation of Charles's actions (this owing to Puritan convictions), militated against any parallel increase in either political support (across the I—[factor] → G interchange) or authorization of powers of office (across the L—[product] → G interchange). The consequence was that actions undertaken by the government, even if in supposed response to the demands of manufacturing interests, exacerbated the deflation of power and generated a calculating attitude toward political processes among those same people the manufacturing sectors of the economy who were in a situation of goal strain. In chapter 6 we will see how the activation of these two variables (strain at the level of goals and a deflation of power) when coupled with others led to the most important phase of the English Revolution, REVOG.

5. The Coming of the English Revolution

> The alignment of forces of 1640 was quite different
> from that of 1642, by which time a large block of for-
> mer Parliamentarians had moved over to reluctant
> Royalism; it was different again in 1648, when the con-
> servative element among the Parliamentarians, mis-
> leadingly known as Presbyterians, swung back to the
> side of the King.... One of the major causes of the mud-
> dled thinking about the causes of the English Revolution
> has arisen from the failure to establish precisely which
> stage of the Revolution is being discussed. Since each
> stage was triggered off by different immediate issues,
> since each was made possible by different longterm
> movements of society and ideology, and since each was
> directed by a different section of society, these distinc-
> tions are vitally important. It is a measure of the insular-
> ity of English historians that they have failed to profit
> from the lessons to be drawn from studies on the French
> Revolution, where the need for strict periodization
> when advancing theories of social causation has been
> obvious for over a century.
>
> (Stone 1965*b*: xviii, reprinted in 1972*a*: 34)[1]

Chapters 5, 6, and 7 have been written to serve two functions. They
may be read in context as empirical adjuncts to chapter 3, as one
basis in terms of which chapter 3 may be evaluated or they may be
read as an introduction to the book as a whole, providing an entrée
into the more technical theoretical discussions, making them more
intelligible in light of a case study. I have endeavored to make these
chapters (5–7) as self-contained as possible, enabling the historian
whose primary interest is seventeenth-century England to read this
relatively nontechnical discussion in order to determine whether the
experience of dealing with theoretically processed history is sufficiently rewarding to master the formal theory within which the
processing has occurred.

   In writing chapters 5 through 7 I have tried to minimize the use
of technical terms; in those instances where the circumlocution
necessary to avoid these terms was too offensive or too time-

consuming, I have had recourse to the vocabulary introduced in the earlier chapters. In either case, the entire logic of my argument derives from the previous chapters. I hope that this is clear even in those descriptions where a translation has been made into more substantive vocabularies. The utility of this book is found in the explanations it provides, and while the technical terms of the explanation may be translated for each case studied, it is the technical theory that allows for the translation in each case.

Hegel has written,

> At first ... logic must indeed be learnt as something which one understands and sees into quite well but in which, at the beginning, one feels the lack of scope and depth and a wider significance. It is only after profounder acquaintance with the other sciences that logic ceases to be for subjective spirit a merely abstract universal and reveals itself as the universal which embraces within itself the wealth of the particular—just as the same proverb, in the mouth of a youth who understands it quite well, does not possess the wide range of meaning which it has in the mind of a man with the experience of a lifetime behind him, for whom the meaning is expressed in all its power. Thus the value of logic is only appreciated when it is preceded by experience of the sciences; it then displays itself to mind as the universal truth, not as a *particular* knowledge *alongside* other matters and realities, but as the essential being of all these latter.   (1969:58)

If the study of "logic" becomes concrete only with a study of the special sciences, so much more must a study of the special sciences gain in power in a study of their objects (cf. Hegel 1969:57). Chapters 5 through 7 begin this process of enrichment. But insofar as science must constantly refer back to its constituted object, these chapters are a tentative conclusion. Their truth lies in the theory they manifest; the theory's movement to truth lies in the events it portrays, and then in the events the theory helps to create (see the preface, above).

A historian expert in seventeenth-century English history will find in chapters 5 through 7 no description of phenomena that are unfamiliar to her. I have drawn on the standard histories of the period. But if facts are "empirically verifiable statement[s] about phenomena in terms of a conceptual scheme" (Parsons 1949:41, quoting L. J. Henderson), she will find many new facts. These are based on, embedded in, the processing of these standard histories in terms of the theoretical chapters of this book, which the reader has already encountered (chaps. 1, 2, and 3). It is my hope that after reading chapters 5, 6, and 7 the reader's conception of the "facts" of seventeenth-century English history will have altered, and that this alteration will reveal that the theory that has preceded this discussion "is a universal which embraces within itself the wealth of the particular."

Lawrence Stone wrote the words that head this chapter in 1965, in an introduction to a widely used collection of articles and documents, *Social Change and Revolution in England 1540–1640*. Prior to reading Stone but inspired by a knowledge of Lefebvre's masterful *The Coming of the French Revolution*, I began exploring the stage sequential development of the English Revolution from 1640 to 1649. This chapter and the two that follow endeavor to explain the genesis of the English revolutions, recognizing that the generating conditions differ both substantively and theoretically between stages and recognizing that many of the theoretically defined variables are substantively overdetermined (see chap. 3).

In chapter 4 I characterized prerevolutionary seventeenth-century English society as a transitional social formation. A manufacturing mode of production was shown to be economically predominant, and this economic organization was seen to be, at least in essential areas of its functioning, legitimized by that system of value commitments Weber labeled "the Protestant Ethic," and thus animated by "the spirit of capitalism" in a drive toward capital accumulation. It was further shown that the political structure that governed this economic formation was patrimonial in nature. While political actors sought legitimation for their actions in traditional values, they constantly endeavored to extend their powers beyond their traditional scope. This entailed the imposition of nonrational controls on economic activities, controls that were arbitrary in terms of the extant economic structure as legitimized in terms of Puritan rationality. In addition it was shown how the tendential development of this system gave rise to certain variables that led to what I have earlier in this book, in chapter 3, characterized as a rebellion (REVOG), an attempt to redefine the collectivity structure of the polity.

Chapters 5 through 7 show that this rebellion was one of four attempted structural transformations within the polity during the period 1640–49, and they explicate the generating conditions of each (attempted) transformation. In an appendix to chapter 7 I will argue that the Restoration of 1660 returned the political system to the point reached after the first completed revolution (REVOF), and that this REVOF did not adequately deal with the strains inherent in the structural development of seventeenth-century English society, thus setting the stage for the Revolution of 1688 (another REVOG).

My arguments in chapters 5 through 7 are limited in scope and coverage. I concentrate almost entirely on the English political system and the "disorderly movements" that endeavored to transform that system during the seventeenth century. Within this context it will be necessary to emphasize certain political movements, referred to as "riots" in chapter 3, which paralleled the major revolutions and in certain instances were integral components of the revolutions, making the latter possible. This section, emphasizing mass participation in the revolutions, is briefer than I originally intended. The appearance of Manning's *The English People and the English Revolution* has allowed me to shorten the substantive aspects of this discussion.

The appendix to chapter 7 discusses, all too briefly, the religious movements that occurred in seventeenth-century England. My emphasis here is almost entirely on their interrelationships with and effects on the previously discussed political transformations. This appendix is much briefer than an adequate treatment of these movements would be, but is included in order to make more intelligible the comments on religion that continually intrude in the main body of the text.

In 1628 Parliament passed the Petition of Right demanding redress for a series of grievances. The Petition was based on the assumption that only a reconfirmation of traditional "right" or "privileges" was desired.[2] Commons sought to prevent the king from issuing taxes without parliamentary consent, to prevent arbitrary arrest, the billeting of soldiers without consent, and also the revocation of commissions for the implementation of martial law (Gardiner 1906:69; cf. Ball 1964; Berkowitz 1975; Flemion 1973; Foster 1974*a*, 1974*b*; Guy 1982).

There is no need to repeat the analysis just presented in chapter 4, where the necessity of an increase in the scope of governmental activities in a "manufacturing" society was analyzed. The Petition of Right may be taken as a symbol of the conflict over the nature of this expansion which came to fruition in mid-seventeenth-century

English society. It was not a question of the monarchy making demands on the economy which the latter subsystem was incapable of fulfilling in the aggregate; rather it was a question of the nature of those demands and of their consequences for the functioning of the economy. This contradiction, and thus the resistance of the Commons to the monarchy's policies, resulted in a parliamentary opposition that articulated its grievances in a series of Parliaments from the latter part of the reign of Queen Elizabeth (Gardiner 1883–84; Judson 1949; Moir 1958; Mosse 1968; Neale 1966; Notestein 1966, 1971; Roberts 1966; Ruigh 1971; Russell 1971, 1976, 1979*a*, 1979*b*; Sharpe 1978; White 1979*b*; Zaller 1971).

In this conflict a parliamentary opposition developed which focused not simply on a series of issues, but came to form a loosely organized Country faction. Centering in the House of Commons, although often supported by and sometimes led by a significant faction of the Lords, it based its actions upon its own interpretation of the law, but at the same time it began to view itself as the representative of the nation's public interest. (See, e.g., Judson 1949: 279ff.; Gunn 1969.) It was this opposition, about which I will have much more to say later, which passed the Petition of Right, and which precipitated Charles's reaction, the endeavor to rule the country without Parliament, the eleven years of "personal rule."[3]

The King's "REVOF"

I have spoken of revolutionary actions as those that violate the institutionalized authority code within the polity and attempt to redefine at least one component of the political structure (role definitions, collectivity organization, norms, or values). One can argue whether the king's actions during the decade of his personal rule constituted a revolution in these terms; they certainly appeared as such to the parliamentary opposition, or to put it more accurately, these actions were an integral aspect of the genesis of the Country (Judson 1949: 349ff.), the parliamentary opposition that would undertake the first stage of the English Revolution.

In content, insofar as they were revolutionary (see, e.g., Elliot 1973: 249), the king's actions constituted, like the reaction they were to provoke, a facilitory rebellion (REVOF), a redefinition of political roles within extant collectivity structures. What Charles endeavored to accomplish was a "misuse" of existing organizations to appropriate facilities as political resources. The ambiguous legality of his actions is crucial.

"The great difference between the two absolutisms [Tudor and Charles's] ... was that the first worked because it had the support of the people, while the second failed because it was opposed by the people" (Hulme 1960: 115; cf. Gardiner 1884, 6: 314–15; Russell 1979*b*: 51; Russell 1982, 1984). As Charles's policies differed from the perceived interests of the vast majority of the political nation, conflicts arose between his patrimonial regime and the societal community. At first both sides sought to routinize these conflicts in the context of established institutional frameworks.

I will discuss at some length the specific policies Charles sought to implement when I look at the generating conditions for the first stage of the revolution; here it is important to notice the institutional terrain upon which the battle was fought. Charles sought to expand the scope of his prerogative powers, and further, sought legal justification for this expansion, a justification that involved their permanent routinization in the constitution, and which would have had as its consequence his capacity to rule, at least in circumstances of peace, without Parliament.

While the Tudors had maintained a clear separation between government, the sphere of their absolute power, and law, the Stuarts tried to have their absolute powers written into law. This justification was necessitated by the growing strength of the forces they sought to combat; the alliance between the Commons and most common lawyers was a strong foe continually gaining in strength. To combat them the Crown and its allies made use of an ideology legitimizing the Stuart interpretation of the monarch's prerogative powers, and sought to incorporate this ideology into the law.

This was a period when varying notions of the divine right of kings had wide acceptance. In its extreme form these commitments implied not only that monarchy was divinely ordained and that the incumbent king was divinely chosen but that "law cannot exist independently of some lawgiver, and that the ultimate legislative authority in any state is necessarily above all positive law" (Figgis 1965: 145–46). The monarch was seen as this lawgiver, and he was seen as accountable only to God for the nature and consequences of his rule. This point of view was propagated by the Laudian wing of the Church of England after they gained organizational control within the church owing to Charles's preferments.

What was more important than the extreme form in which Charles's prerogative was sometimes supported (see Weston and Greenberg 1981 : chap. 2) was his willingness to test these powers in the courts. As Gardiner puts it, "Ostensibly, at least, Charles's government was a legal one. He was ready at any time to submit his pretensions to the judges, though he had taken good care that no judge likely to dispute his will should have a seat on the Bench" (1884, 8:182). Although in the later years of his personal rule Charles did meet opposition from the bench, the Crown won every major legal decision in the early seventeenth century (see, e.g., Jones 1971).

The doctrine implicit in certain of these decisions "was nothing less than the full-blown theory of absolutism" (Gardiner 1884, 8:182). The nature of these justifications varied even within the legal system. Justice Berkeley said "that there was a rule of law and a rule of government, and that many things which might not be done by the rule of law might be done by the rule of government" (quoted in Gardiner 1884, 8:103). This implied that Charles's actions were not bound by law; Berkeley, an extreme monarchist, maintained "that since king and law were identical, all the king's actions were legal" (Judson 1949:137, and more generally, all of chap. 4. Both of the quoted statements concerned ship money, but in different contexts. Judson's comment refers to Berkeley's final decision, which is reprinted [in part] in Gardiner 1906:115–24; Gardiner discusses the judgement in 1884, 8:277ff.).

The decision declaring ship money legal (I will explicate the term *ship money* later in this chap.) implied the possibility of a regular tax levied solely on the authority of the king without the sanction of Parliament. As Chief Justice Finch had written, "Therefore Acts of Parliament to take away his royal power in the defence of his kingdom are void.... They are void Acts of Parliament to bind the King not to command the subjects' persons and goods, and I say their money too" (as reprinted in Kenyon 1966:116; the excision in the text is Kenyon's). If Charles could regularly take his subjects' money without their consent in Parliament, the personal rule, a Stuart patrimonialism, would be secure (see Gardiner 1884, 8:270ff.; Hill 1966:55).

The consequence of the ship money and other decisions was that in certain crucial areas, areas related specifically to property, the only safeguard against the arbitrary extension of the king's powers was his goodwill.

> By extending the emergency and discretionary power of the king and by
> enlarging his trust, they [the royalists] so exalted the absolute power
> that little room was left for the subjects' rights and property, and they so
> tipped the scales in favor of the prerogative that the old balanced con-
> stitution no longer prevailed.   (Judson 1949:153; see also Wedg-
> wood 1966b:60–61)

It is clear then, even from this cursory survey, that the king endeavored to redefine the powers of the Crown vis-à-vis the Parliament;
at least this was how his opponents saw his actions (Ashton
1978:17).

If we change our perspective somewhat the next task is to examine the conditions, many of them constituted by the king's own
actions, which generated the first stage of the English Revolution.
In fact, the very nature of Charles's actions and the relative success
he had in formally justifying, if not in implementing, his programs,
generated an opposition to his rule which was both broad and
strong (see Judson 1949:249ff.; Koenigsberger 1974:102–3).
Wilson has summarized the consequences of the courts' decisions:

> It was now clear that there was, in practice as well as in theory, a short
> answer to the question—"when is a tax not a tax?" It was: "when it is
> an act of policy, deemed to be in the national interest." And to the
> question, "who determines when such an act is necessary?" the answer
> was shorter still. "The King." Where mutual confidence was already
> weak, such a demand for a blank cheque could only destroy it utterly.
> (1965:100)

These consequences were of primary importance in the articulation
of the Court versus the Country split that defines the participants in
the first of the English revolutions in the seventeenth century. In
what did this revolution consist?

REVOF

After the passage of the Petition of Right, Parliament drew up a
remonstrance against the illegal levy of tunnage and poundage,
forms of customs taxes. This led to the prerogation of Parliament.
In January of 1629 Parliament was reconvened, only to endeavor,
once again, to come to the aid of those merchants who had failed to
pay tunnage and poundage and whose goods had been seized in

consequence. This led to the dissolution of the Parliament; but while the speaker was forcibly held in his chair, the Commons proceeded to pass resolutions sponsored by Sir John Eliot. These declared that anyone who sought to introduce innovations in religion, who urged the levy of tunnage and poundage, or whoever voluntarily paid tunnage and poundage levied without parliamentary approval, was an enemy of the kingdom. The resolutions precipitated the arrest of nine members of the Commons, including Eliot. The dissolution of Parliament began the eleven years of personal rule.

By the meeting of the Long Parliament things had changed. "Before the close of the year [1641] it had become clear that the demands and behaviour of this Parliament were different from those of its predecessors. They had attacked the King's policy; this Parliament was attacking the King's position" (Wedgwood 1966b: 346). The first session of the Long Parliament met from 3 November 1640 until 8 September 1641, and during this period effected the first stage of the revolution.

When the Irish Revolution broke out in October 1641, the rebels' "first manifesto, issued immediately after the start of the revolt, declared that the 'Puritan faction' and the English Commons had invaded the King's prerogative, usurped his authority, and left him naught 'but the bare name of a King.'"[4] What happened in these few short months was not simply an alteration of programs but a redefinition of roles within the political system. Gardiner tells us that Sandys in 1614 was the first to realize "that, in order to preserve the rights of the subject intact, it would be necessary to make some change in the relations between the authority of the Crown and the representatives of the people" (1883, 2: 240). It was this alteration, set in motion twenty-five years later, which defined the Country's "faciliatory rebellion," REVOF.

A REVOF in seventeenth-century England involved a restructuring of role expectations within the context of existing collectivity structures in the polity, and most especially, at Westminster, Parliament's claiming unjustifiable powers of office. These revolutionary actions were in violation of the normative code of the institutionalized authority structure; the violation of this code led to retaliatory actions on the part of the previous claimant to such authority, the monarch.

During the first session of the Long Parliament,

a revolution in government had already taken place. Parliament had ceased to be a body that from time to time met at the king's behest, brought him the petitions and the subsidies of those of his people it represented, and gave—or occasionally withheld—its assent to the legislation devised by his ministers. It had become the effective ruler of the country.   (Pennington 1970:24; see also Wedgwood 1966*b*:331–32, 392)

Pennington, exaggerating somewhat, tells us that the one crucial piece of legislation passed in this session was the bill prohibiting the dissolution of Parliament without its own consent (Pennington 1970:28–29; this bill applied only to the Long Parliament). This act and the Triennial Act, mandating the automatic calling of Parliament every three years, seemed to insure that parliament would become a permanent aspect of the political system (Hexter 1978:46). The first step was to insure the existence of Parliament; the second was to delineate its powers regarding the monarch.

It is important to realize that the Country party, which made the facilitory rebellion, were monarchists.

Right up to the moment when the civil war broke out, the leaders of the parliamentary opposition and Puritan preachers joined with royalist supporters and Anglican clergy in proclaiming the divine origin and sanction of kingly authority and the superiority of the monarchical form of government to all other forms.   (Judson 1949:19)

But,

The parliamentary opposition ... was not content to limit the king's prerogatives when they encroached upon the rights of the subject. They wished also to control the policies of the king in realms belonging to him and generally accepted by law and practice as within his jurisdiction. This desire could only be realized by political, not legal means— by the effective control of parliament over government.   (Judson 1949:225)

It was this control that the Parliament succeeded in obtaining in the first session of the Long Parliament; it was a control that left the monarchical government altered but intact.

The work of parliament's first ten months meant a historic reversal of the relation between monarchy and subject. It took from the crown almost all the powers which enabled the Tudor rulers to exercise their unrivalled mastery. Although the king would continue to govern, his administration would be subject to new and unprecedented restrictions. (Zagorin 1969:244)

In these few months the financial and administrative base of the monarchy was removed; Parliament impeached many of Charles's most loyal servants, and in removing Strafford by attainder took a major if inconclusive step toward insuring some form of ministerial responsibility. Among the other bills passed were an act placing tunnage and poundage under the permanent control of Parliament and an act declaring ship money illegal; additional acts struck at other arbitrary exactions of funds instituted or increased during the previous fifteen years, including exactions under the forest laws, purveyance, and the Crown's ability to collect knighthood fines, among others. In addition, monopolies were proscribed (Ashton 1978:135ff.). All of these acts struck at the capacity of the Crown to assure the king's financial independence.

Parliament also attacked the Crown's control over its own bureaucracy. The prerogative courts were abolished, which Stone sees as the main achievement of the Long Parliament's first year (1972a:104). For Hill, "The destruction of the royal bureaucracy in 1640–1 can be regarded as the most decisive single event in the whole of British History" (Hill 1969b:98, 135).

In sum, Parliament had secured the political nation's property rights, secured her persons from arrest without trial, and secured control over what they perceived as the arbitrary administration of the king. They began the task of destroying a patrimonial political structure in order to ensure their own control over policy and its implementation. When Charles left England for Scotland (in August 1641), he in effect left Parliament and her committees in control of the government of the nation (Snow 1970:273ff.; Gardiner 1884, 10:3ff.). A revolutionary redefinition of powers had been effected, that is clear. We must now ask by whom, and under what conditions did this revolution occur?

Strain at the Level of Facilities (SF)

"The story of the failure of personal monarchy in England—a story which also has its continental parallels—is essentially one of how the regime succeeded in alienating one section of the community after another until it was left without any visible means of support" (Elliot 1973:255). The answer to the question, who made the facilitory rebellion? "Already by the end of 1641, when the Royalist and Parliamentarian parties emerged, a considerable constitutional revolution had taken place, pushed through against the wishes of the King, by the virtually unanimous forces of the political nation represented in Parliament" (Corfield 1973:203). Until the adjournment of the first session of the Long Parliament Charles stood almost alone against the political nation. "On the political questions before the House, on the impeachment of Strafford and Finch, on the condemnation of ship-money, and on the necessity of defensive measures against the Catholics, the House was practically unanimous" (Gardiner 1884, 9:247, see also 264–65). The House was also unanimous in voting to impeach Laud (296). Unanimity also reigned regarding the necessity of limiting royal forests, for abolishing knighthood fees, and for the abolition of the Courts of the Star Chamber and the High Commission (383). The House passed, "without the faintest opposition," ordinances to secure Hull and the munitions gathered there and to secure the Tower (Gardiner 1884, 10:5).

Gardiner has written:

> The day on which the adjournment [of the Long Parliament's first session] was voted was indeed memorable in English history. It was the last time when the two parties into which the House of Commons was divided loyally co-operated with one another. Whatever had been done so far by the Long Parliament stood the test of time. The overthrow of the special courts, by which the prerogative had been defended under the Tudors and the first two Stuarts, together with the abandonment by the King of all claim to raise taxes without the consent of Parliament, was accepted as the starting-point of the restored monarchical constitution in 1660.   (1884, 10:10–11)

This division, which left the king standing nearly naked until the end of 1641, has come to be referred to as "The Court and the Country."

In chapter 3 I argued that the component of the political system subject to attack was determined by the location of strain within the societal system. I also contended that it was possible to differentiate between those groups participating in the movement and those abstaining from participation depending upon the locale of a particular type of strain within the system. Strain involves a lack of coordination between the components of social action—roles, collectivities, norms, and values—which impinges on some group and affects its social performances. Strains tend to focus at one of the components.

Strain at the level of facilities involves a disjunction among the components of social structure which precludes the production and/or allocation of the facilities perceived as necessary for adequate role performance. Strain at the level of facilities is, I have argued, a necessary condition for the genesis of a facilitory rebellion. It should therefore be possible to differentiate between Court and Country by identifying the foci of strain at the level of facilities within prerevolutionary English society.

It is important to recognize that there was more than one variety of facilitory strain operating in 1640, and this in two respects. First, the substantive manifestations of SF impinging on one group were often different from those operating on other groups. Second, more than one type of strain at the level of facilities was often present for a group. For the moment, while recognizing the existence of other manifestations of SF, I will focus on the facilitory strain generated by the crown's fiscal policies. This concentration enables us to confine our immediate attention to the political nation, those men of property able to participate in the election of representatives to the Commons. By the 1640s this was not an insignificant number of men, even if they were only a small percentage of the total population. Hirst has estimated that those holding the franchise after the Long Parliament's early franchise decisions may have constituted between 27 and 40 percent of the adult male population (1975: 105; cf. Plumb 1969a).

"The government was brought down by a revolt of the taxpayers. In 1639, encouraged by the presence of the Scottish army, they went on strike; and the government was shown to be unable to exist without their goodwill" (Hill 1966: 107). In chapter 4 I have shown that the disjunction between the needs of the English monarchy and the resources that the monarchy controlled without the aid of Parliament was tendentially widening. In this chapter we have begun to explore the "REVOF" instituted by Charles in an attempt to institutionalize his personal rule. A consequence of this attempt was a structured facilitory strain throughout most of the political nation; when the government's financial position became acute owing to the Scottish invasion, and when this strain was in consequence exacerbated, the Country's revolution was the result.[5]

Charles had instituted a series of measures aimed at generating sufficient income to stave off the necessity of calling a Parliament. The logic of the situation was, however, that owing to his lack of political support at the onset of this period, these exactions were viewed as arbitrary and illegal by almost everyone subject to them. With the exception of those few who were their direct beneficiaries, they had the consequence of accelerating the decline in political support for him.

Clarendon, no radical, and at the time he wrote these words a firm supporter of the monarchy (see Wormald 1951), wrote as follows:

> For the better support of these extraordinary ways [referring most especially to ship money], and to protect the agents and instruments who must be employed in them, and to discountenance and suppress all bold inquirers and opposers, the Council-table and Star-chamber enlarge their jurisdictions to a vast extent, "holding" (as Thucydides said of the Athenians) "for honourable that which pleased, and for just that which profited" ... so that any disrespect to acts of state or to the persons of statesmen was in no time more penal, and those foundations of right by which men valued their security, to the apprehension and understanding of wise men, never more in danger to be destroyed.

He goes on to say that men often gave voluntarily to the king,

> and all assuring themselves that when they should be weary, or unwilling to continue the payment, they might resort to the law for relief and find it. But when they heard this [ship money] demanded in a court of law as a right, and found it by sworn judges of the law adjudged so, upon such grounds and reasons as every stander-by was able to swear was not law, and so had lost the pleasure and delight of being kind and dutiful to the King; and instead of giving were required to pay, and by a logic that left no man any thing which he might call his own; they no more looked upon it as the case of one man [Hampton] but the case of the kingdom, nor as an imposition laid upon them by the King but by the judges; which they thought themselves bound in conscience to the public justice not to submit to.   (1888, 1:86–87)

Charles's problem was a relatively simple one from our perspective; it was intractable from the perspective of a patrimonial monarch. Charles's capacity to raise adequate revenue depended on the support he generated in Parliament; the support he generated in Parliament depended on the nature of his policies; he could not garner this support insofar as he followed the policies he enunciated. The disjunction was not so much one of the substantive nature of the policies articulated, although this was important; it was more a matter of who controlled these policies, and a matter of their formal rationality (see Weber 1968). The problem Charles confronted was that in the social situation of a growing manufacturing economy *his* policies were arbitrary, as they were not subject to adequate control. Control did not necessarily imply the immediate and direct determination of policies; rather it was coming to mean justification in the context of a formal, procedural rationality (see chap. 4, above; and Hirshman 1977).

English taxes were not high, when compared to continental standards. Hill tells us that in France the *gabelle* in 1641 brought in two times as much as the total English revenue; and more important, in France approximately eight to ten shillings per person were collected each year, while the comparable figure in England was about two and a half shillings. (Hill 1966:51; see Stone 1972*a*:123; Hill 1969*b*:chap. 6; Hill 1971:287, where the same general point is also made about tithes.) The consequence of the revolution was a severe increase in taxation, not a decrease.

The problem was thus not the absolute amount of taxation, it was the arbitrary nature of the taxes and the dangers of their being accepted as justified. In general ship money was paid when it might be viewed as a temporary expedient. But with the third writ of ship money, on 9 October 1636, it was no longer possible to view the tax as temporary; clearly it was Charles's intention to routinize the tax. Here the opposition was no longer sporadic but national, organized, and led by men of "worth and standing." The special danger of ship money and the reason it became the special focus of controversy was that, once routinized, it bore more than a family resemblance to a parliamentary grant, and in this respect it differed significantly from the Crown's other fiscal expedients. By 1640 it was almost impossible to collect ship money; less than 25 percent was remitted to the Crown's agents. (See Gardiner 1884, 7:366ff.; Gardiner 1884, 8:77ff., 85, 103–5, 200, 269; Pennington 1970: 26–27; a good description of the situation in the country is provided for Somerset by Barnes, 1961:chap. 8; for Gloucestershire, see Willcox 1940:122ff.)[6]

Ship money was only one of many financial expedients instituted by the government, expedients viewed as arbitrary, expedients that touched almost all who owned property. The fiscal crisis was long

in germinating; it was no doubt made worse by the prolonged inflation of the sixteenth century, though mitigated by the seizure and
sale of monastic properties. It appears that only one of the Crown's
sources of revenue, the customs, kept its worth throughout the inflationary period. This made the refusal of Charles's first Parliament (1625) to grant him tunnage and poundage for life a severe
blow. In this case, however, the king simply fixed the rate of the
customs payment and continued to collect the taxes. If the parliamentary opposition could not be ignored, it was rendered relatively ineffectual during the first six or seven years of the personal
rule.

The other exactions fell into three broad categories: loans, often
arbitrary, often forced; the revival of obsolete feudal practices; and
the attempt to extract money from manufacturing processes by use
of the prerogative. I will defer comment on the first, for the loans
occupy a special position in the king's fiscal policy, as ultimately
Charles's credit deteriorated to the point where he could only
borrow from his own creatures, monopolists and tax farmers, no
longer even from the corporation of London (see Ashton 1960).

The Court of Wards provided a steady and increasing source of
income. When feudal tenures were the foundation of the king's
army and the army the king's major recompense for the land, there
might have been a logic to granting the monarch control over the
land in case a death left a minor as heir. The Crown served as or
appointed a guardian until the heir reached majority, and in loco
parentis arranged for a suitable marriage. When in the seventeenth
century the feudal system that supported and justified this arrangement was no longer intact, when feudal tenures were no longer the
basis of the king's army, this arrangement amounted to a form of
swindle, allowing for the mismanagement of estates for short-term
profits, destroying many families; it could not be defended as a
method of insuring the fulfillment of a vassal's obligation.[7] All
owners of land with any feudal encumbrance had to fear for the
well-being of their posterity, and wardship was a major issue in the
Commons during the post-1604 period, peaking before the revolution.

Clarendon comments of Cottington's tenure as Master of
Wards, that he

> had raised the revenue of that court to the King to be much greater than
> it had ever been before his administration [March 1635 to May 1641];[8]

by which husbandry, all the rich families of England, of noblemen and gentlemen, were exceedingly incensed, and even indevoted to the Crown, looking upon what the law had intended for their protection and preservation to be now applied to their destruction; and therefore resolved to take the first opportunity to ravish that jewel out of the royal diadem, though it was fastened there by the known law upon as unquestionable a right as the subject enjoyed any thing that was most his own.   (1888, 1:198–99)

Wardship was acknowledged to be legal, if obsolete; the same was true of the requirement of knight's service. The king was able to demand of everyone owning land worth 40 pounds per year that he be knighted. The first summons to knighthood was made in January 1630; by Michaelmas of 1631, 115,000 pounds had been collected (Gardiner 1884, 7:167). Those who fell within the proper categories of wealth were fined for failing to assume a knighthood at Charles's coronation. Ten pounds was the minimum fine, but in Yorkshire squires "had to pay £50, £60, or, exceptionally, even more" (Cliffe 1969:141).

To recompense the damage the Crown sustained by the sale of old lands, and by the grant of new pensions, the old laws of the forest are revived, by which not only great fines are imposed, but great annual rents intended and like to be settled by way of contract; which burden lighted most upon persons of quality and honour, who thought themselves above oridinary oppressions, and therefore like to remember it with more sharpness.   (Clarendon 1888, 1:85)

The revival of the forest laws, which Clarendon quite correctly sees as a major strain on the country, involved the reclamation as forest of much land that had long been used for pasture or tillage by private parties. The forests had once provided game for the court; now they provided a source of fines on those unfortunate enough to have "trespassed" on these royal lands. The fines levied and sometimes collected by the Crown were substantial; they may have amounted to 300,000 pounds in Essex alone (Ranke 1875, 2:34). The Venetian ambassador thought that the "king hoped to exact 20 percent of the value of the land from its owners in compensation." (Hunt, 1983:268; see also Hammersley 1957; Sharp 1980. For comparable events in the Fens, see Lindley 1982; Kennedy 1983.)

These abuses and others (for example, purveyance; see Aylmer 1957) including ship money, involved the revival of what were seen as obsolete feudal claims as rights under the prerogative. Another form of abuse involved the control over manufacturing processes, both industrial and agricultural. Within the context of industry the Crown generated facilitory strain in two ways:[9] the first involved the granting of patents to certain groups allowing for the sole manufacture or sole right to transport a specified product. These patents, in effect monopolies, inevitably led to an increase in price, and often to a decrease in quality. They invariably served two purposes, substituting for direct subsidies to courtiers, and raising money for the Crown. Their consequence was to provide another generator of strain at the level of facilities, both for consumers and for prospective competitors.

Another fiscal expedient involved the sale of incorporations, grants to groups of craftsmen allowing for the organization of one or another form of manufacturing. These allowed the Crown to both profit from and indirectly control branches of manufacturing. Almost inevitably one consequence of these incorporations was higher prices for various manufactured goods, another was a stifling of industrial enterprise.

The government's agricultural policies, focusing especially on enclosures, also served to arouse significant sections of the political nation. While the Crown itself was following a policy of enclosing its own lands, Laud, in the commission on enclosures, was prosecuting others for enclosing their lands. The consequence of these prosecutions was generally that the offender paid a fine.

> From 1633 onwards, when the government was ruling without Parliament, depopulators were prosecuted. Six hundred persons were fined for enclosure between 1636 and 1638: twenty-three out of forty-six members, returned to the Long Parliament from five Midland counties, came from families which has suffered.   (Hill 1966:18)

Within this context it is important to note that the major goal of all of these policies was fiscal; the Crown used them to either raise money directly or to reward favorites, or to shore up the position of certain groups on which the monarch depended for financial assistance. Corfield outlines the three bases of Stuart economic policies: The first was a fundamental social and economic conservatism, striving to maintain a status quo based on a functionally defined hierarchy, trying to prevent disruptions within that hierarchy. This latter was especially pronounced in the Crown's endeavors to avoid unemployment and the riots consequent on unemployment.

Second, in dealing with the new manufacturing, the Crown sought to ally itself with the largest business interests, those that had a vested interest in the status quo, as defined by Crown policy, and that were prepared to pay for privileges and protection. This is often viewed as a form of "Colbertism." Third, the policies were often dominated by fiscal considerations (Corfield 1973:203 and passim). One consequence of this situation was a lack of calculability within the manufacturing economy (see chap. 4, above), but of more direct relevance here was the fact that people came to see this whole series of regulations "as yet another devise whereby the country was bled white by the court" (Ashton 1970:98).

The king's two closest advisors followed policies in Ireland and Scotland which not only helped to provoke revolutions in these two "colonies," but served to affirm the propertied Englishmen's worst fears. Charles directly attacked the property rights of lay proprietors in Scotland in seeking to regain control over church lands. The Act of Revocation of 1625 sought to regain all church lands granted to laymen in Scotland since 1542; simultaneously a commission was set up to repurchase tithes that had been surrendered to lay impropriators. The compensation offered for both was inadequate. One can almost feel today the chill these and Laud's subsequent actions sent up the spines not only of the Scots but of their English "cousins" (Hill 1971:332–34, 325; Stevenson 1973:35ff.; Stone 1972a:132).

Similar things occurred in Ireland, where Strafford was seen to be treading property rights under his boot. Strafford attacked Irish common law, a bulwark of property rights, and the English knew that the Irish and English common law were one (Ives 1968:120). "The rights of the Crown and Church, Strafford told Laud, could not 'be recovered unless a little violence and extraordinary means be used for the raising again as there has been for the pulling down.' Strafford was as good as his word, and violence and extraordinary means were extensively used" (Ranger 1967:297, quoting from Strafford's letter to Laud, 10 March 1635). Strafford and Laud came to personify the attack on property. This attack unified disparate groups into the Country opposition, and when the war with Scotland both increased the fiscal demands of the Crown and made necessary the calling of Parliament, the stage was set for a revolution of the notables. It now remains to see who sided with the king against this revolution.

It is, I hope, obvious that the policies that Charles endeavored to implement were natural within the context of a patrimonial political system. He sought to incorporate control over crucial sectors of the economy and governmental administration under the rubric of his personal, prerogative powers. In so doing he sought to legitimize his actions in terms of a series of traditionally defined commitments, and he argued that his actions were not innovations but that they fell within the scope of these personal, traditionally accepted powers. His quest for greater powers was precipitated by the greater responsibilities government was expected to meet in a new social situation. It was the disjunction between the economy and the polity which precipitated Charles's actions. The consequences of his actions increased this disjunction, as they involved an even greater imposition of nonrational controls on an economic structure constructed in terms of a formal rationality. In endeavoring to maintain the king's traditional role in an altered society, Charles helped to generate the reaction in which his powers were first circumscribed, and later (even excluding the stage of the revolution based on his execution) effectively eliminated.

The Crown's attack on property in a society where property was not the monopoly of any class united a broad and diverse movement behind the aristocratic opposition. But not even at this stage did the movement have unanimous support; the first reason for the lack of unanimity involved inhibitions to the pervasiveness of facilitory strain. For example, Supple, in an article discussing the diverse nature of merchant enterprise in the early seventeenth century, comments as follows:

> And even when they [merchants] might have been reacting in ways determined by their economic interests, these interests ... were too diversified to lead to any class unity in action. If most traders objected to higher customs duties not approved by any parliamentary sanction, there were sufficient wealthy merchants who had invested in the farming [i.e., subcontracting] of customs collection to break any absolutely united front.   (Supple 1968:141)

This is only one of many examples indicating that the very same conditions that created strain at the level of facilities for one group led to economic advantage for another, in this case a much smaller group, the Court.

Stone tells us:

The courtiers ... [may be] lumped together with the royal officials, some lawyers, the higher clergy, the customs farmers, and the monopoly merchants of the capital to form a single group whose interests were diametrically opposed to those of the rest of the population, the clash between the two being the basic cause of the domestic upheavals in some many countries in Europe in the middle of the seventeenth century.   (1967: 34)

Later in the same work Stone comments:

From one point of view government may be regarded as a device for the redistribution of wealth from the taxpayers to privileged favourites and officials. By the early seventeenth century men were becoming increasingly aware of the polarization of interest between those who ate the King's bread and those who paid for it, a polarization accentuated by the progressive diminution in the share of the tax burden borne by the aristocracy and the Court.   (277)

Clearly the division between the Court and the Country involved a split between those suffering from infringements on their property and those benefiting from those infringements. In the first stage of the revolution, the Court party included those who controlled economic concessions and those who purchased these concessions, "patents of monopoly, patents conferring rights of regulation in economic matters, farms of the royal customs, and export licenses, to cite but a few examples" (Ashton 1970:98).

Merchants split between those owing success to Charles's favor and the majority of others. But as Ashton has recently argued, even among those merchants based in the privileged companies, the arbitrary nature of the king's policies generated disaffection. As long as Commons was hostile to them, they remained relatively loyal to the king, but as Commons' hostility was mitigated and Charles's prodigality increased, a considerable portion of this merchant community opposed the Crown's policies.

In the early years of Charles I, when the issue of the non-parliamentary levying of tonnage and poundage was added to that of impositions, the whole question of the unparliamentary exaction of customs duties became a rallying cry which linked for the first time the interests of many of the chartered companies—and notably the Levant Company and the Merchant Adventurers—with those of the leaders of the parliamentary opposition.   (Ashton 1979:129)

For many, this tie continued into the REVOF. (See also Howell 1967; Pearl 1961; Brenner 1970, 1973. The pictures in these and other discussions are sometimes blurred by a failure to distinguish between the various stages of the revolution; Ashton's discussion, however, attempts to distinguish between my REVOF and REVOG in assessing the loyalties of the privileged merchants.)

Levack tells us:

> The Court comprised all those men, both in London and the shires, who held offices of profit under the Crown and who depended, therefore, upon the central government for at least a portion of their incomes. The Country, on the other hand, were those members of landed society who did not hold remunerative positions in the service of the King and who spent the greater part of their time managing their estates and participating in local government.   (1973:7)

Most agree that most officers of the county governments occupying unpaid and, during the personal rule, burdensome positions, fall into the Country faction. (There are many studies of local government; see Zagorin's summary statement, 1969:41; Ashton 1971 and Russell 1979*b*:6 take issue with the complete exclusion of the county government from the Court.) The court included those who were royal officials dependent on the king's patrimony:

> All the organs of central and regional government, all who had to do with the ceremonial position of the monarch as the fountain of honour and head of his people, all who served him as the greatest landowner and chief feudal lord of the realm. Thus, the Privy Council, the secretaries of state with their staff, the diplomatic personnel, and great departments such as the Exchequer and Court of Wards were part of the Court; so were the courts of common law and equity and the prerogative tribunals—the Star Chamber and the High Commission; so too were the King's household and the households of the Queen and the Prince of Wales. Beyond the seat of government at London, the Court swept out to include officials in every area of the kingdom: receivers of royal revenue and feodaries of the Court of Wards in the counties; persons connected with the Admirality, the customs, the Duchy of Lancaster, the Councils of the North and in Wales; keepers and surveyors, constables, stewards, and under-officers of royal castles, manors and forests. All these, in the capital and in the countryside, were the ministers, officials, and servants of the prince, receiving by his authority the fees and perquisites of their places.   (Zagorin 1969:41)

These offices were all thought to be pieces of property, yielding an income. "Court offices" yielded a direct income compensating for and often dependent on the infringement of Country rights. As such, court officials and those dependent on their favors were, in general, monarchists from the beginning; it was they who opposed the first stage of the revolution. (For a detailed analysis of *The King's Servants*, see Aylmer 1961.) Within the Long Parliament these men had little voice, for two reasons. Most were unsuccessful when they endeavored to run, and as Clarendon reminds us, "no person, how lawfully and regularly soever chosen and returned, should be and sit as a member with them [in the Long Parliament] who had been a party or a favourer of any project, or who had been employed in any illegal commission" (Clarendon 1888, 1:228). In short, those men who participated in or who supported the king's attempted REVOF were almost completely unrepresented in the Parliament, and the first stage of the revolution was carried out in virtual unanimity by the remainder of the political nation.[10]

There was one set of major exceptions to this generalization— the peerage, those entitled to a seat in the House of Lords. It is of enormous import that the peers, whatever their de facto position, were not de jure able to evade taxes. An attack on property was de jure an attack on the property of the nobles, and as Firth informs us, a "Country party," an opposition, formed among the peers in the early part of the seventeenth century (Firth 1910:37–38; cf. Hill 1981:104). While the position of the Lords was ambivalent even in the first stage of the revolution, Parliament *as a whole*, in defending its own privileges to control the amount and type of taxation, was able to pose as the defender of the people under the name of the inviolability of property. This could not happen where the Crown's attack was simply on the privilege of the ruling class to avoid paying taxes, for such an attack had to be welcomed by a significant section of the Commons. In England, however, the "notables," including a significant number of lay peers, could help to develop an ideology that could later be applied more generally (see Manning 1967; Cooper 1960:78).

It is very difficult to determine the relative balance between privilege and grievance among the nobility. It is clear that many nobles suffered from the king's revival of the forests and from his uses of the court of wards, and more generally from the prerogative courts

(Manning 1973*a*: 37, where he quotes the relevant passages from Clarendon, and Firth 1910: 56). It is also clear that rich landowners, including the peers, were under-assessed for their taxation payments. From the time of Elizabeth the peerage "was progressively evading its share of taxation.... In their financial relations with the Government the aristocracy would appear to have been almost entirely the beneficiaries, while making very little monetary contribution to the running of the State" (Stone 1967: 227–28). Stone goes on to tell us that this impression is partially false owing to the peers' contributions toward maintaining court luxury, but nonetheless the impression is conveyed that most benefited more than they suffered from the court. And thus it is not surprising to learn that "the opposition in the Upper House cannot have numbered much more than thirty peers" (Firth 1910: 77). We will see when we discuss the next phase of the revolution that this number remained stable.[11]

In my opinion Hill is either exaggerating or speaking too loosely in referring to what I have called the REVOF as a revolt of the nobles (1966: 104; 1969*b*: 127). Likewise Farnell, in my opinion, exaggerates the importance of the Lords' leadership of the Commons by, among other means, patronage—although the Lords certainly played a more important role than in Notestein's traditional picture (Farnell 1972; Notestein 1966; cf. the special issue of *The Journal of Modern History* 44: no. 4; and Hexter 1978; Hirst 1978). It is clear nonetheless that the revolt of the Country, at least in terms of the actions that directly constituted the facilitory rebellion, was a revolt from within the political nation. Why?[12]

Opportunity Structure (Og)

Lindley paints a picture of Fenland Riots, focusing on the actions of small and medium commoners (although often acting with the overt or covert support of higher strata, including gentry, who at least refused to crush them), as fluctuating with what I have called facilitory strain. The riots coincided with the money-making projects initiated or encouraged by Charles as fiscal expedients. These undertakings impinged on the livelihood of the fenmen and challenged their property rights (Lindley 1982: 1). Sharp portrays food riots and riots against disafforestation as conducted by an almost propertyless rural proletariat. "In an age of rapidly rising food prices, those growing for the market or living from economic rents prospered, while those who depended on the market for food and on nonagricultural employment for income were at the mercy of natural calamities and the fluctuation of a mercantile economy" (Sharp 1980:7). Thus these riots, which he sees as occurring without gentry support (but also without their effective action to suppress them, see 116ff.), were also in response to facilitory strain. "The status of the vast majority of rural and small-town artisans [a skilled proletariat] suggests that propertylessness was at the root of their involvement in disorders. The wages earned in manual trades virtually their sole support, in standard of life little removed from [unskilled] laborers, artisans (especially those in the cloth industry) were squeezed by depression, unemployment, declining wages, and sharp rises in the price of food in the market" (173). As Russell has commented, "outbursts of hostility to authority among the lower classes ... [were] associated with bad economic years, and it is impossible to understand the years 1640–42 without remembering that they were bad years in the cloth industry" (Russell, 1973a: 26). (For more on Sharp and Lindley see n. 22, below in chap. 6; see also Kerridge 1958 for a different view of some of the riots Sharp discusses, and Manning 1976.) These riots were an integral part of the revolution (chap. 6) but the rioters were not the actors who made the revolution at the level of facilities. They had no opportunity to do so.

A facilitory rebellion involves the redefinition of existing political role positions within the context of a given organizational structure. To do this necessitates access to those positions. Kamen reminds us that the European revolutions of the seventeenth century were played out within existing "representative bodies" (1971:328). England, at least in the first stage of her revolution, that phase most like the other revolutions of the period, was no exception.

In chapter 3 I explained that facilitory strain was a necessary but insufficient condition for the genesis of a REVOF. The next condition is an open illegitimate opportunity structure; this involves access to roles allowing for the mobilization of the facilities necessary for (1) the formation of a revolutionary subculture, and (2) if the revolution is to be successful, for the institutionalization of the revolution. This access was severely limited.

The reader of Brunton and Pennington's *Members of the Long Parliament* or Mary Keeler's *The Long Parliament* has a fairly detailed impression of who these men were. Here it suffices to say that most were leading members of their communities; they were among the socially and economically privileged—three-fifths were gentlemen bearing the titles of baronet, knight, esquire gentleman, or courtesy lord; many were lawyers, and about 10 percent were men of trade (Keeler 1954:21). As such they were in a position to command respect, and as parliamentarians were authorized to command their constituents' obedience and their economic resources. Acting in Parliament with the Lords, and having received the king's approval for most of their actions—even though this sanction was given under great duress—they were in a position to routinize the alterations they effected.

This situation, where the revolutionaries occupied those political roles recognized by the vast majority of the nation as commanding obedience and economic facilities for governmental use, explains the Country's ability to seize the initiative against the king, to formulate programs seeking to redress grievances, but it does not explain the revolutionary (rather than what we might call "reformist") nature of their actions. It does not, in other words, differentiate their actions from those of previous parliaments. (See, among many other general treatments, Notestein 1966; Russell 1971; Loades 1974; Aylmer 1965; Davies 1959; Tanner 1928. There are books on the Parliaments of 1603–10: Notestein 1971; the Parliament of 1614, the Addled Parliament: Moir 1958; the Parliament of 1621, Zaller 1971; the Parliament of 1624, Ruigh 1971; and the Parliaments of 1621–1629, Russell 1979*b*. The classic treatment remains Gardiner 1883–84, 10 vols.)

Neutralizing Beliefs (NB)

Considered as a whole, the opposition engendered by the rule of Charles I was not an organized affair…. Acts of disobedience were frequently spontaneous or due to the force of example, a product of common grievances and sympathies, rather than of planning and calculation.

But at the centre of the Country was something more. Here a definite organization existed: a group united by conviction, linked through family and friendship, meeting to concert the tactics of opposition. In structure an informal alliance of like-minded men, this group was the nucleus of the Country.   (Zagorin 1969:99)

These passages describe what I earlier referred to (in chap. 3) as the subculture of revolution and the revolutionary subculture. The first consists of those groups in situations where strain (at the level of facilities), an open illegitimate opportunity structure, and a neutralizing belief place the actors in a state of drift, where given the opportunity they will commit riotous and/or revolutionary actions. The inner core of the subculture of revolution is the revolutionary subculture, comprised of those actors who have legitimized the commission of revolutionary actions and are capable of organizing and leading the revolution.

In the terms used in chapter 3, a neutralizing belief was generated during the period of the personal rule; this belief implies a calculating orientation toward the institutionalized authority system and a nonnegative attitude toward the specific (set of) revolutionary act(s) capable of combating (here) facilitory strain. The former of these two aspects of a neutralizing belief may be discussed under the rubric of a deflation of power (see chap. 3 and chap. 2, above).

There are many conditions under which a deflation of power will appear. A model capable of analyzing these was presented earlier in this book (chap. 2) and I will not repeat what was said there. Each of these conditions eventuates in a situation where the government's capacity to implement some set of programs exceeds the effective support offered to that government, where the scope of real power is in excess of the symbolic scope of power. Charles's policies, especially during the years of personal rule, went well beyond the level of support he was capable of garnering; within this situation what I earlier referred to as a "paradox of thrift" was generated.

In chapter 2 I showed how a series of inputs to the polity from other societal subsystems could be compared to a series of analogous variables in conventional macroeconomic theory. We saw that the three product inputs to the polity were (1) political authorization, which defines the scope of legal powers of office (political investment) (2) political control over economic resources in assuming operative responsibility for the implementation of political policies (political savings) and (3) political support (political consumption). When in balance these three product inputs to the political system yield an equilibrium formally much like the one isolated by Keynes among investment, savings, and consumption. As in the economic

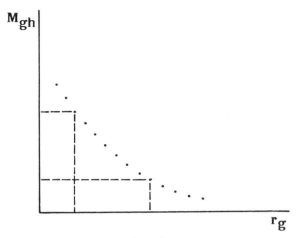

Figure 28. Allocation of surplus economic resources.

case, an autonomous increase in political savings, control over economic productivity (including services), yields a "paradox of thrift," that situation where the scope of political output decreases; and paradoxically, occurring parallel to this decrease is a decrease in savings (political control over economic productivity).

Within the more complex version of the model discussed in chapter 2 it can be shown that a similar result occurs from an autonomous increase in the level of surplus economic product allocated to the polity, for example, in the form of an increase in taxation. If one begins at this point, with an increase in taxation, it is apparent—referring to figures 28, 29, and 30 (figures 17, 19, and 20 in chap. 2)—that such an increase moves the M_{gh} curve (allocation of surplus economic resources) up and to the right (in figure 28) and the LM curve (those combinations of political income and legitimacy which result in an equilibrium of the power market, where the total amount of power equals the power demanded) up and to the left (in figs. 29 and 30). The two most apparent consequences of this movement are (1) that the scope of political output will decrease and (2) that the level of political alienation (r_g in figs. 29 and 30) will increase. As was pointed out in chapter 2, an increase in the rate of political alienation is equivalent to a loss of legitimacy for the government in power.

It is important that in the English case the deflation of power was

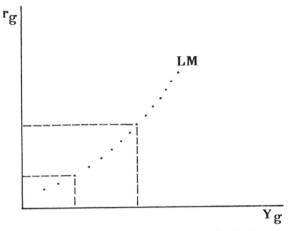

Figure 29. For a given stock of power and a fixed ratio between the amount of power controlled and the capacity to secure available intrinsic satisfiers, the combinations of r_g and Y_g which yield and equality of M_{gs} and M_{gd}.

generated by both movements, an autonomous increase in the government's control over economic productivity and services ("the thorough" at the local level and economic regulations at the national level) and by an autonomous increase in taxation (as discussed below). Neither of these shifts was precipitated by an increase in demands for political action, although, perhaps paradoxically, the decrease in political output left many interest demands unmet (see fig. 30 and chap. 2). But it is important to note that the increase in legitimacy that would be expected from a decrease in output owing to the "paradox of thrift" (a decrease in Y, political output, and r_g, political alienation, on fig. 30) was more than offset by the decrease in legitimacy owing to the arbitrary increases in taxation, and by the short-term capacity of the government to maintain output through the use of coercion.

> The reputation of the Crown was deeply involved with its resources because the measures taken to increase the royal revenues were a principal reason for the dwindling respect in which the government was held. A constant need for money hampered and deformed the King's policy, and the methods he chose to raise it were unpopular and corrupt.   (Wedgwood 1966*b*: 143)

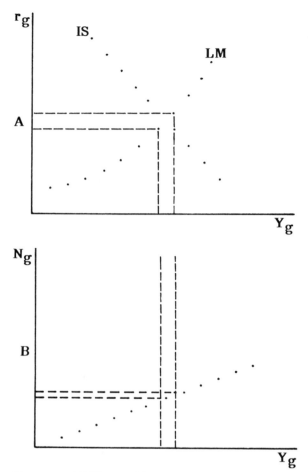

Figure 30. (A) The equilibrium of power and production markets; (B) Scope of implemented interest
demands.

The government had demanded arbitrary and relatively large tax
increases (in a variety of forms and with a variety of attempted
justifications). As Hawkins points out, it was not so much that
these demands were new departures that mattered; what was important is that they revealed the narrowing of the government's
political support (1973 : 56–57).[13]

Thus the government, in the person of Charles and his agents but not including either the Commons or the Lords, endeavored to raise taxes not justifiable before the nation as a whole. The government in the person of Charles and his agents attempted to exert point-by-point control over the enforcement of law within the counties. The actions taken under the Books of Orders, especially with respect to its central concern, the poor laws, may be taken as indicative. Hill, generally following Barnes, emphasizes three aspects of these reforms: inclusiveness, intensiveness, and duration. The Crown put unheard-of pressure on its country servants in an assumption of operative responsibility for the implementation of governmental policies (Barnes 1961; L. M. Hill 1973; Sharp 1984). As we have seen, these policies led to a deflation of power and to a disrespect for the court and a lack of trust in the king (see, e.g. Gardiner 1884, 8:223; Judson 1949:161; Stone 1972a:79, 88ff., 116; Stone 1967:9–10, 351). This lack of respect tended to center at those positions within society where facilitory strain was most severe; this tendency was worsened by another facet of the Court-Country split.

The court suffered most from two associations: with Catholicism and with corruption, the latter both venal and spiritual. Without elaborating on the reasons, Charles and Laud were seen as liable to reintroduce Roman Catholicism to England. As such they aroused the animosity of all Protestants of any Puritan tinge, and of many Protestants who viewed themselves as loyal Anglicans. Their fears were reinforced by what was perceived as Charles's pro-Catholic foreign policy, and by Laudian innovations that were perceived as Catholic in inspiration (see, e.g., Clifton 1971, 1973; Clarendon 1888, 1:194–95, 380; Hibbard 1983; Hill 1971; Morrill 1984). This fear was overlaid by and associated with perceptions of corruption in the court (see Stone 1967:230–31).

Venal corruption was simply another form of taxation. Small gifts to officials were an accepted practice, and fees for services rendered were an integral part of the compensation received by Crown officials. Aylmer estimates that these fees and gratuities totaled between 250,000 and 400,000 pounds per year in the 1620s and 1630s; this in a context where "total royal revenue, omitting extraordinary taxation and capital gains, averaged only c. £618,000 a year in the early 1630s" (Aylmer 1961:248). It is this situation about which Stone has written in commenting on the distinct weakening of the moral integrity of the courtiers. He traces this from the 1590s, and comments that "it was the impact of merchant capital on a venal court and official world which so gravely accelerated the drift up to and beyond the acceptable threshold of corruption" (Stone 1967:224).

Smelser treats corruption as "above all a matter of exchanging sanctions or rewards among two or more parties: as a prototypical example, the public official agrees not to enforce a law (a political sanction) if he receives a sufficiently generous bribe from a businessman (an economic sanction)" (1971:13). As such it involves inappropriate demands for economic resources, and in consequence will yield or in this case magnify the political deflation of power. "The greatest casualty of this development [of corruption] was public respect for the highest officers of the state" (Stone 1967:224). Although venal corruption was important in the growing split between Court and Country, the perceived moral corruption of the court was equally so.

The court had an evil reputation. "Incalculable harm was done to the prestige of monarchy by the gold-rush atmosphere of gambling, sex and drink created by the lavish generosity and the genial tolerance of King James" (Stone 1967:187–88). Although the accuracy of this image might have altered somewhat during Charles's personal rule, when many nobles and gentry were forcibly expelled from London, the image remained (Ashton 1978). The court was associated with gambling, stage-plays, drunkenness, promiscuity, and worse, homosexuality.

> Throughout the whole of this period [the early seventeenth century] archidiaconal courts and town magistrates had been treating the sexual peccadilloes of the lower orders with extreme severity, and the discrepancy between the generally enforced moral code and the licence of the Court became an established part of public belief. Impinging upon the puritan conscience, this was a powerful factor in undermining the moral authority of both the peerage and the Court.   (Stone 1967:301)

This odium that fell upon the court was rooted in the Country opposition.

The major consequence of this lowering of moral legitimacy was a contraction in the legitimate political power available to the court. The scope of legitimate authority available to mobilize collective action in adherence to the "authorized power" of Crown officials shrank with the diminution of the nation's value commitment to the Crown and the Court. This shrinkage increased the other pressures toward a deflation of power within the system.[14]

One consequence of the deflation of governmental power was the adoption in the Country of a calculating attitude toward those who were empowered.

> Criticism and propaganda expose the *arcana imperii* to the light of common day. Subjects ask if they should obey, and whom, and why. Authority is constrained to plead its case with reasons or impose itself by violence. In either instance it has lost its virtue: for while authority remains itself, it neither argues nor coerces, but merely speaks and is accepted. (Zagorin 1969: 198)

The fact that the king had won each of the disputed taxation cases placed before the courts was relevant, but as Gardiner points out, the victory in the ship money case, which appeared to seal the doom of Parliament, was actually the beginning of the end for the government. It was an indication of the level to which the debate between Court and Country had been carried. The capacity of the court to maintain the formal authorization of the powers of office it claimed simply raised the level of political alienation in the country. The formal legality of the Crown's arbitrary actions was not accepted as legitimate, and when possible the Crown's decrees were evaded. Only if positive rewards followed or negative sanctions were to be avoided would persons obey these decrees. Their violation, owing in part to their "legality," increased in importance.

Thus one half of the neutralizing belief was present, a calculating attitude toward the Court; the second involves either a positive or neutral attitude toward the specific actions under consideration. This neutralization was substantively an integral part of the set of beliefs which legitimized the REVOF, and as such it will be treated in more detail in what follows. Here it is only necessary to note that, as Walzer puts it, in devaluing traditional authority and the status quo, in insisting on the responsibility of private persons for the creation of the kingdom of God on earth, in emphasizing the legitimacy of resistance if led by lesser magistrates (in England, Parliament), Calvinism made revolution available to the English in the seventeenth century (Walzer 1968).

By the end of Charles's personal rule the Country was in a state of drift, suffering under strain at the level of facilities, having access to an open illegitimate opportunity structure, occupying roles wherein a deflation of power was operative, and at the very least neutral toward the actions that would constitute their facilitory rebellion. These men were the subculture of revolution and from them would emerge, was emerging, a revolutionary subculture.

Bacon, writing in the 1620s and quoting Tacitus, observed, "And such was the state of men's minds, that though few dared to commit this worst of crimes [sedition], many desired it, and all acquiesced in it" (1924:67). Given an appropriate precipitant, the country was ready to make what I call a facilitory rebellion; those who did not actively participate would remain neutral, and as we shall see below, those who did participate had no difficulty in legitimizing and routinizing their actions.

Precipitating Factor (P_g)

As was noted in chapter 3, it is easier to identify a precipitant of revolutionary actions after the fact than it is to predict what it will be prior to its occurrence. Often a precipitating factor serves to accentuate strain, an open illegitimate opportunity structure, or neutralizing beliefs. It might also create the conditions in which one or more of these variables might be manifested.

The precipitating factor of the revolution was the Scottish revolution. The revolution in Scotland was provoked by Laud's attempts to recapture church lands and by his imposition of the Book of Common Prayer in Scotland. (The most comprehensive introduction to the events in Scotland is Stevenson 1973.) This revolution led to the First Bishops' War, with the Scottish covenanters endeavoring to consolidate their position and Charles endeavoring to regain control over one of his three kingdoms. Charles was forced to call the Short Parliament in order to raise money to support his war effort.

The Short Parliament focused primarily on policies and not on institutions. Nonetheless, in demanding redress of grievances prior to supply (in demanding that Charles respond to their complaints prior to their granting him funds), it signed its own death warrant. It lasted from 13 April to 5 May 1640.

The failure of the Treaty of Berwick, which had ended the First Bishops' War, led to a successful Scottish invasion of northern England in the Second Bishops' War. By and large the English refused to fight; in a situation of drift they were being asked to go to war against their fellow religionists on behalf of religious innovations they viewed as approaching papacy. "Most Englishmen were so discontented, said the earl of Northumberland, that they 'will be readier to join with the Scots than to draw their swords in the King's service'" (Zagorin 1969:115). Defeated by the Scots at Newburn on the Tyne on 28 August 1640, Charles came to terms on 26 October, and in the Treaty of Ripon agreed to pay the Scots 850 pounds per day until a final settlement was reached.

Strapped for funds in times of peace,

> in these distractions and discomposures, between an enemy proud and insolent in success, an army corrupted or at best disheartened, a country mutinous and inclined to the rebels, at least not inclined to reduce them, and a Court infected with all three, the King could not but find himself in great straits; besides that his treasure, which had hitherto kept that which was best from being worse, was quite spent ... and the borrowing so much money for the raising and supplying this latter army had drawn assignments and anticipations upon the revenue to that degree that there was not left wherewithal to defray the constant necessary expense of the King's household. (Clarendon 1888, 1:192–93)

The king first called a Great Council of Peers, but in these circumstances a parliament was inevitable. The Long Parliament was constituted on 3 November 1640.

Called to alleviate the king's financial plight, this Parliament came

> after ten years in which they [the English] had submitted to persistent interference, to the irritation of knighthood fines, of petty prosecutions for enclosure, of prohibitions, licences and regulations affecting their closest interests, they saw themselves faced with the heavy trouble and not inconsiderable expense of making the largest levy of troops within the memory of man. And for what? For a war on their Protestant neighbours and fellow-subjects, provoked by the Archbishop [Laud]. (Wedgwood 1966b:304)

Now they had to fund not only Charles, but the Scottish army that had defeated Charles; facilitory strain, both as arbitrary and as exorbitant, was magnified to a breaking point.

In addition, the war had the consequence of reopening the opportunity structure for a facilitory rebellion. With the calling of Parliament, the Country once again had access to the institutional structure within which it could mobilize the nation for a revolution. This moment of access occurred at the same time as an acute strain at the level of facilities; in addition, the war had exacerbated the deflation of power, and respect for and trust in the government was at a nadir. So the Second Bishops' War magnified all three prior variables; the calling of the Long Parliament occurred in a situation of acute financial strain on the executive (not only was Charles broke and in debt but his debts to the Scots mounted with each passing day), and the dissolution of the Parliament was almost impossible. With the meeting of the Long Parliament the immediate opportunity for the revolution had arrived; almost immediately the revolution was to begin.

As I have described it, in 1640 the Country was in a state of drift, and the calling of the Long Parliament consequent on the Second Bishops' War with the Scots provided the immediate opportunity for them to implement revolutionary actions. But as we have seen in chapter 3, this situation is one where a calculating attitude dominates, where a weighing of positive and negative sanctions occurs. The English government was expected to shoulder a major responsibility for the well-being of the nation; although there was significant controversy over the definition of the appropriate policies, there was no controversy about the necessity of governmental action. For Parliament, acting on its own, in its perceived—even if incoherently and too often inconsistently perceived—self-interest, and acting against the executive branch, rewards were certain to accrue. The reassertion of parliamentary control over taxation was seen as certain to yield significant benefits, but this reassertion was possible, as we will see in more detail later, because it could not yield significant punishments.

We have seen earlier the events that constituted the facilitory rebellion. The prerogative was the focus of the attack, and the prerogative courts that had instituted and justified the king's usurpations were destroyed as Parliament redefined its role within the political system. It only remains, in our discussion of this first phase of the revolution, to explore the basis of the formation of the revolutionary subculture that guided the revolution and the basis upon which the members of this subculture legitimized their actions.

Legitimizing Beliefs (LB_g REVOF)

There are three questions that require examination if we are to understand the capacity of the rebels to legitimize and institutionalize their actions. First, it is necessary to examine the specifics of the beliefs and symbols that were used to legitimize the facilitory rebellion. Second, we must examine how these beliefs were connected with a transformation from one stage of social structural development to another. Third, it is essential to gain some understanding of the forms of social organization and social relationship that facilitated the communication essential to affecting this transformation and its legitimation. Ordinarily we would want to be very careful to separate "what really was happening" from the revolutionaries' rhetoric; here we will find that the conflation between the two is an essential clue to the former.

"Nothing could be more misleading than to picture the vehement assertion of the antiquity of English laws and liberties as an inert acceptance of 'traditional society'" (Pocock 1975:341). While the first stage of the English Revolution was legitimized almost entirely under the rubric of tradition and law, or when the two were merged, in terms of a restoration of the ancient constitution,[15] it is essential to recognize that the revolutionaries used "tradition" as precedent, to legitimize innovations outside the traditional order. In Walzer's words, precedent "suggests the rational use of historical example to underpin political innovation" (1968:77).

The ambiguity of this position is almost unconsciously articulated by Zagorin. He emphasizes that the Country produced "no original political doctrine of its own," and tells us that this was

> a result of their political mentality, and, as such, [is] highly revealing.
>
> The Country was a conservative opposition. Its adherents had no prejudice in favour of change. Certainly, in contesting with James I and Charles I, they did not set out to alter the government. They felt no necessity to rationalize a new version of the state or the English constitution because they conceived themselves defenders of an immemorial legal order of rights and liberties against which the King was the transgressor. He, not his antagonists, was the innovator—so it seemed to the Country. (1969:83; see also Ashton 1978; Christianson 1976; Russell 1979*b*)

Later in the same work, however, in a discussion of Strafford's impeachment, Zagorin tells us, "With praiseworthy effort they [Pym and his colleagues] excavated the mines of precedent to the depths to prepare their case. Yet that case rested on a principle really revolutionary in nature" (217). This point might well be generalized to the sum of those actions that we have called the facilitory rebellion; while legitimized in terms of the law and ancient constitution, much the same ideology as held by the truly conservative opposition throughout the century, these actions were revolutionary in nature. (See Gardiner 1884, 8:155; Pocock 1967.)

Never before 1642 did the Parliament admit that the law was insufficient to legitimize their actions (Judson 1949:415; Mendle 1973:226, 231). It is clear, as we will see in discussing the movement into the next phase of the revolution, that it was this appeal to law which allowed moderates (like Hyde, Falkland, and Culpepper [Colepeper] to support the first phase of the revolution (Judson 1949:267). We will also see how the king, under Culpepper's and later Hyde's direction, provided the archtypal legitimating document for this phase of the revolution (his reply to the nineteen propositions).

In chapter 4 I emphasized that this ability to use tradition to legitimize innovation was an attribute of patrimonial systems. If the REVOF we have discussed marked a point of transition between patrimonial structures and those more closely approximating legal rationality, we should be able to spot some distinctions between the constitutional arguments put forward even at this early period of the revolution and those of previous times. This difference was necessary, if only because the king, as a patrimonial ruler, also legitimized his actions by precedent. It was this alteration by Parliament of the bases of its legitimacy which provided the foundation for subsequent constitutional developments. Here I will only suggest a few distinctions (see chap. 8, below).

The new element seems to have been interjected by Puritanism. Puritanism involved, in the first instance, a devaluation of tradition (see Walzer 1968:chap. 5). But this devaluation was not simply passive; it occurred within the context of an ethical prophecy, demanding the reordering of this world. As Little puts it, ethical prophecy implied a this-worldly asceticism that in turn implied the active participation of all believers in the construction of both the temporal and the spiritual worlds (cf. Little 1969:21–22; Weber 1958; Gardiner 1884, 8:308–9; Hill 1969c:214–15). The Puritan God was transcendent, but he expected men and women to act as his agents. Like Knox, many Puritans were driven "to an explicit denial of two traditional political ideas: that the magistrate was the only public person and that private men were politically irresponsible" (Walzer 1968:106).

By 1640 Puritan preachers set forth the ideas "by which the king was made subject to God and His laws, to man and his rights, and to man's necessary consent to government. The need for action—and drastic action—had been stressed, and often the necessity as a last resort of armed resistance had been suggested" (Judson 1949:348). Thus while it might be argued that the dominant view in the Lords was reactionary, desiring that the polity revert back to a system in which the king was simply the first among equals, one among many nobles, sitting at the top of a hierarchy at the pinnacle of the great chain (cf. Snow 1962), clearly the Commons' opposition (including those peers who joined with them) even at the stage of the facilitory rebellion had different consequences. They had learned from a Puritanism that centered the authority to make and implement decisions first in a transcendent God and second in the elect. In this world, therefore, legitimacy flowed upward from individual believers to their church or state government. The consequences of this pattern of beliefs took a long time to work out, as they were embedded in a series of inconsistent assumptions. But these beliefs provided a possible basis on which to legitimize actions necessary to avert manipulation from above.

In contrast to these beliefs that emphasized the importance of ordinary men, James had helped to refine and develop the theory of the divine right of kings (see James I 1965; Figgis 1965). A king who governed by divine right might claim to be bound by the law, but such divinely sanctioned powers placed him outside the bounds of an "organic state" (McIlwain 1910:345ff.). In combating the king and resisting his pretensions, Parliament invoked the doctrine of an unchanging fundamental law (see Gough 1971), but interpreted it as justifying their own position as responsible to the nation (see Judson 1949:351; cf. McIlwain 1966:113ff.; Kenyon 1966:24ff.). They appealed to tradition and law against the prerogative, but even so, they implicitly in the REVOF and later explicitly attacked the traditional mode of legitimizing power (of which divine right was a subgrouping).

The Tudor and early Stuart state was a patrimonial structure cybernetically controlled by a complex ideological system that mixed organic and hierarchical principles. The well-ordered state was seen as a series of elements rank-ordered in a descending chain

(Pocock 1975:349; Hanson 1970:4) and as we have seen, the
king's position in this chain allowed for his attempts to expand the
scope of his uncontrolled power. "So long as descending authority
met with ascending custom, the king's obligation to respect the
privileges of his subjects remained prudential; it was not the consequence of a division and sharing of authority between him and
them" (Pocock 1975:357–58). The facilitory rebellion began the
process of institutionalizing a division of powers (Hexter 1978:
46–47) which in effect began to transform the developmental level
of the English political system (see chap. 8, below).

"The important point ... is that a normative theory of balanced
or mixed government was incompatible with Tudor [and Stuart]
notions of descending authority, and that the elements of republican theory were therefore best adapted to dealing with imperfectly
legitimized situations" (Pocock 1975:355). Or put somewhat differently: in order to combat a prerogative legitimized by divine
right, the Parliament had to take the first steps toward a theory of
popular control, toward a mode of legitimizing authority which
ascended first from Parliament and later, as we will see, from the
people (see Weston and Greenberg 1981). The older rhetoric remained, not, as Pocock has it, because the English were "monarchical and customary animals by nature" (1975:365), but because
at first there was no other rhetoric, and because another rhetoric
would have destroyed the unity necessary to insure the success
of the facilitory rebellion. When this unity was dissolved, when
Charles adopted the facilitory rebellion as his own, another rhetoric
slowly evolved.

It is most interesting that it was Charles and Hyde who put the
final stamp of approval on the facilitory rebellion, and thus helped
to institutionalize a new order. Weston tells us that theories of
mixed government arose in Tudor England and that

> the cardinal document in the history of the theory of mixed government
> in modern England and a document of the first importance in the con-
> stitutional conflicts of the seventeenth century was the Answer to the
> Nineteen Propositions, issued by King Charles I in June 1642, on the
> very eve of the first Civil War.   (Weston 1965:5)

The first printed version of this document, apparently written by
Culpepper and Falkland, referred to the king, lords, and commons
as the three estates. Hyde objected to this as lowering the king from

his position above the three estates: lords spiritual, lords temporal, and commons. Further editions of the answer printed in 1643 either omitted the offending passage (which was penned by Culpepper) or the entire section devoted to the constitution (Weston 1965:23–28).

In the original, the king was one of three balanced estates. The answer assumes their relative positions after the first session of the Long Parliament.

> The king based his rejection of the Nineteen Propositions on the ground that the two Houses, because of the constitutional reforms that had been completed by August 1641, possessed sufficient power to prevent the growth of royal tyranny and that further concessions [like those demanded in the Nineteen Propositions, a classic document of the REVOG (reprinted in Gardiner 1906:249–54)] would upset the destruction of the mixed and balanced government that he was describing.   (Weston 1965:24)

Perhaps the best name for this "mixed government" is a "regulated monarchy," the phrase that Charles uses to describe it in the answer (as reprinted, in the relevant parts, in Kenyon 1966:21–23; Weston 1965:263–65). Even in Culpepper's version, the document leaves the king in control over executive powers; the government is entrusted to the king,

> the House of Commons (an excellent convener of liberty, but never intended for any share in government, or the choosing of them that govern) is solely entrusted with the first propositions concerning the levy of money (which is the sinews as well of peace as of war), and the impeaching of those who for their own ends, though countenanced by any surreptitiously gotten command of the King, have violated the law, which he is bound (when he knows it) to protect; and to the prosecution of which they are bound to advise him, at least not to serve him to the contrary.   (Kenyon 1966:22)

This document is clearly intended to sanction the REVOF, already completed, and to combat the REVOG, already underway. But this understates its importance. For as Pocock says "it was, in a very short time, so widely accepted and so diversely employed as to present us with a clear case of paradigmatic innovation—here, we must believe, was a new formulation of a kind for which many men had been searching for many reasons" (1975:361).

The king—as his adversaries remarked with glee and his friends with dismay—was here made to describe himself as a part of his own realm, one of three "estates" between which there must be a balance and (it followed) proportionate equality.[16] But the implications of the language ... reach farther still. Government in England is no longer a direct emanation of divinely or rationally enjoined authority; it is a contrivance of human prudence, blending together three modes of government —the only three that can exist—each of which possesses its characteristic virtues and vices.... The government of England, in short, without ceasing to manifest the element of monarchy, is being presented as a classical republic (Pocock 1975:362–63).

I have quoted Pocock at such length because he states the argument so well, even if he exaggerates a bit. The point is that if accepted, Charles's argument tends toward the point where it becomes republican in content. Here it remains within the bounds of a regulated monarchy, but the logic of legitimation for that monarchy is, in a fundamental respect, no longer hierarchical, no longer descending, and no longer based on a transcendent view of authority (see chap. 8, below).[17]

The foundation on which a notion of ascending authority was constructed was Puritanism, but this religious conviction also provided the assurance of success needed to enable "common men" ("Commons") to challenge their social superiors.

Puritanism provided the certainty of moral righteousness in opposing corruption, the certainty of God's favor and thus the certainty of success. "Without absolute confidence in the rectitude of their cause, which nothing other than Puritanism could have given, the Parliamentary leaders of the 1640s would have been unable to bring themselves to the pitch of defying the King and levying war against him" (Stone 1972a:101). Rebellion was not simply a political necessity, it was a religious duty (Zagorin 1969:197). The doctrine of providence, held by most Puritans, "carried an assurance of success" (Russell 1973a:24). Or most eloquently,

In the great revolution which was approaching, it was Puritanism which was to play the part of the motive power. It was not enough that men should hold theories about liberty. What was needed was that there should be found those who were ready to dare anything and to suffer anything on behalf of Him whom they called the Lord; men who could confront kings, as being themselves the servants of the King of kings. (Gardiner 1883, 4:171)

Practical men in considerable numbers can be persuaded to commit themselves to fight for a faith and a program when they can be induced to believe in the inevitability of a favorable outcome. If, however, some are predestined to win, some must be equally sure to lose. If any are elect, others must be damned. The certainty of election and reprobation was, then, an indispensible theme in the arguments of the Puritan preachers prior to [and after] 1640.   (Haller 1957: 169; see Hill 1969c: 241–42)

This surety of salvation was articulated within the context of a theologically defined discipline (see Hill 1969c: chap. 6). This discipline was one basis within which the parliamentary party was able to organize itself. Puritanism was a foundation on which the Country party could organize; in part this was because it provided the focus around which revolved an English nationalism and an English anti-Catholicism. But most important, it provided one of the organizational structures that could be adapted to political functions.

I argued in chapter 3 that the commission of revolutionary actions generates the necessity of legitimizing those actions. We have seen some of the forms that those legitimations took; it now behooves us to explore the networks within which this legitimation took place, to attempt to understand the channels within which a revolutionary subculture was formed from among those in the subculture of revolution.

Certain aspects of the beliefs just discussed were present prior to the revolution, but insofar as they were accepted it was among those persons who were to spearhead the facilitory rebellion, persons legitimizing prior actions deemed by the king to be in violation of his authority. When these beliefs were acknowledged as the basis of a commitment to a reconstructed political system it was in order to legitimize the Country's facilitory rebellion. At the core of this revolution the participants were organized, at least in a rudimentary fashion. There is a great deal of evidence concerning this grouping, which had its political roots in earlier Parliaments. There is, however, considerable controversy over the degree and nature of its organization.

Firth tells us that there was a more or less organized party from 1614 (1910: 37; see Snow 1970: 102–3); Gardiner speaks of the meetings Commons leaders held to organize the opposition during the Parliament of 1628 (1884, 6: 230ff.), and Mitchell attempts to trace the opposition from 1603, emphasizing and overestimating its

degree of organization in 1628, which "showed at last a true opposition organization" (1957:xvi. Others have tried to trace the
genesis of specific factions, for example, the "middle group," into
the 1620s; see Thompson 1972). Christianson argues that a "network" existed prior to the Long Parliament which quickly took
control to effect what I've called a REVOF. He suggests "that peers
may well have led" this network, but provides little evidence of
their control (1977:599 and passim; cf. Hexter 1978:15ff.).

Others have suggested that these images are overdrawn (see the
citations in n. 3, this chap.). There clearly was not an organized
parliamentary opposition preparing for a revolution. "What they
[the so-called "revisionists"] expose as misguided is the extreme
notion of 'a deliberate opposition with constitutional aims,' 'with
long term constitutional objectives about the power of Parliament,'
which engaged in 'the pursuit of supreme power'" (Rabb 1981:
65). Perhaps the most judicious assessment is Hexter's:

> Now in all these instances [of opposition to the king in the early 1600s]
> the men placed under duress had just been doing something the king did
> not like, was opposed to; and conversely, to judge by what they said and
> did, the king was doing things they were against, opposed to, in opposi-
> tion to. Moreover, this opposition had two kinds of continuity. In the
> first place, a continuity of leadership. Not that the Houses of Parliament
> had the same leaders from the accession of James to the Civil War.
> Rather, it was the kind of continuity that Wittgenstein describes, the
> continuity of a rope, which does not require that any single strand be
> continuous from the beginning of the rope to the end.... Besides the
> continuity of leadership there was continuity of issues. Not that all par-
> ticular issues or grievances recurred in Parliament after Parliament;
> here, too, the continuity was that of rope. But particular grievances
> tended to be subsumed under and seen as mere examples of general
> wrongs that could be righted only by opposing them and by opposition
> to the king's government that inflicted them.   (1978:27; the striking
> image of the rope is found in Selden, comparing a ship to common law,
> in his critical note on Fortescue's *De Laudibus*, cited in Tuck 1979:84,
> 132)

By the meeting of the Long Parliament we have evidence of an
organization within the Country, as manifest in the petitions delivered to Parliament. Further, there is evidence of the organized control exerted by the Parliament's leaders from the beginning of the
session (Zagorin 1969:200–202, 207:10). We know, for example,

of meetings including members of the Lords and Commons in 1640 (e.g., Manning 1973a:41ff.; Clarendon 1888:242–43). These early meetings led to a petition for a new Parliament (Gardiner 1884, 9:198–99). Between the Short and the Long Parliaments, "Pym's energies throughout the summer and autumn months of 1640 were devoted to the organization of the first electoral campaign that England had ever seen" (Newton 1966:294). Newton also reminds us here that this involved a "tortuous web of intrigue that at any moment might lead him to the block." Many undertook actions prior to the first session of the Long Parliament which needed legitimation in ways not acceptable to the king. These actions prefigured the facilitory rebellion that was to enlist the participation of a much wider body of people, as the revolutionary subculture was broadened to include a considerable segment of the subculture of revolution.

As in a broken crystal, these political fissures appeared along predetermined lines.

> Fundamental differences separated the nobility from the towns [in Prussia]: in England, on the other hand, the gentry and the urban middle classes were linked by strong religious, social, economic and political ties, and both were driven into a united opposition by the policy of the Stuarts.   (Carsten 1954:277; see Moore 1966; Carsten's is one of the books on Germany which serves as a substitute for a "Germany chapter" in Moore's study)

This compatibility of interest was manifest in many areas:

> The intimate business alliance of such members of the Upper House as Warwick, Saye, and Brooke with great London merchants is prominent throughout our pages and we must recognize that these commercial bonds are of great importance in the history of the time [the early seventeenth century], as rendering it easier for great nobles and wealthy country gentlemen to unite with city merchants and to work side by side with them in the constitutional struggle against the crown. Such a union would have been impossible at an earlier period.   (Newton 1966:39; cf. Brenner 1970; Rabb 1967; Manning 1967; among many other sources)

Various commercial ventures provided the foci around which the Country was organized. The best example is the Providence Island Company, around which Pym's middle group organized. The company undertook the colonization of the islands of Provi-

dence, Henrietta, and Association in the West Indies, but as Newton puts it: "The work of the Long Parliament, that broke forever
the power of absolute monarchy in England ... was begun in the
courts of the Virginia, the Saybrook, and the Providence companies" (1966:2). The Providence maintained its continuity during
the 1630s (Hunt 1983:266) and served as a base of organization at
the beginning of the Long Parliament. It was, for example, at a
supposed meeting of the company that a request for Scottish intervention was drawn up, to be signed by seven leading peers: Essex,
Bedford, Warwick, Brooke, Saye, Mandeville, and Saville; the last
later claimed that the letter was a forgery (Snow 1970:230ff.).

There were bases of organization within each local community,
but these familial and parochial ties (analyzed and emphasized
by Brunton and Pennington 1968 and more specifically in many
studies of local areas cited in the references) were welded together
by certain centrifugal forces. Puritanism was the strongest of these
forces. (See, e.g., Hexter 1968:67; Walzer 1968:261.) As Stone
puts it, the Puritans provided "an embryo organization out of
which grew true radicalism" (1972a:103).

The importance of this focus is accentuated by the disciplined
nature of Puritan congregations. The organization implicit in the
"godly discipline" was utilized not only to organize a preaching
ministry, the feoffees, but to provide the basis for political organization. (All descriptions of Puritanism stress the discipline and organization found in its multitudinous varieties; on organization
around the feoffees see Hill 1971:263.)

Thus we have seen that facilitory strain, an open illegitimate
opportunity structure, and a set of neutralizing beliefs put the country into a state of drift; the Second Bishops' War and the calling of
the Long Parliament precipitated the facilitory rebellion. This rebellion was legitimized largely in terms of precedents, the framework
of a newly defined "regulated monarchy." It remains only to ask
why it succeeded; in the first instance, why wasn't it crushed?

Inflation of Power

It has often been pointed out that the English monarchy lacked a standing army or any extensive local bureaucracy with which to back its inter-
ventionist aims ... but, as we have stressed, its strength rested on its
close sympathies with the locally influential.... This local bureaucracy

was only partly under government control, which did not matter as long as it was asked to do only what it wanted, but became crucial if the central government found itself forced into policies unwelcome to the locally influential.... [For example] the non-payment [of ship money] eventually became substantial, and revealed clearly the fragile administrative basis for any attempt by the government to pursue what the localities regarded as innovatory policies. In short, the lack of a local bureaucracy became crucial when confidence had already been lost. It did not cause the government's weakness, though it certainly ensured that the collapse was rapid when it came. (Hawkins 1973:44–45)

Hawkins, adopting a position he shares with many, puts it more cogently than most. When the crown controlled no police force, had no standing army, and only the smallest paid bureaucracy, which did not extend into the country, it required the confidence and support of the political nation. (See Elliot 1973; Stone 1972a:116, 133–34; Hill 1966:30–31.) This situation, in the theoretical argot of this book, is much like the economic condition we have recently learned to label stagflation. Here where, as Bacon pointed out, those who had a voice in making the laws in Parliament were the same men enforcing them in the country (as cited in Cooper 1960:87–88; see also Russell, 1979b:3), a deflation of power affecting the political nation necessarily became an inflation of power when the executive endeavored to enforce his "decrees."

A situation of deflation, owing to its focus among those who provided services for the polity, became a situation of inflation, a situation where the symbolic scope of power of office exceeded the officials' capacity to assume operative responsibility for the implementation of executive policies. Hobbes pointed out shortly after the revolution that obedience allows the sovereign to do his office (1969:144); here the sovereign's officials were among those refusing to obey (Holmes 1980b:133–34; Fulbrook 1982:255).

By mid-1640 a tax strike coupled with the refusal of the local officials to collect ship money brought on the disintegration of the king's power (Zagorin 1969:116; L. M. Hill 1973:86). Charles had no standing army, and the army raised against Scotland was unreliable and mutinous (Clarendon 1888:340; Russell 1973a: 26; Wedgwood 1966b:307; Gardiner 1884, 9:159, 172; Stone 1972a:135). This inflation of power meant that the Country could disobey the king with impunity (see Willcox 1940:120–31). It meant that in calculating the possibility of making a revolution, the traditional constraint, the resort to violence by the government in a situation of power deflation, was a most unlikely possibility. Thus with Parliament able to garner the economic resources, the political support, and the legitimation necessary to make and institutionalize a facilitory rebellion, the king's legislation guaranteed its success.[18]

6. REVOG: The Rebellion

It is a commonplace in the historiography of the seventeenth century that the series of revolutions which broke out throughout Europe were in some sense generated by arbitrary taxation emanating from the central authorities.[1] Trevor-Roper's discussion is one of the most interesting. He argues that central governments were expanding from the sixteenth century, but only in the 1620s, a period of economic stagnation, did this result in a relative increase in taxation and therefore in anticourt parties throughout Europe. He includes Laud as one of these "Puritan" oppositionists, seeking to reform the court, and if we allow for a warp in our perspective, viewing Laud within the context of the "king's REVOF, and RELIGF" (see chap. 5 and the appendix to chap. 7), this makes more sense than seems apparent at first glance.[2]

If taken alone, this point of view is extremely misleading. It implicitly attempts to explain the three phases of the English revolution plus the Leveller movement in the context of a variable appropriate only to the first phase. Such explanations, even when coupled with some form of breakdown theory, are able to "explain" only that aspect of the English Revolution closest to the other European rebellions. (See Elliot 1963; Forster and Greene 1970; Mousnier 1970; Porshnev 1963; Coveney 1977; Moote 1971; Salmon 1967; Zagorin, 1982. Many of these authors, beginning with Merriman, recognize England's unique place among the seventeenth-century revolutions.) In this chapter I will try to remedy this error, in the context of an explanation of the second phase of the English Revolution, the phase most closely related to the tendential development of seventeenth-century English society (see chap. 4, above).

The first thing that must be pointed out is that the previous chapter may have created some confusion. I have treated all of the revolutionaries alike and have made no attempt to differentiate groups within the Country. Now, in explaining why some progressed into participation in REVOG, and why some fell back into neutrality or became partisans of the king, fissures present all along will become visible.

The necessary and sufficient conditions for the genesis of a rebellion, a REVOG, are strain at the level of goals, an open illegitimate opportunity structure, neutralizing beliefs (including a deflation of power), and a precipitating factor. Once revolutionary actions are committed, if they are to be routinized they must be legitimized.

REVOG

The now-completed facilitory rebellion redefined the balance of powers between governmental collectivities. Under great duress Charles had acceded to these transformations. Unfortunately for him, both his sincerity in so doing and the legitimacy of his actions were questionable. The queen told the papal agent that consent under duress was no consent at all (Gardiner 1884: vol. 4, 404) and Pym, along with other Parliamentarian leaders, was clearly aware that Charles was simply biding his time. (See, e.g., Wedgwood 1966b: 393ff., 414; Zagorin 1969: 225–26, 245ff.). In addition, the belief was widespread, and an integral part of the "divine right of kings" ideology, that the king could not cede any part of his sovereign authority (Figgis 1965: 5ff.). Hobbes, emphasizing a similar point although writing from a very different perspective, commented that

> by the law of equity, which is the unalterable law of nature, a man that has the sovereign power, cannot, if he would, give away the right of anything which is necessary for him to retain for the good government of his subjects, unless he do it in express words, saying, that he will have the sovereign power no longer.   (Hobbes 1969: 118)

We will see later how Parliament's insecurity was a major factor in its seizure of executive authority in redefining the collectivity structure of the polity.

The debate over the Grand Remonstrance may be taken as symbolic of the start of a new quarrel; it was the focal point around which the Royalist party was formed, and was a test of strength between Hyde, who joined the king, and Pym, whose "reign" began with this victory over the king (Gardiner 1884, 10:60; Stone

1972a:140–41; Wormald 1951:22ff., 28, 31; Zagorin 1969:301, 265 n. 3; Hill 1980a:14). With its contestation and passage the opposition we have called the Country broke up into two parts; one came to side with the king, one remained loyal to the Parliamentarian cause. Both were fragmented, and in the pages that follow we will analyze the major fissures within the Parliamentarian party.

The Grand Remonstrance may also be taken as symbolic of the nature of the revolution begun by the Parliamentarians. In chapter 3 I defined a "rebellion," REVOG, as an attempt to redefine the collectivity structure of the polity. As I noted then, this involves a seizure and perhaps a restructuring of what Easton calls the "government," but not an attempt to redefine either the political regime or the political community (respectively the focus of political norms and values). The central foci of governmental powers involve the specification and implementation of "executive decisions" and control over "police" powers. An attempt to redefine the organizational focus of these powers is a rebellion when that attempt is in violation of the constituted authority structure of the polity under examination.

In a series of ordinances passed during the second session of the Long Parliament, those who were in rebellion against the king's authority deprived the monarch of control over the government and gained this control for themselves.

> Perhaps the framers of their manifestoes did not perceive that under colour of declaring law they introduced the greatest innovation ever made in England's government. If so, the King at any rate knew better. In a critical review of the Houses' claims, he taxed them with making themselves absolute so as to become the sole disposers of all law and public matters by majority vote. He was not wrong.   (Zagorin 1969: 311–12)

Between the passage of the Grand Remonstrance and the beginning of the Civil War, Parliament laid claim to "annex both the recognized attributes of monarchical supremacy and a legislative power as well which the King had never possessed" (Zagorin 1969:311).

Parliament did not assert that it was sovereign (cf. Ashton 1978:179); to do this would have implied an attempt to redefine the political regime, the normative basis of the political system. Instead the parliamentary party adopted a series of evasions that provided them with de facto control, leaving de jure responsibility in the king's hands. One evasion involved a distinction between the king's personal and his regal capacities, between his person and his office. Parliament "asserted that kings are in conscience obliged to assent to bills offered them by Parliament in the name and for the good of the whole kingdom; Parliament is the fittest judge of whether or not a bill is for the common good" (Wormuth 1939: 111). As Wormuth goes on to say,

> This insistence that "his Majesties Authority is more in his Courts without his person, then in his person without his Courts" barely falls short of an absolute claim of power to govern without the king. What was lacking was pieced out by the doctrine of emergency. In cases of "extreme danger" the two houses might by ordinance legislate without the king.   (112)

Such a doctrine, while seemingly leaving the constitution intact, implied that the king, himself, might act illegally, but that in so doing he was separating himself from his office. Resistance therefore implied support for the monarchy, as the disobedience would be only to the person of Charles Stuart (Zagorin 1969: 281).

During the period of the revolution characterized by the rule of the Parliamentarians,[3] Parliament's rule remained, at all times, provisional.

> In March 1642 it was resolved by both houses that parliament, as "the supreme court of judicature in the Kingdom," would declare what the law of the land was, and that any questioning, contradiction, or command to disobey such law was "a high breach of the privilege of Parliament." Yet, from the time of the break with the King in 1642, through January 1649, laws were designated by parliament as ordinances, not Acts, thereby noting that the assent of the king was lacking.   (Hast 1972: 39; cf. Gardiner 1884, 10: 176; Clarendon 1888, 1: 594)

In short, Parliament attacked the king, but not the monarchy (Judson 1949: 18ff., 379; Schwoerer 1971: 72). The evasion was so great as to enable Parliament to claim royal authority for orders directly opposed to the king's orders (Judson 1949: 375ff.; Gardiner 1884, 10: 200–201).[4] From 1642 Parliament engaged in actions in direct opposition to the king's will and in clear opposition to the constitution (Gardiner 1884, 10: 176).

The Grand Remonstrance was a lengthy document covering much ground. (It is reprinted in Gardiner 1906: 202–32.) For our purposes, its major import was that it demanded parliamentary

control over the appointment of the king's ministers; it was therefore a major step in establishing parliamentary control over the
king (Coates 1932:9–10; Wedgwood 1966b:438; Gardiner 1884,
10:63–64). It passed by only eleven votes in Commons, and it was
submitted for printing and distribution to the people without the
concurrence of the Lords or, of course, Charles Stuart. This appeal
to the people against the king helped to open the breach with the
quickly constituted Royalist party (Pennington 1970:33–34).
There was, as Coates has pointed out, no legal justification for
either the main clauses of the Grand Remonstrance, or for the
Commons' appeal to the people (Coates 1932:15). Nonetheless,
the appeal to the people was important in creating a new justification for Parliament's actions.

Coates has suggested that the main proposals of the Remonstrance, "parliamentary control of the executive and the appeal to
the people," had not previously been considered revolutionary by
most members of the Commons (1932:16–17). Perhaps not, but
within this context, and with the imminent need to establish parliamentary control over the militia because of the Irish revolution,
their evolutionary consequences were obvious.

Judson defines three categories of the king's prerogative: "(1) the
special privileges accorded the king in law courts; (2) his prerogatives as chief feudal lord in the kingdom; (3) his prerogatives as
head of the government of the commonwealth" (1949:23). In 1642
Parliament worked to transform the nature of the third component
of the prerogative; originally this transformation centered around
control over the militia. The power over the militia was a central
component of sovereign power; for Hobbes it was the whole
of sovereignty (1969:79, 80, 98, 102; cf. Zagorin 1969:273).
Schwoerer agrees: "The heart of the issue was not just command of
the militia, but sovereignty in the state. When 'push came to shove'
who held ultimate power: the King or Parliament?" (1971:66; cf.
Weber 1968, 1:54). While one can argue with Hobbes and Schwoerer, it was true that for Clarendon, and for Charles, without this
control one could not be king (Clarendon 1888, 1:566, 590).
Charles was willing to assent to the exclusion of the bishops from
the Lords, which barred his most consistent supporters from Parliament, but he would not put control over the militia in the hands of
Parliament (Clarendon 1888, 1:566). He vetoed the militia bill,
which mandated parliamentary control. It was passed and im-

plemented as an ordinance. The Lords, with many absences, agreed to this, and Parliament put the kingdom in a state of defense (Gardiner 1884, 10:185; Snow 1970:293ff.; Zagorin 1969:301ff.).

> The assumption of military authority by the Lords and Commons in the King's name, against his expressed will, settled three issues in a stroke. The royal veto was swept aside. The military powers of the King—historically undoubted prerogatives—were disposed of as the two houses saw fit. Finally, the body was set to resist the forces of the King. (Mendle 1973:231)

Parliament viewed the ordinance as law; the king countermanded this claim and Parliament proclaimed those who disobeyed its will to be traitors. (The most important documents are reprinted in Gardiner 1906:245ff.) From this point civil war seemed inevitable (Schwoerer 1971:75) as a situation of dual power was established (Ashton 1978:140, 160). It remained for the Parliamentarians to consolidate their power.

The next months and years until 1649 allowed for only partial consolidation. Parliament endeavored to codify its control over the king's advisors. If the Nineteen Propositions had been accepted, something akin to a ministry responsible to Parliament would have resulted (Zagorin 1969:318–19; cf. 216–17, 247). Instead this consolidation of a Parliament-controlled executive within an integrated monarchy was "completed" only with the institutionalization of the REVOG in the period following 1688; during the 1640s Parliament was fighting the king; it did not control his actions. Thus the Houses had to establish their own executive arm.

On 3 January 1642, Charles had tried to arrest Pym, Hampden, Haselrig, Holles, Strode, and Lord Kimbolton for treason. The Commons refused to order their arrest and they fled to the sanctuary provided by the city of London. Charles, having failed in this coup, left London on 10 January 1642. He was never to return of his own volition. In the following months Parliament passed and declared law a number of ordinances, neither sanctioned by the king nor certified with the great seal.[5] And in July a committee of public safety was appointed, marking the first stage in the institutionalization of an executive controlled by Parliament.

"At the beginning of the English Civil War parliament had to create for itself, without precedent, an executive which was efficient for war, responsible to parliament and easily dismissed when no longer needed" (Glow 1965*b*: 289). This committee, the Committee of Safety, "developed into the first true parliamentary executive" (Zagorin 1969: 321). Previously the Houses had appointed committees to fill in as the king's power disintegrated, and to maintain control during the previous parliamentary recess. But the Committee of Safety, made up of ten members of the Commons and five members of the Lords, directly subordinate to the two Houses and charged with the defense of the kingdom, provided Parliament with "the rudiments of a Government" (Gardiner 1884, 10: 209).

In January 1644 the king convened a Royalist Parliament at Oxford. In February, Parliament joined by the Scots formed the Committee of Both Kingdoms.

> To the constitutional historian the ordinance by which it was appointed is important as containing not only the first germ of a political union between England and Scotland, but also the first germ of the modern Cabinet system. As far as the English members of the Committee were concerned, it was a body composed of members of both Houses, exercising general executive powers under responsibility to Parliament, and not merely, like the old Committee of Safety, a mere channel to convey information to Parliament and to take its orders.   (Gardiner 1893, 1: 307; cf. Firth 1910: 138ff.)

This committee, in April 1644, produced peace proposals that demanded Royalist capitulation. "Perhaps the biggest stumbling block to having the proposals considered seriously was the Committee's insistence on naming a day for His Majesty's return, failing which an alternative was to be found for governing without him" (Glow 1969: 7). Thus Parliament had established an executive, which proceeded to carry out the war with considerable vigor, defining as its goal a set of conditions which necessitated the consummation of a rebellion, REVOG, the restructuring of the collectivity structure of the polity (Kishlansky 1979*a*: 20, 105).

Parliament was to raise money without the consent of the king as early as June 1642 (Zagorin 1969: 323; and, more generally, on Pym's role, Hexter 1941: chap. 1). It was to establish its own administration in the counties (see among the many discussions Everitt 1973; Holmes 1974), and to raise its own army. It was not only to claim control over the king's counsellors but had instituted its own committees to govern in his stead, and in opposition to his expressed will. In the facilitory rebellion "Parliament" had included the king, and the balance between the Houses and the monarch had been redrawn. In the rebellion under the provisional government, "the Houses claimed the responsibility of parliament for themselves alone" (Zagorin 1969:309). At this point Parliament appeared to be the innovator and a Royalist party was formed; opposition to the king was no longer "unanimous" (Manning 1957:278; Judson 1949:43ff.; Wormald 1951:217ff.; Wormuth 1939:119). We must now ask what groups supported this new revolution, and why.[6]

Strain at the Level of Goals (SG)

This section begins to provide an explanation of the conditions under which a group supported Parliament's REVOG. I try to differentiate these groups from those that remained supporters of the king, the Court, and from those that became supporters of the king in opposition to Parliament's rebellion, the Royalists (a term that includes the Court).[7]

In this section I obfuscate the alliances that formed among the "Presbyterians" (those persons who supported the REVOG, but not the REVON), and between certain of them and those who were to emerge as "Independents" (those persons who supported the REVON). I say little about the War and Peace parties, about the Presbyterian and Independent parties, about the Middle Group, and about the Radical and Moderate parties discussed at great length by others (see n. 6, this chap.). Here I need only note that with the exception of those members of the War, Independent, or Radical parties who later became "Independents," all of these groups fall within my category "Presbyterian." I will later explain why certain members of these more radical alliances within the rebellion supported the next phase of the revolution, a REVON, and why most persons halted their revolutionary progression. I will also have something to say about those who remained neutral in the conflict between the king and his Parliament.

In chapter 4 I have written of prerevolutionary England as predominated by a "manufacturing" system. I argued that the tendential development of this system gave rise to key variables necessary for the genesis of a rebellion, and that one consequence of this rebellion and its institutionalization in 1688 was the natural development of English capitalism (see chap. 9, below). I further argued that one cannot point to a specific, static group and say that they made the revolution. On the contrary, a class, or any other social group, is constituted in its interactions with other groups. These interactions are structured, and the patterns that constitute these structures delimit, at any time, the groups in a society. In a historical analysis the concern must be the tendential development of this structure, and therefore of the constitution of those groups which make history. But one must not reify any group and attribute to it a conscious intention. Classes do develop (in accordance with the model presented in chap. 8, below), but the structure of this development is what constitutes the class.[8]

A social group is constituted in its actions, its interactions with other groups. But these actions are not arbitrary; they are delimited as a patterned set of constraints. This pattern is the social structure under examination. In this section I will try to determine the positions within this structure where revolutionary actions were undertaken. It is hypothesized that the theory outlined in chapter 3 identifies the conditions under which a rebellion will occur, and that the theory outlined in chapter 4 and here partially recapitulated specifies the locations where the tendential development of a manufacturing structure will generate these conditions.[9]

There is considerable agreement about the broad divisions to be used to categorize Royalist and Parliamentarian support. Most agree that there was a geographic division, with the southeast and east supporting the Parliament, the southwest, west, and north supporting the king. The former regions were economically more "advanced," and were supplemented by most ports, except those in Cornwall and Wales, and by most towns dependent on manufacturing. For example, "in Yorkshire, Lancashire, and Sussex there was a clear division between Parliamentarian industrial areas and Royalist agricultural areas" (Hill 1966:121–22). London sided with Parliament.

There is also considerable agreement that most nobles sided with the king; most, but a smaller proportion of the gentry sided with the king, but the nature of their distribution will be found to be crucial. The middle sort, those who made up an "independent middle class"—most yeomanry in the country and most domestic merchants, shopkeepers, small masters and their apprentices in the towns—supported Parliament.[10] Most below these groups in the stratification system either followed those on whom they were dependent, usually into the Royalist camp, or remained neutral. For example, Underdown has found evidence that in the arable areas of

downland Dorset and south Wiltshire, the common people "shared
(or followed) the neutralist or mildly royalist bent of the gentry"
(1981:76). But he also notes variations in this pattern and concludes
that "variations in popular political behaviour may be related to
plebian culture as well as to patrician leadership" (1981:90; cf.
Malcolm, 1983; Hutton, 1982).

Underdown emphasizes that "armies were recruited from the
poor and the marginal, and this seems to have been particularly
true of the King's army" (1981:83). In the recruitment of soldiers
he finds that "Parliament did best in the clothing towns, the King ...
in economically depressed market towns. It [his statistical evidence]
certainly demonstrates the continuing force of social deference in
places with a strong aristocratic presence" (1981:83). Likewise, a
protracted period as a garrison seems to have helped the king's re-
cruiting. In his summary he comments that "It is enough to conclude
that, for whatever reasons, industrial development and the kind of
society it produced can be associated with parliamentarian loyalties" (1981:84–85; Underdown 1985 appeared too late to be
analyzed in this context).

It must be emphasized that many in and on the fringes of the
political nation were neutral; even at the height of contention this
percentage might well have constituted a majority of each group,
excepting the nobility. (For summary statements see, among many
others, Brailsford 1961:6–7; Gardiner 1893, 1:11; 33ff.; Hill
1966:119–26; Howell 1983; Kamen 1971:312; Manning 1957:
383; Underdown 1971:11–13; Woolrych 1968:2–22). Finally,
we will later find that religious differences were also significant in
dividing the nation.

There is no question that ad hoc conjunctures were relevant to
the genesis of the conditions leading certain groups and persons to
support either the king or the Parliament. But if the predominant
tendency of development in prerevolutionary society was constituted by an incipient capitalist organization, the reality of this
tendency should be manifest in its consequences at the time of the
rebellion. It is important to understand that this tendency was predominant both in the countryside and in the towns, but that its
structures were not evenly distributed throughout the country. The
distributions of groups just outlined is explicable if we analyze how
the tendential development of manufacturing structures resulted in
strain at the level of goals for those embedded in it.

"It can hardly be an accident that the first of the 'Great Revolutions' in the history of the West should have occurred in one of the two societies in which protocapitalism was most highly developed" (Stone 1972a:71). It is likewise hardly a coincidence that those groups associated with the rise of the gentry, and the development of what Everitt has called a "pseudo-gentry," "that class of leisured and predominantly urban families who, by their manner of life, were commonly regarded as gentry, though they were not supported by a landed estate" (1966:71), supported Parliament's rebellion. In order to understand the REVOG it is essential to recognize that these groups of rising gentry, professional classes, and independent manufactures and merchants in London, the towns, and the countryside shared a common set of interests derived from their position in a common manufacturing structure, and that this common position was manifested in an impairment of the relationships between components of the social structure in which they were embedded. I do not wish to minimize controversies that might have been and which were to develop in this disparate group, but here it is my contention that their common position defined the structural basis on which strain at the level of goals developed.

Strain at the level of goals (SG) is most readily understood as a form of relative deprivation. If an actor, in comparing herself to another, finds that she has been unequally rewarded for "equivalent" performances, or unfairly rewarded in terms of her ascribed position, SG results. The existence of this deprivation is thus dependent on the standards used in making these evaluations and on the group selected for comparison.

In the terms presented in chapters 2 and 3, SG is manifested as an impairment of output across the factor boundaries of the polity (or some other "goal attainment subsystem"), that is, as an inadequate opportunity for economic performance, inadequate implementation of political responsibilities, or inadequate fulfillment of interest demands for the determination of governmental policies. As was the case for strain at the level of facilities, goal strain may be overdetermined, present in more than one substantive form, for any given collectivity.

One economically rising group, the merchants, felt themselves denied social prestige, and resented the affront. Other economically advancing groups, the successful lawyers and the greater squires, felt themselves

excluded from power by the Court, and also resented the affront....
Those nearest London felt the resentment most keenly, since they were
most aware of the discrepancy in opportunities. Though the gentry
in the home counties were better off economically than those of the
north and west they were more bitter since they knew what they were
missing.   (Stone, 1966:49)

These groups were rising as they were among those caught up in the
manufacturing system, either in country or town. These were men
who were advancing economically within the context of prerevolutionary society, men whose advance was in some sense threatened
by the king.

As I have argued elsewhere (in chaps. 4 and 8), an essential attribute of a "manufacturing" society is that the structure of actions
changes, while the structure of the beliefs legitimizing these actions
lags behind. Thus the ideals embedded in a stage four patrimonial
structure (see chap. 8) demand customary legitimation for the routinization of actions corrosive of custom. One consequence of this
discrepancy will be an emphasis on order and stability in the dominant ideology, an emphasis stemming from a dearth of both in
society (see Stone's comments in the selection cited under the title
"Social Mobility: A Conference Report," 1965:10; and 1966;
Hexter 1963; cf. Stone and Stone 1984:281, n. 17). A second
consequence will be an insecurity of those advancing into new positions in the stratification system. They will demand the perquisites
of their new positions, and they will demand control over policies
and programs necessary to insure and institutionalize their new
positions.

The rise of the gentry in the hundred years preceding the English
Revolution may be taken, insofar as anything about seventeenth-
century England may be taken, as established (Tawney 1954a,
1954b; Stone 1965a, 1966, 1972b; Thompson 1966; Stone has
edited and written an introduction for a collection of essays dealing
with the question, 1965). But this rise was not uniform; most did
not markedly improve their position. This differentiation is
reflected in the fact that the majority of the gentry appear to have
supported the king; evidence suggests that those most deeply
embedded in a manufacturing mode of production, producing
iterative surplus value, were most likely to rise, to be in a situation
of goal strain, and to support Parliament against the king. One
manifestation of this strain was a form of status anxiety.

Stone has commented that

> Given the traditional and conservative value system of the age, the great increase in mobility of all kinds in the hundred years from 1540 to 1640 probably created discontent rather than satisfaction, due primarily to the wide discrepancies which developed between the three sectors of wealth, status and power. (1966: 48–49; this confusion and the anxiety it often created has also been stressed by others: Ashton 1969: 316–17; Everitt 1969a: 30; Walzer 1968: 247–52)

In the latter part of this period, the personal rule marked a period of political and ideological retrenchment of the old order.

> This ideological pattern [emphasizing hierarchy, privilege, and position] and these measures designed to freeze the social structure and emphasize the cleavages between one class and another were introduced or reinforced at a time when in fact families were moving up and down the social and economic scale at a faster rate than at any time before the nineteenth and twentieth centuries. (Stone 1967: 22)

Thus those who "rose" within the context of an economic structure not fully institutionalized within the society were in a position of status anxiety or frustration. Their insecurity was exacerbated by an inflation of honors consequent on the Crown's selling honors under the pressure of fiscal needs (Stone 1965a: chap. 3). With this devaluation of one source of prestige, people searched for secure sources of status, the most obvious being ownership of land. In addition, in a society where "nobility" was no longer associated with military prowess but more closely associated with office, office in either local or national government certified one's position in addition to allowing for control over what might otherwise appear as the arbitrary policies of a patrimonial government (Stone, in "Social Mobility: A Conference Report," 1965: 10; Stone 1965a; Hexter 1963: 142ff., 1968); we will see below that these arbitrary policies were themselves an additional source of goal strain.

Aylmer has told us that office-holding implied an increase in status, but that while there were approximately sixteen thousand gentry there were only about eight hundred suitable offices available for them (Aylmer 1959: 235–36; cf. Stone 1967: 213–14). L. M. Hill writes that "the honour attendant upon being named to the commission [of the peace] was so great in the eyes of county gentry as to make them keenly aware when one of their number was overlooked" (1973: 67; cf. Mathew 1948: 44ff.). Hawkins has emphasized, "For an important, and perhaps growing part of the political nation, the central government was the focus of personal aspirations." He goes on to comment that while the governmental structure was not large enough to satisfy demands for jobs and perquisites, "it was not insignificant enough for such demands to be unrealistic and thus be dropped" (1973:45, 64). Hill emphasizes the financial benefits stemming from offices and indicates that their relative dearth, for those who saw themselves as the country's natural rulers, involved an "alienation" within the gentry (Hill 1966:70-71).

The strain involved in failing to secure an office might be paralleled by the threat to the political rights controlled by the gentry, perhaps even including those in office. Thus while Wormuth argues that "the ambition of the country gentry to attain a position in political life commensurate with their economic importance" was more prominent in setting the temper of the Long Parliament than a concern over property or religion (1939:18), Hawkins emphasizes, in this context, that "the thorough" led to a diminution of gentry control at the country level. He specifically notes the consequences of Laud's visitation policy, seen as a direct attack on the gentry's control over local parishes (1973:61-62). This local insularity and the desire to retain control over county affairs is stressed in almost all of the local histories of the period. For example, Sherwood writes that the "sections of the gentry class [of the Midlands], who in the exercise of local power enjoyed a degree of autonomy, resented the encroachment upon their political and judicial liberties by the government, which was the logical outcome of the King's centralizing policies" (1974:13; cf. Ashton 1978:chap. 3).

I am not the first to emphasize that the theory of relative deprivation may be applied to political goods, to shares in decision making; Stone has previously argued in the same vein, emphasizing that such deprivation was felt by many of the gentry owing to an attack on their authority at both the national and local levels (the personal rule and the thorough) (1972a:124–25, 132). There are a number of consequences we might draw from these arguments. First we would expect that those whom Trevor-Roper has categorized as mere gentry, men of relatively secure, stable, and limited social position, ought to be less likely to be in a situation of strain at the level of goals than those rising in status and thus insecure in their social position. Second, we expect that those closer to the fount of authority might be more likely to feel relatively deprived than those farther away, as the relevant reference group would be closer at hand; thus proximity to London and Westminster ought to be relevant. Third, we would assume that those entangled in a manufacturing economy would be more likely to be in a situation of goal strain than those isolated in more traditional counties, this for two reasons: (1) they would be more likely to be rising in wealth and therefore desirous of certifying their status in office; (2) the arbitrary nature of crown policies, for example regarding enclosure, would place them in a position of goal strain. Their structured interest demands, relatively congruent with those of more purely mercantile interest, would be frustrated by the inconsistent programs of Stuart partrimonial rule (see chap. 4, above, and the discussion of merchants later in this chapter). Each of these expectations is fulfilled.

As I have noted, the majority of the gentry appear to have sided with the king. It is the exceptions to this rule which are of interest. For example, Everitt has emphasized in a number of publications that counties with high percentages of new gentry tended to support Parliament; further, in other counties not dominated by a new, rising gentry, "there was also a marked tendency for the older, more deeply-rooted families to support the king, and the new gentry to side with parliament" (Everitt 1969b: 18ff.; 1966: 64; 1960: 21). The bases of these divisions are of even greater interest.

> The great exception to this general rule of gentry royalism is the south-east. In Puritan East Anglia, in counties within the orbit of London, such as Buckinghamshire, the royalist gentry were in a marked minority though there is Baxter to remind us that this may reflect the harsh realities of military power. (Underdown 1971: 28)[11]

The area around London is a paradigmatic case of the commercialization of agriculture. While it is conceivable that this commercialization could have occurred via a reintroduction of feudal mechanisms, it did not happen this way. Instead, here and in other commercial areas,

> there was a massive shift away from a feudal and paternalist relationship between landlord and tenant, towards one more exclusively based on the maximization of profits in a market economy.... The shift to economic rents was accompanied by a reorganization of property rights, by which more and more land fell into private control through

enclosures of both waste and common fields. As a result of this process and of the engrossing of farms into larger units of production, there began to emerge the tripartite pattern of later English rural society, Landlord, prosperous tenant farmer, and landless labourer. (Stone 1972*a*: 68).

The home counties developed a manufacturing organization in part owing to the pull from London.[12] It is not surprising then to find that these areas were heavily for Parliament.[13] Nor is it surprising to find reference to the economic effects of other cities.

> The growth of a larger and more diversified urban population in the later seventeenth century was a sign of economic growth in the economy as a whole. Urban development depended upon an increasingly efficient and productive agricultural system; it was linked with the growth of inland trade and the great expansion of England's overseas trade in the later seventeenth century; and it also reflected the strengthening of the country's manufacturing base. (Corfield 1976:231; see also Thirsk, 1967:211)

Finally, we find references to the political consequences of these developments. For example, in Nottinghamshire most of the gentry rallied to the king, "of that small number of gentry who declared for parliament, practically all came from the area within an eight mile radius of Nottingham" (Manning 1957:59). They found support among "'the middle sort, the able substantial freeholders, and other commons, who had not their dependence upon the malignant nobility and gentry'" (Manning 1957:59, quoting Lucy Hutchinson; see also Ashton 1978:84–85; Underdown 1981:84–85; Blackwood 1978; Heaton 1920:208; Mann 1971:4; Manning 1975:149; cf. Cliffe 1969:339–40).

In his "Note on Statistics and Conservative Historiography" Moore (1966:513) pleads ignorance in avoiding a thorough explanation of the differences between regions supporting the king and the Parliament (as indicated by the actions of the members of the Long Parliament). Unfortunately the issue remains unclarified. Although two very important books have been published since the appearance of Moore's essay (Thirsk ed. 1967; Kerridge 1968), my knowledge of English geography and of the exact relationships between types of husbandry and forms of economic organization is not adequate to allow a detailed analysis. In addition we are plagued by a dearth of information concerning the nature of the

Table 2. *Members of the Long Parliament 1640–42*

Areas of Parliamentary strength:

	East		Midland		Southeast	
	No.	%	No.	%	No.	%
Royalist	14	20	32	37	28	27
Parliamentarian	55	80	51	59	70	68

Areas where Parliamentarians were in a minority:

	North		West		Southwest	
	No.	%	No.	%	No.	%
Royalist	37	55	43	67	82	50
Parliamentarian	28	42	20	31	78	48

Source: Moore 1966, p. 512. Adapted from Brunton and Pennington 1968.

participation in the rebellion of various groups in various locales. The preceding arguments and those that follow are, then, consistent with what we know, but less detailed and systematic than I would like.

Moore prints a table that he constructed utilizing data taken from Brunton and Pennington (1968). The table, reprinted above, shows a clear division among the members of Parliament; those from the broad areas we might label as dominated by manufacturing structures supported, with large majorities, Parliament. Those from areas less developed were more likely to support the king.

Both Manning and Hirst have warned of attempting political delineations between Royalist and Parliamentarian areas purely in terms of the activities of representatives to the Commons; Hirst emphasizes the difficulties for the period 1640–42. Both add the additional warning that we cannot understand an M.P.'s actions without recognizing the pressures he might be under from his constituents (Manning 1954:74; Hirst 1972:196, 207; the second argument, while its relevance has been questioned in Pennington 1954:85, has recently been reaffirmed in Russell 1979*b*). These warnings are both well taken, and they make me reluctant to place great emphasis on the type of figures Moore cites. The consequences of the first argument, however, ought to imply the lesser importance of the relationship between the specifics of an individual M.P.'s actions and the nature of the locale from which he serves. The second ought not to affect Moore's breakdown of the figures, as it should "cut both ways." If it does distort the figures,

Table 3

	Members with Upward Economic Mobility		Total Membership of Long Parliament	
	Number	Percentage	Number	Pecentage
Parliamentarian	103	70	302	55
Royalist	39	27	215	39
Not ascertainable	4	3	30	6
Total	146	100	547	100

Source: Antler 1972, p. 155.

it should also diminish the relationship. Thus the relationships ought to be stronger than indicated, not false.

Our confidence in these relationships is built by other bits of information. Antler has provided figures, basing his tabulations on Keeler's data (1954), indicating that "members known to have increased their estates in the years before the Long Parliament" were more likely to emerge as Parliamentarians than Royalists. He also provides the information that members with downward mobility were more likely to support the king than Parliament.

Antler's information is interesting, and conforms to my predictions, but it too must be viewed with some restraint. His upwardly mobile group includes members known to have increased their estates by any means: marriage, enterprise, or via some undisclosed method. Those among this group who did not significantly alter their position within their county may well not have experienced goal strain; certain of them may have had a previously experienced goal strain alleviated in their successful quest for a seat in Parliament. Without more details than Antler and Keeler provide, all that we can say for certain is that their data appear to support our suggested hypotheses.

"The original conflict developed because men who were strong in wealth and local power, but who felt their advance hindered by some of the state's activities, wanted to increase their share of central authority at the expense of the king and his narrow circle of courtiers and administrators" (Pennington 1954:89). This argument is true not only for the gentry, but also for "mercantile interests" in general. Many have argued that for segments of the gentry and merchants, interests were the same (Stone 1966:29, 52; Stone 1972a:69; Tawney 1954a:175; Hill 1969b:76; Wadsworth and Mann 1968:56). One must circumscribe such a generalization for both merchants and gentry, but it is the case that, while Brunton and Pennington tell us that it would be impossible to draw up a list of gentry whose activities placed them on the fringe of the merchant class, among country families it is easier to find Parliamentarian supporters "exploiting local assets and opportunities," and Royalists supplementing income through "connections at Court and in the capital" (1968:66–67). Keeler's figures show that 72 percent of the merchants supported Parliament, 23 percent the king (Antler 1972:155). Brunton and Pennington's figures indicate that "all London Merchants sitting in Parliament, and all merchants representing places in the Eastern Association were Parliamentarians, while the merchants from the less economically advanced areas were divided between the two parties" (Manning 1954:75). In addition, while monopolist merchants supported the king, colonial merchants supported Parliament (Manning 1954:71; Pennington 1954:86; I will say more about these merchants later when I discuss Brenner's work). Can we explain these divisions in terms of strain at the level of goals for the merchants, as we have endeavored to do for those gentry embedded in a manufacturing system?

The merchants, like the rising gentry, were anxious about their position within society. Zagorin notes that there were numerous interrelationships between merchants and the gentry, and that the status ideology and snobbery that went with them denigrated merchants in relation to their landed countrymen. This led, he concludes, to a self-justifying attitude on the part of the merchants (1969:119ff.). Walzer confirms this status anxiety (1968:248), while many local histories directly or indirectly remark on it (e.g., Andriette 1971:21; Barnes 1961:6). In noting that "by and large, commercial and manufacturing interests seem to have been opposed to the King," Corfield indicates that their social position was not guaranteed by the dominant social structure. The status accorded to these men was not consonant with their wealth. She concludes, "These men had nothing to gain from the King and much to lose from his arbitrary policies. Those with liquid assets were highly vulnerable to the depredations of an impecunious monarchy" (1973:216–17). It is the last statement that is of special importance.

Almost all who write about economic questions are in agreement concerning the necessity of a formally rational governmental policy if capitalism is to grow and develop.[14] Lack of this capacity to intelligently calculate Crown policy was manifested at two levels: the first was a feeling of discrimination vis-à-vis those merchants who were favored by the Crown. The second and in the long run more important level was the general incapacity to have needed opportunities provided and essential demands fulfilled.

Pearl in her study of London and Howell in his study of Newcastle have shown the existence of divisions among the merchants, between those included in Crown privileges and concessions, and those jealous of these privileges (Pearl 1961; Howell 1967). This division was also seen in differing policy positions. For example, Supple remarks on the divide between those who opposed higher customs duties not approved by Parliament against those who had invested in the farming of customs; or between those in London who objected to Charles's pressures to raise money on the eve of war versus those who were prepared to lend more, in part, one assumes, although Supple does not indicate this, to protect their previous "investments" (Supple 1968:141; cf. Ashton 1960). These divisions appear to mirror the Court-Country boundary, until we recall Ashton's arguments (see chap. 5, above). Many and perhaps most of the merchants in privileged companies did not escape the facilitory strain associated with the REVOF, and in consequence supported this stage of the revolution. But they were not in a situation of goal strain; in fact, regarding them, other merchants were in a position of relative deprivation.

Brenner provides substantial evidence that those merchants who were members of privileged companies supported the King. He goes so far as to refer to the Levant-East India complex as "Court Merchants" (1973:74). The overwhelming majority of the members of these companies were constitutional Royalists in 1641–42: "Thus, of 78 men who traded in currants [within the Levant Company] in 1634, 1638 and 1640 and who were alive in 1641–2, a total of 48 can be identified as to political orientation; and of these, 34 were constitutional-royalists, 11 parliamentarian, and 3 left contradictory evidence" (1973:75). Brenner succeeded in identifying a total of 53 Levant merchants who allied themselves with the Crown. He is less clear about the nature of support for Parliament, as the other major group on which he focuses, the colonial merchants, while within a situation of SG, were not the major "Presbyterians" among the merchants. They actively participated in the REVON, while domestic merchants formed the backbone of the "Presbyterian" revolution (Brenner 1973 : 86ff.).

This distinction between privileged merchants and domestic merchants may be related to the different types of mercantile capital. As I have noted in chapter 4, mercantile capital may live as a parasite off a precapitalist mode of production, in which case it may reinforce the extant productive structure. Comparable to this were the merchants whose enterprises were based on patrimonial privileges; they were not an integral part of the manufacturing system even though they fed off it. On the other hand, domestic merchants were integral to the manufacturing system and must have developed interests consonant with those of the capitalists of that system. This appears to be the case; one can find in Pearl's analysis of the revolution in London through 1643 evidence that it was these domestic merchants who held the leading positions in the city's revolution that paralleled the national REVOG, and who provided the backbone of the city's support for Parliament (Pearl 1961).[15]

In chapter 4 I argued that one of the clearest attributes of most patrimonial systems is the patronage links the government develops between itself and supportive sectors within the economy. While it would be an exaggeration, ignoring the structural underpinnings upon which these ties rested, to say that the government created the economic organizations that then provided it with the adaptive resources necessary to continue functioning, the government did aid in the creation of such organizations. (See, e.g., Weber 1968; and for a brief statement concerning England, Tawney 1947: 196ff.) Also, its policies, whether consciously or not, channeled the economy in certain directions. In Tawney's incisive phrase, prior to 1640 English mercantilism was imposed by government on business; after, on government by business (quoted in Hill 1969b: 17). The earlier governmental imposition made impossible a rationalization of governmental policies in the interest of a wider business community.[16]

In the terms I have used in chapter 2, the possibility of Charles garnering political support from the mercantile-manufacturing community depended on the imposition of universal criteria defining opportunities for economic effectiveness, or else, if these criteria were particularistic, for them to cast a net wide enough to include those interests necessary for the continued development of the economy. Thus the interest demands of the manufacturing community could only be fulfilled when the level of opportunity provided to actors within the economy was sufficient to engender their support for the government in power. When this support was not adequate, a situation for the polity comparable to equilibrium unemployment for the economy resulted, only in this instance the consequence was not, as in the case of the economy, unemployment, but unfulfilled interest demands. This dearth of policy decisions, below a political "full employment" level, involves goal strain across the G—(factor)$\rightarrow I$ boundary, a goal strain structured into the situation by the king's need to provide policies favorable to the particularistic interests on which his government rested. The need was, of course, exacerbated during the period of the personal rule, but had been present throughout the reigns of both James and Charles, to say nothing of the Tudor dynasty.[17]

I have emphasized the unified interests within the English manufacturing economy. The consequences of the particularistic and therefore seemingly arbitrary nature of Charles's policies may serve to highlight this unity. Wilson has written, for example, that

> There was no official recognition, much less encouragement, of enclosure until after the Restoration. But since what was official was by no means always what was practicable, some enclosure did go on, by voluntary agreement, by stealth, by violence or simply by that flagrant inconsistency which was perhaps the leading characteristic of Stuart attempts at social and economic planning.   (1965:34)

If, in this quotation, stress is placed on an agricultural question, it is obvious that enclosures affected the health of English "industry," whether via the availability of wool or via the price of grain (and therefore wages); uncertainty regarding Crown policies was a hindrance to all economic development, and was found in almost all economic sectors (see Supple 1959: Introduction; on this general question, Nef 1964 is valuable).

Supple, focusing directly on the years 1640–41, argues that

> The crisis of mercantile confidence which, in these years, produced widespread dislocation in an already weakened economy, was largely due to the direct interference of the Crown under the stress of its financial needs, and to the sweeping public resistance to its political and religious policies.   (1959:125)

Supple emphasizes the Crown's tampering with the monetary system and the consequences of this tampering not only for London but for the outlying areas dependent on London for their own sustenance (124ff.; Corfield 1973:217). A salient theme in Corfield's essay on the "Economic Issues and Ideologies" involved in the origins of the Civil War is the arbitrary nature of Crown policies. (I have discussed many of these as they affected landowners under the rubric of SF.) She also emphasizes those policies that, while not confiscatory, involved economic dislocation. The regulation of industry fell under the rubric of the prerogative, and she emphasizes that this regulation created uncertainty even for those it benefited. The Crown was, for example, prepared to sell exemptions from monopolistic control to rival groups (1973:210–11). It was not necessarily that the Crown's and Parliament's policies would differ significantly in substance, although she at times underestimates these differences, but rather that Parliament was accountable; "the King on the other hand was not accountable and in his efforts to find an extra-parliamentary source of revenue had resorted to arbitrary measures, which threatened property rights and undermined business confidence" (1973:215). Those merchants who supported Parliament wanted a consistent policy aggressively pursuing their interests. "Consistency, except in the pursuit of fiscal expedients, was not the hall-mark of the Personal Rule, but there was an almost consistent reversal of the 1622 commission's recommendations" (Cooper 1970:85); that is, the recommendations of a parliamentary commission that studied the consequences of the depression of 1621, and which represented the interests of clothiers and landowners against the Merchant Adventurers who then were the dominant monopolistic trading company (Brenner 1970:48–49).[18]

The consequent goal strain for the merchants, excluding those dependent on benefits derived from the crown's prerogative, and for the gentry embedded in a manufacturing structure, led in the first instance to the Grand Remonstrance. Many of the grievances of those in the manufacturing economy were addressed in this document, but more important, these men went on to carry out a revolution that when institutionalized after 1688 enunciated policies that were broadly in their interest, within the context of a political system they could control. No longer was there to be a gap between their interest demands and governmental policies.[19]

The actions of the nobility allow us to reaffirm our explanations. The major pressures leading the approximately thirty nobles who supported Parliament into their actions (Firth 1910:77, 115, 153; Snow 1970:414; Stone 1972a:144) appear to have stemmed from their exclusion from position and therefore from control over policy decisions; it further appears that those so excluded were among the more economically enterprising of the nobility.

After the 1580s a noble's advancement lay in the court (Stone 1967:75–76, 191ff., 218; Stone 1965a:402ff.). This was the case not only for those aspiring to high office, but as Stone commented, "Every peer thought himself entitled by virtue of his dignity to a share in at any rate the more decorative offices of state or court, and when rebuffed he tended to join the country party out of pique" (1967:58). This assumption, that a lucrative and perhaps powerful or influential office was his by right, confronted serious obstacles in Stuart England. A lower proportion of the nobility held office under Charles than under Elizabeth. These diminished prospects were the natural result of the inflation of numbers within the peerage (Stone 1965a: appendices V, VI) and the much slower increase in jobs under the first two Stuart rulers. Consequently, unless the crown were to have adopted a deliberate policy of selecting peers for offices, the prospects of any securing a job were proportionately less than was previously the case. This was especially so for born peers, as against new creations who might have been elevated as a reward for prior service in office. While the ratio of suitable noble applicants to jobs was two to one under Elizabeth, only 33 percent of born peers took office under Elizabeth. The comparable figures for the early Stuarts are one in three and 22 percent (Stone 1967:214–15; the one in three figure comes from Ashton 1969:316, and is for the reign of Charles I). Thus at the very time when the noble was turning to the court to provide him a career (Stone 1967:215), his prospects were diminished. This lack of success was, no doubt, even more annoying as it became apparent that the distribution of offices was in the hands of cliques, and that offices were distributed in an inequitable fashion (Stone 1967:220ff., 228–29, 232). Kamen and Stone have both pointed out that rebellions have often been generated at least in part by the thwarted ambition of those who felt themselves to be deserving (Kamen 1971:160; Stone 1967:220). But the strain caused by this exclusion was increased when the clique in control was itself hated and deserving of little respect.

Buckingham had monopolized patronage until his death in 1628. Hexter has commented,

> If Stone's figures are even approximately correct, the channels of large-scale favor open to English peers, scandalously broad after the accession of James, became even more scandalously narrow twelve years later and remained so for about another twelve. During that relatively short time the Duke of Buckingham may have been the beneficiary of offices and rewards equal to those enjoyed by the entire Elizabethen peerage through the whole of the Queen's forty-five-year reign. (1968:57–58, citing Stone 1967: Appendix III, C, 775)

This largesse to Buckingham and his control over offices led to the exclusion of many qualified peers; two of the clearest examples are Essex and Bedford (Snow 1962:230; 1970:223–24, 235, 241, 300).

These tensions were, as already noted, increased by the creation of a large number of new peers. These men were seen not only as competitors but as social upstarts (Stone 1967:chap. 3; Gardiner 1883, 4:39). Newcastle advised Charles II,

> Making so many peers made the Upper House more factious than the Lower House. Nay, the House of Commons had not been factious but for them. For as soon as even one is made a Lord he thinks himself capable of the greatest place in England, though most unfit (partiality hath such force), and if he be denied, he grows factious, and makes parties, and joins with the House of Commons to disturb your Majesty's government. (Quoted in Firth 1910:3; Stone 1967:58–59)

Newcastle's observations were acute, except that it was not primarily the new peers who were rebellious, but rather a faction of the old peers, excluded from office and in a situation of goal strain. Firth wrote that

> It was observed, too, that there was a distinct divergence in political opinion between the two sections of the peerage; the old peers were generally disposed to stand up for the constitution against the court, the new were generally subservient to the King and the favourite [Buckingham], though there were marked exceptions in both classes. (1910: 20)

This divergence, with many exceptions, remained at the time of the Civil War. We can construct the following table showing this discrepancy.

Revolution in the Development of Capitalism

Table 4

	Old[a]	New
Parliamentarian[b]	14	8
Royalist[c]	34	65

a. Noble positions created in 1603 or later (Stone 1965a; index and appendices V and VIII–C).

b. The 22 peers present at Westminster on 22 January 1644, in reaction to the king's convening a new Parliament at Oxford (old: Northumberland, Warwick, Essex, Pembroke, Rutland, Kent, Lincoln, Bolingbroke, Nottingham, Suffolk, Willoughby, North, Wharton, and Hunsdon. new: Stamford, Manchester, Salisbury, Denbigh, Saye and Sele, Grey [of Warke], Howard, and Bruce) (Snow 1970:414; Stone 1965:index and appendices V and VIII–C).

c. The total number of peers in 1641 (NB the earlier date) minus the number of parliamentary peers; all those not listed as Parliamentarians are listed as Royalists.

Note: These figures are somewhat arbitrary. Snow lists 4 additional peers (Clare, Kingston, [Snow's index lists him as Robert Pierrepoint, but Stone's index tells us that Robert Pierrepoint died in 1643, and he must therefore be Henry Pierrepoint], Westmoreland, and Conway) who subsequently "showed their colors for Parliament," each of whom was a new peer (Snow 1970:414). Another possible list to draw from is the record of 29 peers qualified to vote in the House during the summer of 1646. This collection includes all of the names listed as Parliamentarians in table 4, excludes Snow's 4 vacillating members, and adds an additional 7 names (old: Berkeley, Dacres [Dacres of South], and Mulgrave. new: Robartes, Maynard, Middlesex, and Montagu) (Gardiner 1893, 3:105 n. 3; Firth 1910:153, where one additional name is added to Gardiner's list, Bruce). Of these additional 7, 4 were new creations. The inclusion of either or both of these additional sets of names would weaken the relationship seen in table 4.

We have previously seen that the old peers resented the new, but this does not adequately explain the relationship found in table 4 (where 29 percent of the old and only 11 percent of the new peers sided with Parliament), or the many exceptions found to that pattern.[20] Generally, Hexter tells us that the main economic innovators among the peers were pre-Stuart peers, our "old" nobility (Hexter 1968:28–29, commenting on Stone 1965a:chap. 7). But we must be wary of this kind of statement, as most such innovation was "speculative," not "capitalist" (Stone 1967:182). It also appears that there was a presumably noncoincidental conjuncture of three factors among those peers who supported Parliament: they were economically active, religious Puritans and excluded from office.

Stone tells us that

> Among the substantial minority of 25 percent who sided with Parliament, and so gave the cause its essential elements of patronage and respectability, there were relatively few new men or small men. Only one came from a family in economic decline over the previous forty years, and the majority were from active, enterprising, and economically advancing families. (1972a:144)[21]

These men also appear to have been Puritans (Stone 1972a:144; Zagorin 1969:92–96). Stone tells us that "an abnormally high proportion" of rack-renters in the Stuart period were Puritans, and such stringency regarding rents was an indication of a new mode of relationship in agrarian organization (Stone 1967:143, 156). Stone goes on to point out that Puritanism, in countering the traditional values of idleness and over-consumption, made a significant contribution to nascent capitalism (159). We can assume, I think, that these nascent capitalists among the peerage were overrepresented among those enterprising nobles who supported Parliament's cause. It should be emphasized that these are assumptions; I am not able to draw precise one-to-one connections.

> The great Puritan peers had had a considerable stake at Court in the first thirty years of Elizabeth's reign, and had still been influential for most of the reign of James. In the 1630s both groups [Puritan peers and the greater gentry] were deprived of powers which they had come to regard as a right. (Stone 1972a:125)

It has been pointed out by many observers who disagree about almost everything else that the nobility was of the same class as the gentry (Trevor-Roper 1953:9; Stone 1967:31–32; Hexter 1961: 128; Hill 1948:138–39; Mathew 1948:39–40). Given our previous arguments, then, we would expect to find strain at the level of goals present among those nobles situated within what appears to be a manufacturing system, especially wary of the uncertainties created by the personal rule, and excluded from any significant role in decision making. As far as we can tell from the data available, this seems to be the case.

There are two additional groups about which I want to say a few words: lawyers and "the middle sort." It is generally agreed that lawyers split into two camps; almost all civil lawyers supported the Crown, and although common lawyers divided, a significant group supported the Parliament (Levack 1973:1–3, 7–8; Wormuth 1939:5–6; Prest 1972). Civil lawyers were dependent on and thus firmly attached to the Crown; the common lawyers, following considerable controversy with the Crown, were free to select sides on other grounds when by 1642 the main constitutional struggles were over. There were seventy-five barristers in the original Long Parliament; thirty-three sided with the king, forty-two with Parliament, approximately equivalent to the breakdown of the House as a whole (Brunton and Pennington 1968:7).

We know that many common lawyers favored business interests (Ives 1968:117). This adherence was based on their integration into the propertied classes; the successful entered the gentry, and in general they were socially intertwined with the gentry (Stone 1967:23; Stone 1966:27ff.; Manning 1967:274). We would then suspect that their participation would mirror the divisions of the gentry, and this hypothesis gains some credence by the fact that Stone includes them among the rising groups who felt excluded from power, and notes that those nearest London felt this exclusion most keenly (1966:49). This view is reinforced when it is considered that the number of former members of Lincoln's Inn to sit as judges and barons of the Exchequer and sergeants fell markedly between 1625 and 1640. Lincoln's Inn provided the greatest support for Parliament's cause and had a markedly Puritan reputation (Prest 1972:225, 237).

It is very hard to gather evidence about the common people and their attitudes toward the rebellion. What evidence there is appears to be consistent. Generally when they took sides, the "middle sort" supported Parliament. (This is questioned by Morrill 1977.) Ranging from domestic merchants to masters and artisans and including yeomen and independent tenant farmers, an independent middle class was well developed in both country and town in seventeenth-century England. (Demographic breakdowns of the population are given in Laslett 1965; MacPherson 1962; Tawney and Tawney 1934.)

> In the middle class I include most merchants, richer artisans, the independent peasantry (yeomanry) and well-to-do tenant farmers. These were differentiated from the landed gentry and the ruling oligarchies of London and the bigger towns, on the one hand, by their lack of privilege; and from the mass of the rural and urban poor and vagabonds, on the other, by the possession of enough property to be economically independent.   (Hill 1969b:54; see Manning 1976:152ff.)

Although not very precise, this description will have to do for our purposes.

Manning has emphasized the consequences of the middle ranks' lack of privileges. He uses as his major example what he sees as a widespread antagonism toward ship money; among the middle sort this antagonism was not manifest simply as strain at the level of facilities, but was one indication of goal strain, here generated by the inequitable apportionment of taxes. He quotes a pamphlet from 1641: "The poorer sort cannot pay the King: the greater sort, as having the law in their own hands, will pay but what they please, but the middle sort, they must and shall pay; and in such a disproportion as is insufferable" (1973b: 108; in addition see his discussion in 1976: 154–56). This misallocation of financial burdens was also manifest for yeomen and farmers in church taxation, the tithes (1973b: 109; 1976: 156; cf. Hill 1971: chaps. 5, 12).

In an ordered society, where governmental policies had great impact on their economic well-being, the middle sort clamored for greater power. Manning goes so far as to comment that

> For the middle rank of the people the civil war came at the climax of a struggle for a greater measure of democracy in local affairs, parliamentary elections and ecclesiastical government—a democracy not extending so far as to include the mass of the poor (servants, labourers, paupers), but confined to the better-off farmers and craftsmen.   (1973b: 110; see 1976: 158ff.)

He further emphasizes that this movement was more radical in the towns, where they fought for a voice in local governments dominated by oligarchies, than in the countryside. He attributes this to the fact that the middle rank in the countryside had better established positions within a firm status system (cf. Campbell 1960) and had a share in running their own village.

Manning emphasizes one additional foundation of what I have called goal strain. He notes that the years of Charles's personal rule saw an increase in class jealousy and a fierce reaction against social mobility (1976: 156–58). The yeomen, for example, appear to have improved their financial prospects, primarily at the expense of husbandmen, during the sixteenth and seventeenth centuries (Campbell 1960; Portman 1974; Russell 1973a: 9; Trevor-Roper 1953: 9; Thompson 1966: 515). During most of this period their social advance and, if they were wealthy enough, their absorption into the gentry appear to have been relatively easy (Stone 1967: 122; cf. 1966: 34). With the ossification of the stratification system and the reimposition of traditional values for establishing prestige in communities (Hill 1969b: 68; Stone 1967: 19), goal strain was a real possibility. Those who were able to improve their position were relatively deprived compared to previous status incumbents who were used as a reference group; those who failed to improve their position were relatively deprived compared to those whose position improved.

> The small merchants, tradesmen, shop-keepers, artisans and appren-
> tices tended to be Puritan in sympathy and Parliamentarian in alle-
> giance, with a view to breaking the ramparts of privilege which pro-
> tected the entrenched oligarchy. In so far as these groups were able to
> seize power, which they did in London and Newcastle, they turned
> the resources of the city over to the Parliamentary forces.   (Stone
> 1972a: 145; see also Pearl 1961; Howell 1967)

This phenomenon should have been most extreme, I would predict, in situations where the social structure was least fixed, where old standards were breaking down and new standards were not yet capable of ordering actions of community members (cf. Thomas 1971: especially chaps. 13, 17; MacFarlane 1970).

About this, as about so much else, our evidence is imprecise and impressionistic. Because it has recently been summarized by Manning there is no need for me to cover the same ground. His conclusion is that

> In the extreme north of England and the extreme south-west, in Wales
> and the border counties, the ruling classes were mostly royalists and in
> these areas the king's authority remained intact. But in other parts
> of the country the king's cause collapsed when the royalist leaders were
> attacked by hostile crowds.   (1976: 166; see Hill 1969b: 131–34)

Thus those areas where the old social structure was more or less intact remained loyal to the Crown; in those areas, in town and country, where a manufacturing economy was dominant, the middle sort were effective supporters of Parliament. This statement is surely much too simple, if only because it ignores the many within all ranks who sought to remain neutral, but as a general summary it appears reasonably accurate. (For Manning see 1976: 166ff.; also 1957: 57ff.; 1970; 1973: chap. 3, and for an interesting general argument, 1967; for another brief summary see Underdown 1971: 11ff., chap. 2; 1981, 1985.)

No one has yet written a book entitled *The Crowd in the English Revolution.* In chapter 3 I stressed the complex, multi-faceted nature of any major revolution. I emphasized that under the rubric of what we label a revolution there are many movements of diverse cause and complex effect, and that many of the participants within these movements might have been chagrined at the real consequences of their actions. Here there is no space to provide a description of these diverse movements, many of which would fall under the conceptual category of a riot, making no attempt to redefine the political system, rather than a revolution (see Charlesworth 1983; Lindley 1982; Sharp 1980; Underdown 1979).[22] Instead I want to say a few words about those popular movements within the context of the REVOG which most directly affected the course of this revolution. I will thus overemphasize events in London and Westminster.

Within this context three different consequences of the popular agitations that complemented the Long Parliament might be mentioned. The crowds pressured the king and his supporters, as well as both the Lords and the Commons. Regarding the king, the fact that London was controlled by Parliamentary partisans and the fact that these partisans actively controlled the streets of the city forced Charles to flee his capital (see Clarendon 1888, 1:486; Hobbes 1969:27; MacCormack 1973:57). Russell calls this Parliament's first crucial victory, and it rested on the support of tradesmen and artificers who effectively controlled the streets of the city, and who were to form the backbone, along with their counterparts in the countryside, of the Parliamentary armies (Russell 1973a:8–9).

Many people have pointed to the split within the political nation over the mounting political action of their social inferiors. Hill has long suggested that the Parliamentary party was from the first dependent on the actions of their social inferiors, those he has called the "industrious sort." He has recently emphasized that "whatever the original intentions of Parliament, other wills took over from 1642–43," noting that clothiers in the West Riding and "common people" in Lancashire forced the pace by insisting on fighting (Hill 1980a:115). As Holmes has commented, "Unless the existence of groups of peasants and craftsmen who were perfectly capable of forming political opinions, and of expressing them forcibly in action, independent of the gentry, is recognized, events during the early stages of the Civil War in many areas—Somerset, the West Riding—are inexplicable" (1980a:72).[23]

Russell has commented that one point of distinction between Royalist and Parliamentarian involved their attitude toward the

people; the Parliamentarians reacting as "benevolent paternal-
ists," the Royalists with fear and anger. It is clear that one of the
crucial aspects of the Grand Remonstrance, that aspect that some
see as irrevocably dividing the two parties, was its appeal to the
populace, to the lower orders, instead of to the monarch (Russell
1973*a*: 10–11; Manning 1976: 49ff.). Manning goes so far as to
label the division between these two parties as between "The Popular Party and the Party of Order" (1976: chap. 3). Although this
may be an exaggeration in the connotations it evokes of later times
and different places, it is clear that one basis on which the Royalist
party was formed was a fear of the way the people were using their
newfound liberty (Hill 1969*b*: 128, 133; Ashton 1978: 152ff.).[24]

This fear and the capacity to manipulate it also had effects on the
ongoing process of the revolution itself. These effects were of two
sorts: the Parliamentary party within both Commons and Lords
came to depend on the popular support they received as a basis for
further actions, and this support was used to manipulate the fears
of certain recalcitrant members, especially within the House of
Lords. The first and perhaps most illustrative instance of this pressure on the Lords concerns the bill of attainder against Strafford
and has been vividly described by Clarendon:

> The next day [3 May 1641] great multitudes of people came down to
> Westminster, and crowded about the House of Peers, exclaiming, with
> great outcries, that "they would have justice;" and publicly reading the
> names of those who had dissented from that bill in the House of Com-
> mons as enemies to their country; and as any lord passed by, called,
> *Justice, justice!* ... This unheard-of act of insolence and sedition con-
> tinued so many days, till many lords grew so really apprehensive of
> having their brains beaten out that they absented themselves from the
> House, and others, finding what seconds the House of Commons was
> like to have to compass whatever they desired, changed their minds....
> (1888, 1: 337)

Gardiner informs us that these demonstrators were primarily merchants and shopkeepers (1884, 9: 350). Zagorin comments, "The
crowds were estimated at five or six to ten thousand. They consisted of shopkeepers, craftsmen, apprentices, and many citizens 'of
very good account ...'" (Zagorin 1969: 223 n. 5). Many agree that
it was the pressure of these demonstrations which dictated Strafford's fate (Gardiner 1884, 10: 108; Snow 1970: 263–64; Zagorin
1969: 225–26; cf. Firth 1910: 86ff.; Pearl 1969: 216–17), although

Hulme indicates that he feels the crowd would have been satisfied without Strafford's death (1960:118).

There were a number of other examples of this use of the power of the people of London; MacCormack informs us that the Lords were threatened into the attainder for Laud (1973:52) and Zagorin argues that they forced the exclusion of the bishops from the House of Lords (1969:299). These demonstrations were earlier integral to eleven bishops protesting that the sitting of the House of Lords was under duress and that its actions ought to be voided; these bishops were, in consequence, impeached (Gardiner 1884, 10:120ff.). But the most important instance of popular pressure during the early years of the revolution focused around parliamentary control over the Tower and over the militia.

In this situation we are able to get a reasonably clear view of how M.P.s in Commons utilized their popular support to impose a decision on the Lords. The disturbances that followed Charles's naming Colonial Thomas Lunsford, "only known as a debauched ruffian, who was believed to be capable of any villany" (Gardiner 1884, 10:108), as Lieutenant of the Tower have been described in some detail by Manning (1976:chap. 4). These demonstrations were interlaced with others aiming at different but complementary goals, for example a thirty-thousand-signature petition was presented to the Commons asking for the rooting out of Episcopacy on the 23d of December, the same day Lunsford was appointed to his position. The intent of these demonstrations was to put pressure on the Parliament to implement specific policies. These demonstrations were followed by others, no less specific in intent, but with different consequences.

At the end of January and the beginning of February 1642, a new series of demonstrations occurred. These were basically generated by the economic paralysis that plagued London, a paralysis that the Parliamentarians blamed on the uncertain state of the government. Thus when hundreds, and then thousands of artificers, apprentices, and other poor persons, both men and women, marched on Parliament during these days, they provided Pym and his supporters with the leverage to secure parliamentary control over the Tower, the militia, and the exclusion of the Bishops from the House of Lords.

Pym, in a conference with the Lords, warned of "tumults and insurrections of the meaner sort of people" (Manning 1970:11) caused by want of trade and consequent economic pressures. Later Holles was sent to the Lords to inform them of a petition protesting the decay of trade, said to be caused by the bishops, papists, and others in the malignant faction in the Lords. While complaining of the participation of such persons in parliamentary affairs, Holles warned, "They have not bread to put in their mouths," and noted that they were a sleeping lion that must be put to work; this, he said, could only be done by settling the affairs of the kingdom. This appeal was followed by hundreds of women, on the next day, besieging the Houses for bread, and on the following day, a petition was delivered representing fifteen thousand poor laboring men, porters; they warned of their poor economic situation, noting that "they would be forced 'to extremities, not fit to be named, and to make good that saying, "That necessity hath no law"; it is true, that we have nothing to lose but our lives'" (Manning 1970:12).

> Under this pressure the conservative majority in the House of Lords collapsed on 1 and 2 February and the peers joined with the Commons in a petition to the king 'to put the Tower of London, and all other forts, and the whole militia of the kingdom, into the hands of such persons as shall be recommended unto your Majesty by both Houses of Parliament....' From this moment the parliamentarians dominated both Houses. (Manning 1970:12)

The importance of this victory is obvious, coupled as it was with the Lords' passage of the Bishops Exclusion Bill (5 February). (The preceding three paragraphs are based on Manning 1970:10–13; cf. Manning 1976:106ff.; Mendle 1973:241–44; Zagorin 1969: 298–300.)

It is important to note that these victories were possible because the Parliamentary party was able to utilize, and to control, demonstrations within the city, demonstrations that were only partly directed to the Parliamentarians' aims.

> In dealing with this crucial question of the control of the forts and the militia, the minds of members of both Houses were directed to the economic crisis, with its attendant risks of popular disorders, rather than to the constitutional and political issues involved in the actual demand made by the two Houses. It was the apparent worsening of the economic crisis that provided the growing pressure for agreement between the two Houses, for the crisis was thought to have been caused by their disagreements. (Manning 1970:12)

The Parliamentarians had controlled the city streets from the beginning of the revolution. The populace's demonstrations against Strafford were crucial in leading to his attainder. By means of petitions, demonstrations, the activities of Puritan preachers and tavern clubs, they "created a movement which made a considerable contribution, underestimated by historians, to Pym's victory over the crown" (Pearl 1969:236; cf. Russell 1973a:29–30). The victory was cemented when the Parliamentarian party took over the City Common Council and gained Pym the backing of an effective armed force, the City Trained Bands (Pearl 1969:224–25; Fisher 1968:86).

Pearl traces the organizational ties linking Parliament and the city populace (1969:chap. 6); here I want only to reemphasize this case as an example of an ancillary movement to the parliamentary revolution, a movement facilitating that revolution and perhaps making it possible. The Parliamentarians in the person of Holles, a moderate, had actually presented to the Lords a petition exploiting the peers' fear of a popular rising (Pearl 1969:227), and although the moderates were soon themselves backtracking in fear of the people, they had made their point. When Charles refused to accept Parliament's petition concerning control over the militia and fortresses to persons trusted by Parliament, the Civil War became inevitable, and certain of the populace had the opportunity to coalesce and press for further gains.

Only one more set of variables must be mentioned prior to concluding this already overly long section. I have emphasized those structural conditions that underlie the genesis of strain at the level of goals. This goal strain was overdetermined within the context of the king's actions taken during the revolution, although the bases upon which these actions were interpreted were long-standing. Primarily these conditions indigenous to the revolution involved the genesis of a distrust of Charles, and a consequent fear for personal safety.

Englishmen in the early seventeenth century were conscious of the progress of absolutism on the continent (Cooper 1960:73). They saw themselves on the defensive, fighting against Catholicism and absolutism, and the loss of Parliament after 1629 confirmed them in their fears (Elliot 1973:253). They were further aware of the nature of both Laud's policies in Scotland and Strafford's in Ireland, and they feared these as precedents for what might happen in England (Hill 1971; Gardiner 1884, 9:222; Ranger 1967). Within this context, when Charles prevaricated by calling certain trusted members to serve in his Privy Council and then failed to entrust them with power, goal strain naturally resulted (Clarendon 1888, 1:174, 260–61; Manning 1973*a*:64–65; Snow 1970:249). When on top of this Charles sought to arrest five members of Commons and one peer, distrust for the Court was magnified a thousandfold (Clarendon 1888, 1:479, 583–84; Gardiner 1884, 10:129ff.; Hulme 1960:119–20; Snow 1970:290; Woolrych 1968:18; Wormald 1951:41ff.; Zagorin 1969:278ff.). The members of the Parliament recognized that Charles had the power to charge them with treason (Judson 1949:370), and at this time the Court "resorted openly to measures to overthrow men whom it regarded as its enemies" (Wormald 1951:44; see the series of actions, along with the distrust they provoked, herein described: 56, 59, 67, 81, 90, 113, 120, 125, 132. Cf. Hexter 1941:198). The emerging Parliamentary party saw themselves as forced to secure executive control, control over the executive, if only to secure their own persons from danger (Judson 1949:370ff.; Schwoerer 1971: 49, 57, 61). The possible use of force by the king made all granted thus far worthless (Gardiner 1884, 10:405; Hobbes 1969:133; Zagorin 1969:199; cf. Daly 1966). Thus the structured goal strain, delimited by the Parliamentarians' positions within English social structure, was over-determined by the king's actions within the context of the revolution itself.[25]

Opportunity Structure (O_g, REVOG)

Strain at the level of goals (SG) is a necessary but not sufficient condition for the occurrence of a rebellion (REVOG). The next necessary condition is an open illegitimate opportunity structure available to those in a situation of goal strain. Such a structure was available to those members of the Houses of Commons and Lords who supported the parliamentary rebellion.

In the first instance this structure was the same as that present for the facilitory rebellion (REVOF). As Members of Parliament, potentially rebellious persons had the opportunity to command the resources under the control of Parliament. The opportunity came to fruition as they succeeded in mobilizing a majority of the members of Commons, and as they succeeded in ensuring a majority of those present in Lords (by purging the House of Bishops and by coercing a significant number of the peers to flee Westminster). In a situation of dual power, the rebels controlled a major governmental institution and were able to issue ordinances that possessed a certain authority within the country. They were thus able to issue tax ordinances with some expectation that they would be paid. In addition, as Stone reminds us, exaggerating somewhat, "The list of leaders and active supporters of the parliamentary cause in 1642 ... reads like a roll call of the most important county families" (1967:9). These men were clearly in a position to use preexisting ties to mobilize support for the cause. And as Gardiner reminds us, from almost the beginning of the Civil War "England was divided by an undulating line, which left only the less wealthy and the less thickly populated districts of the North and West to Charles" (1893, 1:34). Although the king had considerable support outside these boundaries, clearly the Parliament controlled sufficient wealth and manpower to mount a good fight.

In addition, and perhaps as important, Parliament controlled London. Pearl has described in detail the tactics used by Parliamentarians within the city in financing Parliament's actions and in withholding support for policies likely to benefit the king (1969: 198–210, 226). Further, once Parliamentarians gained control over the city's government, they controlled the City Trained Bands, the only effectively organized armed force extant within the country (Pearl 1969:224–25).

Thus Parliament possessed the capacity to mobilize both the financial resources and personal services necessary to routinize a government. This is not to say that the king was incapable of doing likewise; clearly once the REVOG began he was able to mobilize a considerable party that supported his cause (Hutton 1981, 1982, 1983; Malcolm 1981; Warklyn and Young 1981). We will see that after the first Civil War this party increased in size and in strength as it came to encompass the "Presbyterian" wing of the Parliamentarian movement (see n. 3 this chap.). But just as clearly, it was possible for the Parliamentarians to not only mount a movement to make a rebellion, but to institutionalize this movement, if only in a provisional fashion, as the government of England.

Neutralizing Belief (NB$_g$, REVOG)

In analyzing the facilitory rebellion that divided the Country from the Court I emphasized the distinction between the subculture of revolution, those individuals in a state of drift owing to the presence of strain, an open illegitimate opportunity structure, and a set of neutralizing beliefs, and those individuals within a revolutionary subculture. While the former are available for the commission of revolutionary actions, the latter have legitimized the commission of these actions. The same division is found in the REVOG, only here the mode of strain, at the level of goals, limits the nature of revolutionary actions liable to be undertaken to those that seek redefinition of the collectivity structure of the political system.

Here we are concerned with the genesis of the set of neutralizing beliefs. These consist of two components, a calculating attitude toward the authority system of the society and the neutralization of barriers to the commission of the specific types of activities integral to the revolutionary actions undertaken. The former has as its social structural counterpart a deflation of power. When these neutralizing beliefs are present, along with goal strain and an opportunity to commit revolutionary actions, actors will calculate the positive versus the negative sanctions involved in the commission of these revolutionary actions. If the actions are to be regularized, they must be legitimized; in many revolutionary circumstances most people viewed as supportive of the revolution, and perhaps most viewed as opposed to the revolution, will be in a state of drift, neither actively and regularly supporting nor actively and regularly opposing the revolution.

We saw earlier how the king was able to gather a party by posing as the legitimate representative of the constitution.

> When the civil war finally came in 1642, the king, following the wise advice of Clarendon, made himself the guardian of the subjects' rights and property. Now many moderates cast their lot with the king, believing that their property rights and their traditional form of government were better maintained under the king than under parliament, which by 1642 was claiming complete control over the subjects' rights and taxing their property with little regard for their consent. (Judson 1949:43)

For these persons not in a situation of goal strain, the actions of the Parliamentarians generated a deflation of power within the authority structure constituted by the Houses similar in nature to the deflation of power generated by Charles during his personal rule. The Houses, in seeking an autonomous increase in their control over the economic resources of person and property, created in the minds of many a calculating attitude toward parliamentary power and a regeneration of the king's power. No concomitant authorization of the redefined powers of office claimed by Parliament was forthcoming among those not in a situation of strain at the level of goals.

For those persons (located primarily in the context of a manufacturing economy) in a situation of goal strain, the events of 1642 reinforced the deflation of power they experienced vis-à-vis the Crown. While in my opinion overemphasizing the role of monetary factors, Supple's summary description of this period is useful and worth quoting at length:

> The depression which settled on the economy in 1641–2 owed little to purely economic factors. In 1642 the "want of money" was seen as "an epidemical disease raging like the sweating sickness of late years over the whole land"; and it is clear that the constitutional crisis did have precisely this effect. By directly and indirectly reducing confidence it also increased the liquidity preference of merchants, and this must have manifested itself as a shortage of cash, a restriction of credit, and a reduction in demand.   (1959:131)

Here we see how the original deflation of power helped to generate an economic crisis via a reduction of economic opportunities (A—[factor] → G), and how this rebounded by accelerating the deflation of power.

This connection between economic well-being and the status of the political system will become clearer if we take a step back and view the situation from a wider perspective. In chapter 4 I argued that those components of the English economy dominated by manufacturing as a mode of production were producing iterative surplus value. Thus expanded production, within the context of an emergent capitalist economy, produced a significant increase in the absolute amount of surplus value. A consequence of this development was a transformation of the nature of expectations placed on the government concerning its economic activities. Within both Tudor and Stuart patrimonial regimes, the government was expected to ensure the stable functioning of a well-ordered society, and this included the economy. This expectation was a development from, while remaining within, a traditional ideology. With the genesis of Puritanism and the concomitant growth of a manufacturing economy, expectations naturally changed.

If in any system both economic and governmental actions are judged in terms of their own criteria of rationality (Hill 1969c; Offe 1973, 1974, 1975a, 1975b), as the structure of the system alters the nature of successful policies will also alter. Within the patrimonial regime that existed prior to the revolution, the small group of privileged concessionaires, the "Court faction," exercised great influence over governmental policy because of their capacity to withhold credit from the Crown. Their considerable control over the input of fluid economic resources to the polity (A—[factor] → G) gave their interest demands (I—[factor] → G) considerable weight (Stone 1966:28, 52). These policies were not necessarily in the interest of the wider manufacturing community, from which these patrimonial economic organizations often diverged (Nef 1957: 55).[26]

If we assume that at least in the long run, members of the political nation evaluate policy decisions and opportunities for effective economic and political performances in terms of a more or less rationally perceived self-interest, it is relatively easy to see how a diminution of economic activities, coupled with controls impelling the economy to produce ever more surplus value, would result in a diminution of support for the government held responsible for effective leadership.[27] We will see below how this deflationary spiral was crucial to the progressive decomposition of the king's government. And while it is very difficult to secure evidence about the distribution of this power deflation, it seems reasonable to assume that it, like the goal strain it appears to be correlated with, centered in those areas most directly affected by the spreading manufacturing economy, and thus those areas most directly affected by the commercial depression of 1641–42. As we have seen for London, these circumstances led to demands on Parliament to solidify its rule, and thus, via a transfer of political support from the king to the Houses, to the concomitant growth of parliamentary power, while the power of the Crown was progressively deflated.

If my previous analysis is correct (in chap. 4), these tendencies (embedded in a manufacturing mode of production) had long been present in English society; they came to a head for those situated in a manufacturing economy and thus in a situation of goal strain,

when exacerbated by the deflationary pressures generated by the
personal rule. At the crucial juncture of 1641–42 these tendencies
were increased by the commercial depression. At this point a split
occurred between those, on one side, suffering goal strain, possessing an open illegitimate opportunity structure and toward whom
the king's power was deflated, and on the other side, those who
were sympathetic to the emerging Royalist party. These two groups
were contentious factions, each seeking to dominate the government.

Thus there was a full-fledged situation of dual power, where the
Royalists owed their allegiance to the king, and where the Parliamentarians supported the actions of the two Houses. As Baltzell has
stated, "Viable civilizations, are, almost literally, *clothed* in authority; and when the emperor's clothes are removed his only recourse
is the exercise of *naked* power [force]" (Baltzell 1972:210; cf. Parsons 1967:chap. 9; Robertson 1968). In this situation, loyalists to
one cause caught within the net of the other were subject to coercion. Further, each side had to endeavor to establish its control
within the territorial limits of the kingdom, and this could only be
done through the use of force, in war. As Harrington argued, it was
the dissolution of the government that led to war, not war to the
dissolution of the government (Kamen 1971:328; MacPherson
1962:65 n. 5; Stone 1972*a*:48, 56–57).

In addition to a deflation of power, the revolutionary situation
called for the use of force against the king. The difficulty in neutralizing such actions may perhaps be most cogently illustrated by
quoting Manchester, who in 1644, while commanding a Parliamentary army, is reported to have commented, "If we beat the King
ninety and nine times yet he is king still, and so will his posterity be
after him; but if the King beat us once we shall be all hanged, and
our posterity made slaves" (Gardiner 1893, 2:59).[28] Manning has
pointed out that "when the King and Parliament appealed to arms
against each other each individual had to decide his course of action
in his own conscience. The first question on which he had to satisfy
himself was whether the use of force was justified" (1957:205).
Manning argues that there was little pacifist sentiment during the
early seventeenth century (206): "Scruples of conscience at taking
up arms against their fellow men were much less powerful in early
seventeenth century England than scruples of conscience at taking
up arms against their king" (207–8). The latter scruples were,

however, deeply internalized by many. The incapacity to at least neutralize this reluctance to coerce the king led many to either remain neutral or to join the king.

It is difficult to determine the source of this neutralization of the fear of using violence against the monarch. It was, no doubt, in part literally neutralized; that is, violence was used in fear of the consequences of the king's regaining control over the government. This situation is manifest in Manchester's statement, "but if the King beat us once we shall be all hanged, and our posterity made slaves." The justifiable lack of trust in the king, which we have seen was present for most Parliamentarians, continued for most until the completion of the first civil war, in 1646. Clearly, many men in this circumstance felt themselves to be in a situation where they could not win, and these men sought to refrain from action. Others, under more direct pressures, supported Parliament; some fought for Parliament, but not in good conscience.

There was, however, one source of beliefs which made palatable the use of force against the king.

> If indeed men did not dream of peaceful change, if they had been brought somehow to view violence and systematic warfare as the necessary price of reformation, this was because of the training that Calvinism provided. The traditional mentality, for which such a struggle might well have been inconceivable, was slowly worn away and finally altogether replaced by the collective and modernist conscience of the saints. (Walzer 1968:21)

Calvinism asked that force be used under the tutelage of lesser magistrates, and these aristocrats were at hand to command the Parliamentary armies. When this condition was present it was possible for Puritan ministers to justify forcible resistance to the king. The first such lecture, before the Artillery Company of London, was preached by Dr. Calybute Downing in 1641: "There is in England, he told his congregation, a 'Jesuited faction' which must be destroyed as the Israelites of old righteously destroyed their persecutors, the Amalekites." After this lecture Downing was forced to leave the city; he fled to the Earl of Warwick's house in Essex (Zagorin 1969:144–45; see also Walzer 1968:chap. 8; Hill 1971: especially chap. 3). Charles's association with the Irish intensified arguments of this type (see Clarendon 1888, 1:399–400 for an early, October 1641, indication of the volatility of this issue, and Gardiner 1893, 1 : 245–46, for a later example, in October 1643) and made many recognize the need to coerce the king.

"In 1629 no quarrel, however bitter, between king and parliament would have led to fighting because neither side held such a thing to be within the bounds of practical politics" (Pennington 1970 : 36). Prior to the end of the personal rule, deflation of power was not widespread in England. Thus animosities were deflected.

> It might logically be argued that by the end of 1627 Englishmen should have lost faith in their King and should have turned any love they had for him into hatred. But that was not the case. The vast majority of the land still venerated their sovereign, still respected him. Rightly or wrongly, they placed the blame for all the errors in government on the despised Duke of Buckingham.   (Hulme 1960 : 99)

After the calling of the Long Parliament, in a situation of power deflation, it was possible for revolution (REVOF) to break out, and to be supported by the vast majority of the populace. In 1642–43, for many of those in a situation of goal strain, this deflation of power worsened. Gardiner focuses on Waller's plot, the king's plan to seize the major military positions in London and to imprison Lord Mayor Pennington, Pym, and Hampden, among many others. When this plot became known, it was also known that Charles was in direct communication with the Irish rebels, and Pym's report to the Houses on 6 June 1643 generated great indignation and directed that indignation against the king, who was seen "no longer as a sovereign led astray by evil counsellors, but as a conspirator against the peace and safety of the nation."[29] The consequence of this episode was the adoption of a Parliamentary Covenant, binding those who took it "to support the forces raised in defence of Parliament against those raised by the King, 'so long as the Papists now in open war against the Parliament shall by the force of arms be protected from the justice thereof'" (Gardiner 1893, 1 : 148–49).[30]

Thus goal strain and an open illegitimate opportunity structure were placed in conjunction, where they were joined with a deflation of the king's power and a neutral attitude toward the use of force. While it is not possible to provide clear ecological and demographic data to display this overlap, the presence of each variable seems to be most pronounced in places characterized by a manufacturing economy, which was itself intertwined with an ascetic Protestant religious ideology (see chap. 4, above).

Precipitating Factor (P_g, REVOG)

On 1 November 1641 the House of Commons was scheduled to discuss the Grand Remonstrance. This was also the day that Westminster received word that the Native Irish were staging a revolution (Gardiner 1884, 10:43). This revolution and the necessity to react to it served as the precipitant of Parliament's rebellion.

In chapter 3 we saw that the precipitating factor can operate in a number of ways. Often one of its consequences is to reinforce already extant variables, and often it helps to create a conjuncture in which action is mandated and in which, for those in a state of drift, revolutionary actions are possible. The Irish revolution did both of these things.

In the first instance it magnified the country's fear of Catholicism (Clifton 1973). In consequence it magnified the opposition's fear of Charles, "for the Irish rebels falsely claimed his sanction for their seizure of protestant property" (Woolrych 1968:17). The association between Charles and Catholicism had always been close in the minds of many of his subjects; among other things his wife was Catholic and his archbishop was seen as introducing innovations that seemed closer to Catholicism than to "true religion." The Irish revolution reaffirmed this linkage in the minds of many, reinforcing the fear of the king felt by many and intensifying loss of respect for the monarchy.

These consequences, although severe, were magnified in importance by the necessity of reaction to the Irish revolution.[31]

> Ever since the collapse of the government in 1640, there had been a vacuum of power, a situation which, had it not been for the Irish Rebellion, might have been allowed to continue for some time until the political crisis had been settled. But now there arose the necessity of raising an army, and therefore the question of who was to control it.   (Stone 1972a:138)

The immediate issue that led to the Civil War was the question of who would control the militia (Underdown 1971:9; Schwoerer 1971) and this became the crucial issue when the Irish rebelled.

Clearly the king could not be trusted with control over an army capable of subduing the Irish, and Pym began demanding control over the king's advisors. The Additional Instruction was Pym's immediate response to the Irish rising. "Undoubtedly no proposal of so distinctly revolutionary a character had yet been adopted by the Commons.... The Additional Instruction seized upon the executive power itself, so far at least as Ireland was concerned" (Gardiner 1884, 10:57). A little more than three weeks after notice of the Irish revolution, the Grand Remonstrance was passed and Parliament's rebellion was in the making, while the country slowly began preparing for the Civil War many now viewed as inevitable.

Legitimizing Beliefs (LB$_g$, REVOG)

In discussing the legitimation of Parliament's rebellion we confront the same issues as in the discussion of the facilitory rebellion: the specifics of the beliefs that were utilized in order to legitimize Parliament's actions, the relation of these beliefs to the transformation from one stage of social development into another, and the organizational context within which these beliefs grew. It is important to note in regard to both the first and the second of these areas that we are dealing with the establishment of a provisional government and that the commitments that legitimized this government were not articulated within a systematic framework. What we find, instead, are utterances that are often ad hoc legitimations and descriptions of the revolutionary events. As this stage of the revolution did not directly attack either norms or values within the polity, these statements were, in general, made within the context of prior tradition. This should not mislead us with regard to the radical disjunction between them and the commitments embedded in that tradition (Schwoerer 1971:63).

"It was the Long Parliament that accomplished the decisive alteration when it divorced the king's natural capacities from his political capacities and itself absorbed the latter" (Hanson 1970:312). With the articulation of this distinction, substantively similar to the fourteenth-century treason of the Despensers (1970:313), Parliament put itself in a situation where it might act to preserve the safety of the state and the welfare of the nation. If only Parliament could legitimize its assumption of a power that was in fact, if not in name, sovereign, the Despensers' doctrine appeared capable of legitimizing its actions within the context of prior English political tradition.

During the first civil war, Parliament never abandoned the attempt to legitimize its actions in terms of the law and constitution. They argued that they, as the highest court in the land, were the true interpreters of the law, and basing their contention on the separation of the king's personality from his role, claimed that they were acting in the name of the king. Nonetheless, "Hyde's straightforward declarations presenting the king's case had made it all too evident that the king had now [after 1642] become the guardian of the law and constitution which parliament had broken" (Judson 1949:379). The king's resistance to Parliament's claim of acting in his name, supported by legal arguments, had commanded a considerable following, and the Houses found themselves justifying their claim to issue ordinances in the name of the king on (what were implicitly) political grounds. Between 1642 and 1649 Parliament never fully rationalized these arguments (Franklin 1978: chap. 2), but it is possible to show that the arguments made by Parliament during the REVOG are structurally different from the traditional arguments within a patrimonial system; in other words, it will be possible to show that Parliament's arguments in support of its actions were coherent only within a normative structure radically different from that legitimizing a patrimonial system. The new structure will be shown to be intelligible only within the context of a cultural logic defined in terms of religious beliefs.

> More and more in the Long Parliament the arguments became political, as the aggressive demands and desires of the leaders increased. Their growing claims, beginning with the Grand Remonstrance, and continuing right up to the Nineteen Propositions [and beyond], could not be presented on the basis of the law and constitution, but only on the basis of their responsibility to the nation.   (Judson 1949:226)[32]

While not abandoning the fight for the law and the constitution, Parliament had to find a political defense for its own guardianship of that law and that constitution; these arguments involved legitimizing fundamental transformations in both. Parliament defined its role as serving the welfare of the people and assuring the safety of the state; these roles were justified through a theory that articulated Parliament's trusteeship for the people. The implications of this theory were that Parliament was a contrivance created in the people's name and representing the people's will in government. A consequence of this theory was to be the definition of the sovereignty of Parliament.

> If a legal argument could be used, it was employed. When, however, the law supported the claims of the royalists, as it often did, the more ardent parliamentary leaders refused to accept a legal defeat, but pushed forward as representatives of the nation at large, claiming that parliament, and particularly the house of commons, was entrusted with the responsibility for the general welfare of the commonwealth. (Judson 1949: 275)

It was as custodians of the nation's welfare that Parliament justified its assumption of the king's rights. The assumption of this trust was legitimized as necessary to protect the safety of the people and the state.

Wormuth tells us that Parliament's argument passed through three stages: the claim of exclusive right to counsel the king; the adoption of the Despensers' argument, separating the role of the king from his person, and the adoption of the emergency doctrine (1939: 109ff.). "In cases of 'extreme danger' the two houses might by ordinance legislate without the king, and the ordinance of the militia was only the first exercise of legislative power under the pretense of necessity" (Wormuth 1939: 112). The primary basis the Parliament adopted to legitimize its actions was the doctrine of necessity on behalf of the general welfare, the same argument they had attacked the Crown for employing (Judson 1949: 364–66; Wormuth 1939: 113–14). In a pamphlet published in 1642, Charles Herle brought the argument full circle. He maintained that Parliament's resistance to the king, itself justified by the necessity of a secure and safe state,

> was "legal," i.e., according to the original law and constitution. When the king would not act to save the state, then the people in parliament might act alone, against the king's personal wishes, because the constitution provided and allowed for resistance by parliament. The people set up government and gave to parliament the legal constitutional right to resist the king. (Judson 1949: 420)

Herle's argument seems persuasive, but in fact it is as arbitrary as the king's. Its success against the king and his progeny depended on a fundamental transformation of the logic by which statements legitimizing and justifying political power were made. I have discussed this logic in chapter 8, below; here I will only sketch the high points of that discussion as they are directly related to the arguments of the 1640s.

Against the Parliament's claim that it was the guardian of the nation's safety and welfare, Charles commented that

> he had often heard of the great trust that by the law of God and man was committed to the King for the defence and safety of his people, but as yet he never understood what trust or power was committed to either or both Houses of Parliament without the King; they being summoned to counsel and advise the King. But by what law or authority they possess themselves of his majesty's proper right and inheritance, he was confident that as they had not, so they could not shew.   (Quoted in Clarendon 1888, 2: 58)

Charles's reply rests upon the law and constitution of his realm. To simplify greatly, authority descends from above and is vested in the king; he may share that authority, if he chooses, with Parliament, but the safety and welfare of the kingdom are entrusted to him as the apex of a pyramid that defines English social structure.

Parliament's reply was as follows:[33]

> There must be a Judge of that Question wherein the safety of the Kingdom depends (for it must not lie undetermined). If then there be not an agreement between his Majestie and his Parliament, either his Majestie must be the Judge against his Parliament, or the Parliament without his Majestie.... Besides, if his Majestie in this difference of opinions should be Judge, he should be judge in his own Case, but the Parliament should be Judges between his Majestie and the Kingdom, as they are in many, if not in all cases.... And if the Kingdom best knows what is for its own good and preservation; and the Parliament be the Representative Body of the Kingdom, it is easy to judge who in this case should be the Judge.... We do not say this, as if the Royall Assent were not requisite in the passing of Laws nor do, as ever did we say, that because his Majesty is bound to give his consent to good Laws, presented to him in Parliament: that, therefore they shall be Laws without his consent or at all Obligatory. Saving only for the necessary preservation of the Kingdom whilst that necessity lasteth, and such consent cannot be obtained. (As quoted in Wormuth 1939: 112)

I have quoted this passage at such length as it is an especially clear indication of the nature of the assumptions Parliament made in defending its position. Its authority was as a representative of the kingdom, which is assumed to know its own interest. Such statements make sense only within a specific context.

After quoting a passage where the Houses "claim" sovereign power to issue a militia ordinance, while at the same time they "refuse to claim such a power," Zagorin comments that

> underlying their arguments was the notion that they, as the kingdom's representative body, were entitled to declare the law and to determine public policy in the commonwealth's interest. It was therefore the idea of the Houses as representative—as being, quintessentially, the community itself—that constituted the tacit theoretical basis of the Parliamentarian case.   (1969:310)

This assumption, that the houses were entrusted by the kingdom to act in its name, was often found in its declarations.

In her analysis of three parliamentary thinkers, Hunton, Herle, and Parker, Judson helps us to see the dilemma confronted by Parliament (see also Franklin 1978:chap. 2). Hunton articulated a cogent and coherent theory of mixed monarchy. For him the power of legislation "(the supreme or sovereign power) was in 'three distinct concurrent Estates, the consent and concourse of all most free, and none depending on the will of the other' was 'in the very modell of it ... a mixed constitution'" (Weston 1965:36, quoting Hunton, "A Treatise of Monarchie," 1643). Because he was a consistent thinker, this analysis created a problem for him. If correct, there could be no resolution to the question of which branch of government was supreme in case of conflict, and Hunton insisted that this was so. If one power was supreme, then the government was not mixed, but rather one power absolute. Hunton criticized both Royalists and Parliamentarians for claiming this power for their agent.

Nonetheless, Hunton was an active, if unrewarded, supporter of Parliament (Judson 1949:384 n. 2, 405–6). If neither estate could be allowed supremacy, and if the estates were deadlocked, and if what we have referred to as a situation of dual power was extant, then "in this case, which is beyond the Government, the Appeal must be to the Community, as if there were no Government" (Hunton, "A Treatise," as quoted in Hanson 1970:317–18). Thus it was the community, which was "prior" to government, which was vested with the power to decide between the contending estates. Hunton believed that the community ought to support Parliament.

He argued that "the judgment of the two houses ... is better than the judgment of private men, for it is made 'by the best eyes of the Kingdom.' Private men should therefore be guided by that judgment." The Houses were acting to preserve and save the kingdom, and each individual must make the individual judgment to support their cause (Judson 1949:405–6, quoting "A Treatise").

Although Hunton allowed for an appeal to the people, he was not capable of rationalizing their decision. It was no coincidence that he was not rewarded by Parliament; his arguments were too neutral, and although, as we will see later, they would have made sense to most Puritans who sided with Parliament, they were too indecisive about crucial issues. Hunton's judgment on the basis of conscience reduces itself "to the judgment of heaven as expressed in the outcome of a trial by battle" (Pocock 1975:368). And once again, while this argument would have made sense to most of his Puritan readers, who shared this view, and while it may have been the basis upon which he was able to support Cromwell, it was not satisfactory in and of itself as a legitimation for Parliament's actions (on Hunton as a supporter of Cromwell, see Judson 1949:384 n. 2; on Cromwell, see Hill 1972*a*:chap. 9). Hunton provides a cogent rationalization for the REVOF, but his arguments for the REVOG had to be carried further than he was desirous of taking them. As Judson comments, his legal and constitutional views were "really outdated ... before he wrote his *Treatise of Monarchie* [in 1643]" (1949:408 and 425).

We will find in chapter 7 that an argument like Hunton's might have radical consequences. He may be read as vesting ultimate control within a community extant prior to the government. In this case neither the king nor Parliament possesses the final decision, but rather this control is vested in the people. This point of view allowed for the development of a more democratic theory than most Parliamentarians were desirous of supporting; it also made the final decision as to which party merited the people's support arbitrary, decisionistic (cf. Habermas 1974:265, on decisionism; Hanson 1970:318; Pocock 1975:367–68, on Hunton). It further made the type of government men might establish an arbitrary decision (Judson 1949:397–98). What was needed, however, was a set of arguments capable of legitimizing the revolution Parliament was undertaking against the king. Such arguments were provided by Parker and Herle (Judson 1949:407ff.).

Both Parker and Herle were aware that legal arguments were insufficient, and both saw the people as the source of government's power. Parker explicitly recognized the prior existence of the people, but this prior existence resembled Hobbes's state of nature; out of necessity men created government. This is crucial, for it necessitated the establishment of a sovereign capable of wielding an arbitrary power.[34] Thus while government was based on popular consent, sovereignty was lodged with Parliament. "The two houses actually claimed sovereign power for themselves and *exercised it in the part of the nation under their control* [italics mine]" (Judson 1949:377).

"Both Parker and Herle gave sovereign power to the two houses of parliament, and both emphatically denied that the people possessed such power out of parliament. To both men parliament and people were identical for all political purposes" (Judson 1949:429; cf. Weston and Greenberg 1981:292 n. 5). Both were therefore forced to view Parliament's power as arbitrary, and in the last instance as absolute; the people were not capable of resisting any of its actions. "According to Herle, parliament cannot be resisted, even if it should 'enact Paganisme itselfe'" (Judson 1949:431). Parliament was the "'essence' of the people; its actions, even against the king and law, could not be questioned, for it was acting for the welfare of all" (417, quoting Parker; the above two paragraphs are based on Judson 1949:407ff.).[35]

Judson comments that with Herle and Parker "the transition from the medieval to the modern became explicit. With them the pendulum definitely swung away from God and His law, reaching down and guiding man, towards man and his concerns and actions as the central and guiding force in state life" (1949:423). Both men's writings were embedded in a problematic that differentiated between government and people; that is, the societal community was assumed to be differentiated from the government. For both God was transcendent, not directly involved in the direction of government. The form of government was legitimated from below, and at least for Parker, was derivative from the people. Government was premised on the capacity of the people to arbitrarily select its form, and it was empowered to arbitrarily determine policy. Parker moved close to arguing that reason, not precedent, was decisive in determining the nature of government and its policies, but neither he nor Herle completely formulated an image of natural, law-like movement of civil society (the economy plus the societal community) and neither was an egalitarian, basing decisions on a procedural, formal rationality that differentiated between constitutive and constituted rules. But within the parliamentary rebellion we come close to the genesis of commitments justified by formally rational norms (see chap. 8, below), and we do find a legitimation for vesting in Parliament, as the embodied people, wardship over the redefined law and constitution. If we examine the ways in which these commitments were overdetermined, it will be possible to briefly articulate a little of the religious structure that made them intelligible.

To make statements that assume that the people exist prior to the constitution of government, that authority ascends from the people, and that a government entrusted with sovereign authority wields arbitrary powers, is to deny the traditional-hierarchical normative structures associated with stages three and four in our model of societal development. It is not yet to articulate a coherent vision of procedural egalitarianism, as in stage five (see chap. 8, below). For these arguments to be intelligible they must rest on some prior consensus that specifies the context within which they are articulated. This consensus was defined, for seventeenth-century Englishmen, by Puritanism.

In chapter 4 I noted the effects of Puritanism on the tendential development of English society and specified certain of the ideational characteristics of Puritanism which controlled these tendencies. I do not want to repeat that analysis. Instead I want to show that Puritanism provided the context within which the revolutionary political actions that comprised Parliament's rebellion took place. Unfortunately the data are not available to make a crucial discrimination; it is impossible to determine empirically whether Puritans tended to support the Parliament because their beliefs made intelligible the arguments Parliament used in support of its actions, or whether Puritans supported Parliament because the social networks that constituted Puritan organization were the basis on which Parliament's forces were mobilized. There is every reason to suspect that there was no clear-out discrimination between the two; certain persons supported Parliament because its actions and arguments made sense to them; this sense was reinforced because those near to them capable of wielding a "personal influence" (Katz and

Lazerfeld 1955) on them also supported Parliament (see chap. 3, above). In any case, almost all the evidence we possess indicates that Parliament's support, both at Westminster and in the counties, came from the Puritan faction.[36]

> The overwhelming majority of the members who remained at Westminster after 1642 were Puritans in the broad, undifferentiated moral sense used by Baxter. They took religion seriously, disliked sabbath-breaking, stage plays, church-ales and long hair, wished to purge the Church of England of the "popish" innovations introduced by the Arminians, and to have no more of episcopacy as practised in the 1630s. They were not necessarily opposed to bishops in principle ... but by 1643 the case for episcopacy had gone by default, for the choice was between Laudian bishops and none at all.   (Underdown 1971:15–16, where he cites Hexter 1963:177; see also Yule 1958:32–33)

In his general survey *The Revolt of the Provinces* Morrill comments:

> What emerges quite clearly from a study of the activists in the summer of 1642 (those who pushed themselves forward) is that, for them, religion was the crucial issue. Quite simply, in most counties the active royalists are the defenders of episcopacy who saw in puritanism a fundamental challenge to all society and order, and the parliamentarians are those determined to introduce a godly reformation which might, for a few of them, leave room for bishops, but in most cases did not. What the puritan activists did agree on, however, was the need to go beyond a restoration of traditional pre-Laudian erastian anglicanism to create a new, militant evangelical Church.   (1976:47)[37]

At both the center and the periphery support for Parliament, especially among activists, was linked to Puritanism.

Stone argues that Puritanism made two contributions to the rebellion.[38] It provided a theoretical justification for a challenge to the existing political system, and in so doing created a feeling of moral rectitude for the opposition (1972a:100ff.), and it provided the foundations of an organization within which the Parliamentarian cause could develop. One component of this organization was the leadership provided by the Puritan faction in the English Church (Stone 1972a:103; see Hunt 1983). In fact, the two contributions were closely related, as the nature of Puritan organization was defined by the nature of Puritan beliefs.

Puritanism called for Christians to engage in the struggle against Antichrist, a struggle that was defined as the responsibility of each individual. Without repeating what was argued elsewhere, Puritanism also provided the impetus to rationalize one's life into a disciplined routine, calculated to attain some sought-after goal (see chap. 4, above). In so doing it provided not only disciplined organizations but also the ultimate certainty of success that is necessary for the triumph of any revolution, but especially necessary in circumstances where common men were challenging a king, and where their leaders were not questioning the status system extant in their society. Walzer has commented that "opposition in practice required something else [other than solidity and seriousness], some more special preparation—a peculiar certainty, a willfulness, almost a fanaticism. This was exclusively a Puritan product" (1968 : 257). In the first instance this "fanaticism" allowed men to follow lesser magistrates in reordering this world; later it allowed "the godly sort" to challenge even these lesser magistrates in an attempt to complete the process.

If Puritanism provided an ideology, accessible to all, which demanded active participation in the reordering of this world, it also provided the organizational context within which the mobilization of the "saints" occurred. Hill has commented, "Among the many historical achievements of Puritanism was the fact that it gave men an abstract ideal to be loyal to, in place of the previous personal and local loyalties" (1971 : 23). While this is no doubt true, Puritanism also defined a supralocal, supraparticularistic focus around which the networks of local ties could be organized (cf. Hughes 1985). Often it was parochial groups, based on familial or other particularistic allegiances, which participated in actions organized under the legitimation of Puritan beliefs.

Brunton and Pennington emphasize personal and local factors in accounting for the distribution of men into the Royalist and Parliamentarian camps. But at the same time they recognize that these personal ties were themselves organized. In the south and east "the tightly-bound nuclei of the Parliamentarian cause—the family groups round the Fienneses, the Hampdens and others, the colonizing ventures, and the Puritan congregations—mainly developed" (1968 : 179).[39] London served as the focus for the opposition leaders, and Parliament itself was one of the bases on which they organized themselves (Fisher 1968 : 83–84; Hexter 1968 : 62–64).

But most important, Puritanism served as the basis on which communication between local areas might be developed. Haller comments that one section of

> the landed gentry, growing into something like a party conscious of interests it had to protect and extend, grew active in assisting promising youths to obtain education, education which in the ordinary course would lead them to the service of religion, that is to say into the work of guiding and forming the public opinion of a new day. (1957:39; cf. Hill 1971:59)

These Puritan preachers not only helped to rally and support their co-religionists in Parliament (Wilson 1969; Spalding 1967; Trevor-Roper 1968:chap. 6) but served as the nodes of a network mobilizing support for Parliament in London and throughout the country.

> The main strength of the Parliamentary armies came from the South and East of England, especially from godly and self-respecting volunteers in the urban and Puritan areas. But there were pockets of support for Parliament in the North and West. "In whatever considerable village there was a Puritan preacher," says the historian of Puritanism in Lancashire [R. Halley], "he found adherents to the parliamentary cause among the yeomanry and traders of his neighborhood." (Hill 1963:101)

It was among these that "Puritanism taught men to stand on their own feet: it established a higher duty to God which could override feudal loyalties" (101). As the preachers before Parliament stressed, a nation returning to God deserved and received God's blessing and approbation.

Manning has commented in a review of Brunton and Pennington (1968) that "the important connexions were not merely family interests, they were groups of relations and dependents united by a wider purpose intimately connected with local and national politics. The Providence connexion was united by its interest in colonisation, but most connexions simply revolved around patronage" (1954:72). Brenner emphasizes the importance of colonial ventures in the development of a coalition between merchants and "aristocrats."

> In their American projects the new merchants and the opposition aristocrats explored their very considerable grounds of common interest and orientation, and learned to work together to achieve their common

goals. As they soon discovered, their basis for common action was not confined to the sphere of colonization, but extended to politics as well. (1970:234–35)

The Providence Island Company may be taken as exemplifying the intertwining of familial networks with economic and religious networks.

Newton, whose work documents the importance of the Providence Island Company, has written that

> the adventurers in the company included amongst their number almost every important member of the inner circle of the leaders in opposition to the arbitrary rule of Charles I.... The eleven years of the company's activity ... coincide almost exactly with the eleven years of Charles I's autocracy. This coincidence will seem the more striking when we show that between 1636 and 1640 many of the plans of opposition to the government were matured in security under cloak of the company's meetings. (1966:2–3)

Thompson, in an article tracing the lineage of the parliamentary "Middle Group," Pym's political organization, tells us that "by 1629, the delicate web of friendship and common political [and religious] conviction upon which the Providence connexion rested had been spun" (1972:86). Thus the Providence Island Company, organized to establish a plantation in the West Indies, provided one organizational node for the construction of the Parliamentary party (Hunt 1983:266). This group of Puritans, friends, and relatives shared common commercial interests, and their organization to further these interests, while economically not a success, provided the executive leadership for the party that led the REVOG.[40]

Thus the Parliamentary party was able to build on preexisting ties. As the oppositionist and the Puritan causes merged, organizations constructed to further religious principles assumed political responsibilities. Thus the Feoffees for Impropriations, a group organized to help purchase places to support a godly and preaching ministry, served as a focus for the opposition to Charles prior to the Providence Island Company (Hill 1971:263; Zagorin 1969:142–43). Particularistic ties, often stemming from family connections, provided the foci within which oppositionist tactics were planned. The oppositionist peers had long used their London homes as meeting places for anti-Court leaders (Snow 1970:239) and there is evidence that a series of meetings occurred at the homes of peers between the first and second sessions of the Long Parliament to plan strategy (Manning 1973*a*:72–73; Wedgwood 1966*b*:409–10). It appears that Pym and Hampden kept a common table at Westminster (Brailsford 1961:7), where the meetings of Parliament and the London trade provided opportunities for solidifying ties stemming from other connections.

These organizational ties among Calvin's "lesser magistrates" penetrated downward; Pym is said to have had a tavern devoted to his interests in every ward of the city (Brailsford 1961:25). Pearl has shown the importance of the city members in Parliament in organizing popular support for the Parliamentary cause in London (1961:especially 228ff.). In the counties, the opposition often was able to take over the local administration and place it at the service of Parliament; at first this was accomplished, as in Suffolk, through the good offices of the county gentry (Everitt 1960:16–17). In addition, local bodies were utilized to construct support for Parliament, as when Quarter Sessions and Grand Juries at Assizes were used as representative bodies (Manning 1957:4, 23). These actions were legitimized within the context of a rapidly developing body of political theory, but the acceptance of this theory was greatly facilitated by the prior existence of Puritan beliefs. Puritan ministers provided the leadership within which a country-wide party emerged. Puritan beliefs made the goals of that party intelligible (see Hill 1969*c*:241–42 and the two books by Haller which he cites, 1957, 1963). These men were fighting the Antichrist; Charles's association with Catholics reinforced the righteousness of their cause and assured them of God's favor (Clifton 1971, 1973; Manning 1957:290ff.; Judson 1949:321, 327; Walzer 1968:294ff.).[41] These legitimations were reinforced within other sections of the culture by, for example, prophecies that were treated as legitimations for both Parliament and the king (Rusche 1969; for the context within which such prophecies were accepted see Thomas 1971: chap. 13).

In a recent article Christianson tells us, "Having examined all the works collected by Thomason before 1 November 1642 looking for a revolutionary ideology, the author was shocked when none appeared" (1976:50 n. 27). My readers ought not to be shocked at this discovery. Prior to the actions that constituted the parliamentary rebellion, legal arguments incapable of legitimizing a REVOG were dominant. It was only after the Grand Remonstrance, with its appeal downward, the Militia Ordinance, and the assumptions of executive powers by Parliament, that a commitment to beliefs capable of legitimizing these actions was established. These beliefs were intelligible owing to the prior existence of Puritanism within English culture, and Puritanism provided the foundation of a social network within which these beliefs were transmitted.

The REVOG was never institutionalized. Almost from the rebellion's inception Parliament found itself locked in a civil war with the king's forces; the culmination of this stage of the revolution was a more radical revolutionary movement carried out under the impetus of Parliament's own army.

This is not the place to assess the reasons for the king's failure in crushing the rebellion. Unlike during the first phase of the revolution (REVOF), however, Charles was able to raise a party and establish an alternative government capable of effectively challenging Parliament's forces. In the end Parliament won because of its control over greater economic resources than the king, and because of its capacity to mobilize not only a significant portion of the political nation but also those men and women of the middle sort who fought for Parliament out of conviction, loyalty to their patrons, and for wages and plunder. Some of these men were to seek an extension of the revolution beyond the point where the vast majority of the political nation was willing to follow.

7. REVON and REVOV: The Normative and the Attempted Total Revolution

My discussion of the remaining two stages of the English Revolution will be considerably briefer than that of the first two stages. Although the "normative revolution," REVON, which was formally begun in 1649, and the "total revolution," REVOV, which was crushed, represent portents of things to come in English history, it was the REVOG that was the culmination of the tendential development of prerevolutionary English social structure. Neither a REVOF, a REVON, nor a REVOV was capable of long-term routinization in seventeenth-century England, although the Restoration period from 1660–1688 was defined within the mold of the REVOF.

REVON

The necessary and sufficient conditions for the generation of a movement seeking a normative revolution are strain at the level of norms, an open illegitimate opportunity structure, deflation of power coupled with a neutral orientation toward the specific actions that constitute the revolution, and a precipitating factor. If the revolutionary actions are to be regularized, a commitment must be generated to a framework of beliefs legitimizing them. If the movement is to succeed, it must occur in a situation of power inflation. It is important to reemphasize the multivariable nature of this theory. For example, strain at the level of norms, if not coupled with appropriate legitimizing beliefs, will not result in regularized actions entailing a normative revolution. All of the relevant variables must be present for the specified action to occur.

The division of the houses and the country into parties between

1642 and 1649 and the changing nature of the alignments has been subject to much controversy among historians. Much of the debate has focused on the religious affiliations of various categories of actors, and almost as much on the genesis and demise of the contending parties, especially on the survival of the so-called Middle Group. Fortunately, with the exception of the relationship between politics and religion, which sorts itself out quite nicely when the question is properly posed, we will be able largely to ignore these disputes.

Our task will not be to differentiate between the contending parties within the REVOG but to attempt to determine which groups participated in making the REVON that succeeded the parliamentary rebellion. We are not concerned with the basis of differentiation between the Independent and Presbyterian parties in the House, or with the bases on which the Presbyterian party generally supported the king in the second civil war, or with the prolonged negotiations with the king leading to the development of a group of men and women willing to support his trial and execution and the termination of the monarchy itself. Instead we will focus on those persons Underdown labels "revolutionaries," those members of Commons most instrumental in making the REVON. It is these persons and their supporters whom I label "Independents," always in quotation marks. Those who held back, who refused support for the normative revolution, I label "Presbyterians," again in quotation marks. Within the house, all members of the Presbyterian party opposed the REVON; they are therefore categorized as "Presbyterians." The Independent party split, its more radical members supporting the normative revolution, its less radical members stepping back; thus the Independent party divides into "Presbyterians" and "Independents."[1]

There were a series of crucial events setting the stage for the REVON. On 26 June 1647 eleven members of the Presbyterian party in Commons withdrew from the House. The army had demanded their suspension, and while the Commons had refused to remove them, their retreat was necessitated by army pressure. They were later charged with negotiating to reinstate the king on their own terms (Gardiner 1893, 3:304, 322–23).

These eleven members were recalled on 1 August 1647, but only after the two speakers, eight peers, and fifty-seven Independent members of Parliament were forced to flee Westminster as the city demonstrated for the reinstatement of the eleven and for peace with the king. "Another sixteen or twenty quickly signified their approval of the [withdrawal] action, by subscribing the *Engagement* of 4 August to this effect" (Underdown 1971:83). The Independents found sanctuary with the army, and Parliament placed itself under the protection of the city militia and prepared to defend itself in any confrontation with the army. Instead, the city was surrendered and occupied and the Independent members were restored to Parliament (Gardiner 1893, 3:chap. 53; Underdown 1971:chap. 4).

The remainder of 1647 saw considerable maneuvering within Parliament and fluctuating majorities for either the Presbyterian or Independent factions. The Presbyterians had a majority, but Cromwell, using the army to threaten the House, secured the voiding of actions between 26 July and 6 August, when the Independents were not seated, and in consequence large numbers of Presbyterians withdrew (Gardiner 1893, 3:351–52). Even so, the Presbyterians maintained a majority in a "full house" (Gardiner 1893, 4:114).

It is too simple to view the second civil war as constituted by the Scots, Royalists, and Presbyterians against the Independents and their more radical supporters. This view is unacceptable, if only because of the influence the Presbyterians continued to wield after its culmination in favor of the Independents, and because of the anti-Scot feeling that led to a certain rallying of support for the Independent-controlled army.[2] The continued Presbyterian influence was manifested, in part, because the war was located in a different conjuncture than was the first civil war; it was, as Underdown has pointed out, between the army and the county communities (1971:98). As the Independents went back to their local bases to organize the fighting, the Presbyterians emerged in control of Parliament (1971:101).

We need not discuss the battles of the second civil war. The Independent army led by Cromwell succeeded in crushing both the Scots and the pro-Presbyterian (and pro-Royalist) rebels in the country. But this victory led not to an immediate settlement but rather to continued wrangling between the king and a parliament not desirous of imposing a settlement on him. Parliament voted 129 to 83 to accept the king's response to the Houses' propositions of Newport as the basis for a settlement.[3]

The army's verbal response to these actions was its *Remonstrance*. It demanded a purge of Parliament and the trial of the king (Underdown 1971:117–18). The army's *Remonstrance* was based on two fundamental beliefs: "the sovereignty of the people, buttressed by representative government, and a contract between ruler and ruled, and secondly the use of divine providence as proof of the godliness or otherwise of any given course of action" (Underdown 1971:123–24; see Gardiner 1893, 4:chap. 67). The army's actual response came in Pride's Purge, when those who voted for the motion accepting the agreement at Newport, "and/or one against the August motion declaring those who assisted the Scots invaders rebels and traitors" were barred from Parliament (Underdown 1971:141, and chap. 6).

The army carried out the purge, leaving only a remnant of the original Long Parliament. The Rump Parliament was under the firm control of the army; together they enacted the REVON. On 4 January 1649 the Commons established a High Court of Justice to try the king. When the Lords demurred, the Commons gave their own actions the force of law. The court's deliberations began on the 8th; on the 27th the king was sentenced and on the 30th he was executed. Then in short succession the House of Lords and the monarchy were abolished. The Council of State was created as Parliament's executive. "With *Salus Populi* echoing from their lips, the revolutionaries began the unprecedented transformation of a kingdom into a commonwealth. God's people, Capt. George Joyce told the Army Council, were about 'such things as were never yet done by men on earth'" (Underdown 1971:173; see Wedgwood 1966a; Walzer 1974).

The previous stages of the revolution had left the nature of the regime intact. This stage redefined the set of norms that internally justified political actions; it thus altered the nature of the regime, in this instance from a monarchy to a republic. When the king was executed, the Commons, as Hobbes succinctly put it, challenged "the sovereignty in plain terms, and by that name" (1969:27). Clearly the rules of the game had been altered. The question we must pose is by whom, and under what conditions?

A number of summary statements about activists and supporters in the REVON have been argued. There seems to be considerable agreement that in general they were more likely to be lesser than greater gentry, of lower income and rank than those who participated in the REVOG. Gardiner commented about the divisions leading to the king's execution: "In Scotland, as in England, the question of the supremacy of the King or Parliament was giving

way to a strife of classes" (1893, 4:192). There are three locales at
which this characterization may be examined: in the counties, in
the split between the army and Parliament, and within Parliament
itself.

In an essay entitled "The County Community at War," Pennington summarizes his argument as follows: he contends that the split
everywhere was between those who wanted to fight to secure a
peace settlement within the old forms of society (our REVOG), and
those who wanted to win the war and throw out those who monopolized power at the center and in the counties.

> Localism, compromise, and social conservatism opposed centralism,
> militancy, and revolutionary Puritanism. One of the most consistent
> claims in the propaganda of the conservative Parliamentarians was that
> the radicals were "mean, petty fellows," a gang of unheard-of climbers
> motivated only be greed, jealousy, and ambition. In fact there were
> plenty of both types on both sides; but there is little doubt that in gen-
> eral there were significantly more from the old ruling groups and the
> richer families on the side of peace than on the side of war, and more of
> the "new men" among the militants and later Cromwellians. Indeed it
> seems likely that this social division within the parliamentary side, *more
> apparent at the level of the county than of parliament* [italics mine], is
> more marked than the differences between roundhead and cavalier.
> (Pennington 1968:73–74)

I will defer comments on the army-Parliament split until we discuss illegitimate opportunity structures. Here I endeavor to specify
one of the reasons certain of the "outs" supported the REVON.
Unfortunately, the best and most easily summarized data comes
from an analysis of members of Commons. In dealing with these
materials we would be wise to heed Underdown's warning concerning these materials: "Once more it should be stressed that we are
dealing with M.P.s, men of a governing class, most of whom shared
a common educational experience [and a common socioeconomic
past]" (1971:226). If I overemphasize the M.P.s in what follows, it
is because Underdown has provided us with considerable statistical
material relating to them, and because I believe that the conclusions
I draw from these materials have wider applicability. It must be
emphasized, however, that most who supported the REVON did
not come from this privileged ruling class of M.P.s, and that the
victory of army over Parliament and the consequent execution of
the king were brought about primarily by the yeomen, that very
group who, as Engels emphasized, were to be destroyed by the con-

Table 5

Group	Secure/Established	Others
R	25 (12)	46 (18)
C	24 (11)	59 (23)
A, S, I	160 (77)	157 (60)
Totals	209	262

Source: Underdown 1971, table 10a, 405.
Key: R = revolutionaries, C = conformists, A = abstainers, S = secluded, I = imprisoned.
Note: Percentages in parentheses.

sequences of the revolution (see Engels, in Marx and Engels 1968:389; Hill 1948; Moore 1966).

Underdown divides the members of the Long Parliament alive in December 1648 (N = 471) into five categories:

> the active revolutionaries [R, N = 71, % = 15] who openly committed themselves to the revolution while it was in progress during December and January; the conformists [C, N = 83, % = 18] who avoided formal commitment at that time, but accepted the *fait accompli* in February, when they could no longer be incriminated in the execution of the King; the abstainers [A, N = 86, % = 18], who were not actually secluded, but showed their opposition by staying away from Parliament at least until the spring of 1649; the victims of the Purge who were secluded [S, N = 186, % = 39]; and the hard core of the Army's enemies, who suffered imprisonment as well as seclusion [I, N = 45, % = 10].   (1971: 210–11ff.)

We will see in the analysis that follows that the crucial categories are the revolutionaries, those who made the REVON, and the combination of abstainers, secluded and imprisoned, those who opposed the REVON.

Underdown draws a distinction between secure, established families, "those of the greater and county gentry of Tudor or earlier origin, not in decline by 1640," and insecure or unestablished families, "those of the lesser gentry, the new gentry [established since 1603] and the declining gentry, with the addition of the merchants" (1971:239). He finds that those "insecure" members in the House were more likely to support the revolution than were the secure members (see table 5). Underdown comments:

There was ... a definite connection between status and political behaviour in the revolution of 1648–9. This rough-and-ready analysis
does not prove that the Rs were a party of *nouveaux riches*, declining or
lesser gentry and merchants. But it does suggest that the revolution had
more appeal to men of such descriptions than it had to the greater and
county gentry.   (1971:239)

Although there is no clear relationship between simple status
and actions in the REVON (see Underdown 1971:236–38 and
table 10b, 405), there does appear to be some relationship between
what might be called an ambivalent status position and participation
in the revolution.

In chapter 3 I argued that there was a relationship between strain
at the level of norms, the situation in which an actor is confronted
with conflicting expectations, and participation in revolutionary
movements directed toward the redefinition of the norm component of the polity. One possible manifestation of normative strain is
status inconsistency, when an actor's ranks on different ladders
(situses) in a stratification system differ. If an actor is ranked very
highly on a prestige scale measuring social status but has an income
insufficient to act out her status position, she might be in a situation
of normative strain. Likewise, if her situation is reversed and she
has income in excess of her status she might experience normative
strain.[4] If we can develop a measure of this inconsistency, it could
serve us as a makeshift indicator of normative strain.[5]

Underdown divides the M.P.s into five categories, which loosely
indicate their status:

The greater gentry [GG] include the sons of peers, baronets and their
sons, and members of families which had provided knights of the shire
in the century before 1640, thus demonstrating their roles as leaders of
their counties. The county gentry [CG] are the men slightly below this
level: knights and their sons, members of families which had provided
M.P.s for borough seats, or had filled such county offices as high sheriff
or deputy lieutenant. The lesser gentry [LG] are those at the next level,
whose families had aspired to nothing higher than producing an occasional J.P.; this definition, it should be stressed, is somewhat broader,
and includes men of somewhat higher status than that which equates
the lesser gentry only with the very small parochial gentry. Merchant/
gentry [MG] are the men whose main occupation was trade, but who
were of recent gentry origins ... the term merchant [M] is used here in a
very broad sense, and includes all the M.P.s who were not of recent
gentry origin.   (1971:236–37)

Although these categories are not precise, they are serviceable; their ambiguity ought to strengthen our belief in any relationship we might discover, most especially as there is no fear of my having unconsciously miscategorized persons to support my theoretical arguments.

Underdown also divides the M.P.s into three income levels: (1) a prewar income of over 1,000 pounds per year; (2) between 500 and 1,000 pounds per year and (3) less than 500 pounds per year. He finds a slight relationship between relative poverty and revolutionary activity (see 1971:241–43 and table 11). From these two indicators, status and income, we are able to construct a crude measure of status inconsistency.

If we group Underdown's five status categories into three groups—(1) GG + CG; (2) LG and (3) MG + M—one indicator of status inconsistency and thus normative strain will be a discrepancy between status and income, for instance, any incongruity in rank between positions 1 and 3 on the status and positions 1 and 3 on the income hierarchies will be taken as an indicator of SN. For example, an M.P. categorized as CG with an income of 750 pounds per year will be deemed in a situation of SN; an M.P. categorized as M with an income below 500 pounds per year will not be so categorized.

I have added one additional criterion of SN, also taken from Underdown's data. He provides us with a category of "declining or new [post-1603] families," and another of "serious pre-war debt." It seems reasonable that when these two categories are taken in conjunction SN would be manifest. An established and wealthy family with a serious debt ought to understand how it is supposed to act; but a mobile family with such a debt, at whatever level of status and income, ought to be in a state of confusion. Thus SN includes cases of status inconsistency and cases where the family is declining or rising and in serious prewar debt.[6]

The results of this analysis may be seen in table 6. If we exclude the conformists from both tables 5 and 6, and if we arrange table 5 in conformity with table 6, we have tables 7 and 8. The Q is a simple measure of association, showing the strength of the established relationship.[7] It is clear from these tables that the relationship between normative strain and participation in the REVON is considerably stronger than that between insecurity and active par-

Table 6

Group	SN	$\overline{SN}$
R	41	13
C	34	25
A, S, I	99	132

Source: Underdown, Appendix A.
Key: R = revolutionaries, C = conformists, A = abstainers, S = secluded, I = imprisoned; SN = strain at the level of norms, $\overline{SN}$ = absence of strain at the level of norms.

Table 7

Group	Others (insecure)	Secure/Established
R	46	25
A, S, I	157	160

Note: Q = .15
Key: R = revolutionaries, A = abstainers, S = secluded, I = imprisoned.

Table 8

Group	SN	$\overline{SN}$
R	41	13
A, S, I	99	132

Note: Q = .62
Key: R = revolutionaries, A = abstainers, S = secluded, I = imprisoned; SN = strain at the level of norms, $\overline{SN}$ = absence of strain at the level of norms.

ticipation. Given the nature of our data, the relationship between SN and the making of REVON is remarkably strong.

While this analysis is interesting, I must warn the reader against allowing it to mask the underlying conditions that generated these strains. In aggregating our data we will often miss important relationships. Let me cite only one example: Brenner has shown that the English merchants who supported the REVON came from specific organizational contexts. While the REVOG was dominated by domestic merchants (see also Pearl 1972:34), the one merchant group that supported the REVON was made up largely of the "colonial-interloping complex." "Only the new merchants were prepared to ride to power on the backs of the Army after many years in the political wilderness" (Brenner 1973:92, and for a more complete picture, 1970).[8] This crucial distinction between categories of merchants is necessarily blurred in the analysis I have presented, yet it too is essential in explaining the REVON.

With the coming of the second civil war the party alignments within the revolution once again underwent alteration. With the changing of loyalties the institutional bases of the combatants also altered. The more radical members in Parliament found that their traditional sources of support had eroded. For example, they no longer controlled London. Demonstrations in the city had forced the Independents to flee to the army; the reformados (disbanded soldiers) demonstrated in favor of the Presbyterian party, demanding, for example, the reinstatement of Holles in the Commons; in general from 1646 the demonstrations in the city were for peace with the king; they forced the repeal of a militia ordinance that had removed Presbyterians from the city militia, and urged that Charles be invited to the city (Firth 1910:169–70; Gardiner 1893, 4:98, 127–28, 133ff., 140–42, 146, 210–11; Underdown 1971:83; and for the most comprehensive discussion, Pearl 1972).

Those who wanted to push the revolution forward were isolated in London. They would find that when push came to shove the peers would unanimously refrain from committing themselves to the execution of the king. Fortunately for them, however, they had one important base of operations, the New Model Army. They recognized themselves to be a minority in Commons, and all recognized that their power rested in the army.

> The New Model army was rightly regarded by all factions as the mainstay of radical power, and its political significance now [in 1646 according to MacCormack] came into sharp focus. To disband it was the devout wish of the Holles group [moderate Presbyterians]; to maintain it in full battle array, the firm resolution of the radicals.   (MacCormack 1973:128; Pearl 1972:42–44)

There is considerable controversial literature concerning the New Model Army, and this is not the place to evaluate those discussions. I do not believe, though, that there is any controversy concerning its importance in defeating the Royalists. In was instrumental in winning the first civil war; it won the second civil war. It also provided a focus for the lesser gentry who dominated its officer corps (Yule 1958:60, 80) and for the journeymen and yeomen who dominated its fighting forces (Hill 1969*b*:55; Russell 1973*a*:8–9; Shaw 1968:22–26; Brailsford 1961:146; and more generally, Solt 1959; Firth 1962; cf. Morrill 1976:62–63, n. 37; Kishlansky 1979*a*). Even though over one-half of its infantry were pressed (Brailsford 1961:147; Firth 1962:36), and although it is possible to exaggerate the importance and level of its Puritan devotion, it was a more disciplined army than any other on the field and it did fight with great success (cf. Morrill 1976:63). Likewise, although it is possible to overstate its radicalism, it was the major actor in effecting the REVON (see Kishlansky 1979*a*; and the review in Holmes 1981).[9]

Unlike the Royalists and Parliamentarians the Independents apparently did not stem from closely knit local ties, at least not among the M.P.s. "Independency in its various forms was established at the centre, in a Parliament and an Army whose members had had many years in which to develop new friendships and associations" (Brunton and Pennington 1968:133). While the Independents were a minority in Parliament, by 1647 they controlled the army and the Independents in Parliament remained in close contact with their compatriots in the army (Hexter 1961:178–79; Yule 1958:58–59). When confronted with a Presbyterian attack, the Independents in the army and the House grew even closer, and the army itself closed ranks, uniting its three disparate elements, the Independents and the Levellers with those simply desirous of maintaining the army in order to secure their pay (see Kishlansky 1979*a*:chaps. 7, 8).

> In March 1647, so that they might be upon a nearer level with the Parliament, the army made choice of a number of such officers as they liked, which they called *The General's council of officers*, and were to resemble the house of peers; and the common soldiers made choice of three or four of each regiment, most corporals or sergeants, and none above the degree of an ensign, who were called *Agitators*, and were to be as a house of commons to the council of officers.   (Clarendon 1888, 4:220)

It was from this organizational base that the Independents moved. As Hill has simply and lucidly stated, "Army and Parliament now existed side by side as rival powers in the State" (1955:49). Hobbes had personified the same thought:

B. Now that there was peace in England and the King in prison, in whom was the sovereign power?

A. The right was certainly in the King, but the exercise was yet in nobody; but contended for, as in a game at cards, without fighting, all the years 1647 and 1648, between the Parliament and Oliver Cromwell, lieutenant-general to Sir Thomas Fairfax.   (1969:135)

This was a situation of dual power which lasted until the more radical among the Independents, the "Independents," purged Parliament and made the REVON.

The army's position was complicated. While the Levellers, as we will see below, were willing to make a reasonably clean break with the past, the "Independents" were never willing to contemplate a total revolution. They always remained within the context of prior political values. It was therefore difficult for them to legitimize their position as claimants for sovereign power. During the Putney Debates Cromwell argued: "Either they are a Parliament or no Parliament. If they be no Parliament they are nothing, and we are nothing likewise. If they be a Parliament, we are [not to proceed without them in our plan for settlement, but—A.S.P.Woodhouse] to offer it to them." He goes on to add, "If I could see a visible pressence of the people, either by subscriptions or number [I should be satisfied with it—A.S.P.Woodhouse]; for in the government of nations that which is to be looked after is the affections of the people. And that, [if—A.S.P.Woodhouse] I find [it—A.S.P.Woodhouse], would satisfy my conscience in the present thing" (Woodhouse 1938:97). It was Cromwell's misfortune to commit a series of actions for which he could not command popular support, actions that, while committed in the name of a (purged) Parliament, were contrary to the will of that (unpurged) body. The question is, then, how were these actions, and especially the execution of the king, possible?

In July 1647, the army had enunciated in "The Heads of the Proposals" "a constructive policy for a political settlement" (Aylmer 1972:6. The "Proposals" are reprinted in Gardiner 1906: 316–26). Gardiner discusses Charles's reactions to these proposals, citing Sir John Berkeley's *Memoirs* of his meeting with the king. Cromwell had assured Berkeley that the army wished "for no more 'than to have leave to live as subjects ought to do and to preserve their consciences,' and more than this, 'that they thought no man could enjoy their estates quietly without the King had his rights.'" Nonetheless, when Berkeley saw the king, Charles informed him that with the exception of one officer, he distrusted the entire army. "The reason given by Charles for his distrust of all the other officers was that they had been backward in asking him for personal favours. The whole secret of the failure of these negotiations on which Cromwell was about to enter is written in these words" (Gardiner 1893, 3:318). While Gardiner no doubt exaggerates, in effect he is pointing out that the army officers were not determined in their actions by a situation dominated by either facility or goal strain. On the contrary, in order for them to find a peaceful settlement normative changes would have to be effected in the nature of the political system. While these might be rhetorically defined so as to include a monarch, it was clear that the role this monarch would assume was incompatible with the role Charles defined for himself. The second civil war was inevitable.

Negotiations continued with the king, focusing on "The Heads of Proposals," and on various parliamentary proposals. But all negotiations broke off on 3 January 1648 with Parliament's vote of "no address." The king had signed an accord with the Scots; he would allow Presbyterianism in both countries for three years; they would invade England in order to replace him on his throne. For the only time prior to the Purge the Independent party mustered a majority in the Commons and the second civil war was formally a parliamentary war against king and Scots. During the war the Presbyterians regained control over the Commons, and at its culmination another set of hesitations appeared in Parliament's dealings with the king.

It is clear that for the Independents there was no longer a legitimate source of authority, although the Declaration of the Army (June 1647) had attempted to establish the army's right to speak for, in effect to govern in the name of, the people (Gardiner 1893, 3:293). After the war, the Army Remonstrance argued

> against the Treaty [of Newport] . . . on the contention that Charles I has broken the original contract, under which he had "a limited power to rule according to laws . . . with express covenant and oath also, obliged to preserve and protect the rights and liberties of the people." Repeated breaches of faith have shown that the King cannot be trusted. There is no sign of remorse for past misconduct, his principles are irreconcilable with those of Parliament (there can be no reconciliation "of light with darkness, of good with evil"), and experience shows that princes never

observe agreements limiting their powers. . . . The conclusion was
obvious: to break off this "evil and most dangerous treaty", and bring
"the capital and grand author of our troubles" to justice.   (Underdown
1971:124–25, quoting the "Remonstrance," which is reprinted, in
part, in Woodhouse 1938:456–65; and in full in The Parliamentary or
Constitutional History of England, xviii, 161–238)

The consequence of this situation, in which normative strain was
coupled with an illegitimate opportunity structure in a situation of
power deflation, was the REVON. It was clear that the king would
have to be deposed, and the logic of the situation implied that the
monarchy would have to be terminated. There were, however, differential capacities to legitimize these actions, and an understanding
of two separate modes of legitimation will help us to understand
the behavior of Underdown's revolutionaries and conformists.

> The Presbyterians had done their work. They had overthrown the
> monarchy, never, in the sense in which Charles understood the word, to
> rise again in England. In accomplishing this they had called forth an
> army which had translated their phrases into action, and the virtual
> head of that army was a statesman as well as a soldier.   (Gardiner
> 1893, 3:191)

So writes Gardiner; with the death of Charles, he quotes Frederic
Harrison: "'The true monarchy of England ceased to reign.' If,
however, the act was the act of the Independents, the mental preparation for it was the work of the Presbyterians, even more than they
were themselves aware of" (Gardiner 1893, 3:191 n. 1; in our
terminology he is speaking of the Presbyterians and the "Independents," see chap. 6 n. 3, below). That which was inconceivable in
1640 came to pass in 1649. The man who could be defeated a hundred times and remain king lost his head because of the truth of this
statement (cf. Walzer 1974).

The Rump had to govern the country without the enthusiastic
support of the vast majority of the old political nation. It relied on
local supporters, who, Underdown tells us, were the informal counterparts of the French *Intendants*. They were able to rule because
they could count on three things: the power and prestige of Parliament, the army, and "the passive obedience of the acquiescent
majority, who still preferred peace to disorder" (1971:307). This
latter group formed the subculture of revolution, either tentatively
supporting the revolution when such actions seemed beneficial, or

remaining neutral and passive in the face of the revolution. In Zagorin's terms, they appear to have justified their actions and their reluctance to act in terms of an "unofficial" ideology. The revolutionaries, those who actively participated in the revolution from the first and who took responsibility for the king's execution (Underdown 1971:215), appear to have legitimized their actions in terms of the "official" ideology of the revolution.

Zagorin distinguishes between two theoretical doctrines that endeavored "to vindicate obedience to a political order that was without any precedent in the historic constitution." The unofficial doctrine "asserted simply that any *de facto* power is entitled to obedience." In opposition to this view, the official theory, which Cromwell and his close supporters entertained, "employed the repertoire of conceptions clustering round the belief in the people's right to call rulers into account" (Zagorin 1954:63).

Implicit in the Army Remonstrance are two fundamental beliefs: "First, the sovereignty of the people, buttressed by representative government and a contract between ruler and ruled, and secondly the use of divine providence as proof of the godliness or otherwise of any given course of action" (Underdown 1971:124). Earlier "The Declaration of the Army" enunciated "for the first time the modern political doctrine that the people themselves are the source of power, and that there is no appeal from their decision when expressed through Parliaments recently chosen" (Gardiner 1893, 3:294). These were principles, although no doubt influenced by the Levellers, on which the "Independents" could stand (cf. Tuck 1979:148).

"The concept of popular sovereignty was the main prop of Regicide theory" (Salmon 1959:103; Zagorin 1954:73). Nonetheless, when on 4 January 1649 the Rump declared itself sovereign as the representative of the people, no one accepted its claim. In fact the Rump sought, at least in part, to avoid the implications of its claim: "That the people are under God the original of all just power: that the Commons of England in Parliament assembled being chosen by and representing the people, have the supreme power in this nation" (quoted in Brailsford 1961:98). As Underdown put it, "By declaring themselves the repositories of that sovereignty they had at once sought to escape from the dangerous logic of their own principles" (1971:263). Theoretically the Rump was omnipotent as a representative of the people, but factually it represented only a

small percentage of the population (Firth 1910:217). Commonwealth theorists sought to bridge this gap.

The key term in reconciling the Rump's position was "necessity."

> The chief theme was that the purge of Parliament and the removal of
> kingship and the House of Lords arose from an unavoidable necessity
> which forced the army, acting as the sovereign people's representative,
> to exercise its right of calling a bad ruler and his accomplices to
> account.   (Zagorin 1954:80)

Given the fact, however, that the new government was narrow, that
the majority of the population had not given its consent to the
Purge and the Rump's consequent acts, and that the majority of the
population probably opposed these actions (Zagorin 1954:80), the
notion of "necessity" had to fulfill a second role. Zagorin uses John
Goodwin to illustrate this amended official doctrine.

Goodwin argues, in a traditional Calvinist fashion, that when
higher magistrates act contrary to the welfare of the people, lower
magistrates may remove them. In his eyes, the army fulfilled the role
of these lower magistrates. Admitting that the army had no formal
call from the people, he indicates that it nonetheless represented the
people, and was forced to act out of necessity.

> A sincere believer in the people's right to remove unfaithful magistrates,
> he [Goodwin] was certain that the army had acted as the people's repre-
> sentative and in their interest. Yet what if the people did not consent? No
> matter, he replied, extreme necessity justifies what has been done. His
> final appeal, therefore, was to necessity, which he accorded precedence
> even over the sovereign people.   (Zagorin 1954:82)

This moved very close to the "Cromwellian Rationalization" (Salmon 1959:105) of Marchamont Nedham, and the other exponents
of the unofficial view.[10]

It might be argued that if the "Independents" had followed the
logic of their ideas they would have enunciated Leveller doctrine.
It is clear that in retreating from these implications—Cromwell
crushed the Levellers—they enunciated a doctrine capable of justifying anything (Zagorin 1954:83). This arbitrariness (Hexter
1978:15), here an unintended consequence, was very nearly the
central goal of certain "unofficial theorists."

Skinner points out that the new government was aware of the
need to provide a basis for its own legitimation. It did so in "The
Declaration of the Parliament of England," which

reflected the most characteristic political belief of the Independents: that the origin of any lawful government must lie in a decision by the people to consent to its establishment. The execution of Charles I was thus vindicated with the claim that it represented the removal of a tyrant and the reassertion of the people's right to set limits to the power of government.   (Skinner 1972:79–80. In our terms Independents should be "Independents.")

Skinner goes on to point out that while this argument might convince those already within the ranks, it would not convince Royalists, Presbyterians, and others outside the "Independent" party. Thus the development of the "Engagers" (after the Engagement controversy: whether persons should engage to be loyal to the commonwealth), or as Skinner calls them, "the *de facto* theorists," Zagorin's "unofficial" theorists.

The specific nature of the justifications of obedience provided by the de facto theorists varied, but they all argued that even usurping powers ought to be obeyed. Francis Rous, a Presbyterian, based his arguments on the Pauline injunction of submission to authority. He had in common with John Dury his belief that the commonwealth government was both in power and dispensing justice, protecting those giving it allegiance and commanding nothing unlawful. Anthony Ascham secularized these arguments; for him obedience was mandated not from providence but in order to protect men from their fellow men. The function of political society was the maintenance of order, and even if the government was a usurper, it was in the interests of the people to obey its commands in order to preserve order and to stifle anarchy. He also argued that even if the government was not legal in origin, in its actions it might establish a prima facie legality meriting allegiance. Nonetheless, in effect he agreed with Nedham and others in arguing that if the government provided protection it deserved obedience. Nedham concluded, more directly, that the successful preservation of order entailed the fact that the government was just and equitable. (This paragraph is based on Skinner 1972 and Zagorin 1954:chaps. 5, 10; see also Judson 1980).

In sum, the unofficial theorists of the revolution justified obedience to those actually empowered to rule. The rationale of their arguments varied from providence to utilitarian benefit, but all of their arguments lacked persuasiveness as they tried to bridge the gap between an obedience based on prudence and one based on commitment. They were on surer ground when they touched on the necessity of such a government obeying positive law. As Pocock says, in referring to a true "independent," Ireton, "It should be stressed that the necessity being imposed upon the individual is in an important sense more formal than specific: an obligation to respect *some* system of law and property, rather than *the* specific system now obtaining" (1975 : 376). As one moved further toward the conservative direction of the political spectrum, as it became necessary to generate support from among the uncommitted on the "right" when the "left" had been crushed, these norms became more specific and more in accord with previous common law development.

Underdown (1971) and Worden (1974) have provided detailed analyses of the retreat of the revolutionaries as they tried to consolidate support for their new regime. "By encouraging as many M.P.s as possible to align themselves with the Commonwealth, even if in their hearts they did not believe in it, the original Rumpers themselves helped to destroy what impetus the revolution possessed" (Underdown 1971 : 262). They made pragmatic appeals for obedience, and they were joined by many who acted as if their motives were to restrain and retard the revolution. While I cannot provide evidence that these two groups, first revolutionaries and second conformists and neutrals, adopted different modes of legitimation, it will be useful to briefly explore the religious contexts within which they acted.

Underdown tells us that Presbyterian ministers preached against the Purge, and this is not surprising when we learn from Pearl that there had long been an alliance between religious Presbyterians and the Peace Party (Underdown 1971 : 163, 176ff.; Pearl 1972 : 35ff., 54–56). Nor should we be surprised when Underdown informs us:

> Not all the preaching and praying ... was against the Purge. For the Puritan Saints, the extreme Independents, sectaries and millenarians of various hues, this was the dawn of a new day, the last chance of completing the Godly Reformation, the rule of the Saints, perhaps even the Fifth Monarchy itself.   (Underdown 1971 : 163–64)

It is not possible to determine whether these distinctions were held in the country, but Underdown does provide us with information concerning the religious beliefs of the M.P.s. He divides the M.P.s into four categories: (1) with the Presbyterians he includes moderate or covert Episcopalians; he draws a distinction between

Table 9

Group	Sectaries, Indeps., and Pres-Indeps.	Presbyterians	Unknown
R	37	9	25
C	21	23	39
A, S, I	13	146	158
Total	71	178	222

Source: Underdown 1971, table 9a, 404.
Key: R = revolutionaries, C = conformists, A = abstainers, S = secluded, I = imprisoned.
Note: Excluding conformists and unknown: Q = .96, standard error = .05; Y = .74, standard error = .05.

two groups of Independents, (2) Congregational Independents and (3) "Presbyterian Independents," who were in Walker's term "congregational Presbyterians" who differed little from Independents. He also includes among the Presbyterian-Independents "those who moved from Presbyterian to Independent without clearly demonstrating that they were either" (1971:234 n. 62, and 18). These distinctions appear to parallel Woodhouse's between separating and nonseparating Congregationalists (1938:34), whom he groups together as a Centre party between the Presbyterians and the sectarian Levellers. Underdown's final category, (4) the sectaries, is used broadly to include Baptists, Deists, and freethinkers.

It would be nonsensical to assume that religious categories were rigid. Clearly persons' religious affiliations changed, perhaps especially among the Independents and sectarians who gained in strength throughout the revolutionary period. But it is nonetheless reasonable to assume that religious persuasion might provide a context within which one might legitimize or be capable of legitimizing political actions. This is apparently what happened, as we can see in table 9.

We cannot conclude from this table that religious Independents supported the REVON as "Independents" owing to their acceptance of the "official" commonwealth theory, but it does seem reasonable that men whose religious beliefs stressed individual autonomy and the individual's authority to make religious decisions might well have accepted parallel arguments in the political realm. Likewise, it seems reasonable that men more disposed toward a religious system creating a religious hierarchy within an established church would find such arguments more difficult to accept. In any case, we find that the Independent party of the middle 1640s split over the REVON, and those members who supported this step of the revolution were likely to be either religious Independents or their more radical separatist, sectarian brethren.

Another possible interpretation of these data must be indicated. Underdown's categorizations of religious allegiance appear to derive from data varying in time. It is thus quite possible, and theoretically intelligible, that "conversion" to religious Independency may have followed participation in the REVON. In this case, religious beliefs were not the cultural context within which certain political legitimations were meaningful, but rather among the legitimations for political actions. This appears especially likely in the seventeenth century, when the neat division we tend to draw between religion and politics was blurred.

Our theory explaining the genesis of revolutions is multivariable. It thus behooves us to put our various statistics together to see if we can better explain the behavior of our circumscribed group of M.P.s. If the theory is correct, we would expect that both normative strain and, if we take this as a crude index of capacity to legitimize actions within the REVON, "radical" religious beliefs (Presbyterian-Independent, Independent, and Sectarian) would be necessary to enable active and sustained revolutionary action. Table 10, again based on Underdown's data, is taken from our tables 8 and 9:

It is true that these data reveal twenty-one (20 + 1) erroneous predictions and that many cases were excluded for lack of information, but given the quality of the data this performance of the theory is adequate. I should note that much of this success comes from the connection between politics and religion, and as we will see in the appendix to this chapter, this entails a certain conflation of variables, as we would expect SN to be related to Independency as a religious preference. But even with this caveat, it seems clear from our tables that predictions based on the theory hold up.

It is possible to add one further conjecture in conclusion. One might assume that those who were likely to conform to the commonwealth would have been those who were subject to disorder because of the REVON itself. Thus these men, many of whom had participated in the Independent party prior to 1649 (Underdown 1971:table 8) remained within a subculture of revolution, and

Table 10

Group	SN and S, I and P-I	SN and Pres.	$\overline{SN}$ and Unknown Relig., S, I, P-I, P.	SN and P. Unknown Relig.	Unknown Strain and P
r	21	5	13	15	2
c	5	7	25	22	7
a, s, i	1	40	132	58	38
Total	27	52	170	95	47

Key: r = revolutionaries, c = conformists, a = abstainers, s = secluded, i = imprisoned; SN = strain at the level of norms, $\overline{SN}$ = absence of strain at the level of norms; S = Sectaries, I = Independents, P-I = Presbyterian-Independents, P = Presbyterians.

Table 11

Group	SN and S, I and P-I	SN and P; or $\overline{SN}$ and Unknown Relig., S, I, P-I and P; or Unknown Strain and P.
r	21	20
a, s, i	1	210
Total	22	230

Note: Q = .99, standard error = .01; Y = .88, standard error = .06.
Key: r = revolutionaries, a = abstainers, s = secluded, i = imprisoned; SN = strain at the level of norms, $\overline{SN}$ = absence of strain at the level of norms; S = Sectaries, I = Independents, P-I = Presbyterian-Independents, P = Presbyterians.

while incapable of legitimizing the REVON, this temporary strain allowed them to justify their own complicity with the revolution. It is hard to prove this contention, but it seems supported by the particularly high percentage of merchants among the conformists; these would have been men especially sensitive to the disorders of the times (Underdown 1971: table 10b, 405).[11]

REVOV

The "Independents," even at their most radical, remained within the context of the traditional value patterns. While restructuring the political regime, the normative component of the polity, they endeavored to retain the polity's extant value system. A significant part of their difficulties in legitimizing their actions stemmed from their refusal to follow their actions to their logical consequences. In other words, the actions they undertook were capable of rationalization only within a commitment to a pattern of value orientations they refused to adopt. It was the Levellers who sought to complete the English revolution, to make a total revolution (REVOV) by redefining the polity's central values in order to legitimize the construction of a political system derivative from and responsible to a sovereign people (cf. Pease 1965 : 120).

My discussion of the Levellers will be brief. This group, drawn primarily from just below the middle sort, from skilled craftsmen and small farmers, was the only organized political group with any significant impact on the events of the revolution which was not led by the "gentle" (Walzer 1968 : 267). It was also the most significant revolutionary grouping not to take power; unlike in the French Revolution, here the "final phase" of the revolution was crushed by force of arms. As Manning has emphasized, an analysis of seventeenth- and eighteenth-century English history must be based on the understanding that "it was not the ideas of the Levellers that made the American and British constitutions, it was the crushing of the Levellers that made the American and British constitutions" (1969 : 132), and the British economic system (Brailsford 1961 : XII, 13, 442; Hill 1969*b*: 15, 170).

With the Levellers we cannot assess and explain what they did in making a revolution; we can only try to assess their programs and the conditions under which these programs were advocated. As their actual actions in making a revolution do not define a standard for our use, it is often difficult to disentangle what was representative of a sometimes heterogeneous political movement. In what follows I focus on what I take to be typical of the Levellers as actors seeking to make a REVOV.[12]

The Levellers in a series of manifestos and in the writings of prominent spokesmen articulated a set of beliefs that amounted to a party program. Their central concern was with the capacity of the sovereign people to find political expression, whatever the form in which the expression was manifest. While not consistent in their advocacy, in essence they were concerned to establish a democratic republic. Unlike less radical theorists, for the Levellers the people could delegate the responsibility to govern, but the people nonetheless retained control and responsibility for the government.

> During the years of civil war a large number of writers turned to the people as the final authority in government, and some of these theorists proved to be better democrats than Parker or Herle, for they did not assume that parliament spoke for the people. John Lilburne, Richard Overton, and other Levellers actually went from parliament to the people themselves for the final sanction in government. They are the writers in whose works the full meaning of parliament's earlier appeal to the nation is first truly realized.   (Judson 1949:416)

For the Levellers, political power, even the power of Parliament, was a trust from the people; if this trust was broken, power was to be reclaimed by the people themselves (see Schenk 1948:56). In fact, this was especially the case for Parliament, for while the king's power might be seen as derivative from law, for the Levellers the authority of Parliament was solely "derived from the people's trust, and designed for the people's welfare. When on such terms the Commons claimed supremacy, they empowered the people to revoke their trust if it was abused" (Pease 1965:182).

There is considerable controversy concerning the foundations of the Levellers' beliefs. Some attribute a greater influence to their sectarian religious background than do others, although no one, to my knowledge, denies this background (cf., among many others, Brailsford 1961:33, 84, 314, 367; Higgins 1973:216; Solt 1959: 66, 68, 70; Underdown 1971:44; Woolrych 1970:61–62; Yule 1958:4, 68; Thomas 1972:60; Woodhouse 1938:Introduction; Davis 1973). In addition, no one denies that the Levellers were concerned with effecting a separation of Church and State. "The Levellers made the final breach with theocracy, when they advanced from a plea for religious toleration to a complete divorce between religion and the state. Theirs is the distinction that they were the first party in the modern world to call for a secular republic" (Brailsford 1961:550; see also 56, 65, 90, 120; Woolrych 1970:62; Hill 1972*b*:30). This call entailed a transformation of the values used to legitimize political action, and within this context it is permissible to focus on the structure of their new orientation, even if my analysis makes it appear more systematic than it was in their own writings.

The Levellers were individuals who believed in a transcendent "God," "Reason." They broke down all mediations between this god and man, viewing each person as equal in his (and sometimes her) capacity to commune with this god. Thus each person was capable of discovering truth, although this discovery was to be "corrected" and no doubt molded via a process of free discussion within the context of sectarian congregation and political meetings. The people, defined as autonomous and equal, retained control over their government, and the interests of the people controlled the actions of the government, that is, the government had to act according to right reason. While they wavered, according to circumstance, from their favor for republican forms, they almost never wavered from their belief in civil liberties; these liberties were essential to enable the quest for truth and the people's interest to continue. It was essential that autonomous men, equal in the eyes of God, had the capacity to carry out "the progressive interpretation of truth" (Woodhouse 1938:45–47, 53, 76). Ideologically they assumed conditions of equality; programmatically they sought to preserve such conditions where they existed and to create them where they were denied (Manning 1968:154; Hill 1955:21–22, 51; Thomas 1972:77). It is essential to realize that the principles of equality, individualism, right reason and the consent of a sovereign people were for the Levellers interrelated into a coherent whole.

In 1646, on the occasion of the imprisonment of Lilburne, certain Levellers issued a "Remonstrance of Many Thousand Citizens and other Free-born People of England to their own House of Commons." (The "Remonstrance" is reprinted in Wolfe 1944:113–30): "Wee are well assured," they began,

> yet cannot forget, that the cause of our choosing you to be *Parliament-men*, was to deliver us from all kind of Bondage, and to preserve the Common-wealth in Peace and Happinesse: For effecting whereof, we possessed you with the same Power that was in our selves, to have done the same; For wee might justly have done it our selves without you, if we had thought it convenient; choosing you (as Persons whom wee thought fitly qualified, and Faithfull,) for avoiding some inconveniences.
>
> But ye are to remember, this was only of us but a Power of trust, (which is ever revokable, and cannot be otherwise,) and to be imployed to no other end, then our owne well-being ... Wee are your Principalls, and you our Agents ... yee were chosen to worke our deliverance, and to Estate us in naturall and just libertie agreeable to *Reason* and common *equitie*; for whatever our Fore-fathers were; or whatever they did or suffered, or were enforced to yeeld unto; we are the men of the present age, and ought to be absolutely free from all kindes of exorbitancies, molestations or *Arbitrary Power*, and you wee chose to free us from all without exception or limitation, either in respect of Persons, Officers, Degrees, or things.   (Wolfe 1944:113–14; see Brailsford 1961:

96–97, where he discusses this document, and where he also finds it impossible to resist quoting it at some length.)

We have here an enormous shift from Cromwell's fear that the army was nothing without Parliament (Woodhouse 1938:97). For the Levellers, the Parliament was nothing without the consent of the people (Brailsford 1961:261; Manning 1968). The final judge of a government's actions was the law of reason; the interpretation of this law fell not to one component of government, Parliament, but rather to the people (Pease 1965:138–39), and thus the Levellers were to be disturbed by Cromwell's desire to present a plan of settlement to Parliament instead of to the people (Woodhouse 1938:97; Gardiner 1893, 4:3–4).

The standard by which the Levellers came to evaluate governmental actions was equity and right reason. They came to judge the structure within which government occurred not in terms of the ancient law, but in terms of a rationality transparent, or at least available, to every man. Hill distinguishes between two opposed theories of the Norman Yoke: the first insists that the common law is a continuation of Anglo-Saxon law, subtly effaced since the Norman conquest. While the Levellers sometimes wrote in sympathy with this argument, usually they viewed the common law itself as an alien imposition. In this voice, the Magna Carta itself was viewed as a "beggarly thing" (Brailsford 1961:100–101; Hill 1964:60, 71; cf. 78ff.; Thomas 1972:64). While the Levellers did not differentiate, as this essay has, between norms and values and between political and integrative processes, much of their attack on the traditional definition of political action, and their contrasting of these traditions with right reason, may be interpreted as an attack on English political values, values accepted by those who made the REVON, as well as an attack on the values of the English legal system.[13]

Hill retells a story originally related by Aubrey (1962:194) concerning the shift from arguments based on faulty history to arguments based on the rights of man, and though the story concerns Marten, a "republican" who sometimes worked in alliance with the Levellers (Brailsford 1961:46), it is worth quoting:

> Henry Marten introduced a Remonstrance into Parliament, probably in 1649, in which he spoke of England being "*restored* to its ancient government of a commonwealth." When challenged on his history, "H. M.,

> standing up, meekly replied that 'there was a text had much troubled his
> spirit for severall dayes and nights of the man that was blind from his
> mother's womb whose sight was restored at last'—i.e., was restored to
> the sight which he should have had."   (Hill 1964:79, quoting Aubrey)

In other words, the Levellers moved "from the recovery of rights
which used to exist to the pursuit of rights because they *ought* to
exist" (Hill 1964:75). This was a monumental transition (cf. Hill
1969*a*:238, 242; Schenk 1948:30–31).

One of the bases of the Levellers' confrontations with the Independents concerned the primacy of the law of man versus the law of
nature. It is essential, if we are to understand this controversy, to
recognize that it defined the difference between a constitution based
on property and status and a constitution based on person and the
equality of autonomous individuals. Cromwell, during the Putney
Debates, expresses his fear of the great alterations demanded in
the Levellers' Agreement of the People. He emphasizes that it
alters the form of government possessed by the kingdom since it
was a nation, and he asks, "How do we know if, whilst we are
disputing these things, another company of men shall [not—
A.S.P.Woodhouse] gather together, and put out a paper as plausible perhaps as this" (Woodhouse 1938:7). As both he and Ireton
make clear later in the debate, only within the established political
values, the established contract of government, will property be
secure.

> For matter of goods, that which does fence me from that [right—
> A.S.P.Woodhouse] which another man may claim by the Law of
> Nature, of taking my goods, that which makes it mine really and civil-
> ly, is the law. That which makes it unlawful originally and radically is
> only this: because that man is in convenant with me to live together in
> peace one with another, and not to meddle with that which another is
> possessed of. . . .   (Ireton, in Woodhouse 1938:26–27)

The discussion at Putney was obscured by a confusion between
two points: the necessity, according to the Grandees, the Indepe-
dents, of adhering to the specific contracts made with Parliament
and the necessity, again according to the Grandees, of adhering
to the more fundamental contract establishing the nature of the
English political system. This latter at various times includes, or is
exhausted by, the right of property as established by positive laws.
This property right is built into the basic structure of the constitu-

tion when property becomes the foundation on which the vote is distributed.

> I think that no person hath a right to an interest or share in the dispos-
> ing of the affairs of the kingdom, and in determining or choosing those
> that shall determine what laws we shall be ruled by here—no person
> hath a right to this, that hath not a permanent fixed interest in this
> kingdom and those persons together are properly the represented of this
> kingdom, and consequently are [also—A.S.P.Woodhouse] to make up
> the representers of this kingdom, who taken together do comprehend
> whatsoever is of real or permanent interest in the kingdom. . . . This
> is the most fundamental constitution of this kingdom and [that—
> A.S.P.Woodhouse] which if you do not allow, you allow none at all.
> This constitution hath limited and determined that only those shall have
> voices in elections. . . . And if we shall go to take away this, we shall
> plainly go to take away all property and interest that any man hath
> either in land by inheritance, or in estate by possession, or anything
> else—[I say—A.S.P.Woodhouse], if you take away this fundamental
> part of the civil constitution.   (Ireton, in Woodhouse 1938:53–55)

In fact Ireton was arguing that the franchise was the property of a limited number of persons with a fixed interest in the nation. To redefine the basis of this property, of the franchise, would be to allow for a redefinition of the grounds of all property.

> Now I wish we may all consider of what right you will challenge that all
> the people should have right to elections. Is it by the right of nature? If
> you will hold forth that as your ground, then I think you must deny all
> property too, and this is my reason. For thus: by that same right of
> nature (whatever it be) that you pretend, by which you can say, one man
> hath an equal right with another to the choosing of him that shall
> govern him—by the same right of nature, he hath the same [equal—
> A.S.P.Woodhouse] right in any goods he sees—meat, drink, clothes—
> to take and use them for his sustenance.   (Ireton, in Woodhouse 1938:
> 58)

It is the Leveller response to this contention that we must endeavor to understand. Clarke, during the Putney Debates, provides the beginning of an answer:

> . . . whether or no it be the property of every individual person in the
> kingdom to have a vote in election [s—A.S.P.Woodhouse]; and the
> ground [on which it is claimed—A.S.P.Woodhouse] is the Law of Na-
> ture, which, for my part, I think to be that law which is the ground of all

constitutions. Yet really properties are the foundation of constitutions, [and not constitutions of property—A.S.P.Woodhouse]. For if so be there were no constitutions, yet the Law of Nature does give a principle [for every man—A.S.P.Woodhouse] to have a property of what he has, or may have, which is not another man's. This [natural right to—A.S.P.Woodhouse] property is the ground of *meum* and *tuum*. (Woodhouse 1938:75)

In effect, the natural right to property subsumes both *meum* and *tuum* and the franchise.[14]

There has been considerable controversy over the extent of the suffrage that the Levellers demanded, a controversy in part fueled by different persons selecting different texts as the basis of their arguments, but as far as I know, no one has disputed that the Levellers demanded the vote for every man (not women) in control of his own person. It is the limits and nature of this control which is in question; that the Levellers based the franchise on person while the Independents based it on property is not in question.[15]

For the Levellers each

individual has certain rights pertaining to him as a man. This principle leads them to conclude that at the time when individual persons coalesced into a sovereign body politic, each person reserved certain rights which Nature and Nature's God taught him were inalienable—so vital to his safety that if he surrendered them he violated the instinct of self-preservation and committed murder on his own body. (Pease 1965:142)

Thus, as MacPherson argues, the Levellers argue for a natural right to property, including one's self, but unlike MacPherson's argument, the property in one's self which allowed for the possession of the franchise appears inalienable (cf. Brailsford 1961:121; MacPherson 1962:137ff.). It was different from what Marx came to call "labor power," which would be alienated for wages, and closer to "labor," which was alienable only in servitude.

In 1647, a Presbyterian author undertakes to define the difference between the two theories of compact. The defenders of the Parliament against the king understood the law of nature to refer to the right enjoyed by heads of families in a patriarchal society of establishing government over themselves and their households; but the postulate of the radical doctrine is far different, namely the breaking up of patriarchal authority and the setting up of every individual as a member of the sovereign people. (Pease 1965:142–43)

If this interpretation is correct, it casts doubt on Schochet's and Thomas's interpretation of the exclusion the Levellers allow in the franchise as a simple manifestation of patriarchal norms—that those excluded were not heads of families (Thomas 1972:73, 77; Schochet 1969:423 n. 29. This is not to deny that others might justify these exclusions on patriarchal grounds, nor that a latent adherence to such norms was a contributing factor for the Levellers; see Schochet 1975:65–66).

These arguments leave us in a difficult position; while one's birthright to the vote is inalienable, according to some Levellers it was alienated within a series of statuses: for example, beggars, servants (however defined), apprentices, and women. Perhaps one should simply accept Petty's statement: "I conceive the reason why we would exclude apprentices, or servants, or those that take alms, is because they depend upon the will of other men and should be afraid to displease [them—A.S.P.Woodhouse]" (Woodhouse 1938: 83). What is clear is that, with perhaps the exception of apprenticeship, which was transitory, the Levellers sought to eliminate such dependencies (sometimes including the dependent position of women), just as they wanted to eliminate an unequal franchise. The paradox is unconsciously stated by Thomas: "For the Levellers are implausible as prophets of the new age of capitalism and wage-labour. However 'advanced' their constitutional notions, their economic ideas were backward-looking. They wanted to preserve (or rather to create) a world in which every man was an independent proprietor" (1972:77). This is, in a sense, MacPherson's point; whether wage labor robbed persons of their right to the vote or not, the right was inalienable, and the Levellers wanted to (re)create the conditions in which it might be realized.

Implicit in the argument attributed to the Levellers is a belief in the autonomous status of free and equal men. Brailsford notes that it is possible to "distinguish three basic ideas in the web of the Levellers' thought; all the rest is machinery" (1961:461). The first defined the realm of autonomous individuality, circumscribing that area where individual conscience and man's reason enabled him to make his own decisions, and for the Levellers, necessitated that he do so.

The second concerned this individual's right of association with his fellows and included realms of action we label freedom of religion, association, and speech. The third, variously stated and argued, defined these autonomous individuals as equal in the eyes of God and man, and therefore required equality before the law and equality of political power. Ideally for the Levellers this included economic equality sufficient to allow for autonomy, but not, in most instances, entailing an economic leveling, and certainly not any communal effacement of the individual. (For a similar summary see Brailsford 1961:462–63.)

The Levellers postulated that individuals, following right reason, would come to understand their interests within a community of men. They had considerable experience with self-government within their sectarian congregations, where private interpretations of scripture and perhaps private visions were tested via communal discussion (Hill 1972*b*:76–77, 300–302; and for the more general issue of the validity of illumination by the Holy Spirit, Nuttall 1946), and within their local communities where considerable self-determination still existed (cf. Manning 1969, 1973:224–25; Thomas 1972:60). But these were intelligent men and perhaps unconsciously they realized that discussion required freedom and a community of equals. All must have the ability to speak, even to preach, and within the context of such discussions truth would emerge, not the false dogma of imposed authority.[16]

In Parsons's terms (1949) the Levellers removed one horn of the utilitarian dilemma by assuming that a "natural identity of interests" would emerge from the free discourse of autonomous individuals. Living in a pre-Malthusian, pre-Marxian age, the structure of society which distorted these freedoms was not apparent to them, or rather insofar as it was apparent they were content to try to "turn the clock backward" in an endeavor to create economic autonomy and political freedoms. This is the basis of Lilburne's late arguments that a petite jury was capable of defining the law, of determining when an Act of Parliament transgressed the bounds of reason (Brailsford 1961:618–19; Hill 1964). Reason was found in every man, and human law was acceptable only within the bounds of reason. Within a jury, equals stood side by side to discover what was reasonable, and as these men were equal and autonomous their discoveries would be congruent. If men in society had comparable autonomy, political equality would yield comparable results.

For the Levellers the commonwealth was a phony system. "The Republic was established in 1649, but Normanism remained. There had been no fundamental change in the law or in the social relations which the law defended" (Hill 1964:81; Hill 1972*b*:56;

Zagorin 1954:41). The Levellers could not bear a system based on privilege and property, not representative of the people, and not under the control of, and therefore not in the interests of, the people. The Levellers sought a total revolution; they wanted to redefine the entire political system, but the major thrust of their actions focused on political values and involved the creation of an organized movement seeking liberty, equality, and the fraternal interaction of autonomous individuals. As Hill puts it, the Levellers reversed the values of their betters (1964:80).

In attempting to explain the genesis of the Leveller movement we risk arguing in a circle. There is only inferential evidence concerning the presence and location of the variables leading to a REVOV, and while this evidence is consistent with the theory presented in chapter 3, it is by no means conclusive. I will therefore keep these speculations brief.

Part of the problem in providing this explanation comes from a conflation of theoretical perspectives. If we assume that the Levellers were, for the most part, sectarians, it is easy to make intelligible the genesis of strain at the level of values (SV); if, however, one wants to explain sectarianism, a religious movement directed toward religious values, values within the pattern-maintenance subsystem, one's argument may become circular. For example, statements that reflect a situation of value strain are easy to find for both sectarians and Levellers, and very difficult to find for less radical political and religious groups. But we encounter a chicken and egg problem. The theory as argued in chapter 3 tells us that this strain should precede the genesis of a value-oriented movement, but our evidence comes primarily from within the context of the movements themselves. Thus one might argue that the value strain was a product of and not a cause of these movements.

It is possible to conjecture that the conjuncture of two circumstances led to the generation of SV for those who were to become Levellers. The first concerns their social position; they were among those whom Hill labels "common people." They were situated in the social structure below the yeomen and artisan masters but above wage laborers; that is, they were skilled craftsmen and small farmers (Brailsford 1961:9, 99, 104ff., 314–15). Within the context of a more general Puritan tradition, they viewed themselves as in some sense chosen, special, and in comparison with the rich, privileged and important. In addition these men were subjected to the exigencies of a Puritan ideology that demanded "biblical study, formal theological reasoning, and eager and disputatious searching into the purposes of God" (Woodhouse 1938: Introduction, 41). Often, and especially for persons in stable social positions, the opportunity or necessity to question and argue leads to a reaffirmation of prior values; for men of a transitional class it might well lead to a questioning of and alienation from those values. These factors may explain the genesis of SV, even though they fail to explain its exact distribution. Many persons, for example, fall under this description who did not develop value strain.

Puritans were taught that there was no mediator between themselves and God, and as we know from Durkheim (1951), this position may well give rise to "egotism," a situation of extreme individualism. But this condition must not be interpreted as a pathology or as one necessarily leading to individual adaptations. Here it occurred in the context of an ideology mandating the progressive interpretation of and quest for truth, wherein each asserted the right of speaking and thinking for his or herself, but where speech occurred within the context of collective, organized, sometimes highly disciplined movements. The point is that these movements either withdrew from the values of the society in which they were embedded, or else they actively fought to restructure those values (within any one of the society's subsystems).

Ireton speaks of the interest of the kingdom (Woodhouse 1938: 4); the Levellers have a tendency to emphasize the rights of the individual (Pease 1965:113, 141–42, 152). Ireton assumes the validity of extant values; the Levellers assume that ignorance allows these values to retain their force. Education and the appeal to right reason will enable men to distinguish political good from evil (Pease 1965:112). It appears that Leveller ideas were a development from Independent and other progressive ideas; with the Levellers, however, liberalism resulted in the questioning of values, not in their reaffirmation, and this was, I suspect, a function of their social position vis-à-vis the "Independents."

When these men found themselves in a situation in which the sword seemed the only power in the kingdom, they did not rationalize the victory of the strongest. Rather they announced that the kingdom was dissolved into a state of nature. When the House of Commons failed to fulfill the people's trust, this cancelled "its power of attorney; therefore the kingdom was without govern-

ment, and in a state of nature" (Pease 1965 : 179, 180; Hill 1972*b* :
53). But for them, the state of nature was as in Locke, not as in
Hobbes.

> A wider suffrage, annual elections and the fundamentals of the Agree-
> ment of the People were intended to preserve rulers from the tendency
> of power to corrupt. This was a remarkable reversal of hitherto ortho-
> dox conclusions about government drawn from the Fall—that the mass
> of mankind, being wicked, could be restrained only by the law and the
> magistrate. (Hill 1972*b* : 132)

It was no longer the magistrate who was assumed to be divinely
ordained, but rather common men in free communication with one
another and therefore with God. The societal community, civil society, was seen as autonomous from and prior to government.

These beliefs necessitated the delegitimation of the provisional
governments from 1646–49, and of the so-called Commonwealth
of 1649. While no doubt in part generated by economic conditions—"heavy" and inequitable taxation (especially the excise) in a
situation of economic duress—this seems a case like the one described by Habermas, where the structure of values was incapable
of legitimizing a certain form of government, his motivation crisis
(1975). Contrary to Habermas, however, it seems apparent to me
that the basic motor of history is not the autonomous development
of commitment systems, systems of social beliefs, but rather the
integrated, tendential development of entire social structures, conditioned by economic alterations (see chap. 4, above). The Levellers
were, even given their considerable import, not the motor of history; that "honor" belongs to the "Presbyterians," and later to the
descendents of the "Independents."

We must remember that within our context, this organized
group of radicals motivated changes beyond their own actions. It
is clear that their pressure necessitated a radicalization of political
action from the "Independents" and therefore from the "Presbyterians" (Brailsford 1961 : v, xi, 164, 173, 186–88, 195, 206, 223,
267, 274ff.; Hill 1972*b* : 49–51; Thomas 1972 : 57). Like the working class of later times, even in defeat they modified in the direction
of liberty and freedom the consequences of their own and others'
actions. While some of us believe that we have transcended their
political and moral ideals, many of us struggle within the confines
of their liberal, utilitarian beliefs, and others have not yet developed

to the point of certain of Lilburne's more radical friends or even of Lilburne himself: "Lilburne's chief aim, we might sum up, was equality before the law; that of his more radical friends, equality established by the law" (Schenk 1948:79; cf. chap. 8, below).

Appendix

In this appendix I sketch descriptions of three series of events: the religious movements that paralleled the political revolutions just discussed, the restoration of the Stuart monarchy after the Interregnum, and finally the Revolution of 1688. Within the brief compass of this appendix I will not be able to provide elaborate discussions explaining these events, but I will be able to identify their location within the theoretical framework I have laid out (especially in chap. 3) and will, in consequence, have outlined their explanation.

Religious Movements: 1630–49

Between 1630 and 1649 there emerged in England religious disorders (as defined in chap. 3) parallel to and interrelated with the political revolutions (disorders) just discussed. These began with an attempt from within the hierarchy of the Church of England to impose a facilitory transformation ("RELIGF"). This movement is associated with the name of Laud, who had been appointed Archbishop of Canterbury in 1633. The movement had three interrelated foci: instrumental, doctrinal, and organizational; each was relevant to a redefinition of role expectations within the structure of religious institutions.

The Arminian party within the Church of England rejected Calvinist predestination and substituted for it a grace rooted in sacrament (Tyacke 1973). This movement into what has been labeled "Anglo-Catholicism," while firmly rooted in England and not predisposed toward reunification with Rome, exalted the hierarchy of the episcopate and surrounded the newly "raised" priesthood with symbols of their authority. These enhanced the ritualistic nature of the church's religious practice and might be symbolized by the removal of the communion table from the body of the church to the east end of the chancel, where it was enclosed by railings and symbolically exalted above the body of the church's members.

Though a clear minority in the church, the Arminians endeavored to impose their innovations on the laity and the clergy. The High Commission enforced these innovations, and they were codified by the Convocation of 1640 and symbolized in the "et cetera oath":

> In full control during the '30s, the Laudians crowned their dominance by the canons which the clerical convocation passed in the spring of 1640. These enacted their programme into ecclesiastical law binding clergy and laity alike. They prescribed the ceremonial practices the archbishop favoured, and they imposed an oath on ministers and various classes of laymen promising never "to alter the government of this Church by archbishops, bishops, deans, and archdeacons, &c. as it stands now ... and as by right it ought to stand...." (Zagorin 1969:191)

Complementary to these transformations were organizational innovations integral to the imposition of ritualistic conformity on the nation. Within the context of seventeenth-century England's incomplete differentiation of religious and political institutions, these redefined executive powers; the power of both king and church hierarchy, in both state and church, was enhanced to the detriment of the laity, Parliament, the common law courts, and the notables who were accustomed to having considerable say in the control over parish business.

Laud magnified the king above the common law (Gardiner 1884, 6:259–60), and the emphasis on church courts tended to the same end for the clergy. Attempts to regain control over tithes for the church challenged the property rights of lay improprietors (Hill 1971). This was done to reinforce the prestige of the priesthood through a magnification of the power of the hierarchy and in the institutionalization of a clergy suited for the performing of ritual, but not for preaching (a core of its historic function within the church). Further, the hierarchy sought to gain control over the appointment of these clergy, removing this control from lay hands.

In sum, the movement begun by Laud articulated a series of innovations in violation of the structure of religious commitments embedded in church tradition (Tyacke 1973; Clarendon 1888:127, 194; Hill 1969c:489). These violations redefined the organizational powers of the church hierarchy and entailed the enforcement of a religious doctrine that may be characterized as "High Church," or "Anglo-Catholic." In challenging the Elizabethan religious settlement, Charles and Laud forced "Puritans" into opposition.[17] In challenging the property rights of improprietors, Laud alienated almost all sections of the propertied class (Hill 1971:340). Laud's actions thus paralleled and were integral to Charles's "REVOF," and they were in part responsible for a parallel consequence, the genesis of a facilitory religious movement that itself sought to redefine the role structure of the church.

As was the case with the facilitory rebellion (REVOF) that began the English Revolution, the facilitory religious movement (RELIGF) that began the religious disorders of the 1640s occurred within an extant organizational structure. It was concerned with the restructuring of roles within religious institutions.[18] Again parallel to the political movement, this facilitory disorder directed toward religious instructions commanded almost unanimous support in the ecclesia (Christiansen 1977:579).

Perhaps the most adequate characterization of the first phase of religious disorder in 1640–41 (RELIGF) is as "Erastian." It concerned a struggle for control between the Laudian episcopate within the Church of England and lay notables in both national and local spheres of interest. For the latter the question was how to bring the church and the clergy under their own control (Hill 1969b:191).

During the RELIGF "friction between parson and squire was ended by the complete subordination of the former to the latter" (Hill 1971:240). At the national level this fight was carried out in many ways. When in 1641 Parliament abolished the High Commission it destroyed the executive's control over parishes, as church courts ceased to function and ecclesiastical censorship and control over education ceased to exist (Hill 1969b:190; cf. Usher 1968).

> On December 15, 1640, it was resolved in the House of Commons "That the Clergy of *England*, convented in any Convocation, or Synod, or otherwise, have no Power to make any Constitutions, Canons, or Acts, whatsoever, in Matter of Doctrine, Discipline, or otherwise to bind the Clergy, or the Laity, of this Land, without common Consent of Parliament." (Judson 1949:361)

As Clarendon wrote,

> the House of Commons (that is, the major part) made no scruple in that fury to declare that the Convocation House had no power at all of making Canons, (notwithstanding that it was apparent by the law and

the uncontradicted practice of the Church that Canons had never been otherwise made), and that those Canons [promulgated by the convocation] contained in them matter of sedition and reproach to the regal power [n.b.], prejudicial to the liberty and property of the subject and to the privileges of Parliament. (1888, 1:273–74)

The general tenor of this Erastian movement was to reduce the power of the clergy and to transfer part of the king's ecclesiastical prerogative to Parliament (Hexter 1963:178). The movement overlapped with the REVOF insofar as religious and political institutions were not differentiated, and it focused on specifically religious roles insofar as religious and political institutions were differentiated. Like the REVOF, this RELIGF held within it the seeds of its own disintegration.

"More than half the members [of Parliament] would, in the long run, want nothing more in the Church than the abandonment of controversial ceremonies, the retirement of the bishops from secular power and an end to visitations and inquisitions" (Wedgwood 1966b:356). These men were a core within the party that rallied around the king in opposition to the REVOG made by the Parliamentary party. Among those who made the REVOG we find men supporting one or another form of RELIGG.

During the period of the REVOG Parliament abolished the episcopate organization of the Church of England and substituted in its place a form of Presbyterianism. It is important to note, however, that this Presbyterianism was of a very different variety than that found in Scotland. Even when under pressure from the Scots to effect a Presbyterian reform of the church, Parliament resisted implementing a Scottish form of Presbyterianism: in 1642

the Parliament was driven to throw itself unconditionally into the arms of the Scotch, but its whole precedent and subsequent action shows its determination to control the reconstruction of the national Church in its own sense—in a lay sense, in an English sense—by the help of an Assembly of Divines, and with a desire of approximation to the best reformed churches, but none the less with a repugnance to the pure Scotch Presbyterian system. (Shaw 1900, 1:136–37)[19]

Nearly all commentators remark on the Erastian nature of English Presbyterianism. Hill writes that "when a presbyterian system came to be set up in the sixteen-forties, it horrified the Scots by its erastianism: nominated laymen enjoyed a majority over ministers at all levels" (1969c:223). At the top, Gardiner wrote that "to make King and Church responsible to Parliament was the real aim of the Presbyterian party" (1893, 2:67). In other words, those in Parliament instrumental in making the RELIGG wished to "subordinate the regulation of church life and discipline to a hierarchical structure with Parliament at the top as final arbiter" (Glow 1965c:60).[20]

The consequence of this orientation was that Parliament substituted a provisional religious structure for the prior episcopal organization, while remaining within the general normative context provided by the Elizabethan settlement. No codified opinion regarding church organization (the crucial question at this level of religious movement) emerged during the 1640–49 period. Thus while a "presbyterian" government was established as the national church, it was an "aristocracy" of parliamentary and lay control within the context of the extant "monarchical" organization, although the absence of the monarch denuded this of significance during the years of rebellion (REVOG), and even more so, in time, as parliamentary control was institutionalized after 1688 (cf. Solt 1959:70–71; Gardiner 1893, 2:67, and 3:136–37). What remained was an official church capable de jure, if not de facto, of imposing itself on the populace, but it was now a church controlled by Parliament.

The religious Independents went even further; they challenged not only the collectivity organization of the church but also its normative structure. While they did not separate themselves from or challenge the idea of an official church organization (thus retaining the extant notion of a religious community at least equivalent with the society in which they lived) they challenged the capacity of that community to define normative expectations for its individual members. This did not necessarily imply a position in favor of toleration, as the individual unit could be interpreted as encompassing the congregation instead of the individual, but in the English case it almost always did imply great toleration (while excluding Catholics, among others).[21]

It is important to note that while Parliament abolished episcopacy, at no time between 1640 and 1660 did it disestablish the Church (Cross 1972:99). Yule is correct that after 1649 "Independency, if anything, was the established religion" (1958:24, cf. 41, 67). But it is important to remember in what this "establish-

ment" consisted. Cromwell's church, as Cross calls it, had no articles of religion approved by the state and no common liturgy. Instead it established institutions (the tryers, who met to examine all
men seeking to enter the ministry of the national church, and the
ejectors, who removed unworthy ministers in possession of livings)
to oversee the maintenance and the conduct of clergy (paraphrasing
Cross 1972:105). As Yule puts it, "Neither the Republic nor the
Protectorate Parliaments, nor the rule of the Major-Generals, upset
the pattern of a decentralized Calvinist Church organization, the
Puritan-Anglican Church without bishops" (1958:74ff.).

As early as 1643, Independents tried to define themselves as a
middle ground between presbyterianism and sectarianism. In *An
Apologetical Narration* they wrote, "We believe the truth to be and
consist in a middle way betwixt that which is falsely charged on us
Brownism [sectarianism]; and that which is the contention of these
times, the authoritative Presbyterial Government in all the subordination and proceedings of it" (quoted in Kaplan 1969:255).
Thus these men who did not renounce communion in the Church of
England, as did the sectarians, articulated a system of church organization in which each congregation was an autonomous unit, and
in which, "With its emphasis on the congregation as the unit of
discipline and its denial of hierarchical control, would have led even
more than Presbyterianism to a dominance of the industrious sort
and their allies among the gentry over their congregations" (Hill
1969c:224; Brailsford 1961:30).

It was these men who were able to legitimize participation in the
REVON. They abolished the extant mode of hierarchical organization within their church as they did within the state, but in both
circumstances they remained in the context of the patrimonial
values that controlled each institution. They were incapable of
effecting a break with these values, and thus had no reason to reconstruct them. The attempt at reconstruction in both church and
state was left to the sectarians, men and women who broke with
both sets of values, and realized the necessity of differentiating between them in articulating an ideology that demanded the separation of church and state.[22]

A religious disorder directed toward the values institutionalized
within the church may take two forms; it may seek to redefine those
values or may simply involve a retreat from the institutional structure in which those values are defined. In the latter case a religious

subculture will be constructed in which a new set of values will be institutionalized; in the former case, this religious subculture will endeavor to transform the nature of the religious community, including in this attempt a redefinition of the community's values.

The sectarian movements of mid-seventeenth-century England were of both types. All withdrew from the "established church," however that church was defined at the time of withdrawal; some sought only toleration for their particular brand of salvation, others sought, by whatever means, to convert the ecclesia into their own image. A detailed analysis of the substance of these movements is not possible in this context, but a few words about certain of the bonds among these various sectarian groups may be in order.

Writing about various groups involved in the RELIGV, Thomas comments:

> What they had in common was that they all were sects, that is, they believed in a pure Church, they made spiritual regeneration a condition of membership and insisted upon separation from a national Church which contained ungodly elements. More often than not they believed in the complete self-government of individual congregations; they usually thought in terms of direct inspiration by the Holy Spirit; and they tended to depreciate the role of a ministry, of "outward ordinances" and of human learning. Their assertion of the spiritual equality of all believers led to an exalted faith in private judgement, lay preaching, a cult of prophecies and revelations, and culminated in the Quaker doctrine of the spirit dwelling in all men. (1967:335)

For our purposes, the crucial points to highlight are the emphasis placed on the spiritual equality of all believers, on the perceived capacity of individuals within a community of believers to make their own religious "judgments," however these might be rationalized, and on the emphasis in many sects on the necessity of separating church and state. These three facets of English sectarianism must be understood as an integrated whole; though one can imagine and find circumstances where they vary independently, their cohesion in the mid-seventeenth century was a mark of "the world turned upside down" (see Hill 1972*b*).

Within sectarian religious organizations nonnotables took the lead in articulating new organizational forms and new doctrines. Whatever their attitude toward outsiders, within their own organizations sectarians tended to recognize the merit of individual conscience and inspiration, defining each person (often including women) in direct communion with God, and allowing for the corroboration of each person's judgment within the collectivity of her congregation. The authenticity of each judgment was not manifested by the outward show of office or title but by the veracity of one's spiritual experience and faith. The merit of that experience was incapable of coercion, and thus required a division between civil and moral law, between church and state.

Thus within the context of patrimonial institutions, in both church and state, the sects that constituted the RELIGV articulated an ideology and constructed organizational forms based on the equality of all believers and the autonomy of each believer in her dealings with God, an autonomy that did not eliminate the desirability of collective reinforcement of moral action within the congregation, and the autonomy of these congregations from a hierarchical church organization and from the apparatus of the state. From these sectarian organizations came most of the persons who attempted, without success, to make a revolution at the level of values (REVOV). From their ideologies came one source of the beliefs that were used to legitimize this attempted revolution.

The Restoration and the Revolution of 1688

This essay has largely ignored the period from 1649 to 1660, when early attempts to institutionalize a republican form of government (within REVON) backslid into quasimonarchical, but not traditionally acceptable, modes of governance (REVOG). In 1660 these latter regressed further with the restoration of the Stuart monarchy in the person of Charles II, the son of the executed Charles I.

The term "restoration" is ambiguous within this context. What was restored was not the "Stuart monarchy" prior to the revolution, but rather the "Stuart monarchy" after the first phase of the revolution. In other words, the restored state was an institutional structure that had undergone a facilitory rebellion (REVOF).

"In England ... it was not the king that was restored, but the king in parliament" (Ogg 1967:31). As Gardiner put it, "Everything that it had done up to this point [the culmination of the REVOF] with the single exception of the compulsory clauses of the Triennial Act, was accepted at the Restoration and passed into the permanent constitution of the country. The first was the work of the whole Parliament, the second [what the Restoration rejected, the REVOG] was the work of a majority" (1884, 10:34). In other words, in 1660 it was the men who wanted to stop short of the rebellion (REVOG) who emerged, for the moment, as victorious:

> The legislation of 1641 was not the private property of the middle-party men; in it they were but copartners. Men later of the peace party and moderate Royalists of the stamp of Hyde, Falkland, and Southampton had a full share in the early work of the Long Parliament. Of the groups responsible for placing insurmountable obstacles in the path of despotism, the moderate Royalists [who withdrew from the revolution after the culmination of the REVOF] might with some show of reason boast that they had played the wisest part, since in the Restoration settlement they most nearly achieved their avowed ends.   (Hexter 1941:174)

Thus the monarchy was restored, but in a context wherein Parliament's powers were enhanced to the level of eighteen years earlier, to the point of completion of the facilitory rebellion (Stone 1980:50–51). Under these circumstances the king retained control over the militia and thus of the core of executive powers. While it is true that the restoration involved a recognition of a permanent place for Parliament within the polity (even given the repeal of the Triennial Act in 1664; see Roseveare 1969:55), the tendencies that had led to the REVOG in the previous decades continued unabated or actually accelerated in development, and their consequences were exacerbated to the point of diminishing the import of the institutionalization of the REVOF at the Restoration. For example, "in 1660 no one could have foreseen that, with the development of English industry and commerce, the revenue from Customs and Excise would eventually reach such a figure as to make Charles and his successor independent of parliament" (Ogg 1967:158). These pressures, largely a consequence of the continued growth of manufacturing, resulted in the regeneration of the conditions that had earlier led to the REVOG; as we would predict based on our previous analyses, they once again had the same consequence, the REVOG we call the Revolution of 1688.

The period after the Restoration witnessed considerable transformation and economic growth. A clear indication of this growth was increased output in many sectors of the economy, coupled with a decline in prices. In addition there is clear evidence of a growth in English trade internal to the country, and overseas trade in both old and new markets. This growth occurred in the context of developing economic institutions: manufacturing, financial, and commercial institutions. These processes were visible in both agriculture and in industry.[23]

I have argued in chapter 4 that a manufacturing economy went through a long period of gestation in English society. The political movements that were constructed (most especially the REVOG discussed above and the Revolution of 1688) on its foundation had a similar history, reaching back into the reign of the Tudors. More directly relevant to the Revolution of 1688, Gardiner wrote of the Parliament of 1625 that it "opened the floodgates of that long contention with the Crown which was never, except for one brief moment, to be closed again till the Revolution of 1688 came to change the conditions of government in England" (1883, 5:432). Even more directly, Macaulay wrote:

> the leaders of the Roundhead party in 1642 [who made the REVOG], and the statesmen who, about half a century later, effected the Revolution [of 1688], had exactly the same object in view. That object was to terminate the contest between the crown and the Parliament, by giving to the Parliament a supreme control over the executive administration. The statesmen of the Revolution effected this indirectly by changing the dynasty. The Roundheads of 1642, being unable to change the dynasty, were compelled to take a direct course towards their end. (1906, 1: 84)

While seeing their goals more clearly than the actors themselves, Macauley was correct in viewing the Revolution of 1688 as a recapitulation of the Great Rebellion (REVOG).

While this appendix is not the place to enter into an extensive examination of the Revolution of 1688 a few essential points must be made. The Revolution occurred within the context of the traditionally accepted normative framework of the polity. The monarchy as a formal system of government emerged unscathed, and the Revolution itself was legitimized in terms of legal arguments. The marvel of the Revolution was not the diminished power of the executive compared to Parliament. Rather, while it was clear that sovereign control resided in Parliament, the executive also increased in power. As Plumb puts it in assessing the bases of postrevolutionary political stability, "And perhaps the most important of all is the expansion of the executive, which grew, not independently of the legislature, but partly within it" (1969b: 114). While it was clear that no ministry would survive for long without the support of parliament, parliament itself was in part a creature of the executive. This reciprocity allowed for an extraordinary growth in the power of government, as the revolution made clear that "any future ruler would at his peril defy those whom Parliament represented: no ruler did" (Hill 1966:277).

While the monarchy survived, control over government passed into the hands of those men of property who constituted Parliament. The fiction of representation of the people by Parliament later proved to be sufficient to allow for the expansion and reorganization of the political nation and its state without any future revolution.

There were marked differences between the revolution from 1641–49 and the Revolution of 1688. The most obvious and probably the most important involves the role of religion in the two revolutions. In 1688 England was ruled by a Catholic monarch who was at great pains to rehabilitate Catholicism within English life. This rehabilitation involved an infusion of Catholics into secular pursuits, contrary to law. For example, in endeavoring to secure control over the army and thus over a primary institution for the furtherance of his policies, James appointed numerous Catholics as officers.

Ogg labels the remodeling of parliamentary boroughs and a repetition of the Declaration of Indulgence as the immediate causes (precipitants) of the revolution (1969:186). The former brought royal dignity and authority into "grave disrepute by wholesale eviction of men who assumed, without question, a vested and hereditary right to power and pre-eminence in those parts of England where they had their estates" (Ogg 1969:189). The Declarations of Indulgence, while ostensibly allowing for the inclusion of Dissenters into the political nation, were viewed as a ruse allowing for the inclusion of Catholics, and for the undermining of the church in favor of the Catholic religion (and thus, it was thought, in favor of "the Catholic," meaning now the French interest in Europe, and thus in favor of French absolutism at home).

Whatever James's intentions, his religion when coupled with his actions neutralized the church hierarchy and the Tory interest toward the revolution. When he removed himself from England these natural supports of the Stuart monarchy were able to acquiesce in a REVOG, whereas their structured interests would have otherwise limited their participation to a reaffirmation of the Restoration settlement (REVOF). In fact, as was the case in the Rump many years earlier, their tacit support of the revolution served to moderate its consequences (cf. Underdown 1971; Worden 1974).

The apparently fortuitous circumstances that James was a Catholic allowed for the tacit unification of the political nation behind the "Whig Revolution." This circumstance of James's religious beliefs allowed the church hierarchy to act in opposition to him and in consequence to ensure their own legitimacy within the new social formation. Contrary to 1642–49, in 1688 there was no religious disorder running parallel to the political revolution.[24]

8. Theory of Social Development

A societal crisis may be said to exist when there is the possibility that social disorder will lead to the transformation from one stage of social development into another. It is a major contention of this work that a theory of crisis can be successfully enunciated only within a conceptual framework that encompasses three dimensions: the functional, structural, and developmental. I have presented so far a functional theory of internal disorder and a structural model of a manufacturing mode of production. I have argued that the internal dynamic of a manufacturing economy, interpenetrated by rationalizing values and regulated by a patrimonial political structure, generated the key variables leading to a rebellion in early seventeenth-century England. In this chapter I present a theory of stage sequential development that will enable us to argue that the resolution to the societal crisis in Stuart England facilitated the transition from a society grounded in manufacture to one grounded in machine capitalism.

We have discussed social disorders as motivated actions in violation of one or another institutionalized normative code within a society. They may result in attempts to redefine some component of social action or they may be constituted as violations of institutionalized norms without any attempt to reconstruct the system attacked. The revolutionary actions discussed in chapters 5, 6, and 7 were violations of the political authority code that sought to redefine one or another component of the polity (values, norms, collectivities, or role relations). Such attempts at reconstruction need not seek to transform, or result in the transformation of, the stage of social development of the structure attacked.

The term *crisis* may be applied to the social system in which a particular form of disorder is occurring or to the disorder itself. In the latter case, a crisis is something more than a form of social disorder that endeavors to reconstruct the system under attack; in addition, the attempted reconstruction must have as a possible consequence the transformation of the system from one stage of social development into another. Only when this structural development is an objective possibility, whatever the goals of the actors under discussion, will I use the term *crisis*. Thus a crisis is a subset of social disorder; a crisis may be said to occur when there is the possibility that social disorder might lead to the structural transformation of a social system from one stage of social development into another.

The successful articulation of a theory of crisis is dependent on our capacity to integrate functional, structural, and developmental perspectives. A structure describes a tendency of development. Marx, for example, retains the Hegelian "notion" in the context of his analysis of each stage of social development. His characterizations of these stages are tendential, specifying the constrained pattern of development, the logic of progression within a stage. These patterns are, of course, subject to countervailing pressures within the same logic as well as to conjunctural imbalances and exogenous dislocations. Nonetheless, a structural analysis is necessary if we are to assess the constancy of the crisis. Is the conjuncture definitive of the crisis fortuitous and thus capable of successful, long-term amelioration? Or is the crisis a necessary consequence of the natural, patterned unfolding of the structure? In order to determine the answer to these questions we must be capable of specifying the natural, tendential development within the extant structure; this specification is the goal of a structural analysis (see chap. 4).

The next question we must ask concerns the consequences of this tendential development. Will the natural unfolding of the system give rise to social disorder? In order to answer this question we must rephrase it; we may argue that a crisis is present only when the tendential development of a system gives rise to the necessary and sufficient conditions leading to a disorder severe enough to reconstruct the social formation. To make this argument we must have a theory of internal disorder, a theory that is couched in functionally defined concepts and is valid for all social formations. Only with such a theory is it possible to get outside the structural, tendential model, to define the meaning of an irresolvable contradiction.

Without the functionally defined theory there is no way to assess the possible consequences of the structurally constituted tendential development I have presented. From the structural analysis we can conclude that "contradictions" exist in the system, but there is no way to assess the consequences of these contradictions. The logic of structural theory does not allow us to get outside the structure it delimits.

Thus many Marxists have fruitlessly sought for the final crisis of machine capitalism, when they were really looking at a series of business cycles, each of which in time created the conditions for the renewal of economic activity and capital accumulation. If our analysis remains within a structural model we have no way to determine the resolution of events we may label "crises"; we have, in other words, no way to differentiate between crises (as I have used the term in this essay) and cycles, where the latter are integral to the continued tendential development of the system under examination. But even with an integrated structural and functional theory, we still have no way of determining whether the predicted disorder will result in the transition from one stage of social development to another; to determine this we require a developmental theory.

Most social disorders, even if they involve the reconstruction of some component of a social formation, do not lead to the transformation of one type of social formation into another. In order to assess this possibility we need a theory of societal development which allows us to order social formations as stages in the development of societies. Such a theory will allow us to determine when, for example, a revolution might lead into a new stage of society. If this theory is to be of assistance in evaluating the crisis potential of specific conjunctures in capitalist societies, it must be defined within a functionally conceptualized framework.[1]

In generalizing Piaget's discussion of the stages of moral development, the developmental theory I have constructed articulates the structural relationships characteristic of each stage in this sequential progression. In the analysis of both cognitive and social systems the theory focuses on structural relationships, not, as in Kohlberg and Habermas, on normative principles. Here I will present only a very truncated picture of the theory emphasizing its general applicability.[2]

The second half of the chapter takes us back to the seventeenth century. Here I specify the theory of development in an examination of the transformation of the structure of political legitimation which began in earnest with the English revolutions. I focus on the movement from a traditional-hierarchical structure into a rational-egalitarian one. The first half of the chapter enunciates the stage sequence theory by means of an illustration. I try to show how Piaget's discussion of moral development is capable of generalization within the context of Parsonian functionally defined categories. In effect this involves adding a developmental perspective to the conceptual apparatus adopted throughout this book. I have chosen this aspect of Piaget's work as it is easily comprehended and discussed.

It may seem odd to some readers to suddenly enter the world of the moral development of the child. A second reason for selecting this illustration, in addition to its comprehensibility, is that it allows me to emphasize that the theoretical tools used in this book are intended to have broad generality. They apply to all action systems (see Parsons 1977:chap. 10). Parsons endeavors to base this applicability on quasi-metaphysical grounds; my justifications are more pragmatic. I am only concerned with the empirical status of the model. If the use of this model in an analysis of numerous psychological and social situations can be justified, it will be reasonable to use it as a basis for hypotheses in future work. If it is so used, it will be subject to both continued empirical evaluation and refinement.[3]

The final reason for using Piaget's discussion of the development of moral judgment is that it is easily specified to a discussion of political legitimation, the subsumption of political actions within structures of value orientation. Piaget was aware that his analysis recapitulated Durkheim's in *The Division of Labor*. Here I recapitulate Piaget's argument in order to reverse the process, in order to respecify his analysis to the level of collective, normative regulation. It will be easy to show, in at least one context, the power of the developmental model in an area of considerable importance to our historical discussion.[4]

The Theory

At the level of cognitive development, each stage may be understood as specifying a capacity; within each capacity a determinable range of performances are capable of articulation. Practice precedes its codification and routinization in consciousness. Thus while a particular practice need not indicate the existence of a determinate capacity, its routinization alongside comparable performances is intelligible only within the context of the attainment of a specific stage of development. It is possible for a person to function at one level of development within one sphere of activity, and at another level in a second set of activities. In general, when this occurs the capacity to learn at the higher level may be presumed, even if the additional conditions for this learning are not present. It must be understood that no particular substantive activity need be present as marking the attainment of a particular developmental stage. Too often analysts confuse a particular performance with the capacity to assimilate that performance.

At the social system level, a stage is constituted as a set of organizational constraints, of the sort Durkheim spoke of under the rubric of mechanical and organic solidarity. They may be present in a variety of contexts and in a variety of substantive manifestations. Thus one stage may characterize both economic and political development, and two or more substantive varieties of political system may be characteristic of one stage. The autonomy of social systems indicates that they need not all function at the same level of development within a particular system. However, such incongruence may be relevant to the genesis of internal disorder.

Piaget (1962) has discussed seven steps, or stages, wherein children both learn the practice of rules and become conscious of the import and significance of rules. The first stage in each sequence overlaps, and the composite series has six periods.[5]

Stage One: A:

The Practice of Rules, stage one and the Consciousness of Rules, stage one: In the practice of rules there is "A first stage of a purely *motor* or *individual* character, during which the child handles the marbles at the dictation of his desires and motor habits. This leads to the formation of more or less ritualized schemas, but since play is still purely individual, one can only talk of motor rules and not of truly collective rules" (Piaget 1962:26–27).

In a brief summary of the first stage in the development of the consciousness of rules Piaget comments that "during the first stage rules are not yet coercive in character, either because they are purely motor, or else (at the beginning of the egocentric stage [my stage two—M.G.]) because they are received, as it were, unconsciously, and as interesting examples rather than as obligatory realities" (1962:28). As may be obvious even from this brief description, these two stages overlap. Both concern motor functions, an accommodation to and assimilation of new objects within individualized adaptive schema.

At this developmental level behavior is individualized and concerns the attainment of adaptive control over items in the environment. This differs slightly from the Parsonian notion of adaptation in that this set of actions is not yet part of a more encompassing system. The child is not yet concerned with the use of facilities to attain socially defined goals, as there are no socially defined goals. From this perspective, she is the sole unit of a monolithically defined system; her behaviors incorporate both goal-oriented and adaptive behavior as well as, to the degree that ritualization is followed, the maintenance of "traditional patterns."

Stage Two: A—G:

The Practice of Rules, stage two:[6] This stage begins with the child's reception of codified rules, but though she imitates an example, she continues to play by herself, or if with others, without coordinating her actions to theirs. "In other words, children at this stage, even when they are playing together, play each one 'on his own' (everyone can win at once) and without regard for any codification of rules. This dual character, combining imitation of others with a purely individual use of the examples received, we have designated by the term Egocentrism" (27).

This stage concerns the definition of individual goals, but without the coordination of such interests into an integrated game, into an integrated system. It concerns a definition of the importance of facilities for the realization of some goal, but this goal retains its individualistic nature. For example, in a game of marbles, to win "does not mean getting the better of others, but simply playing on one's own" (39). It is quite possible that two children playing in one location (not properly speaking, together) will relate two sets of rules to an observer (40–41). So here we find a specification of goals, but no integration of the individuals' purposive behaviors into a communal social organization.

Stage Three: G—L:

Consciousness of Rules, stage two: "During the second stage [of consciousness, my third stage—M.G.] (apogee of egocentric and first half of cooperating stage) rules are regarded as sacred and untouchable, emanating from adults and lasting forever. Every suggested alteration strikes the child as a transgression" (28).

In this stage rules are accepted as traditionally legitimate. They are attributed to the parent and accepted as if given by divine guidance. If innovations in such rules are accepted it is because the children are not aware that any innovation has occurred (54). Within this context the creation of a new rule is simply viewed as the rediscovery of one already in existence (57).

Piaget distinguishes between constraint and cooperation: the former implies a hierarchically organized, unilateral respect for authority; the latter, an intercourse between equals. Stage three concerns unilateral respect in the generation of a "mystical" attitude toward authority, an attitude *not* necessarily contradictory to the egotism already discussed. Values are seen as emanating from "on high" and are defined at a relatively low level of generality, often having reference to specific situations; as such, they may approximate, or very narrowly control, situationally specific goals. Nonetheless, this is the first stage where an internal social system boundary appears within the interaction sequence, where the social system, as distinguished from the actors who make it up, appears.[7]

Social-structurally, this stage is typified by hierarchical relationships. This child's primary socializing agents are her parents, and the child's attitude toward her parents is one of reverence and subservience. During this stage rules appear as external laws, sacred because they have been laid down by adults (103). In the genesis of moral rules the hierarchy is age-graded; in other contexts the hierarchy is dependent not primarily on age differentials, but rather on differentially ranked social positions. At this point, for the child, the moral constraint of adults leads to heteronomy and consequently to moral realism.

At the level of social systems, we are dealing with the development of mechanical solidarity, and thus emphasis is primarily on segmentation, not differentiation, among individuals (Durkheim 1964; Parsons 1967: chap. 1). Collectivities will be hierarchically organized. The value orientations defining desirable activities, and thus the nature of the desirable community, will appear as external laws; each unit's position with regard to them will be heteronomous. These values will be relatively concrete, and will define fairly narrow ranges of acceptable action for persons within specific status positions.

Stage Four: G—I:

Practice of Rules, stage three: This is the stage of incipient cooperation. Each player in the marble game tries to win, and all concern themselves with the "mutual control and unification of the rules." But the rules are rather vague and different children provide "disparate and often entirely contradictory accounts of the rules obeyed in playing marbles" (Piaget 1962:27). In other words, support is provided for some set of procedures within the context of a game, but the rules themselves are not codified.

Piaget accepts as a criterion of the beginning of this stage the moment when winning refers to getting the better of others. This determines a form of institutionalized conflict within the context of the game (42). The important point is that this is the beginning of harmonized, coordinated activity within the system of reference. Interests are defined within the context of a mutually accepted—if vaguely defined—system.

"Generally speaking, it is a perfectly normal thing that in its beginnings cooperation—on the plane of action—should not immediately abolish the mental states created—on the plane of thought—by the complexis: egocentricity and constraint. Thought always lags behind action and cooperation has to be practised for a very long time before its consequences can be brought fully to light by reflexive thought" (64; see 98, 117, 119, 136–37). In this stage actions in anticipation of the stage of consciousness which follows are found, legitimized within ideas derivative of the stage of consciousness preceding. It therefore marks a disjunction between thought and action. "Since cooperation is a method, it is hard to see how it could come into being except by its own exercise. No amount of constraint could determine its emergence. If mutual respect does derive from unilateral respect, it does so by opposition" (98).

Stage Five: I—A:

Consciousness of Rules, stage three: During this stage "a rule is looked upon as a law due to mutual consent, which you must respect if you want to be loyal but which it is permissible to alter on the condition of enlisting general opinion on your side" (28). Here the rules of the game are no longer viewed as imposed by outside authority, but rather as the outcome of free decisions based on mutual consent; "there are no more crimes of opinion, but only breaches in procedure" (65). In Piaget's terms, autonomy follows upon the veritable elimination of egoism, and "one is struck by the synchronism between the appearance of this new type of conscious-ness of rules and a genuine observation of rules" (70).

This stage concerns the justification of claims, the allocation of decisions within a specified set of procedures. It involves, then, the generation of Durkheim's organic solidarity and the noncontrac-tual elements of contract. In personality terms it marks the integra-tion of the ego and the generation of ego-identity (cf. Erikson 1963, 1968; Habermas 1979). At a societal level it marks the develop-ment of a structurally differentiated societal community (Parsons 1966; Hegel 1967). More generally, it involves the development of formal rationality, the genesis of constitutive rules that define pro-cedures within which decisions (constituted rules) might be arrived at. This occurs through the differentiation of structures between integrative and pattern-maintenance functions. It is essential within this context that we recognize that the latency function does not disappear; on the contrary, the structures that constitute it within stage five will have themselves undergone a process of development, including a generalization of the values embedded in them allowing for the legitimation of a wider set of social relationships. The non-contractual elements of contract, the constitutive rules, are con-trolled by, legitimated by, the value-commitments definitive of the new pattern-maintenance subsystem (cf. Parsons 1967, chap. 1).[8]

Stage five is typified by contractual relationships between equals and a formal equality pertains in the relations that constitute it. Within the context of these social relationships, roles are formally interchangeable, but the substantive status differences between actors remain; the rules formally apply to all, and the proverbial rich and poor men are both forbidden to sleep under the bridge. In consequence, within the strict logic of this stage, formal equality may serve as a mask for a growing substantive inequality (Dur-kheim 1964:374–88; Weber 1968, 2:729–31). What is important in stage five is that each has a formally defined equal opportunity within a mutually agreed-upon framework of cooperation and con-tention.

Stage Six: I—L:

Practice of Rules, stage four: This is the last stage Piaget dis-cusses, and his perception of it seems to be colored by this fact. He emphasized that this stage marks the codification of the procedures governing the game; the code of rules is known by the entire children's grouping. In other words, concern is manifest for the rules themselves, and further, attention is paid to the constitutive rules within which constituted rules are articulated (Piaget 1962:47ff.).

More generally, this stage seems to mark the period of the legitimation of procedures. This is the stage, in Weber's terms, where rational-legal authority as a mode of justification is itself legitimized.[9] Specific collective loyalties are sanctioned in terms of institutionalized values, but if we widen our frame of reference, these values themselves are justified in terms of a cultural meaning system. At this stage the child is capable of evaluating, of justifying, the values she upholds. She can become autonomous and self-critical (cf. Habermas 1979:chap. 2, where he adds a seventh stage to Kohlberg's six-stage model).

This discussion seems acceptable except in one respect. A stage of action is not simply a codification of the past. It ought to imply, in practice, the consciousness of the future. In this respect, it seems to me that Piaget's discussion needs amplification. Instead of endeavoring to do that within the context of stage six, I will proceed to describe stage seven.

Stage Seven: L—G:

Consciousness of Rules, stage four: This discussion is only in part based on Piaget; he does not take his schema past the preceding stage. I have extrapolated within the confines of the logic of the theory, and have based parts of my discussion on other work (dealing especially with the structure of the psychoanalytic relationship, the structure of party-mass interaction in Leninist theory, and the structure of the teacher-student relationship in college classrooms), and based parts of my discussion on other aspects of Piaget's own work. Prominent among the latter is his discussion, in *The Moral Judgement of the Child* (1962), of three stages in the development of distributive justice. The first of these stages concerns a definition of the "just" as that which is commanded by an adult; the second stresses equality, and the third, equity (1962:chap. 3, and for a brief description of the three stages, 284–85, 315–17). It is my view that stage seven is constituted by equitable social organization.

Stage three concerns the institutionalization of hierarchical controls, identified with tradition; stage five concerns the institutionalization of egalitarian controls, identified with rational-legal legislation; stage seven will institutionalize equitable controls, which we will learn to recognize at the societal level as focusing on scientific, nonarbitrary control over decision making.

In stage seven, "in addition to considerations of pure justice, the circumstances of the individual must be taken into account" (272). In other words, equity is not based simply on formal equality; it involves a consideration of the situations in which individuals are actually placed (283, 285, 317). "Instead of looking for equality in identity, the child no longer thinks of the equal rights of individuals except in relation to the particular situation of each.... In the domain of distributive justice it means no longer thinking of law as identical for all but taking account of the personal circumstances of each (favouring the younger ones, etc.). Far from leading to privileges, such an attitude tends to make equality more effectual than it was before" (317).

Thus stage seven involves the transcendence of the hierarchy involved in stage three and the equality of stage five in a new synthesis. Within a more general developmental context, it is essential to stress that each of these stages is defined by organizational constraints.[10] Within an organizational context characterized by equitable relationships, the basis for the evaluation of positions is their performance capacity. The substance of this evaluation, and thus of the ranking of positions, must be specific to the situation under examination. But in every instance the principle of equity must be maintained, and control over a situation vested in those capable of acting in ways capable of successfully implementing system goals.[11] In saying this I do not mean to imply that all organizations will be guided at all times by equitable regulations. Rather, it is clear that there will be situations where hierarchical and egalitarian relationships are appropriate in terms of the performance capacity of the system. In such cases, these relationships will be the natural consequence of equitable structures. What places equity higher on a level of sequential development than either hierarchy or egalitarianism is that the reverse process of genesis is not possible within these earlier structures. When an equitable system has greater performance capacity it will not be generated by either egalitarian or hierarchical systems.[12]

Thus the stages in this model from one to seven are ordered in terms of a hierarchically inclusive progression. I intend this to be a scientific, not a value judgment.[13] It is only necessary to demonstrate that the earlier stages, in social structure and process, are capable of genesis within the latter, but not vice versa, and that according to some criteria of appropriateness, they will be generated in requisite situations.

Here I will simply illustrate this thesis, with reference to the model as already outlined. Within stage five the primary criterion of justification is procedural (rationality); the substantive nature of decisions is unimportant, so long as they do not touch the constitutive procedural rules.[14] Within this system the traditional norms definitive of stage three may be generated, if appropriate, and excluding the constitution of tradition as inviolable, all components of stage three are permissible, and contextually most will be manifest. The reverse is not true. Unless the traditional prescriptions are coincidentally congruent with those formally determined within a procedural rationality, a genesis of the latter is prohibited by the authority of tradition.

In the equitable stage decisions are made based on the performance capacity of the actors, and are structured so as to allow for the evaluation of their consequences and thus of the theory (and persons) informing them. Within this structure there will be situations mandating hierarchical and egalitarian processes. To take a very simple case, imagine a situation requiring the application of some technical skill. In the determination of decisions requiring this skill, the person possessing it may well find herself in a hierarchically superior position to others in the group, especially if her advice has been repeatedly shown to be accurate and beneficial. In a situation involving an "unknown" factor, persons in the group will find themselves in "the same" circumstance, and their discourse will be among formal equals. But both of these circumstances, phenomenologically like hierarchy and egalitarianism, are manifestations of equity, where control over decisions is in the hands of those with demonstrable performance capacity, and where the situation allows for the redemption of presumed expertise or the obverse, the falsification of a presumed, but unredeemable capacity. In an equitable structure a special expertise is vested in those confronting the consequences of such actions. As the "reality" of our first situation involved hierarchical relations, and the "reality" of our second involved egalitarian relations, each was in turn generated, but both were generated within an equitable structure.

This argument might be restated in more technical terms showing that performance capacities generated in the later stages are
transferable to the earlier, but that the reverse is not true. Such an
argument might be based on competence in the performance of
socially defined roles, and it would demonstrate that the personal
ability to support (*tragen*) a role was developmentally generated for
individuals, and that the roles were developmentally patterned in
terms of their structural organization. This formal task need not be
completed in this context (cf. Habermas 1979), as long as the logic
of progression is intuitively understood.

What is essential to realize is that the generative process is not
reversible: a hierarchical system cannot generate egalitarian relationships (in its core components) without ceasing to be a hierarchical structure, and an egalitarian structure cannot generate equitable relationships (within its core components) without ceasing to
be an egalitarian structure. As long as we remain at the level of
words these statements are true by definition. When we enter the
world of social practice, we discover that the patterned constraints
of either a hierarchical or an egalitarian social formation prohibit
these transformations. In order to arrive at the more developed
level, these patterned constraints must be restructured.[15]

The truth of these assertions is perhaps most palpable if we
revert to the level of personal development. Stage three in the
development of individual moral judgment is intrapsychically characterized by heteronomous principles, and interpersonally characterized by hierarchical structures. Stage five is intrapsychically
characterized by autonomous principles and interpersonally characterized by egalitarian relationships. Not only is the natural progression from one to another, but autonomous principles are incapable of generation within hierarchical relationships. The age-graded
progression of an individual is embedded in the developmental progression I have, following Piaget, articulated. This means that the
natural maturation of an individual is constituted by her progression through the seven stages.

The logic of progression in the stage sequence model, if not the
specific content of each stage, may be made apparent in terms of
figure 31. The sequence of development that I have enunciated follows
a clear pattern within the context of the functional model Parsons
has developed (as modified in Gould 1976:470–78).[16] Each stage
focuses on one boundary interchange and thus on the structural pro-

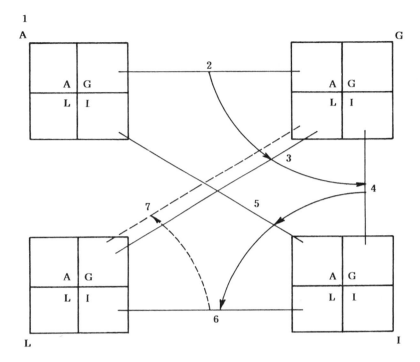

Figure 31.

cesses occurring at that point. The next stage follows in sequence. This is not to indicate that the other functions are dormant in any stage; as Piaget clearly realizes, there is a continuity of function and a transformation of structure (1962:84, 85, 334–35). Each stage emerges, however, in an emphasis on a functionally defined problem, even though each stage involves a "relative transformation" of the entire system.[17]

It is important to note that this presentation of the stage sequential model merely illustrates its construction. I do not mean to imply that stages are to be typified in terms of the level of moral judgment reached by the average actor within some social organization, or by the logic of moral judgment implicit in societal values. Rather I mean this discussion of moral judgment to illustrate the structural mechanisms operative at each stage. These structural mechanisms are definitive of the level of development, and at the societal level must first be applied to the mode of economic organization, either differentiated from or embedded in organizations fulfilling noneconomic functions. Societal stages must be characterized, in the first instance, by the level of economic development, as the economic structure limits the variability of other subsystems.

As I have indicated above, this model must be evaluated in terms of its utility in helping to reconstruct the development of social (and perhaps of personality) systems. Because the model is defined at such a high level of abstraction, it is possible to evaluate it and to improve it in examining a wide variety of contemporary and historical systems. In the next section of this chapter, I will present a brief discussion of that aspect of the model relevant to seventeenth-century English political legitimation.

Structures of Political Legitimation in 17-th Century England

Within the context of our three-dimensional framework we can see why the English revolutions of the seventeenth century had the potential to generate the transformation of one form of social formation into another, more advanced in the system of social development. The manufacturing bourgeoisie (in agriculture and industry) took a leading role in the crucial stage of the revolution. These were the same persons who assumed a leading role in the process of capital accumulation that led to the transformation of manufacture into machine capitalism. While the former was grounded in the formal subsumption of labor under capital, the latter entailed the real subsumption of labor under capital. Machine capitalism involved the revolutionizing of the labor process that constituted the forces of economic production. This development altered the economic foundation that limited the form of political and other social structures that might be constructed on its base.

Crucial in this process of economic transformation was the position of the nascent bourgeoisie. This class's capacity to accumulate capital within the predominant manufacturing economy was constrained by a patrimonial political structure. This impingement helped to generate the conditions necessary and sufficient to motivate revolutionary action. In addition, this developing bourgeoisie constituted a class with a future in the construction of a viable and more advanced social formation. This coincidence did not ensure the progressive nature of their revolution, but it made possible its progressive consequences.

Put somewhat differently, in the seventeenth century the manufacturing bourgeoisie could enunciate its views as universal principles. Because it was a class with a future, its focus was not primarily on the defense of traditional privileges; it could state demands within an unstated problematic that necessitated the eventual articulation of universal rights (even when it was not so used by the revolutionaries themselves). When the necessary and sufficient conditions leading to a revolution impinge on groups with a future in the construction of the next stage in the developmental progression, they may legitimize a revolution in terms of progressive universalistic demands; when they impinge on groups without such a future, they will enunciate reactionary, particularistic demands, usually entailing the preservation of some privilege. The former groups may work toward the reconstruction of the society in a progressive direction; the latter will generally work toward goals that do not have this consequence.

Ideally this chapter ought to conclude with the presentation of a generative model of normative controls specific to stages four and five. I would like to be able to show the coherence, for example, of the model of political legitimation which emerged during the revolutions we have examined, and to distinguish that construction from the one extant prior to these revolutions. Ideally I would like to do this both at the level of a discursive formation and at the level of an underlying structure.[18] Neither task is, unfortunately, within my present capabilities. Instead I will merely outline certain of the dominant characteristics of stage four and five control structures, without pretending that this outline is either complete (closed) or anything more than a few hints pointing in the direction an adequate analysis might follow; in the next pages I focus on the normative logic within which the revolutions analyzed in chapter 5 were legitimized.

In chapter 4 I provided a partial model of a "manufacturing" social formation. There we saw that it involved the emergence of new modes of social action legitimized in terms of traditional patrimonial beliefs. The following diagram partially represents the developmental position of a manufacturing social formation, surrounded by feudal and capitalist social formations.[19]

Stage	three	four	five
mode of legitimation	traditionalism	patrimonialism	rational-legalism
mode of production	feudalism	manufacturing	capitalism
	three	four	five

As the diagram implies, manufacturing is a form of capitalism and patrimonialism is a form of traditionalism.

The development of manufacturing into machine capitalism as the dominant mode of production in English society took decades. It occurred within the context of other social transformations, and along with them necessitated the redefinition of the normative controls within English society, changes that yielded the development of a formally rational, egalitarian, normative structure, from a substantively rational, hierarchical structure.

A major strain of Western social thought sees this movement as one of differentiation within the societal system. In Parsons's terms this differentiation was coupled with three parallel movements: value generalization, inclusion, and adaptive upgrading.[20] Value generalization involves the abstraction of values away from concrete commitments. It allows for an increase in diversity and choice among the roles actors might legitimately follow. Inclusion involves a process concomitant to differentiation when and if the now-differentiated structures are "included within" one system. Concretely it has meant an increasing centralization of powers within nation states, as the nation has risen above particularistic loyalties and ties. Adaptive upgrading is simply an indication of the enhanced performance capacity of the emergent mode of economic production. In fact, each of these terms is a specification of the enhanced performance of the relevant societal subsystem (see Parsons 1961c, 1966, 1971).

This very abstract discussion might be repeated in terms more familiar to the historian of early modern England. In pre-sixteenth-century England, a hierarchically integrated society manifested relatively little structural differentiation of its major institutions. In contrast, the seventeenth century has been characterized as witnessing the emergence of a differentiated economy, the differentiation of political from private and religious roles, the emergence of a societal community encompassing a relatively autonomous legal system and a stratification system open to achievement, where the relevant unit of evaluation more and more came to be the nuclear family or its individual members. Perhaps the easiest way to summarize these arguments is by saying that the seventeenth century saw the emergence and/or consolidation of differentiated institutional complexes, and witnessed greater freedom and choice in how they and the individuals within them might act. It might be argued that the most important of these "institutions" was what has been called "institutionalized individualism" (Parsons 1968).[21]

The emergence of these differentiated institutions demanded the creation of new normative regulations capable of legitimizing their actions. It is insufficient to simply characterize these new structures as abstract (value generalization allowing for the inclusion of diverse groups) and secularized (differentiation allowing for economic efficiency). While these characterizations are accurate to a degree, they miss the logic manifested in these new structures.

In England the logic of this new normative framework was embedded in a set of assumptions concerning the nature of humans and the society in which they lived. These assumptions postulated the autonomy of self-regulating societal subsystems and a specific mode of individual action within and adaptation to the institutions that constituted those systems. The portrait of society constructed in this normative logic transcended even while upholding the "is—ought" dichotomy, arguing for the naturalness and therefore the universality of the picture it portrayed, and in consequence drawing an image of the deleterious consequences involved in any attempt to retouch the portrait.

It is important to note that this set of normative orientations was not fully constituted at the time of the English revolutions of the 1640s or even by 1688. Thus its articulation was not always internally consistent or always coherent. Further, in actual practice the emerging normative framework was corrupted by "residues" from traditional orientations. In the first instance it was articulated within the vocabulary of an older tradition; that is, a new orientation was expressed in the only terms available (cf. Derrida 1978). It is important to remember that this emergent normative structure was capable of considerable variation and capable of generating various points of view (discursive formations) within the context of its "underlying structure."[22]

Against traditional hierarchical images of the social order, the normative framework emerging in the seventeenth century was able to conceptualize social relationships as extant prior to the genesis of social order. Whether in the imagery of Hobbes's war of all against all or of Locke's natural harmony of interests, this "state of nature" featured discrete units acting one "against" the other, from a position of relative equality. While there was an accelerating tendency to view these units as individuals, they did not need to be so conceptualized. They merely had to be discrete units not embedded in an all-encompassing, hierarchically structured totality.[23]

One aspect of their discrete existence was the capacity to formulate autonomous goals. This entailed new modes of imagery to conceptualize the interrelationships between units. The most prominent was the notion of contract, wherein two parties entered into an agreement in order to improve their respective positions. It was understood, however, that the criteria of judgment were fixed and univocal. These criteria emerged with ever-increasing clarity in portraits of men rationally striving for their own self-interest. As Hill has argued, the seventeenth century saw the emergence of a new image of "reasonableness," one manifestation of which we may see characterized in any microeconomics text as defining assumptions about rational action (Hill 1969c; and e.g., Dorfman 1964).

The final key to this complex structure was its assumed transparency. The process of secularization took numerous paths and many detours, but ultimately people came to see a natural order in society; it was not dependent on governmental or divine intervention. This order was codified in the empiricist theories of the Manchester economists, but it has its intellectual roots in the mid-seventeenth century.[24]

It was within this emerging normative framework that the revolutions of the seventeenth century were able to find legitimation, as their legitimation was instrumental in constructing the framework. The root from which subsequent legitimations arose was the normative theory of balanced or mixed government. This theory was paradigmatic for a new stage of societal development, implying that government is not a direct manifestation of an immanent higher authority. In early Stuart England authority descended from God; by the time of the culmination of the English Revolution's first stage, government was seen as a construct of human practice. This construct sought to balance powers of the three principal estates of the realm, treating each as equal and each as a discrete atom. Found in Puritan beliefs, the image of authority constructed to legitimize the REVOF pushed God into the heavens and embedded the state in a structure of authority ascending from a prior community of king, lords, and commons.[25] Within this context each division of the community would seek to maximize its own interest, while the mode of reason used to justify the selection of interest would alter in time. At first closed in by the precedents of prior times, soon the justification of precedent itself would be its reasonableness in attaining sought-after goals.[26]

In the second phase of the revolution (REVOG) authority was vested in Parliament as a representative of the kingdom, which was assumed capable of understanding its own interests. Here there was a differentiation between government and the people, and it was generally understood that the community was prior to the state. Authority was ascending, and the state was constituted out of the need to establish a sovereign in possession of an arbitrary power. Sovereign power was vested in Parliament as the people's representative, not in the people themselves.

We find here a differentiation, more explicit than in the first stage of the revolution, between the societal community and the government. God remains high in the heavens and the value commitments embedded in his image are abstract. People's interests are the determining factor of their actions and government is justified in terms of those interests; it is derived from the people. But we are not at a point where constituted rules protect the people from the arbitrary actions of their government; instead such authority is vested in Parliament. The king as a representative of descending authority is clearly subordinate to the people, although in this phase of the revolution he most often retains his formal status as an equal unit within government, with interests of his own.

In the last phase of the revolution (REVON) and even more clearly in the Levellers' failed revolution, the new stage of normative structure emerges with considerable clarity. The "official" legitimations of the revolution took their cue from the Army Remonstrance, and articulated a view that allowed the people to call their rulers to account. The people were seen as formulating a contract with their rulers, and Parliament's authority was an emanation from the people's sovereignty.[27]

In Leveller ideology things were even clearer. Here the concern was the mechanism allowing for the political expression of a sovereign people. Though the people might delegate the responsibility to govern, they could not abdicate control over or responsibility for government. In addition, among the Levellers it is especially clear that they saw the individual standing alone before a transcendent God, when God entered the picture at all. These individuals were conceptualized as equals (with some exclusions) and their interests, usually justified at the pulpit of reason, were seen as constitutive of the legitimation of government and its actions. Here the public interest reigned supreme.

Among the Levellers we also find the clearest expression of emerging constitutionalism. They sought to formulate a set of constitutive rules defining the formal procedures within which government would have to function. This was an outgrowth of legal arguments demanding an abstract justice defined procedurally within the common law, a justice not subject to the substantive rationality of legal equity but subject to rational calculation. It was the structure of procedures which was in need of legitimation, and within this structure people were able to act in the light of their own reason.

All of these legitimations (sketched in greater detail in chaps. 5, 6, and 7 above) were acceptable within a stage five normative code but not within the patrimonial code, which was a form of traditionalism. Each rests on the assumption of a differentiated societal community made up of autonomous units (usually conceived of as individual personalities); each assumes a God removed far into the heavens and thus an abstraction of values allowing for considerable individual choice concerning personal interest and disallowing the possibility of specifying concrete interests in advance. Each assumes the equal capacity of these units to act rationally in terms of their own interests and provides either an implicit or an explicit theory of contract within which such actions might take place. Finally, each assumes the preexistence of society as a summed set of relationships between discrete units, from which government emerges and to which government is in some sense bound. This community is autonomous and its laws are natural. It is within a normative framework characterized by these attributes that the legitimations of the English revolutions become explicable.[28]

9. Revolution (with)in the Development of Capitalism

> What makes power hold good, what makes it accepted, is simply the fact that it doesn't only weigh on us as a force that says no, but that it traverses and produces things, it induces pleasure, forms of knowledge, produces discourse. It needs to be considered as a productive network which runs through the whole social body, much more than as a negative instance whose function is repression. In *Discipline and Punish* what I wanted to show was how, from the seventeenth and eighteenth centuries onwards, there was a veritable technological take-off in the productivity of power.
>
> (Foucault 1980:119)

This book has focused on the role of revolution (with)in the development of capitalism and has emphasized the fact that so-called bourgeois revolutions occur within an already developed (manufacturing) capitalist social formation. But, and this is the key to understanding the ambiguous nature of the book's title, such revolutions may also be preconditions for the genesis of capitalist social relationships, when the latter are more narrowly understood as constituted in relation to the extraction of relative surplus value, as is machine capitalism.[1]

I have demonstrated, I believe, that the English revolutions of the seventeenth century occurred within the tendential development of English manufacture. It would take another book to demonstrate that one consequence of these revolutions was the progression of manufacture into machine capitalism. This chapter, a conclusion, is a preface to that as yet unwritten book.

It is essential that we recognize that the primary consequences of the English revolutions were political. It was these political transformations that had economic and other effects. The establishment of an institutional structure within which political power could be expanded, with consequent economic benefits, was the primary impact of the revolutions.

In England, owing to an early development of a relatively strong centralized national state, national power grew at the same time as local power. "In the absence of a bureaucratic apparatus of their own, and in fact precisely because of the centralization of administration, the kings were dependent on the cooperation of the notables" (Weber 1968, 3:1280). Or the reverse: "Because of the relatively early centralization of rule in England, and the domestication of the feudal political nobility into a court-oriented aristocracy, English monarchs were able to dispense with the development of a separate state bureaucracy and to rule instead through a decentralized form of local government based on local unpaid officials such as the Justices of the Peace" (Fulbrook 1982:255). Yet Fulbrook does of course agree with Weber: "But their [English monarchs'] apparent strengths involved associated weaknesses. One was ensuring that central orders were effected locally. Local governors could simply ignore, or fail to implement effectively, orders with which they did not agree" (255). Thus the strength of the English state was, from an early point in time, ultimately dependent on the consent of the notables (however the latter might be constituted).

Russell has recently emphasized that the parliamentary legislators in Westminster were the king's executive in the counties (1979*b*:3). This situation provided the potential for resistance to a monarch acting contrary to the notables' interests, but it also provided the foundation for a balanced expansion of power in the postrevolutionary period. The revolutions resulted in a situation where the legislative and executive powers of the English state expanded in tandem. As Western aptly phrased it: "in becoming more powerful the executive also became less independent and more subject to parliamentary restraint" (1972:401). Executive power increased within Parliament as the executive came to exert a powerful de facto control over the Parliament, which came increasingly to gain de jure control over the executive. This parallel growth in power allowed for the emerging sense of possession which the English "oligarchy" felt for its government. It exerted formal control over the government and came, as the institutions of the executive expanded, to support (*tragen*) roles within that government (Plumb 1969*b*:118). Here was, as Weber expected, the plutocratic domination of the state by *honoraitiores* (1968, 3:1091).

The expansion of political power was a consequence of the growing differentiation within English society. It is essential, however, that we not misconstrue this process within zero-sum categories.

Differentiation and the growing complexity of "the division of labor in society" resulted not only in a growth of centralization and state power, but also in a growth in the power of peripheral organizations, governmental and private (including but not limited to economic organizations). In fact it is essential that we realize the mutual dependency of these two processes. Laissez faire may not have been a myth as a characterization of governmental policy (at least in comparison with other polities), but in England this policy was the product of a state organization incomparably more powerful than any early modern absolutism.

This process of accumulating power and the resulting enhancement of political productivity (see chap. 2, above) occurred within the context of the enhanced learning capacity of the political system. The English revolutions were not bourgeois revolutions in the sense that they were made by a bourgeois specifically intent on the furtherance of extant interests. They were bourgeois revolutions, however, in that they resulted in the creation of a political structure that adapted itself to a developing capitalist economy. Again, this process of adaptation was not conscious; it was a natural process resulting from the necessities inherent in an ongoing social formation. To ensure the stable operation of the political system, governmental policies had to be structured so as to avoid contradiction with the immanent logic of a capitalist economy and to secure the support of those with control over that economy (see chaps. 2, 4, above).

This process worked in numerous ways that were triggered, perhaps paradoxically, by a differentiating societal community. Within the context of the genesis of a public sphere empirically separate from the moral community of religious and familial organizations, interest demands and political support were mobilized on behalf of the English state and its constituency. This support was an essential basis of the capacity of the state organizations to adopt flexible policies within the context of a set of constitutive rules. This support, in tandem with emergent common law institutions, provided the basis for the rational-legal justification crucial in controlling the English political and administrative organizations and thus crucial in allowing for (1) the calculability of their actions, and (2) the expansion of their scope of operation without generating a political "paradox of thrift" (see chaps. 2, 3, above).

Behind these processes lay the concomitant differentiation of social and cultural symbolic systems. In Tudor and early Stuart

England law was relatively undifferentiated, as a symbolic system, from cultural symbols. One consequence of this was the somewhat ambiguous doctrine of the fundamental law, which meant, as Gough and others have shown, that laws enacted in Parliament had to conform to notions of reason, nature, and "equity." The reason for this conformity, the reason this conformity was assumed, was that interpretations of the law in violation of the cultural norms defining intelligibility were simply nonsensical, and thus if one was to assume that the members of Parliament were sane, a "statutory" violation of the "law of reason" was literally incomprehensible.

The relatively low level of differentiation of cultural from legal symbolism, coupled with the patrimonial (stage four) structure of Tudor and Stuart England (see chap. 8, above), meant that tradition, while no longer sovereign, had not yielded to cognitive rationality. This meant that the source of the fundamental law was assumed to be given and was thus assumed to be congruent with the common law, the law from time immemorial (cf. Gough 1971; Pocock 1967; for a different perspective, Tuck 1979:83, 133).

The added flexibility generated from the emergence of a public sphere, civil society, within the context of differentiated social and cultural normative systems allowed for the emergence of the public interest, both as a concept and as a reality differentiated from moral obligations. Within the context of constitutive procedures, resources might be mobilized to ensure the realization of this interest through state action, and thus state power might be mobilized to allow for the realization of private interests that were to be rationalized as leading to the maximization of the public interest. This allowed for the reunification, at least ideologically, of what had been differentiated.

This reunification occurred, however, not in the form of a fusion, but rather through a process of integration. Relatively autonomous structures were integrated within a social formation, but the autonomy of, for example, economic, political, and legal organizations enhanced the productive capacity of each separately and also of each when the ensemble of organizations worked in cooperation.

Activities were no longer regulated within a substantively specific set of value orientations. As we saw in chapter 8, the logic of value orientations was itself transformed. While drawing upon earlier traditions, the seventeenth century saw the emergence of and the first steps in the codification of rational egalitarian values. Even if they were neither rational nor egalitarian when first enunciated, their immanent development is clear.[2] Their content was atomistic and assumed that individual agents maximized their own interests. What was desirable came to be understood as the opportunity of actors to maximize their own desires. What came to be politically obligatory was that the procedures within which activities occurred allowed for formal freedom, even while the outcomes were structured in terms of relationships of power and control (in economic, political, and legal activities).[3] This was true, even as the state found it necessary to regulate the attitudes and activities that constituted desire and gained the power to do so. What was important was that the members of the political nation were committed to procedures that suggested that their support for the current government be determined by its success in meeting their interest demands.

Within this context, in assessing the consequences of a revolutionized political structure in the development of capitalism, we might begin by schematically looking in two directions: first at the direct interchanges between the polity and the economy as structured to allow for the emergence of a capitalist economy within a capitalist social formation, and second at the resources that were mobilized by the economy in the process of capital accumulation and structural transformation. Both of these assume the transformation of the nature and scope of noneconomic resources mobilized by the state; both are dependent on the institutionalization of a rational-legal political and normative order capable of adapting to the exigencies of an already constituted manufacturing economy.

What emerged were regulating institutions whose rationality was procedural, not substantive. Their structures were flexible, allowing for learning, as an adaptation to the extant economy. This was of course an adaptation controlled by those in whose interest the economy developed. As this linkage between economic development and interest altered (direct or indirect) control over the state altered in a parallel fashion. Who actually occupied governmental positions was only of limited importance (see chap. 2, above).[4]

The Revolution of 1688 was nowhere more glorious than in its financial impact on the state, and in the effects that fiscal stability and growth had on the economy. This was witnessed by the creation or growth of fiscal institutions, including the Bank of England and the Treasury, and also by the rationalization of old and the introduction of new administrative procedures concerning the government's capacity to collect more and more money, and the polity's (understood as including the central banking structure) capacity to accumulate and distribute liquid resources. In these and in other respects, the postrevolutionary period witnessed a financial revolution (Dickson 1967; Baxter 1957; Clapham 1944; Hargreaves 1930; Roseveare 1969, 1973).

The capacity of the state to recruit the services of persons was enhanced along with its capacity to secure funds. "The number of men employed by the government grew faster between 1689 and 1715 than in any previous period of English history, and perhaps at a rate not to be equalled again until the nineteenth century. The volume of government business grew equally fast, and in so doing touched directly the lives of more people than ever before" (Plumb 1969b:118). While this expansion was lead by the Treasury, it was not limited to it. It included, for example, the navy, and with the growth of the navy (and the army) grew England's capacity to secure overseas opportunities for her manufacturing economy.

One might easily exaggerate the importance of overseas trade for the pre-eighteenth-century growth of English capitalism,[5] but it would be equally foolish to underestimate its importance for eighteenth-century growth. The postrevolutionary period saw the expansion of English trade, an expansion built on the twin foundations of a growing manufacturing economy and a state growing in its capacity to seek and enforce access to international markets and to the productive resources gained from those markets.[6] English development came to be more and more dependent on English economic and political expansion, an expansion dependent on the strength of the English state. This growth in power was a result of the revolutions during the seventeenth century; as Plumb points out, after 1694 the Whig aristocracy was concerned not to limit but to strengthen monarchy and authority (1969b:138),[7] a monarchy it controlled and an authority wielded in its interest.[8]

"By 1714 Britain probably enjoyed the most efficient government machine in Europe" (Plumb 1969b:26). This efficiency, an attribute of the strength of the state, was a consequence of the growth in support allocated to the state, and this support was itself a consequence of the capacity of the state to adapt to the interests of those situated in a manufacturing economy, and to rationalize those interests by mediating between them.

The concomitant development of differentiated political and legal systems subject to control by rational-legal procedures allowed for the rationalization of economic performances in directions consistent with and ultimately patterned by the immanent rationality of capitalist production and exchange (see Weber 1968, 2:698–99). These processes were especially important in the specification of capitalist property and contractual relationships, and the latter was most important in the rationalization of the employment of formally free labor (cf. Weber 1968; Noyes 1936; Schlatter 1951; Commons 1957; North and Thomas 1973). The final point to emphasize in concluding this "preface" is the importance of state power in the extraction of surplus value within the labor process of capitalist production.

The state defines and enforces the rules within which labor power is sold, and the context of those rules is instrumental in defining the value of labor power and acceptable rates of exploitation. To do either or both of these things the state must be accepted as legitimate and must be capable of generating considerable support for its everyday policies and, more important, for its constitutive procedures. Perhaps the greatest legacy of the English revolutions of the seventeenth century was the combination of the general acceptance of the legitimacy of the English state joined to its natural adaptation to the processes of capital accumulation and the exploitation of labor power. These coupled together in a hegemony of capitalist interests, wherein both capital and labor came to legitimize social processes in the interest of capital (defined as the general interest) and only secondarily and in struggle in the interest of labor.

The legacy of the revolution was that an already predominant manufacturing economy was provided with an environment in which it could prosper. Its development was by no means unimpeded, but its growth was self-sustaining and derivatively sustained by the mechanisms of the state.

These comments are no more than assertions, but perhaps their veracity might be hinted at in the following and concluding argument. In chapter 3 I argued that major revolutions tend to begin as facilitory rebellions (REVOF), and that these rebellions are manifest when one group within the political nation usurps the powers of another. Further, I suggested that such rebellions are likely to be successful when the political nation is nearly unanimous in support of—or is neutral in respect to—the actions of the resisters. If this argument is correct, structural arrangements that impede this set of circumstances should impede the possibility of major revolutions. It is possible to point to two examples of structures that seem to inhibit the genesis of this variety of political fissure.

One impediment to the generation of this sort of facilitory rebellion is a viable "parliamentary" system; another is the assurance of the conjunction of the major branches of government, and, most important, the assurance that the executive be selected from the majority party in the legislature, and ultimately be subject to the legislature's control. The first is present in both Great Britain and the United States; the second only in Britain, where both are (indirect) legacies of the seventeenth-century revolutions.

The (appearance of) a viable parliamentary system allows for the hope that present policies are amenable to change, and thus for the possibility of fundamental transformations within the extant system of government. Though this is not a definitive block to revolutionary action, this possibility serves as an inhibition to most persons most of the time (cf. the situation in England after the birth of a Catholic heir in 1687). In addition, it inhibits splits within the government which might allow part of the state system (e.g., Parliament) to legitimize and justify actions taken against another part of the system (e.g., the executive).

It is difficult to imagine a situation in Britain where the Prime Minister loses the "complete support" of the majority party or parties in Commons and is still able to govern. A split between the executive and legislative branches of government is virtually unimaginable in contemporary Britain. This institutional complex, while not the direct result of the seventeenth-century revolutions, was one culmination of the working out of their consequences.[9] It has provided one basis of the relative political stability and transformation that Britain has witnessed for over three hundred years, and has presided over the development of a capitalist social formation in England. It has provided the terrain on which workers could struggle for democratic rights, for procedural equality as citizens, and for economic benefit—all within a relatively stable capitalist social formation capable of considerable social reform (cf. Marshall 1965).[10] This accomplishment has been instrumental in molding the liberal, egalitarian world that some of us are fortunate enough to live in; we would not be wise to sacrifice its benefits simply because they may make it more difficult for us to effect a fundamental transformation of this world into one controlled by equitable procedures. The seventeenth-century English revolutions were instrumental in creating not only the governing liberal political system but also the social formation in which it is situated.

A Recapitulation

The reader who has read this far is now in a position to evaluate the merits of my arguments and the merits of my theoretical strategy in addressing a significant set of historical questions. I suggested earlier in this book that one problem in articulating viable social science theories lay in our tendency to attempt to explain the unexplainable. I want to illustrate this problem with a closing story (which I am repeating from chap. 3, n. 18).

One morning a student of mine awoke to find his automobile's windshield broken. He wondered out loud during a meeting with me why someone had done this, and following a well-trodden procedure we translated his question into a problem: Under what conditions will an actor "break a windshield"?

Our impulse was to treat this action as a form of vandalism and to posit conditions akin to those hypothesized in chapter 3 as explaining deviant aggression, nonutilitarian deviance. It then occurred to us that we could never be successful in explaining why someone would "break a windshield." In considering the following example of this action, my reader will understand why I have adopted the theoretical strategy used in this book.

What of the windshield smasher who lives in a small midwestern town and owns a glazier's shop? Her activity may be a form of utilitarian deviance, what I called "deviant innovation" in chapter 3. Because the explanation for deviant aggression differs from the explanation of deviant innovation, and because the activity we perceive as "breaking a windshield" may be either utilitarian or nonutilitarian, we will be doomed to failure if we try to explain why someone would undertake to "break windshields." A specific action that we commonsensically would label "breaking a windshield" requires reconceptualization as either deviant aggression or deviant innovation (or perhaps as something else) if it is to be successfully and systematically subject to explanation.

If this example sounds far-fetched, the reader should know, by way of conclusion, that students have sent me at least two news clippings relating the activity of glaziers who systematically broke automobile windshields for profit. However, my favorite case is the related one of the English mason who earned himself the name Harvey Wall-Banger before his incarceration. It is situations like the ones epitomized by these examples, in themselves trivial, that impose the necessity of formulating analytical concepts if we are to succeed in formulating viable social theory.

In other words, we must know how to label an event if we are to know how to explain it. We can only learn the nature of events as we formulate their explanations. It is these parallel tasks that I have attempted in this book. It remains for the reader to determine if the functional, structural, and developmental concepts and theories used in this essay merit further consideration.

Notes

Preface

1. This position derives, of course, from the work of Karl Popper, and he is aware of certain difficulties inherent in it. In general, however, the discussions in the social sciences are less complex and much more naive than their counterparts for the natural sciences.

2. Bridgman's original notion of operationalization, where concepts were not operationalized but where the procedure of "measurement" defined the concept, adequately confronted this problem. However, this mode of procedure was soon recognized by both natural and social scientists to be theoretically sterile. Whatever the case within the natural sciences, within the social sciences it leads to a categorization of phenomena in terms of their surface characteristics, and this is often theoretically misleading. (See chap. 3, n. 18.)

3. I ignore arguments that indicate that social science is impossible. Whatever their structure, it seems to me that they are considerably weakened by an explanation of why the social sciences are so ill-developed, and of the conditions of their (potential) future development.

4. In an essay I am currently completing I ground these assertions in argument (Gould, forthcoming).

5. One unintended consequence of this procedure has been to mask my debts to other classical and Marxist authors: Durkheim, Freud, and Lenin being the most slighted. It has also masked part of my debts to more recent writers, of whom there are too many to mention.

6. Some would argue that an elaborate theoretical schema is the worst sort of preconception. I would counter that at least it involves the conscious articulation of assumptions and thus allows for the possibility of weeding out biases that run counter to the data. We all have preconceptions, and as Marshall stated, "The most reckless and treacherous of all theorists is he who professes to let facts and figures speak for themselves" (as quoted in Parsons 1949:10 n. 1; cf. Leibig's comment on the antitheoretical practical man who assumed that, "theorized that," the soil's fertility was inexhaustible; quoted in Krohn and Schäfer 1976:29–30).

7. "In answering the question raised it seemed to us that it was not

enough to adduce facts showing the formation and growth of a home market, for the objection might be raised that such facts had been selected arbitrarily and that facts to the contrary had been omitted. It seemed to us that it was necessary to examine the whole process of the development of capitalism in Russia, to endeavour to depict it in its entirety" (Lenin 1960ff., 3 : 25).

8. This point increases in importance for me as my primary interests focus on the development of an equitable system of societal organization after the demise of capitalism. This has not yet been accomplished, and in order to study the mechanisms of transition, it was necessary to go back in time and to examine the last major societal transformation in man's history, the development of capitalism. While it would be foolish to assume that the theoretical problems relating to the development of an equitable society are equivalent to those concerning the development of capitalism, it may not be too much to hope that we may be able to shed some light on the former in formulating and evaluating theory relevant to the latter.

9. A more important problem is the fact that I have not adequately treated England's relations with Scotland and Ireland.

1. A Sociological Foundation

1. As Lukacs points out, this type of "functional argument" is seen throughout Marx's work; a particularly lucid example is found in *Capital*, vol. 1: "whether a use-value is to be regarded as raw material, as instrument of labour, or as product, this is determined entirely by its function in the labour-process, by the position it there occupies: as this varies, so does its character" (1967: 182).

2. On the many uses of the term *structuralism* see Boudon 1971.

3. "Durkheim's primary interest is in the fact that units agree on norms because they are backed by values held in common" (Parsons 1967: 7). These values are the beliefs and sentiments that made up the *conscience collective*. (See Durkheim 1964: 79.)

4. An actor is said to believe in a value (to be committed to it) and to conform to a norm (Smelser 1962: 29). Insofar as the actor's attitude toward a rule is morally neutral, her attitude is likely to be one of calculation. Where the norm is not legitimized by collective values, sanctions when effectively applied will act as deterrents. In a situation of calculation, the actor will be primarily concerned with maximizing positive sanctions and minimizing negative sanctions in determining her course of action. (See Durkheim 1961: 30–31, 34, 105; and chap. 2 below.)

5. In Parsons's terms all human action, as against human behavior, is culturally mediated.

6. I take the term *support* in this context from Althusser. The Althusse-

rians use the term *support* after Marx's use of the German *Träger*. Cf. Terray where, in the translation from the French, the term *uphold* is used in a parallel context (1972:176).

7. "Action consists of the structures and processes by which human beings form meaningful intentions and, more or less successfully, implement them in concrete situations" (Parsons 1966: 5). The fact that we are dealing with human action is another reason to avoid simplistic behavioristic operationalizations of concepts. We must constantly remember that there is an underlying meaning system within which all action occurs, and our concepts must be formulated with this in mind. Imagine the consequences of an attempt to explain Curt Flood's stealing a base solely in terms of behavioristic observables.

8. To avoid possible misunderstanding let me state that the terms *economy*, *polity*, and *societal community* are used as cognates for the adaptive, goal-attainment, and integrative subsystems at the societal level. They do not refer to economic or political organizations. For example, governmental organizations may have adaptive consequences for the society, and they will then be categorized within the economy, not the polity. It is essential to refrain from reifying these functionally defined categories. (See Parsons and Smelser 1956, for a justification of these usages.)

9. Cf. Bellah 1965:171–72, as quoted below, chap. 3, n. 6.

10. "My suggestion is that there is a very simple paradigm of modes by which one acting unit ... can attempt to get results by bringing to bear on another unit ... some kind of *communicative operation*: call it 'pressure' if that term is understood in a nonpejorative sense" (Parsons 1969:410).

11. The above discussion of the media is obviously very terse and incomplete. The interested reader should consult the works cited for a full elaboration of the crucial concept of symbolic media. I have attempted in another essay (1984) to reconcile certain differences that appear in the work of the two leading media theorists, Parsons and Luhmann. In certain respects I have pushed the discussion of internal disorder beyond the level of sophistication discussed in the following pages (Gould 1977, forthcoming).

2. Systems Analysis

1. This chapter is a revised and somewhat less technical version of an essay written in honor of Talcott Parsons and originally published in J. Loubser et al. 1976. In its original version it contains a justification of the revised format of the systems analysis paradigm used in this chapter (cf. Parsons and Smelser 1956).

2. Throughout this essay I will adopt the following terminological convention: The word *system* will refer to the action system under discussion,

generally to a social system, and most regularly to a society. The word *subsystem* will refer to the four functionally defined subsystems of reference, for example, when the system is a society, to the economy, polity, societal community, and latency subsystems. The word *subsector* will refer to the four functionally defined subsectors of the subsystem of reference.

Symbolically I will adhere to the usage of Parsons and Smelser (1956): A will refer to the adaptive subsystem of the system of reference and A_A to the adaptive subsector of the adaptive subsystem.

3. The preceding discussion is elliptical, referring to functional subsystems as actors. As I do not mean to reify these subsystems, in each instance I should refer to structures and processes classified within these systems (even this is elliptic); to do so, however, would be tedious and pedantic.

4. Terminological difficulties have haunted me in composing this chapter. The economic terms used in certain discussions applicable to all social subsystems were chosen because of their familiarity and because the only alternatives that came to mind were abysmal neologisms. The drawbacks in proceeding as I have are twofold. First, it is difficult to distinguish the general level of reference from the economic. Second, and for the discussions in this chapter, more important, the economic terms have connotations not always appropriate to their political, integrative, and maintenance references. When the latter is the case, I attempt to clarify the points at issue.

5. Both consumption and investment involve the allocation of subsystem-derived income in support of units within the subsystem of reference. The point is that consumed output is utilized in satisfying "immediate" wants (within the time period of reference), while investment involves the provision of media resources for the production of goods to be utilized in the production of future goods (beyond the time period of reference) (cf. Marx 1967: vol. 2; Sraffa 1960). I have chosen the term *consumer support* rather than *consumer demand* because even though there is a type of demand involved in every variety of consumption, the actual allocation of the media resources is a form of support for the producing collectivity. This distinction will be elaborated in the following discussion of the polity.

6. On these points, which require more space than I have here, see Chamberlain 1962 and Baran and Sweezy 1966.

7. The reader will note the similarity between this discussion and Parsons's arguments that at this boundary money appears not as a circulating medium but rather as a measure of value (see Parsons 1967: 373–75). In fact, Parsons is effectively quite correct, especially in noting that "the economist's ideal of free competition is here the limiting case in which influence as an independent factor disappears" (1967: 375). His errors are threefold: first, in his assertions elsewhere that this boundary is the major focal point of the code components of the media, money, and influence;

second, in his sharp division between money as a circulating medium and as a measure of value. As the former it is both; as the latter, actual money is characterized by a high level of liquidity and can circulate; as a simple measure of relative value "money" would not be money but any scale of equivalence and relative difference; for example, Marx's labor unit. Third, at this boundary the "measure of value" aspect of money, insofar as it relates to the value principle of utility, is not relevant. Rather our concern is with the coordination standard of money, solvency, as identified in the factor output from I to A, "standards for the allocation of resources."

"Measure of value" does not directly refer, in the context of the I $\longleftrightarrow$ A boundary, to the value of labor power within capitalist productive relationships. However, the I $\longleftrightarrow$ A product input does concern the ranking of claims made by labor regarding actual wages received in payment for labor power expended (A $\longleftrightarrow$ L). Within the Marxian system there is an ambiguity between the two, as the value of labor power is not accurately specified (as Marx tells us) by physical necessities and thus is very difficult to define unambiguously. An increase in wages might involve an increase in the value of labor power (socially and culturally determined) or a capture of surplus value by workers. In the latter case, even assuming no increase in productivity, no inflation should occur; in the former, unless there is a proportional increase in productivity, a price rise is likely to follow should the rate of surplus value remain equivalent to what it was prior to the increase in the money value of labor power (see Marx 1967, 1:chaps. 17, 18; Gould 1981a). The I $\longleftrightarrow$ A interchange is relevant to the specification of the actual rate of surplus value.

8. (The following is a technical note and may be skipped by the general reader.) Something comparable occurs for each subsystem. The product input to the subsystem which delineates the level of the sending subsystem's saving (e.g., I—[product] $\rightarrow$ A and A—[product] $\rightarrow$ G) is always allocational regarding recipient functions, although not necessarily with regard to the sending product. The product output to the subsystem which defines savings for the outputting subsystem (e.g., A—[product] $\rightarrow$ I and G—[product] $\rightarrow$ A) is always allocational (although not necessarily as a savings input). It always concerns the distribution of the sending subsystem's product among receiving units. This is so even when these allocational priorities become relevant to the determination of the aggregate product for the sender in the next period. And it is also true when this output (to the subsystem that defines total savings) involves the "purchase" of real product from the sending subsystem.

For example, the G product output to A concerns the allocation of fluid resources (I_a) in return for the control of productivity and services (S_g). Here the economy receives from the polity an allocational product, relevant to the distribution of the total political product, not, in this time period, to the scope of political output (see n. 34, this chap.). The return product from the economy is allocational with regard to the mobilization of political resources. It concerns the availability of real economic product in the implementation of the powers inherent in the political subsystem. Thus while the A ⟷ G boundary involves the scope of economic output, the I ⟷ A boundary deals with the distribution of both economic and integrative product. Only in the following periods can this I ⟷ A interchange be determinative of the aggregate level of either economic or integrative output.

9. Let me remind the reader that the term *polity* is functional in reference and includes processes that are not necessarily governmental, for example, certain banking functions. Likewise, not all governmental processes are political in function.

10. To many readers, and certainly to the author, this caveat should be an indication of the necessity of coupling simple functional aggregative analysis with structural and historically specific analyses. Let me provide a simple example: Weber argued that in traditional social systems workers might work less, beyond a specifiable point, if wages were raised (a backward-sloping demand curve). The direction of the aggregative relationship between wages and labor capacity is thus not determined on simple a priori grounds; rather it must be determined within the context of a specific class of social situations. Given the historical, social-structural determination of the slope of certain relationships, general propositions of the type I go on to discuss are presumably valid. A more sophisticated theory would be able to correlate types of historical structure with stages in the development of social systems, thus identifying in general terms, but for a more narrowly delimited range of systems—those categorized within a developmental stage—the specifics of the relationship.

11. In such an analysis the economist hypothesizes that where planned savings equals planned investment an equilibrium situation occurs. Ex ante savings and investment need not be equivalent, even though by definition ex post savings is identical with ex post investment. This is roughly comparable to the situation where desired demand is greater than desired supply, whereas the actual amount of goods sold and purchased must be equivalent. Only where the desired supply equals desired demand is there an equilibrium.

For the economist an equilibrium situation is where all the wants of individuals are satisfied, given the constraints of the system. As Schumpeter puts it (I quote slightly out of context), economic equilibrium "corresponds to a position ... whose constituent parts cannot be altered (if all the data remain the same) without [any] ... individual's having the experience that he is worse off than before" (Schumpeter 1949:40; see also Samuelson 1965; Kuenne 1963; and Smelser 1968). In this condition we are assuming the possibility of a meaningful aggregation of consumer proclivities in a stable curve related to produced output or, equivalently, total income. A change in the slope of the curve as against a move along it for any of the variables would change the equilibrium level of output.

Much of the elegance and power of macroeconomics is based on the possibility of making such assumptions. The existence of singular equilibrium points is based on (1) the ability to measure in ratio scale terms levels of income and (2) the existence of monotonic functional relationships between the processes measured. Although the first is reasonable in economics, the second is based on the often questionable assumption of the sameness of the units aggregated, thus eliminating qualitative jumps across income levels (see Clower 1969 : part III).

Once we leave the realm of utilitarian, psychologistic economics the world of the economy gains in complexity and becomes more difficult to treat "rationally." In this essay I allow the simple assumptions of the economist and further sin (later in this chapter) by making even simpler assumptions about the polity. It should be noted in both instances that empirically the equilibrium points identified are at best approximations allowable within the context of short-term analysis.

12. If the MPC > 1, the model provides no equilibrium condition. This involves dynamic assumptions of a simple lag, consumption behind income (see Ackley 1961 : 326–330, 347ff.). This fact has multiple consequences for internal disorder, especially in precapitalist social formations and most especially in the cognate political case. It consists in the situation where political mobilization far exceeds the capacity of a governmental response.

13. For more detailed discussions of these phenomena see Samuelson 1939.

14. Let me immediately clear up a misconception that might confuse the reader. Interest demands are a factor of political effectiveness, an input of influence to the polity (I—[factor] → G). As such they parallel the factor input of labor capacity to the economy (as will be elaborated below), not the product input of consumer support to the economy, L—[product] → A (not "consumer demand" in part for this reason; rather, in certain contexts, intended support) (see Bronfenbrenner and Holzman 1965 : 53 and footnote, who use the term "aggregate expenditure"). From the societal community the power or product input to the polity is political support (I—[product] → G)—"The product-inputs of power to the polity from its neighboring subsystems thus constitute a mechanism for evaluating past and prospective political performances of collective agencies" (Parsons 1969 : 486)—the accurate theoretical parallel to consumer support. The reader should note the importance of the concepts of "good will," "brand names," and "party loyalty" within this context.

Labor capacity and interest demands are factor inputs processed within the economy and polity; the respective economic and political products— intrinsic satisfiers—are exchanged for product inputs in the broad sense; inputs of support, investment, and consumption. Parsons's views on these matters have been inconsistent; see, for example, "'Voting' and the Equilibrium of the American Political System," reprinted in 1967; "Some Reflections on the Place of Force in Social Processes," reprinted in 1967; "On the Concept of Political Power," reprinted in 1967, especially p. 302; and *Politics and Social Structure*, 1969, especially pp. 489ff. With regard to the last reference, it is especially important to note that interest demands are *not* a component of the so-called "effective demand" of the polity; rather, this term should be "effective support" and encompasses what I will later call $C_g + I_g$, political support plus authorization of powers of office.

The quotation from Marshall in the text blurs the distinction between labor power, the capacity to labor which is purchased on the market in capitalist economies, and labor (work), which must be extracted in the labor process. While labor power is contracted for on the labor market, labor cannot be purchased; it must be motivated. Labor is a variable component within a labor process; the amount of labor extracted varies independently from the amount of labor power hired.

15. My usage of *intentionality* differs from Parsons's in "On the Concept of Influence" and the "Postscript" to it in 1967.

16. Marcuse 1960:7–8. See the discussions in Marx 1975, 1967; Lukacs 1970; and Durkheim 1964. The literature on the processing of interest demands and on the sabotage of policy decisions is voluminous.

17. Pragmatically this task will be much easier with labor capacity than interest demands or policy decisions. Realistically, however, one must remember that the structural location of the intention is very important in determining its productive effect and the return generated. This is as true for labor capacity as it is for interest demands and policy decisions (cf. Granovetter 1981).

18. It does not seem reasonable at this point to engage in an analysis of the controversies monetary theorists have engendered over the notion of the demand for money. Here I assume that this demand is a function of income and opportunity. As will be seen, opportunity is broader than the usual conceptualization of "the interest rate," but for many purposes "the interest rate" is an acceptable surrogate.

Some confusion might arise if I don't explicitly note that an increase in the speculative demand for money—more generally, the demand for money to hold—implies an increase in the amount of money retained in the economy, and therefore a decrease in the amount of money going across the $A \rightarrow G$ and/or the $A \rightarrow L$ factor boundaries (see Leijonhufvud 1968: 29–30 and footnote 35).

19. For clarity's sake much of the preceding discussion utilizes terminology appropriate to a capitalist system. Cognate terms descriptive of the same processes can be found for any economy, although the level of differentiation manifest in a capitalist social formation may not be present.

20. Brief discussions of the model I am utilizing are found in Hicks

1937; Johnson, "Monetary Theory and Keynesian Economics," reprinted in Johnson 1967; Ackley 1961; Allen 1968; and Smith and Teigen 1965. The best source, as Leijonhufvud has emphasized, is Keynes himself. Complicating factors are introduced into the model by both Leijonhufvud 1968 and Horwich 1964, among numerous other recent commentators. Allen provides a brief discussion of two sector models (consumption and investment output) in 1968:150–54. Models including a separate governmental sector can also be constructed.

Before continuing the reader may want to reread the quotation from Keynes which serves as a headpiece for this chapter.

21. Modigliani's term (1944:266).

22. This is put very simply. For discussions of some of the factors I have ignored in the context of the economic theory I have drawn on, see Keynes 1965; Leijonhufvud 1968; Patinkin 1964; Tobin 1947; and, more briefly, Ackley 1961; Allen 1968.

The following equations define the system I have been discussing:

$$I_a = I_a(r_a)$$
$$S_a = S_a(Y_a)$$
$$M_a = M_{at}(Y_a) + M_{ah}(r_a)$$
$$S_a = I_a$$
$$Y_a = Y_a(N_a)$$

For the restrictions on the first four equations yielding an equilibrium value of Y_a and r_a see Allen 1968:chap. 7. Treating investment as a function of Y_a and r_a does not markedly alter the results of our discussion.

23. For a similar analysis using a more complicated graphic model see Ackley 1961:373ff. For cogent, brief, numerical examples see Smith and Teigen 1965:chap. 1.

24. I do not have the space to discuss the complex theory of the supply of money. Within the system paradigm outlined, the supply is treated as specified within the polity. I treat an increase in supply as an increase in the amount of money, yielding in the analysis that follows, except in situations of true inflation, an increase in its scope (Y_a) (see Laswell and Kaplan 1950; Parsons 1969:chap. 15, postscript). This ignores circumstances of stagflation, which can only be analyzed in a disaggregated model.

25. Policy decision is "a process of power output from the polity to its constituencies through the support system.... an output of power to the [societal] community.... The crucial feature of policy decision is the bindingness of policy decisions on all elements obligated to the collectivity as either associational or bureaucratic members. Policies, however, impinge differentially, not equally, on members. They generally favor certain interests over others and impose varying obligations so that they somewhat reallocate resources" (Parsons 1969:334; see also Parsons 1967:321). I

interpret policy decision in the fashion just used, not in the narrower sense of Barnard (see Parsons 1960:28ff.; 1969:344). My meaning is close to Easton's "authoritative statements," as a political output. Likewise, my usage of "operative responsibility" is close to but not so substantive as his "authoritative performances," as output. His "associated outputs" seem to encompass both influence and commitment outputs from the polity (see Easton 1965:chap. 22).

26. See Parsons 1967:chap. 5. The scope of power in any office is related to the concept of discretion, that is, the range within which the incumbent's decision (1) need not be referred to higher authority, (2) need not be referred to a constituency, and (3) need not be referred to adjudication (or in retrospect where adjudication will support the decision as justifiable within the authority structure) (see Parsons 1969, the postscript to chap. 15, pp. 482–85). An increase in the range of discretion for an office, for example, a constitutional increase, would involve an increase in the amount of power and the scope of power within the office, except in the case of true inflation, where only the amount of power would be increased.

27. See Huntington 1968:vii and passim; and Eisenstandt 1963:380: "Institutionalization of powers, i.e., extent of clearcut definition of powers." Note that this usage of "institutionalization" is narrower than the one indicated in chapter 1, above.

28. The term *operative responsibility* often causes confusion: "Operative responsibility ... which is treated as a 'factor of integrity' is responsibility for success in the implementation of the value-principles, not only of collective effectiveness, but of integrity of the paramount societal value-pattern" (Parsons 1967:404; see also 354). I am not directly concerned with bureaucratic responsibility but with police powers: "Police, the French word here [in Montesquieu], referred to the function or branch of government involving the keeping of public order and morality" (Montesquieu 1965:58, ed. n.). I am referring to the assumption of operative responsibility for the implementation of legitimized constitutional powers. The extent of the polity's capacity to implement operative responsibility, in any set of circumstances, is limited by its control over productivity and services.

29. Parsons's arguments in favor of all services passing into the polity confuse the structural concept "collectivity" with the functional concept "polity" (see Parsons 1967:279, 303; 1969:324, 479).

30. Services are allocated "human role-performances to an 'employer,' or contracting agent" (Parsons 1967:303). In quoting out of context I have altered the meaning of Parsons's usage. See Marx 1968:12, addendum: "Productivity of Capital, Productive and Unproductive Labor."

31. Not necessarily. It is possible to imagine a system wherein certain individuals would have a guaranteed income and provide services outside of an occupational category, as in much charity work. Such cases need not

involve dedifferentiation within the economy or categorization within the polity.

32. See Parsons 1967:304. For simplicity's sake I have not analyzed the dependence of economic savings and surplus on granted opportunity. As noted above, such an analysis does not markedly affect the propositions generated, but it does greatly complicate their graphical presentation.

33. See Parsons 1967:329–30; 1969:324. This inequality is certainly the case both with regard to the generation of human capital through educational opportunity and in the opportunity to fill higher appointive office within the polity.

34. The specification of the opportunities for effectiveness (G—[factor] $\rightarrow$ A) is an indication of position within the political system, an output of information relative to power position, not an allocation of an income of power. The allocation of fluid resources (G—[product] $\rightarrow$ A) involves the distribution of political output among economically classified units. Although evincing a reallocation and perhaps an expansion of economic resources within a credit structure organized by the polity, it is not relevant to the immediate scope of political output. In short, at the G $\longleftrightarrow$ A boundary, questions of the scope of power are not at issue; rather it concerns questions of the allocation of the resources available to make good the symbolic definition of that scope (see the following discussion of inflation and deflation).

35. The figure is drawn to indicate that the direction of the relationships is known, but not to indicate ratio scales: all equilibrium conditions will be approximations. The only assumption that the graphical presentations make is that it will be possible to operationalize notions like the scope of power in terms of interval scales. Later, when I speak of the "multiplier," I assume the sensibility of the process of multiplication and thus ratio scales. In the latter case I think it theoretically unlikely that power will ever be operationalized in "stronger than" interval scale terms, and thus some distortion will be introduced in the process of multiplication. In the former, approximations of much utility can be made with indices of only ordinal strength (see Stevens 1968).

36. Let me remind the reader that the latency subsystem (L) refers to a functional subsystem. Not all power allocated as "operative responsibility" need necessarily be utilized as investment. Rather, units within L may redistribute some of it to the societal community (L—[product] $\rightarrow$ G—[factor] $\rightarrow$ I or through dedifferentiation) where it might be utilized as a component of political support. This seems to occur, for example, in situations where administrative workers are expected to campaign and vote for the party in power.

37. The preceding paragraph deals with movements along the drawn curves, not movements in the curves themselves, in which case the equilib-

rium conditions themselves are subject to modification. The study of the movement of the curves is comparable to the economic study of the middle-range theories of consumption and investment.

38. Later in this chapter I will discuss the conditions of inflation and deflation of the generalized media of social action. Deflation of a medium plays an important role in the generation of disorder, inflation in its pro-longation, and in its success if the "disorderly movement" is one that attempts to restructure some component of social action. An increase in political saving might well be the wisest course of action in a situation of power inflation. I will discuss the generating conditions of internal disorder in chapter 3.

39. Political alienation involves a strain at the level of values in cases where units are ambivalent toward or consciously reject what they believe are dominant institutionalized values of their political system (see chap. 3).

40. The rate of alienation is separate from the "alienation of consti-tuent intent."

41. Working within these parameters allows me to blur distinctions between real and medium measures of the variables. I will partially remedy this ambiguity in the next section of this chapter when I discuss questions of inflation and deflation of the media.

42. Here the necessity of disaggregation is of paramount importance. To say that an increase in output implies that more interest demands are met is as obvious as it is trivial. It is not, of course, trivial to know what proportion of interest demands go unsatisfied, but it is also necessary to explicate the notion of "wages of demand," the return of power for influence provided. It is essential to know how policy decisions are dis-tributed within the society, as well as which demands are politically pro-ductive.

43. See Allen 1968:123; and Smith and Teigen 1965:15–18, for intro-ductory discussions of the economic analogies.

44. This might but need not imply a situation comparable to deficit spending of monetary resources by governmental collectivities. It would imply deficit spending, for example, if a constitutional court exceeded the level of provided operative responsibility in its authorization of the powers of elective office. It seems to me that such phenomena have occurred on multiple occasions in the history of the United States and are especially likely to occur in the founding of new states. They may but surely need not involve an inflation of power.

45. Inflation cannot be adequately portrayed on the IS-LM diagram unless we make the inputs to the polity a function of real, nonpower vari-ables, for example, the level of political saving as a function of real output, not measured in terms of power. Then a shift to the left of the LM curve indicates a decrease in the value of power, where a position with a given

level of authorization is, for example, less able to secure and to see implemented binding decisions; the price level is no longer a given. See Allen 1968:147–49 for the economic case.

46. The dictatorship of the bourgeoisie refers to those in whose interest the government must function, not necessarily to who rules. The point is as follows: even if Lenin and Mao were elected president and vice president of the United States, the conditions imposed on political action by a capitalist economy would thwart any electoral transition to socialism and communism. The question is not who governs but rather what are the conditions of successful governance, and therefore, "What must the governor do, what are the constraints on her capabilities in acting?" This is the same question one should ask about economic leaders. Queries concerning their satanic or saintly values are not irrelevant, as the conditions of action do not define the content of action, but we should be especially concerned with the structural constraints on their actions and the limits thereby imposed. Successful governance within a capitalist social formation requires the furtherance of the interests of the bourgeoisie; success in managerial positions in a capitalist economy requires adherence to the rules of capitalist success, solvency and profit (see Gould 1970).

47. A governmental alteration of the basic structure of the economy would create a situation of disorder by doing violence to the property rights institutionalized within the economy. (See Arendt 1965:10: "Cain slew Abel, and Romulus slew Remus; violence was the beginning and, by the same token, no beginning could be made without using violence, without violating." See also Blumer 1955:168ff.) The necessity of using force in such transformations is largely dependent on the response of those expropriated; surely coercion would be essential.

48. These words were originally written in 1971 and were followed, in this place, with the following footnote: "But we may watch Chile if she attempts to implement a communist program." I then cited an article by Sweezy and Magdorf. Unfortunately there is no longer any need to cite a reference.

49. Another aspect of Marx's dictatorship of the bourgeoisie can be made intelligible within the context of power deflation. "Ideally," known violations of the system's authority code are met with coercive reactions, not excepting the case of parliamentary democracy. It was Marx's point that in a capitalist system the rules exist to protect the interests of the bourgeoisie as a class (an empirical question in any society) and that classes that, in a position of deflated power, act in violation of the authority code will be forced to conform. This gains in importance if one accepts the argument, previously made, that communist programs cannot be implemented in a capitalist social formation without generating power inflation. Thus the communists are forcibly attacked when they act as a minority within the polity in seeking to attain their interest demands; and when they wield

sufficient political support to act democratically, their power inflates. Their only alternatives are (1) to wrest control of the economy and polity from bourgeois interests and thus begin the development of a new type of social formation or (2) to give up programs that fundamentally challenge the structure of capital accumulation.

Marx also recognized the validity of these arguments within the context of a socialist economy; economic conditions necessitate the protection of those in whose interest the economy operates. The dictatorship of the proletariat means that the authority code specifies that policies on behalf of the proletariat are acceptable while those on behalf of the bourgeoisie are not acceptable. It defines the rules of the game, which for Marx necessarily (excepting only communist social formations) benefit one class, in socialism the proletariat, and harm another, in socialism the bourgeoisie. Theoretically, the dictatorship of the proletariat need no more lead to totalitarianism than must democratic capitalism, "the dictatorship of the bourgeoisie," lead to fascism. It must, however, rest on a socialist economy that limits policies capable of implementation to those in the longterm interest of the proletariat.

50. Here the assumption of single "rate of alienation," of an aggregate measure of alienation across collectivities, clearly becomes misleading.

51. DeJouvenal (1962) correctly emphasizes the importance of the increasing ability of the political system to control conscription and taxation. It is not fortuitous that the "new type" of revolution that Arendt (1965) analyzes begins with the onset of the increase of such control and thus with the onset of the growing importance of acute power deflation.

52. I regret not having the space to treat the societal community and latency subsystems at length in this essay (a brief discussion of influence is included in chap. 3). My thinking about these subsystems is less developed than that about the polity, but it might help others if I simply indicate symbolically a few parallels, as I tentatively see them:

C_i Leadership responsibility (G—[product] → I)

S_i Justification for allocations of loyalties (I—[factor] → L), extent delimited by grounds for justification of claims (A—[product] → I)

I_i Value-based claims to loyalties (L—[product] → I)

N_i Policy decisions (G—[factor] → I)

M_{it} Transactions demand for influence

M_{ih} Assertions of claims for resources (A—[factor] → I)

O_i Commitment to valued association (L—[factor] → I)

r_i Rate of alienation from commitment to valued association

C_l Commitment to the production of goods (A—[product] → L)

S_l Commitment to valued association (L—[factor] → I), extent delimited by moral responsibility for the collective interest (G—[product] → L)

I₁   Commitments to common value (I—[product] → L)

Nₗ   Consumer income (A—[factor] → L)

M_{lt} Transactions demand for commitments

M_{lh} Operative responsibility (G—[factor] → L)

O₁   Justifications for allocation of loyalties (I—[factor] → L)

r₁   Rate of distrust

I have generally retained Parsons's terminology, which might cause some confusion, especially in the case of commitments. The reader should note that some outputs occupy a double role: $M_{ih} = S_a$, $M_{lh} = S_g$, $O_i = S_l$ and $O_l = S_i$ (see fig. 2). These nodes are, I believe, the keys to integrating the partial theories developed about the subsystems into a total theory of societal scope. (A few comments on the logic of these categorizations will be found in Gould 1976: 505 n. 119.)

3. Toward a Theory of Internal Disorder

1. The strategy outlined in the text follows logically from the criticisms I have made of Popper's theory of science (see Preface, above, and Gould 1977). The reader should also understand that I am here concerned with the construction of propositions and not with their validation. As I indicated in the Preface to this book, while it is possible to refine sociological propositions within the context of essays like the one that follows, ultimately the only adequate testing for sociological theory will be by democratically controlled political movements.

2. Institutional structures are legitimized normative patterns defining regularized expectations for actors in situations where the requisite facilities for performance are provided and where conforming performance is, in the idealized case, rewarded and disorder negatively sanctioned.

3. Cf. Deutsch 1964: 100–111; and also, in the same volume, Eckstein's attempt to delimit the area of study covered by "internal war" as a category of discourse, pp. 8–23.

4. My indebtedness to the work of others is documented in the notes and references that follow. The basis for the theoretical work on deviance is found in Gould 1967, where the interested reader will find a fuller presentation of my debts and my conflicts with the work of others. The reader of that essay will also find survey data strongly in support of some of the hypotheses developed in this chapter. Since he published nothing I can cite, I must record my gratitude to the late Howard Jolly. His importance to sociology is understood only by the many sociologists (and others) who were privileged to learn from him. This essay would have been much improved had he lived to criticize it.

5. Here I assume a simple differentiation of institutional structures by functional subsystem. Where this variety of differentiation is not present, the generating conditions of disorder will be conflated—in a theoretically explicable fashion—and the resultant disorders conflated in a parallel fashion.

In an essay completed after the current chapter I have dropped this assumption, arguing that it is possible to nest structural categorizations of internal disorders within the functional framework (Gould 1977). Farther on in the present chapter I predict which institutional structure will be attacked depending on the location of a medium deflation; in the 1977 essay I assume that media are differentiated along with the differentiation of institutional structures and that more than one institutional structure and therefore more than one medium may be categorized in one functionally defined subsystem. In the 1977 essay I discuss the structure of scientific "revolutions" as a form of disorder within the integrative subsystem. The presence of this type of disorder is seen to be partly determined by a deflation of reputation, a form of influence particular to scientific communities.

6. Cf. Bellah 1965:171–72: "We may consider religion as a set of symbols that may be institutionalized, considered as normative, in a society or internalized in a personality.... Our broadest definition of 'religion' [is] ... a set of symbols providing the most general level of orientation to reality." I use the term *religion* to refer to the institutionalized social structure.

7. Compare this situation with Johnson's self-criticisms of his widely admired typology of revolutions, 1964:30, and with Smelser's more limited goals, 1962:66 and 1969:162–64.

8. Cohen 1965:462. I have added the term *motivated* to Cohen's definition, as my theory does not deal with unmotivated deviant behavior. In general I have used the term *deviant action* instead of the more usual *deviant behavior*. Cf. Becker 1963:1–39; and Blake and Davis 1964: 466–82.

9. There is no assumption that the reaction, even to public acts of deviance, will be comparable across social categories such as class, race, or ethnicity. A separate problem lies in the identification of the actual norms appropriate and in force within a given situation; this problem encompasses questions of jurisdiction and the specification of "covert" norms that may be applicable. It is related to the general issue of the interrelations among legal, political, and economic control within societal systems.

10. At one time I felt that while Durkheim's *Suicide* categorized various types of strain and linked those strains with "deviant action," he was concerned with only one type of response, suicide. I have now come to accept his view that while descriptively, in terms of the dead individual, suicide is one type of event, socially its consequences can and do differ and thus suicides can and should be categorized in many different ways.

11. It is true that many of these youths were at one time involved in

criminal gangs. This involvement was conditioned by strain at the level of facilities (SF), but a necessary precondition for their narcotics use was the development of strain at the level of values. It is of course possible that the use of narcotics was responsible for an accentuation (or development) of SF, in which case, given the other preconditions, utilitarian crime (see above) would continue (or begin).

12. This is a form of strain Cloward and Ohlin mention but do not discuss: the case where persons are oriented to the middle class and feel deprived relative to members of the middle class (Cloward and Ohlin 1960:91–99).

13. Another reason for Smelser's error stems from his view that strain always becomes manifest at the lower levels of the component of action under stress. Further, he assumes that all types of strain give rise to anxiety as their social psychological component. He fails to realize that different social conditions can be manifest in different psychological reactions (but see 1962:29–30); neglecting this possibility, he is able to assume that any variety of strain may yield any variety of collective response—especially since "anxiety, rooted in situations of ambiguity, is a generalized response not tied to precisely definable objects" (1962:89). An indication of the error this involves is manifest in the unintelligibility (at least to me) of a generalized belief focused on facilities reducing the ambiguity stemming from systemic value strain. (For Smelser it is the generalized belief that "determines" the type of collective behavior undertaken.)

14. Smelser's work has always displayed a tendency to confuse functional subsystems with structures classified therein. Thus in *Theory of Collective Behavior* there is a tendency to confuse the structural component of values with the pattern-maintenance subsystem. In *Social Change and the Industrial Revolution*, family structures are "equated" with the pattern-maintenance subsystem.

15. I am certain that a relationship exists between the position of strain within a system and the direction of the response in terms of the functional system "attacked," perhaps delimiting which subsystem or subsector. For example, assuming a deflation of influence and a strain at the level of facilities, the exact location of the strain might determine which "legal system" (of the society, the integrative subsystem, etc.) would be attacked. Here, location might be interpreted either with reference to the functional (sub)-systems or with reference to structurally autonomous systems (cf. Gouldner 1967). Nonetheless, in this book I assume that the location of the strain is irrelevant to the (functionally defined) direction of response, and further, that the response is at the level of the total system. Thus SF is a precondition for deviant innovation (see below), and it is assumed that the normative code deviated from is the "legal" system institutionalized at the societal level, therefore the normative structure within I, the societal

community, not the "legal" code of some subsystem, within its integrative subsector.

16. The version of the model I use in this essay is the one discussed in Gould 1976 and chapter 2, above.

17. Regarding the types of strain, cf. Smelser 1962, where the general categorical schema I use is outlined in some detail.

18. This seems a good place to warn about the behavioristic operationalization of concepts. No one, I would suspect, would object to speaking of stealing as one possible result of strain at the level of facilities. It is intelligible that many forms of theft might result from one or another form of facilitory strain, for instance, under most conditions, robbing a bank. But what about the case of smashing an automobile windshield? Our immediate reaction is to say that this is a form of vandalism, of deviant aggression, not deviant innovation. Under most circumstances, "statistically," we would no doubt be correct, but we might be wrong, subject to what I call the "behavioristic fallacy." Perhaps we are concerned with one action, occurring in a small town; perhaps it was committed by Joe Smith, and perhaps Joe Smith owns the only glazier's store in the town. Under these (admittedly farfetched) conditions, this action, which we would normally assume was nonutilitarian in meaning, appears motivated by utilitarian concerns.

In this example, no doubt a trivial one, the correct conclusion can only be based on a thorough understanding of Joe Smith's social and personal situation, but surely we can avoid many gross misunderstandings simply by being aware of the cultural (meaning) and social contexts within which the actors studied function. We must not simply categorize events according to their phenomenological appearance. Such contextual considerations obviously grow in importance as we begin to study deviance and disorder across societal and cultural boundaries. (The windshield example emerged from a discussion with Charles Heckscher, the afternoon he woke up to find his car's windshield smashed. I place it in a somewhat different context in the final pages of this book.)

19. It should be noted that the role conflict discussed above does not include the conflict each deviant faces in deciding to violate an institutionalized norm.

20. Bay's use of the term *anomie* is not to be confused with Merton's usage of the same term. Merton's usage was outlined in the discussion of SF.

21. I have tried to treat structural strain as a sociological variable. Strain refers to a property of the social system and not to the psychological state of an individual personality. The degree of strain present in a system, however, can sometimes be measured in terms of a rate derived from data gathered about and/or from individuals who experience psychological

strain within the various contexts of social strain. (See Smelser 1962:29–30. The four types of psychological strain differ from these attitudes.) The reader should note that we are at this point concerned with the breadth of strain in a system, not with the strength or intensity of that strain for any unit within the system (cf. Gurr 1970:chap. 3). For simplicity's sake, we here assume a threshold of strain marking its presence or absence.

The following table, assuming that the other preconditions are fulfilled, may be seen as approximating rates of deviance. Treating the other variables in a fashion parallel to the treatment of strain indicated in the table, and overlapping with it, complicates the discussion considerably. (This table, along with parts of my argument in this note, is adapted from Merton 1964.)

| | Types of Collectivity | | |
	I	II	III
Population size	1000	1000	1000
Percentage of individuals under "psychological strain"	75	40	15
Percentage of individuals under "psychological strain" engaging in deviant action	85	50	30
Percentage of individuals not under "psychological strain" engaging in deviant action	25	10	2

22. If this characterization seems excessively broad, it turns out to be amenable to specification once a concrete problem is posed. It is, however, considerably easier to deal with in attempting to explain the genesis of some type of deviant subculture, more difficult in an attempt to predict the occurrence of an already perceived form of deviance, and much more difficult in an attempt to predict the onset of a new form of deviance. It remains the case that a determinate outcome is not readily accessible.

23. Juvenile delinquency is the specific form of deviance over which this argument has taken place, but its relevance can be extended to other forms of deviance and, as we shall see, to other forms of disorder.

24. The reader should note that I have added a sequential assumption to the value-added model. For any set of actors, progression through the neutralizing belief and the actual commission of some disorderly action precede the acceptance of a set of legitimizing beliefs. However, within the social and cultural systems under examination, the legitimizing beliefs

might be present prior to their actual acceptance by any specific group of deviants.

25. See the quotation from Parsons cited above in note 10, chapter one.

26. I have used the term "specifically legal," for both power and value commitments can also serve to obligate actors to obey legal norms. Power and commitments may be so utilized when the societal legal structure is not completely differentiated from the societal morality and/or authority structures. Where the separation has occurred, a dedifferentiation often appears in situations of acute influence deflation.

27. The reader might also note that it is possible within the interchange model to trace the channels of mutual interaction between the four varieties of strain and the eight varieties of media imbalance (inflation and deflation of each medium).

28. These references must remain elliptical in this context.

29. From a perspective different from the one developed in this book, it is possible to isolate three varieties of deviance, each stemming from one of three orientations toward the legal norm violated, only one of which falls directly within the compass of our discussion.

The first violation is of a norm that the person has approached rationally, in an attempt to calculate the positive and negative benefits of compliance versus violation. These individuals develop, in other words, an expedient attitude toward the law stemming either from a societal deflation of influence or a deflation specific to the collectivities in which they are members. For them, a violation of the law is unlikely to provoke guilt feelings because adherence to the legal system is not an internalized value. (This statement is actually much too simple, assuming that "internalization" is an either/or affair; for most persons of this type, dissonance is created in the violation of a legal norm.) Each law must be justified in its own right.

The second type of violation involves a norm legitimized by an internalized value. (The value legitimizing the norm can be one proclaiming the "sanctity" of the legal system, or a non-legal value legitimizing this one law. In many instances, of course, the action will be in violation of both kinds of standards.) This is not relevant to our discussion when the violation is not the result of conscious motivation, where the violation is, for whatever reason, unintentional. Guilt feelings will result, however, when the violation is intentional, or even if it is not, owing to the violation of a moral standard. In this case the person can be called back to society through the reactivation of this commitment to her own internalized standards. (It is assumed that the repercussions of her act will not be widespread enough to weaken the moral integration of the society.) In this type of violation there is little or no possibility of legitimizing continued deviance.

This second form of deviance is relevant to our discussion at the collectivity level, for it can occur in situations of acute reference group pressures in the dynamics of wider subcultural processes. From a sociological point of view, these deviant actions on the fringe of a subculture that has neutralized the norms relevant in understanding the deviance committed can be routinized. Those fringe members, however, for whom these norms are still legitimate can, if separated from the subculture, be recalled to societal values by reactivating retained commitments. The size of this fringe can vary (cf. Merton 1964; and n. 21, this chap.).

The third type of violation occurs when the actions are not simply alternative but are also oppositional (see Williams 1973:11; Yinger 1960), where an attempt is made to redefine the norms violated. Here we come to the situation of movements oriented toward the societal community, where an attempt is made to redefine some component of the legal-stratification subsystem, as against deviance, where no attempt at redefinition is made.

30. Within the context of most work in dissonance theory there is no formal way of identifying dissonant relations between cognitions, or between actions and norms, and so on. Thus the theory as used often verges on a series of tautologies: two cognitions are dissonant if one or another mechanism of dissonance reduction occurs. This fault can be remedied only if the logic that defines contradictory relationships within a given society is specified. This logic is embodied in the cultural meaning system that defines the situation within which the person acts. Delimiting its content is not an easy task, but this is, I think, the task that some ethnomethodologists are attempting. They are generally concerned with what Homans calls "subinstitutional behavior," what I refer to as action unmediated by social structural norms but guided by "cultural norms," norms defining intelligibility rather than "right and wrong." We are also concerned with the cultural meaning—intelligibility—of social norms and the acts they regulate.

31. This is the burden of argument of the "labeling school." Their view of deviance may be simplified and summarized in a quotation from Faulkner which Becker (1963) uses as an epigraph to his book: "Sometimes I ain't so sho who's got ere a right to say when a man is crazy and when he ain't. Sometimes I think it ain't none of us pure crazy and ain't none of us pure sane until the balance of us talks him that-a-way. It's like it ain't so much what a fellow does, but it's the way the majority of folks is looking at him when he does it."

32. An extensive discussion of inflation and deflation of power, with the parallels drawn to influence, is found in chapter 2, above. Here I will only note that it is often the case that inflation and deflation of a medium are found together within the context of one system, and that this seemingly paradoxical situation is one reason why it is often necessary to disaggregate our measures of influence potential within a system.

33. Recall the Arendt quotation from chapter 2: "Cain slew Abel, and Romulus slew Remus; violence was the beginning and, by the same token, no beginning could be made without using violence, without violating" (1965: 10).

34. Cf. Arendt 1970: 56: "Violence appears where power is in jeopardy, but left to its own course it ends in power's disappearance.... Violence can destroy power; it is utterly incapable of creating it." Until the final clause this is correct. Violence, simply because it is in violation of a normative code, can call forth extremely deep beliefs legitimizing its use. These beliefs can become one foundation of a new political order. Cf. below, the discussion of legitimizing beliefs.

35. Not all actions making up a revolution are in violation of the institutionalized authority structure. Lenin, for example, often pointed out that many forms of legitimate action were necessary in the making of a revolution. Here we will be concerned with those participants who, while engaged in legitimate actions seen as furthering the revolution also commit actions in violation of the institutionalized authority structure.

36. There have been many natural history theories of revolution, but the best discussions focusing on a stage sequence version of a revolution are found in Marx 1963 and 1964, and in the work of Lefebvre (see, as an introduction, 1947).

37. In this chapter I treat society as an isolated entity, abstracting it from its interactions with other systems at the same level (e.g., society to society). This abstraction is acceptable at this level of generality, but it often leads to confusion and error in the analysis of historical cases. It also implies an isolated focus on intrasocietal preconditions for revolutions, a misperception of my intent.

I am concerned with isolating the necessary and sufficient conditions for revolution; but just as the fact that I have not analyzed the structured pressures in the genesis of these preconditions does not imply a desire to minimize their importance, likewise a failure to deal with pressures from the international system does not indicate a lack of awareness of their importance. The point I want to make is that in both of these cases, the pressures left undiscussed are relevant in generating the variables I have discussed. The effects of the international system are found, for example, in the generation of certain types of strain within the analyzed society.

38. An extensive discussion of the English revolution is found in chapters 5–7 below, where I point out that Parliament's first steps were in retaliation for comparable actions of the king. It is a debatable question whether the king's actions, in this regard, should be categorized as a form of revolution.

39. Johnson uses a similar categorization of revolutions, but he makes no attempt to identify parallel conditions leading to the occurrence of each

of the movements he identifies (cf. especially Johnson 1966: chap. 7). For a slightly different view of the types of revolt by the same author see Johnson 1964; cf. Lasswell and Kaplan 1950: 268ff.

40. "Social Revolution, that is, the complete overthrow of the established forms of associated human activity" (Kautsky 1909: 1ff; see Marx 1971a: preface).

41. While riots make no attempt to restructure the system attacked, this does not imply that they are not viewed as legitimate within a "riotous subculture." Elaborate moral legitimations have been generated within the context of action we label riotous, and must be generated if riots are to be a regularized activity within a political system (cf., e.g., Thompson 1971).

In practice the distinction between riotous and revolutionary actions is difficult to make. A collectivity of actors may be rioting while some other collectivity is defining the consequences of their (the first collectivity's) actions as revolutionary, and their collective actions may result in a revolution. It is clear that any historical analysis of disorder must examine the actions of specifiable collectivities of actors as well as the "totalistic" consequences of their actions for the system under examination. A large group of rioters may weaken the authority system sufficiently to allow a small group of revolutionaries to assume power.

A similar point should be emphasized regarding the principles of classification of revolutionary actions and revolutions. In any situation, it is quite possible for the vast majority of revolutionary actions to be directed to REVOG, for example, when the actual culmination of these actions is REVOV. This can be the case when mass participation in a revolution leads to the seizure of power by a group of "intellectuals." We must always be aware of the distinction between those who make the revolution and define it and those who participate in the revolution but who do not define it. The intentional thrust of the actions of diverse groups might well be contradictory, and the consequences of the actions of certain of these groups might well be antithetical to their articulated desires.

42. One indication of this conflict and of an attitude toward it is found among those who define collective behavior as an "uninstitutionalized" mobilization for action (for example, Smelser 1962: 71, and much work that is derived, directly or indirectly, from Le Bon). Smelser recognizes that there are institutionalized components within the movements that he studies, but indicates that these components will not be treated in his book (1962: 74–75). This is a caveat that he is unable to follow; perhaps the best single example of his lapse is the discussion of the "bureaucratic" leader within a "norm-oriented movement" (297). He is not able to treat such factors systematically; in his discussion of the derived phases of mobilization in norm-oriented movements he refers to a "period of institutionalization," but does not really come to grips with this phenomenon. Clearly,

his view of the "real and derived phases of mobilization" is a movement toward our distinction between the subculture of disorder and the disorderly subculture, but he never adequately defines the distinction.

43. I am not prepared to outline a set of categories differentiating between the four types of riots. It is my opinion that they are related to the four variables of strain and are akin to the varieties of deviance already outlined. For example, the first no doubt includes looting for gain and the second nonutilitarian aggression. The four types of revolution may make use of any variety of riot in weakening the political order, but the revolutionaries' tactics do not seem to be as substantively constrained as the varieties of riot and deviance.

44. At the point of *first* action, the distinction between the two will not have been made.

45. Cf. Lukacs 1971:317–8. This brilliant book is, even with its many weaknesses, full of insights relevant to our discussion.

It is true, of course, that some individuals develop and adhere to revolutionary ideologies prior to the commission of revolutionary actions. These individuals presumably make some form of decision assuming revolutionary identities and couple this with actions not in violation of the political code. Here, however, I hypothesize that only those who have progressed beyond the point of no return, into violence, violation, are sufficiently committed to be included within the revolutionary subculture. This leads to the apparent paradox that many of those who articulate the beliefs that come to legitimize revolutionary actions will not themselves be categorized as revolutionaries; although it is clear that in many cases their beliefs are sincere, that they will have made sacrifices for their beliefs, and that they may be important in leading to the occurrences of revolution.

Even with the above caveat, the case of the individual who is a committed ideological revolutionist and who then participates in some revolutionary disorder eludes our theoretical net, explicable perhaps in terms of peer or parental socialization in the context of the revolutionary subculture where such beliefs are the norm (cf. n. 21, this chap.).

46. In the case of the polity and the societal community, these two inputs, value commitments and investment, cross over the same boundary; in the case of the economy, over different boundaries. This fact is relevant to an explanation of why, in Weber's view, the constancy of symbolic legitimation is more important for the polity than for the economy. For example, in the case of the genesis of capitalism, the Protestant ethic was more important at the transition point into capitalism than in capitalism's routinization. This question is discussed in more detail, along with a fuller discussion of charisma, in chapter 4, below; cf. Gould 1981*b*.

47. Smelser believes that ambiguity at a higher-level component of social action is always a sufficient condition for lower-level ambiguity, but

not a necessary condition for such ambiguity; while ambiguity at a lower level is not necessarily a sufficient condition for ambiguity at higher levels (Smelser 1962:43–45, 53–54).

48. Here power inflation is a situation in which the symbolic scope of the medium exceeds the available resources necessary to assume operative responsibility for these authorized powers (see chap. 2, above).

49. This radicalization is not necessarily in a politically more radical direction; cf. Marx 1963:42.

50. The developmental model progresses through stages emphasizing the following processes: (1) A; (2) A–G; (3) G–L; (4) G–I; (5) I–A; (6) I–L; (7) L–G. It is with stage three that the necessity for a new basis of mechanical solidarity is established, although the actual value base of the polity is not yet questioned by those controlling the current phase of the revolution. It was only in progressing through stage four, at both the level of societal development and the development of individual revolution, that revolutionaries came to legitimize their actions in terms of a futuristic, non-traditional orientation. (See Arendt 1965, and chap. 8, below.)

4. Manufacturing Social Formation

1. I will endeavor to maintain the following terminological conventions: the term *system* refers to a series of social relationships that maintain a boundary and are open. Its units are treated in an aggregative, macro-functionalist perspective, without regard to their organizational forms (see chaps. 1 and 2). The term *structure* may have two references. More generally it refers to patterns of social interaction in which a violation of the pattern is negatively sanctioned. More concretely and of direct relevance to my current discussion, it refers to the mode of production (pre)dominant (dominant or predominant) within the social system or social subsystem of reference. *Social formation* refers not to the combination of modes of economic production found in an actual society, but rather to the configuration of (pre)dominant modes of production in the four subsystems of a society. In other words, each societal subsystem may be assumed capable of characterization in terms of a (pre)dominant structure or mode of producing the relevant subsystem output; the patterned relationship between the four (pre)dominant structures, modes of production, in the four societal subsystems may be referred to as a social formation. Thus the concept of a social formation involves a nondescriptive characterization of the (pre)-dominant structure within a society.

Society refers to the functionalist, aggregative characterization of "a type of social system, in any universe of social systems, which attains the highest level of self-sufficiency as a system in relation to" other systems (Parsons 1966:9). Thus while *social formation* refers to the configuration of (pre)dominant structures within each of the four societal subsystems, *society* refers to the aggregative characterization of social relations within those four subsystems. (For the difference between predominance and dominance, see below.)

2. I use the word *manufacturing* to label stage four in the development of economic subsystems, and *"manufacturing,"* in quotes, to label stage four in the development of societies. The use of economic terms to categorize types of societies is justified, I believe, by the fact that the structure of the economy sets limits on the scope of variation of the entire societal system.

3. On two occasions it has been suggested to me that the phrase "tendential development" is redundant. Such a view indicates a misunderstanding of my usage. Not all "tendencies" need involve "development." On the contrary, certain tendencies are regressive and others are repeating (in the sense of a static equilibrium). Further, not all development is tendential. All stage sequence development involves a violation of a tendential structure, as I use the term. A "tendential development" is the working out, within a given structure, of some progression. Progression thus implies a direction of movement, which may be structured as a tendency.

4. This distinction, while theoretically accurate, is not so clear-cut in history. As Marx commented, "epochs in the history of society are no more separated from each other by hard and fast lines of demarcation, than are geological epochs" (1967, 1:371).

5. This is not the place to enter into the controversy surrounding Marx's discussion of the tendential decline in the rate of profit, or the more general controversy regarding analyses in terms of "value." I hope to publish in the near future an article outlining my position on these issues; in this essay, even recognizing its failings in certain contexts, I stick reasonably close to Marx's own position. Cf. Steedman 1977, 1980; Van Parijs 1980; Okishio 1961; Roemer 1981; Shaikh 1978, 1980; Mandel and Freeman 1984; Salvadori 1981, among many others of direct and indirect relevance.

6. It is not that the individual capitalist will necessarily follow these laws but rather that determinate consequences will befall her if she fails to obey them.

7. Marx 1967, 1:363. Usually when Marx uses the word *spontaneous* he is referring to a natural process within a constituted tendency. The problem in this case is his failure to establish the structures that constitute the tendency of the "spontaneous" formation of manufacture based on division of labor, the real subsumption of labor under capital, from manufacture grounded in the formal subsumption of labor under capital.

8. Marx recognizes, of course, that the capitalists' revenue tends to increase along with the increase in the amount of surplus value (1967, 1:445–47, 608); Nicolaus (1967) provides a convenient collection of

quotations dealing with this issue and relating it to the growth of a middle class.

9. This form of analysis, which assumes a specific response to a "given opportunity," dominates not only utilitarian economics, but certain writings claiming to be within either a Marxist or social historical tradition. See Brenner 1976 and 1982 for some general comments criticizing demographic and exchange interpretations of economic development, and Brenner 1977; Skocpol 1977; and Dupuy and Fitzgerald 1977 for criticisms of Wallerstein 1974. The Brenner essays are especially valuable in that they stress the importance of agrarian social structure in the development of capitalism, as did Marx, and Lenin 1960ff.: vol. 3.

10. The impression Weber gives in his writings is that he had read everything, forgotten nothing, and was slowly piecing it all together. There are brilliant sketches of the legal, political, and economic bases on which capitalism developed throughout his writings, but the only systematic discussions related to this problem are of religion. For references see bibliography below; a partial exception is Weber 1961, a relatively neglected work meriting considerable study; on pages 208–9 he lists the features of rational capital accounting, which he views as "the most general presupposition for the existence of this present-day capitalism."

11. Weber noted the criticism of circularity (1958: 198 n. 13).

12. A rudimentary manufacturing economy is one characterized by pockets of manufacture, governed by traditional controls and situated within the context of a noncapitalist system. Such pockets are not predominant and whatever their basis show no tendency to develop other than in response to exogenous pressures. They do not, in either the short or the long run, undermine the constitutive structure that surrounds them, even when they are embedded in extensive networks of merchant and/or usury capital.

13. As written this statement is too baldfaced, ignoring as it does other relevant variables.

14. Weber often stresses exchange relationships when discussing capitalism; I have altered this emphasis, focusing on the relations of production. For a justification of this tactic in dealing with Weber, see Gould 1981*b*; more generally see Marx 1973: Introduction.

15. Marx writes (I am tempted to write, following Durkheim 1964) that "just as a certain number of simultaneously employed labourers are the material pre-requisites for division of labour in manufacture, so are the number and density of the population, which here correspond to the agglomeration in one workshop, a necessary condition for the division of labour in society. Nevertheless, this density is more or less relative. A relatively thinly populated country, with well-developed means of communication, has a denser population than a more numerously populated country, with badly-developed means of communication ..." He con-

tinued, "Since the production and the circulation of commodities are the general pre-requisites of the capitalist mode of production, division of labour in manufacture demands, that division of labor in society at large should previously have attained a certain degree of development. Inversely, the former division reacts upon and develops and multiplies the latter" (1967, 1:352–53; see 1976:951).

16. The literature on enclosures is vast, including the following: Tawney 1967; Kerridge 1968, 1969; Thirsk 1958, 1967; Leonard 1905; Slater 1907; Gonner 1912; McClosky 1975a, 1975b, 1976, 1979; Cohen and Weitzman 1975; Wordie 1983, 1984; Chapman 1984; Wilson 1979; Butlin 1979; Yelling 1977, 1982.

17. In this discussion I have slighted the demographics of the growth of the English proletariat. Recent discussions by Levine (1984), for England, and Tilly (1984), for Europe, provide cogent analyses of this issue. Both emphasize the interrelationship between population growth and the development of the economic organization I've called manufacture. Both also discuss the contribution of the expropriation of peasants, especially prior to 1700. Yet both emphasize that in their view the importance of the "natural," internally generated growth of the wage-earning proletariat was paramount.

18. Major aspects of this process of growing differentiation and dependence on wage labor differed between the fifteenth and seventeenth centuries. In the situation of enclosures for pasturage (primarily in the fifteenth and sixteenth centuries), sheep were needed for wool, which was needed as a raw material for England's largest manufacturing industry. The "movement of labour power from agriculture to manufacturing industry is what was then, and since has been, denounced under the name of depopulation. Needless to say, there was no depopulation of the kingdom. Nor, so far as can be judged, was there any depopulation of the plain. Indeed, all of the evidence points to a rapid upsurge of Midland population at this time [and the Midlands were a focal point of enclosure]. Nor, for that matter, does there appear to have been any depopulation of the countryside, for the industries that now grew and developed were mostly rural. What did certainly take place was a depopulation of agriculture, a 'putting down of ploughs', and a reduction of the agricultural work force" (Kerridge 1973:108–9). Thus the roots of the major English industry were intertwined with an alteration in farming organization which lead to the production of wool for market (but not necessarily to manufacture in agriculture) at the same time as it lead to the growth of a formally free labor market.

The major alterations of the seventeenth century (and later) were different, and they transformed the context within which both corn and pasturage farming occurred. "The great agricultural changes increased the demand for wage-labour. Extra hands were needed to form and run the up-and-down farms, to dig marl and cart it to the fields, to drain the marshes, to float the meadows, to hoe the turnips, to mow the hay, and simply to replace petty tenant farmers and share-croppers. In cereal growing the small farm could not compete on equal terms with the large one. The small farmer had higher unit costs and so little money coming in that he could not wait and get the best prices for what he had to sell. As long as a seller's market kept corn prices high, all this did not matter so much, but later on, in the seventeenth century, especially towards the end of it, when a buyers' market developed and prices slumped, many small men had to throw up their farms" (Kerridge 1973:147–48).

19. See Marx 1967, 3:part VI; Marx's discussion of absolute ground rent is problematic in many respects, but these problems are not relevant to our argument and need not detain us here; cf. for varying points of view on Marx's discussion: Hindess and Hirst 1975: chap. 5; Rey 1973; Cutler and Taylor 1972; Cutler 1975; Tribe 1977; Amin 1977.

20. I am, with some reservations, ignoring the legal controls which were demolished in order to allow for leasehold on nondemesne land unobstructed by feudal custom. The nature of this demolition process has been subject to considerable controversy (the two major combatants: Tawney 1967 [1912]; and Kerridge 1969; cf. Thompson 1976), but no one denies that the economic pressures necessitating legal transformations worked with gathering speed from at least the fifteenth century. Feudal tenures and the court of wards were abolished in 1646; this abolition was reconfirmed in 1660 by the Convention Parliament as its second order of business, after agreeing to the restoration of Charles II (Hill 1969*b*:146–48).

21. See Marx 1967, 3:part VI. *Price of production* is the technical term defining the equilibrium price of commodities when competitive pressures equalize the rate of profit; very simply it involves the costs of production plus the average rate of profit on capital invested (see Marx 1967, 3:parts I and II).

22. This paragraph is based on A. Appleby 1978; Bowden 1967:598ff.; Clarkson 1971:34, 218ff.; Coleman 1956; Everitt 1967*a*:424ff., 435; Everitt 1969*a*:32; Hill 1966:24–25; Hill 1969*b*:15, 46, 56, 65, 83ff.; Hoskins 1953–54:98; Kerridge 1973:150–52; Stone 1966:26; Spufford 1974:48; Supple 1959:15.

23. "Least productive" ought not to be interpreted as referring simply to the productivity of land under some pregiven set of conditions, but to the form of production under actual conditions.

24. Jones 1967. Jones tends to downplay the importance of organizational changes in allowing for increased productivity. It is, however, obvious from his own words that the introduction of new techniques was interrelated with organizational transformations. For this argument, and citations from Jones, see Brenner 1976:64 n. 83.

25. Let me emphasize once again that "small holders" were not com-

pletely eliminated; sometimes their position was "merely" transformed as the nature of economic production altered around them and as they were incorporated first into a system controlled by mercantile capital and later by manufacturing capital. What is crucial is that the economic structure was transformed (cf. Moore 1966: 514–17).

26. The above discussion has focused on the production of grain; in forest areas the process was different, involving less differentiation into large and small and more parceling of holdings, often supplemented, as we have seen, with by-employments. For a good description of this process in the early seventeenth century, but only in one circumscribed area, see Spufford 1974: chap. 5.

27. This point requires some clarification. Relative surplus value surely did increase as real wages declined, but this increase was presumably the same for all capitalists. It was not generated by an increase in surplus profits derived from an innovation in the structure of the labor process increasing the productivity of some capitalists' hired labor power, and thus (if this increase in productivity occurred in the production of commodities necessary to reproduce labor power) lowering the value of labor power. While a transformation in the labor process increasing productivity would generate competitive constraints, a decrease in real wages for the entire laboring population would not have this consequence.

28. The major exceptions to this "rule" appear to have been the obvious ones, where production was necessarily tied to a specific location, e.g., coal production. Cf. Langton 1972: 52; Nef 1932, 1964.

29. For this paragraph see Clarkson 1971: 106ff.; Hinton 1955: 282; and most important, Supple 1959, who comments as follows:

Part of the volatile nature of the effects of commercial disruptions was undoubtedly caused by the ease of disinvestment consequent upon the nature of capital at the time. As already intimated, outside a few special trades, the individual entrepreneur had a preponderance of his investment in the form of circulating capital and could therefore withdraw from participation in his activity far more easily than his nineteenth-century counterpart—much of whose capital was immobilized in fixed items of investment. This importance of working capital was matched, given technological poverty, by the significance of labour, whose share as a cost of production was commensurately more significant. Hence, a sudden expansion in output would be secured less by a change in organization or techniques than by an increase in employment and a multiplication of units of production. Conversely, a fall in demand would quickly put pressure on wages and employment. In these circumstances, one marked feature of society— much as a government enamoured of the concept of a stable and

ordered economic framework might dislike it—was a considerable
horizontal and even vertical mobility of capital, entrepreneurial skill
and labour. (Supple 1959:9–10)

30. In this chapter I have largely ignored both "heavy industry" and the
joint-stock companies. Both were gaining in importance, but neither, in my
opinion, controlled the course of English development. In addition, both
were generally organized as manufacture with formal subsumption of
labor to capital and reliance on iterative surplus value. On joint-stock
companies Scott 1968 remains invaluable. Clarkson 1971 contains a good
general bibliography; in addition a number of recent general treatments
have been published, for example, Coleman 1975 and 1977; the latter contains a more limited bibliography, including some more recent citations;
see also Holderness 1976 and Gregg 1976. Unwin 1957 remains an invaluable guide.

31. See also Court 1953:42–43, where he notes credit relationships
and intermarriage between small farmers and industrial workers.

32. R. Davis's suggestion that "more than a quarter of all manufacturing production, [and] a half of the production of woollen goods, was ex-
ported" seems too high to me, even for the second half of the seventeenth
century (1973*a*:8); cf. Chartres 1977*a*; Jones 1967:36; Deane and Cole
1969:41–42.

33. *Calculation* within this context does not refer primarily to rational
cost accounting but rather to a freedom from arbitrary interferences in
running an enterprise. It thus comes to involve either the stability of expectations within a market or the control over expectations via governmental action, for example in dealing with colonies.

Weber, in discussing the importance of calculation, in my opinion over-
emphasizes fixed capital as the foundation of the need for calculability.
This type of predictability became necessary with the development of
manufacture, based on "large" investments of capital, but not necessarily
of fixed capital (cf., for example, Weber 1968, 1:240; Weber 1968,
3:1095 with Weber 1968, 1:152–53).

34. It might be argued that the major lacuna in this essay is the fact that
so little attention is devoted to the emergence of "civil society," a differentiated societal community. While I will say a little about this below, as the
fact of differentiated authorization and support inputs to the polity (across
the L—G and I—G boundaries) is of considerable importance in understanding questions that directly concern us, a systematic discussion of the
emergence of a differentiated societal community will have to await the
sequel (see Hegel 1967; Parsons 1966:chap. 2; Parsons 1971).

35. A monopoly, to follow Coke's definition, was "'an institution or
allowance by the King by his grant, commission or otherwise, to any person or persons, bodies politic or corporate of or for the sole buying, selling,

making, working, or using of anything whereby any person or persons, bodies politic or corporate are sought to be restrained of any freedom or liberty that they had before, or hindered in their lawful trade'" (Foster 1960:59).

36. This is a pattern the development of which will accelerate with the consequent increases in productivity as complex cooperation emerges.

37. In order to save time and space I have used a shorthand in the following discussion. Social processes are functionally categorized within the AGIL functional schema. Thus when I locate "the means of labor" within the goal-attainment subsector of the adaptive subsector of the adaptive subsystem (A_{A_g}), I mean those processes involving control over the means of production that have goal-attainment consequences for the adaptive subsector of the economy, and thus adaptive consequences for the economy and for the society. I do not mean that plows and knitting frames are so classified.

38. The term "nonlaborer" is an ambiguous one. It refers to the persons who live off the surplus produced by others, but it does not imply that these persons must refrain from working. Capitalist entrepreneurs might well work as hard as their hired laborers, but their functionally defined position within the economy nonetheless differs from the laborers' position.

39. Within this frame of reference the term *valorization process* must be understood more broadly than in its context within the capitalist mode of production.

40. If the reader wishes she may trace this from figure 17 to 19 to 20; the M_{gh} curve shifts out and to the right, resulting in a shift up and to the left in the LM curve, and in a consequent decrease in output at the intersection of the LM-IS curves.

41. That is, in figures 19 and 20, the government could not increase the scope of power within the system—in the movement of the LM curve out and to the left.

42. This may be seen in figures 15, 16, and 20. The Crown's demands created a paradox of thrift: the S_g curve shifts up and to the left, the IS curve down and to the left, and intersects with the LM curve at a point defining a lower level of political output and of political savings, economic productivity and services, and thus the capacity to implement policies.

5. Coming of the English Revolution

1. Engels recognized the need for this periodization in 1844, and he explicitly drew parallels to the French Revolution. Unfortunately, the parallels he drew were inaccurate, and he did not endeavor to explain the genesis of either "revolution" (Marx and Engels 1975, 3:472–73; cf. Trotsky 1967, 1:204–5).

2. The Petition is reprinted in Gardiner 1906. I do not intend chapters 5, 6, and 7 to serve as an introduction to seventeenth-century English history. While they are, I hope, intelligible without such an introduction, they will surely be richer in content the deeper one's background in the period. There are a number of books that seek to introduce "the century of revolution" to students: Hill 1966; Stone 1972*a*; Laslett 1965; and Wrightson 1982, among many others. The best overview of the general political scene remains Gardiner 1883–84: 10 vols.

In the discussion that follows I have often focused on certain events, e.g., the passing of the Petition of Right, as exemplifications of the tendencies I am seeking to analyze. I have done this in order to keep the discussions as brief as possible, not because these were the only events available for illustrative purposes. The reader should also be informed about my strategy in citing references. Most of the points I enunciate will not be "factually" controversial, and will go unsupported. Often when I cite a reference it is one of many available. The selection of a particular reference has often been arbitrary.

I discussed in the preface the problem of the validity of certain historical arguments and my inability, in this context, to confront many of the contradictory arguments put forward by historians. In general when a point is in dispute I have cited the source(s) on which I am relying, but usually not opposing positions. Perhaps more dangerous, I have often used and cited arguments out of context, i.e., I have ignored the author's rationale in making them. I hope that this is justified by the sociologist's desire to formulate systematic theory, theory that must be evaluated on its own terms and not as a piece of historiographical controversy. (On these points see the preface, above.)

Finally, it may be worth noting that I have tried to present, in Stone's phrase, "a whole complex of interlocking evidence" (1972*b*: 134) for my crucial contentions. My confidence in the veracity of an argument has increased when a variety of types of evidence from a number of sources could be adduced to substantiate it. For example, while there is no systematic and definitive proof that the predominance of manufacture led to support for the REVOG, I think that the range of evidence I present in chapter 6 makes a very good case for this relationship. In each such contention my standard of judgment can be stated counterfactually. Thus we may conclude a complementary argument with the claim that without the development of manufacture there would not have been a rebellion (REVOG) in England in the mid-seventeenth century.

3. The nature and genealogy of opposition in early Stuart England is a controversial topic among contemporary historians. My view for the later period, from 1630, is in the pages that follow; for the earlier period I feel that there was an opposition, that from the late 1620s it had a central core in Parliament and that it emerged in reaction to Stuart patrimonialism. It

was not an opposition such as we see in modern parliaments nor was it constituted like a contemporary political party. It had no membership and what organization it had fed off an extrapolitical foundation. While it sporadically reacted to perceived violations of "law and property," it was consolidated only when it became apparent that these violations had the potential to be institutionalized. Its actions were legitimized by citing royal innovations and evoking traditional, hierarchical values. Though concerned with local issues, it was not merely localist in its orientation or purpose. Finally, as we will see in the pages that follow, opposition fragmented along predictable lines with the onset of the REVOG.

The highlights of the current controversies may be followed in the following texts: Ashton 1978; Christianson 1976, 1977; Farnell 1977; Fletcher 1981, 1983; Fulbrook 1982; Gruenfelder 1977, 1981; Hexter 1978; Hill 1981, 1983; Hirst 1978, 1980, 1981; Holmes 1980*a*; Kishlansky 1977, 1979*a*; Morrill 1976, 1979; Rabb 1981; Roberts 1977; Russell 1976, 1979*a*, 1979*b*; Underdown 1980; White 1979*a*; Woolrych 1980. Rabb presents a useful summary.

4. Zagorin 1969:259, quoting from "The generall remonstrance ... of the Catholikes of Ireland," 1641. Zagorin 1969 and Fletcher 1981 provide the most complete treatment of the first session of Parliament, but much additional information will be found in Gardiner 1884:vols. 9 and 10; Wormald 1951; Clarendon 1888; Lambert 1984; and for the Lords, Firth 1910; Christianson 1977.

The reader familiar with English history will note that I have ignored the Short Parliament (13 April to 5 May 1640). The meeting of this Parliament was precipitated by the Scottish Revolution. It refused to vote money prior to the settling of grievances and was dissolved.

5. I have not endeavored to discuss the generating conditions for either the Scottish or the Irish Revolution. Both are of interest and consequence and both are much too important to be treated in a cursory fashion. In my opinion, however, neither was essential in generating any phase of the English Revolution except as a precipitant (Rabb 1981:65); as I have shown in chapter 4, tendencies inherent in the English social structure generated the necessary conditions for the most crucial phase of the English Revolution; the events in Scotland and Ireland helped to define, in exacerbating these variables, the moment when the preconditions would come together and thus the time of the first two phases of the English Revolution. Stevenson 1973 deals with *The Scottish Revolution, 1637–44*; there is, to my knowledge, no comparable book for Ireland. My understanding of the Irish events has been aided by a seminar paper written by Francesca Jessup.

6. Russell has recently emphasized that parliamentary subsidies, Parliament's major provision of extraordinary supply, were "scandalously underassessed" (1979*b*:49) and in any case were, as voted, totally in-

adequate to meet the Crown's fiscal needs. What he doesn't adequately comprehend, in my opinion, is why Parliament was reluctant to vote additional sums and why the people were reluctant to pay what was voted (Russell 1979*b*:49ff., 64ff.).

Russell tends to view Parliament's action as manifesting an unwillingness to take responsibility for the policies they advocated. He doesn't sufficiently emphasize their lack of trust of both James I and Charles I. He underplays the importance of the illegality of Stuart levies (1979*b*:51) and of Parliament's fears for its own survival (51–52). The tenor of his argument is perhaps clearest when he comments: "In 1628, Sir Edward Coke was full of regret that no bill had ever been passed to give legal authority to the lieutenantcy, but in the twenty-seven intervening years [from 1601 when Lords, but not Commons, passed such a bill], he made little attempt to remedy the omission" (1979*b*:76). It is as if the problematic nature of the Crown's activities would be eliminated if only Parliament would have legalized the "illegal" actions undertaken by the Crown. Surely there were reasons for Coke's reluctance to legitimize a Stuart-controlled militia, just as there were reasons Parliament was unwilling to provide James and Charles with sufficient monetary resources (for similar comments, see Hirst 1980:461).

7. I should note that the king did, in 1640, summon those who held tenancies in knight service to follow him in battle against the Scots. Clearly, however, this was, in addition to the composition for knighthood, an attempt to collect fines in lieu of service. See Gardiner 1884, 9:170; and Firth 1910:63–64.

8. The receipts from wardship had trebled during the personal rule. See Stone 1972*a*:122, and the sources he cites.

9. It is important to note that the regulations discussed below had other consequences in addition to their manifestations as facilitory strain. These are discussed in their appropriate places, especially where I discuss strain at the level of goals.

10. This discussion ignores two important groups: first, those who were not part of the political nation, who will be discussed below, and second, those who were at least passive Royalists, even though in a situation of strain at the level of facilities (including many Catholics and most civil lawyers), who even if not always part of the Court (many civil lawyers were), nonetheless did not fall within the compass of one or more of the other variables to be enunciated as necessary conditions for participation in the revolution.

11. It is very difficult to determine the relationship between specific strains and specific actions among the peers from secondary sources, because these do not make a clear distinction between the phases of the revolution and because they do not discuss the peers in my terms. Thus I can

provide no direct evidence that it was those peers who were in a situation of facilitory strain who participated in the REVOF.

It must also be noted that the peers' actions were often directed toward different goals than the actions of their counterparts in the Commons; especially during the first session of the Long Parliament many clearly sought to mediate between the Commons and the king, and many saw this conflict as an opportunity to (re)institute a form of councillor government with the nobility (re)assuming their rightful place at the king's right hand. We will also see in chapter 6 how many of the peers' actions as a group in the Lords were coerced by popular pressure.

12. Perhaps it is important that I reinforce a general methodological point. The explanations I am providing for the events of the English Revolution are couched in sociological terms; they are not intended to capture the activities of any given individual. This is true for two fundamental reasons: first, some individuals will participate in revolutionary actions even if they do not personally fall within the variables defined as necessary and sufficient in leading to these actions. These persons may be simply conforming to demands made on them within their social environment (see chap. 3, n. 21). Second, and more substantively, an individual may fall under the rubric of this discussion, but other variables applicable to her (perhaps idiosyncratically) might counterbalance the specifics I have discussed for her as a member of a general category; for example, a member of the Country category who has received special benefits from the Crown owing to some factor not considered, or a member of the Court who has lost the benefits of office owing to some factor specific to her relationship with the king. They must not be treated as counterexamples but simply as an indication that (this operationalization of) the sociological categories cannot capture the fine grains of individual action.

13. Hawkins goes on to say that the government's intervention in the economy "passed the indefinable line between public and private interest" (1973:57). We will see below that the development of a notion of the "public interest" was a crucial aspect of the revolutionary period, and that the incapacity of the government to justify its actions in the name of that public interest, as against the concept of a hierarchically ordered society where each person had his or her place, was crucial to the dissolution of the government.

14. On figures 29 and 30 this diminution of power as a generalized medium is shown by a movement of the LM curve to the left.

15. During the period of the term *revolution* was often used in the sense of "motion returning to its point of origin" (Zagorin 1969:13). See in addition to Zagorin: Snow 1962; Rosenstock-Huessy 1938; and Griewank 1966.

16. This might have been a logical consequence of the argument and it

was quickly read into it (see Weston 1965; Weston and Greenberg 1981), but substantively it is not explicit in Charles's document.

It should be noted that Weston and Greenberg also see the document "stressing an equal partnership among the three estates" (1981:36). They emphasize the following statement: "'In this kingdom the laws are jointly made by a king, by a house of peers, and by a house of commons chosen by the people, *all having free votes* and particular privileges'" (1981:36, their italics). Emphasizing the emergence of legislation as the primary focus of sovereignty, they underemphasize the importance of the king's retention (within the document) of "Government (*gubernaculum*) [which] was the king's preserve. He made treaties of war and peace, created peers, chose officers and councillors for state and judges for law, named commanders of forts and castles, gave commissions for raising men to fight wars abroad and prevent insurrections at home, exercised the power of pardon, etc.... To prevent the abuse of these powers or the exploitation of the king's authority in matters of public necessity for the gain of favorites, the house of commons was empowered to raise money and impeach. But it was barred from one important area: it had no share in government or in selecting those who governed" (1981:37). The civil war was, of course, most directly a fight over who controlled the "government."

17. Pocock's book traces this development through Renaissance political thought, and in this process greatly overestimates, in my opinion, the Renaissance's importance for English political thinking. Conversely, he underestimates, in my view, the importance of the Reformation, religious thought, and Calvinism in particular for this development. In addition, without taking into account the stream of influences stemming from the Reformation there is no way to explain the commitments that sanctioned these arguments and which led persons to act in perilous situations to enforce them (cf. Weber 1958:197).

18. Koenigsberger, in a review of Stone's *The Causes of the English Revolution*, dissents from this type of argument, asserting that a standing army and paid bureaucrary were not crucial. He based this conclusion on the fact that continental officials purchased their offices and thus were also independent of the Crown (for similar comments regarding England see Hill 1966:70; Hawkins 1973:46). He argues that it was the breadth of the English opposition which was crucial. Clearly both factors were important. Here, the essential point to emphasize is that Charles's army and officials were his enemies (at least during the facilitory rebellion). They could act with nearly complete confidence once united; this was not the case to as great an extent anywhere in Europe. In England the Crown was dependent on Parliament, which granted support only if granted local control, and this led to a parallel growth of local and central power (see Stone 1972a:63–64). This was crucial, in my opinion. (Koenigsberger 1974: 104–6; 1972; and for Stone's reply, Stone 1974.)

6. REVOG

1. In addition to the citations above regarding England, this point has featured in almost all the comparative treatments of the seventeenth-century revolutions, from, for example, Merriman 1938:89, one of the first books to treat the *Six Contemporaneous Revolutions*, to Kamen 1971:79, one of the better recent texts.

2. Trevor-Roper 1967a, especially 84ff. The cited paper has been extensively and justifiably criticized on many points. Some of the more interesting criticisms are reprinted in Aston 1967; see also Lublinskya 1968. I will discuss Hobsbawm's essay on the crisis in this chapter.

3. I have adopted the following terminological conventions in this book. Those who supported the REVOF are labeled the Country, those who opposed this first stage of the revolution, the Court. Those who supported the REVOG are refered to as Parliamentarians, those in opposition as Royalists. Those who supported the REVON (see chap. 3, above, and below, chap. 7) are labeled "Independents," with the term always placed within quotation marks to differentiate them from both the religious Independents and from the Independent party within the REVOG. Among those who supported the REVOG, the Parliamentarians, I will emphasize two groups, those who failed to support the REVON, the "Presbyterians," with the term always in quotation marks, and the Independents. It must be noted that the "Presbyterians" include members of the so-called Independent party of 1644–45 to 1649. The relationship between these political groups and their religious counterparts will be made apparent as we proceed and in the appendix to chapter 7. The relationship between these political groups and the Presbyterian and Independent parties of 1644–5 to 1649 will also be clarified.

4. "It is acknowledged that the King is the fountain of justice and protection, but the acts of justice and protection are not exercised in his own person, nor depend upon his pleasure, but by his courts and by his ministers, who must do their duty therein, though the King in his own person should forbid them; and therefore, if judgments should be given by them against the King's will and personal command, yet are they the King's judgments." "Declaration of the Houses in Defence of the Militia Ordinance," 6 June 1642 (27 May 1642), reprinted in Gardiner 1906:254–58; see McIlwain 1910:352; Latham 1945:43.

5. "On November 11 [1643], by authorizing the use of the new Great Seal, they [Parliament] laid claim to possess the highest symbol of sovereignty" (Gardiner 1893, 1:250). One party to the dialogue in the *Behemoth* asks, "Was not the making of a new Great Seal a sufficient proof that the war was raised, not to remove evil counsellors from the King, but to remove the King himself from the government?" (Hobbes 1969:128).

6. Thus far I have only typified certain of the actions that substantiate

my characterization of the period from 1642–49 as a REVOG; I have not, of course, presented anything resembling a comprehensive picture of the period. An adequate picture of the political history of the period emerges from the relevant books and articles by Gardiner, Hexter, MacCormack, Wedgwood, Roots, Kaplan, Pearl, Glow (= Mulligan), Underdown, and Zagorin, cited in the references.

One set of events, important to the specification of the concept of REVOG, has not been touched upon. One suggested method of dealing with Charles Stuart was to replace him with one of his sons, or with a monarch from a different dynasty. See, for example, Gardiner 1893, 4:49, 99; Glow 1969:8–9; Hexter 1941:106; MacCormack 1973:103–4, 115, 161ff., 197; Underdown 1971:96, 183. For an argument against the existence of a plot to depose Charles in 1644, but one that is faulty in consistently confusing what I have called a REVOG with a REVON (a redefinition of the political regime), see Kaplan 1971. MacCormack comments on this argument in 1973:33 n. 51; again Kaplan 1976:56 and n. 82. This resolution to the problem, the removal of Charles in favor of another monarch, would fall under the rubric of a REVOG. In most instances those who contemplated such coups intended them as a redefinition of the polity which placed control over the executive in the two Houses.

7. There are hints in the literature that some who were supporters of the king in the REVOF supported Parliament in the REVOG. Cf. Woolrych 1968:19.

8. This image of social groups has always seemed to me to be the "orthodox" interpretation of role theory (cf. Parsons 1951 and Goodenough 1963), with a developmental dimension added. For me, this image of concept formation comes from an analysis of Hegel's concept of "notion." One consequence of this interpretation is that one cannot understand a structure without an analysis of its tendential development. Although it is true that this development is complex in "space" as well as "time," and that in certain places Hegel reduces each phase in a tendential development to an undetermined point, what the Althusserians call an "essential section," and that contradiction is therefore located only in time and not in space, it nonetheless remains the case that if one reads Hegel and not the "Hegelian Marxists" there is much to learn on these questions from the great philosopher. The Althusserian argument can be found in Althusser and Balibar 1970; Althusser 1970, 1971, 1972; Poulantzas 1973, 1975; and Godelier 1972. See also Thompson 1963.

9. It is perhaps important to reemphasize what was said in chapter 1, that this "positional definition" does not exhaust the "subject." Personalities, to take the easiest case, not only exist but exist as autonomous systems that cannot be reduced to the sum of the roles an individual actor occupies. The error of reducing personalities to social structures is every bit as absurd as the error of reducing social structures to psychological processes. Each

personality system must be studied in and for itself, and the specification of theory to it is as complex as the specification of theory to a society, thus the necessity of a detailed "case history," as in psychoanalysis.

An understanding of the interaction that occurs between personality and social system is essential to a complete understanding of any historical process, and one reason that this essay is incomplete is that we do not attempt this analysis for even a single concrete personality system. This lacuna is one reason the persons constructed in social history often appear to be paper men and women, mechanical and dry. One hopes this "error" is one of omission, not of commission.

Another blank place in this analysis is manifest at a different level. There are intracollectivity processes that are of considerable importance, processes that are sometimes taken as constitutive of the collectivity studied. These are largely ignored in this book in favor of specifying certain of the contexts within which these collectivities are constituted. Thus my descriptions must seem sparse, schematic, and incomplete.

10. Ashton's characterization of the geographic divisions and their implications is typical: "Although Marxist historians quite properly lay stress on the fact that the part of the country from which the parliamentary cause drew its chief strength was the economically advanced south and east, while the royalist strength lay more especially in the more economically backward north and west, the available evidence does not suggest any uniform identification of any of the competing groups with any identifiable economic or social interest" (1978:79). He comments later that "all classes were to be found on both sides [in the Civil War, but] both Cavalier and Roundhead gentry were acutely aware of a common interest arising out of the danger that the lower orders might use the war as the occasion of an attack on the property of enemies, which might all too easily spill over into an attack on property in general" (1978:271).

No one should expect to find uniform political allegiance or action from the members of any social group, for any cause, certainly not if that group is a class grounded in economically productive social relations. Divisions are especially likely when common interests, here fear of the "lower orders," define a commonality of interest for a status group encompassing more than one class category. In addition, there are always (1) overlapping considerations that define membership in the relevant groups and (2) other variables that are relevant in the determination of political action. What one would expect to find is what Morrill suggests is the case for the "economically backward" north and west:

> I have no doubt that in the North and West of England, the committed Royalists would appear as powerful groups of leading gentry, including dominant elements within the ruling élite, bound together by a fear of social revolution from below and the need to preserve hierarchy in

Church and State, allied, with differing degrees of discomfort, to leading recusant families; and that the parliamentarian radicals would be
led by one or two leading gentry, but otherwise dominated by gentlemen of middling wealth, often kept just outside the governing circle,
often of recent gentry origin, with very strong commitment not simply
to a reversal of Laudian innovation, but to the radical reform of the
Elizabethan settlement and to the creation of a society influenced by
godly Christian values and integrity....

These 'honest radicals' were drawn not only from amongst the gentry
but also from amongst the yeomen and urban 'middling sorts.' And
they call into question an *assumption* ... that it is the gentry alone who
determine the political alignment of a county in the Civil War.
(1979:83–84; but cf. 1983*b*)

We will see that those persons who supported Parliament were likely to
be in a situation of strain at the level of goals; they come primarily from
those areas where manufacture was predominant or, in the north and west,
from the groups most likely to be embedded in the not yet predominant
manufacturing structure.

11. The harsh realities of military power were determined by whom a
given area supported, and while perhaps relevant to the actions of specific
individuals or isolated locales (see below) cannot be taken as determinative
of the support of an area for one side or the other (cf. Morrill 1983*b*:12–
13; Hughes 1985).

We will see in the pages that follow that Puritanism also was relevant to
the legitimation of the rebellion.

12. Fisher 1935, 1948, 1968, 1971. Wrigley 1967, although discussing
a later period, is nonetheless relevant in this context.

In addition to the bases for SG given above, Stone has emphasized that
proximity to London generated deep resentment and envy, as those close to
the capital were more aware of what they were missing. Thus although the
gentry of the home counties were wealthier than those of north and west,
they were more likely to be in a situation of goal strain. See Stone
1972*a*:112.

13. Holmes, writing about East Anglia, has commented: "In the early
seventeenth century much of the industry and agriculture within the region
was becoming increasingly specialized and oriented towards market production, and it can be shown that the concomitant mercantile contacts
resulted in the dissemination of radical political and religious ideas within
the region." He ties this economic development in both agriculture and
industry to the orbit of London (1974:7–8). He makes these points while
noting that the type of "political geography" I indulge in below is unsatis-
factory owing to the absence of detailed comparative studies of the eco-

nomic structure of regions, allowing for impressionistic and therefore elastic categorization. He also points out that areas of "intense commercial
specialization and areas of traditional agrarian practice existed side by side
within" East Anglia (1974:10). From this argument he concludes that to
characterize the division between Parliamentarians and Royalists in terms
of socioeconomic categories is to commit the ecological fallacy. (If area A is
80 percent Protestant and 20 percent Catholic and area B is 20 percent
Protestant and 80 percent Catholic and the suicide rate in area A is 5 per
1000 inhabitants per year and in area B is .01 per 1000 inhabitants per
year, and if you conclude from these figures that Protestants are more likely
to commit suicide than Catholics, you have committed the ecological fallacy. It may be Catholics, in both areas, who are prone to suicide. See Selvin
1957.)

There are a number of responses one wants to make to Holmes. First, I
agree wholeheartedly with his warning about vague and imprecise categorizations and data, and I must admit that this book falls within his stricture.
This is one of the reasons I have stressed its tentative nature. Second, my
concern is, as Tawney's concern was, with geographical divisions insofar as
they may be taken as indicative of (pre)dominant economic structures, and
therefore of "constraints" on the occupants of a region. Tawney writes, "It
[the economic struggle] was primarily a struggle between economies of
different types, which corresponded more closely with regional peculiari-
ties than with social divisions" (1954a:186).

It would be foolhardy to assume that an individual within a specific
category would necessarily undertake particular revolutionary activities,
and this is exactly what I want to avoid. Instead the point is that the transformed social structure of a manufacturing economy in town and country
gave rise to conditions leading to the rebellion. Thus while Holmes provides no evidence that those who supported Parliament were primarily in
the traditional sections of East Anglia and there is much evidence indicating the contrary, from my perspective such a finding would not refute my
argument concerning the impact of a predominant social organization if it
could be shown that those who supported Parliament fell within the orbit
of the "constraints" defined by that social organization. It should be noted,
however, that I've placed the word constraints in quotation marks; I've
done this to indicate that we are not talking about the much more stringent
constraints of competition under machine capitalism. Here the "constraints" are closer to economic (religious and perhaps political) demonstration effects. Thus we would expect to find uneven development and the
retention of noncapitalist production techniques even in those areas where
manufacture was predominant.

The thesis of Holmes's book is that the homogeneity of East Anglia is a
myth and that this supposed homogeneity cannot therefore be used to explain the success of the Eastern Association. It is clear that the formation of

the Association was no knee-jerk reaction to prior homogeneity; no social movement is ever this. It is also clear that many residents remained neutral, and finally, as we may glean from this analysis, that most persons were in a state of drift prior to acting on behalf of Parliament, and that they had to be mobilized into action. But none of this refutes the contention that the social structure in which they lived conditioned and controlled their actions, and that these structures were determinate in generating the conditions resulting in the dominance of actions in support of Parliament throughout East Anglia.

14. Weber, though he misunderstands the possible genesis of formal rationality within a common law system, emphasizes this necessity and indicates the impossibility of formal rationality under Stuart patrimonialism (see Weber 1968; cf. Marx 1963, 1973. From a neoclassical perspective, this theme is dominant in North and Thomas 1973).

15. These arguments are not affected by Ashton's criticisms of Pearl and Brenner, as he agrees with their characterization of what I've labeled the REVOG. His contention is that the City of London's government and the (patrimonial) mercantile interests it represented supported the REVOF (unlike the monopolists and customs farmers), but he is in agreement that the by then pro-Royalist municipal government had to be captured for Parliament once the REVOG began (1979:203, 220 and passim). Thus while during the REVOF many within the city government opposed the king, within the context of the Parliament's rebellion they were the privileged reference group that smaller merchants sought to overthrow (cf. Stone 1972a:145).

16. This impossibility was true for England, "the first new nation," the first nation to develop a capitalist system, not for those that followed.

17. I hope that this paragraph is intelligible to the reader who had begun her sociological reading with chapter 5. The framework which it is defined is found in chapter 2, except for the definition of SG, which is found in chapter 3. This use of the model is not explicitly discussed in either context.

18. The Merchant Adventurer's economic situation was perilous by 1640, and they appear to have split in their support for Parliament or the king; perhaps as a consequence of the support of some of their members, their charter was renewed by Parliament in 1643. See Brenner 1973, and for a more comprehensive look, 1970; cf. Ashton 1979.

19. "After the civil wars, successive governments from the Rump onwards, whatever their political complexion, gave much more attention to the interests of trade and colonial development in their foreign policies. It was the Rump government, too, which in 1651 promulgated the famous Navigation Act, in the interests of English shipping. This Act marked the culmination of some thirty years' concern for the development of English

maritime strength. It also laid the basis of the 'old colonial system', in which English shipping eventually enjoyed a monopology position within the nascent overseas Empire" (Corfield 1973:215).

20. As I mentioned earlier in this essay, when dealing with aggregate data culled from the status and actions of individuals one must expect exceptions to identifiable relationships. Here we are looking for the structural bases of SG, and when this is translated to individual actors there will of necessity be mitigating circumstances for many individuals, as well as other bases on which SG was generated for other individuals. In this case it seems, however, that we can at least tentatively specify additional factors generating SG for those who supported Parliament.

21. To support this statement Stone cites the work of W. S. Schumacker. Upon my inquiry Stone wrote informing me that "Mr. Schumacher did the research I refer to in a seminar paper for me, which he has never revised for publication. He is now out of the academic profession and working for the government" (personal letter of 1 June 1976). I thus do not know exactly to whom Stone is referring. But if one looks at Stone's appendix VIII-C one finds that the categories of peers analyzed in table 4 are not differentiated from the norm in terms of their gross rentals.

22. Two recent books provide pictures of riots in response to disafforestation (Sharp 1980) and the draining of the fens (Lindley 1982). Both see the riots as a response to governmental policy, creating what I've called facilitory strain, and both see them as concerned almost entirely with local issues. While Lindley sees them as facilitating the revolution in the creation of disorder, both see them as facilitated by the disorder the revolution created.

Neither sees the participants as politically motivated: Sharp writes that they focused, not on the gap between Parliamentarian and Royalist, but on the gap between the propertied and powerful and the poor and powerless, emphasizing a skilled, almost propertyless rural proletarian among the participants and leaders. In fact, he finds some rioters voicing opinions bordering on class hatred. He finds no evidence of gentry participation among the rioters, and attributes this to the fact that forest enclosures seem to have been done with the consent of those holding substantial property and thus substantial legal rights (cf. Kerridge 1958). It was the almost landless cottagers (holding under ten acres), with almost no legal right to compensation for the loss of common rights and dependent on wage labor in manufacturing, who rioted. It is unclear from Sharp's account what actions his rioters might have taken regarding the civil war, apart from the riots; what is clear is that by the time of the Protectorate, the government was adopting forest policies very similar to those of the personal rule and generating similar responses.

Lindley finds the draining of the fens to have aroused more widespread opposition. The fenmen sought to defend their traditional economy against innovation, and were supported and to some degree led by the gentry and supported by more substantial commoners, whose property rights were also infringed on by the king and his courts. In fact, Lindley finds that in the absence of gentry participation opposition was muted and less violent. As the revolution progressed the fenmen found the Lords seeking to restore order (assuming the role of the abolished prerogative courts—as they did during the forest riots), while the Commons, except in one area, provided them with guarded support, at least avoiding pro-undertaker stances. (Sharp is unclear regarding the Common's position concerning disafforestation.) While focusing on specific grievances in their riots, the commoners were also distinctly pro-Parliament in most areas. Even though drawing this conclusion, Lindley is careful to emphasize that their position was not an ideological stance supportive of the constitutional policy enunciated by Parliament. Often it was a matter of the specific conjuncture; in fact, when possible during the personal rule, they claimed royal sympathy. When Parliament and the Protector defended the undertakers, they became the objects of the fenmen's scorn.

23. It is important to note that the major consequence of the peoples' differential attitude toward the two parties came when there was need for armies to be raised. Hunt comments as follows:

> The strength of Parliament lay in its ability to call on these reserves of popular energy to carry through the great destructive ordinances of 1640–1642. Pointing to Pym's manipulation of the London crowd in support of the Grand Remonstrance, some historians have concluded that the rank and file were merely passive tools in the hands of the opposition leadership. Richard Baxter, however, saw it the other way around. In his view "the headiness and rashness of the younger inexperienced sort of religious people made many Parliament men and ministers overgo themselves to keep pace with these hot spurs." It is best to think of a constant interplay between the action of the opposition at Westminster and a relatively autonomous (and heterogenous) popular movement in the country at large. The influence was reciprocal. (1983:288–89)

Later he asks an important question:

> But why had the king no army in Essex? In large part because more men chose to obey the Militia Ordinance than the Crown's Proclamation. This was one of those occasions when the beliefs of ordinary people really made a difference. Charles had aristocratic supporters everywhere in England, but his writ ran only where his agents could exact compliance. (1983:307)

Even Morrill suggests, within the context of a discussion arguing that the breakdown of the "middling sorts" between Royalists, neutrals, and Parliamentarians was "broadly similar to the proportion amongst the gentry," that "there is evidence that the parliamentarians recruited *volunteer* soldiers more easily in 1642 than did the king. [He cites an incomplete Brandeis Ph.D thesis by Joyce Johnson; see now, Malcolm (= Johnson) 1978; Malcolm 1983; cf. Wanklyn and Young 1981; Hutton, 1982; and Underdown 1981.] Those parliamentarians committed to a vision of a godly reformation and uncorrupt commonwealth were probably the most highly motivated men on either side, and may well have been drawn heavily from the middling sorts, but they were a tiny minority" (1977: 231). It was, in other words, the Puritan middling sort who most readily moved from the subculture of revolution into a revolutionary subculture.

24. It is hard from a contemporary perspective to realize what a remarkable period this was in human history. For one of the first times common people formed active and coherent political movements and were able to propagandize their beliefs. One of the things that makes this period so fascinating is that it is possible to read the words of a great variety of people in the many tracts and pamphlets which literally littered the streets of the country from 1640–60. It is one of the strengths of Hill's work to constantly emphasize this fact.

25. It has been argued that one major differentiating factor between the Peace Party and the Middle and War Parties was the fact that the former felt greater trust in the king (Hexter 1941: 55; Manning 1970: 2–3; 1957: 180–81; Pearl 1969: 89; Stone 1972a: 138; Zagorin 1969: 219, 245, 295, 312).

26. It should be noted that the king's policies did not always follow the advice and/or interest of the privileged merchants on whom he depended and who depended on him. In the early seventeenth century Cockayne's Project was a clear indication of this divergence, but it was scrapped soon after it began. For an extensive discussion see Ashton 1979: chaps. 3 and 4.

27. It must be emphasized that the "more or less rationally perceived self-interest" was structured for the actors in question in terms of a manufacturing system interpenetrated with the "rationalizing values" of the Protestant ethic.

28. Cromwell is reported to have responded, "My Lord, if this be so, why did we take up arms at first? This is against fighting ever hereafter. If so, let us make peace, be it never so base" (Gardiner 1893: vol. 2, 59).

29. If it is true, as I believe it is, that a deflation of power for the system is dependent on a perception of the system as inflexible, this shift of responsibility from counsellor to king is crucial. It is clear in a parliamentary democracy that distrust tends to focus on the person of the president or prime minister in anticipation of her removal from office. Counsellors were also subject to removal from office, either by the mechanism of impeach-

ment (Tite 1974) or at the king's discretion. But the king and his posterity
rule forever. We will see later in discussing the Revolution of 1688 that the
existence of this posterity can be a crucial variable in the genesis of a rebellion; there was no question about the existence and health of Charles's
heirs.

30. There is nearly unanimous agreement that the most general attitude
assumed by the English populace was the desire to remain neutral in the
face of conflict. This neutrality is not the equivalent of what I've called
neutralization, as it often didn't involve the presence of all of the variables
outlined in the text, e.g., the relevant strain or a neutral attitude toward
bearing arms against the king. Nonetheless, it constituted something akin
to a subculture of revolution, the ocean within which the revolutionary fish
could swim. This was especially important for the Parliamentarians, as it
resulted in reluctance on the part of most people to take up arms on behalf
of the king or to provide any material assistance to him; it also entailed
tolerance of those who fought against the king. The importance of this
unusual position is easily underestimated. Widespread neutrality allowed
the revolution to occur and provided the breeding ground on which the
revolution could grow and develop. When constituted in terms of the relevant strain, an open illegitimate opportunity structure, deflated power,
and a neutral attitude toward the use of force against the king, it provided
the foundation for the construction of the revolution. On the depth and
forms of neutralism see Manning 1957; Andriette 1971:53ff., 64; Blackwood 1978:38, 48; Brailsford 1961:13; Cliffe 1969:336; Coates 1963:
107; Everitt 1968:49; Everitt 1969a:47; Gardiner 1893, 2:8; Holmes
1980b:148–49; Howell 1983; Hunt 1983:295, 306–7, 311; Morrill
1976; Stone 1972a:143; Underdown 1971:25ff, 1979; Woolrych 1968:
19; Zagorin 1969:340ff.

31. The Levellers, whom we will discuss below, were the only (non-
Catholic) group in England who manifested any understanding of the rebels' plight, and consequently they were the only group of Englishmen who
were not desirous of imposing English rule on them.

32. A bit later in the paragraph, after noting that Charles tried to define
himself as the guardian of the law and the constitution, Judson continues,
"Nevertheless, even after the civil war broke out, some of the champions of
the parliamentary cause presented their case in the following semi-legal and
constitutional way. Parliament, they claimed, was acting as the guardian of
law and right, as the interpreter of the constitution, as the last remaining
constituted authority in the realm able to save the country from the misuse
of the king's powers and from the dissolution of all government and authority" (1949:226; see 377ff.).

33. Chronologically the king's reply was to a parliamentary declaration
defending Sir John Hotham's refusal to allow his majesty entrée into Hull.
In that declaration they had defended Hotham as following their orders,

issued "in discharge of the great trust that lies upon us, and by that power which in cases of this nature resides in us" (Clarendon 1888, 2:56–57). The parliamentary declaration of 2 November 1642, labeled "Parliament's reply" in the above text, is from some months later, and is not a direct reply to the king's statement concerning Hull.

34. There are two logics within liberal thought: one stems from Hobbes and is based on an assumption of disorder and thus on the necessity of coercion; the second stems from Locke and is based on the assumption of consensus and thus of order. A more sophisticated version of liberal thought transcends utilitarianism and merges the two dimensions; this version is dominant in classical sociological theory: in Weber, Durkheim, Parsons, and so on (cf. Parsons 1949:chaps. 2, 3). Marx can be shown to have transcended liberal thought in that his theories assume the possibility of transcending disorder within a rational consensus, grounded in truth, as determined through theoretically guided action. The natural order that Locke assumes and Durkheim finds in an arbitrary morality can be shown, under specifiable structural conditions, to be capable of generation within the context of scientifically guided practice.

35. Following Judson, I have largely ignored the differences between Herle and Parker. I want, however, to comment on one point of divergence which she mentions. Herle, while recognizing the necessity of undivided sovereignty, and of political instead of legal arguments in favor of Parliament, indicated (1) "that in England government had risen through the 'consent of *both* [italics mine] King and People'" (Judson 1949:419, quoting Herle), and further, Herle "maintained that parliament's resistance was 'legal,' i.e., according to the original law and constitution" (Judson 1949:420). These points differentiate him from Parker, and perhaps explain why he found it impossible to support the execution of the king. If government was constituted in the name of *both* king and people, and if Parliament had the right to act to preserve these interests, even against the personal will of the king and the people, then surely the government must not destroy either party to the agreement.

In contrast, Parker had argued "that Princes were created by the people, for the peoples sake, and so limited by expresse Laws as that they might not violate the peoples liberty" (quoted in Judson 1949:417–18). As we have seen, for Herle a mixed government was set up by the king and the people as independent agents, and even if an ultimate and arbitrary power rested in Parliament, one must assume that this power did not include the destruction of the two parties to the agreement. Herle still had one foot stuck in the past (cf. Weston and Greenberg 1981:292 n. 58).

36. This type of statement is plagued by our lack of a precise definition of the word *Puritan*, and by the difficulty of identifying just who was a Puritan. This problem is exacerbated by the political connotations the word had for contemporaries; there is a danger in assuming that anyone

who supported Parliament's cause was a Puritan, no matter what his or her religious orientation. In this section I am largely limited in my usage by the (implicit) definitions of the authors from whom I draw my information. In general I am including under the rubric of Puritanism those "Calvinists" who wanted to reform the church from within—the Presbyterians, English style, and the Independents—and those separatists who retained a theology derivative from Calvinism. In the appendix to chapter 7 these three groups are discussed.

37. This statement comes two paragraphs after Morrill has commented that in both county and town "side-taking for the great majority was largely arbitrary" (Morrill 1976:46). If this comment is intended to reinforce the truth of the neutralism of many in England, it is acceptable; if it is meant to imply that the divisions between Parliamentarian and Royalist were random, it is clearly absurd. We will see below that the emphasis of conservative historians on the local, familial, and religious networks that were activated in the genesis of support for these two sides is quite correct; what they too often fail to see, however, is that the distribution of these networks is itself explicable. As I have previously argued, our task is not to explain the actions of individuals, where we will find many contradictions in the correlation of attributes and revolutionary activities, but rather to explain why those in certain structurally defined locations generally supported one side or the other. See the following discussion of the interrelationship between the set of variables discussed in chapters 5–7 and participation in various phases of the revolution.

38. Puritanism, here interpreted to mean no more than generalized conviction of the need for independent judgment based on conscience and bible reading. The quintessential quality of a Puritan was not the acceptance of a given body of doctrine, but a driving enthusiasm for more improvement in every aspect of life, "a holy violence in the performing of all duties," as Richard Sibbes put it. In practice this zeal found expression in a desire to simplify the services of the Church and to improve the quality of its ministers, to reduce clerical authority and wealth, and most significant of all, to apply the strictest principles of a particular morality to Church, society and State. (Stone 1972a:99)

This definition, especially its first phrases, leads Stone to emphasize the radical consequences of Puritanism, which I will analyze below. In this context I am only concerned with its consequences for REVOG.

39. In discussing the southwest they comment: "It included strongly Royalist and strongly Puritan [sic] districts" (Brunton and Pennington 1968:130).

40. See, in addition to Newton, Hexter 1941:76ff.; Wedgwood 1966b:122–24, 289; Stone 1972a:130; Glow 1965c:52; and Snow

1970:23ff. I have not discussed either the Saybrook or the Massachusetts Bay Companies, both of which also played a part in this mobilization process. See Hexter 1941:77ff.; the works he cites; and Brenner 1970.

41. Hunt's summary comments, even if he exaggerates the level of comfort across class lines, are appropriate:

> It was puritanism that inspired godly aristocrats to transcend those venal and parochial concerns to which historians are rightly devoting more attention, but which could never, in themselves, have triggered a major revolution. It was puritanism and anti-Catholicism that brought those aristocrats into a temporary coalition with disaffected members of the middle and lower classes. Without that unstable, ephemeral, but historically decisive alliance, it is doubtful that a county like Essex could have been secured for Parliament or that a civil war could have been waged, let alone have been won, by the rebels. But for a moment—the Puritan Moment—class resentments and fears could be forgotten by men and women who believed, with Stephen Marshall, that "the question in England is whether Christ or Antichrist shall be Lord." (1983:313)

As he earlier commented:

> It may well be true that most men and women—even in Essex at the height of the Puritan Moment—were indifferent or self-interested. It is not news that history is often made by minorities; but this is hardly a reason to ignore the history that minorities do in fact make. (1983:311)

7. REVON and REVOV

1. I am aware that the use of the same terms to categorize three different if overlapping groups of people may be misleading. But I decided on this course of action so as to avoid the even greater confusion of making up new terms (see chap. 6 n. 3, above).

2. Those who see the continued existence of the Middle Group through 1648 view the invasion of the Scots in April of that year as the precipitant of its separation from the Independent party. The more moderate members of the Middle Group sided with the Presbyterians in the coming struggle (Underdown 1971:96–97ff., where the consequent actions of the Middle Group are traced; for a different view see MacCormack 1973).

3. Underdown in describing this vote treats it as a vote for the Restoration, which was to follow in eleven years. It is difficult to categorize such a decision, based as it was on a written document, but in our terminology it

seems closer to a vote to stabilize the revolution at REVOG: the Restoration, as we will see, retreated to REVOF. Two problems with the Treaty were that its solutions were short term, e.g., the militia was to be removed from the king's control for twenty years, and its resolution of the conflict was dependent on the king's willingness to adhere to his agreements. The final settlement of the REVOG after 1688 was not so dependent on personalities (see Underdown 1971 : 139, and chap. 5; Ranke 1875, 2 : 530ff.).

4. Strain at the level of norms is not always a consequence of status inconsistency. There are circumstances in which either status position or income, especially the latter, may define clear norms of action. In situations of social transition where customary status is in doubt, this incongruity will almost certainly yield normative strain (cf. Walzer 1968 : 312, 315).

5. The virtue of statistical analysis is that it allows us to draw (tentative) conclusions from inadequate data, inadequately analyzed. In what follows I will tacitly assume that the index of status inconsistency is a valid measure of normative strain; the reader should not forget, however, that such strain might well be manifest for certain M.P.s in ways not measured by my indicator; thus certain cases listed in the not SN (strain at the level of norms) rows on my tables may well be in a situation of normative strain.

6. One assumes that most of the second-category families will be declining.

7. I am using Yule's Q as it is the simplest measure of association I know. There is always a temptation to overanalyze one's data, making it appear that the presented argument is stronger than the data will bear. I have tried to resist this temptation.

For the following table,

	X	$\overline{\text{X}}$
Y	a	b
$\overline{\text{Y}}$	c	d

$$Q = \frac{ad - bc}{ad + bc}$$

with a standard error of

$$\left(\frac{1 - Q^2}{2}\right)\sqrt{\frac{1}{a} + \frac{1}{b} + \frac{1}{c} + \frac{1}{d}}$$

In the above two examples (table 7 and table 8), the standard errors are .13 and .09, respectively. We can be reasonably certain that the correct value lies within two standard errors of the calculated value; while this considerably reduces our confidence in table 7, table 8 holds up reasonably well.

Let me add one final comment regarding measures of association. Yule also developed an additional measure:

$$Y = \frac{1 - \dfrac{bc}{ad}}{1 + \dfrac{bc}{ad}}$$

This calculates to .16 and .67 for our two examples. Its standard error equals

$$\frac{1 - Y^2}{4} \quad \frac{1}{a} + \frac{1}{b} + \frac{1}{c} + \frac{1}{d}$$

In our two examples the standard error for Y is .07 and .05. In the tables that follow I will give both the Q and Y numbers, as Y discriminates more clearly at high levels of association. The reader should note that these two measures differ and comparisons should only be made within the same statistic; the reader should also avoid attributing any metaphysical import to the numbers themselves.

8. Farnell in making a similar argument about the Navigation Act of 1651 comments:

> The royal governments had occasionally wavered in their support of established monopoly companies as in the temporary favouring of the projects of Alderman Cockayne and Sir William Courteen, but on the whole monopoly principle in overseas trade and the paramountcy of the venting of woollen cloth had been adhered to by the monarchy. The substantial London merchants who supported the Long Parliament expected these policies to be continued without the speculative flings which had marred the governments of James and Charles. But the Independent regime of 1649 allowed another group of merchants to suggest policies [basically Brenner's colonial interlopers]." (1964: 454)

9. While Kishlansky and I differ over many details concerning both the New Model Army and Parliamentary activity, he would not disagree that the New Model was the crucial actor making what I've labeled a revolution at the level of norms. He even comments, "The symbol of the Army's revolution was not the King executed, but the Parliament eclipsed" (1979a: 11).

10. Nedham is a more complicated case than some of the others, and Zagorin treats him separately from the "unofficial commonwealth theorists," but for our purposes we may group them together.

11. I am made somewhat queasy by the loose definitions of categories provided by Underdown and by the fact that he was willing to move men within these categories on "arbitrary" grounds, meaning on the basis of his

own very considerable knowledge or on the advice of other experts (see, e.g., 1971:237). I would be more queasy about this manipulation if I had done it; but as Underdown had no knowledge of the theoretical framework I have elaborated one must assume that any errors were nonbiased relative to this framework. In any case, as is obvious from the preceding pages, his excellent book has been of great value in this essay.

12. There is considerable literature on the movement; the following works focus on the Levellers, narrowly conceived: Wolfe 1944; Haller and Davies 1964; Woodhouse 1938; Brailsford 1961; Frank 1969; Pease 1965; Bernstein 1963; Schenk 1948; Zagorin 1954:chap. 2; MacPherson 1962:chap. 3; Aylmer 1970, 1975; Shaw 1968; Hill 1972*b*, 1964:chap. 3; Davis 1968, 1973; Manning 1968; Morton 1970:especially chaps. 6 and 7; Howell and Brewster 1970; Thomas 1972; Kishlansky 1979*b*. There has been much written on the religious background of the Levellers; see in particular Troeltsch 1960:vol. 2; Haller 1963; and Jordan 1965, especially vols. 3 and 4.

13. I have said almost nothing about the attempts to reform the English legal system which were coincident with the political revolution. They are, I believe, explicable within the "internal disorder" model discussed in chapter 3 above, and run parallel to the political movements discussed in chapters 5–7. Discussions of law reform may be found in Veall 1970; Prall 1966; and Cotterell 1969.

14. Clarke goes on to argue that disputes must ultimately be settled by the sword, "which is the wrath of God" (Woodhouse 1938:75). Later in the debates Wildman indicates that he cannot find the will of God in civil matters, and that they must therefore look to the safety of the people, which is the will of God (Woodhouse 1938:108). Such arguments were no doubt what frightened Ireton. If the safety of the people required the seizure of property, would not such a seizure be justifiable? For most Levellers the answer was no, but Ireton had reason to fear that some might not be so (un)reasonable.

15. Lilburne had indicated in 1646 that the seats in Commons ought to be distributed according to taxation rates. Six weeks later he had either changed his mind, as Brailsford argues, or simply indicated that the poorest as well as the richest had a right to vote. This need not have implied anything about the distribution of the seats for which men voted (cf. Brailsford 1961:15–17). In any case, the basis of the franchise was almost universally, in Leveller writings, the natural and equal right of each autonomous man (not person) to a voice in the selection of his government.

The controversy concerning the suffrage was sparked by MacPherson 1962:chap. 3; a list of references is provided by Thomas 1972:208, to which one might add MacPherson's rebuttal of Laslett, in 1973:chap. 12, and Hirst 1975, an extended discussion of the electorate in seventeenth-century England.

16. All of this sounds much like Habermas's theory of distortion-free

communication, and fits well within the classical liberal image of the desirability, even the necessity of freedom of speech if truth is to be found (cf. Habermas 1970, 1979, 1984; Mill 1961; Woodhouse 1938:Introduction 77–80).

The status of women was often defined by the Levellers as inferior to that of an autonomous male individual. Sex was an inalienable status, but for half the population it was often viewed as a bar to autonomy.

17. "In classifying as 'Puritans' many who in the previous reign would have been bishops, and some who already were bishops, the Caroline government made potential rebels of many natural supporters of the political establishment" (Russell 1973a:19).

18. In chapter 3 the reader will find an outline of the necessary and sufficient conditions for the occurrence of religious disorder; they include for facilitory movements strain at the level of facilities and a deflation of value commitments (the generalized medium operative for religious institutions categorized within the pattern maintenance subsystem). In this appendix I am primarily concerned with the set of religious disorders that attempt to redefine rather than simply attack religious institutions.

19. Gardiner comments about this assembly: "Composed of 120 clerical and 30 lay members, the latter having been selected from the two Houses, it was the creature of Parliament, and was only authorized to give advice upon subjects on which Parliament desired its opinion" (1893, 1:232; see also 1893, 2:66–67; cf. Cross 1972:100–101).

20. Readers of Glow's article should note that she attributes Presbyterian religious affiliation on the basis of exclusion at Pride's Purge, thus biasing her conclusions concerning the congruence of political and religious activity.

21. An idea of the type of discussions which occurred at this time may be gained from the following quotation:

> The basis on which ordinary Presbyterianism rested was parochial. Every person living within certain geographical limits was to take his place in the parochical organization, and to submit to the parochial authorities. Each parish was to take part in the choice of representatives to sit in the superior assemblies of the Presbytery or of the national Church, and no ecclesiastical community except that of the parish was to be allowed to exist. It was now urged on behalf of the Dissenting Brethren [in Commons, December 1644] that the basis of Presbyterianism to be established should be congregational; that is to say, that, in addition to the parochial churches, there should be a toleration of congregations voluntarily formed by persons living in different parishes, and that such congregations should be exempted from parochial jurisdiction, but should be subordinated to presbytery and assembly, to which larger gatherings they were to send respresentatives.
> The scheme thus proposed was one which, at least for a time, might

have bridged over the gulf which separated the two Puritan parties. Neither of them, however, would have anything to say to it. It was too lax for the Presbyterians, too strict for the more pronounced Independents. (Gardiner 1893, 2:109)

The position of Parliament had changed considerably because of army pressure by December 1647:

> in its plan for an agreement with Charles ... for the establishment of Presbyterianism it included the provision "that all such persons as shall not conform to the said form of government and divine service shall have liberty to meet for the service and worship of God, and for the exercise of religious duties and ordinances ... so as nothing be done by them to the disturbance of the peace of the kingdom." (Cross 1972:103)

22. In this discussion I have sketched an ideal typical distinction between Presbyterian and Independent, based primarily on the actions of the two groups when they were empowered to act. For a brief description of the elusive "Presbyterian-Independents" (Congregational Presbyterians) see Underdown 1971:18, and more concretely in his own data, 234 n. 62. Nuttall has sketched the differences between Presbyterian and Congregationalist, dividing the latter into left- and right-wing factions (1964).

23. The above paragraph is based on a wide variety of sources; summaries may be found in Clarkson 1971; Coleman 1977; Hill 1969b; Holderness 1976; C. Wilson 1969, among many others. A recent article argues the case for "significantly more rapid growth [in agricultural productivity] after 1650 than before" (Olsh 1977:460).

24. These factors were all exacerbated with the birth of a healthy heir to the throne. The belief that the normal course of things would lead to the ascension of a Protestant monarch was crushed as it became clear that the normal course of things would bring instead the institutionalization of a form of patrimonialism legitimized by the Catholic religion.

8. Theory of Social Development

1. If a theory of social development is formulated within a functionally defined framework it will be possible to find empirical anticipations of postcapitalist societies in social systems of smaller scope than societies, social systems conceptualizable within the same framework we use to analyze societies. Thus it will be possible to formulate a quasi-empirical theory of future events, events of which we have no societal examples. It will in other words be possible for us to specify the type of social organiza-

tion which would have to be created to secure the institutionalization of a new social order, an order marking an evolutionary development in the adaptive capacity of the system.

2. In this chapter I present a very tentative and abbreviated formulation of a theory of stage sequential development. This simplified version of the theory leaves many problems untouched. I have not, for example, included a discussion of the relationships between long and short cycles, neither have I distinguished between the formation of a new system and the reconstruction of an old system. I have not analyzed the fit of developing institutions within a larger system context, or somewhat different, the alteration of the model when applied to dependent societies within an "international, intersocietal system," where different units are at different stages of development and where the greater development of one unit may be constructed on the retarded development of other units. These and other problems must be dealt with in detail.

In this simple presentation of the model it may appear that I am arguing that development is unilineal and successively "progressive." I mean to imply neither and am well aware that the theory must consider various forms of stagnation, regression, and debilitating breakdown, as well as incorporate a model of nonunilinear time. The theory involves no evaluative judgments concerning progress but it does imply a progression of development. Here I need only note that this progression is not a necessary one; the movement from one stage into another will occur only under determinate and, one hopes, specifiable conditions. If I say very little about these mechanisms of transformation in this chapter it is because so much of the remainder of the book focuses on them.

3. If the applicability of this conceptual schema to a wide variety of systems can be empirically shown an analysis of social development (and perhaps psychological development) may be grounded in empirical materials whose progression has moved beyond the development of any societal system. If this is the case, an analysis of these more developed, relatively autonomous systems (e.g., the structure of experimental and clinical science) will provide hypotheses with which to approach the postcapitalist development of societal systems. In other words, as I've previously noted, one of the virtues of Piaget's work is that it lets us push beyond the stage we substantively label a capitalist social formation (see Gould 1983).

4. In another context I would feel compelled to justify my reliance on Piaget in the face of the work of Kohlberg and the dependence on Kohlberg's work of my former colleagues at the Marx-Planck-Institut, Starnberg (most readily available in Habermas 1979). Here I need only note that while Kohlberg's work usually involves the articulation of normative principles, what become for Habermas principles of organization, Piaget almost always provides a structural analysis of the patterned constraints definitive of the relationships between identifiable units. Parsons

has also too often fallen into the trap of identifying structure with norm (see Gould 1981c). In this essay the reader must always be clear, even if I write elliptically, that a structure is a patterned—not necessarily normative—and sanctioned set of constraints between the components of action, at whatever level of analysis. Thus norms become one of the patterned units within the structure. These structures are definitive of stages of development; thus chapter 4 in this book is a partial analysis of stage four in the sequence of societal development.

5. Piaget's substantive reference is usually to children's games of marbles.

The careful reader of Piaget will have noted a problem of confusion between system levels in his discussion of system development. He often fails to distinguish between the cognitive and the social systems under discussion and he fails to provide a coherent model of their interaction. He does not indicate, for example, the possibility that an individual at stage five might function within a social system at stage four, that is, that there need be no absolute correlation between "personality" and social system development. In this brief presentation I have also taken the liberty of conflating system levels and the reader should be aware of the consequent simplification (I hope not obfuscation) of the model.

6. Here and throughout the discussion of development the listing of subsystems is without arrows and in the order of development, not of cybernetic control.

7. It is necessary to be careful here; when we shift to a discussion of social systems, it will be necessary to categorize these systems within the first two stages. This is possible as each may develop to a point, in terms of its substages, where an organized system emerges. Nonetheless, these systems will manifest the properties outlined within the present context.

With regard to short and long cycles within the context of substages, the phenomenon of "repetition" should be considered. Here we confront the interesting point that each stage undergoes a sequence of stages in its development. I believe that this sequence repeats the larger system (with some modifications). Here we find the context of an explanation of a stage of medicine approximating magic (Fox 1976), and a stage of magic approximating science (Levi-Strauss 1966). These are simply indications of repetition and functional performance within different contexts: the first probably 6_2, the second probably 2_6, in the development of a certain type of institutional structure. (John Titcomb, a former student, suggested the utility of using numbers as symbolic referents for stage and substage development. I have adopted a system based on sevens: $STAGE_{SUBSTAGE}$, N_n, where $N = 1, 2 \ldots 7$; $n = 1, 2, \ldots 7$. Rich Garfunkel, another student, caught my error of using a capital N for both stage and substage, thus vitiating the possibility of portraying autonomous substage development within a given stage).

8. Piaget writes on occasion so as to imply that this stage is the first point where rules become introjected (see 1962:71). In my opinion this is not correct; the rudiments of a superego were formed at stage three, but owing to the heteronomy characterizing this stage, a child at stage three will act in an "infantile" fashion. It appears that the processes articulated in this early version of a superego are capable of generating guilt, but not of effectively controlling behavior. The "mature" superego, coordinated with the ego and capable of autonomous control over action, appears in stages five and six; a superego capable of making nondecisionistic determinations appears only in stage seven.

9. Justification occurs through the process of inclusion in the purview of a set of norms and legitimation occurs through the specification of a set of values; on the difference, see Parsons 1967:284–86; Parsons 1977: 190–91, 358 n. 10.

10. Jan Loubser and I once had a vehement argument over Parsons's formulation of the phase of socialization he (Parsons) calls studentry (Parsons and Platt 1970, 1973). I argued that Parsons was correct in believing that studentry involved hierarchical ties between teacher and student. Loubser argued that it involved the progressive equalization of ties. We were both correct, or both in error; when successful, it involves the institutionalization of equitable ties.

11. In the preface to this book I asserted my belief that a viable social theory will develop only within an equitable social organization. In a social system characterized by equitable relations, if we might imagine a most simplified scenario, a "theorist" will be able to put forward a piece of social theory and it will be available for evaluation and criticism. If within the context of such discussion a determination is made to act on this theory, such actions will be carried out within the context of a continued assessment of their consequences, and thus in a continued assessment of the theory guiding them. These evaluations will be made by the persons best able to judge, those on whom the consequences of the theory impinge. Thus the efficacy of the evaluations will be dependent on the knowledge and therefore the performance capacity of those in a situation of "democratic control." It is only in this situation, where "experiments" are constantly undertaken and where new experiments are molded based on the consequences of the old, that a recursive development of social scientific theory will occur. This process will only be possible within an equitable society that does not seek to efface relevant expertise but rather lets it control the decisions that fall within its purview. Political decisions will therefore rest in the hands of those affected by them, and as a result of these repeated evaluations informed consensus based on the unity of theory and action and not simply on discussion among "equals" will emerge.

12. This is not the place for a more extensive discussion of stage seven, but I cannot refrain from pointing out its similarity to the Marxian notion

of communism. If one looks at figure 31 it is apparent that stage seven marks the final point of development; and stage eight simply involves the resumption of the process from "the beginning." In one interpretation this is the end of history; in a more optimistic and in my opinion more accurate interpretation it marks the beginning of people's control over our own history. Social relations will not remain static within stage seven—quite the contrary. They will be in constant flux, but what will remain static are the equitable relations that entail the scientific evaluation and control of social and political organizations. Ideally, decisions will not be based on the arbitrary determination of the majority, but as in scientific communities, on the consensus of all rational women and men; when this ideal is incapable of realization, a regression will occur into formally democratic procedures. This is not to say that distortions will not enter into these processes; clearly they will. It is to suggest that the processes are capable of realization (see Gould, forthcoming).

13. I do not believe it legitimate to evaluate, on moral grounds, one form of social formation as superior to another. To do so necessarily involves the acceptance of the moral standards of one or another system. What I want to argue is that such a moral judgment is unnecessary. With one exception, the choice of life or death (cf. Durkheim 1964: 34–35), the judgment between types of social formation may be grounded in scientific criteria, that is, in the structure of constraints operative at the equitable stage. The choice to deny these criteria is in my opinion *ultimately* a choice of suicide. Marx did not write that socialism was inevitable but rather that the choice was between socialism and barbarism.

14. The situation is actually a bit more complex than this. Both the procedures and the decisions made within them are subject to questions concerning their legitimacy. In other words, they are subject to evaluation in terms of rational-egalitarian values. What precludes the necessity of substantive differences between stages three and five is the formal nature of equality in the latter stage. Egalitarian values are capable of generating and legitimizing hierarchical organizational forms (Gould 1983).

15. This demonstration is in itself one aspect of selecting scientific, i.e., equitable, criteria as those relevant in the construction of our evaluations. The ultimate rationale of these criteria would come in a demonstration that there are circumstances in which an equitable organization results in, or might result in, performances likely to ensure the survival of the social system, whereas an egalitarian or hierarchical system might succumb to disorder in comparable circumstances. A weaker form of this argument (again, both are embedded in the scientific criteria of an equitable society) simply involves the demonstration of the greater performance capacity of an equitable system within some set of situations.

16. This diagram also allows us to see that the culmination of any stage's development is also the beginning of its decline and transformation

(with the exception of stage seven). This makes it obvious that stages, even when typified as structures, merge in the "real world" one into another, and while it may be possible to define the point of transition the empirical demarcations are never transparent and clear-cut.

17. I have used the phrase "relative transformation" because stages of action exist in the context of normative frameworks taken from the previous stage of consciousness. We have seen in chapter 4 that stage four at the societal level is characterized by a manufacturing system as the predominant mode of economic production, and that one characteristic of such an economic system is that it does not necessarily encompass all productive relationships. Thus the stage is altered in the sense that the structure of relationships it typifies are transformed, but individual units within this structure may retain their previous phenomenological appearance and perhaps even their function.

18. "Whenever one can describe, between a number of statements, such a system of dispersion, whenever, between objects, types of statements, concepts, or thematic choices, one can define a regularity (an order, correlations, positions and functionings, transformations), we will say, for the sake of convenience, that we are dealing with a *discursive formation*" (Foucault 1972:38, and more generally, chap. 2).

An underlying structure defines the acceptability of certain actions, including the actions of a discourse, but it does not seek to define the coherence of the actions actually performed. In other words, it defines the limits of permitted actions (actions not in violation of the structure), but makes no attempt to define the nature of the actions performed. A discursive formation is thus a coherence model of practice, an underlying structure a coherence model of competence, using the latter term more broadly than does Chomsky.

19. The terms used in this diagram are all subject to reevaluation. Perhaps the most misleading is "feudalism," for which Amin suggests "tributary mode of production" (1976:chap. 1).

20. The literature on these matters is voluminous and for the most part very misleading. Too often there is a tendency to define differentiation as a master concept and to trace the progressive differentiation of social structures from more monolithic structures as a unilinear and continuing process. This image has gained credence by the fact that empirical analyses are usually carried out in examinations of the emergence of capitalism, where, with significant modifications of its cruder portrayals, it holds up. Here I will not mount an attack on this mode of analysis; the reader must understand, however, that I am using it to characterize the movement from stage four to stage five and not as a general theory of social change or development.

21. Lest this sound as if freedom came to reign supreme in the emerging system, three oft-repeated comments bear repeating once again. In the first

instance the freedoms that one associates with individualism were for most persons, most of the time, "formal," in the sense of a formally free labor market. Constraints too often determined which choice had to be selected. Second, the division of labor that emerged with greater differentiation involved the growing interdependence of units on one another. Thus the (economic) autonomy of relatively self-sufficient units was replaced with networks of mutual dependence. These networks were often the basis of the constraints demanding the choice of one alternative over others. Third, the development of these formal freedoms took a very long time and required a great deal of struggle; even today, their realization is by no means completed.

22. When providing a structural model of English syntax one has immediately accessible a criterion by which to evaluate the model. If an opponent utters an acceptable English sentence and if your model is incapable of generating that sentence, the model fails. If she utters the sentence "I eat correction speak humpledink you," and claims the inadequacy of your model because it is incapable of generating this sentence, the correct response is that her sentence is not acceptable within everyday English syntax. Both the successful counterargument and the successful rebuttal derive from the authority of a native-born speaker and will be confirmed by all native-born speakers of English. The competence that defines the empirical structure in need of modeling is pregiven and assumed as the correct empirical authority.

A structural analysis of the discourse of legitimation in seventeenth-century English revolutionary politics is not so simple. I must admit that utterances were made which contradict my structural model. Though these utterances were intelligible to the men of those times, I nonetheless want to label them "residues." Unfortunately there is a danger that the criterion I will use in so labeling them will be the very model I wish to evaluate; thus I run the risk of circular argument: "That utterance is a residue," and then the unspoken justification, "as I cannot explain it with my model." Such arguments preclude the possibility of invalidating the model. In fact this invalidation is possible only in the context of a detailed analysis of the historical continuity (tendential development) of legitimizing discourse, an analysis not provided in this book.

There is no simple solution to this problem. Here I rely on the good judgment of my reader to correct me when I go astray, and especially on the judgment of those readers more expert than I in English constitutional and political history. As a preliminary step, however, each reader might ask herself whether my arguments make sense of the materials discussed in chapters 5, 6, and 7, while remembering that those materials were selected and organized by the same writer making the current argument.

23. I do not mean to imply that these notions were absent from pre-seventeenth-century discourse, only that the revolutions precipitated their

consolidation and that they then provided a new basis on which political policies and structures might be legitimized. See Appleby 1978; Brown 1965; Franklin 1969, 1978; Gierke 1957, 1958; Greenleaf 1964; Gunn 1969; Hanson 1970; Hirshman 1977; Judson 1949; MacFarlane 1979; Maitland 1908; McIlwain 1910; MacPherson 1973; Pocock 1967, 1975; Salmon 1959; Skinner 1978; Tuck 1979; Weston and Greenberg 1981.

24. The importance of Calvin and Calvinism in the articulation and dissemination of this structure is still in my opinion underemphasized by most observers. This failure to realize the importance of Calvin is clearest, perhaps, in our failure to recognize his important place in the genesis of modern social theory. A persuasive argument could be made that he provided the paradigmatic framework within which modern social theory has been working for over 300 years.

25. Often "the new theory further damaged royal authority by the assertion that a particular form of government was a human ordinance although political authority, indeed authority in general, came from God" (Weston and Greenberg 1981:83).

26. Very simply tradition may be divided into three types: the tradition of "traditional legitimation," marking a relative stasis of action and legitimation; the tradition of precedent, using the legitimation of time to rationalize innovation; and finally, the tradition of "modern" conservatives, legitimizing the precedent of the past as the most rational way to enter into the future. Schematically each may be identified with a stage of development: three, four, and five respectively. But the reader should be aware that stage five, for example, undergoes a substage development that recapitulates stages three and four, albeit within a different structural context and with different consequences.

27. More conservative theories were also propounded and in fact came to dominate. In these the Parliament assumed sovereignty as the representative of the people.

28. In Parsons's terms these attributes are atomism, the "randomness of ends," rationality, and empiricism (1949:chap. 2; these attributes are reformulated in Gould 1981*c*).

9. Revolution (with)in the Development of Capitalism

1. I do not want to make the argument that revolution is a necessary precondition for the development of machine capitalism. Instead I argue that the English revolutions were integral in the genesis of conditions necessary for its development. This does not prejudge the possibility of these conditions originating from another form of social action, either in (a counterfactual) England or in some other country.

2. Every aspect of religious phenomena that points beyond evils and

advantages in this world is the work of a special evolutionary process, one characterized by distinctively dual aspects. On the one hand, there is an ever-broadening rational systematization of the god concept and of the thinking concerning the possible relationships of man to the divine. On the other hand, there ensues a characteristic recession of the original, practical, and calculating rationalism [where "the normal situation is that the burden of all prayers, even in the most other-worldy religions, is the aversion of the external evils of this world and the inducement of the external advantages of this world"]. As such primitive rationalism recedes, the significance of distinctively religious behavior is sought less and less in the purely external advantages of everyday economic success. Thus, the goal of religious behavior is successively "irrationalized" until finally otherwordly non-economic goals come to represent what is distinctive in religious behavior. (Weber 1968, 2:424; the excerpt in brackets is from the same page)

The rationalization of religion allowed for the secularization and formal rationalization of the secular world.

3. The most poignant discussions of these processes are found not in Marx but in Weber. See 1968, 1:150ff.; 1968, 2:585, 698–99, 729–31, 814.

4. As Weber commented, "Calculability and reliability in the functioning of the legal order and the administrative system is vital to rational capitalism. This need led the bourgeoisie to attempt to impose checks on patrimonial monarchs ... by means of a collegial body in which the bourgeois had a decisive voice, which controlled administration and finance and could exercise an important influence on changes in the legal order" (1968, 1:296).

Weber's understanding of the import of common law was uncertain; he failed to adequately appreciate that it was both formally, procedurally rational, and substantively rational in its adaptation to capitalist development. While he recognized that the needs of the "bourgeoisie" for "'calculable' law" "may be gratified quite as well, and often better, by a formal, empirical case law [than by a purely formal law]" (1968, 2:855), and while he recognized that "the consequences of the purely logical construction [in formal law] often bear very irrational or even unforeseen relations to the expectations of the commercial interests" (1968, 2:855), he also commented that "it may indeed be said that England achieved capitalistic supremacy among the nations not because but rather in spite of its judicial system" (1968, 2:814).

5. "Foreign trade hallucinated the imagination and bemused so many minds that its importance has been overrated. The old patterns of trade—European and domestic—were still (in 1688) the country's life blood, particularly the latter" (Plumb 1969b:17).

6. "Every expansion of a country's power sphere increases the profit potential of the respective capitalist interests" (Weber 1968, 1:346).

7. In the seventeenth and eighteenth centuries a form of power comes into being that begins to exercise itself through social production and social service. It becomes a matter of obtaining productive service from individuals in their concrete lives. And in consequence, a real and effective "incorporation" of power was necessary, in the sense that power had to be able to gain access to the bodies of individuals, to their acts, attitudes and modes of everyday behaviour.... But at the same time, these new techniques of power needed to grapple with the phenomena of population, in short to undertake the administration, control and direction of the accumulation of men (the economic system that promotes the accumulation of capital and the system of power that ordains the accumulation of men are, from the seventeenth century on, correlated and inseparable phenomena): hence there arise the problems of demography, public health, hygiene, housing conditions, longevity and fertility. And I believe that the political significance of the problem of sex is due to the fact that sex is located at the point of intersection of the discipline of the body and the control of the population. (Foucault 1980:125)

8. For the enormous importance of production for overseas markets and of international trade in the transformation from manufacture to machine capitalism see Schumpeter 1960: Deane and Cole 1969; Coleman (ed.) 1969; Davis 1967, 1973a; Heckscher 1955; Minchinton (ed.) 1969; Thomas and McClosky 1981; and the sources cited in these works.

9. Even about the king Stone can write that "the Act of Settlement of 1701, by which the succession was deliberately altered by mere fiat of Parliament ... meant that after the death of Anne, England was to be openly ruled by a King chosen by Parliament, and thus ruling on sufferance" (1980:69).

10. "Since the great object of social reform is to prevent a fundamental change in class relations, sensible reformers must fight on two fronts within the ruling class. They must fight against those reactionaries who cannot understand the need for secondary, although not necessarily trivial, change in order to prevent deeper change; and they must fight against cheerful fools who think that change is intrinsically wonderful and who therefore cannot distinguish between the safe and the dangerous" (Genovese 1976: 49).

Bibliography

The following list of references has grown to the point where stringent measures were required to keep it to a reasonable length. Citations were, in general, limited to those noted in the text. While a few uncited references of specific relevance to my discussion have been included, I have for the most part excluded references to detailed monographs or articles on, for example, specific industries, geographical areas, or persons. By and large references to theoretical materials were dropped and I have largely ignored in this bibliography countries other than England. The references were confined to the narrow band of time discussed in the text. Excluding theoretical, comparative, and developmental perspectives from the bibliography gives a misleading impression of the sources on which I have based my discussion, but given space constraints, these exclusions seemed unavoidable.

Abbreviations Used in the Bibliography

AgHR	Agricultural History Review
AJS	American Journal of Sociology
ASR	American Sociological Review
BIHR	Bulletin of the Institute of Historical Research
EcHR	Economic History Review
EHR	English Historical Review
JBS	Journal of British Studies
JEcH	Journal of Economic History
JModH	Journal of Modern History
P&P	Past and Present
THJ	The Historical Journal
TRHS	Transactions of the Royal Historical Society

Abel, Wilhelm
 1980   *Agricultural Fluctuations in Europe From the Thirteenth to*
 [1978]   *the Twentieth Centuries.* Trans. Olive Ordish. New York: St.
          Martin's.

Ackley, Gardiner
  1961   *Macroeconomic Theory.* New York: Macmillan.
Aiken, William, and Basil Henning, eds.
  1960   *Conflict in Stuart England.* London: Jonathan Cape.
Allan, D. G. C.
  1952   "The Rising of the West: 1928–1931." *EcHR* 2d ser. 5:76–
          85.
Allen, R. G. D.
  1968   *Macro-Economic Theory: A Mathematical Treatment.* New
  [1967] York: St. Martin's.
Allison, K. J.
  1960   "The Norfolk Worsted Industry in the Sixteenth and Seven-
          teenth Centuries: The Traditional Industry." *Yorkshire Bulle-
          tin* 12:73–83.
  1961   "The Norfolk Worsted Industry in the Sixteenth and Seven-
          teenth Centuries: the New Draperies." *Yorkshire Bulletin*
          13:61–77.
Althusser, Louis
  1970   *For Marx.* Trans. Ben Brewster. New York: Vintage Books.
  [1965]
  1971   *Lenin and Philosophy and Other Essays.* Trans. Ben Brewster.
          London: New Left Books.
  1972   *Politics and History.* Trans. Ben Brewster. London: New Left
          Books.
Althusser, Louis, and Étienne Balibar
  1970   *Reading Capital.* Trans. Ben Brewster. London: New Left
  [1968] Books.
Amin, Samir
  1976   *Unequal Development.* Trans. Brian Pearce. New York:
  [1973] Monthly Review Press.
  1977   *Imperialism and Unequal Development.* Trans. Alfred Ehren-
  [1976] feld and Joan Pinkham. New York: Monthly Review Press.
Anderson, Perry
  1974a   *Lineages of the Absolutist State.* London: New Left Books.
  1974b   *Passages from Antiquity to Feudalism.* London: New Left
          Books.
Andriette, Eugene A.
  1971   *Devon and Exeter in the Civil War.* Newton Abbot: David
          and Charles.
Antler, Steven D.
  1972   "Quantitative Analysis of the Long Parliament." *P&P* 56:
          154–57.
Appleby, Andrew
  1975   "Agrarian Capitalism or Seigneurial Reaction? The Northwest

of England, 1500–1700." *American Historical Review* 80: 574–95.

1978   *Famine in Tudor and Stuart England*. Stanford: Stanford University Press.

1979   "Grain Prices and Subsistence Crises in England and France, 1590–1740." *JEcH* 39:865–88.

Appleby, Joyce Oldham

1978   *Economic Thought and Ideology in Seventeenth-Century England*. Princeton: Princeton University Press.

Arendt, Hanna

1965   *On Revolution*. New York: Viking Press.

1970   *On Violence*. New York: Harcourt, Brace and World.

Ashton, Robert

1960   *The Crown and the Money Market 1603–1640*. London: Oxford University Press.

1969   "The Aristocracy in Transition." *EcHR* 2d ser. 22:308–22.

1970   "The Civil War and the Class Struggle." In *The English Civil War and After, 1642–1658*, ed. R. H. Parry. Berkeley, Los Angeles, London: University of California Press.

1971   "[Review of] Zagorin. *The Court and the Country*." *EcHR* 2d ser. 24:144–46.

1978   *The English Civil War*. London: Weidenfeld and Nicolson.

1979   *The City and the Court 1603–1643*. Cambridge: Cambridge University Press.

1983   "From Cavalier to Roundhead Tyranny, 1642–1649." In *Reactions to the English Civil War*, ed. J. S. Morrill. New York: St. Martin's.

Aston, Trevor, ed.

1967   *Crisis in Europe 1560–1660*. Garden City, N.Y.: Anchor.
[1965]

Aubrey, John

1962   *Aubrey's Brief Lives*. Ed. Oliver Lawson Dick. Ann Arbor: University of Michigan Press.

Aylmer, G. E.

1957   "The Last Years of Purveyance 1610–1660." *EcHR* 2d ser. 10:81–93.

1959   "Office Holding as a Factor in English History, 1625–42." *History* 44:228–40.

1961   *The King's Servants*. New York: Columbia University Press.

1965   *The Struggle for the Constitution*. Rev. ed. London: Blandford.

1970   "Gentlemen Levellers?" *P&P* 49:120–25.

1972   "Introduction: The Quest for Settlement 1646–1660." In *The Interregnum*, ed. G. E. Aylmer. London: Macmillan.

Aylmer, G. E., ed.
  1972   *The Interregnum.* London: Macmillan.
  1975   *The Levellers and the English Constitution.* Ithaca: Cornell
          University Press.
Bacon, Francis
  1924   *The Essayes or Counsels Civil and Moral.*
  [1625] London: Philip Allan.
Baker, Alan, and Derek Gregory, eds.
  1984   *Explorations in Historical Geography.* Cambridge: Cam-
          bridge University Press.
Ball, J. N.
  1964   "The Petition of Right in the English Parliament of 1628."
          Album E. Lousse 4:43–64.
Ball, R. J., and P. Doyle
  1970   *Inflation.* Baltimore: Penguin.
Baltzell, E. Digby
  1972   "Epilogue: To Be a Phoenix—Reflections on Two Noisy Ages
          of Prose." *AJS* 78:202–20.
Banaji, Jarius
  1976   "Summary of Selected Parts of Kautsky's *The Agrarian Ques-
          tion.*" *Economy and Society* 5:1–49.
Baran, Paul
  1968   *The Political Economy of Growth.* 2d ed. New York: Month-
  [1957] ly Review Press.
Baran, Paul, and Paul Sweezy
  1966   *Monopoly Capital.* New York: Monthly Review Press.
Barber, Bernard, and Alex Inkeles, eds.
  1971   *Stability and Social Change.* Boston: Little, Brown.
Barnes, Thomas
  1961   *Somerset 1625–40.* Cambridge: Harvard University Press.
Baxter, Stephen
  1957   *The Development of the Treasury, 1660–1702.* London:
          Longmans, Green.
Bay, Christian
  1965   *The Structure of Freedom.* New York: Atheneum.
Becker, Howard
  1963   *The Outsiders: Studies in the Sociology of Deviance.* New
          York: The Free Press.
Beckett, J. V.
  1977   "English Landownership in the Later Seventeenth and Eight-
          eenth Centuries: The Debate and the Problems." *EcHR* 2d ser.
          30:567–81.
Beer, George Louis
  1959   *The Origins of the British Colonial System: 1578–1660.*

[1908]   Gloucester, Mass.: Peter Smith.
Bellah, Robert
    1957   *Tokugowa Religion*. New York: The Free Press.
    1965   "Epilogue: Religion and Progress in Modern Asia." In *Religion and Progress in Modern Asia*, ed. R. Bellah. New York: The Free Press.
    1967   "Civil Religion in America." *Daedalus* 96 : 1–21.
Berg, Maxine, et al.
    1983   "Manufacture in town and country before the factory." In *Manufacture in Town and Country Before the Factory*, ed. Maxine Berg et al. London: Cambridge University Press.
Berg, Maxine, et al., eds.
    1983   *Manufacture in Town and Country Before the Factory*. London: Cambridge University Press.
Berkowitz, David
    1975   "Reason of State in England and the Petition of Right." In *Staatsrason: Studien zur Geschichte eines politischen Begriffs*, ed. Roman Schnur. Berlin.
Bernstein, Eduard
    1963   *Cromwell and Communism*. Trans. H. J. Stenning. New York:
    [1895]   Schocken.
Blackwood, B. G.
    1978   *The Lancashire Gentry and the Great Rebellion 1640–60*. Atlantic Highlands, N.J.: Humanities Press.
Blake, Judith, and Kingsley Davis
    1964   "Norms, Values and Sanctions." In *Handbook of Modern Sociology*, ed. Robert E. L. Faris. Chicago: Rand McNally.
Blanchard, Ian
    1978   "Labour Productivity and Work Psychology in the English Mining Industry." *EcHR* 2d ser. 31 : 1–24.
Blumer, Herbert
    1955   "Collective behavior." In *Principles of Sociology*, ed. Alfred M. Lee. New York: Barnes and Noble.
Bogucka, Maria
    1980   "The Role of the Baltic Trade in European Development from the XVIth to the XVIIIth Centuries." *Journal of European Economic History* 9 : 5–20.
Bonney, Richard
    1980   "The English and French Civil Wars." *EHR* 65 : 365–82.
Bouch, C., and G. P. Jones
    1968   *A Short Economic and Social History of the Lake Counties,*
    [1961]   *1500–1830*. New York: Kelley.
Boudon, Raymond
    1971   *The Uses of Structuralism*. Trans. Michalina Vaughan. Lon-

[1968]   don: Heinemann.
Bowden, Peter
  1967   "Agricultural Prices, Farm Profits, and Rents." In *The Agra-
            rian History of England and Wales*. Vol. 4, ed. Joan Thirsk.
            Cambridge: Cambridge University Press.
  1985   "Agricultural Prices, Wages, Farm Profits, and Rents." In *The
            Agrarian History of England and Wales*. Vol. 5, ed. Joan
            Thirsk. Cambridge: Cambridge University Press.
Brailsford, H. N.
  1961   *The Levellers and the English Revolution*, ed. Christopher
            Hill. Stanford: Stanford University Press.
Braverman, Harry
  1974   *Labor and Monopoly Capital*. New York: Monthly Review
            Press.
Brenner, Robert
  1970   Commercial Change and Political Conflict: The Merchant
            Community in Civil War London. Ph.D. diss., Princeton Uni-
            versity.
  1972   "The Social Basis of English Commercial Expansion, 1550–
            1650." *JEcH* 32:361–84.
  1973   "The Civil War Politics of London's Merchant Community."
            P&P 58:53–107.
  1976   "Agrarian Class Structure and Economic Development in Pre-
            Industrial Europe." *P&P* 70:30–75.
  1977   "The Origins of Capitalist Development: A Critique of Neo-
            Smithian Marxism." *New Left Review* 104:25–93.
  1982   "Agrarian Class Structure and Economic Development in Pre-
            Industrial Europe: The Agrarian Roots of European Capital-
            ism." *P&P* 97:16–113.
Bridbury, A. R.
  1974   "Sixteenth-Century Farming." *EcHR* 2d ser. 27:538–56.
Brighton Labour Process Group
  1977   "The Capitalist Labour Process." *Capital and Class* 1:3–26.
Brinton, Crane
  1965   *The Anatomy of Revolution*. Rev. and exp. ed. New York:
  [1938]   Vintage.
Bronfenbrenner, M., and S. Holzman
  1965   "A Survey of Inflation Theory." Reprinted in *Surveys in Eco-
            nomic Theory*. New York: St. Martin's.
Brown, K. C., ed.
  1965   *Hobbes Studies*. Oxford: Basil Blackwell.
Brunton, D., and D. H. Pennington
  1968   *Members of the Long Parliament*. Hamden, Conn.: Archon.
  [1954]

Bücher, Carl
  1968   *Industrial Evolution*. Trans. S. Morley Wickeff. New York:
  [1900] Kelley.
Burawoy, Michael
  1985   *The Politics of Production*. London: Verso.
Butlin, R. A.
  1979   "The Enclosure of Open Fields and Extinction of Common
          Rights in England, *circa* 1600–1750." In *Change in the Coun-
          tryside: Essays on Rural England, 1500–1900*, ed. H. S. A.
          Fox and R. A. Butlin. London: Institute of British Geog-
          raphers.
Campbell, Mildred
  1960   *The English Yeoman*. London: Merlin.
  [1942]
Capp, B. S.
  1972   *The Fifth Monarchy Men*. London: Faber and Faber.
Carsten, F. L.
  1954   *The Origins of Prussia*. London: Oxford University Press.
Carus-Wilson, E. M., ed.
  1954   *Essays in Economic History*. 3 vols. New York: St. Martin's.
  1962
Chalklin, C. W., and M. A. Havinden, eds.
  1974   *Rural Change and Urban Growth 1500–1800*. London:
          Longman.
Chamberlain, E.
  1962   *The Theory of Monopolistic Competition*. Cambridge: Har-
  [1933] vard University Press.
Chambers, J. D.
  1957   *The Vale of Trent 1670–1800*. EcHR, Supplement 3.
Chapman, John
  1984   "The Chronology of English Enclosure." *EcHR* 2d ser. 37:
          557–59.
Chapman, S. D.
  1967   *The Early Factory Masters*. New York: Kelley.
  1972   "The Genesis of the British Hosiery Industry." *Textile History*
          3:7–50.
Charlesworth, Andrew, ed.
  1983   *An Atlas of Rural Protest in Britain 1548–1900*. Philadelphia:
          University of Pennsylvania Press.
Chartres, J. A.
  1977a   *Internal Trade in England 1500–1700*. London: Macmillan.
  1977b   "Road Carrying in England in the Seventeenth Century: Myth
          and Reality." *EcHR* 2d ser. 30:73–94.
  1985   "The Marketing of Agricultural Produce." In *The Agrarian*

History of England and Wales. Vol. 5, ed. Joan Thirsk. Cambridge: Cambridge University Press.

Chayanov, Aleksandr
1966   *The Theory of Peasant Economy.* Trans. from the Russian. Homewood, Ill.: Irwin.

Christianson, Paul
1976   "The Causes of the English Revolution: A Reappraisal." *JBS* 15:40–75.
1977   "The Peers, the People and Parliamentary Management in the First Six Months of the Long Parliament." *JModH* 49:575–99.

Clapham, John
1944   *History of the Bank of England.* London: Cambridge University Press.
1949   *A Concise Economic History of Britain From the Earliest Times to 1750.* Cambridge: Cambridge University Press.

Clarendon (Edward Hyde, Earl of)
1888   *History of the Rebellion and Civil Wars in England,* ed. W. Dunn MacRay. 6 vols. London: Oxford University Press.

Clark, Alice
1982   *Working Life of Women in the Seventeenth Century.* Boston:
[1919] Routledge.

Clark, Peter
1976   "Popular Protest and Disturbance in Kent, 1558–1640." *EcHR* 29:365–82.
1977   *English Provincial Society from the Reformation to the Revolution: Religion, Politics and Society in Kent 1500–1640.* London: Harvester.

Clark, Peter, ed.
1981   *Country Towns in Pre-Industrial England.* New York: St. Martin's.
1984   *The Transformation of English Provincial Towns.* London: Hutchinson.

Clark, Peter, and Paul Slack
1976   *English Towns in Transition, 1500–1700.* London: Oxford University Press.

Clark, Peter, Alan Smith, and Nicholas Tyacke, eds.
1979   *The English Commonwealth 1547–1640.* New York: Barnes and Noble.

Clarkson, L. A.
1960   "The Organization of the English Leather Industry in the Late Sixteenth and Early Seventeenth Centuries." *EcHR* 2d ser. 13:245–56.
1965   "English Economic Policy in the Sixteenth and Seventeenth

Centuries: The Case of the Leather Industry." *BIHR* 28:149–62.

1966   "Leather Craftsmen in Tudor and Stuart England." *AgHR* 14:25–39.

1971   *The Pre-Industrial Economy in England 1500–1750*. London: Batsford.

Clay, C. G. A.

1984   *Economic Expansion and Social Change: England 1500–1700*. 2 vols. London: Cambridge University Press.

1985   "Landlords and Estate Management in England." In *The Agrarian History of England and Wales*. Vol. 5, ed. Joan Thirsk. Cambridge: Cambridge University Press.

Cliffe, J. T.

1969   *The Yorkshire Gentry from the Reformation to the Civil War*. London: Athlone.

Clifton, Robin

1971   "The Popular Fear of Catholics During the English Revolution." *P&P* 52:23–55.

1973   "Fear of Popery." In *The Origins of the English Civil War*, ed. Conrad Russell. London: Macmillan.

Clinard, Marshall, ed.

1964   *Anomie and Deviant Behavior*. New York: The Free Press.

Cloward, Richard, and Lloyd Ohlin

1960   *Delinquency and Opportunity*. New York: The Free Press.

Clower, R. M., ed.

1969   *Monetary Theory*. Baltimore: Penguin.

Coate, Mary

1963   *Cornwall in the Great Civil War and Interregnum 1642–*
[1933]   *1660*. Truro: D. Bradford Barton.

Coates, Willson H.

1932   "Some Observations On 'The Grand Remonstrance.'" *JModH* 4:1–17.

Coates, Willson, Anne Steele Young, and Vernon Snow, eds.

1982   *The Private Journals of The Long Parliament 3 January to 5 March 1642*. New Haven: Yale University Press.

Cohen, Albert

1955   *Delinquent Boys: The Culture of a Gang*. New York: The Free Press.

1965   "The Study of Social Disorganization and Deviant Behavior."
[1959]   In *Sociology Today*, ed. Robert Merton et al. New York: Harper Torchbooks.

Cohen, Jon S., and Martin L. Weitzman

1975   "Enclosures and Depopulation: A Marxian Analysis." In *European Peasants and Their Markets*, ed. William Parker and

Eric L. Jones. Princeton: Princeton University Press.

Coleman, D. C.

1956   "Labour in the English Economy of the Seventeenth Century."
        EcHR 2d ser. 8:280–95; reprinted in *Essays in Economic
        History*. Vol. 2, ed. E. M. Carus-Wilson. New York: St. Mar-
        tin's.

1967   *The Domestic System in Industry*. London: The Historical
[1960] Association.

1969   "An Innovation and its Diffusion: The New Draperies." *EcHR*
        2d ser. 22:417–29.

1973   "Textile Growth." In *Textile History and Economic History*,
        ed. Harte and Ponting. Manchester: Manchester University
        Press.

1975   *Industry in Tudor and Stuart England*. London: Macmillan.

1977   *The Economy of England 1450–1700*. London: Oxford Uni-
        versity Press.

1983   "Proto-Industrialization: A Concept Too Many." *EcHR* 2d
        ser. 36:435–48.

Coleman, D. C., ed.

1969   *Revisions in Mercantilism*. London: Methuen.

Coleman, D. C., and A. H. John, eds.

1976   *Trade, Government and Economy in Pre-Industrial England*.
        London: Weidenfeld and Nicolson.

Collins, Randall

1980   "Weber's Last Theory of Capitalism." *ASR* 45:925–40.

Commons, John R.

1957   *Legal Foundations of Capitalism*. Madison: University of
[1924] Wisconsin Press.

Cooper, J. P.

1960   "Differences Between English and Continental Governments
        in the Early Seventeenth Century." In *Britain and the Nether-
        lands*, ed. Bromly and Kossmann. London: Chatto and
        Windus.

1967   "The Social Distribution of Land and Men in England, 1436–
        1700." *EcHR* 2d ser. 20:419–40.

1970   "Economic Regulation of the Cloth Industry in Seventeenth-
        Century England." *TRHS* 5th ser. 20:73–99.

Cope, Esther

1981   "The Inconveniences of Long Intermissions of Parliament and
        a Remedy for Them." *Albion* 13:1–11.

Corfield, Penelope

1973   "Economic Issues and Ideologies." In *The Origins of the
        English Civil War*, ed. Conrad Russell. London: Macmillan.

1976   "Urban Development in England and Wales in the Sixteenth and Seventeenth Centuries." In *Trade, Government and Economy in Pre-Industrial England*, ed. D. C. Coleman and A. H. John. London: Weidenfeld and Nicholson.

Cotterell, Mary
1969   "Interregnum Law Reform: The Hale Commission of 1652." *EHR* 83:689–704.

Court, W. H. B.
1953   *The Rise of the Midland Industries*. London: Oxford Univer-
[1938] sity Press.

Coveney, P. J.
1977   *France in Crisis 1620–1675*. London: Macmillan.

Cross, Claire
1972   "The Church in England 1646–1660." In *The Interregnum*, ed. G. E. Aylmer. London: Macmillan.
1976   *Church and People 1450–1660*. London: Fontana.

Cust, Richard
1985   "Charles I, the Privy Council and the Forced Loan." *JBS* 24:208–35.

Cust, Richard, and Peter Lake
1984   "Sir Richard Grosvenor and the Rhetoric of Magistry." *BIHR* 54:40–53.

Cutler, A.
1975   "The Concept of Ground-Rent and Capitalism in Agriculture." *Critique of Anthropology* 4 & 5:72–89.

Cutler, Anthony, and John Taylor
1972   "Theoretical Remarks on the Theory of the Transition From Feudalism to Capitalism." *Theoretical Practice* 6:20–30.

Daly, J. W.
1966   "Could Charles I Be Trusted? The Royalist Case, 1642–46." *JBS* 6:23–44.

Davies, Godfrey
1955   *The Restoration of Charles II 1658–1660*. London: Oxford University Press.
1959   *The Early Stuarts*. 2d ed. London: Oxford University Press.

Davis, J. C.
1968   "The Levellers and Democracy." *P&P* 40:174–80.
1973   "The Levellers and Christianity." In *Politics, Religion and the English Civil War*, ed. Brian Manning. London: Edward Arnold.

Davis, Ralph
1962   *The Rise of the English Shipping Industry*. Newton Abbot: David and Charles.
1967   *A Commercial Revolution*. London: The History Association.
1973*a* *English Overseas Trade 1500–1700*. London: Macmillan.

1973*b*   *The Rise of the Atlantic Economies.* Ithaca: Cornell University
          Press.
Deane, Phyllis, and W. A. Cole
1969   *British Economic Growth 1688–1959.* 2d ed. London: Cam-
        bridge University Press.
DeJouvenal, Bertrand
1962   *On Power.* Trans. J. F. Huntington. Boston: Beacon.
[1945]
Denison, E.
1962   *The Sources of Economic Growth in the United States.* New
        York: The Committee for Economic Development.
1967   *Why Growth Rates Differ.* Washington: The Brookings In-
        stitution.
Derrida, Jacques
1978   *Writing and Difference.* Trans. Alan Ball. Chicago: University
        of Chicago Press.
Deutsch, Karl
1964   "External Involvement in Internal War." In *Internal War,* ed.
        Harry Eckstein. New York: The Free Press.
Dickson, P. G. M.
1967   *The Financial Revolution in England.* London: Macmillan.
Dietz, F. C.
1932   *English Public Finance, 1558–1641.* New York: Century.
Dobb, Maurice
1976   *Studies in the Development of Capitalism.* Rev. ed. New York:
[1947] International.
Dobb, Maurice, et al.
1976   *The Transition from Feudalism to Capitalism.* London: New
[1954] Left Books.
Dore, R. N.
1966   *The Civil Wars in Cheshire.* Chester: Cheshire Community
        Council.
Dorfman, Robert
1964   *The Price System.* Englewood Cliffs, N.J.: Prentice-Hall.
Downes, David
1966   *The Delinquent Solution: A Study in Subcultural Theory.* New
        York: The Free Press.
Dupuy, Alex, and Paul Fitzgerald
1977   "A Contribution to the Critique of the World System." *Insur-
        gent Sociologist* 7:113–24.
Durkheim, Emile
1951   *Suicide.* Trans. John Spaulding and George Simpson. New
[1897] York: The Free Press.
1961   *Moral Education.* Trans. Everett K. Wilson and Herman

[1925]   Schnurer. New York: The Free Press.
1964   *The Division of Labor in Society.* Trans. George Simpson.
[1893]   New York: The Free Press.
1965   *The Elementary Forms of the Religious Life.* Trans. Joseph
[1912]   Ward Swain. New York: The Free Press.

Easton, David
    1965   *A Systems Analysis of Political Life.* New York: John Wiley.

Easton, David, ed.
    1966   *Varieties of Political Theory.* Englewood Cliffs, N.J.: Prentice-
             Hall.

Eckstein, Harry
    1964   "Introduction. Toward the Theoretical Study of Internal
             War." In *Internal War,* ed. Harry Eckstein. New York: The
             Free Press.

Eckstein, Harry, ed.
    1964   *Internal War.* New York: The Free Press.

Eisenstadt, S. N.
    1963   *The Political Systems of Empires.* New York: The Free Press.

Elliot, J. H.
    1963   *The Revolt of the Catalans.* London: Cambridge University
             Press.
    1969   "Revolution and Continuity in Early Modern Europe." *P&P*
             42:35–56.
    1973   "England and Europe: A Common Malady?" In *The Origins
             of the English Civil War,* ed. Conrad Russell. London: Mac-
             millan.

Elton, G. R.
    1974   *Studies in Tudor and Stuart Politics and Government.* Vols. 2
    1982   and 3. London: Cambridge University Press.

Engels, Frederick
    1975   "The Condition of England: The Eighteenth Century." Re-
    [1844]   printed in *Collected Works,* Marx and Engels. New York: In-
             ternational Publishers.

Erikson, Erik
    1963   *Childhood and Society.* 2d ed. New York: Norton.
    1968   *Identity, Youth and Crisis.* New York: Norton.

Everitt, Alan
    1966   "Social Mobility in Early Modern England." *P&P* 33:56–73.
    1967a   "Farm Labourers." In *The Agrarian History of England and
             Wales.* Vol. 4, ed. Joan Thirsk. Cambridge: Cambridge Uni-
             versity Press.
    1967b   "The Marketing of Agricultural Produce." In *The Agrarian
             History of England and Wales.* Vol. 4, ed. Joan Thirsk. Cam-
             bridge: Cambridge University Press.

1968   "The County Community." *The English Revolution 1600–1660*, ed. E. W. Ives. London: Edward Arnold.

1969a   *Change in the Provinces: The Seventeenth Century.* Dept. of English Local History, Occasional Papers 2d ser. 1. Leicester: Leicester University Press.

1969b   *The Local Community and the Great Rebellion.* London: The Historical Association.

1973   *The Community of Kent and the Great Rebellion 1640–1660.*
[1966]   Leicester: Leicester University Press.

1979   "Country, County and Town." *TRHS* 5th ser. 29:79–108.

Everitt, Alan, ed.

1960   *Suffolk and the Great Rebellion 1640–1660.* Vol. 3, Suffolk Records Society.

Fanon, Franz

1966   *The Wretched of the Earth.* Trans. Constance Farrington.
[1961]   New York: Grove.

Farnell, James E.

1964   "The Navigation Act of 1651, the First Dutch War, and the London Merchant Community." *EcHR* 2d ser. 16:439–55.

1972   "The Aristocracy and Leadership of Parliament in the English Civil Wars." *JModH* 44:79–86.

1977   "The Social and Intellectual Basis of London's Role in the English Civil Wars." *JModH* 49:641–60.

Feiling, Keith

1950   *A History of the Tory Party 1640–1714.* London: Oxford
[1924]   University Press.

Festinger, Leon

1962   *A Theory of Cognitive Dissonance.* Stanford: Stanford Uni-
[1957]   versity Press.

Figgis, John Nelville

1965   *The Divine Right of Kings.* New York: Harper Torchbooks.
[1914]

Finch, M. E.

1956   *The Wealth of Five Northamptonshire Families, 1540–1640.* Vol. 19, Northamptonshire Record Society.

Firth, C. H.

1910   *The House of Lords During the Civil War.* London: Long-man.

1962   *Cromwell's Army.* 3d ed. London: Methuen.
[1921]

Fisher, F. J.

1935   "The Development of the London Food Market: 1540–1640." *EcHR* 5:46–64. Reprinted in 1954, *Essays in Eco-*

nomic History. Vol. 1, ed. Carus-Wilson. New York: St. Martin's.

1948　"The Development of London as a Centre of Conspicuous Consumption in the Sixteenth and Seventeenth Centuries." *TRHS* 4th ser. 30:37–50; reprinted in 1962, *Essays in Economic History*. Vol 2, ed. Carus-Wilson. New York: St. Martin's.

1968　"The Growth of London." In *The English Revolution 1600–1660*, ed. E. W. Ives. London: Edward Arnold.

1971　"London as an 'Engine of Economic Growth.'" In *Britain and the Netherlands*. Vol. 4, ed. J. S. Bromley and E. H. Kossmann. The Hague: Nijhoff.

Fisher, F. J., ed.

1961　*Essays in the Economic and Social History of Tudor and Stuart England*. Cambridge: Cambridge University Press.

Flemion, J. S.

1973　"The Struggle for the Petition of Right in the House of Lords: The Study of an Opposition Victory." *JModH* 45:193–210.

1976　"The Nature of Opposition in the House of Lords in the Early Seventeenth Century: A Reevaluation." *Albion* 8:17–34.

Fletcher, Anthony

1975　*A County Community in Peace and War: Sussex 1600–1660*. London: Longman.

1981　*The Outbreak of the English Civil War*. London: Edward Arnold.

1983　"Parliament and People in Seventeenth Century England." *P&P* 98:151–55.

1984　"Natural and Local Awareness in the County Communities." In *Before the Civil War*, ed. Howard Tomlinson. New York: St. Martin's.

Forster, Robert, and Jack P. Greene, eds.

1970　*Preconditions of Revolution in Early Modern Europe*. Baltimore: Johns Hopkins Press.

Foster, Elizabeth Read

1960　"The Procedure of the House of Commons Against Patents and Monopolies, 1621–1624." In *Conflict in Stuart England*, ed. W. Aiken and B. Henning. London: Jonathan Cape.

1974*a*　"Petitions and the Petition of Right." *JBS* 14:21–45.

1974*b*　"Printing the Petition of Right." *Huntington Library Quarterly* 28:81–83.

1977　"The House of Lords and Ordinances, 1641–1649." *The American Journal of Legal History* 21:157–73.

1983　*The House of Lords, 1603–49*. Chapel Hill: University of North Carolina Press.

Foster, Stephen
    1969   "The Presbyterian Independents Exorcized. A Ghost Story for Historians." *P&P* 44: 52–75.
    1970   "A Rejoinder." *P&P* 47: 137–46.
Foucault, Michel
    1972   *The Archeology of Knowledge.* Trans. A. M. Sheridan Smith.
    [1969] London: Tavistock.
    1973   *The Order of Things.* Trans. from the French. New York:
    [1966] Vintage.
    1977   *Discipline and Punish.* Trans. Alan Sheridan. New York:
    [1975] Pantheon.
    1980   *Power/Knowledge.* Trans. Colin Gordon, Leo Marshall, John Mepham, Kate Soper. New York: Pantheon.
Fox, Renée C.
    1976   "Medical Evolution." In *Explorations in General Theory in Social Science,* ed. Loubser et al. New York: The Free Press.
Frank, Joseph
    1969   *The Levellers.* New York: Russell and Russell.
    [1955]
Franklin, Julian
    1978   *John Locke and the Theory of Sovereignty.* Cambridge: Cambridge University Press.
Franklin, Julian, ed.
    1969   *Constitutionalism and Resistance in the Sixteenth Century.* New York: Pegasus.
Freud, Sigmund
    1965   *New Introductory Lectures on Psychoanalysis.* Trans. James
    [1933] Strachey. New York: Norton.
Friedman, Milton
    1970   "A Theoretical Framework for Monetary Analysis." *Journal of Political Economy* 78: 193–238.
Fulbrook, Mary
    1982   "The English Revolution and the Revisionist Revolt." *Social History* 7: 249–64.
Furniss, Edgar S.
    1920   *The Position of the Laborer in a System of Nationalism.* Boston: Houghton Mifflin.
Gamson, William
    1968   *Power and Discontent.* Homewood, Ill.: Dorsey.
Gardiner, Samuel Rawson
    1883–84 *History of England from the Accession of James I to the Outbreak of the Civil War 1603–42.* 10 vols. London: Longman.
    1893   *History of the Great Civil War 1642–49.* 4 vols. New ed., London: Longman.

Gardiner, Samuel Rawson, ed.
1906   *The Constitutional Documents of the Puritan Revolution 1625–1660.* 3d ed. London: Oxford University Press.
Genovese, Eugene D.
1976   *Role, Jordan, Role.* New York: Vintage.
[1974]
George, C. and K.
1961   *The Protestant Mind of the English Reformation 1570–1640.* Princeton: Princeton University Press.
Giddens, Anthony
1979   *Studies in Social and Political Theory.* London: Hutchinson.
[1977]
Gierke, Otto
1957   *Natural Law and the Theory of Society 1500 to 1800.* Trans.
[1913]   Ernest Barker. Boston: Beacon.
1958   *Political Theories of the Middle Ages.* Trans. Frederic William
[1881]   Maitland. Boston: Beacon.
Gleason, J. H.
1969   *The Justices of the Peace in England 1558 to 1640.* London: Oxford University Press.
Glow, Lotte
1964   "Pym and Parliament: The Methods of Moderation." *JModH* 36:373–97.
1965a   "The Committee-Men in the Long Parliament, August 1642– December 1643." *THJ* 8:1–15.
1965b   "The Committee of Safety." *EHR* 80:289–313.
1965c   "Political Affiliations in the House of Commons after Pym's Death." *BIHR* 38:48–70.
[Glow] Mulligan, Lotte
1969   "Peace Negotiations, Politics and the Committee of Both Kingdoms, 1644–1646." *THJ* 12:3–22.
1975   "Property and Parliamentary Politics in the English Civil War, 1642–6." *Historical Studies* 16:341–61.
Godelier, Maurice
1972   "Structure and Contradiction in *Capital*." Reprinted in *Ideology in Social Science*, ed. Robin Blackburn. London: Fontana.
Goldstone, Jack
1983   "Capitalist Origins of the English Revolution." *Theory and Society* 12:143–180.
1984   "Urbanization and Inflation: Lessons from the English Price Revolution of the Sixteenth and Seventeenth Centuries." *AJS* 89:1122–60.
Gonner, E. C. K.
1912   *Common Land and Inclosure.* London: Macmillan.

Goodenough, Ward
1963   "Rethinking 'Status' and 'Role.'" In *The Relevance of Models for Social Anthropology*, ed. Michael Banton. London: Barnes and Noble.

Goodman, David, and Michael Redclift
1981   *From Peasant to Proletarian: Capitalist Development and Agrarian Transitions*. Oxford: Blackwell.

Goodwin, Albert
1966   *The French Revolution*. Rev. ed. New York: Harper Torchbooks.

Goody, Jack, et al., eds.
1976   *Family and Inheritance*. London: Cambridge University Press.

Gough, J. W.
1971   *Fundamental Law in English Constitutional History*. London:
[1955] Oxford University Press.

Gould, Mark
1967   A Theory of Deviant Behavior: The Use of Psychedelic Drugs by College Students. B.A. thesis, Reed College, Portland, Oregon.

1970   "On Michael Harrington, *Toward a Democratic Left*." *Sociological Inquiry* 40: 169–74.

1976   "Systems Analysis, Macrosociology and the Generalized Media of Action." In *Explorations in General Theory in Social Science*, ed. Loubser et al. New York: The Free Press.

1977   Development and Revolution in Science. MS, Max-Planck-Institut, Starnberg, West Germany.

1981a   "The Devaluation of Labor-Power." *Berkeley Journal of Sociology* 26: 139–155.

1981b   "Marx ≟ Weber: The Role of Ideas in Social Action." Paper delivered at the 1981 meeting of the American Sociological Association, Toronto, Ontario, Canada.

1981c   "Parsons Versus Marx: 'An earnest warning ...'" *Sociological Inquiry* 51: 197–218.

1983   "Egalitarian Values: Some Unintended Consequences, Some Equitable Remedies." Paper delivered at the 1983 annual meeting of the Eastern Sociological Society, Baltimore, Maryland.

1984   "Parsons and Luhmann: Relations Between Macrosocial and Microsocial Treatments of the Media." Paper delivered at a Spenser Foundation Sponsored Conference on "Generalized Symbolic Media," Philadelphia, Pennsylvania.

1985   "Prolegomena to Any Future Theory of Social Crisis." In *NeoFunctionalism*, ed. J. Alexander. Beverly Hills: Sage.

forth-   Science and Society: Development and Revolution.
coming

Gouldner, Alvin
1967   "Reciprocity and Autonomy in Functional Theory." Re-
[1959]   printed in *System, Change and Conflict*, ed. N. J. Demerath III
         and Richard Peterson. New York: The Free Press.

Gramsci, Antonio
1971   *Selections from the Prison Notebooks*. Trans. and ed. Quintin
         Hoare and Geoffrey Nowell Smith. New York: International.

Granovetter, Mark
1981   "Toward a Sociological Theory of Income Differences." In
         Sociological Perspectives on Labor Markets, ed. Ivar Berg.
         New York: Academic.

Grassby, Richard
1969   "The Rate of Profit in Seventeenth Century England." *EHR*
         84:721–51.
1970   "The Personal Wealth of the Business Community in Seven-
         teenth Century England." *EcHR* 2d ser. 23:220–34.

Greenleaf, W. H.
1964   *Order, Empiricism and Politics*. London: Oxford University
         Press.

Gregg, Pauline
1976   *Black Death to Industrial Revolution*. London: George
         Harrap.

Gregory, Derek
1982   *Regional Transformation and Industrial Revolution: A
         Geography of the Yorkshire Woollen Industry*. Minneapolis:
         University of Minnesota Press.

Griewank, Karl
1966   "Emergence of the Concept of Revolution." Trans. Heinz
[1955]   Lubasz. In *Revolutions in Modern European History*, ed.
         Heinz Lubasz. New York: Macmillan.

Grigg, D. B.
1980   *Population Growth and Agrarian Change*. Cambridge:
         Cambridge University Press.

Gross, Neal, et al.
1958   *Explorations in Role Analysis: Studies of the School Superin-
         tendent*. New York: John Wiley.

Gruenfelder, John
1977   "The Electoral Patronage of Sir Thomas Wentworth, Earl of
         Strafford, 1614–1640." *JModH* 49:557–574.
1981   *Influence in Early Stuart Elections 1604–1640*. Columbus:
         Ohio State University Press.

Gunn, J. A. W.
  1969   *Politics and Public Interest in the Seventeenth Century.* Lon-
            don: Routledge & Kegan Paul.
Gurr, Ted Robert
  1970   *Why Men Rebel.* Princeton: Princeton University Press.
Guy, J. A.
  1982   "The Origins of the Petition of Right Reconsidered." *THJ*
            25:289–312.
Habakkuk, H. John
  1953   "Economic Functions of English Landowners in the Seven-
            teenth and Eighteenth Centuries." *Explorations in Entre-
            preneurial History* 6:92–102. Reprinted in 1968, *Essays in
            Agrarian History*, vol 1, ed. Minchinton. Newton Abbot:
            David and Charles.
  1965   "La disparition du paysan anglais." *Annales* 20:649–63.
  1979–81 "The Rise and Fall of English Landed Families." *TRHS* 5th
            ser. 29–31: in three parts.
Habermas, Jürgen
  1970   "Toward a Theory of Communicative Competence." In *Re-
            cent Sociology, No. 2*, ed. Hans Dreitzel. New York: Mac-
            millan.
  1974   *Theory and Practice.* Trans. John Viertel. London: Heine-
            mann.
  1975   *Legitimation Crisis.* Trans. Thomas McCarthy. Boston:
  [1973]   Beacon.
  1979   *Communication and the Evolution of Society.* Trans. Thomas
  [1976]   McCarthy. Boston: Beacon.
  1984   *Theory of Communicative Action*, Vol. 1. Trans. Thomas
  [1981]   McCarthy. Boston: Beacon.
Haller, William
  1957   *The Rise of Puritanism.* New York: Harper Torchbooks.
  [1938]
  1963   *Liberty and Reformation in the Puritan Revolution.* New
  [1955]   York: Columbia University Press.
Haller, William, ed.
  1934   *Tracts on Liberty in the Puritan Revolution.* 3 vols. New
            York: Columbia University Press.
Haller, William, and Godfrey Davies, eds.
  1964   *The Leveller Tracts 1647–1653.* Gloucester, Mass.: Peter
  [1944]   Smith.
Hammersley, G.
  1957   "Crown Woods and their Exploitation in the Sixteenth and
            Seventeenth Centuries." *BIHR* 30.

Hanson, David
1970   *From Kingdom to Commonwealth*. Cambridge: Harvard University Press.
Hargreaves, E. L.
1930   *The National Debt*. London: Arnold.
Harte, N. B., and K. G. Ponting, eds.
1973   *Textile History and Economic History*. Manchester: Manchester University Press.
Hast, Adele
1972   "State Treason Trials During the Puritan Revolution, 1640–1660." *THJ* 15:37–53.
Havinden, M. A.
1967   "Agricultural Progress in Open-field Oxfordshire." Reprinted
[1961]   in *Agriculture and Economic Growth in England 1650–1815*, ed. E. L. Jones. London: Methuen.
Hawkins, Michael
1973   "The Government: Its Role and Its Aims." In *The Origins of the English Civil War*, ed. Conrad Russell. London: Macmillan.
Heaton, Herbert
1920   *The Yorkshire Woollen and Worsted Industries*. London: Oxford University Press.
Heckscher, Eli
1955   *Mercantilism*. 2 vols. Trans. Mendel Shapiro. Rev. ed. Ed.
[1931]   E. F. Sönderlund. New York: Barnes and Noble.
Hegel, G. W. F.
1949   *The Phenomenology of Mind*. Trans. J. B. Baillie. New York:
[1807]   Humanities Press.
1967   *The Philosophy of Right*. Trans. T. M. Knox. London: Oxford
[1821]   University Press.
1969   *The Science of Logic*. Trans. A. V. Miller. New York: Huma-
[1812]   nities Press.
Herrup, Cynthia
1983   "The Counties and the Country: Some Thoughts on Seventeenth Century Historiography." *Social History* 8:169–81.
Hexter, J. H.
1941   *The Reign of King Pym*. Cambridge: Harvard University Press.
1963   *Reappraisals in History*. New York: Harper and Row.
[1961]
1968   "The English Aristocracy, Its Crisis and the English Revolution, 1558–1660." *JBS* 8:22–79.
1970   "Presbyterians, Independents and Puritans: A Voice from the

Past." *P&P* 47:134–36.

1978   "Power Struggle, Parliament, and Liberty in Early Stuart England." *JModH* 50:1–50.

Hibbard, Caroline M.

1983   *Charles I and the Popish Plot.* Chapel Hill: University of North Carolina Press.

Hicks, J. R.

1937   "Mr. Keynes and the 'Classics': A Suggested Interpretation." Reprinted in 1966, *Monetary Theory and Policy*, ed. R. Thorne. New York: Random House.

Higgins, Patricia

1973   "The Reactions of Women, with Special Reference to Women Petitioners." In *Politics, Religion, and the English Civil War*, ed. Brian Manning. London: Edward Arnold.

Hill, Christopher

1948   "The English Civil War Interpreted by Marx and Engels." *Science and Society* 12:130–56.

1955   *The English Revolution 1640.* 3rd ed. London: Lawrence and
[1940]   Wishart.

1963   "Puritans and the 'Dark Corners of the Land.'" *TRHS* 5th ser. 13:77–103.

1964   *Puritanism and Revolution.* New York: Schocken Books.
[1958]

1966   *The Century of Revolution: 1603–1714.* New York: Norton.
[1961]

1969a   "'Reason' and 'Reasonableness' in Seventeenth Century England." *British Journal of Sociology* 20:235–52.

1969b   *Reformation to Industrial Revolution.* Baltimore: Penguin.
[1967]

1969c   *Society and Puritanism in Pre-Revolutionary England.* Lon-
[1964]   don: Panther.

1971   *Economic Problems of the Church.* London: Panther.
[1956]

1972a   *God's Englishman.* Harmondsworth: Penguin.
[1970]

1972b   *The World Turned Upside Down.* London: Temple Smith.

1975   *Change and Continuity in Seventeenth-Century England.* Cambridge: Harvard University Press.

1980a   "A Bourgeois Revolution?" In *Three British Revolutions: 1641, 1688, 1776*, ed. J. G. A. Pocock. Princeton: Princeton University Press.

1980b   *Some Intellectual Consequences of the English Revolution.* Madison: University of Wisconsin Press.

1981   "Parliament and People in Seventeenth-Century England."
        P&P 92:100–124.
1983   "A Rejoinder." *P&P* 98:155–58.
1985   *The Experience of Defeat.* New York: Penguin.
[1984]
Hill, L. M.
1973   "County Government in Caroline England 1625–1640." In
        The Origins of the English Civil War, ed. Conrad Russell.
        London: Macmillan.
Hindess, Barry, and Paul Hirst
1975   *Pre-capitalist Modes of Production.* London: Routledge &
        Kegan Paul.
Hinton, R. W. K.
1955   "The Mercantile System in the Time of Thomas Mun." *EcHR*
        2d ser. 7:177–90.
Hirshman, Albert O.
1977   *The Passions and the Interests.* Princeton: Princeton Universi-
        ty Press.
Hirst, Derek
1972   "The Defection of Edward Dering, 1640–41." *THJ* 15:193–
        208.
1975   *The Representative of the People?* London: Cambridge Uni-
        versity Press.
1978   "Unanimity in the Commons, Aristocratic Intrigues, and the
        Origins of the English Civil War." *JModH* 50:51–71.
1980   "Parliament, Law and War in the 1620s." *THJ* 23:455–61.
1981   "Revisionists Revisited: The Place of Principle." *P&P* 92:79–
        99.
Hobbes, Thomas
1969   *Behemoth or the Long Parliament.* Ed. Ferdinand Tonnies. 2d
[c. 1668] ed. M. M. Goldsmith. New York: Barnes and Noble.
Hobsbawm, E. J.
1960   "The Seventeenth Century in the Development of Capitalism."
        Science and Society 24:97–112.
1967   "The Crisis of the Seventeenth Century." Reprinted in *Crisis
        in Europe 1560–1660*, ed. Robert Aston. New York: Anchor.
Holderness, B. A.
1976   *Pre-Industrial England.* Totowa, N.J.: Rowman and Little-
        field.
Hollaender, A. E. J., and William Kellaway, eds.
1969   *Studies in London History.* London: Hodder and Stoughton.
Holmes, Clive
1974   *The Eastern Association in the English Civil War.* London:

Cambridge University Press.

1980*a*   "The County Community in Stuart Historiography." *JBS* 19:54–73.

1980*b*   *Seventeenth Century Lincolnshire*. Vol. 7 of *History of Lincolnshire*. Lincoln: History of Lincolnshire Committee for the Society of Lincolnshire History and Archeology.

1981   "New Light on the New Model." *THJ* 24:505–8.

Homans, George

1940   "The Puritans and the Clothing Industry in England." *New England Quarterly* 13:519–29.

1969   "The Explanation of English Regional Differences." *P&P* 42:18–34.

Horwich, George

1964   *Money, Capital and Prices*. Homewood, Ill.: Irwin.

Hoskins, W. G.

1953–54 "Harvest Fluctuations and English Economic History, 1480–1619." *AgHR* 2:28–46. Reprinted in 1968, *Essays in Agrarian History*, vol. 1, ed. W. E. Minchinton. Newton: Abbot: David and Charles.

1965*a*   *The Midland Peasant*. London: Macmillan.
[1957]

1965*b*   *Provincial England*. London: Macmillan.
[1963]

1968   "Harvest Fluctuations and English Economic History, 1620–1759." *AgHR* 1:14–31.

Howell, Roger

1967   *Newcastle-upon-Tyne and the Puritan Revolution*. London: Oxford University Press.

1979   "The Structure of Urban Politics in the English Civil War." *Albion* 7:111–27.

1983   "Neutralism, Conservatism and Political Alignment in the English Revolution: The Case of the Towns, 1642–9." In *Reactions to the English Civil War*, ed. Morrill. New York: St. Martin's.

Howell, Roger, Jr., and David Brewster

1970   "Reconsidering the Levellers: The Evidence of *The Moderate*." *P&P* 46:68–87.

Hudson, Pat

1983   "From Manor to Mill: The West Riding in Transition." In *Manufacture in Town and Country Before the Factory*, ed. Berg et al. London: Cambridge University Press.

Hughes, Ann

1981   "Militancy and Localism: Warwickshire Politics and Westminster Politics, 1643–1647." *TRHS* 5th ser. 31:51–68.

1982   "Warwickshire on the Eve of the Civil War." *Midland History* 7:42–72.

1985   "The King, the Parliament and the Localities during the English Civil War." *JBS* 24:236–63.

Hulme, Harold

1960   "Charles I and the Constitution." In *Conflict in Stuart England*, ed. Aiken and Henning. London: Jonathan Cape.

Hunt, William

1983   *The Puritan Moment: The Coming of Revolution to an English County.* Cambridge: Harvard University Press.

Huntington, Samuel

1968   *Political Order in Changing Societies.* New Haven: Yale University Press.

Hutton, Ronald

1981   "The Structure of the Royalist Party, 1642–6." *THJ* 24:553–69.

1982   *The Royalist War Effort 1642–1646.* London: Longman.

1983   "The Royalist War Effort." In *Reactions to the English Civil War*, ed. Morrill. New York: St. Martin's.

Hymer, Stephen, and Stephen Resnick

1969   "A Model of an Agrarian Economy with Nonagricultural Activities." *American Economics Review* 59:493–506.

Ives, E. W.

1968   "Social Change and the Law." In *The English Revolution 1600–1660*, ed. Ives. London: Edward Arnold.

Ives, E. W., ed.

1968   *The English Revolution 1600–1660.* London: Edward Arnold.

James I

1965   *The Political Works of James I.* New York: Russell & Russell.
[1616]

James, Margaret

1930   *Social Problems and Policy During the Puritan Revolution 1500–1640.* London: Oxford University Press.

James, Mervyn

1974   *Family, Lineage and Civil Society: A Study of Society, Politics and Mentality in the Durham Region, 1500–1640.* London: Oxford University Press.

John, A. H.

1960   "The Course of Agricultural Change 1660–1760." In *Studies in the Industrial Revolution*, ed. L. S. Pressnell. London: Athlone. Reprinted in 1968, *Essays in Agrarian History*, vol. 1, ed. W. E. Minchinton. Newton Abbot: David and Charles.

1962   "Aspects of English Economic Growth in the First Half of the

Eighteenth Century." *Essays in Economic History*, vol. 2, ed.
E. M. Carus-Wilson. New York: St. Martin's.

1967   "Agricultural Productivity and Economic Growth in England
              1700–1760 (with a Postscript)." Reprinted in *Agricultural and
              Economic Growth in England 1650–1815*, ed. E. L. Jones.
              London: Methuen.
1976   "English Agricultural Improvement and Grain Exports 1660–
              1765." In *Trade, Government and Economy in Pre-Industrial
              England*, ed. D. D. Coleman and A. H. John. London:
              Weidenfeld and Nicolson.
Johnson, A. H.
1963   *The Disappearance of the Small Landowner*. London: Merlin
[1909]   Press.
Johnson, Chalmers
1964   *Revolution and the Social System*. Stanford: Hoover Institu-
              tion Press.
1966   *Revolutionary Change*. Boston: Little, Brown.
Johnson, Harry
1967   "Monetary Theory and Keynesian Economics." Reprinted in
[1958]   *Money, Trade, and Economic Growth*. Cambridge: Harvard
              University Press.
1969   *Essays in Monetary Economics*. Cambridge: Harvard Uni-
              versity Press.
Jones, E. L.
1967   "Editor's Introduction." In *Agriculture and Economic
              Growth in England 1650–1815*, ed. E. L. Jones. London:
              Methuen.
1968   "The Condition of English Agriculture, 1500–1640 [a review
              of Thirsk (ed.), 1967]." *EcHR* 2d ser. 21:614–19.
1974   *Agriculture and the Industrial Revolution*. New York: John
              Wiley.
Jones, E. L., ed.
1967   *Agriculture and Economic Growth in England 1650–1815*.
              London: Methuen.
Jones, W. J.
1971   *Politics and the Bench*. London: Allen and Unwin.
Jordan, W. K.
1965   *The Development of Religious Toleration in England*. 4 vols.
[1932]   Gloucester, Mass.: Peter Smith.
Journal of Modern History
1977   "Special Issue on the English Revolution." 49:no. 4.
Judson, Margaret
1949   *The Crisis of the Constitution*. New Brunswick, N.J.: Rutgers
              University Press.

1980   *From Tradition to Political Reality: A Study of the Ideas Set Forth in Support of the Commonwealth Government in England, 1649–1653.* Hamden, Conn.: Archon.
Kamen, Henry
1971   *The Iron Century: Social Change in Europe 1550–1660.* London: Weidenfeld and Nicolson.
Kantorowicz, Ernst
1957   *The King's Two Bodies.* Princeton: Princeton University Press.
Kaplan, Lawrence
1969   "Presbyterians and Independents in 1643." *EHR* 84:244–56.
1970   "The Steps to War: The Scots and Parliament 1642–43." *JBS* 9:50–71.
1971   "The Plot to Depose Charles I in 1644." *BIHR* 44:216–23.
1976   *Politics and Religion During the English Revolution.* New York: New York University Press.
Katz, Elihu, and Paul Lazersfeld
1955   *Personal Influence.* New York: The Free Press.
Kautsky, Karl
1909   *The Social Revolution and On the Morrow of the Social Revolution.* Trans. J. B. Askew, rev. by Kautsky. London: Twentieth Century.
1970   *La Question Agraire.* Trans. Edgard Milhaud and Camille
[1898]   Polack. Paris: Maspero.
Keeler, Mary Frear
1954   *The Long Parliament, 1640–1641.* Philadelphia: The American Philosophical Society.
Kellenbenz, Hermann
1977   "The Organization of Industrial Production." In *Cambridge Economic History of Europe*, vol. 5, ed. E. E. Rich and C. H. Wilson. Cambridge: Cambridge University Press.
Kellett, J. R.
1958   "The Breakdown of Gild and Corporation Control Over the Handicraft and Retail Trade in London." *EcHR* 2d ser. 10:381–95.
Kennedy, Mark
1983   "Charles I and Local Government: The Draining of the East and West Fens." *Albion* 15:19–31.
Kennedy, William
1913   *English Taxation 1640–1799.* London: Bell.
Kenniston, Kenneth
1965   *The Uncommitted: Alienated Youth in American Society.* New York: Harcourt, Brace and World.
Kenyon, J. P.
1977   *Revolution Principles.* London: Cambridge University Press.

1978   *Stuart England.* Harmondsworth: Penguin.
Kenyon, J. P., ed.
  1966   *The Stuart Constitution.* London: Cambridge University Press.
Kerridge, Eric
  1953   "The Movement of Rent, 1540–1640." *EcHR* 2d ser. 6:16–
            34. Reprinted in *Essays in Economic History*, vol. 2, ed.
            Carus-Wilson. New York: St. Martin's.
  1958   "The Revolts in Wiltshire Against Charles I." *The Wiltshire
            Archaeological and Natural History Magazine* 57:64–75.
  1968   *The Agricultural Revolution.* New York: Kelley.
  [1967]
  1969   *Agrarian Problems in the Sixteenth Century and After.* Lon-
            don: Allen and Unwin.
  1973   *The Farmers of Old England.* London: Allen and Unwin.
Ketton-Cremer, R. W.
  1970   *Norfolk in the Civil War.* Hamden, Conn.: Archon.
  [1969]
Keynes, John Maynard
  1965   *The General Theory of Employment, Interest and Money.*
  [1935]   New York: Harcourt, Brace and World.
Kishlansky, Mark
  1977   "The Emergence of Adversary Politics in the Long Parlia-
            ment." *JModH* 49:617–40.
  1978   "The Case of the Army Truly Stated: The Creation of the New
            Model Army." *P&P* 81:51–74.
  1979a   *The Rise of the New Model Army.* Cambridge: Cambridge
            University Press.
  1979b   "The Army and the Levellers: The Roads to Putney." *THJ*
            22:795–824.
  1982   "What Happened at Ware?" *THJ* 25:827–39.
  1983   "Ideology and Politics in the Parliamentary Armies, 1645–9."
            In *Reactions to the English Civil War, 1642–1649*, ed. Mor-
            rill. New York: St. Martin's.
Kobrin, Solomin
  1951   "The Conflict of Values in Delinquency Areas." *ASR* 16:653–
            61.
Koenigsberger, Helmut
  1972   "Revolutionary Conclusions." *History* 57:394–98.
  1974   "Early Modern Revolutions: An Exchange [a review of Stone,
            The Causes of the English Revolution]." *JModH* 46:99–106.
  1977   "Cominium regale or dominium politicum et regale? Monar-
            chies and Parliaments in Early Modern Europe. In *Der
            moderne Parlamentarismus and seine Grundlagen in der*

ständischen Repräsentation, ed. Karl Bosl. Berlin: Duncker and Humblot.

Krantz, Frederick, and Paul Hohenberg, eds.

1975   *Failed Transitions to Modern Industrial Society*. Montreal: Interuniversity Centre for European Studies.

Kriedte, Peter, Hans Medick, and Jürgen Schlumbohm

1981   *Industrialization Before Industrialization*. Trans. Beate
[1977]   Schempp. London: Cambridge University Press.

Krohn, Wolfgang, and Wolf Schäfer

1976   "The Origins and Structure of Agricultural Chemistry." In *Perspectives on the Emergence of Scientific Disciplines*, ed. Lemaine et al. Chicago: Aldine.

Kuenne, R. E.

1963   *The Theory of General Economic Equilibrium*. Princeton: Princeton University Press.

Kula, Witold

1970   *Théorie économique du système féodal*. Trans. from the
[1962]   Polish. Paris: Mouton.

1976   *An Economic Theory of the Feudal System*. Trans. from the
[1962]   Italian edition by Lawrence Garner. London: New Left Books.

Kussmaul, Ann

1981   *Servants in Husbandry in Early Modern England*. Cambridge: Cambridge University Press.

1985   "Agrarian Change in Seventeenth Century England: The Economic Historian as Paleontologist." *JEcH* 45 : 1–30.

Lambert, Sheila

1984   "The Opening of the Long Parliament," *THJ* 27 : 265–87.

Lamont, William M.

1969   *Godly Rule*. London: Macmillan.

Langton, John

1972   "Coal Output in South-West Lancashire, 1590–1799." *EcHR* 2d ser. 25 : 28–54.

Laslett, Peter

1965   *The World We Have Lost*. New York: Scribners.

Laswell, Harold, and Abraham Kaplan

1950   *Power and Society*. New Haven: Yale University Press.

Latham, R. C.

1945   "English Revolutionary Thought, 1640–60." *History*, n.s. 30 : 38–59.

Lefebvre, George

1947   *The Coming of the French Revolution*. Trans. R. R. Palmer.
[1939]   Princeton: Princeton University Press.

Leijonhufvud, Axel
  1968   *On Keynesian Economics and the Economics of Keynes.* New York: Oxford University Press.

Lemert, Edwin
  1964   "Social Structures, Social Control and Deviation." In *Anomie and Deviant Behavior,* ed. Clinard. New York: The Free Press.
  1967   *Human Deviance, Social Problems and Social Control.* Englewood Cliffs, N.J.: Prentice-Hall.

Lenin, V. I.
  1960ff. *Collected Works.* Vol. 3, *The Development of Capitalism in*
  [1899] *Russia.* London: Lawrence and Wishart.

Leonard, E. M.
  1905   "The Inclosure of Common Fields in the Seventeenth Century." *TRHS,* n.s. 19:101–46.

Levack, Brian P.
  1973   *The Civil Lawyers in England 1603–1641.* London: Oxford University Press.

Levine, David
  1977   *Family Formation in an Age of Nascent Capitalism.* New York: Academic.
  1984   "Production, Reproduction and the Proletarian Family in England, 1500–1851." In *Proletarianization and Family History,* ed. David Levine. Orlando, Fla.: Academic.

Levine, David, ed.
  1984   *Proletarianization and Family History.* Orlando, Fla.: Academic.

Lévi-Strauss, Claude
  1966   *The Savage Mind.* Trans. from the French. Chicago: Universi-
  [1962] ty of Chicago Press.

Levy, F. J.
  1982   "How Information Spread Among the Gentry, 1550–1640." *JBS* 21:11–34.

Lidz, Victor
  1981   "Conceptions of Value-Relevance and the Theory of Action." *Sociological Inquiry* 51:371–408.

Lindberg, Leon, et al., eds.
  1975   *Stress and Contradiction in Modern Society.* Lexington, Mass.: Lexington Books.

Lindert, Peter H.
  1980   "English Occupations, 1670–1811." *JEcH* 40:685–712.

Lindley, Keith
  1982   *Fenland Riots and the English Revolution.* London: Heinemann.

Lipson, E.
1959, *The Economic History of England*. Vol. 1, 12th ed.; Vols. 2
1956 and 3, 6th ed. London: Adam and Charles Black.
1965 *The History of the Woollen and Worsted Industries*. London:
[1921] Frank Cass.
Lis, Catharina, and Hugo Soly
1979 *Poverty and Capitalism in Pre-Industrial Europe*. New York: Humanities Press.
Little, David
1969 *Religion, Order and Law*. New York: Harper and Row.
Loades, D. M.
1974 *Politics and the Nation 1450–1600*. London: Fontana.
Loubser, Jan, et al., eds.
1976 *Explorations in General Theory in Social Science*. 2 vols. New York: The Free Press.
Lublinskya, A. D.
1968 *French Absolutism: The Crucial Phase, 1620–1629*. Trans. Brian Pearce. London: Cambridge University Press.
Luhmann, Niklas
1974 "Sociology of Political Systems." In *German Political Studies*, vol. 1, ed. Klaus von Beyme. Beverly Hills: Sage.
1976 "Generalized Media and the Problem of Contingency." In *Explorations in General Theory in Social Science*, ed. Loubser et al. New York: The Free Press.
1979 *Trust and Power*. Trans. Howard Davis, John Raffan, and
[1973] Kathryn Rooney. New York: John Wiley.
[1975]
Lukacs, George
1970 "The Dialectics of Labor: Beyond Causality and Teleology." Trans. A. Gucinski. *Telos* 6:162–74.
1971 *History and Class Consciousness*. Trans. Rodney Livingstone.
[1922] Cambridge: MIT Press.
[1967]
Macauley, Thomas Babington
1906 *History of England*. 4 vols. London: Everyman.
[1849–61]
McCloskey, Donald
1975a "The Economics of Enclosure: A Market Analysis." In *European Peasants and Their Markets*, ed. Parker and Jones. Princeton: Princeton University Press.
1975b "The Persistence of English Common Fields." In *European Peasants and Their Markets*, ed. Parker and Jones. Princeton:

Princeton University Press.

1976   "English Open Fields as Behavior Towards Risk." In *Research in Economic History*, vol. 1, ed. Paul Uselding. Greenwich, Conn.: JAI.

1979   "A Reply to Professor Charles Wilson." *Journal of European Economic History* 8: 203–7.

McClosky, Herbert and John Schaar

1965   "Psychological Dimensions of Anomy." *ASR* 30: 14–30.

MacCormack, John R.

1973   *Revolutionary Politics in the Long Parliament.* Cambridge: Harvard University Press.

MacFarlane, Alan

1970   *Witchcraft in Tudor and Stuart England.* New York: Harper Torchbook.

1979   *The Origins of English Individualism.* Cambridge: Cambridge
[1978] University Press.

McIlwain, Charles Howard

1910   *The High Court of Parliament and Its Supremacy.* New Haven: Yale University Press.

1966   *Constitutionalism: Ancient and Modern.* Rev. ed. Ithaca: Cor-
[1940] nell University Press.

MacPherson, C. B.

1962   *The Political Theory of Possessive Individualism.* London: Oxford University Press.

1973   *Democratic Theory.* London: Oxford University Press.

Maitland, F. W.

1908   *The Constitutional History of England.* Cambridge: Cambridge University Press.

Malamet, Barbara

1967   "The 'Economic Liberalism' of Sir Edward Coke." *Yale Law Journal* 76: 1321–58.

Malamet, Barbara, ed.

1980   *After the Reformation.* Philadelphia: University of Pennsylvania Press.

Malcolm, Joyce

1978   "A King in Search of Soldiers: Charles I in 1642." *THJ* 21: 251–73.

1983   *Caesar's Due: Loyalty and King Charles 1642–1646.* New Jersey: Humanities Press.

Mandel, Ernest

1967   "The Labor Theory of Value and 'Monopoly Capital.'" *International Socialist Review* July–August: 29–42.

Mandel, Ernest and Alan Freeman, eds.

1984   *Ricardo, Marx and Sraffa.* London: Verso.

Mann, Julia de L.
    1971   *The Cloth Industry in the West of England from 1640 to 1880*. London: Oxford University Press.

Manning, Brian
    1954   "Review Article: The Long Parliament." *P&P* 5:71–76.
    1957   Neutrals and Neutralism in the English Civil War 1642–1646. Ph.D. diss., Oxford University.
    1967   "The Nobles, The People and the Constitution." Reprinted in *Crisis in Europe 1560–1660*, ed. Aston. Garden City, N.Y.: Anchor.
    1968   "The Levellers." In *The English Revolution 1600–1660*, ed. E. W. Ives. London: Edward Arnold.
    1969   "[Review of Wolfe (ed.)]." *EcHR* 2d ser. 22:131–32.
    1970   "The Outbreak of the English Civil War." In *The English Civil War and After 1642–1658*, ed. R. H. Parry. Berkeley, Los Angeles, and London: University of California Press.
    1973*a*   "The Aristocracy and the Downfall of Charles I." In *Politics, Religion and the English Civil War*, ed. Manning. London: Edward Arnold.
    1973*b*   "Religion and Politics: The Godly People." In *Politics, Religion and the English Civil War*, ed. Manning. London: Edward Arnold.
    1975   "The Peasantry and the English Revolution." *Journal of Peasant Studies* 2:133–58.
    1976   *The English Revolution and the English People*. London: Heinemann.

Manning, Brian, ed.
    1973   *Politics, Religion and the English Civil War*. London: Edward Arnold.

Mantoux, Paul
    1962   *The Industrial Revolution in the Eighteenth Century*. Trans.
    [1927]   Marjorie Vernon. New York: Harper Torchbooks.

Mao Tse-Tung
    1965   *Selected Works*. 4 vols. Peking: Foreign Language Press.

Marcuse, Herbert
    1960   *Reason and Revolution*. 2d ed. Boston: Beacon.

Marglin, Stephen A.
    1974   "What Do Bosses Do? The Origins and Functions of Hierarchy in Capitalist Production." *Review of Radical Political Economics* 6:60–112.

Marshall, Alfred
    1920   *Principles of Economics*. 8th ed. London: Macmillan.

Marshall, Gordon
    1980   *Presbyteries and Profits: Calvinism and the Development of*

  Capitalism in Scotland, 1560–1707. Oxford: Oxford University Press.

Marshall, T. H.
  1965   *Class, Citizenship and Social Development.* Garden City, N.Y.: Anchor Books.

Marx, Karl
  1963   *The Eighteenth Brumaire of Louis Bonaparte.* Trans. from the
  [1852]   2d German ed. New York: International Publishers.
  [1869]
  1964   *Class Struggles in France (1848–1850).* Trans. from the Ger-
  [1850]   man. New York: International Publishers.
  [1895]
  1967   *Capital.* 3 vols. Trans. Samuel Moore and Edward Aveling et
  [1867]   al. New York: International Publishers.
  [1885]
  [1894]
  1968   *Theories of Surplus Value,* part [vol.] one. Moscow: Progress
            Publishers.
  1971a   *A Contribution to the Critique of Political Economy.* Trans. S.
  [1859]   W. Ryazanskaya. London: Lawrence and Wishart.
  1971b   *Un chapitre inédit du Capital.* Paris: Union Générale d'Edi-
            tions.
  1973   *Grundrisse.* Trans. Martin Nicolaus. Harmondsworth: Pen-
  [1939]   guin.
  1975   "Economic and Philosophic Manuscripts of 1844." In *Col-
            lected Works,* Vol. 3, Marx and Engels. New York: Interna-
            tional Publishers.
  1976   *Capital,* vol. 1. Trans. Ben Fowkes. Harmondsworth: Penguin.
  [1867]
  1978   *Capital,* vol. 2. Trans. David Fernbach. Harmondsworth: Pen-
  [1885]   guin.
  1981   *Capital,* vol. 3. Trans. David Fernbach. New York: Vintage.
  [1894]

Marx, Karl, and Fredrick Engels
  1964   The German Ideology. Trans. S. Ryazanskaya. Moscow: Pro-
  [1845   gress Publishers. A revised version appears as vol. 5 of the
  –6]   *Collected Works,* 1975ff.
  1968   *Selected Works.* New York: International Publishers.
  1975   *Collected Works.* (Publication in progress.) New York: Inter-
            national Publishers.

Mathew, David
  1948   *The Social Structure in Caroline England.* London: Oxford
            University Press.

Mathias, Peter
  1959   *The Brewing Industry in England, 1700–1830.* London:
          Cambridge University Press.
Matza, David
  1964   *Delinquency and Drift.* New York: John Wiley.
  1969   *Becoming Deviant.* Englewood Cliffs, N.J.: Prentice-Hall.
Matza, David, and Greshem Sykes
  1961   "Juvenile Delinquency and Subterranean Values." *ASR* 26:
          664–70.
Meillassoux, Claude
  1981   *Maidens, Meal and Money.* Trans. from the French. Cam-
  [1975] bridge: Cambridge University Press.
Mendels, Franklin
  1972   "Proto-Industrialization: The First Phase of the Industrializa-
          tion Process." *JEcH* 32:241–61.
Mendle, M. J.
  1973   "Politics and Political Thought 1640–1642." In *The Origins
          of the English Civil War*, ed. Conrad Russell. London: Mac-
          millan.
Merleau-Ponty, Maurice
  1970   "Western Marxism." *Telos* 6:140–61.
Merriman, Roger B.
  1938   *Six Contemporaneous Revolutions.* London: Oxford Univer-
          sity Press.
Merton, Robert
  1957   *Social Theory and Social Structure.* Rev. ed. New York: The
          Free Press.
  1964   "Anomie, Anomia and Social Interaction: Contexts of Deviant
          Behavior." In *Anomie and Deviant Behavior*, ed. Clinard.
          New York: The Free Press.
Mill, John Stuart
  1961   "On Liberty." Reprinted in *The Philosophy of John Stuart
  [1859] Mill.* New York: Modern Library.
Millward, R.
  1981   "The Emergence of Wage Labor in Early Modern England."
          Explorations in Economic History 18:21–39.
Milson, S. F. C.
  1969   *Historical Foundations of the Common Law.* London: Butter-
          worths.
Minchinton, W. E., ed.
  1968   *Essays in Agrarian History.* 2 vols. Newton Abbot: David and
          Charles.

1969   *The Growth of English Overseas Trade.* London: Methuen.

1972   *Wage Regulation in Pre-Industrial England.* Newton Abbot: David and Charles.

Mitchell, Williams M.

1957   *The Rise of the Revolutionary Party in the English House of Commons 1603–29.* New York: Columbia University Press.

Modigliani, F.

1944   "Liquidity Preference and the Theory of Interest and Money." Reprinted in 1969, *Macroeconomic Theory: Selected Readings,* ed. Williams and Huffnagle. New York: Appleton-Century-Crofts.

Moir, Thomas

1958   *The Addled Parliament of 1614.* London: Oxford University Press.

Montesquieu

1965   *The Greatness of the Romans and Their Decline.* Trans. D. Lowenthal. Ithaca: Cornell University Press.

Moore, Barrington, Jr.

1966   *Social Origins of Dictatorship and Democracy.* Boston: Beacon.

Moote, A. Lloyd

1971   *The Revolt of the Judges.* Princeton: Princeton University Press.

Morgenstern, Oskar

1965   *On the Accuracy of Economic Predictions.* 2d ed. Princeton: Princeton University Press.

Morrill, J. S.

1972   "Mutiny and Discontent in English Provincial Armies, 1645–47." *P&P* 56:49–74.

1974   *Chesire 1630–1660: County Government and Society During the English Revolution.* London: Oxford University Press.

1976   *The Revolt of the Provinces.* London: Allen and Unwin.

1977   "Provincial Squires and 'Middling Sorts' in the Great Rebellion." *THJ* 20:229–36.

1979   "The Northern Gentry and the Great Rebellion." *Northern History* 15:66–87.

1983*a*   "The Church in England, 1642–9." In *Reactions to the English Civil War, 1642–1649,* ed. Morrill. New York: St. Martin's.

1983*b*   "Introduction." In *Reactions to the English Civil War, 1642–1649,* ed. Morrill. New York: St. Martin's.

1984   "The Religious Context of the English Civil War." *TRHS* 5th ser. 34:155–178.

Morrill, J. S., ed.
  1983   *Reactions to the English Civil War, 1642–1649.* New York:
           St. Martin's.
Morton, A. L.
  1970   *The World of the Ranters.* London: Lawrence and Wishart.
Mosse, George
  1968   *Struggle for Sovereignty in England.* New York: Octagon.
  [1950]
Mousnier, Roland
  1970   *Peasant Uprisings in Seventeenth Century France, Russia and*
  [1967]   *China.* Trans. Brian Pearce. New York: Harper Torchbook.
Mueller, M. G., ed.
  1966   *Readings in Macroeconomics.* New York: Holt, Rinehart and
           Winston.
Mulligan [Glow], Lotte
  1969   "Political Affiliations in the House of Commons after Pym's
           Death." *BIHR* 38:48–70.
  1975   "Property and Parliamentary Politics in the English Civil War,
           1642–6." *Historical Studies* 16:341–61.
Neale, J. E.
  1966   *Elizabeth I and Her Parliaments 1584–1601.* New York:
  [1958]   Norton.
Nef, John
  1932   *Rise of the British Coal Industry.* London: Routledge.
  1957   *Industry and Government in France and England 1540–1640.*
  [1940]   Ithaca: Cornell University Press.
  1964   *The Conquest of the Material World.* Chicago: University of
           Chicago Press.
Newton, Arthur P.
  1966   *The Colonizing Activities of the English Puritans.* Port
  [1914]   Washington, N.Y.: Kennikat.
Nicolaus, Martin
  1967   "Proletariat and Middle Class in Marx." Reprinted in *For a*
           New America, ed. James Weinstein and David Eakins. New
           York: Vintage Books.
North, Douglas, and Robert Paul Thomas
  1973   *The Rise of the Western World.* London: Cambridge Universi-
           ty Press.
Notestein, Wallace
  1966   "The Winning of the Initiative by the House of Commons."
  [1924]   Reprinted in *Studies in History*, ed. Lucy S. Sutherland. Lon-
           don: Oxford University Press.
  1971   *The House of Commons 1604–1610.* New Haven: Yale Uni-
           versity Press.

Noyes, C. Reinold
 1936 *The Institution of Property*. New York: Longmans, Green.
Nuttall, Geoffrey
 1946 *Holy Spirit in Puritan Faith and Experience*. Oxford: Black-
    well.
 1957 *Visible Saints*. Oxford: Blackwell.
 1964 "Relations between Presbyterianism and Congregationalism
    in England." In *Studies in the Puritan Tradition* (a joint Sup-
    plement of the *Congregational Historical Society Transactions*
    and the *Presbyterian Historical Society Journal*), 1–7.
Offe, Claus
 1973 "The Abolition of Market Control and the Problem of Legi-
    timacy." Part I in *Kapitalistate 1* and Part II in *Kapitalistate 2*.
 1974 "Structural Problems of the Capitalist State." In *German
    Political Studies*, ed. Klaus von Beyme. Beverly Hills: Sage.
 1975a "Introduction to Part II[I]." In *Stress and Contradiction in
    Modern Society*, ed. Lindberg et al. Lexington, Mass.: Lexing-
    ton Books.
 1975b "The Theory of the Capitalist State and the Problem of Policy
    Formation." In *Stress and Contradiction in Modern Society*,
    ed. Lindberg et al. Lexington, Mass.: Lexington Books.
Ogg, David
 1967 *England in the Reign of Charles II*. 2d ed. London: Oxford
 [1956] University Press.
 1969 *England in the Reigns of James II and William III*. Rev. ed.
 [1955] London: Oxford University Press.
Ogilvie, Charles
 1958 *The King's Government and the Common Law, 1471–1641*.
    Oxford: Blackwell.
Okishio, Nobuo
 1961 "Technical Change and the Rate of Profit." *Kobe University
    Economics Review*. 7:85–99.
Olsh, John Lindsay
 1977 "The Growth of English Agricultural Productivity in the
    Seventeenth Century." *Social Science History* 1:460–85.
Olson, Mancur
 1971 *The Logic of Collective Action*. Cambridge: Harvard Universi-
 [1965] ty Press.
Ormrod, David
 1975 "Dutch Commercial and Industrial Decline and British
    Growth in the Late Seventeenth and Early Eighteenth Centu-
    ries." In *Failed Transitions to Modern Industrial Society*, ed.
    Krantz and Hohenberg. Montreal: Interuniversity Centre for
    European Studies.

Outhwaite, R. B.
  1969   *Inflation in Tudor and Early Stuart England.* London: Macmillan.
Overton, Mark
  1979   "Estimating Crop Yields from Probate Inventories: An Example from East Anglia, 1585–1735." *JEcH* 39:363–78.
  1984   "Agricultural Revolution: Development of the Agrarian Economy in Early Modern England." In *Explorations in Historical Geography,* ed. Baker and Gregory. Cambridge: Cambridge University Press.
Palliser, D. M.
  1982   "Tawney's Century: Brave New World or Malthusian Trap?" *EcHR,* 2d ser. 35:339–53.
Palmer, William
  1982   "Oliver St. John and the Middle Group in the Long Parliament, 1643–1645: A Reappraisal." *Albion* 14:20–26.
Parker, Geoffrey, and Lesley M. Smith, eds.
  1978   *The General Crisis of the Seventeenth Century.* London: Routledge and Kegan Paul.
Parker, William, and Eric L. Jones, eds.
  1975   *European Peasants and Their Markets.* Princeton: Princeton University Press.
Parliamentary or Constitutional History of England, The
  1761–63 2d ed. London.
Parry, R. H.
  1970   *The English Civil War and After, 1642–1658.* Berkeley, Los Angeles, London: University of California Press.
Parsons, Talcott
  1949   *The Structure of Social Action.* New York: The Free Press.
  [1937]
  1951   *The Social System.* New York: The Free Press.
  1959   "General Theory in Sociology." In *Sociology Today,* ed. Robert Merton et al. New York: Basic Books.
  1960   *Structure and Process in Modern Societies.* New York: The Free Press.
  1961a   "Culture and the Social System." In *Theories of Society,* ed. Parsons et al. New York: The Free Press.
  1961b   "An Outline of the Social System." In *Theories of Society,* ed. Parsons et al. New York: The Free Press.
  1961c   "Some Considerations on the Theory of Social Change." *Rural Sociology* 26:219–39.
  1964   *Social Structure and Personality.* New York: The Free Press.
  1966   *Societies: Comparative and Evolutionary Perspectives.* Englewood Cliffs, N.J.: Prentice-Hall.

1967   *Sociological Theory and Modern Society*. New York: The Free
            Press.
1968a   "Emile Durkheim." In *International Encyclopedia of the So-
            cial Sciences*, ed. Sills. New York: Macmillan and The Free
            Press.
1968b   "Social Systems." In *International Encyclopedia of the Social
            Sciences*, ed. Sills. New York: Macmillan and The Free Press.
1969   *Politics and Social Structure*. New York: The Free Press.
1971   *The System of Modern Societies*. Englewood Cliffs, N.J.:
            Prentice-Hall.
1977   *Social Systems and the Evolution of Action Theory*. New
            York: The Free Press.

Parsons, Talcott, et al., eds.
1961   *Theories of Society*. New York: The Free Press.

Parsons, Talcott, Robert Freed Bales, and Edward Shils
1953   *Working Papers in the Theory of Action*. New York: The Free
            Press.

Parsons, Talcott, and Gerald Platt
1970   "Age, Social Structure and Socialization in Higher Educa-
            tion." *Sociology of Education* 43 : 1–37.
1973   *The American University*. Cambridge: Harvard University
            Press.

Parsons, Talcott, and Neil Smelser
1956   *Economy and Society*. New York: The Free Press.

Patinken, Don
1951   "Price Flexibility and Full Employment." Reprinted in 1966,
            Readings in Macroeconomics, ed. Mueller. New York: Holt,
            Rinehart and Winston.
1964   *Money, Interest and Prices*. 2d ed. New York: Harper and
            Row.

Patten, John
1978   *English Towns 1500–1700*. Hamden, Conn: Shoe String
            Press.

Pearl, Valerie
1961   *London and the Outbreak of the Puritan Revolution*. London:
            Oxford University Press.
1966   "Oliver St. John and the 'middle group' in the Long Parlia-
            ment: August 1643–May 1644." *EHR* 81 : 490–519.
1968   "The 'Royal Independents' in the English Civil War." *TRHS*
            5th ser. 18 : 69–96.
1969   "London Puritans and Scotch Fifth Columnists: A Mid-
            Seventeenth Century Phenomenon." In *Studies in London His-
            tory*, ed. Hollaender and Kellaway. London: Hodder and
            Stoughton.

1970   "Exorcist or Historian: The Dangers of Ghost-Hunting."
        P&P 47:122–28.
1972   "London's Counter-Revolution." In *The Interregnum*, ed.
        Aylmer. London: Macmillan.
Pease, Theodore Calvin
1965   *The Leveller Movement.* Gloucester, Mass.: Peter Smith.
[1916]
Pennington, Donald
1954   "Communication: The Long Parliament." *P&P* 6:85–89.
1968   "The County Community at War." In *The English Revolution
        1600–1660*, ed. Ives. London: Edward Arnold.
1970   "The Rebels of 1642." In *The English Civil War and After,
        1642–1658.* Parry, ed. Berkeley, Los Angeles, London: Uni-
        versity of California Press.
Pennington, Donald, and Keith Thomas, eds.
1978   *Puritans and Revolutionaries.* Oxford: Oxford University
        Press.
Phillips, C. B.
1978   "The Royalist North: The Cumberland and Westmoreland
        Gentry, 1642–1660." *Northern History* 14:169–92.
Piaget, Jean
1962   *The Moral Judgment of the Child.* Trans. Marjorie Gabain.
[1932] New York: Collier Books.
Pinchbeck, Ivy
1981   *Women Workers and the Industrial Revolution.* London:
[1930] Virago.
Plumb, J. H.
1969a   "The Growth of the Electorate in England From 1600 to
        1715." *P&P* 45:90–116.
1969b   *The Growth of Political Stability in England 1675–1725.*
[1967] Harmondsworth: Penguin.
Plunknett, Theodore
1956   *A Concise History of the Common Law.* 5th ed. Boston: Lit-
        tle, Brown.
Pocock, J. G. A.
1967   *The Ancient Constitution and the Feudal Law.* New York:
[1957] Norton.
1975   *The Machiavellian Moment.* Princeton: Princeton University
        Press.
Pocock, J. G. A., ed.
1980   *Three British Revolutions: 1641, 1688, 1776.* Princeton: Prin-
        ceton University Press.
Porshnev, Boris
1963   *Les Soulèvenments Populaires en France de 1623 à 1648.*

[1948]   Trans. from the Russian. Paris: S.E.V.P.E.N.; partially trans-
          lated into English in 1977, *France in Crisis 1620–1675*, ed.
          Coveney. London: Macmillan.
Portman, Derek
    1974   "Vernacular Building in the Oxford Region in the Sixteenth
            and Seventeenth Centuries." In *Rural Change and Urban
            Growth 1500–1800*, ed. Chalklin and Havinden. London:
            Longman.
Poulantzas, Nicos
    1973   *Political Power and Social Classes*. Trans. Timothy O'Hagan.
    [1968]   London: New Left Books.
    1975   *Classes in Contemporary Capitalism*. Trans. David Fernbach.
    [1974]   London: New Left Books.
Prall, Stuart
    1966   *The Agitation for Law Reform during the Puritan Revolution,
            1640–1660*. The Hague: Nijhoff.
    1972   *The Bloodless Revolution*. Garden City, N.Y.: Anchor.
Prest, Wilfred R.
    1972   *The Inns of Court under Elizabeth I and the Early Stuarts
            1590–1640*. London: Longman.
Rabb, Theodore K.
    1967   *Enterprise and Empire*. Cambridge: Harvard University Press.
    1981   "Revisionism Revised: The Role of the Commons." *P&P*
            92:55–78.
Ramsay, G. D.
    1965   *The Wiltshire Woollen Industry*. 2d ed. London: Frank Cass.
    1982   *The English Woollen Industry, 1500–1750*. London: Mac-
            millan.
Ranger, Terence
    1967   "Strafford in Ireland: A Revaluation." Reprinted in *Crisis in
            Europe 1560–1660*, ed. Aston. Garden City, N.Y.: Anchor.
Ranke, Leopold von
    1875   *A History of England Principally in the Seventeenth Century*.
            6 vols. Trans. from the German. London: Oxford University
            Press.
Rey, Pierre-Philippe
    1973   *Les alliances de classes*. Paris: Maspero.
Roberts, Clayton
    1966   *The Growth of Responsible Government in Stuart England*.
            London: Cambridge University Press.
    1977   "The Earl of Bedford and the Coming of the English Revolu-
            tion." *JModH* 49:600–16.
Robertson, Roland
    1968   "Strategic Relations Between National Societies." *Journal of*

Conflict Resolution 12:16–33.

Roemer, John
    1981   *Analytical Foundations of Marxian Economic Theory.* London: Cambridge University Press.

Roots, Ivan
    1966   *Commonwealth and Protectorate.* New York: Schocken.

Rosenstock-Huessy, Eugen
    1938   *Out of Revolution.* New York: Morrow.

Roseveare, Henry
    1969   *The Treasury.* New York: Columbia University Press.
    1973   *The Treasury 1660–1870.* London: Allen and Unwin.

Rowlands, Marie
    1975   *Masters and Men in the West Midland Metalware Trades Before the Industrial Revolution.* Manchester: Manchester University Press.

Ruigh, Robert E.
    1971   *The Parliament of 1624.* Cambridge: Harvard University Press.

Rusche, Henry
    1969   "Prophecies and Propaganda, 1641–1651." *EHR* 84:752–70.

Russell, Conrad
    1971   *The Crisis of Parliaments.* London: Oxford University Press.
    1973*a*   "Introduction." In *The Origins of the English Civil War*, ed. Russell. London: Macmillan.
    1973*b*   "Parliament and the King's Finances." In *The Origins of the English Civil War*, ed. Russell. London: Macmillan.
    1976   "Parliamentary History in Perspective, 1604–1629." *History* 61:1–27.
    1979*a*   "The Parliamentary Career of John Pym, 1621–9." In *The English Commonwealth 1547–1640*, ed. Clark, Smith, and Tyacke. New York: Barnes and Noble.
    1979*b*   *Parliaments and English Politics 1621–1629.* Oxford: Oxford University Press.
    1982   "Monarchies, War and Estates in England, France, and Spain, c. 1580–1640." *Legislative Sciences Quarterly* 7:205–20.
    1984   "The Nature of Parliament in Early Stuart England." In *Before the Civil War*, ed. Tomlinson. New York: St. Martin's.

Russell, Conrad, ed.
    1973   *The Origins of the English Civil War.* London: Macmillan.

Salmon, J. H. M.
    1959   *The French Religious Wars in English Political Thought.* London: Oxford University Press.
    1967   "Venality of Office and Popular Sedition in Seventeenth Century France." *P&P* 37:21–43.

Salvadori, Neri
   1981   "Falling rate of profit with a constant real wage. An Exam-
             ple." *Cambridge Journal of Economics* 5:59–66.
Samuelson, Paul
   1939   "Interactions between Multiplier Analysis and the Principle of
             Acceleration." Reprinted in 1966, *Readings in Macroeconom-
             ics*, ed. Mueller. New York: Holt, Rinehart and Winston.
   1965   *Foundations of Economic Analysis.* New York: Atheneum.
   [1947]
Schenk, W.
   1948   *The Concern for Social Justice in the Puritan Revolution.* Lon-
             don: Longman.
Schlatter, Richard
   1951   *Private Property: The History of an Idea.* New Brunswick:
             Rutgers University Press.
Schochet, Gordon
   1969   "Patriarchalism, Politics and Mass Attitudes in Stuart Eng-
             land." *THJ* 12:413–41.
   1975   *Patriarchalism in Political Thought.* New York: Basic
             Books.
Schofield, R. S.
   1965   "The Geographical Distribution of Wealth in England, 1334–
             1649." *EcHR* 2d ser. 18:483–510.
   1975   "Quantitative Analysis of the Long Parliament." *P&P*
             68:124–29.
Schultze, Charles
   1959   Recent Inflation in the United States. Study Paper 1, U.S. Con-
             gress Joint Economic Committee, Study of Employment,
             Growth, and Price Levels.
   1967   National Income Analysis. 2d ed. Englewood Cliffs, N.J.:
             Prentice-Hall.
Schumpeter, Elizabeth
   1960   *English Overseas Trade Statistics, 1697–1808.* Oxford: Ox-
             ford University Press.
Schumpeter, Joseph
   1949   *Theory of Economic Development.* Trans. R. Opie. New
   [1934]   York: Oxford University Press.
Schwoerer, Lois
   1971   "'The Fittest Subject for A King's Quarrel': An Essay on the
             Militia Controversy 1641–1642." *JBS* 11:45–76.
Scott, William Robert
   1968   *The Constitution and Finance of English, Scottish and Irish
   [1912]   Joint-Stock Companies to 1720.* 3 vols. Gloucester, Mass.:
             Peter Smith.

Seaver, Paul S.
  1970   *The Puritan Lectureships*. Stanford: Stanford University Press.
Seaver, Paul S., ed.
  1976   *Seventeenth-Century England*. New York: Franklin Watts.
Selvin, Hannan
  1957   "Durkheim's Suicide and the Problems of Empirical Re-
          search." *AJS* 63:607–19. Reprinted in a revised version in
          Emile Durkheim, ed. Robert Nisbet. Englewood Cliffs, N.J.:
          Prentice-Hall, 1965.
Selznick, Philip
  1960   *The Organizational Weapon*. New York: The Free Press.
  [1952]
Shaikh, Anwar
  1978   "Political economy and capitalism: notes on Dobb's theory of
          crisis." *Cambridge Journal of Economics* 2:233–51.
  1980   "Marxian competition versus perfect competition: further
          comments on the so-called choice of technique." *Cambridge
          Journal of Economics* 4:75–83.
Shakle, G. L. S.
  1961   "Recent Theories Concerning the Rate of Interest." Reprinted
          in 1966, *Monetary Theory and Policy*, ed. Thorne. New York:
          Random House.
Sharp, Buchanan
  1980   *In Contempt of All Authority: Rural Artisans and Riot in the
          West of England, 1586–1660*. Berkeley, Los Angeles, Lon-
          don: University of California Press.
Sharpe, Kevin
  1984   "The Personal Rule of Charles I." In *Before the Civil War*, ed.
          Tomlinson. New York: St. Martin's.
Sharpe, Kevin, ed.
  1978   *Faction and Parliament: Essays on Early Stuart History*.
          Oxford: Oxford University Press.
Shaw, Howard
  1968   *The Levellers*. London: Longman.
Shaw, William A.
  1900   *A History of the English Church During the Civil Wars and
          Under the Commonwealth 1640–1660*. 2 vols. London:
          Longman.
Sherwood, R. E.
  1974   *Civil Strife in the Midlands, 1642–51*. London: Phillimore.
Shils, Edward
  1961   "Centre and Periphery." In *The Logic of Personal Knowledge:
          Essays Presented to Michael Polanyi*. London: Routledge and
          Kegan Paul.

1965   "Charisma, Order and Status." *ASR* 30:199–213.

Short, James F., Jr., and Fred C. Strodback
1965   *Group Process and Gang Delinquency.* Chicago: University of
        Chicago Press.

Sills, David, ed.
1968   *International Encyclopedia of the Social Sciences.* New York:
        Macmillan and The Free Press.

Simpson, Alan
1961   *The Wealth of the Gentry, 1540–1660.* Chicago: University of
        Chicago Press.

Skinner, Quentin
1965   "History and Ideology in the English Revolution." *THJ* 8:51–
        78.
1972   "Conquest and Consent: Thomas Hobbes and the Engage-
        ment Controversy." In *The Interregnum*, ed. Aylmer. London:
        Macmillan.
1978   *The Foundations of Modern Political Thought.* 2 vols. Cam-
        bridge: Cambridge University Press.

Skipp, Victor
1978   *Crisis and Development.* London: Cambridge University
        Press.

Skocpol, Theda
1977   "Wallerstein's World Capitalist System: A Theoretical and
        Historical Critique." *AJS* 82:1075–89.
1979   *States and Social Revolutions.* Cambridge: Cambridge Uni-
        versity Press.

Slater, G.
1907   *The English Peasantry and the Enclosure of Common Fields.*
        London: Constable.

Slicher van Bath, B. H.
1963   *The Agrarian History of Western Europe A.D. 500–1850.*
        London: Edward Arnold.

Smelser, Neil
1959   *Social Change in the Industrial Revolution.* Chicago: Universi-
        ty of Chicago Press.
1962   *Theory of Collective Behavior.* New York: The Free Press.
1968   *Essays in Sociological Explanation.* Englewood Cliffs, N.J.:
        Prentice-Hall.
1969   "Some Personal Thoughts on the Pursuit of Sociological Prob-
        lems." *Sociological Inquiry* 39:155–68.
1971   "Stability, Instability and the Analysis of Political Corrup-
        tion." In *Stability and Social Change*, ed. Bernard Barber and
        Alex Inkeles. Boston: Little, Brown.

Smith, C. T.
1978   *An Historical Geography of Western Europe before 1800.*
[1967]   Rev. ed. London: Longman.
Smith, Page
1973   "Intelligence Systems Can Never Work." *Philadelphia Inquir-
er,* 29 August.
Smith, Richard
1984   "'Modernization' and the Corporate Medieval Village Community in England." In *Explorations in Historical Geography,*
ed. Alan Baker and Derek Gregory. Cambridge: Cambridge
University Press.
Smith, W., and R. Teigen, eds.
1965   *Readings in Money, National Income and Stabilization Policy.*
Homewood, Ill.: Irwin.
Snow, Vernon
1962   "Essex and the Aristocratic Opposition to the Early Stuarts."
JModH 32:224–33.
1970   *Essex the Rebel.* Lincoln: University of Nebraska Press.
Social Mobility: A Conference Report
1965   *P&P* 32:3–11.
Solt, Leo F.
1959   *Saints in Arms: Puritanism and Democracy in Cromwell's
Army.* Stanford: Stanford University Press.
Sorel, Georges
1961   *Reflections on Violence.* Trans. T. E. Hulme and J. Roth. New
[1906]   York: Collier Books.
Spalding, James
1967   "Sermons before Parliament (1640–49) as a Public Puritan
Diary." *Church History* 36:24–35.
Spufford, Margaret
1974   *Contrasting Communities: English Villagers in the Sixteenth
and Seventeenth Centuries.* London: Cambridge University
Press.
Sraffa, Piero
1960   *Production of Commodities by Means of Commodities.* Cambridge: Cambridge University Press.
Steedman, Ian
1977   *Marx After Sraffa.* London: New Left Books.
1980   "A note on the 'choice of technique' under capitalism." *Cambridge Journal of Economics* 4:61–64.
Stephens, W. B.
1958   *Seventeenth-Century Exeter.* Exeter: University of Exeter
Press.

1969   "The Cloth Exports of the Provincial Ports, 1600–1640."
        EcHR 2d ser. 22:228–48.
1971   "Further Observations on English Cloth Exports, 1600–
        1640." *EcHR* 2d ser. 24:253–57.
Stevens, S. S.
1968   "Measurement, Statistics and the Schemparic View." *Science*
        161:849–56.
Stevenson, David
1973   *The Scottish Revolution 1637–1644*. Newton Abbot: David
        and Charles.
Stone, Katherine
1974   "The Origins of Job Structures in the Steel Industry." *Review
        of Radical Political Economics* 6:113–73.
Stone, Lawrence
1964   "The Educational Revolution in England, 1560–1640." *P&P*
        28:41–80.
1965a   *Crisis of the Aristocracy*. London: Oxford University Press.
1965b   "Introduction." In *Social Change and Revolution in England
        1540–1640*, ed. Stone. London: Longmans.
1966   "Social Mobility in England, 1500–1700." *P&P* 33:16–55.
1967   *Crisis of the Aristocracy*. Abridged ed. London: Oxford Uni-
        versity Press.
1972a   *The Causes of the English Revolution 1529–1642*. London:
        Routledge and Kegan Paul.
1972b   "Counting Manors Again: a Reply to Mr. Thompson." *EcHR*
        2d ser. 25:131–36.
1974   "A Reply [to Koenigsberger]." *JModH* 46:106–12.
1977   *The Family, Sex and Marriage In England 1500–1800*. Lon-
        don: Weidenfeld and Nicolson.
1980   "The Results of the English Revolutions of the Seventeenth
        Century." In *Three British Revolutions: 1641, 1688, 1776*, ed.
        Pocock. Princeton: Princeton University Press.
1983   "Interpersonal Violence in English Society 1300–1980." *P&P*
        101:22–33.
Stone, Lawrence, ed.
1965   *Social Change and Revolution in England 1540–1640*. Lon-
        don: Longmans.
Stone, Lawrence, and Jeanne C. Fawtier Stone
1984   *An Open Elite? England 1540–1880*. Oxford: Oxford Uni-
        versity Press.
Sullivan, Richard
1985   "The Timing and Pattern of Technological Development in
        English Agriculture, 1611–1850." *JEcH* 45:305–14.

Supple, Barry

    1959   *Commercial Crisis and Change in England 1600–1642*. London: Cambridge University Press.

    1968   "Class and Social Tension: The Case of the Merchant." In *The English Revolution 1600–1660*, ed. Ives. London: Edward Arnold.

    1977   "The Nature of Enterprise." In *The Cambridge Economic History of Europe*, vol. 5, ed. E. E. Rich and C. H. Wilson. Cambridge: Cambridge University Press.

Sutherland, Edwin H.

    1956   *The Sutherland Papers*. Ed. Albert Cohen, Alfred Lindesmith, and Karl Schuessler. Bloomington: Indiana University Press.

Sutherland, Lucy S.

    1966   *Studies in History*. London: Oxford University Press.

Swart, Koenraad Wolter

    1949   *Sale of Offices in the Seventeenth Century*. The Hague: Marinus Nijhoff.

Sweezy, Paul, and Harry Magdorf

    1971   "Review of the Month: Peaceful Transition to Socialism?" *Monthly Review* 22:1–18.

Sykes, Greshem, and David Matza

    1957   "Techniques of Neutralization: A Theory of Delinquency." *ASR* 22:664–70.

Takahashi, Kohachiro

    1976   "A Contribution to the Discussion." Reprinted in *The Transi-*
    [1952] *tion from Feudalism to Capitalism*, Dobb et. al. London: New Left Books.

Tanner, J. R.

    1928   *English Constitutional Conflicts of the Seventeenth Century 1603–89*. London: Cambridge University Press.

Tawney, A. J., and R. H. Tawney

    1934   "An Occupational Census of the Seventeenth Century." *EcHR* 5:25–64.

Tawney, R. H.

    1947   *Religion and the Rise of Capitalism*. New York: Mentor.
    [1926]

    1954*a*   "The Rise of the Gentry." Reprinted in *Essays in Economic*
    [1941] *History*, vol. 1, ed. Carus-Wilson. New York: St. Martin's.

    1954*b*   "The Rise of the Gentry: A Postscript." *EcHR* 2d ser. 7:91–97.

    1962   "Introduction." In *A Discourse upon Usury*, Thomas Wilson, ed. R. H. Tawney. London: Frank Cass.

    1967   *The Agrarian Problem in the Seventeenth Century*. New York:

[1912]   Harper Torchbooks.
1972   "The Assessment of Wage in England by the Justices of the
        Peace." Reprinted in *Wage Regulation in Pre-Industrial Eng-
        land*, ed. Minchinton. Newton Abbot: David and Charles.
Teigen, R.
1965   "The Demand for and Supply of Money." In *Readings in
        Money, National Income and Stabilization Policy*, ed. Smith
        and Teigen. Homewood, Ill.: Irwin.
Terray, Emmanuel
1972   *Marxism and 'Primitive' Societies*. Trans. Mary Klopper. New
[1969]   York: Monthly Review Press.
Thirsk, Joan
1958   *Tudor Enclosures*. London: Historical Association.
1961   "Industries in the Countryside." In *Essays in the Economic
        and Social History of Tudor and Stuart England*, ed. Fisher.
        Cambridge: Cambridge University Press.
1963   "Introduction," to A. H. Johnson, *The Disappearance of the
        Small Landowner*. London: Merlin Press.
1967   "Enclosing and Engrossing." In *The Agrarian History of Eng-
        land and Wales*, vol. 4, ed. Thirsk. Cambridge: Cambridge
        University Press.
1973   "The Fantastical Folly of Fashion: The English Stocking Knit-
        ting Industry, 1500–1700." In *Textile History and Economic
        History*, ed. Harte and Ponting. Manchester: Manchester Uni-
        versity Press.
1976   "Seventeenth Century Agriculture and Social Change." Re-
[1970]   printed in *Seventeenth-Century England*, ed. Seaver. New
        York: Franklin Watts.
1978   *Economic Policy and Projects*. Oxford: Oxford University
        Press.
1985a   "Agricultural Innovations and Their Diffusion." In *The Agra-
        rian History of England and Wales*, vol. 5, ed. Thirsk. Cam-
        bridge: Cambridge University Press.
1985b   "Agricultural Policy: Public Debate and Legislation." In *The
        Agrarian History of England and Wales*, vol. 5, ed. Thirsk.
        Cambridge: Cambridge University Press.
1985c   "Introduction [to Part I]." In *The Agrarian History of England
        and Wales*, vol. 5, ed. Thirsk. Cambridge: Cambridge Uni-
        versity Press.
1985d   "Market Gardening in England and Wales." In *The Agrarian
        History of England and Wales*, vol. 5, ed. Thirsk. Cambridge:
        Cambridge University Press.
Thirsk, Joan, ed.
1967   *The Agrarian History of England and Wales*. Vol. 4 *1500–*

1640. Cambridge: Cambridge University Press.

1985 *The Agrarian History of England and Wales.* Vol. 5 (in two parts), *1640–1750*. Cambridge: Cambridge University Press.

Thomas, David

1984 "Financial and Administrative Developments." In *Before the Civil War*, ed. Tomlinson. New York: St. Martin's.

Thomas, Keith

1964 "Work and Leisure in Pre-Industrial Society." *P&P* 29:50–63.

1967 "Women and the Civil War Sects." Reprinted in *Crisis in Europe 1560–1660*, ed. Aston. Garden City, N.Y.: Anchor.

1971 *Religion and the Decline of Magic.* New York: Scribners.

1972 "The Levellers and the Franchise." In *The Interregnum*, ed. Aylmer. London: Macmillan.

Thomas, R. P., and D. N. McClosky

1981 "Overseas trade and empire 1700–1860: a survey." In *The Economic History of Britain Since 1700*, ed. R. Floud and Donald McClosky. Cambridge: Cambridge University Press.

Thompson, Christopher

1972 "The Origins of the Politics of the Parliamentary Middle Group, 1625–1629." *TRHS* 5th ser. 22:71–86.

Thompson, E. P.

1963 *The Making of the English Working Class.* New York: Vintage Books.

1967 "Time, Work-Discipline and Industrial Capitalism." *P&P* 38:56–97.

1971 "The Moral Economy of the English Crowd in the Eighteenth Century." *P&P* 50:76–136.

1976 "The grid of inheritance: a comment." In *Family and Inheritance*, ed. Goody et al. London: Cambridge University Press.

Thompson, F. M. L.

1966 "The Social Distribution of Landed Property in England since the Sixteenth Century." *EcHR* 2d ser. 19:505–17.

Thorne, R., ed.

1966 *Monetary Theory and Policy.* New York: Random House.

Thorner, Daniel

1962 "Peasant Economy as a Category in Economic History." In *Second International Conference of Economic History*, vol. 2. Paris: Mouton.

Tilly, Charles

1973 "Do Communities Act?" *Sociological Inquiry* 43:209–40.

1975 "Revolution and Collective Violence." In *Handbook of Political Science*, vol. 3, *Macropolitical Theory*, ed. Fred I. Greenstein and Nelson Polsby. Reading, Mass.: Addison-Wesley.

484

Bibliography

1978　　*From Mobilization to Revolution.* Reading, Mass.: Addison-Wesley.

1984　　"Demographic Origins of the European Proletariat." In *Proletarianization and Family History*, ed. Levine. Orlando, Fla.: Academic.

Tite, Colin

1974　　*Impeachment and Parliamentary Judicature in Early Stuart England.* London: Athlone.

Tobin, James

1947　　"Money Wage Rates and Employment." Reprinted in 1966, *Readings in Macroeconomics*, ed. Mueller. New York: Holt, Rinehart and Winston. Also reprinted in 1969, *Macroeconomic Theory: Selected Readings*, ed. Williams and Haffnagle. New York: Appleton-Century-Crofts.

Tomlinson, Howard, ed.

1984　　*Before the Civil War.* New York: St. Martin's.

Trevor-Roper, H. R.

1953　　The Gentry 1540–1640. EcHR Supplement 1.

1962　　*Archbishop Laud: 1573–1645.* Hamden, Conn.: Archon.
[1940]

1967a　　"The General Crisis of the Seventeenth Century." Reprinted in *Crisis in Europe 1560–1660*, ed. Aston. Garden City, N.Y.: Anchor.

1967b　　"[Reply]." Reprinted in *Crisis in Europe 1560–1660*, ed. Aston. Garden City, N.Y.: Anchor.

1968　　*The Crisis of the Seventeenth Century.* New York: Harper and Row.

Tribe, Keith

1977　　"Economic property and the theorization of ground rent." *Economy and Society* 6:69–88.

Troeltsch, Ernst

1960　　*The Social Teachings of the Christian Churches.* 2 vols. Trans.
[1911]　　Olive Wyon. New York: Harper Torchbooks.

Trotsky, Leon

1967　　*History of the Russian Revolution.* 3 vols. Trans. Max East-
[1930]　　man. London: Sphere Books.

Tuck, Richard

1974　　"Power and Authority in Seventeenth Century England." *THJ* 17:43–61.

1979　　*Natural Rights Theories: Their Origin and Development.* Cambridge: Cambridge University Press.

Tyake, Nicholas

1973　　"Puritanism, Arminianism and Counter-Revolution." In *The*

         Origins of the English Civil War, ed. Russell London: Macmillan.

Underdown, David

1964   "Independents Reconsidered." *JBS* 3:57–84.

1968*a*   "The Independents Again." *JBS* 8:83–93.

1968*b*   "Party management in the recruiter elections, 1645–1648." *EHR* 83:135–64.

1970   "The Presbyterian Independents Exorcized: A Brief Comment." *P&P* 47:128–30.

1971   *Pride's Purge.* London: Oxford University Press.

1973   *Somerset in the Civil War and Interregnum.* Newton Abbot: David and Charles.

1978   "'Honest' Radicals in the Counties 1642–1649." In *Puritans and Revolutionaries*, ed. Pennington and Thomas. Oxford: Oxford University Press.

1979   "The Chalk and the Cheese: Contrasts Among the English Clubmen." *P&P* 85:25–48.

1980   "Community and Class: Theories of Local Politics in the English Revolution." In *After the Reformation*, ed. Malamet. Philadelphia: University of Pennsylvania Press.

1981   "The Problem of Popular Allegiance in the English Civil War." *TRHS*, 5th ser. 31:69–94.

1985   *Revel, Riot, and Rebellion: Popular Politics and Culture in England 1603–1660.* Oxford: Clarendon Press.

Unwin, George

1957   *Industrial Organization in the Sixteenth and Seventeenth Cen-*
[1904] *turies.* 2nd ed. London: Cass.

1958   *Studies in Economic History.* 2d ed. Ed. R. H. Tawney. New York: Kelley.

Usher, Roland G.

1968   *The Rise and Fall of the High Commission.* London: Oxford
[1913] University Press.

Van Parijs, Philippe

1980   "The Falling-Rate-of Profit Theory of Crisis: A Rational Reconstruction by Way of Obituary." *Review of Radical Political Economics* 12:1–17.

Veall, Donald

1970   *The Popular Movement for Law Reform 1640–1660.* London: Oxford University Press.

Vries, Jan de

1972   "Labor/Leisure Trade-off." *Peasant Studies Newsletter* 1.

1974   *The Dutch Rural Economy in the Golden Age, 1500–1700.* New Haven: Yale University Press.

1976   *The Economy of Europe in an Age of Crisis, 1600–1750.* London: Cambridge University Press.

Wadsworth, Alfred, and Julia De Lacy Mann
1968   *The Cotton Trade and Industrial Lancashire 1600–1780.*
[1965]   New York: Kelley.

Wagner, Donald O.
1935   "Coke and the Rise of Economic Liberalism." *EcHR* 6:30–44.

Wallerstein, Immanuel
1974   *The Modern World-System.* New York: Academic Press.
1980   *The Modern World-System II.* New York: Academic Press.

Walter, John, and Keith Wrightson
1976   "Dearth and the Social Order in Early Modern England." *P&P* 71:22–42.

Walzer, Michael
1968   *Revolution of the Saints.* New York: Atheneum.
[1965]
1974   *Regicide and Revolution.* London: Cambridge University Press.

Wanklyn, M. D. G., and Brigadier P. Young
1981   "A King in Search of Soldiers: Charles I in 1642: A Rejoinder." *THJ* 24:147–54.

Weber, Max
1946   *From Max Weber: Essays in Sociology.* Trans. and ed. H. H. Gerth and C. Wright Mills. New York: Oxford University Press.
1958   *The Protestant Ethic and the Spirit of Capitalism.* Trans.
[1904–5] Talcott Parsons. New York: Scribners.
1961   *General Economic History.* Trans. Frank Knight. New York:
[1923]   Collier.
1968   *Economy and Society.* 3 vols. Ed. Guenther Roth and Claus
[1925]   Wittich. Trans. various. Kansas: Bedminster.
1976   *The Agrarian Sociology of Ancient Civilizations.* Trans. R. I.
[1909]   Frank. London: New Left Books.
1978   "Anticritical Last Word on *The Spirit of Capitalism*." Trans.
[1910]   Wallace M. Davis. *American Journal of Sociology.* 83:1110–31.

Wedgwood, C. V.
1966a   *A Coffin for King Charles.* New York: Time-Life Books.
[1964]
1966b   *The King's Peace.* London: Fontana.
1966c   *The King's War.* London: Fontana.

Western, J. R.
1972   *Monarchy and Revolution.* London: Blandford.

Weston, Corinne Comstock
1965   *English Constitutional Theory and the House of Lords, 1556–1832.* New York: Columbia University Press.
Weston, Corinne, and Janelle Greenberg
1981   *Subjects and Sovereigns: The Grand Controversy over Legal Sovereignty in Stuart England.* Cambridge: Cambridge University Press.
White, Peter
1983   "The Rise of Arminianism Reconsidered." *P&P* 101:34–54.
White, Stephen
1979a   "Observations on Early Stuart Parliamentary History." *JBS* 18:160–70.
1979b   *Sir Edward Coke and 'The Grievances of the Commonwealth,' 1621–1628.* Chapel Hill: University of North Carolina Press.
Willan, T. S.
1938   *The English Coasting Trade 1600–1750.* Manchester: Manchester University Press.
1964   *River Navigation in England 1600–1750.* London: Frank Cass.
1976   *The Inland Trade.* Totowa, N.J.: Rowan and Littlefield.
Willcox, William Bradford
1940   *Gloucestershire: A Study in Local Government 1590–1640.* New Haven: Yale University Press.
Williams, H., and J. D. Huffnagle, eds.
1969   *Macroeconomic Theory: Selected Readings.* New York: Appleton-Century-Crofts.
Williams, Raymond
1973   "Base and Superstructure in Marxist Cultural Theory." *New Left Review* 82:3–16.
Wilson, Charles
1965   *England's Apprenticeship 1603–1763.* London: Longmans.
1969   *Economic History and the Historian.* New York: Praeger.
1979   "A Letter to Professor McCloskey." *Journal of European Economic History* 8:193–201.
Wilson, John F.
1969   *Pulpit in Parliament.* Princeton: Princeton University Press.
Wilson, R. G.
1971   *Gentlemen Merchants: The merchant community in Leeds 1700–1830.* New York: Kelley.
Wilson, Thomas
1962   *A Discourse upon Usury.* Ed. R. H. Tawney. London: Frank
[1572] Cass. First Tawney edition, 1925.

Wolf, Klaus
    1963   "Stages In Industrial Organization." *Explorations in Entre-
            preneurial History* 2d ser. 1:125–44.
Wolfe, Don M., ed.
    1944   *Leveller Manifestoes of the Puritan Revolution.* New York:
            Nelson.
Wood, Alfred C.
    1971   *Nottinghamshire in the Civil War.* East Ardsley, Wakefield,
    [1937]   Yorkshire: S. R. Publishers.
Woodhouse, A. S. P., ed.
    1938   *Puritanism and Liberty.* London: Dent.
Woodward, Donald
    1971   "Agricultural Revolution in England 1500–1900: A Survey."
            Local Historian 9:323–33.
    1981   "Wage Rates and Living Standards in Pre-industrial England."
            P&P 91:28–46.
Woolf, Stuart
    1970   "The Aristocracy in Transition: A Continental Comparison."
            EcHR 2d ser. 23:520–31.
Woolrych, Austin
    1968   "The English Revolution: an Introduction." In *The Eng-
            lish Revolution 1600–1660,* ed. Ives. London: Edward
            Arnold.
    1970   "Oliver Cromwell and the Rule of the Saints." In *The English
            Civil War and After, 1642–1658,* ed. Parry. Berkeley, Los
            Angeles, London: University of California Press.
    1980   "Court, Country and City Revisited." *History* 65:236–245.
    1982   *Commonwealth to Protectorate.* Oxford: Oxford University
            Press.
Worden, Blair
    1974   *The Rump Parliament.* London: Cambridge University Press.
Wordie, J. R.
    1983   "The Chronology of English Enclosure, 1500–1914." *EcHR*
            2d ser. 36:483–505.
    1984   "The Chronology of English Enclosure: A Reply [to Chap-
            man]." *EcHR* 2d ser. 37:560–62.
Wormald, B. H. G.
    1951   *Clarendon: Politics, History and Religion 1640–1660.* Lon-
            don: Cambridge University Press.
Wormuth, Francis
    1939   *The Royal Prerogative, 1603–49.* Ithaca: Cornell University
            Press.
Wrightson, Keith
    1982   *English Society 1580–1680.* London: Hutchinson.

Wrightson, Keith, and David Levine
    1979   *Poverty and Piety in an English Village, Terling, 1525–1700.*
            New York: Academic.
Wrigley, E. A.
    1967   "A Simple Model of London's Importance in Changing Eng-
            lish Society and Economy 1650–1750." *P&P* 37:44–70.
    1972   "The Process of Modernization and the Industrialization of
            England." *Journal of Interdisciplinary History* 3:225–60.
Wrigley, E. A., and R. S. Schofield
    1981   *The Population History of England 1541–1871.* Cambridge:
            Harvard University Press.
Yablonsky, Lewis
    1966   *The Violent Gang.* Baltimore: Penguin.
    [1962]
Yamamura, Kozo
    1979   "Pre-Industrial Landholding Patterns in Japan and England."
            In *Japan: A Comparative View*, ed. Albert Craig. Princeton:
            Princeton University Press.
Yelling, J. A.
    1977   *Common Field and Enclosure in England 1450–1850.* Ham-
            den, Conn.: Archon.
    1982   "Rationality in the Common Fields." *EcHR* 35:409–15.
Yinger, Milton J.
    1960   "Contraculture and Subculture." *ASR* 25:625–35.
Yule, George
    1958   *The Independents in the English Civil War.* London: Cam-
            bridge University Press.
    1968   "Independents and Revolutionaries." *JBS* 7:11–32.
    1970   "The Presbyterian Independents Exorcised: A Brief Com-
            ment." *P&P* 47:130–33.
Zagorin, Perez
    1954   *A History of Political Thought in the English Revolution.* Lon-
            don: Routledge and Kegan Paul.
    1969   *The Court and the Country: The Beginning of the English
            Revolution.* London: Routledge and Kegan Paul.
    1982   *Rebels and Rulers 1500–1660.* 2 vols. Cambridge: Cambridge
            University Press.
Zaller, Robert
    1971   *The Parliament of 1621.* Berkeley, Los Angeles, and London:
            University of California Press.
    1980   "The Concept of Opposition in Early Stuart England." *Albion*
            12:211–34.
    1983   "Edward Alford and the Making of County Radicalism." *JBS*
            22:59–79.

Index

Absolutism, 190, 191–192, 267–268
Accelerators. *See* Precipitating factors
Accumulation. *See* Capital, accumulation of
Action, xviii, xxiv, 8, 339; human, 12; rational, 132–133, 354; social, 9, 10, 241. *See also* Revolutionary actions
Act of Revocation (1625), 203
Aggression, deviant, 76, 77, 366
Agriculture, 139, 143; capital accumulation in, 151, 153–154; Charles I on, 202; class differentiation in, 160; commercialized, 247–248; competition in, 150–151, 152, 154; consolidation in, 153–154; crises in, 146–147, 152–154, 162; debt in, 152, 159; grain production in, 162–163; industry and, 161–162, 163; inflation in, 148–149; innovation in, 145, 146, 151; landowning separate from, 137–138; manufacture in, 122–123, 124, 135–136, 137, 144–146, 153–154; prices in, 148–149, 150; productivity in, 144–146, 162–163; prosperity in, 148–149; revolution in, 137–138, 150–151, 163; surplus profits in, 147–148; wages in, 149. *See also* Enclosure

Alienation, political, 46, 47, 49, 50, 54, 56, 57
Allocation: of resources, 11, 21–22, 24, 25, 31, 32, 39, 45–46, 76; of surplus, 26, 212
Ambiguity, 76–77, 391–392 n. 47
Amin, Samir, 152–153
Anglo-Catholicism, 324, 325
Anomie, 71, 73, 74
Antler, Steven D., 250
Anxiety, 112, 244, 245, 251
Arendt, Hanna, 100, 381 n. 51
Aristocracy. *See* Nobility; Peers
Arminianism, 324, 325
Army: authority of, 306; and Charles I, 231, 237, 238, 302–304, 412–413 n. 23; Clarendon on, 301; control of, 237, 238, 263, 265, 267, 276–277, 294, 301, 412–413 n. 23; Declaration of, 303, 305; on divine providence, 294, 305; Heads of Proposals of, 302, 303; and Independents, 293, 301; New Model, 300–301; Parliament's, 237–238, 263, 265, 267, 412–413 n. 23; v. Parliament, 292–294, 295, 301–302; on popular sovereignty, 294, 305; recruitment of, 242; Remonstrance of, 293–294, 303–304, 305
Ascham, Anthony, 307
Ashton, Robert, 203, 205, 252, 407–408 n. 10

State, xviii, 44. *See also* Government; Patrimonialism/patrimonial polity; Polity

Status, 83; anxiety, 244, 245, 251; inconsistency, 111, 297, 298; of M.P.s, 296–297; and office-holding, 245–246; and REVON, 296–297

Stone, Lawrence, 105, 142, 246, 262, 269, 276; on agriculture, 247–248; on class mobility, 245, 256; on court, 204–205, 215–216; on gentry, 243–244; on lawyers, 260; on Parliament, 195, 258; on peers, 208, 258; on Puritans, 230, 259, 285

Strafford, Earl of (Thomas Wentworth), 195, 196, 203, 264, 267

Strain: and deviance, 71, 72, 73, 76, 77, 78; facility, 74–75, 76, 95–96, 195–208, 209, 219, 252; at goals (*see* Goal strain); and internal disorder, 66–68; and juvenile delinquency, 71, 72; location of, 68, 73–76; at norms, 76–77, 97, 291, 297, 298–299, 303–304; response to, 68, 71–72, 73–74, 75, 76, 95–99, 208–209; and retreatism, 72; and revolutionary actions, 94–99; role, 76–77; society controls, 90; structural, 71–78, 94–99; at value level, 72, 77–78, 97–99, 321–322

Structure, 392–393 n. 1; analyzed, 3–5; compatable, 115; model of, 116–118; strain on, 71–78, 94–99; theory of, 337–338. *See also* Society, structures in

Stuarts, 172, 190, 202–203. *See also* Charles I; Charles II; James I; James II

Subculture: counter-, 66; criminal, 71, 72; deviant, 79, 80, 81, 89; of deviancy, 80–81, 89; retreatist,

71, 72; revolutionary, 99, 100, 101, 109, 111–112, 211, 270; of revolution, 99, 100, 101, 102–103, 109, 211, 270, 304–305; socialization into, 79–80

Supple, Barry, 157, 159, 204, 252, 254–255, 271

Surplus value, xiv, 25, 45; absolute, 122, 123, 125, 126, 127; allocated, 26, 212; in capitalism, 122, 127–129; determinants of, 149; extracted, 115, 123, 125, 126, 128–129, 141–142, 364; increases, 126, 127; iterative, 126, 127, 129, 130, 133, 180; of labor, 119, 120, 121; in manufacture, 122; Marx on, 121–122, 127–128, 129; relative, 115, 122, 123, 125, 126, 127

Sutherland, Edwin H., 79–80

System, 5, 392–393 n. 1; analysis of, 16–63

Tawney, R. H., 149, 154–155, 253

Taxation, 46, 170, 199, 212; as corruption, 215; king's power to, 191, 192; and legitimacy, 213–214; as polity input, 46; and revolution, 199, 233

Textiles, 156–157, 158, 159, 160

Thirsk, Joan, 144–145, 158

Thomas, Keith, 319, 330

Thomason tracts, 100, 289

Thompson, Christopher, 288

Thrift. *See* Paradox of thrift

Tilly, Charles, 92, 93, 112

Tower of London, 196, 265, 266

Tradition, 311–312, 354, 429 n. 26; legitimizes, 221–222; in patrimonial polity, 114, 170, 172; Puritans on, 222–223; in values, 168, 170, 172

Trevor-Roper, H. R., 233

Triennial Act, 194, 332

Triggers. *See* Precipitating factors
Tudors, 172, 190, 256
Tunnage and poundage, 192, 193, 195, 200

Underdown, David, 241–242; on gentry, 247, 296–297; on M.P.s, 295, 296–299, 308–309, 310; on Puritans, 285; on revolutionaries, 292, 308; on second civil war, 293; on support for Parliament, 247, 304, 305, 308
Universals, xiii, 4, 16, 60, 64, 118
Urban development, 248. *See also* London
Usury, 124, 158

Valorization process, 120, 180. *See also* Surplus value
Value, 323; -added model, 69–71; attacked, 315; commitment, 17, 78, 107–108, 134, 387 n. 26; generalization, 352; of "Independents," 311–312; of labor, 46, 119, 120, 121, 364; legitimizes, 8; Levellers on, 315; and loyalty, 84; money as, 371–372 n. 7; v. norms, 6, 8, 10; orientation, 361–362; rationalizing, 181; strain, 72, 77–78, 97–99, 321–322; traditional, 168, 170, 172; use-, 128
Violence: and dissonance, 108; legitimized, 108–109; in revolution, 92, 177

Wage, 156; agricultural, 149; labor, 135–141, 142–143, 248

Waller's Plot, 275
Wallerstein, Immanuel, xxiv
Walzer, Michael, 217, 221, 223, 251, 274, 286
Weber, Max, 8, 107, 345, 359; on calculation, 170, 171; on capitalism, 131–135; on patrimonial polity, 168–172; on Protestant Ethic, 131–135, 187; on rationalization, 132–133, 171; on social transformation, 70; on tradition, 170
Wedgwood, C. V., 193, 213, 219, 327
Western, J. R., 359
Weston, Corinne, 224–225
Wilson, Charles, 160, 192, 254
Winstanley, Gerrard, 113
Wolfe, Don M., 314
Woodhouse, A. S. P., 302, 309, 316, 317, 319
Worden, Blair, 308
Wormuth, Francis, 236, 246, 279, 280
Wrigley, E. A., 144

Yule, George, 328, 329

Zagorin, Perez, 210, 226, 239; on authority, 217; on Country faction, 221; on court, 206; on Goodwin, 306; on Laudians, 325; on merchants, 251; on obedience, 305; on Parliament, 194–195, 235, 264, 281, 306; on Scottish Revolution, 219